The George Bell-Gerhard Leibholz Correspondence

The Selected Letters and Papers of George Bell, Bishop of Chichester

GEORGE KENNEDY ALLEN BELL (1883–1958) was a figure of distinctive importance in many of the great political and religious landscapes by which we have come to recognize the history of the European twentieth century. He was a priest of the Church of England, a chaplain to an Archbishop of Canterbury, a Dean of Canterbury and then, for almost thirty years, Bishop of Chichester. Bell played a significant role in the development of that church, but his most distinctive contribution lay in the evolution of the international ecumenical movement. Bell became a leading light in the Life and Work movement and then the World Council of Churches, and a crucial bridge not only between the Church of England and other churches but between British Christianity and the churches of the world at large. In this context he came to know intimately such luminaries as Nathan Söderblom, Dietrich Bonhoeffer, Willem Visser't Hooft and Eivind Berggrav.

In the context of the unfolding history of the Third Reich, Bell worked to support the persecuted, playing an important part in the German Church Struggle and also organizing relief to support refugee families who sought to escape abroad. He saved many lives. During the Second World War Bell repeatedly challenged British military and diplomatic policy, particularly over the obliteration bombing of German cities, and by his own secret initiatives he became a ready emissary of the German resistance against Hitler. Throughout his life Bell also sought to promote a new relationship between religion and the arts, commissioning work from the composer Gustav Holst and new drama from John Masefield, T.S. Eliot and Christopher Fry. He was, at the last, a figure of the twentieth-century world, a friend of Gandhi and Radhakrishnan, of the pastor Martin Niemöller, the constitutional lawyer, Gerhard Leibholz and the artist Hans Feibusch.

The Selected Letters and Papers of George Bell, Bishop of Chichester seeks to represent the many, interrelating dimensions of the career of a man whom the German pastor Heinrich Grűber considered as great a presence in his lifetime as Albert Schweitzer, Martin Buber and Martin Luther King.

Forthcoming:

The Speeches, Writings and Selected Sermons of George Bell, 1929–1958,
edited by Andrew Chandler
The George Bell-Alphons Koechlin Correspondence, 1933–54,
edited by Andrew Chandler and Gerhard Ringshausen

The George Bell-Gerhard Leibholz Correspondence

In the Long Shadow of the Third Reich, 1938–1958

Edited by
Gerhard Ringshausen and Andrew Chandler

BLOOMSBURY ACADEMIC
LONDON • NEW YORK • OXFORD • NEW DELHI • SYDNEY

BLOOMSBURY ACADEMIC
Bloomsbury Publishing Plc
50 Bedford Square, London, WC1B 3DP, UK
1385 Broadway, New York, NY 10018, USA
29 Earlsfort Terrace, Dublin 2, Ireland

BLOOMSBURY, BLOOMSBURY ACADEMIC and the Diana logo are trademarks of
Bloomsbury Publishing Plc

First published in Great Britain 2019
Paperback edition published 2021

Copyright © Gerhard Ringshausen and Andrew Chandler, 2019

Gerhard Ringshausen and Andrew Chandler have asserted their right under the Copyright,
Designs and Patents Act, 1988, to be identified as Editors of this work.

For legal purposes the Acknowledgements on p. viii constitute an extension of
this copyright page.

Cover design: Adriana Brioso
Cover images © [left] Gerhard Leibholz (© The estate of Marianne Leibholz);
[right] George Kennedy Allen Bell by Howard Coster
(© National Portrait Gallery, London).

All rights reserved. No part of this publication may be reproduced or transmitted
in any form or by any means, electronic or mechanical, including photocopying,
recording, or any information storage or retrieval system, without prior permission
in writing from the publishers.

Bloomsbury Publishing Plc does not have any control over, or responsibility for, any
third-party websites referred to or in this book. All internet addresses given in this
book were correct at the time of going to press. The author and publisher regret any
inconvenience caused if addresses have changed or sites have ceased to exist, but
can accept no responsibility for any such changes.

A catalogue record for this book is available from the British Library.

A catalog record for this book is available from the Library of Congress.

ISBN: HB: 978-1-4742-5766-4
PB: 978-1-3502-7095-4
ePDF: 978-1-4742-5767-1
eBook: 978-1-4742-5768-8

Series: The Selected Letters and Papers of George Bell, Bishop of Chichester

Typeset by Deanta Global Publishing Services, Chennai, India

To find out more about our authors and books visit www.bloomsbury.com
and sign up for our newsletters.

I am a learner from you, but I agree whole-heartedly with you.
George Bell to Gerhard Leibholz, 11 December 1942

I really think you are the living Christian conscience of this country and I only feel it a little painful that the other acting Archbishops and Bishops have not taken the opportunity of openly supporting you in a matter which concerns them too. In any case, at a time when the political leaders are obviously not able to see the implications of their policy it is a comfort to know that there are in this country personalities who have the courage to stand up against public opinion and to warn the nation in a truly prophetic way of the dangerous road they are taking.
Gerhard Leibholz to George Bell, 14 February 1944

Contents

Acknowledgements	viii
Introduction	ix
The Text: Editorial Conventions	xxvii
The Letters	1
Appendices	455
Bibliography	465
Index	469

Acknowledgements

The editors are glad to acknowledge with gratitude a gift from the late Hans Florin and his wife, Ev. It is this that has made possible the publication of the complete correspondence of George Bell and Gerhard Leibholz.

We remember with gratitude Marianne Leibholz, who kept her father's letters to George Bell for many years and gave permission for their publication, and who died in Göttingen on 30 January 2017.

We owe much to the kindness of the archivists and librarians of Lambeth Palace Library in London and of the Bundesarchiv in Koblenz. We also wish to thank the staff at the World Council of Churches archive in Geneva and the Evangelisches Zentralarchiv in Berlin. We are also grateful to the librarians at Leuphana University of Lűneburg and the University of Chichester for their continuing support.

Gerhard Ringshausen thanks the Deutsche Forschungsgemeinschaft for a grant to support his research work in Lambeth Palace Library.

We are truly grateful to Rhodri Mogford, our admirable editor at Bloomsbury, and to the meticulous, and patient, staff at Bloomsbury.

It is a pleasure to express our continuing gratitude to our wives and families, to Ellen Ringshausen in Lűneburg and to Alice Chandler in Tangmere.

Introduction

At the end of August 1938 the bishop of Chichester, George Bell, received a letter from his German friend, the young German pastor Dietrich Bonhoeffer. By this time they had come to know each other well, as friends but also as fast allies. Their paths had first crossed at a meeting of the Universal Christian Council for Life and Work in Novi Sad at the end of 1933, but it was when Bonhoeffer had come to London to be the pastor of a German congregation in Forest Hill that their relationship had assumed a far greater importance in the context of the unfolding German Church Struggle. This was now an intimate connection which showed the many proofs of a personal rapport and a creative moral affinity.

Before 1933 George Bell had cultivated close links with German theologians and scholars both within the contexts of the Life and Work movement, in which he had soon become a leading light, and within an occasional, though purposeful and productive, series of Anglo-German exchanges between 1927 and 1930. While these expressed an emerging ecumenical consciousness they also represented a contribution to the ongoing labours of men and women of goodwill in both Britain and Germany to foster the harmony of two nations only recently embroiled in a catastrophic war. It was a war in which George Bell had lost two brothers.

Bell was no Germanist: he did not speak or read German and his sense of German theology, philosophy and thought at large was not profound. But if the interior theological world of German Protestantism remained, to a certain extent, obscure to him, a public crisis of Church and State was something that he, like many other British Christians, intuitively recognized. Bell was in no doubt that this is what he saw at work in Germany after January 1933, the month which brought Adolf Hitler and the National Socialist movement to power. Four days after Hitler had been appointed chancellor of a coalition government, and on Bell's fiftieth birthday, the Executive Committee of the Universal Christian Council for Life and Work met in Berlin. It is difficult not to wonder at the conversations which must have occurred between the formal sessions of this gathering. For already the atmosphere was one precariously poised between moods of popular excitement and of public dread. National Socialism had many admirers in provincial life, but many critics in Berlin itself, a diverse, creative city which would never be profoundly reconciled to its principles or manifestations. Bell's first impressions of National Socialism were early ones, and vivid ones too.

The National Socialist state almost at once threw up a plethora of new, and often intense, fears, and not only in Germany. Across Europe observers viewed the coming of this new power as a danger to the security of nations and also a threat to the idea of democracy at large. For all its protestations of 'national revolution', the fundamental reality of the new regime was that of persecution: of political opponents, of pacifists and, above all, of Jews. Unscripted acts of hostility by party zealots were now purposefully reinforced by legislation passed by a new, supportive Reichstag. On 21 March 1933 a Malicious Practices Act was passed to license the detention of critics. On 1 April 1933 a boycott of Jewish businesses was imposed. In the same month the Reichstag passed the law for the Restoration of the Civil Service which removed from their positions all German Jews. It would be the first of a succession of 'Aryan paragraphs' which would seek to classify Jews as 'full or half non-Aryans' and enforce discrimination against them across German society. In April 1933 limits were imposed on the number of places allowed to Jewish students in German universities while Jews working in the medical or legal spheres faced growing penalties and even found that they could no longer practice at all. In the new climate further laws against German Jews accumulated across the provinces. Such measures identified and ostracized countless numbers of what had until 1933 been a secure and prosperous middle class. It was inevitable that thousands of German-Jewish families began to ask if they had a future in Germany at all. The numbers of those escaping into exile began to rise.

No one could deny that this national drama represented a new international crisis in the Europe created by the Versailles settlement. Democracy was again seen to be retreating; the politics of self-determination were now to provide the grammar for a ruthless new imperialism. After January 1933 politicians, journalists, intellectuals and humanitarians recognized that the world in which they lived had become more brutal and more dangerous. In such a context the churches, too, sensed new responsibilities. Christian institutions and charitable organizations of all kinds stirred into life, some of them philanthropic and others committed to protest. George Bell became a leading figure in this response, both within the international forms of the ecumenical movement and the national landscape of Britain itself. By the summer of 1933 he was widely regarded as an authoritative voice on the crisis in the German churches and on the plight of the persecuted Jews. For the next six years these preoccupations would fundamentally reconfigure his priorities as a bishop, his labours, his hours and days. Much of what he now did was practical: in the archive at Lambeth Palace no less than five stout volumes document his patient endeavours for refugee families as they sought to negotiate the difficulties of bureaucracy and the many practical obstacles of migration and settlement.[1]

It was in such a context that Bell encountered the beleaguered figures of Gerhard and Sabine Leibholz. A *Volljude*, Leibholz was married to Sabine Bonhoeffer, the twin sister of Bell's friend Dietrich Bonhoeffer. It was Bonhoeffer who in September 1938 asked Bell to assist the couple. On 2 September 1938 Bell replied, eagerly: 'I am *delighted* to act as a reference for your brother-in-law *Professor Leibholz*: and to do anything I can to help him'. The letters which followed from this undertaking bring to life not merely a relationship of two individuals, brought together in a haphazard world of many dangers, but a civilization of ideas and endeavours, in which the intricate, daily uncertainties and frustrations of diasporic existence became intertwined with

---

[1] See Ronald C.D. Jasper, *George Bell, Bishop of Chichester* (London, 1967), pp. 135–7; also Andrew Chandler, *George Bell, Bishop of Chichester: Church, State and Resistance in the Age of Dictatorship* (Grand Rapids, 2016), pp. 42–61.

sophisticated intellectual argument, high personal drama, political intrigue and public endeavour. This was, arguably, a meeting of minds quite unique in the tumultuous history of the European mid-twentieth century.

Leibholz's life until 1938

Gerhard Leibholz[2] was born on 15 November 1901 in Charlottenburg, since 1920 a part of Berlin. His parents came from wealthy Jewish families; they were highly assimilated and the religious atmosphere at home was secular and liberal. Like his two brothers Gerhard was baptized in the Lutheran Church. In 1916, as a candidate for confirmation, he became a friend of the young Hans von Dohnanyi who introduced him to Klaus Bonhoeffer, an elder brother of Dietrich, and Justus Delbrück. These friendships led to marriages: in 1925 Hans von Dohnanyi married Christine Bonhoeffer and in 1930 Klaus Bonhoeffer married Emmi Delbrück, while it was in 1926 that Leibholz married Sabine Bonhoeffer (1906–99). They had two daughters, Marianne, born in 1927, and Christiane, born in 1930.

In 1919 Leibholz finished school at the humanist Mommsen Gymnasium and began to study philosophy, law and political economy at Heidelberg University. Here he fell under the influence of the liberal democrats, Richard Thoma and Gerhard Anschütz. It was under Thoma's auspices that Leibholz completed his doctorate in 1921, a discussion of the German idealist Johann Gottlieb Fichte and the 'Idea of Democracy' which showed his interest in the law as it may be viewed in ideological and political contexts. In the same year Leibholz returned to Berlin and finished his academic studies with the First State Examination, duly awarded in 1922. Heinrich Triepel now became Leibholz's doctoral supervisor and Triepel was also responsible for his postdoctoral lecturing qualification. His doctoral thesis sought to interpret the principle of 'Equality before the Law' in a contemporary context in which the discussion of constitutional law[3] had come to involve debates about the legitimacy and character of the law itself, not as something given but as something which might support a contemporary, value-orientated interpretation. For Leibholz the principle of equality was not a formal, theoretical condition which silently underlay the enactment of laws but an actual, practical demand which must be acknowledged by legislative authorities as they worked. He argued that equality was a basic element of justice itself,[4] and while the idea of justice was not natural and bound to eternal values, its properties must be specified according to contemporary circumstances. The 'suum cuique', or just

---

[2] See Manfred H. Wiegandt, *Norm und Wirklichkeit: Gerhard Leibholz (1901–1982): Leben, Werk und Richteramt* (Baden-Baden, 1995); also 'Gerhard Leibholz (1901–1982)', in Jack Beatson, Reinhard Zimmermann (eds.), *Jurists Uprooted. German-speaking Émigré Lawyers in Twentieth-century Britain* (Oxford, 2004), pp. 535–81.
[3] See Peter C. Caldwell, *Popular Sovereignty and the Crisis of German Constitutional Law* (Durham, 1997).
[4] See M.H. Wiegandt, 'Antiliberal Foundations, Democratic Convictions. The Methodical and Political Positions of Gerhard Leibholz', in Peter C. Caldwell and William E. Scheuerman (eds.), *From Liberal Democracy to Facism* (Boston, 2000), pp. 106–35.

judgement, must express the 'common legal consciousness of the people'.[5] 'In reality', wrote Leibholz, 'laws given by the political powers become right in a material sense only by the legal consciousness that subsists in the concrete community of the people, which accepts the law as motivated by justice and legitimates it as just law'.[6]

From 1926 to 1928 Leibholz pursued his research at the Kaiser Wilhelm Institute for Foreign and Public International Law, work which culminated in his inaugural lecture at the university, a discussion of the 'Problems of Fascist constitutional law'. His analysis of the authoritarianism of Mussolini's Italy was explicit: Fascism, he argued, 'tries to combine the petrified common interest with vivid individuality'.[7] Separation from liberal democracy seemed to be the current trend in a time of 'striving for being embedded in a new Absolute'.[8] In 1929 Leibholz's postdoctoral thesis, 'The Essence of Representation with a Special Focus on the Representative System',[9] examined ways in which parliamentary representation in Germany had evolved from a system which counted the votes of individual representatives to one in which those representatives had become dependent on political parties. Leibholz believed that such a transformation meant that while the practices of the German republic were legal, and in accordance with the wording of the 1919 Constitution, they had lost a vital legitimacy. In this he showed the influence of his friend and near-contemporary, the jurist and political theorist Carl Schmitt. Manfred Wiegandt has observed, 'Much of Leibholz's analysis of the crisis of the representative system and of his understanding of the representative principle was nurtured by Schmitt's ideas'.[10] Leibholz and Schmitt were to remain friends until 1934, though by then their paths had clearly diverged.[11]

Leibholz had certainly won for himself an enviable reputation. He was not quite twenty-eight years old when, in 1930, he secured the chair in public law at Greifswald University. Only a year later he accepted the newly created chair for public law at Göttingen University. But the arrival of the National Socialist state was soon to catch up with him. At first he evaded the 'Law for the Restoration of the Professional Civil Service' because he had participated in the activities of the 'Free Corps' after the war. But in January 1935 the leading figure in the 'National Socialist Lecturers Association', and future dean of the university, proposed to the political authorities that the law

---

[5] 'Rechtsbewusstsein des Volkes', in: Gerhard Leibholz, *Die Gleichheit vor dem Gesetz* (Berlin, 1925; 2nd ed., Munich, 1959), pp. 61, 77.
[6] Leibholz, 'Begründet der in den verschiedenen Verfassungen ausgesprochene Grundsatz der Gleichheit aller vor dem Gesetze durchsetzbares subjektives Recht?' (1931), in Leibholz, *Die Gleichheit*. (2nd edition), p. 218.
[7] Leibholz, *Zu den Problemen des faschistischen Verfassungsrechts* (Berlin, 1928), p. 41. Leibholz corrected the proofs. See Reinhard Mehring, *Carl Schmitt. Aufstieg und Fall* (München, 2009), p. 241.
[8] See Leibholz, *Die Auflösung der liberalen Demokratie* (Munich-Leipzig, 1933), p. 55.
[9] Leibholz, *Das Wesen der Repräsentation unter besonderer Berücksichtigung des Repräsentativsystems* (Berlin, 1929). See Reinhard Mehring, *Carl Schmitt. Aufstieg und Fall* (Munich, 2009), pp. 232, 638 (note 51).
[10] Wiegandt, *Gerhard Leibholz*, p. 543. When Carl Schmitt wrote a review of Erwin von Beckerath's *Wesen und Werden des faschistischen Staates*, Leibholz corrected the proofs. See Mehring, *Carl Schmitt*, p. 241.
[11] The information here is from Marianne Leibholz. It was the increasingly anti-Semitic Schmitt who ended the friendship. See Mehring, *Carl Schmitt*, p. 316.

faculty be purged of three 'non-Aryan' members: Julius von Gierke, Franz Gutmann and Leibholz himself. Indeed, Leibholz looked increasingly vulnerable: a month later the National Socialist Students' Association organized a campaign against him. It was because of this that he was required by the Minister of Science to take leave on 1 April 1935. The public career in which he had taken such pride had ended ignominiously and abruptly.

The Leibholz family now faced clearly the prospect of exile. Yet they were reluctant emigrants: their ties to the Bonhoeffer family in Berlin were precious and Leibholz also knew how difficult it was for German lawyers to secure employment abroad. When his brother-in-law, Hans von Dohnanyi, informed him of government plans to stamp the passports of German Jews with a 'J' he knew that he must decide. On 9 September 1938 the family said their farewells to Göttingen. Leaving their children in Berlin, Gerhard and Sabine Leibholz travelled via Switzerland to Britain in search of the bishop of Chichester. The family was now almost without means. The German government would no longer pay Leibholz a pension. Because he had left the country without official permission, his assets were frozen.

A life in exile

On 8 November 1938, three days after the Leibholzes arrived in London, Sabine reported to her twin brother their first contacts with members of his old congregation in the German Lutheran parish in Forest Hill.[12] Evidently the couple were still gaining confidence: 'Gert', reported Sabine to her twin brother, 'is still very inhibited in speaking. He does not yet want to visit uncle G[eorge]. I doubt that he will do much more in the next fortnight'.[13] Bonhoeffer, however, urged them not to postpone the visit too long.[14] It was not until the beginning of the new year that Leibholz first wrote to Bell, who answered promptly, inviting the family for a weekend in the middle of January 1939.[15]

These days in Chichester, later remembered fondly and vividly by Sabine Leibholz,[16] were the beginning of what would become an intensive collaboration between the English bishop and the German professor. Yet for the first two years their correspondence was largely a discussion of personal practicalities. Bell did his best to secure for Leibholz a stipend from the World Council of Churches (then 'in process

---

[12] See Sabine Leibholz-Bonhoeffer, Vergangen – erlebt – überwunden (Gütersloh, 1976), pp. 119–21. A photograph of them intently at work in a guesthouse in Forest Hill was taken soon after their arrival: see Eberhard Bethge, Renate Bethge and Christian Gremmels (eds.), Dietrich Bonhoeffer: A Life in Pictures (London, 1986), p. 169.
[13] 'Gert ist noch sehr gehemmt im Sprechen. Er will auch noch nicht gern Onkel G. besuchen. Ich bezweifle, das er in 14 Tagen viel mehr können wird.' Sabine Leibholz to Dietrich Bonhoeffer, 8 November 1938, in: Dietrich Bonhoeffer Works 15, p. 76.
[14] See Dietrich Bonhoeffer to Sabine and Gerhard Leibholz, 10 November 1938, in: DBW 15, p. 78; also Bonhoeffer to the Leibholzes, 5 December 1938, ibid., pp. 85–6.
[15] Bell to Leibholz, 9 January 1939.
[16] See Leibholz-Bonhoeffer, Vergangen, pp. 128–30. But for an English version, taken from the new edition of 1994, see Appendix 2.

of formation') and then another, from Magdalen College in Oxford.[17] Together with a grant from the Society for the Protection of Science and Learning Leibholz was able to cobble together a modest financial basis of £350 a year on which a family might live in London. The WCC stipend required that he give 'a good portion of [his] time to the production of materials for the Study Department' in Geneva, particularly 'on the question of the "Corpus Christianum" and on "The Christian Conception of Freedom"'.[18] In various ways this task would dominate Leibholz's research work and publications in the years to come.

The stay in London did not last long. It was in the shadow of war that the Leibholz family first moved to the town of St. Leonards on Sea, a resort on the south coast, where the vicar, Cuthbert Griffiths, was an ally of Bell and where a house owned by the parish had been turned into a hostel for refugees.[19] This at least brought them within the borders of the diocese of Chichester. The Bells, meanwhile, moved out of the Bishop's Palace in November 1939 and set up a home in nearby Hove. It soon became clear that this move out of London placed the Leibholzes in what became, virtually, a new front line of the unfolding war. The German invasion of the Netherlands and Belgium, and then the dramatic fall of France, provoked an invasion scare in Britain and the government responded with an often chaotic policy, first to clear the south coast of possible fifth columnists, then to classify foreign nationals as 'aliens' of one sort or another and intern those who had come from enemy states, whether they were sympathizers to the Nazi state or refugees from it. On 12 May 1940 Gerhard Leibholz was taken to the internment camp at Huyton in Lancashire. For ten days his wife did not even know where he was and a host of anxious letters of enquiry followed.[20] Sabine Leibholz and the two girls were duly removed to Willand, a village in Mid Devon; a few weeks later they moved to Oxford. It was largely due to Bell that Leibholz was released on 26 July.

The experience of internment affected Leibholz deeply and strengthened his longing for a secure basis in Britain. Yet his financial situation remained precarious and his search for an academic position was frustrated. In Oxford he applied for a university lectureship and an official college fellowship, but to no avail. Like so many other thwarted intellectuals he began to look towards the United States. The energetic Presbyterian ecumenist William Paton made inquiries and, with the help of Reinhold Niebuhr in New York, Leibholz secured an invitation to the Episcopal Theological School at Cambridge, Massachusetts, in September 1940 and a further invitation to the Union Theological Seminary at New York in May 1941. The correspondence between Leibholz and Bell shows how strenuously and patiently a number of committed friends had to work in order to obtain such opportunities. But all of this could still be vulnerable to unavoidable financial obstacles: the Leibholz family needed money for the journey across the Atlantic and for the costs of living once they were there.

---

[17] See Bell to W.A. Visser 't Hooft, 24 April 1939, and following letters, in: Gerhard Besier, *Intimately Associated for Many Years: George K.A. Bell's and Willem A. Visser 't Hooft's Common Life-Work in the Service of the Church Universal – Mirrored in their Correspondence* (Part One, Newcastle upon Tyne: Cambridge Scholars Publishing, 2015), pp. 112–14; Bonhoeffer to Bell, 22 July 1939, in: *DBW* 15, pp. 252–3.

[18] W. A. Visser 't Hooft to Bell, 19 April 1939, in: Besier, *Intimately Associated for Many Years*, p. 115.

[19] See Leibholz-Bonhoeffer, *Vergangen*, pp. 149–51.

[20] Many letters to Sabine Leibholz may be found in BA, N 1334.

This made a fellowship from the Rockefeller Foundation and the transfer of Leibholz's WCC stipend all the more precious. Yet, for all these efforts, the American ambition would remain unfulfilled. In February 1941 Leibholz managed to meet the first official requirements that were made, but negotiations with the American Consulate began to drag on. Meanwhile, the shipping companies made their own demands. The whole plan was eventually destroyed by new developments in the war itself. When German forces attacked the Soviet Union in June 1941 the American government issued new consular regulations and opportunities to travel by trans-Atlantic liners diminished.

These vicissitudes in themselves left a profound, if not exhausting, impression. But by this time Leibholz had begun to find in Bell not merely a practical, but an intellectual and political *alter ego*. Their friendship had ripened and to the Leibholz family Britain had become a new home. In November 1941 Leibholz acknowledged to Bell: 'In any case it would not be easy, under the present circumstances, to leave this country where we have met with so much kindness and above all to lose you, my Lordbishop. You have cheered us up so often and have given us again and again not only help and protection whenever we needed them (and I needed them continuously) but also new hope and courage'.[21] The entry of the United States into the war on 11 December had also raised a great many new uncertainties about what a future in that country might actually bring. Would Leibholz himself be interned once again? In January 1942 he wrote, 'On the one hand I should like to go to America (especially with regard to the future after the war); on the other hand, I fully realize the risks and uncertainties as the result of the incalculable consequences of the new situation'.[22]

In wartime Bell had begun to extend his existing commitments in international and ecumenical affairs and to fashion a bold, new role in British public life. In particular he increasingly used the place in the House of Lords which, in July 1938, he had been given as a senior bishop of the Church of England. Leibholz, the sympathetic, principled German constitutional lawyer now offered exactly the intellectual company that he needed. If Bell wished to be anything at all in such a context it was a thinker who could articulate not a national but an international argument, and one which rested on solid European foundations. In many ways Leibholz confirmed in Bell many ideas and understandings which were already his own. But he also contributed a new substance and weight, and not least a far more secure German dimension, developing his arguments critically and doing much to lift Bell out of clerical company into the richer perspectives of a wider civil society. Although Bell found a handful of allies to guide him in all that he said, it speaks volumes that the friend with whom he enjoyed the greatest rapport in these intense debates was not an eminent British churchman, politician or scholar, but a barely known refugee lawyer, exiled from the very state with which his own country was now at war.

The first fruits of this entente could be seen in the opposition to the policy of internment in 1940, a campaign which was widely judged to be successful – for the government was embarrassed time and again in both houses of parliament and eventually forced to disband what was widely condemned as illogical and compromised.

---

[21] See Leibholz to Bell, 18 November 1941.
[22] See Leibholz to Bell, 27 January 1942.

For his part, Bell knew that as a refugee Leibholz had much to fear from obscurity in a new land. He searched out opportunities for employment, introduced him to new circles in which his ideas could feel the influence of other minds and grow, and also to the many editors and publishers who were known to him. In short, Bell did much to give Leibholz confidence that he did indeed have a place in his adopted country, and a voice too. Above and beyond all such things it is clear that the two men knew, intuitively, how to value each other.

Although he never secured an academic position at Oxford, Leibholz had very probably come to the right place. Bell himself had been a student at Christ Church and he retained a relationship with his old college and with the Oxford scene. A.D. Lindsay, a scholar who played a prominent part in contemporary political debates, was Master of Balliol; Leibholz had met William Beveridge on a visit to the city in March 1939. The Roman Catholic thinker Christopher Dawson, never more eminent than now, lived nearby. The Regius Professor of Moral and Pastoral Theology, Leonard Hodgson, was a prominent member of the Faith and Order movement and had corresponded, if not quite fruitfully, with Dietrich Bonhoeffer in 1935 and again in 1939.[23] It was when Hodgson heard Leibholz speak at a conference of the 'Christian Fellowship in Wartime' that he had invited him to give four lectures on 'Christianity, Politics and Power' at Christ Church in January and February 1942.[24] These found him to be very much more than an authority on the letter of the Law. In the same year Leibholz contributed a paper, 'Christianity, Justice and Modern Society',[25] to a discussion of Natural Law at St Deiniol's Library in Hawarden,[26] a residential institution which was now run by the erudite and internationally minded scholar-priest, Alec Vidler. In all of this Leibholz showed not only that he had won confidence and clarity in the English language but also a measure of respect and recognition from his peers.

Thinking together

Both Bell and Leibholz were fortunate in finding a place in a flourishing world of writing, publishing and reading, where informed opinion found plenty of room for expression on all manner of subjects. The Victorian age had produced a great wealth in periodical literature, much of which still remained alive and available. Journals like the *Fortnightly Review*, the *Round Table*, the *Nineteenth Century* (which had become the *Nineteenth*

---

[23] See Eberhard Bethge, *Dietrich Bonhoeffer. Theologe – Christ – Zeitgenosse* (9th ed., Gütersloh, 2005), pp. 548–50, 722–3.

[24] Published in the series 'Christian News-Letter Books', reprinted in Gerhard Leibholz, *Politics and Law* (Leyden: A.W. Sythoff, 1965), pp. 91–132.

[25] Revised version: 'The Foundation of Justice and Law in the Light of the Present European Crisis', reprinted in Leibholz, *Politics and Law*, pp. 253–70. In his autobiography, Vidler recalls Leibholz and also Karl Mannheim, the sociologist Georg Misch and Hans Ehrenberg. See *Scenes from a Clerical Life: An Autobiography* (London: : SCM Press, 1977), pp. 102–3.

[26] See Alec Vidler and Walter A. Whitehouse (eds.), *Natural Law: A Christian re-consideration* (London: SCM Press, 1946). Leibholz regularly took part of this ecumenical group (see Leibholz to Bell, 27 January 1944).

Century and After) and the *Contemporary Review* presented to the interested private reader new and diverse expositions by authors from all corners of public and private life, unfettered by specialization and the rigidities of academic disciplines. They were the forums of British democracy. Articles in such publications were widely read and could prove influential. Bell's important essay, 'The Church's Function in Wartime', appeared in the *Fortnightly Review* in November 1939. A month before Leibholz had already published his first English article, 'National Socialism and the Church', in the *Contemporary Review*. This was soon the world of a newcomer, the *Christian News-Letter*, a striking venture pioneered by Bell's ally J.H. Oldham, which offered information and comment on the great issues of the moment in a form easily pocketed and passed on in a society which was mobilized for a national campaign and often to be found in uniform. At the same time many other publishers were eager for new work that offered distinctive ethical and religious perspectives on the contemporary drama. It was Bell who wrote what became the first Penguin Special, *Christianity and World Order*, in 1940.[27] This sold 80,000 copies.

Leibholz's new British publications were concerned with the exploration of three propositions: the political task of Christianity and the Church, the foundation of human order by Natural Law, and the character of the totalitarian systems of the day. In 'National-Socialism and the Church' he adopted firmly the term 'totalitarianism', then widely accepted in critical British circles, but also introduced it to the less widely favoured term, secularization, which was only steadily gathering ground in the debates of the ecumenists. 'Under totalitarian governments', Leibholz wrote, 'such phenomena as class, race, the people in its biological sense, and the State as a realistic concept are deified'.[28] National Socialism was a materialistic conception of the people, of its biological existence, and this idea was a result of 'the revolutionary process of general secularisation'.[29] He proceeded, 'At the end of this development stands the man who deifies himself, no longer the servant of God, but the lord of the world, the self-appointed judge in the last resort over good and bad'.[30] Such an assumption of power must involve the denial and destruction of absolute values: both reason and spirit had been 'dethroned'. Christianity and National Socialism represented two different religions and now Europe as a continent was divided into two camps: 'We now approach an epoch more closely akin to that of the religious wars than to one which professes to be characterised by the principle of the nation state'.[31] In Germany itself the Confessing Church had understood its struggle not as a political confrontation but, primarily, as one involving the maintenance of Christian integrity within the Church. Such a view had never been comprehensible in Britain. Leibholz showed that

---

[27] Bell's Foreword to *Christianity and World Order*, pp. vii–viii, names only Hans Ehrenberg as a German adviser. For Visser 't Hooft's assistance see Bell to Hans Schönfeld, 29 March 1940, also his (and surely not Visser 't Hooft's) synopsis of 'The Church and World Order', in Besier, *Initimately Associated for Many Years*, pp. 183–95.
[28] Leibholz, 'National-Socialism and the Church', reprinted in Leibholz, *Politics and Law*, pp. 201–9; here p. 202.
[29] Ibid., p. 201.
[30] Ibid., p. 203.
[31] Ibid., p. 208.

he agreed with British critics when he asserted unequivocally the utter dominance of politics: 'For Christianity', he argued, 'has nothing in common with the quasi-religious needs of National-Socialism. . . . Nor can the Church to-day afford to live in self-contained seclusion, and to limit its activities to the proclamation of the Gospel. . . . Where every sphere of life is in the grasp of the politician, every attempt to escape must itself become political'.[32]

But in one particular matter public opinion was fast altering. Bell was insistent that a distinction must be drawn between the German people at large and the state which governed them. Such a view had been conventional in Britain in September 1939 but by the summer of 1940 defeat in France had provoked a far more rigid, and bitter, view. It was in 1941 that a former Permanent Under-Secretary for Foreign Affairs at the Foreign Office, Sir Robert Vansittart, broadcast a series of lectures over the BBC which saw prompt publication as a pamphlet. This was *Black Record*, a powerful polemic against the historical, contemporary, moral and spiritual, military and perennially troublesome German nation. Vansittart had certainly found an audience. Within a month of its first publication *Black Record* had been reprinted six times.

Bell was sure that what soon became known as Vansittartism must be repudiated. Vanisttart himself was a powerful adversary, for his own public record was an impressive one and it was by no means clear that his views did not represent the mind of the government itself. Because Vansittart was, like Bell, a member of the House of Lords it was in this context that they confronted each other, time and again, throughout the war. This debate drew Bell and Leibholz still more closely together. Leibholz showed Bell how National Socialism might be distinguished from traditional nationalism. Moreover, he insisted that the Nazi regime could not 'be considered as an embodiment either of the spiritual or social forces of Prussianism'.[33] Because of this, Leibholz argued, 'it is not so surprising that the opposition [to Hitler] has drawn relatively greater strength from the "reactionary" old-Prussian forces than from former liberals, and that the army was and is regarded as a moderating influence against the Regime, and that to a certain extent hopes of a change of regime in Germany have been placed in the Army or in certain army circles'.[34] Leibholz admired Bell's *Christianity and World Order* as 'a most admirable and illuminating book'.[35] In a review which he wrote of it he drew particular attention to Bell's insistence 'that the West does not desire to crush Germany', and that it 'must aim at rebuilding the Christian civilisation of Europe upon planned co-operative lines, based on justice and truth. In a peace to come, each nation must play its contributory part'.[36]

Leibholz's writing implied a differentiation of Germans and Nazis. The experience of internment in 1940 must certainly have sharpened these perspectives. Bell

---

[32] Ibid., p. 201.
[33] Leibholz, 'Germany, the West and the Possibility of a New International Order' (1940), reprinted in Leibholz, *Politics and Law*, p. 164.
[34] Ibid., pp. 164–5.
[35] Leibholz, 'Christianity and World Order', in *Christian Fellowship in Wartime*. Bulletin of 15 February 1941, reprinted in *Politics and Law*, p. 133; see Appendix 1. See too Leibholz to Bell, 12 November 1940.
[36] Bell, *Christianity and World Order*, pp. 95 and 88, quoted by Leibholz, 'Christianity and World Order', in *Politics and Law*, p. 138.

had also insisted on this; so too his friend, the first general secretary of the World Council of Churches in Geneva, Willem Visser 't Hooft.[37] As Leibholz explained in a memorandum discussing international affairs in 1940, it was its totalitarian structure which distinguished National Socialism from traditional nationalism. Equally, the Nazi regime could not be considered 'as an embodiment either of the spiritual or social forces of Prussianism'.[38] If such an insistence was looking increasingly out-of-favour in wartime Britain, where strains of Vansittartism were often accommodated and fostered, they found a home, and a resonance, in the arguments of international ecumenism. Yet it was difficult not to sense that the dominant mood was set against them. British policy had hardened. Bell's public interventions became more and more those of a critic. The publication of the Atlantic Charter of the Western powers on 14 August 1941 provoked a letter to the *Times*, published five days later. Here Bell repeated the view of British church leaders at large that only the principles of the Christian religion could yield a solid foundation for national policy and for a permanent peace in Europe.[39] Leibholz agreed, adding that the 'final destruction of Nazi tyranny' as the main war aim 'goes farther than the Versailles Treaty in so far as in it a promise of general disarmament was held out. Herewith not only a Nazi regime but also any regime of military or conservative kind or tincture will be ruled out for Germany in future'.[40] To this Bell replied: 'Our present official Government policy tends to the fixing of the old plan of separate alliances with the certainty of a new war in the end and probably the division of Europe, as you suggest, into a Communist camp versus an Anglo-Saxon one. I myself cannot help thinking that it might be the Churches' special task to keep the idea of the family of nations very much alive, and to give it concrete expression as against the idea of separate alliances'.[41] Leibholz argued that British policy should 'treat an Anti-Nazi government which may come out of an Anti-Nazi revolution and has not a communist character in the same way as Russia would treat a communist Germany'.[42]

In his lectures 'Christianity, Politics and Power', given at Christ Church, Oxford, in January 1942, Leibholz fortified and developed these ideas about the 'intimate connexion between religion, theology and politics'.[43] When they were published in a series of extended studies under the aegis of the *Christian News-Letter*, the references showed that the company in which the author was to be found was not merely national. Here he was seen to be rubbing shoulders with Archbishop William Temple, A.D. Lindsay, Michael de la Bedoyère, Nathaniel Micklem, Christopher Dawson, Arnold Toynbee, Alec Vidler, J.H. Oldham, Jacques Maritain, Reinhold Niebuhr, Karl Barth ('a modern Calvinist'), Oliver Quick, Leonard Hodgson, William Paton and Bell himself. Leibholz demanded a political answer by the Church: 'the Christian faith is of incalculable political value', while an 'unpolitical faith ... enables totalit[arian]ism to

---

[37] See W. A. Visser 't Hooft's memorandum, 'Germany and the West', quoted by Bell in *Christianity and World Order*, pp. 94–5.
[38] Leibholz, 'Germany, the West and the Possibility of a New International Order', reprinted in Leibholz, *Politics and Law*, p. 164.
[39] See Bell's letter to the editor of *The Times*, published 19 August 1941.
[40] Leibholz to Bell, 19 August 1941.
[41] Bell to Leibholz, 27 August 1941.
[42] See Leibholz to Bell, 2 September 1941.
[43] Leibholz, 'Christianity, Politics and Power', reprinted in *Politics and Law*, p. 91.

put God and His commandments aside'.[44] Equally, political thought needed 'a revival through the Christian creed' because 'all true political questions are religious'.[45] He granted that the worlds of politics and religion were distinct: 'the earthly city cannot be governed solely by the principles of the Kingdom of God'.[46] He saw, too, that the Christian was a member of two orders, but these orders need not be in conflict, for both were created by God and both 'are related to the same ultimate end – the glory of God'.[47] 'The world', Leibholz insisted, 'is called upon to testify to the sovereignty of God'. It was when authority did not acknowledge this that it became tyranny. In such a context moral obligations were reordered: 'Man's spiritual integrity and his fellowship with God take precedence of his citizenship'. Such a vision certainly gave the Church much to do in the world: it was 'powerfully and repeatedly to press into national and international life Christian principles such as the sacredness of the human personality, the sovereignty of God above all nations, the universal brotherhood of men, the Christian power of love and forgiveness and the existence of universal moral laws'.[48] Such claims were themselves 'totalitarian', but not in any sense that could threaten 'true human nature' or challenge or subdue the State itself. They were indeed essential to principles of 'justice, goodness and decency' which were absolute and eternal. But here was no case for a Christian State.

Leibholz's thought was indeed changing, and the alteration was to be found most of all in his retrieval of the idea of Natural Law. Gone was the argument that the 'common legal consciousness of the people' must be the foundation, and authorization, of justice.[49] Now he wrote, 'the principles of Natural Law which every kind of human order must respect are inherent elements of justice and ultimately of Christianity'[50]; moreover, 'those principles of law which are an inherent element of divine justice must also find their expression in the various forms of positive law'.[51] Leibholz looked to Aquinas and to Luther, and among his contemporaries he may well have been influenced by Temple. Certainly he found himself at odds with his eminent brother-in-law in Germany. Even so, political totalitarianism, he maintained, expressed no authentic natural law at all, but replaced it with an invention of its own in 'a new quasi-religious content'.[52] In the totalitarian state law was merely 'the expression of the naked will of man, and not the expression of justice and reason and of the transcendent will of God'. Because of this such a state could accept no other foundation: there was no room left for a religious sphere and especially none for Christianity. 'At bottom', concluded Leibholz, 'the deliberate adoption of the belief in force and power is nothing

---

[44] Ibid., p. 102.
[45] Ibid., p. 95.
[46] Ibid., p. 92.
[47] Ibid., p. 94–5.
[48] Ibid., p. 102.
[49] Later, in 'Public Opinion', in August 1944, Leibholz gave a short summary of the changes since liberalism and the need for a 'new spiritual realism'. See *Politics and Law*, pp. 81–7
[50] Leibholz, 'The Foundation of Justice and Law in the light of the present European Crisis', reprinted in *Politics and Law*, p. 258. This paper was first given at St Deiniol's Library and subsequently published *The Dublin Review*, of which Christopher Dawson was the editor, in January 1943. See Bell's similar position in *Christianity and World Order*, pp. 65–6.
[51] Ibid., p. 264.
[52] Leibholz, 'The Foundation of Justice and Law', in *Politics and Law*, p. 259.

but the creed of nihilism in action'. This new international war was a conflict 'between two principles, two attitudes towards the world, two schemes of human values. It is a struggle for the control of the human mind'. Furthermore, 'the Western countries are actually fighting the present war for universal principles, ideas and values. This is why the present conflict has been compared to a kind of crusade, or to a holy war, or to a war of religion'. Modern liberal democracy represented an absolute contradiction of the political structure of modern totalitarianism. It is difficult to know how influential such ideas became, but Leibholz could at least be sure of one sympathetic reader. In December 1942 Bell wrote to him, 'I agree whole-heartedly with you. I am sure that the position which you put before your readers is one which ought to be put forth on a large scale by the churches just now wherever they can find an opportunity'.[53]

The destruction of the German Resistance

Since 1942 both Bell and Visser't Hooft had, in effect, become active ambassadors of the resistance in Germany, a direct consequence of their support for the Confessing Church before September 1939.[54] Bell's visit to Sweden in May/June that year, and his astonishing encounter with Dietrich Bonhoeffer and Hans Schönfeld at Sigtuna, proved a fundamental turning point. In this many of the arguments which had come to define the Bell-Leibholz correspondence, and which had remained thinly substantiated and even speculative, came suddenly into an intense focus. What followed from this is well known: Bell brought his message to Whitehall, met the Foreign Secretary, Anthony Eden, and received the judgement that it was not in the national interest that any reply should be made to such an overture.[55] Bell never ceased to regard this as a blunder. But it was the announcement of a policy of 'unconditional surrender' at the Casablanca conference of January 1943 which showed decisively that Bell and Leibholz were now standing against a very powerful tide indeed. Whatever Churchill's private misgivings, this declaration set the will of the Allied powers in stone. Both Bell and Leibholz believed that such a policy offered Germans only a counsel of despair. Leibolz was at once fearful that such a policy now made far more distinct the prospect of a communist Germany. Bell agreed with him.

Any direct reports of developments in Germany itself remained sporadic. Even the channels kept open by international ecumenical agencies provided little information. For the most part both Bell and Leibholz were wholly in the dark. News of the arrest and incarceration of Bonhoeffer and Hans von Dohnanyi on 5 April 1943 did not reach them at all. But news of the final attempted coup d'état on 20 July 1944 came suddenly and loudly, and from a variety of sources, not least official ones in Germany itself. With this calamity all hope was dashed: it was now a matter of watching bleakly as British

---

[53] Bell to Leibholz, 11 December 1942.
[54] See Gerhard Ringshausen, 'Gerhard Leibholz: Bonhoeffers Schwager als Vertreter des Widerstands in England', in Andrew Chandler, Katarzyna Stoklosa and Jutta Vinzent (eds.), *Exile and Patronage. Cross-cultural negotiations beyond the Third Reich* (Berlin, 2006), pp. 91-107.
[55] Eden to Bell, 17 July 1942, to be found in *DBW* 16, p. 343.

newspapers reported how participants in the German resistance were arrested, tried and executed. The dismay of Bell himself is vividly exposed by his letters to Leibholz, and also revealed by a desperate letter to Anthony Eden pleading that every effort be made to rescue any member of the resistance still at large. But in Britain official opinion was, at best, ambivalent. Churchill had been dismissive of the conspiracy and there were many sceptics besides. It was in this context that Bell and Leibholz now worked to present an account of the resistance which represented its integrity and resolve.[56] As the war moved inexorably towards its conclusion they were left to fear not only for those who may have fallen into the hands of the Nazi state, but for the material well-being of other family members and friends. The letters of the last year of the war are fraught with anxious waiting, and peace itself would bring no easy resolutions. It was only in October 1945, and in the midst of the new divisions of the Cold War, that Bell was able to take off for Germany and find Bonhoeffer's parents in Berlin.

Planning the future of Germany

Early in the war Gerhard Leibholz had seen that a post-war Europe would be dominated by the antagonism between the Western understanding of freedom and the ideology of Communism in the East. The unfolding debate about the terms of a future peace acknowledged that in some way or other the mind of Germany must be altered, if not converted. Any policy that made this more difficult must fail to satisfy the many demands which the future itself must make, not least for international security. But what could this actually mean? Already in June 1944, Leibholz was profoundly pessimistic. In a new article on 'Education in Post-war Germany' he criticized plans for a re-education of the German population as 'bound to fail in the end',[57] and wondered whether 'the Western conception of life possesses enough strength in itself to be able to be transplanted into other countries'. This was not merely a political but a religious task, for it would be 'an impossible undertaking to change the minds of a nation of more than 70 million people by the traditional methods of power politics' with 'a flavour of totalitarianism'.[58] Furthermore, it must be carried out not by the victors but the vanquished: 'A people can repent only of his own accord'.[59] Leibholz saw, too, that those 'thousands' who had refused to accept Nazism and had known 'all the fires of persecution' might now offer 'the basis for the spiritual regeneration and the rebuilding of life in Germany'.[60] By the autumn of 1944 these apprehensions had crystallized. To J.H. Oldham he wrote, 'Security and reconversion of Germany must be organically linked up with each other. In other words, the security policy itself must take on an ideological character. It is impossible to expect a reconversion of Germany with the

---

[56] See Leibholz, 'The Opposition Movement in Germany', in: *The New English Weekly*, 19 October 1944, reprinted in *Politics and Law*, pp. 210–3.
[57] Leibholz, 'Education in Post-war Germany', reprinted in *Politics and Law*, pp. 194–200; here p. 198.
[58] Ibid., p. 196.
[59] Ibid., p. 198.
[60] Ibid., p. 199.

help of the most drastic means of a national power policy'.⁶¹ Yet he looked still to the vision of a united Europe, 'based not on power, but on the free consent and voluntary cooperation of the nations'.⁶² As the war neared its end it became more than ever clear to him that the policy of the Allied powers simply created division, and a division which must see an expansion of Soviet Communism. There soon lay before them no better prospect than an immense ideological confrontation in which 'the Great Powers seek to secure spheres of influence and regimes which are akin to them. I hope', Leibholz added to Bell, 'that they will not be the strategical positions for the next war'.⁶³

Though the great tide of affairs did almost nothing to justify their hopes, both Bell and Leibholz looked earnestly beyond it towards an eventual vindication. In February 1945 Leibholz wrote to Bell that he had 'not the slightest doubt that the time will come (even if it be too late) when the policy which you have advocated with such an admirable steadfastness and courage and with so great political wisdom in the last few years will one day be recognised as the only truly European policy'.⁶⁴ But the stings of the present were still sharp. When the victorious Allied powers met at Potsdam in July and August 1945 Leibholz found their agreed statement a 'phantastic and absurd document'.⁶⁵ Europe was now to be broken into two antagonistic regions and Germany itself would know half-a-century of tragic division.

For Bell this new peace brought many tasks, none of them simple. The World Council of Churches at last stirred to life with an eloquent gathering in Geneva in 1946 and then a vast General Assembly in Amsterdam in 1948. The reconstruction of Germany itself became a fundamental preoccupation. Bell was deeply immersed in charitable enterprises but there were also more controversial initiatives. He intervened on behalf of those accused of war crimes at Nuremberg, at times led by his contacts to justify defendants whose record would turn out to be, at best, compromised. He looked for the vindication of his wartime arguments and vindication, when it came, was partial, late and even hollow. His old adversary, Robert Vansittart confessed in 1951 that much in his earlier views had been mistaken, as Bell reported to Leibholz himself. By then British policy towards Germany had altogether altered: the Federal Republic was now admitted as a partner in the coalition of Western powers.⁶⁶ Churchill, too, had changed his tune. By this time Leibholz had come to support the austere, but constructive, policies of reconstruction framed by Konrad Adenauer.

The return to Germany

A good deal of the new Germany was in May 1945 to be found in Britain. In 1946 Leibholz accepted an offer by the British Foreign Office to give lectures on politics in prisoner-of-war camps, a task which he accepted readily. But, even though family

---

[61] Leibholz to Oldham, 16 October 1944.
[62] Leibholz, 'The Unity of Europe', reprinted in his *Politics and Law*, pp. 241–9; here p. 242.
[63] Leibholz to Bell, 11 December 1944.
[64] Leibholz to Bell, 3 February 1945.
[65] Leibholz to Bell, 4 August 1945.
[66] Bell to Leibholz, 15 February 1951.

members in Germany itself were still fearful of retaliation against those who had resisted the Hitler regime and firmly sought to discourage him from going back to Germany, the prospect of a return did not wane.[67] Gerhard Leibholz had never become deeply rooted in the country of his exile. It was still in Germany that he felt essentially at home. In November 1945 a colleague in Göttingen had asked him privately if he would consider returning to his old position there. Another invitation came in March 1946, this time from Hannover. It was with Bell's assistance that he went to Göttingen with Sabine in June 1947, a visit which made possible a diversion to Berlin to see, at last, the Bonhoeffer family. His naturalization as a British subject in April 1948 showed him still to be straddling two worlds and he had hopes that his future would lie in the promotion of Anglo-German understanding in this emerging, new Europe. On 15 April that year he presented a paper on international law in an age of ideologies to a conference of public and international lawyers in Hamburg.[68] A return was now almost inevitable, but the actual terms of it took some time to settle. Leibholz would turn down no less than six chairs at various German universities, evidently preferring emeritus positions and visiting as a guest lecturer.[69]

After 1948 the correspondence between Bell and Leibholz became, naturally, more sporadic. They were both men almost wholly given to their work, and now their different spheres would only touch occasionally. In that year Bell had become chairman of the Central Committee of the World Council of Churches, a demanding position which he held from the first General Assembly of the Council, in Amsterdam in 1948, to the second in Evanston, Illinois, in 1954. It was in appreciation of his friendship for Germany, his international ecumenical work and, in particular, his support for the pastors of the Confessing Church that the Theological Faculty of Göttingen University conferred upon him an honorary doctorate in June 1949. Bell would present his lecture *The Church and the Resistance Movement* at Göttingen in May 1957, fifteen years after his conversation with Bonhoeffer and Schönfeld in Sweden. This was the last time that the bishop of Chichester and the eminent German lawyer met but their collaboration was not quite at an end. Their last campaign was to press together for the release of the much-entangled figure of Otto John, once the friend and wartime ally of Klaus Bonhoeffer. Within months of his retirement as bishop in January 1958 Bell died at Canterbury on 3 October.

As for Gerhard Leibholz, the Federal Minister of Justice in Bonn had invited him to accept an appointment as a judge in the newly created Federal Constitutional Court at Karlsruhe in March 1951. After an initial refusal, in view of the compatibility of such a position with his continuing obligations in Göttingen, he yielded. On 4 September 1951, he was elected for a term of four years to the Second Senate. One of his first tasks was to clarify and strengthen the position of the Court, placing it on the same

---

[67] Leibholz to Bell, 2 November 1945.
[68] Although Leibholz himself was not personally present. See Leibholz, 'Zur gegenwärtigen Lage des Völkerrechts', in *Archiv des Völkerrechts* Vol. 1, 1948, pp. 415–23. It may be noted that Leibholz favoured a 'revival of the constitution through faith', because 'the liberal democracy of the West needs new justification', in Leibholz, 'Die Struktur der neuen Verfassung' (1948), in his *Strukturprobleme*, pp. 63–70; here p. 65.
[69] See Leibholz to Bell, 30 May 1948.

level as the government and the legislature. In the years to come many decisions of the Court would show the influence of his ideas, particularly drawing from his doctrine of equality and his insistence on the role of the political parties as integrative, and necessary, components of the constitutional framework. In such work the young Leibholz re-emerged: his wartime debates about a Christian basis of state and law had all but vanished.[70]

Gerhard Leibholz was re-elected to the Federal Constitutional Court in 1955, and again in 1963. But the work of the Court did not utterly absorb him. He remained a visiting professor at Göttingen University and, from 1953, also lectured on comparative constitutional law at the European College in Bruges. When, in the spring of 1957, the Faculty of Political and Social Studies at Cologne University asked him to succeed the former Reich chancellor Heinrich Brüning as professor of political science, the Minister of Science in the state of Lower Saxony established a new chair of political science for him in the law faculty. Leibholz continued to act as the principal of the Institute for Political Science and the General Theory of the State even after his retirement from academic life, in March 1970. In that year the European College in Bruges awarded him an honorary professorship. He finally retired from the Federal Constitutional Court in December 1971.

In his later years Leibholz was regarded as a founding father of the Federal Republic, and was much honoured. He remained proud of the work of the years of his exile and in 1965 published a collection of his British writings, dedicating it to the memory of Dietrich Bonhoeffer and George Bell, 'the late bishop of Chichester'. On his sixty-fifth birthday, in 1966, a two-volume festschrift, *Die moderne Demokratie und ihr Recht*, was published, a formidable testimony to the weight and extent of his national and international reputation, and not only among lawyers and scholars of the law.[71] On the occasion of his eightieth birthday Hannover University awarded him an honorary doctorate and his old institute in Göttingen honoured him with a symposium on the equality clause of the constitution, attended by Constitutional Court judges and eminent academics.

Gerhard Leibholz died in Göttingen on 19 February 1982. His place in German history was assured. In Britain his name remained an obscurity. He and his family had simply come as refugees and, for the most part, known little more than a precarious, private existence there. In Oxford the surviving houses in which they took rooms, on Banbury Road, Linton Road, Beechcroft Road and Lincoln Road, today present no acknowledgement that for a few, successive years they were the homes to such immense arguments, endeavours and hopes, and the places where such waiting and longing, such loss and grief, was known.

Although both George Bell and Gerhard Leibholz took care to preserve their letters, it is unlikely that either of them considered their correspondence to be, in itself, a considerable literary or intellectual achievement. Yet it may justly be seen in such

---

[70] Mentioned, though without emphasis, in Leibholz, 'Die Gleichheit vor dem Gesetz und das Bonner Grundgesetz' (1951), in *Gleichheit*, pp. 251–2.

[71] It is significant that one of those responsible was the great contemporary historian, Karl Dietrich Bracher: see Karl Dietrich Bracher et al. (eds.), *Die moderne Demokratie und ihr Recht* (2 vols., Tübingen, 1966).

terms and the claim that it makes on the attention of historians is a powerful one. The letters represent a rare, and perhaps unique, meeting of two European minds caught up in the turbulence of the Second World War, a model of alternative political and moral realism, and a critical and idealistic reflection on the tragic realities of that age. Both men sought to maintain an insistence that all the diplomatic, military and political issues which emerged before them must be located in the context of a just, and constructive, Christian sensibility. Moreover, they were wholly at one in acknowledging, and sharing, the tragic costs of that conviction.

The Text: Editorial Conventions

The letters of George Bell and Gerhard Leibholz were, for the most part, typed by assistants (in Bell's case his long-term secretary, Mary Balmer Joice). But a high proportion of their letters were personal, and handwritten. To read the handwriting of both writers requires some care and art: both sets of correspondence show evidence of the tussles of earlier transcribers, most likely Eberhard Bethge and Ronald Jasper, whose fine selection and translation of the letters, *An der Schwelle zum Gespalteten Europa: Der Briefwechsel zwischen George Bell und Gerhard Leibholz (1939-1951)*, was published by Kreuz Verlag in Stuttgart in 1974. Editorial interventions have been kept to the minimum. Where doubts remain an editorial suggestion, made to maintain the apparent sense of the sentence, has been placed in square brackets.

With the exception of superfluous, and obscuring, commas, all punctuation marks are preserved. In his handwritten notes Bell's expression loosens. He made particularly heavy use of colons and hyphens. Very occasionally commas have been placed in square brackets to ensure clarity of the meaning. Bell's abbreviations have been preserved where the full word is obvious to the reader: for example, where '&' is written for 'and', 'vy' for 'very', or 'affly' for 'affectionately'. At large, underlinings have been replaced with italics and titles (of publications of various kinds) have been italicized. Occasional inconsistencies or simple errors in the spellings of names do occur in the text and for the most part these have been corrected for the sake of clarity. Bell was very uneasy with German and, while his command of English very quickly became fluent, Leibholz here is certainly writing in a second language. Where meaning is obscured by expression the smallest interventions have been made in square brackets, or simply noted as follows: [sic]. Additions, often made by hand to typescripts, have been indicated as follows: ªaddition or insertionª. The headline gives the usual information about date, form and archive of the following document. It should be noted that the letters in the Bundesarchiv are not yet paginated.

It is worth noting that both Bell and Leibholz wrote of the 'German Confessional Church'. Historians have since used the term 'Confessing Church'. The latter term has been adopted in the Introduction and the critical apparatus.

The letters make numerous references to the speeches, articles and assorted published writings of both men. In the case of Bell these may be found in the second volume of this series. In the case of Gerhard Leibholz they may be found in the volume of his collected writings in English which he published later in his life: *Politics and Law* (A.W. Sytoff, Leyden, 1965).

There are now two editions of the *Dietrich Bonhoeffer Works*, in German and in English. In this volume the editors have referred primarily to the former but it is important to note that the latter contains additional, and significant, critical apparatus.

The Letters

1938

11 March	German forces occupy Austria; the Anschluss of the two states is declared two days later.
16 April	The British and Italian governments conclude a settlement whereby the annexation of Abyssinia by Italy is recognized.
27–9 April	British and French representatives meet in London to ensure a closer collaboration of the general staffs of both countries in all questions of mutual defence.
September	The German Government threatens Czechoslovakia over the Sudetenland.
15 September	The British prime minister, Neville Chamberlain, meets with Hitler at Berchtesgaden.
22–3 September	Chamberlain and Hitler meet again, at Bad Godesberg.
26 September	President Roosevelt appeals to Hitler and the Czechoslovak president Benes for peace.
29 September	The Munich settlement signed by Germany, France, Britain and Italy; on the following day Chamberlain and Hitler sign a resolve for peace between the two countries.
2 October	Polish forces occupy the Teschen area of Czechoslovakia.
9/10 November	*Reichskristallnacht*, an orchestrated anti-Jewish pogrom, takes place across Germany and Austria.

Bell to Dietrich Bonhoeffer, 2 September 1938, BA, N 1334 (handwritten)

I write from holidays in Ireland. Your letter only came this morning.

My dear Bonhoeffer,
It was a real pleasure to hear from you, and I need not tell you that I am *delighted* to act as a reference for your brother-in-law *Professor Leibholz*: and to do anything I can to help him in the matter about which you write, and to serve him in every way possible way to enable him to settle in England.[1] I will write personally to the Home Office in the next few days. And I hope we may have the pleasure of seeing your brother-in-law & his wife and two children at Chichester. Tell him to write to me at any time he thinks I can help.

―――――

You are often in my thoughts – as I have a special regard and friendship for you, and [watch] you and any worry I can hear with sympathy and admiration. It has always been a joy to see you at Chichester. And I should love to see you in Germany, when I come again, though I know not when that is [sic].

Yours most sincerely,

[1] See Sabine Leibholz-Bonhoeffer, V*ergangen – erlebt – überwunden* (Gütersloh, 1976), pp. 112–17; Eberhard Bethge, *Dietrich Bonhoeffer. Theologe – Christ – Zeitgenosse* (9th ed., Gütersloh, 2005), pp. 711–13.

1939

14 March	German, Hungarian and Rumanian forces occupy Prague and the remainder of Czechoslovakia. Slovakia becomes an independent state.
16 March	Bohemia and Moravia become protectorates of Germany; Slovakia becomes a protectorate of Germany on the following day.
22 March	Germany and Lithuania sign a non-aggression pact whereby Memel is ceded to Germany.
31 March	Chamberlain announces that Britain and France will come to the assistance of Poland if it is attacked.
1 April	General Franco announces the end of the Spanish civil war.
6 April	Chamberlain announces a formal agreement of mutual aid between Poland, Britain and France, pending the conclusion of a formal treaty.
7 April	Italian forces invade Albania.
13 April	The governments of Britain and France guarantee the borders of Greece and Rumania.
14 April	President Roosevelt appeals to Hitler and Mussolini for ten years of peace.
28 April	The German government ends a ten-year non-aggression treaty with Poland, signed in 1934, and demands the return of Danzig from Poland.
23 August	Germany and the Soviet Union sign a pact of non-aggression.
24 August	President Roosevelt issues a further appeal for peace.
25 August	Britain and France sign a treaty of mutual assistance.
1 September	German forces invade Poland and encounter firm resistance.
3 September	Britain declares war on Germany; France declares war a day later.
16 September	Soviet forces invade eastern Poland.
28 September	The German and Soviet governments agree the partition of Poland and new borders. The Estonian and Soviet governments sign a mutual assistance pact.
1 November	The Polish Corridor, Posen and Upper Silesia are annexed by Germany; two days later the Soviet Union annexes Polish Western Ukraine and Western White Russia.
4 November	The Neutrality Act is approved by Congress in the United States.
30 November	Soviet forces invade Finland.

Bell to Leibholz, 9 January 1939, BA, N 1334 (typewritten)

Dear Dr. Leibholz,

Many thanks for your letter.[1] It would give Mrs. Bell[2] and me great pleasure if you and Mrs. Leibholz could come and stay with us for next weekend, Saturday to Monday. It is the only chance of a weekend in the near future, I fear, as all our next three weekends are engaged away from Chichester, so I do hope this will be convenient for you.[3]

Yours sincerely,

---

[1] Leibholz's early letters to Bell are lost.
[2] Henrietta Bell, née Livingstone (1884–1968); she had married George Bell on 8 January 1918.
[3] See Sabine Leibholz to Dietrich Bonhoeffer (n.d. but probably the end of January 1939, in: *Dietrich Bonhoeffer Werke* (hereafter *DBW*) Vol. 15, p. 118: 'Von unserem Weekend beim Onkel [= Bell] sollte ich Dir natürlich sehr viele schöne Grüße sagen. Ich habe mich sehr wohl gefühlt. Das ist schon ein menschenwürdiges Dasein. Auch die Tante G. [= Henritta Bell] gefällt mir sehr. Die Kinder benahmen sich gottlob sehr gut. Onkel und Tante haben sich viel von ihnen vorsingen lassen und rühmen Mariannes pronunciation. Dieses lernen Kinder eben doch noch viel besser'. See Sabine Leibholz-Bonhoeffer, *Vergangen – erlebt – überwunden* (Gütersloh, 2005), pp. 128–9. On 28 August 1939 Bonhoeffer wrote to the Leibholzes: 'Fahrt doch eventuell noch mal zu George [Bell] wegen Eures Ferienaufenthaltes. Er kann Euch bestimmt gut beraten und Empfehlungen geben'. *DBW* 15, p. 261. Since the end of 1938 Bonhoeffer had been planning a journey to England (see *DBW* 15, pp. 93–4., 100, 117). He stayed there together with Eberhard Bethge from 13 March to 13 April and during that time met Bell; see *DBW* 15, pp. 156–64; see too Bethge, *Dietrich Bonhoeffer*, pp. 716–8; also Holger Roggelin, *Franz Hildebrandt. Ein lutherischer Dissenter im Kirchenkampf und Exil* (Göttingen, 1999), pp. 190–2. Their last meeting in Britain took place on 6 June when Bonhoeffer travelled on to the United States. See *DBW* 15, pp. 180–2. Returning to Britain he was able only to meet the family of his sister: a visit to Bell was impossible.

Bell to Leibholz, 15 November 1939, BA, N 1334 (typewritten)

My dear Leibholz,

Very many thanks for your letter and for the news of Dietrich.[1] Yes, I got your article about the German Church question[2], and was very glad to have it, and liked it, and also the letters, which are always a pleasure to receive.

I hope you and your wife and the two girls are well. I shall be very much interested to hear when you have more news of Dietrich. He cannot, as you say, be an Army Chaplain.[3]

Yours ever,

---

[1] See Eberhard Bethge and Ronald C. D. Jasper (ed.), *An der Schwelle zum gespaltenen Europa. Der Briefwechsel zwischen George Bell und Gerhard Leibholz 1939-1951* (Stuttgart, 1974), p. 14. Bethge and Jasper suspected that this news of Dietrich came via pastor Erwin Sutz in Zurich. Bonhoeffer himself was in Berlin from August to the end of October 1939, when the new term of the preachers' seminary at Sigurdshof began.
[2] 'National Socialism and the Church', in *The Contemporary Review*, 1939, No. 886, pp. 444–5, reprinted in Gerhard Leibholz, *Politics and Law* (Leyden, 1965), pp. 201–9. In his letter to Sabine Leibholz on 25 February 1941, Bonhoeffer wrote from Zürich, that this 'paper of 1939 has made a great impression on many people here'; *DBW* 16, p. 158 (erroneously note 13 here refers to Leibholz, 'Germany, the West and the Possibility of [a] New International Order').
[3] See Eberhard Bethge, *Dietrich Bonhoeffer*, pp. 748–9.

1940

12 March	The conclusion of the Soviet-Finnish war.
9 April	German forces invade Denmark and Norway.
9–10 May	German forces invade the Netherlands, Belgium and Luxembourg.
10 May	Winston Churchill becomes prime minister of Britain; Britain occupies Iceland.
15 May	The Dutch government surrenders. German forces now cross the Meuse into France.
19 May	German forces reach the English Channel.
28 May	The Belgian government surrenders.
9 June	Norwegian forces end hostilities.
10 June	The Italian government declares war on Britain and France.
14 June	German forces occupy Paris.
15 June	Soviet forces invade Lithuania.
22 June	France and Germany sign an armistice; Britain will fight on. France is now divided between an area governed by a collaborationist government under Marshall Petain and an area under direct German military occupation.
5 July	The Petain government breaks off relations with Britain.
25 August	Estonia, Latvia and Lithuania become incorporated into the Soviet Union.
2 September	The American and British governments arrange for 50 American destroyers to be given to Britain in return for military bases under 'Lend Lease'.
27 September	The governments of Germany, Italy and Japan sign a military and economic alliance in Berlin, creating a new Axis.
28 October	Italian forces invade Greece.
20–24 November	Hungary, Rumania and Slovakia sign 'protocols of adherence' with the Axis powers.

Bell to Leibholz, 24 January 1940, BA, N 1334 (typewritten)

My dear Leibholz,

I am ashamed of myself for not having written before now to thank you for your kind and most welcome letter.[1] I am greatly interested to hear of the invitation which you received from Oxford before Christmas to lecture about questions of democracy. I very much wonder whether you have actually gone forward with them. It would be an interesting experience if you were able to get the time for the work, with the other things you have to do.

I was talking the other day to the Professor of International Law at Cambridge, Dr. Gutteridge[2]. I told him about you, and if you are in Cambridge, he would be glad to see you. He said that in England little work has really been done on the subject of canon law. He wondered whether some of the German scholars who had come to this country were interested in that subject. I said I did not know but that I would bear it in mind, and I mentioned your special lines as known to me. He is of opinion that canon law had much more to do with English law than English lawyers usually acknowledged, and that there is a good deal of research work waiting to be done in this field. I thought I would just mention this matter in case in was of interest to you.

[. . .][3] letter marked 'please forward', it would get to me.

I am so happy about the Christmas tree being liked by the children. I do hope that you and Mrs. Leibholz and the children are well. It would be a great pleasure to see you all again one of these days. I often think of Dietrich. He is much in my mind and my thoughts. I appreciate your wishes for Christmas and the New Year. May I in my turn wish you and your wife and family a greater happiness.

Yours very sincerely,

[1] On 6–7 January 1939 Bell participated an ecumenical meeting in the Netherlands; see Armin Boyens, *Kirchenkampf und Ökumene 1939–1945: Darstellungen und Dokumentation unter besonderer Berücksichtigung der Quellen des Ökumenischen Rates der Kirchen* (Munich, 1973), pp. 66–77.
[2] Harold Cook Gutteridge (1876–1953), lawyer and Professor of Comparative Law at Cambridge University (1930–41).
[3] The last lines of the preceding page have been removed.

Bell to Leibholz, 15 February 1940, BA, N 1334 (typewritten)

My dear Leibholz,

Very many thanks for both your letters. Your first letter, in answer to my enquiry, was very valuable and I appreciate very much the point you make. I am very glad you had a conversation on these lines with Sir John Hope-Simpson,[1] from whom also, as it happens, I heard today.

I think it likely that I shall call a few Germans and Britishers to a small informal conversation on the matter in London, quite early in March, and I very much want you to come, for I am sure that exchange of views between like-minded Britishers and Germans on this subject would be very much to the good.

It is extremely good of you to think of my birthday. Yes, your wife and Dietrich and I have the same natal day;[2] it gives us an extra link, and I am very thankful for it.

I do so greatly appreciate what you say and your good wishes and your sympathy, and your prayers for a blessing. I feel that I don't deserve these things, but I am grateful all the more.

Yours very sincerely,

---

[1] Sir John Hope Simpson (1868–1961) was a Liberal politician and governmental administrator. He was widely known for his work on the question of refugees, a commitment which he shared with Bell. It is likely that the conversation to which Bell refers therefore concerns refugee matters. See, for example, Bell's maiden speech in the House of Lords, in *Hansard*, House of Lords Debates, Fifth Series, Vol. 110, cols. 1206–16 (27 July 1938); also his Lucien Wolf Memorial Lecture of 1 February 1939, reprinted in G.K.A. Bell, *The Church and Humanity 1939-1946* (London, 1946), pp. 1–21. For Bell's speech in the House of Lords on internment see Hansard, HL Deb., Vol. 116, cols. 543–8 (12 June 1940).
[2] 4 February.

Bell to Leibholz, 22 April 1940, BA, N 1334 (typewritten)

My dear Leibholz,

I am delighted to get your letter and the message from Dietrich.[1] Please give him, when you have the opportunity, my affectionate remembrance and the assurance of my deep fellowship with him and with his friends.

I should very much like to have an English translation of your memorandum on Dr. Visser 't Hooft's[2] article on *Germany and the West*.[3] I have read 't Hooft's article and I have seen Ehrenberg's comment upon it.[4] I should particularly value the sight of yours.

We did not get very far at our informal conference in London.[5] Two or three drafts have come in since, and I have had a talk with Visser 't Hooft about it. But at the moment there is a pause. I should very much like a talk with you one of these days about the situation generally. If we cannot arrange it before, perhaps we could meet on Sunday morning, June 9th, when I am in St. Leonards for a Church Parade with the Royal Air Force at 10.00. I could, I think, get to see you at your address fairly soon after 11.00, before going on to Battle. If I see a prospect of an earlier meeting all the better. I am actually in Battle itself for an Ordination on Trinity Sunday, May 19th at 11.00. but I do not know whether it will be possible to meet anywhere that afternoon.

I am delighted to have the copy of your letter to *Onlooker*. Unfortunately I did not listen that evening. But what you tell me of this Broadcast is most refreshing and I am quite sure that he will be greatly encouraged not only by the gratitude, which you show in your letter to him, but by the reasoning, which your letter contains, which is unanswerable. On the strength of your letter I am venturing to write Mr Birkett[6] myself. I did have something to do with him two or three years ago.

With warmest greetings to your wife and you and the girls from Mrs. Bell and myself,

Yours very sincerely,

1. Dietrich Bonhoeffer was staying in Berlin from 15 March to the beginning of May 1940.
2. Willem A. Visser 't Hooft (1900–85), Dutch theologian who became a leading figure in the international Student Christian movement, became the first Secretary General of the WCC (in Process of Formation) in 1938 and the first secretary general of the WCC in 1948. He retired in 1966. According to his letter to Bell on 24 February 1940, Visser 't Hooft planned to stay in London on 7, 8 and 11 March 1940; Gerhard Besier, Besier, *Intimately Associated for many Years: George K.A. Bell's and Willem A. Visser 't Hooft's Common Life-Work in the Service of the Church Universal – Mirrored in their Correspondence* (Part One, Newcastle upon Tyne: Cambridge Scholars Publishing, 2015), p. 182. But on 13 March he met Leibholz and Carl Schweitzer; see B.W. Colls to Leibholz, 8 March 1940 and also Leibholz's answer, 9 March 1940; WCC 303_35_8_6.
3. See 'Germany, the West and the Possibility of a New International Order', reprinted in Leibholz, *Politics and Law*, pp. 154–73. In his letter to Sabine Leibholz, 25 February 1941, Bonhoeffer wrote from Zürich, that this paper 'has made a great impression on many people here'; *DBW* 16, p. 158.
4. See 'Germany and the West', WCC 301_9_1; see too Boyens, *Kirchenkampf und Ökumene*, pp. 200–1. Hans Ehrenberg (1883–1958) finished his studies as Dr. rer. pol. in 1902 and Dr. phil. in 1909 and was awarded his postdoctoral university teaching qualification in 1910 at Heidelberg University. He converted to the protestant Church in 1909, studied Theology in 1922–4 and became pastor at Bochum in 1925. After the passing of racial legislation in 1933 he lost his university position and, subsequently, his pastor's office in 1937. After 'Kristallnacht' in November 1938 he was incarcerated in Sachsenhausen for five months but with Bell's assistance he emigrated to Britain in the following year. Ehrenberg went on to work for the WCC and in 1943–5 he taught at the new philosophical institute in London. In 1947 he would return to Germany. See Hartmut Ludwig and Eberhard Röhm (eds.), *Evangelisch getauft – als "Juden" verfolgt. Theologen jüdischer Herkunft in der Zeit des Nationalsozialismus. Ein Gedenkbuch* (Stuttgart, 2014), pp. 86–7. (p. 410: Literature).
5. See Bell to Leibholz, 15 February 1940.
6. William Norman Birkett (1883–1962), Liberal politician, Methodist lay preacher and eminent British barrister. Birkett would be appointed to the High Court of Justice in 1941, joining the King's Bench Division. During the Nuremberg Trials he served as the alternate British judge. He became 1st Baron Birkett in 1957.

Bell to Sabine Leibholz, 13 May (1940), BA, N 1334 (handwritten)

My dear Mrs Leibholz,

Thank you for your letter. I feel very much for you.[1] And I do hope that soon those so absolutely loyal to England as your husband may be freed.

I shall be with you on Sunday after three. Love to the girls

Yours very sincerely,

1. On 12 May 1940 Gerhard Leibholz had been interned at Huyton camp; see Leibholz-Bonhoeffer, *Vergangen*, pp. 152–4; see Charmian Brinson, 'Please Tell the Bishop of Chichester: George Bell and the Internment Crisis of 1940', in Andrew Chandler, *The Church and Humanity: The Life and Work of George Bell, 1883–1958* (Farnham, 2012), pp. 77–88.

Bell to Sabine Leibholz, 19 June 1940, BA, N 1334 (typewritten)

My dear Mrs. Leibholz,

Many thanks for your letter of the 16th June, written from Willand.[1] I am trying to find out where you are; I fancy it is Oxford, and I hope this may reach you. I had a letter from your husband today in which he asks me to give you news of him, and to [say] that he is well,* though of course you and I know the difficulties under which he labours through being interned.

I was in Bloomsbury House² yesterday and saw Miss Bracey³, and a deputation is waiting on the Home Secretary very shortly, led by Miss Rathbone⁴, a member of Parliament. There is a possibility of a few persons being released in special categories,⁵ and I am doing what I can to put your husband's case once again before the Home Secretary. If you are in position to go to America, so far as the visa is concerned, I should say that it was far wiser for you to go. This would make it possible for your husband to be released and start afresh. What facts have you got with regard to the particulars of the application? It is a point which we could take up personally with the Consul. Is it the situation that you could get a visa now by applying for it on your husband's behalf, and that the visa would have four months validity from the date of being granted? Would it cover you and your husband and children? I believe he is in the Isle of Man. I do myself think it would be wise in all the circumstances to take this chance.

Yours very sincerely,

[*] ªHis words are 'Give her my sincerest love and, please, tell her that I am very well'.ª

1. A village in Devon where the Leibholz family stayed for some weeks while Gerhard Leibholz was interned; see Leibholz-Bonhoeffer, *Vergangen*, pp. 157–8. Afterwards Sabine Leibholz and the children moved to Oxford.
2. Bloomsbury House was at this time the seat of a number of welfare organizations for the refugees such as the Jewish Refugee Committee, the Church of England Committee for Non-Aryan Christians, the Catholic Committee for Refugees from Germany and the Refugee Children's Movement.
3. Bertha Bracey (1893–1989), British Quaker. In 1933 Bracey had become the Secretary of the Germany Emergency Committee whose relief work provided support for political prisoners and for Christians who were partly of Jewish background (often in Britain called 'non-Aryan' Christians). In London the Germany Emergency Committee (later renamed the Friends Committee for Refugees and Aliens) was at first based at Friends House. In February 1939 the Committee had moved to Bloomsbury House. An outstanding example of Bracey's many activities came with the 'Kindertransport' of 1938–9, which saved 10,000 German children of Jewish descent, but she also saved the lives of many children left in German concentration camps after the war.
4. Eleanor Florence Rathbone (1872–1946); independent member M.P. for the Combined English Universities (1929–46) who set up the Parliamentary Committee on Refugees in 1938. A life-long social reformer she was also instrumental in advancing the political rights of women.
5. The internees were categorized as A-cases (a high security risk), B-cases (some doubts about loyalty and therefore still subject to restrictions), C-cases (no doubts; clearly the refugees of Nazi racial or political persecution).

Bell to Sabine Leibholz, 24 June 1940, BA, N 1334 (typewritten)

My dear Mrs Leibholz,

I have more than one of your letters to acknowledge but my time has been very fully occupied. I am keeping a special watch for a favourable moment to make a special application for especial terms for your husband. You will I know understand that in the present grave position it is not easy to expect much, but I have good hopes that my opportunity will come. Meantime I know that you will do your best to have patience and courage. The weather is good and the Isle of Man is a very good climate.

Both things to be glad for. Also I believe things will be more comfortable there.[1] I am afraid only men in 'key' positions have been released so far.

Your letter about the American Visa has just come. I think that we must have a little patience until we hear from your husband whether he wishes to apply or not. And then we shall have to see if the boats will book passages or not.

Have good courage, dear friend, God has kept you and yours so far and you must trust him.

Always yours sincerely,

---

[1] At the meeting of the Church of England Committee for Non-Aryan Christians, 14 June 1940, Bell 'reported that he had seen the Dean of Liverpool [Frederick William Dwelly] who was much concerned about conditions at the Huyton camp. He had urged that the local Medical Officer of Health should be called in to inspect the sanitation, and that arrangements should be made for the publication of an official news sheet to counteract the alarming spread of rumours. The Dean has expressed his willingness personally to finance and organize the distribution of such [a] sheet. The Chairman [Bell] also raised the question of pastoral ministration in the camps. He hoped that the German pastors now interned would be distributed so as to provide at least one minister for each camp. He also suggested that a pastor and his wife might do valuable work in the women's camp.' Minutes of the meeting of 14 June 1940, Bell Papers Vol. 35, fols. 151–3.

Bell to Sabine Leibholz, 26 July 1940, BA, N 1334 (typewritten)

ªMyª dear Mrs. Leibholz,

Many thanks for your letters. I have just received one from your husband which he asks me to hand to you. So here it is. I don't think it would be sufficient to give you legal authority, for that has to be done through a solicitor, with a regular form giving power of attorney, but it may be sufficient for immediate purposes.

The party of Pastors' wives[1] was held yesterday at the German Church in Montpelier Place, London. But I found that only those who lived in London were invited; there were about fifty or sixty people present; it was not possible to extend the invitation to those from a distance. I told those present something about the conditions in the Camp.[2] It would have been very nice to have seen you, had you been there, but you will understand the difficulties once people outside London are invited.

With regard to your husband's health. He seemed to me to be pretty well, but undoubtedly there is everything to be said for his release, and this is being pressed constantly to the Home Office authorities. I realize what your father says, and I hope we shall not have to wait long for a Home Office decision.

Yours ªveryª sincerely,

---

[1] The wives of 'non-Aryan' Christian pastors were now interned by the British government.
[2] On 18 July Bell had visited the internment camps on the Isle of Man. See Bell Papers, Vol. 51 (1), fols. 229–348, esp. fol. 231: Bell to the Revd. C.C. Griffiths, 23 July 1940: 'I had a very good day at Huyton on Thursday [18 July], from 11 a.m. to 8 p.m. and saw about fifty people, including, of course, Oelsner, Gordon, Thur, Ehrhardt, Hopf, Krebs, Leibholz, Ehrenberg, Schweitzer, Majut, Carlebach, and many more. They were, except Hopf, and to a lesser extent Leibholz, well. And they were patient too; but one could not resist the feeling of injustice about it all. I am going to meet the wives and relatives of some of the interned men on Thursday at the German Church, Montpelier Place.

I am also going to the Isle of Man at the weekend to see the Women's Camp and the Men's Camp.' Bell Papers, Vol. 278: Huyton, July 18, 1940, remembering Leibholz (fol. 13) and Ehrenberg (fol. 14). See too Hildebrandt's report on Bell's visit in: Leibholz-Bonhoeffer, *Vergangen*, pp. 166–7. Beside Leibholz the mentioned 'non-Aryan' persons were pastors or students of theology; see Ludwig and Röhm, *Christlich getauft*, pp. 72–3, 86–7, 88–9, 134–5, 184–5, 230–1, 260–1, 318–19, 346–7.

Bell to Leibholz, 3 August 1940, BA, N 1334 (handwritten)

My dear Leibholz

I am overjoyed.[1] May God bless you, and yours, and keep you all safe, well, and together. I am just back from the Isle of Man.[2]

Yours ever,

[1] On 26 July 1940 Leibholz was released; see Leibholz-Bonhoeffer, *Vergangen*, p. 168.
[2] Bell's second visit to the Isle of Man internment camps, 28–31 July. In the House of Lords Bell criticized the internment of refugees on 6 August 1940: Hansard, Vol. 117, cols. 120–8; reprinted in Bell, *The Church and Humanity*, pp. 38–47; see in particular pp. 41–3.

Bell to Leibholz, 10 August 1940, BA, N 1334 (typewritten)

My dear Leibholz,

Very many thanks for your letter. I am so happy that you are free and re-united. I do understand what you say about U.S.A. and I think it is well for Paton[1] to start the enquiries. With regard to the fellow internees about whom you write, I am writing to the Dean of Liverpool[2] as he is on the spot. I think that what is wanted is speeding up the applications for release, if it has already been recommended by the Camp Medical Officer. I appreciate the point about "B" cases.[3]

If you have reflections to offer me, which would impress the Release Committee presided over by Mr. Justice Asquith[4], whom I am seeing on Wednesday, as to Grounds of Release, I should be very grateful for them. I want, of course, particularly to stress the point that a refugee has a legal status of his own and very different from that of an enemy alien and that internment should be the exception rather than the rule. I wonder whether you have precedents which could be usefully put, or arguments from the constitutional or political, or any other angle, which might weigh.

Please give the enclosed letter to Irmgard Behr.[5] Please give my love [a]and my wife's[a] to your wife and daughters.

Yours ever,

[1] William 'Bill' Paton (1886–1943) served as the first secretary of the National Christian Council of India, 1922–6. He then succeeded J. H. Oldham as secretary of the International Missionary Council (1927–43), as the latter became more involved with the Life and Work movement. Paton played a vital role in the creation of the WCC and in 1939 became secretary alongside W.A. Visser 't Hooft. Paton's premature death in 1943, at the height of his career, came as he was participating in discussions about the reconstruction of Europe.
[2] Frederick William Dwelly (1881–1957), with whom Bell had developed a close rapport.

3. That is, cases where there may only be some doubts about loyalty and where some restrictions still applied.
4. Cyril Asquith, since 1951 Baron Asquith of Bishopstone (1890–1954), Justice of the King's Bench 1938–46.
5. Irmgard Behr had worked for Pastor Gerhard Jacobi in the offices of the Protestant Church in Berlin and was now a refugee in Britain.

Leibholz to Bell, 20 August 1940, Bell Papers 30, fol. 172 (typewritten)

My Lordbishop,

I thank you very much for your letter and your enquiry in Huyton you kindly made on behalf of the five ill people. Cohnstaedt[1] was released two days ago and I hope the others will follow soon. I wrote to them that the remainder of 'medical cases' will be now settled speedily.

Gordon wrote to me this morning that the brethren you invited, my Lordbishop, to come over with their families are going to be grouped together for release.[2] May I tell you in this connection, confidentially and openly, that I have doubts in the political reliability of Wegner[3]. You will understand, my Lordbishop, that it is very painful for me to tell this, particularly as he is also a colleague of mine and I have nothing against him personally, but I feel bound to do so with regard to our friendship and for the sake of the common cause. Your goodness and generosity are so great that it would be a cause for serious worry for me if you should be disappointed in future in any way. I became acquainted with Wegner not before Huyton, but I know that his former political attitude was ªalsoª rather labil [unstable] and strange. In any case, I think you must know this and I may assure you this is not only my personal view.

I am very glad to know that the notes I sent you on your request, my Lordbishop, were not quite useless. Mr T. S. Eliot[4] wrote to me a few days ago that he will make some use of a letter I sent Dr. Oldham[5] about this matter in the next issue of the *Christian News-Letter*.

As to the White paper of the Home Office there is perhaps possible a comparison. The new regulation is based on the utilitarian principle to release a small number of refugees who might be useful to this country. No scope is left to deal with the case of internees according to their loyalty. In Germany of today the Jews, for instance, who are engaged with war work are being kept separated from other workers and wear an armlet with the inscription 'Useful Jew'. Is this not the same principle?[6]

We are so thankful to be reunited and are daily thinking of you. Particularly I am so deeply grateful that the heavy mental strain has been taken from my wife by your great help.

Yours most sincerely,

1. Unidentified.
2. The White Paper on Release from Internment proposed new categories: Category 18 (Cases of extreme hardship) and Category 19 (public and prominent activity against the Nazi system). (See Bell Papers Vol. 31, fol. 343; see too Bell to Sir Cecil J. B. Hurst, 3 October 1940, in which he presents a table of 37 applicants, none of them ministers of religions, for release under Category 19. Category 16 was definitely intended to exclude German pastors of German congregations in this country. See Memorandum, ibid, fol. 117; see too Bell to H.P. van Dusen, 29 August 1940, Bell Papers Vol. 30, fol. 209: 'Kahle, Leibholz, and Ehrenberg, are the three most urgent cases'.

³ Arthur Wegner (1900–89) was the professor of criminal law at Breslau University (1926–34) and – transferred for disciplinary reasons – Halle University (1934–7). Wegner lost his position because of his 'non-Aryan' wife and emigrated in 1938 to Britain; here, and later in Canada, he was interned. From the 1920s to 1939 Wegner had pursued theological studies to become a missionary, and in 1942 he converted to Roman Catholicism. In 1946 he would return to Germany where he became professor at Münster University. In 1963 he took a position again at Halle University, now in the German Democratic Republic.

⁴ Thomas Stearns Eliot (1888–1965), American-born poet, critic and playwright, was at this time living in Oxford. He had become a British citizen in 1927 and subsequently became an Anglican. Bell knew Eliot well.

⁵ Joseph Houldsworth Oldham (1874–1969); prodigious Scottish missionary who played a major role in the formation of the WCC. At the end of the First World War he was a Secretary of the Emergency Committee of Co-operating Missions, chaired by John R. Mott, before becoming Secretary of the International Missionary Council, 1921–38. In 1934–8 he was also chairman of the research department of Life and Work and in 1942–7 head of a further, British-based body, the Christian Frontier Council. From 1938 to 1947 he convened 'The Moot', a Christian think tank concentrating on the problem of post-war reconstruction. In 1939–49, he was the editor of the *Christian Newsletter*.

⁶ This paragraph is marked by a pencil line at left.

Bell to Leibholz, 23 August 1940, BA, N 1334 (postcard, handwritten)

Very many thanks for your letter of 20th. I quite agree about our friend W. I have not included him in the list of those for whom I am appealing. Indeed before he was interned he told me that he would regard internment as the best thing for him if he could not get to China. I am grateful too for your pointing out the tragic similarity between the government line and the '*useful* Jew'.

All best remembrances to your wife¹

¹ An addition on the top of the card.

Liffman to Leibholz, 15 September 1940, BA, N 1334 (telegram)

NIEBUHR¹ ARRANGED POSITION THEOLOGICAL SCHOOL LETTER FOLLOWS TRANSFER MY ACCOUNT TO HOLMES PERSONALLY I CABLE HIM INSTRUCTIONS = LIFFMAN +

¹ Reinhold Niebuhr (1892–1971) had since 1928 lectured at the Union Theological Seminary, New York, becoming in 1930 Professor of Applied Christianity there. Niebuhr had urged Bonhoeffer to migrate to the United States and helped Paul Tillich to do so.

Bell to Leibholz, 7 October 1940, BA, N 1334 (handwritten)

My dear Leibholz,

You and your wife will I know be happy to see this telegram from Dietrich, which arrived last night.¹ I have replied –

'Sister husband and children all well Oxford stop pastors well though several away from home² please give inquirer affectionate greetings, reaffirming ecumenical faith and fellowship'

It is a precious link, and I am most thankful it is so strong!
Greetings and remembrance to you all

Yours very sincerely,

[1] W. A. Visser 't Hooft to Bell, 6 October 1940, BA, N 1334 (telegram), printed in: *DBW* 16, p. 64.
[2] The pastors were interned mostly as B-cases in camps and would be released in the next few weeks.

Leibholz to Bell, no date (October 1940), BA, N 1334 (handwritten draft on the back of Visser 't Hooft's telegram; fragment)

My Lordbishop,

We were really very happy indeed to have your letter and the telegram from Dietrich and are deeply moved by your great kindness. We are so thankful that these bonds of firm friendship and fellowship based on a common faith and sympathy are stronger than all destructive forces which are unloaded in this time. I trust that in better days, which are to come, the new life will be built up on these only [solid] grounds in this world.

We are just moving to 100 B[unbury] Road and I [will] write to you again shortly.

Bell to Leibholz, 22 October 1940, BA, N 1334 (handwritten)

My dear Leibholz

Just a line to thank you warmly for your letter, your news of the two girls (tell me about their fees)[1] and your inquiries about my wife and myself. We have just moved house,[2] and now have our own books and furniture, which is more like home. And we are both very well.

Oelsner[3] is free.

No news got of Hildebrandt[4] & Rieger[5] but *I hope*; and am confident of Hildebrandt anyhow.[6]

Do please send me the memorandum when ready.[7]

I have further news of possibilities in U.S.A. but I am not very sure how practical they are. Miss Roberts will write to you.

Warmest greetings from us both to you all.

Yours vy. sincerely,

[1] Marianne and Christiane had just been admitted to the Oxford High School for Girls.
[2] The Bells had now moved to 22 The Droveway, Hove, near Brighton.
[3] Willy Oelsner (1897–1983) served as minister at St. Thomas in Berlin 1932–8 moving because of his Jewish descent and his ecclesiastical views. In 1939 he emigrated to Britain. He was re-ordained as an Anglican priest in December 1940 by Bell. In 1941–50 he was curate at St. Andrews in Brighton and in 1950–71 at the Holy Trinity Church in Hove.
[4] Franz Hildebrandt (1909–85) had met Bonhoeffer in 1927; in 1933 they worked closely together against the German Christians. It was because of his Jewish descent that in 1933 Hildebrandt became pastor to Bonhoeffer's German parish at Forest Hill, London. Back in Germany in 1934, he worked in the Confessing Church, also lecturing at the theological college at Berlin in 1935.

In 1937 he immigrated to Britain, becoming a curate to Julius Rieger in London. Between 1939 and 1946 Hildebrandt served as pastor to the Refugee Congregation at Cambridge. In 1944–6 he was district secretary of the British and Foreign Bible Society. Hildebrandt later became an eminent Methodist.

[5] Julius Rieger (1901–84) was pastor of St. George's German Lutheran Church at London, 1930–53. Influenced by Bonhoeffer he took the side of the Confessing Church and mobilized the German parishes of London against the Deutsche Christen-dominated Reichskirche and its Foreign Office, under Bishop Heckel. After Bonhoeffer's return to Germany Rieger was the 'principal source of all information to the churches in this country about the church struggle', as Bell remembered in 1939. Together with Bell he helped 'non-Aryan' pastors and others to remain in his parish. After the war he was directed by the German Evangelical Church (EKD) to serve as supervisor of the spiritual welfare of German Prisoners of War in British camps.

[6] As an internee Hildebrandt was placed in Category B because of his relations with Rieger, who found himself placed in Category A. On his third visit to Huyton in September 1940 Bell found only Franz Hildebrandt in the internment camp. He was released on 17 November 1940. See Roggelin, *Franz Hildebrandt*, pp. 195–7.

[7] The translation of 'Germany, the West and the Possibility of a new International Order'; see Bell to Leibholz, 22 April 1940.

Bell to Leibholz, 3 November 1940, BA, N 1334 (handwritten)

My dear Leibholz,

Just a line to enclose the *Hansard*[1]. My only copy, so please let me have it back when done with (no special hurry). I had a good talk with Miss Roberts[2] about the USA offer on Friday. She is consulting Paton – and we are asking USA for more facts before advising acceptance.

I wrote to Mrs. Adams.

All best wishes. All well here.

Yours always,

I am sending you my *Penguin*[3] this week.

[1] Hansard, H.L. Deb., 5 s., Vol. 117 (6 August 1940); for Bell's speech in the debate about internment of aliens, see cols. 120–8.
[2] Helen Roberts was secretary of the Church of England Committee for Non-Aryan Christians in Bloomsbury House. Bell brought her from the Chichester diocese.
[3] G.K.A. Bell, *Christianity and World Order* (Harmondsworth, 1940). This was the first 'Penguin Special'. See too Philip Coupland, 'George Bell, the Question of Germany and the Cause of European Unity, 1939–1950', in Chandler, *The Church and Humanity: The Life and Work of George Bell*, pp. 109–28.

Leibholz to Bell, 12 November 1940, Bell Papers 40, fols. 1–2 (handwritten); BA, N 1334 (copy)

My Lordbishop,

I did not write to you before, because I wanted to read your book, my Lordbishop, first. I read it in the last few days not only with great admiration but also with a deep sense of gratitude that this book has been published just now and has been written just by you, my Lordbishop. It is the most important book I read about the whole matter up-to-now and I pray that this book may also be the stimulus to the realization of our hopes for building up a new world order and for creating a stronger Christian unity than before.¹

I am in complete agreement with you, my Lordbishop, about the issue and the analysis of the present world crisis and the conditions in which Europe finds itself today. Particularly, I agree ᵇwithᵇ if you emphasize, that we have to be aware that Christianity also means a translation from the spiritual into the material. It is a great and fatal mistake indeed, made also by many churchmen, that it might be possible to keep religion out of public life. In truth, the Church cannot afford today to live in self-contained seclusion and to limit its activities to the proclamation of the Gospel, as the totalitarian States would like them to do.

On the contrary, the Christian church must be a political reality and have to will to make itself absolute, also in the actual life of today. It must reach into the realities of life here below. There is no sphere of life, which can refuse this claim of the Church. In other words, as you, my Lordbishop accentuate, Christians must apply the principles of their faith to the actual problems of life and 'live the Christian life', and that just now according to the commandments of the Gospel. We have to be a witness to our belief in God and our love of our neighbour. I remember the last pronouncement of the Confessional Church before the outbreak of war: 'The Christian is not a private matter, nor does it occupy some particular part of the life and heart of man. God's word claims the whole man'.²

The whole situation would probably not be today so critical as it is, if there were more boldness and less weakness and opportunism in the organised Church too. These general human³ shortcomings are here of special weight and have a more resounding effect. Therefore, to my mind, one of the most urgent problems in this connection is in future that of selection and to put the best men in the right places.

Further, I should like to add to your arguments about modern secularism another one:

I agree with you, my Lordbishop, that it is not possible to identify Christianity with Western Civilisation – in spite of the fact that Christianity is the basis of modern civilisation too. For, in a long run, the secular character of modern civilisation is responsible for the situation of today. I think, the totalitarian anti-liberal State is to a certain extent the continuation of the secularising process which began in the Renaissance and in humanism, passed through the age of enlightenment and of natural law and reached its earlier development in politics, in liberal democracy. That was, therefore, no accident that at the time of the emergence of the bourgeoisie, in the 18th and 19th centuries, the secularising process together with the liberation of reason had led to some conflict with Christianity, and that at that time the Christian churches were often the rallying-point for action against the forces of enlightenment, nationalism⁴ and humanism.

But the present situation presents in so far a graver conflict as the increasing secularisation in the totalitarian states has called in question also the basic principles of humanism, nationalism and political liberalism no less than that⁵ of Christianity itself. The secularisation of Christian thought was formerly bound to Christianity in so far as there was a belief in the unity of the human species and spirit, but now it is just this decisive belief, which is questioned by the new radical secularisation and the increasing materialism of modern thought. This is why Christianity and modern Western civilisation hold common ground to a certain extent today.

As to the question of Germany and the West, I tried to point out in a memorandum what I think it would be perhaps right to say to the admirable paper of Dr Visser 't Hooft.[6] It was just finished when I was interned. I enclose it as I do not know whether you ever received it. It may perhaps be of interest to you. I am going to make a few supplements and additions to this memorandum, but I think now after having read your book to re-write the whole part about the future international order – under the new aspect you, my Lordbishop, have given us.

May I thank you at the same time for your last letter which deeply moved me again by your great goodness I know I do not deserve. I can hardly tell you how greatly I appreciate your kindness. I am so glad to know that it is possible to clear up the open questions before we shall take a final decision.[7] I was hesitating to make a similar proposal, i.e. not to press the matter, but I thought it would not be possible to delay the answer without looking impolite or ungrateful. I do not know, whether it is right, my Lordbishop, to write to the Dean[8] now and to thank him for the invitation, meanwhile, or to wait until we shall have received an answer and we shall be able to overlook the whole matter better.

In any case I should very much like to keep up the contact with the World Council in the present form or in another one, because I feel I am intimately attached to the work of the World Council. I should be glad and grateful if this could be arranged.

My wife who is, unfortunately, very ill the last few days, gives Mrs Bell and you, my Lordbishop, her warmest greetings and remembrances.

Yours ever,

---

[1] See Leibholz, 'Christianity and World Order', Appendix 1 here.
[2] The source of this quotation is unknown, but corresponds strikingly to the Theological Declaration of Barmen, 31 May 1934.
[3] Copy omits: human.
[4] Possibly a copy mistake and typed instead of rationalism; see the translation of Bethge and Jasper, *Briefwechsel*, p. 19.
[5] Copy: 'those'.
[6] See Bell to Leibholz, 22 April 1940.
[7] See Bell to Leibholz, 3 November 1940.
[8] Angus Dun (1891–1971) was a tutor, assistant professor and professor of theology at Episcopal Theological School, Cambridge, Mass., USA, 1920–40. As Dean (1940–4) he invited Leibholz to come to Cambridge. Between 1940 and 1962 he was Bishop of the Episcopal Diocese of Washington in Washington, DC.

Bell to Leibholz, 20 November 1940, BA NL 1334 (typewritten); Bell Papers 40, fol. 3 (carbon)

My dear Leibholz,

I am much touched by your kind and most interesting letter about my *Penguin*. I am very much flattered that you should think so well of it. I do so strongly agree with what you say; and further the fresh argument which you add to mine about modern secularism. I am very glad to have your memorandum and to think that is possible that you may find some of the remarks in my book of service in a revision.

I will let you know, of course, as soon as I hear from Dean Angus Dun. I think it would be a good plan if you were to write a friendly letter to the Dean now and thank him for the invitation and saying that you understand that I have written to him for the elucidation of some matters of importance and therefore you are waiting before writing quite definitely, but that you are much attracted by the post and would like to come if it could be arranged.

I do hope your wife is better. Mrs Bell and I send you all our warmest remembrances.

Yours very sincerely,

Bell to Leibholz, 18 December 1940, BA, N 1334 (handwritten)

My dear Leibholz

I am so very sorry your wife has had measles. I do hope she is well again now, and you also. Don't worry about asking Mr. Griffiths[1] – it is perfectly right; and I understand your feelings. I am seeing what I can do about Mr. Horrwitz[2]. It would help very much if some very well known German lawyer could write about his qualifications as a legal scholar. Would *you* write a memo. about him which I could forward? and does Dr. Alfred Kauffmann[3] know him? His word might help. One wants to make the dossier as strong as possible.

May God be with you and your wife & Dietrich & the girls this Christmas.

Yours ªveryª sincerely,

---

[1] Cuthbert Griffiths, a firm local ally of Bell, was Rector of Christ Church, St. Leonards on Sea, Rural Dean of Hastings and secretary of the Committee for Non-Aryan Refugee Pastors.
[2] It is unclear whether Bell here refers to Rechtsanwälte Hugo Horrwitz or Dr. Walter Horrwitz from Berlin.
[3] Dr. Alfred Kauffmann, a board member of the Association of Jewish Refugees in Great Britain which came to life in June 1941.

1941

1 March	German forces occupy Bulgaria.
11 March	Lend-Lease is approved by President Roosevelt.
25 March	The German government extends its theatre of war beyond Iceland.
27 March	Coup d'état in Yugoslavia by anti-Axis forces; by 5 April a pact has been signed with the Soviet Union.
6 April	German forces invade Yugoslavia and Greece; on 17 April Yugoslavia capitulates; on 27 April German forces occupy Athens.
27 May	Roosevelt declares a state of 'unlimited national emergency' after all remaining foreign diplomats are ordered to leave Paris and the S.S. *Robin Moor* is sunk in the Atlantic.
18 June	The German and Turkish governments sign a ten-year pact of friendship at Ankara.
22 June	German forces invade the Soviet Union and the German and Italian governments declare war; the governments of Finland, Hungary and Albania declare war against the Soviet Union on 26, 27 and 28 June while other Axis client states proceed to break off diplomatic relations with it.
12 July	The British and Soviet governments sign a mutual assistance agreement in Moscow.
2 August	The governments of the United States and the Soviet Union exchange notes undertaking economic assistance.
14 August	Churchill and Roosevelt announce the Atlantic Charter.
4 September	The USS *Greer* becomes the first American ship to fire on a German vessel.
17 November	Congress repeals articles of the 1939 Neutrality Act.
6 December	The British government declares war on Finland, Hungary and Rumania.
7 December	Japanese forces attack Pearl Harbor; the Japanese government declares war on the United States and Britain. A day later the governments of the United States and Britain declare war on Japan.
11 December	The governments of Germany and Italy declare war on the United States; Washington reciprocates.

Leibholz to Bell, 14 January 1941, Bell Papers 40, fol. 4 (typewritten); BA, N 1334 (copy)

My dear Lordbishop,

May I ask you for your advice again. At the beginning of October last the Editor of the *Journal of Education* wrote to me at my inquiry that he would be very glad to publish an article on 'Christianity, Totalitarianism and Democracy'[1], which I wrote on about the same lines as the contribution I made to our discussion at our meeting in June last.[2]

Today I have a letter from him saying that he has so many articles in hand that he cannot make any definitive promise as to date of publication but that he would be glad if he could hold the article for some time longer.

As I have [had] twice the experience that it is not unusual definitely to accept articles or even to ask for them and then later to say that it would still take some time until publication were possible and finally to return the Ms. (The paper shortage may contribute to this practice) I do not know whether this letter is to mean the same. In this case I would be very sorry as, in the meantime, I refused in view of the editor's acceptance two other possibilities of having published the article in *Hibbert Journal* and Dawson's *Review*.

Therefore, I should very much like to ask you whether you would kindly drop a line to the Editor and tell him how things stand. I feel sure that if the Editor realizes that you, my Lordbishop, are taking an interest in the matter he will publish the article soon. I venture to trouble you with the matter as you had the chair when I made my humble contribution. I should be very grateful to you, my Lordbishop.

As to the study about 'The internment policy and the Refugee problem'[3] I had recently a letter from the Editor of the *American Journal of International Law* saying that he would be very glad if he could have the Paper. Under the present circumstances I think this will be the best solution.

Yours ever,

The Editor of the Journal of Education is E. Salter Davies, CBE, MA (address: 40 Walton Crescent, Oxford)[4].

---

[1] Not published, but contained in 'Christianity, Politics and Power' in Leibholz, *Politics and Law*, pp. 91–132.
[2] According to Bethge and Jasper (*Briefwechsel*, p. 21), this was not the meeting announced in Bell's letter to Leibholz, 22 April 1940, but a meeting of the German pastors in Britain.
[3] A manuscript later published in a Festschrift for Ernst Rabel on his seventieth birthday, 1944; in German under the title 'Die völkerrechtliche Stellung der Refugees im Kriege'; in *Christian Fellowship in Wartime* Bulletin 1948, Nr. 18, pp. 2–4; in part reprinted in Leibholz, *Politics and Law*, pp. 314–16.
[4] Ernest Salter Davies (1872–1955), Welsh teacher, editor of the *Journal of Education*, a man much involved in the work of several trusts and institutions.

Leibholz to Reinhold Niebuhr, 2 February 1941, Bell Papers 40, fol. 6 (copy)

Dear Professor Niebuhr,

Not before yesterday I received your letter 16th December and that of Dr. Johnson[1]. I deeply regret their contents, as I was rather optimistic about the chances of getting a

Fellowship after all I heard from you and a few colleagues of former German nationality. I felt the more sure as there was to read in our papers a few months ago that not two but [a] hundred Fellowships should newly be granted to refugees. I do not think to be mistaken supposing that among the German refugees who may have been consulted by Dr. Johnson one or another may have been opposed to the granting a Fellowship to me owing to my divergent political, religious and learned views on many phenomena of the present world crisis.[2]

If Dr. Johnson is writing 'that there are at least a dozen whose claims are stronger than my own ones' I may perhaps say that I was professor designatus in Berlin before Hitler came to power (and that was the best academic position which was possible to get for my subject) and that at the age of 31 when I held the professorship at Göttingen and that a considerable part of my works has been translated in more than twelve languages. I doubt whether among the refugees who form the staff of the New School today [there] are many people who are in a position to base their claims on stronger academic and learned reasons than I put forward. But there may be other reasons as, for instance, such of humanitarian kind, which may have been of more weight for the decision Dr. Johnson has taken. This seems to me to be confirmed by the fact that I just heard from a young scientist who is staying at Oxford and is well known to me that he got such a fellowship. He was formerly a lecturer in Germany but has his family in America.

I thank you that you will kindly keep on trying. May I say that a few friends of former German nationality who have now got posts over there are prepared to give you all help they can give in case you need them. These are Professor J. Franck, Chicago, University (Physicist)[3]; Professor M. Rheinstein, University, Chicago (Lawyer)[4]; Prof. A. Bergstraesser, California (Historian)[5]; Prof. K. Loewenstein, Amherst College, Amherst (Political Science)[6].

Yours sincerely,

---

[1] Very likely Mordecai Johnson (1891–1976), pastor and preacher, influential educationalist and the first African American President of Howard University in Washington, D. C., from 1926 to 1960.

[2] See Bell to Paton, 23 January 1941, Bell Papers 24 (I), fol. 444: 'I am sending my latest letter from *Leibholz*. He seems to think there is some personal difficulty with regard to himself and the Rockefeller Foundation, on account of a colleague of his. Niebuhr has encouraged him to hope.'

[3] James Franck (1882–1964) was a German physicist who won the 1925 Nobel Prize for Physics with Gustav Hertz. In 1920, he became professor of experimental physics and Director of the Second Institute for Experimental Physics at Göttingen University while Max Born held the chair of theoretical physics. In 1933 he resigned his position in protest against the dismissal of fellow academics although he, as a veteran of the First World War, was exempt from the Law for the Restoration of the Professional Civil Service. After a year at the Niels Bohr Institute in Denmark, he moved to the United States, where he worked at Johns Hopkins University in Baltimore and then the University of Chicago.

[4] Max Rheinstein (1899–1977) was scientific referent at the Kaiser-Wilhelm-Institute of Foreign and International Private law, 1927–34, where Leibholz knew him. Qualified as a professor in 1931 he emigrated to the United States in 1933 because of his Jewish descent and his membership of the Social Democratic Party. After two grants he became Max Pam Professor for American and Foreign Law and Professor of Political Science at the University of Chicago.

[5] Arnold Bergstraesser (1896–1964) held a chair on Auslandskunde at Heidelberg University, 1928–36. In 1937 he emigrated to the United States because of his Jewish descent, although in the beginning he had some sympathies for the Nazi dictatorship. He lectured in German literature and history in a succession of universities. In 1954 he returned to Germany and became one of the founding fathers of political science in the Federal Republic, holding a chair at Freiburg University.

[6] Karl Loewenstein (1891–1973) philosopher and political scientist, regarded as one of the most prominent figures of Constitutional Law in the twentieth century. Qualified as a professor by the Law Faculty of Munich University in 1931 he lost his position in October 1933 and emigrated to the United States, where he lectured at Yale University and, after 1936, at Amherst College, Massachusetts. His return to Munich in 1956 proved troubled because of the opposition of former Nazi colleagues. Because of this he was only allowed to lecture for one term.

Bell to Sabine Leibholz, 3 February 1941, BA, N 1334 (handwritten)

My dear Mrs Leibholz,

This is to wish you every blessing on your birthday, and to tell you how specially I shall remember Dietrich also on this day, praying that he may be kept safe, and protected through all the difficulties and struggles of a time which must be so full of pain and anxiety for him. Let us hope and pray that this year may be made a year of deliverance from Hitler and from war. And I also trust that you and your husband's plans may be helped to greater clearness for the future – meantime faith and content be with you. The £16 (if it has not come for the girls from Miss Roberts)[1] is on its way.

Yours vy sincerely,

[1] Leibholz's daughters now received a grant from the Church of England Committee for Non-Aryan Christians.

Bell to Leibholz, 5 February 1941, BA, N 1334 (handwritten)

My dear Leibholz,

I have just this moment had the enclosed from Angus Dun.[1] It looks much more hopeful. Please tell me how it strikes you *prima facie*. Paton is away – but I should like him to see the dossier and advise next week. Please return these, after considering.

Yours ever,

[1] A letter now lost.

Leibholz to Bell, 5 February 1941, Bell Papers 40, fol. 5 (typewritten)

My Lordbishop,

May I thank you very much for your kind letter. My wife also enjoyed very much your birthday-letter and your good wishes, just at a time where her parents, brothers and sisters are hindered to say what they wish and feel. I know that they all would join your and our own wishes. My wife will herself thank you soon.

I got from Mr Griffith £16 together with your kind letter on your and my wife's birthday. I am very glad to have them in order to cover the education-expenses for the children in this term. Many thanks for the renewed great help.

In the meantime I got a letter from Niebuhr with an attached letter from Professor Johnson. I enclose both together with a copy of my answer.[1] I think there must have been a hitch. But it is rather difficult to judge its character from here.

Further I got a letter from Dean Dun this morning the copy of which I enclose as well. It is rather difficult to know what to do now. I am afraid that it will not be possible to live on $1000 with a family of four. The Rockefeller Fellowships are not below $2000 and as far as I heard this is a minimum for a couple without children. On the other hand, Dean Dun may be quite right in writing that the certainty of having friends is more important than the financial question.

I should think one could perhaps find a solution if it were possible to maintain the contact with the World Council of Churches about which I am very much concerned. I venture to hope this as you, my Lordbishop, took a rather optimistic view about this possibility but, of course, I do not know whether this is the case now. I should think that Dr Visser 't Hooft would agree with this suggestion as well. I enclose his last letter[2] in which he also mentions a few subjects in which I am engaged – apart from my main subject about Christianity and international Law. All this work is going on but of course in consequence of the war not so quickly as I should like to. If Dr Paton were kind enough to do something for keeping the contact with the World Council in U.S.A. on the same or similar lines as in the past I could go on with my work and combine it with [a] new academic task. ªThen, the present obstacles would be cleared away.ª I should think that in this case also the American Consulate General could not r[a]ise any objections under the financial point of view. As at any rate some and perhaps many months will elapse till it will be possible to arrange all preparations it would perhaps be possible to accept the invitation in principle and to try to settle the other question in the meantime. But all depends on you, my Lordbishop, and I do not know whether you agree with [all] that I tried to express – probably in a not very intelligible way.

Please kindly forgive for this letter.
With very kind regards
Yours ever,

Five enclosures

ªP.S. I am just reading that Niemöller is reported to have turned Roman Catholic.[3] Is this report confirmed, my Lordbishop?ª

---

[1] A letter not traced in the Bell Papers.
[2] A letter now lost.
[3] Martin Niemöller (1892–1984) became renowned for the leading role which he assumed as the vicar in Dahlem in the Confessing Church. Although the trial against him ended in 1937 with an acquittal, he was taken as a personal prisoner of Hitler into Sachsenhausen concentration camp and in 1941 transferred to Dachau. It appears that in 1940/41 Niemöller was prepared to embrace Catholicism but any such idea foundered, probably in discussions with his wife and three Roman Catholic priests in Dachau. After the war, in 1945, he became councillor of the Evangelical Church in Germany and head of the Office of Foreign Affairs. In 1947–64 he was president of Evangelical Church of Hessen-Nassau. Politically he was engaged in criticism of Adenauer's Western orientation of the Federal Republic and its rearmament policy as well as becoming involved in the peace movement.

Episcopal Theological School to Leibholz, 8 January 1941, Bell Papers 40, fol. 6 (copy)

Dear Dr Leibholz,

I have just sent a letter to the Bishop of Chichester, renewing the offer made to you in the previous letter, and enclosing the affidavit required by the American Consul.

The main change in the present offer is that we are now undertaking to pay you $1000 in cash per year. I have explained to the Bishop of Chichester that while this amount would not be fully sufficient for the needs of your family, we are confident that those interested in assisting refugees in their problems here will be able to find ways of supplementing the resources provided by the School. Naturally, this will involve many uncertainties for you all, and will require a willingness to adapt yourselves to the best possible solution. At least, we can assure you that you will be among friends who will do all in their power to help you and your wife work through to a satisfactory adjustment.

Renewing the hope that you may find it possible to accept our offer,

Very sincerely yours,

Sig. Angus Dun, Dean of the Episcopal Theological School, Cambridge, Massachusetts, U.S.A.

Leibholz to Bell, 20 February 1941, Bell Papers 40, fol. 8 (typewritten)

My Lordbishop,

I thank you very much for your letter I received this morning. I shall turn over in my mind all you kindly wrote to me. Please kindly allow me to give my definite answer to the offer of the Dean Dun a little later.

First of all, I am very grateful to you, my Lordbishop, and Dr. Paton that you kindly offer to continue the World Council stipend for a year. I only hope that the Americans will be able to accept your proposal. Otherwise, I cannot quite see the substantial improvement in the offer of Dean Dun, as the main change is the undertaking to pay $1000 in cash instead of the hospitality offered. But, unfortunately, I am afraid that there is no doubt about the impossibility to live on the sum mentioned, even on modest terms. This would not put me in a position to live with my family as a professor in America as you, my Lordbishop, wished in your very kind letter of November last. For, I should be compelled to try earning additional money and, therefore, able neither to carry on my research work within the framework of the World Council nor to fill up my new post in a satisfactory way.

Naturally, I highly appreciate the great kindness and friendship of Dean Dun and I also hope very much that Dr. Paton might be right that the contingencies the Dean mentions may become realities. However I feel sure you will understand, my Lordbishop, that taking into account all circumstances it is very difficult to me to take a personal decision of such vital importance for us loaded with so many uncertainties. I remember, for instance, that Niebuhr failed in his very kind endeavours of getting a Fellowship although he was quite safe to get such [a] one for me.

I only mention this in order to show you, my Lordbishop, the direction of my considerations and doubts, which press hard upon me at present. If I were alone

I should not hesitate to accept the offer at once but I realize, at the same time, that I have to bear a great responsibility for my wife and the children.

I am looking forward very much [to] seeing you, my Lordbishop, on Sunday.

Yours very sincerely,

Leibholz to Bell, 25 February 1941, Bell Papers 40, fol. 9 (typewritten)

My Lordbishop,

I am so glad and thankful to have seen you and spoken to you, my Lordbishop, last Sunday.[1] I feel sure the whole congregation will have highly appreciated your kind visit and been much impressed by the especially beautiful sermon you delivered and which was so full of understanding of the many and various sorrows of the congregation. I think all who attended the service will never forget it.

I am also so grateful to know that you kindly understand my rather difficult position and my scruples in accepting the American invitation and, of all, I thank you once again that you will kindly write to Dean Dun on the lines you mentioned.

Provided you would agree I should think it would perhaps be not inexpedient to hand in the invitation of Dean Dun to the American Consulate for examination, in the meantime. I think this would have various advantages.

Firstly, it would show Dean Dun that I am actually considering seriously his invitation and that I am willing to close with his offer as soon as I received a more positive answer to our questions.

Secondly, I should perhaps be able, in the meantime, to settle the first formalities, which at any rate, in my view, require a great deal of time. Then, in case we should get a satisfactory answer from Dean Dun we could make our final arrangements more quickly.

Further, in case the American Consulate lets me know the papers are in order this would only mean that I can get an appointment if I am able to produce the passage tickets for all of us. To get these is, however, a special difficulty nowadays. For instance, Dr. and Mrs. Horrwitz booked tickets on 2nd of August last and so far they have no prospects of getting them. Therefore in case Dean Dun's answer were not positive and we could not make up our mind to accept the offer, but the formalities should have been satisfactorily prepared with the American Consulate (which I do not think probable) there is nothing to do but not to provide us with passage tickets.

The main advantage of this additional proposal seems to me to be that I do not lose time in case the project should be practicable in course of the next few months. In these uncertain days in which one does not know what will happen next this may perhaps be of importance, especially if one is taking into account that the invitation is limited to the 1st of October and it will be, in any case, difficult to settle the matter within the fixed time, even if the answer of Dean Dun were positive.

Therefore, in case you should agree, my Lordbishop, I should like to ask you kindly to send the Affidavit to Miss Roberts or myself. Then, I should thank Dean Dun for his kind letter as well and referring to your letter, my Lordbishop. I should write to him on the same lines as you, my Lordbishop. I should say that I hope to be able to accept finally the offer in case he could dispel our apprehensions or diminish the uncertainties and that I were already going to prepare for the settlement of the formalities.

I enclose a letter of Niebuhr.[2] If I am not mistaken I received another one from him in October last, which was still more positive than this one. But I could not find it out so far.

In case you should not need, my Lordbishop, the original letters of Niebuhr, Johnson and Visser't Hooft I enclosed in one of my last letters I should be grateful if you, my Lordbishop, could kindly return them.

Please forgive me for troubling you so much with this matter. But it is so difficult to do the right thing in this time. It is good that there are limits for all our doing and planning. But one likes to do one's best within the limits given one lest it is necessary to reproach oneself later on with having missed any opportunity.

I hope very much that Mrs. Bell is better now. Please give her our best wishes for speedy recovery and our kindest regards.

Yours ever,

[1] Bell visited Oxford on the weekend 22–3 February 1941, evidently preaching at Pusey House on the Sunday.
[2] Niebuhr's letter is to be found in neither archive.

Leibholz to Bell, 5 March 1941, Bell Papers 40, fol. 10 (typewritten)

My Lordbishop,

May I enclose a letter from Niebuhr I received this morning. It confirms my belief that the additional proposal I put forward in my last letter may be right. I should be glad, therefore, if you, my Lordbishop, could kindly comply with my request.

Then we can see whether the American Consul General will be prepared at all to consider the invitation financially sufficient what I am afraid he will not do. [sic] Otherwise – in case we should get a more satisfactory answer from Dean Dun in course of the next few months – it may be that the time limit of the invitation will expire before being able to settle the formalities. I just heard from another colleague who has got a call to the United States that he is trying in vain for six months to settle his things. And as the difficulties will probably increase during the next few months, it will be, in my view, no risk to hand in the affidavit to the American Consul General for a previous examination and to wait for a final decision till an answer of Dean Dun to the letter kindly suggested by you, my Lordbishop, is available.

In case you have written to Dean Dun I should be grateful if you would kindly give me an idea of what you wrote. Then I shall be better able to answer Dean Dun's letter to me of 8th of January.

I am writing to London because I learned from Hopf[1] that you, my Lordbishop, are staying there this week.

With very kind regards, also from my wife and the children.

Yours very sincerely,

¹ Konstantin Hopf (1911–71), exiled German pastor, had been arrested for preaching two allegedly treasonable sermons and held without trial between 15 June and Christmas Eve 1937; he had been released conditionally, but lived under close surveillance until friends arranged his escape to Switzerland in April 1938. When he and his new wife were warned of possible kidnapping they flew to Croydon on 17 January 1939. Bell promptly adopted them. By April Hopf was studying at Ridley Hall in Cambridge. He was re-ordained as an Anglican priest in August 1943. Later, in 1949, the Hopfs changed their name to Hope. Hopf contributed an article, 'Lutheran influences on the Baptismal Services of the Anglican prayer Book of 1549', to the festschrift *And Other Pastors of Thy Flock': A German Tribute to the Bishop of Chichester* (Cambridge, 1942, pp. 61–100)), edited by Franz Hildebrandt. See Nicholas Hope, 'Travels around my Father: Clergy in the Third Reich', in *Humanitas: The Journal of the George Bell Institute*, Vol. 7, No. 1 (October 2005), pp. 37–60.

Niebuhr to Leibholz, 28 January 1941, Bell Papers 40, fol. 11 (copy)

Dear Dr. Leibholz:

You will have received my letter before this. I haven't the slightest idea why the special Fellowship Committee of the Rockefeller Foundation rejected my application on your behalf, except of course that they had hundreds of applications for the hundred fellowships available. What you say about H. Kelsen[1] may be the explanation. I have used every possible pressure without success thus far. If the position of the Episcopal Seminary offers even the barest means of subsistence I would accept it, in the hope that by coming over here you could personally achieve results which cannot be achieved by mail.

Sincerely yours,

¹ Hans Kelsen (1881–1973), lawyer and philosopher, emigrated to the United States in 1940. Kelsen was the author of *Reine Rechtslehre* (1934; translated in the United States as *The Pure Theory of Law*), an influential work which criticized a meta-juridical foundation of justice and insisted on the absolute separation of law and morality. In 1942 he became established in his new country and remained a prominent thinker at the University of California at Berkeley for the rest of his life.

Bell to Dean Dun, 7 March 1941, Bell Papers 40, fol. 12 (copy)

My dear Dean Dun,

Very many thanks for your letter, and for the invitation which it contained to Professor Leibholz. I appreciate the very real consideration which has enabled you to make the offer in the terms in which it is made, with a thousand dollars in cash as well as your own personal undertaking that you would see that Professor Leibholz, his wife and his two daughters, do not find themselves stranded at any time once they have arrived in the U.S.A. and are installed in your College.

I have had a good talk with Professor Leibholz personally. I have also seen Dr. Paton whom you know well. I further made enquiries into shipping possibilities for these are material in present circumstances.

Professor Leibholz would much like to accept your offer and he very greatly appreciates the kindness with which you have made it to him. His whole future, of course, is at stake. And not only his, but that of his wife and children. He feels confident (and you will appreciate that he must necessarily think about this) that once he is in the U.S.A. with you his position, not only in the immediate present, but for such an extended period as, in the present state of the world, it is reasonable to contemplate, is as adequate to his needs as his position in England today. You are much better able to say whether the 1.000 dollars, together with your personal assurances, and with the World Council stipend for another year and a half in the background (either in whole or half, according as you are able to arrange at your end) will enable him to live in a modest way with sufficient security. The point which in a way makes him, after his experience of internment in this country, hesitate a tiny bit, is whether, supposing America came right into the war, there would be a similar internment policy in the U.S.A., the result of which would be his own internment once more. Dr. Paton thought this was a point, which required a little thought, and promised to take it up with Dean Van Dusen[1]. I have had the opportunity of a conversation about Professor Leibholz and this particular point, with the Rev. Edgar Chandler[2], this week.

We are, in the meantime making enquiries about shipping possibilities, though it is clear from the enquiries already made that it must be several months before a passage can be obtained.

I am sending this by air mail and should be grateful for a reply by airmail so that I may tell Professor Leibholz what you say.

With much gratitude,
Yours very sincerely,

---

[1] Henry Pitney van Dusen (1897–1975) was University Trustee of a dozen institutions, including the Rockefeller Foundation, and at Princeton. He began his career at Union Theological Seminary as an instructor in 1926, becoming Roosevelt Professor of Systematic Theology in 1936, and tenth President in 1945. He was prominent in the founding of the WCC.

[2] Edgar H. S. Chandler (1904–88); Congregational minister; U.S. Navy chaplain during the Second World War. He directed the WCC refugee service in Geneva, 1949–60.

Bell to Sabine Leibholz, 25 March 1941, BA, N 1334 (typewritten)

My dear Mrs Leibholz,

I sent a message with your love to Dietrich by telegram in answer to his. I have now just received a letter from him, I enclose a copy, and I am sure you will be happy to have it.[1]

I wonder if you know who Pfarrer Sutz is?[2] I do not quite know whether one is allowed to write to him direct or through Pfarrer Sutz, so I am writing to Pfarrer Sutz himself in the first instance and will see what happens.

Dietrich does not say whether he is remaining in Zurich.[3] That was the Post Mark on his letter.

Please keep the copy of the letter.

My love to the children and your Husband.

Yours very sincerely,

---

[1] Bonhoeffer to Bell, 28 February 1941, in: *DBW* 16, pp. 158–9 (with incorrect date).

[2] Erwin Sutz (1906–87) had been a friend of Bonhoeffer's since his studies at Union Theological Seminary 1930. As minister in Wiesendangen (1933–40) and Rapperswil (SG)

(1940–6) he served as Bonhoeffer's letterbox for contacts in Britain especially during his stay in Switzerland.
3 During his first visit to Switzerland Bonhoeffer stayed at Zurich from 25 February to 2 March 1941.

Bell to Leibholz, 7 April 1941, BA, N 1334 (typewritten)

ªMyª dear Leibholz,
Very many thanks for your letter and also for the memorandum which you have sent.[1] I am delighted to have this and look forward to reading it this week or next. I am going to Chichester today and shall try and get a few days quiet.

I cannot trace at present the letter from 't Hooft,[2] but I will have another look. I am glad to get the news of Dietrich.

With best wishes to you all for Easter,
Yours ªveryª sincerely,

[1] G. Leibholz, 'The internment policy and the Refugee problem', an extract of this is reprinted in Leibholz, *Politics*, pp. 314–16; see Bell to Leibholz, 25 April 1941 and Leibholz to Bell, 29 April 1941.
[2] Probably W.A. Visser 't Hooft to Bell, 19 March 1941, to be found in Besier, *Intimately Associated for Many Years*, pp. 209–10.

Bell to Leibholz, 17 April 1941, Bell Papers 40, fols. 14–15 (carbon)

My dear Leibholz,
I have just received two very important letters which refer to you from America. I am sure you will treat them as confidential and forget all about others who may be mentioned in them, and also remember that the letters are written to me and are part of a general correspondence. But it does look very much as though the American offer to yourself is a very genuine one, and obviously they are most anxious that I should give a definite reply at the earliest possible moment. It does certainly look to me from what Dean Dun says that he is prepared to take full responsibility.

I am, of course, very ready to take up the matter with the representative of the Rockefeller Trust in England, though I do not know where he is to be found at the moment.

Would you very kindly think the matter over carefully and let me know as soon as you can.

Dr. Paton will be in Oxford from Monday to Wednesday next at a Conference at Balliol College of the Church Commission for International Friendship.[1] I am telling him that I have written to you and given him your address. I would suggest your writing to him yourself at Edinburgh House, 2, Eaton Gate, asking whether you might see him. Unfortunately I cannot be at Oxford myself for these meetings.

I would call special attention to the sentence in the first paragraph of Van Dusen's letter beginning – 'It is very clear…'

It does, I confess, seem to me that the double call and situation as described by Van Dusen and Dun makes acceptance the right course. There must necessarily be a time of waiting for passages and so on, but in my opinion you would be wise, subject to facts, which I do not know, to accept the offer.

Of course if you want to see me and talk over any points, which are not clear, I would gladly see you. It is possible that I may be in London on Friday, April 25th, though not by any means certain, but the sooner I am able to cable a reply to Van Dusen the better. If, therefore, you are in a position to let me know at Hove on Tuesday or Wednesday next what your decision is it would be of great satisfaction.

Yours ever,

[1] This meeting of the Church Commission for International Friendship took place on 21–3 April 1941.

H. P. Van Dusen to Bell, 28 March 1941, Bell Papers 40, fol. 13 (copy)

My dear Bishop:

I have recently had a number of urgent inquiries from Dean Angus Dun as to the likelihood that Dr. Leibholz might accept his invitation, which he tells me he renewed in letters to you and to Leibholz under date of January 8th, offering Leibholz the appointment to a lectureship for a two-year period beginning in the next academic year with renewal of stipend of $1,000 a year. It is very clear that Dean Dun is sincerely interested in Leibholz and eager to assure his coming to this country. I hope we shall not have to disappoint him and thus lose the advantage of his very generous call.

In going through my correspondence file, I noted afresh that in your letter of 4th May, 1939, you referred to a communication you had received from Tracey Kitteredge[1], at that time Paris representative of the Rockefeller Foundation, in which he expressed special interest in Leibholz, offering to commend any application on his behalf to the Rockefeller Foundation in New York. Since Kitteredge is now in the New York office, I have reached him by phone. He was not very encouraging, saying that there was some feeling that scholars at present in England had better be supported there rather than brought to this country. However, he promised to give a special attention to whatever we might lay before him and possibly to advise their London representative to take some favourable action regarding Leibholz. Accordingly, I have just written Mr. Kitteredge the enclosed letter. If it is possible for you, might it not be advisable to establish contact with the Rockefeller Foundation representative in London at the present time and see if his interest can be enlisted in Leibholz's behalf? In the event that it is not possible to work out with Leibholz an arrangement which will be satisfactory for his acceptance on the basis of the $1,000 a year from the Episcopal Theological School, plus such World Council stipend as you and Paton are able to allocate to him, plus whatever help – if any – you might be able to secure from the Rockefeller Foundation representative in London. I have raised the question with Dean Dun of whether he might be willing to transfer his invitation in the same terms to Ehrenberg for whom, of course, we still have the probability of the $1,500 a year grant from the Rockefeller Foundation.[2] I have gathered he would be favourably disposed to this suggestion. But he naturally wants to be certain that Leibholz has definitely and finally declined his invitation before transferring the invitation to Ehrenberg.

Under all these circumstances I am hopeful that you will be able to advise us by cable at the earliest possible moment after receipt of this letter on the several possibilities here outlined so that we can without fail bring either the Leibholz or Ehrenberg call (and I shall hope ultimately both of them) to a favourable conclusion.

I shall shortly be writing Paton in some detail about the most recent developments on the very difficult feeding problem and shall ask him to share this information with you.

Faithfully yours,

---

[1] Tracy Barrett Kittredge (1891–1957) was member of the American Commission for Relief in Belgium (1914–19), archivist and statistician at the US Naval Reserve Force (1919–20) and served on the staff of the League of Red Cross Societies (1920–30). He was consultant, administrator and assistant director in the Fellowship Program for the Social Sciences in Europe for the Rockefeller Foundation (1930–42), during which time he was based in Paris. In 1942–6 he worked with the Staff of Admiral Harold R. Stark, American Naval Headquarters in London.

[2] Like Leibholz, Ehrenberg decided not to go to the United States.

Bell to Paton, 17 April 1941, Bell Papers 40, fols. 16–17 (carbon)

My dear Bill,

Leibholz: I have received three important letters, one on top of the other. Two from Van Dusen dated March 28th and April 1st and one from Angus Dun dated April 1st. The most important is that of March 28th from Van Dusen of which I enclose you a copy. I have sent a copy to Leibholz as well.

The net result is that Angus Dun's offer does seem to me to be an offer which meets all reasonable requirements. The fact that the letter is phrased as it is in reply to a letter from myself pointing out the natural hesitation of a man who within his modest limits is certainly safe in England for the next year or so hesitates before completely breaking away to new country, which he does not know the conditions more than a little time ahead [sic]. But you will see what Van Dusen says, and I have sent the other letters direct to Leibholz at Oxford. I think there is little in them, which it would be unwise for him to see, but I have made a copy of the most important letter for you as well as Leibholz, particularly because of the reference to the representative of the Rockefeller Foundation. Do you know where the Rockefeller Foundation in London is? If so, perhaps you could see your way to getting into touch with him personally.

On reflection I think I had better send you and not Leibholz the original letter from Van Dusen to the one of April 1st, together with a copy of his letter to Tracey Kitteredge of March 28th. There is something in the latter letter, which it would never do for Leibholz to see. But I have no idea what the reaction to which objection is taken can be. Leibholz wrote in the *Contemporary Review* but there is not the slightest doubt of his being completely anti-Nazi. How nervous these refugees are [with] regard to what others say.

The point of this letter really is to say that Leibholz lives at 100, Banbury Road, Oxford. I have suggested that he should try and get into touch with you during the meetings at Balliol next week. I have, therefore, suggested his writing to you asking for an appointment. I believe if you could see him and he would show you the letters, which I have let him see from Van Dusen and Dun, it would not be difficult to give him a definite advice.

Most unfortunately I cannot be at Oxford after all myself. I am taking a short holiday. It is my only chance, of a few days in Devonshire. I return to Hove on Tuesday evening, April 22nd, but I have to make a speech next day at Brighton. If Leibholz will tell me on Tuesday or Wednesday what his decision is I can cable it immediately. I am myself in favour of Leibholz accepting, subject to your own views and better information of the situation over there.

Yours ever,

Leibholz to Bell, 20 April 1941, Bell Papers 40, fols. 18–19 (typewritten)

My Lordbishop,

I thank you warmly for your kind letter of 17th of April I received yesterday together with the enclosures and with another letter from Dean Dun to me written on the same lines as the Dean's Letter to you, my Lordbishop.

I have also the impression that it does look very much as though the offer is a very genuine one, but please forgive me one point [which] seems to me to be not quite clear. Prof. v. Dusen and Dean Dun obviously take it for granted that at least a certain amount of the World Council stipend will be continued in the United States. Prof. v. Dusen speaks of an arrangement 'on the basis of the $1,000 a year from the Episcopal Theological School, plus such World Council stipend as you and Dr. Paton are able to allocate to him, plus whatever help – if any – you might be able to secure from the Rockefeller Foundation representative in London'. Dean Dun writes in his letter to me: 'It seems to me that the $1000 a year, which we are able to guarantee, plus a whole or a part of the World Council stipend for the initial period should be sufficient to meet your essential needs'. But the only thing I know about it is that you, my Lordbishop, and Dr. Paton are in agreement to continue the World Council stipend, 'on the understanding that the Americans will do their level best to find additional money'. When we talked over the matter here I had the impression it would be doubtful whether the Americans could really find this additional money. I do not know what the situation is like today. I shall try to talk over the matter with Dr. Paton here in one of the next few days and I am writing to him to Balliol, as a letter addressed to him to London would not reach him in time.

I think this point is of considerable importance. Of course the refugee Committee in Cambridge might be right that many people have not the same sum guaranteed for two years. But, on the other hand, I may say we are four persons and have unlike most of the emigrants no relatives and friends over there who would help us from the financial point of view. In so far our position is a quite different one. When Ehrenberg called on me a few weeks ago and we talked over our possible going over to the United States he also told me that as a matter of fact an amount of $2000 to 2500 for a family of four would be the minimum to meet the essential needs and that he would base his decision on this fact and that although his brother[1] is living over there. I gather from the letters of Prof. v. Dusen and Dean Dun, especially from the sentences quoted, that they obviously take the same view.

I have shortly received a letter from a colleague of mine in Chicago including a letter from Dr. Kittredge on the lines mentioned in the letter from Prof. v. Dusen. He writes:

'I wish to thank you for your letter of January 27th providing further information concerning the present position of Dr. G. Leibholz. His case might perhaps be considered by one of the institutions in England with which he has no doubt been in contact. One of my colleagues is expecting to go to London in the near future and will there discuss with representatives of certain British institutions the suggestions, which they have submitted, that the Foundation might make available certain funds in Great Britain to permit scholars in the position of Dr. Leibholz to continue their scholarly activities in England ... It might be useful, if Dr. Leibholz could inquire as to whether any arrangement might be made, which would permit him to continue his scholarly work in England'.

I gather from the letter of Dr. v. Dusen that the representative of the Rockefeller Foundation is in London at the present time. I should think if the Rockefeller Foundation were prepared to make a grant in this country it ought to be possible considering the offer made by the Episcopal school to secure the same amount for the United States.

I may perhaps also say, in this connection, that there were some negotiations about my case between the Master of Balliol and the Warden of Nuffield College on the one hand and the Rockefeller Foundation on the other hand shortly before the outbreak of war. Because of the war these plans could not be followed up. I have also still an introduction from Mr. Kittredge addressed for the acting Director of the Rockefeller Foundation in New York in my hands (from the time when I called Dr. Kittredge in Paris).

You will understand, my Lordbishop, that under these circumstances it is, unfortunately, very difficult to come immediately to a definite decision. I would, on principle, gladly accept the offer if either the assumption of Prof. v. Dusen and Dean Dun regarding the World Council stipend were to prove right or an additional grant by the Rockefeller Foundation could be secured. As to the World Council stipend you, my Lordbishop, and I hope also Dr. Paton can certainly tell me how the position is. As to the Rockefeller Foundation I will try to find out the address of its representative. I feel sure our position here would be much stronger if we can say that the offer has not yet been accepted because the financial basis is such a weak one. Otherwise I am afraid the R. Foundation would lose interest in making a grant [a]and I think I cannot afford to lose the chance of getting the help of the R. Foundation in this time without at least having the certainty that the World Council stipend can be continued for a limited time.[a]

My request for a short delay is perhaps all the more justified as Prof. v. Dusen wrote to you, my Lordbishop, before your letter of 7th March reached Dean Dun and further Dr. Dusen's letter arrived here very quickly taking into account the present circumstances. There would also not be a loss of time because I am already formally registered with various steamship-lines for some time.

If you would like to see me to talk over the matter I need not say to you that I should come to see you with greatest pleasure at any time.

> With my warmest thanks for all your great goodness and kindest regards
> Yours ever,

[1] The historian Paul Ehrenberg, the youngest brother of Hans Ehrenberg, had first migrated to Britain in 1939.

Leibholz to Bell, 23 April 1941, Bell Papers 40, fol. 21 (typewritten)

My Lordbishop,

I had a good talk with Dr. Paton about the Cambridge-offer at Balliol yesterday evening.

Unfortunately, it seems to me to be wise not to reckon on getting the World Council stipend in America. First a transfer of the stipend from this country to America is not possible because of the regulations, secondly as, under the present circumstances, some months will elapse till it will be possible to sail, the chance of getting the stipend would at best be confined to a few months and thirdly even as to this there is no security of getting it as the matter has only been discussed with the Americans who have, however, promised nothing. I am afraid, therefore, the assumption of Dean Dun and Dr. van Dusen concerning the World Council stipend is not well founded in the facts.

The financial basis of the offer seems to me, therefore, to be extremely weak although it may be generous from the point of view of the Episcopal School. Actually there is nothing certain but $1000 a year for a period of two years for a family of four. And the prospect of burning the boats in this country in which I have great and true friends and of being dependent on a local refugee committee is, if I may say this, not too attractive. I think there are no university people who went to America for taking up a post there and who are compelled to seek considerable help from a local refugee committee which has usually to deal with other people.

There is of course the chance of getting the grant from the Rockefeller Foundation. But I think it will take some time till it will be possible to clear the situation. The dilemma is that Dr. van Dusen wishes to have a cable at the earliest possible moment. I do not know whether he thinks just so still now after your last letter, my Lordbishop, has reached Dean Dun. If this were so and I am, therefore, compelled to take a decision I should suggest to overcome the difficulty by cabling about:

> On principle disposed (or if it seems to be better, prepared or willing) to accept the offer. As transfer of the World Council Stipend not possible trying to come into contact with the Rockefeller Foundation for reaching an additional arrangement.

If you, my Lordbishop, do not agree with the proposal, we must change it. I think such a cable would be acceptable for the Americans as well as for us because we do not weaken our position for the negotiations to come with the Rockefeller Foundation by accepting the offer without reservations.

If you think, my Lordbishop, it would make a good impression to advise our friends over there that I am already registered with different steamship lines we could perhaps do so.

The proposal mentioned was the suggestion I eventually made yesterday to Dr. Paton.

I sincerely ask you to forgive me all the trouble I am causing you, my Lordbishop. I feel sure you will do so as it is a vital and difficult decision – also for my wife and the children – from many points of view, and it may also be that the Rockefeller Foundation may perhaps be only prepared to make a grant for me as long as I am staying in this country. I ask you, therefore, very much, my Lordbishop, to excuse my being frank.

Yours ever,

Bell to Leibholz, 25 April 1941, BA NL 1334 (typewritten); Bell Papers 40, fol. 22 (carbon)

My dear Leibholz,

Many thanks for your letter. I am very glad you had such a good talk with Dr Paton. I have not yet heard from him myself, but, subject to anything that he may say to the contrary, I agree that the cable, which you propose should be sent to Van Dusen, is a right one and I agree with your feelings in the matter. I certainly did not realize that there was going to be a difficulty about the transfer of the World Council stipend, in whole or part, from this country to the U.S.A. It seems to me to be a new and unexpected complication.

As I am writing I should like to tell you how much I have enjoyed reading your report on the Status of the Refugee.[1] I read it a few days ago and was greatly struck by the argument and the whole point of view. If I may say so, it was not only very well informed, but very lucidly and persuasively presented.

I gladly enclose a copy (which you can keep) of Visser 't Hooft's letter to me about Dietrich.[2]

Yours very sincerely,

[1] G. Leibholz, 'The Internment Policy and the Refugee Problem', extract reprinted in Leibholz, *Politics and Law*, pp. 314–16.
[2] W. A. Visser 't Hooft to Bell, 19 March 1941, Bell Papers, Vol. 104 (typewritten); BA, N 1334 (copy) see *DBW* 16, pp. 163–4.

Bell to A. Dun, 29 April 1941, Bell Papers 40, fol. 23 (carbon)

Dear Dean Angus Dun,

On getting your further letter, making the offer to Dr. Leibholz of an appointment to a lectureship for a two-year period with a stipend of 1,000 dollars a year, I immediately got into touch with Dr. Leibholz and Dr. Paton. Fortunately Dr. Paton was in Oxford at the very time when your letter arrived and was able to have a full talk with Dr. Leibholz. The result of that talk I cabled to Van Dusen in the following form:

LEIBHOLZ STRONGLY DESIROUS ACCEPT INVITATION ANXIOUS SECURE ROCKEFELLER ADDITIONAL HELP EXPLORING MATTER HERE WILL CABLE AGAIN.

Dr. Paton is making enquiries of the representative here of the Rockefeller Foundation. There is a very great difficulty in the transfer of the money to America. The Bank of England is severer about sending sterling to America and Canada than to any other part of the world. This affects the World Council stipend, hence it is very important to secure the additional help from the Rockefeller Foundation or other source of which the money is realisable in the U.S.A., before Leibholz can accept, as he very much wants to do.

I feel sure that you will appreciate this. I am most grateful for all you are doing.

Yours very sincerely,

Leibholz to Bell, 29 April 1941, Bell Papers 40, fol. 24 (typewritten)

My Lordbishop,
Many thanks for your very kind letter and the telegram you sent to van Dusen. I am so very glad and grateful to know that you understand my feelings in the matter and kindly allow me to be quite frank with you.

I also thank you most warmly for kindly taking up my case with the representative of the Rockefeller Foundation in London. I for my part informed the Society for Protection of Science and Learning[1] of the matter and asked them if possible to support your action, my Lordbishop, by an additional letter. I did so because Dr. Kittredge in his letter to Prof. Kessler[2] in Chicago advised me to get into touch with the Society because of the grant, which the Rockefeller Foundation might possibly be prepared to make to me. I hope you will agree.

I am very much touched by what you, my Lordbishop, say about my essay and I thank you warmly for your words and for having read it in spite of the great strain, which the present time lays upon you. I think of publishing it after Sir John Hope Simpson wrote me I should do so. He told me I should consult the Master of Balliol. I should very much like to know how you think. It may be perhaps better to publish it in the United States as this country is now taken up too much by other concerns and there are also a few other publications about the matter although not from the specific point of view from which I have tried to put forward the case.

In any case if you, my Lordbishop, still have the ms. and do not need it in any way it would be very kind of you if you could let me have it again. Should it be published I will send you a copy immediately.

Many thanks also for the letter from Dr. Visser 't Hooft [which] I am very glad to have.

Yours ever,

[1] In April 1933 William Henry Beveridge (1879–1963) founded the Academic Assistance Council as an answer to the Nazi persecution of scientists. Academics could support the work of the Council by committing a percentage of their own salaries to support the needs of migrating scholars while universities were encouraged to provide positions in their departments. In 1936 this had become the Society for Protection of Science and Learning, based in Burlington House, London. The organization continues to exist as the Council for the Assistance of Refugee Academics. In 1937 Beveridge had become Master of University College, Oxford. His name is indelibly associated with his influential 1942 report *Social Insurance and Allied Services*, which served as a basis for the programme of post-war social reform subsequently achieved by the 1945–51 Labour governments. From 1919 to 1937 he was Director of the London School of Economics and Political Science. In 1946 he became 1st Baron Beveridge.

[2] Friedrich Kessler (1901–98) had worked at the Kaiser Wilhelm Institute for Foreign and International Private Law since 1926 and lectured at the Berlin Handelshochschule between 1931 and 1933. Because of the events of 1933 (his wife was Jewish) he migrated to the United States in 1934. He became assistant professor at Yale Law School (1935–8) and associate professor at the University of Chicago (1938–47).

Bell to Leibholz, 1 May 1941, BA NL 1334 (typewritten); Bell Papers 40, fol. 25 (carbon)

My dear Leibholz,

Many thanks for your letter. The text of the actual cable ᵃdrafted by Dr Patonᵃ, which I sent to Van Dusen on Saturday, is as follows:

LEIBHOLZ STRONGLY DESIROUS ACCEPT
INVITATION ANXIOUS SECURE ROCKEFELLER ADDITIONAL
HELP EXPLORING MATTER HERE WILL CABLE AGAIN

I have followed it up with a short letter, just to repeat the cable. Dr Paton is taking up the matter with the Rockefeller Foundation.

I think it a very good thing that you have informed the Society for the Protection of Science and Learning; but *Dr Paton* is the actual person ᵃ(not myself)ᵃ who is in touch with the Rockefeller Foundation representative. He is in London and is taking the necessary steps.

I am very much interested to hear about Hope Simpson's desire that you should publish the essay. I think it would be a very good thing; and I think it would be a good thing to publish it in England, if one could get a publisher. I will try a bow at a venture and write to Sir Humphrey Milford[1] who is head of the Oxford University Press, London offices, to see if there would be any chance of his publishing this as a pamphlet in the series of *Oxford Pamphlets on World Affairs*, 3d. each. I will tell him what Hope Simpson says so that he can take the matter up with him. It would be an excellent series in which to publish.

Do you want your paper back *immediately*? If so, you shall, of course, have it. But this question of the status is becoming more and more important and I am seriously thinking of, either raising it, or trying to get it raised, in the House of Lords some time this month, probably on the anniversary of the internment policy, making it, not the only matter of raising, but an important matter in the general position of refugees at this date.[2]

I think that, in a way, you might postpone consulting the Master of Balliol[3] until we hear what Sir Humphrey Milford says. It is, of course, very likely that he will consult the Master, as it may well be that this series is edited by Lindsay[4] and others.

Yours ever,

---

[1] Sir Humphrey Sumner Milford (1877–1952), knighted in 1936, publisher and editor who from 1913 to 1945 was publisher to the University of Oxford and head of the London office of Oxford University Press. Bell knew Milford well, not least because he had been personally involved in the publication in 1935 of his monumental life of Archbishop Davidson.

[2] It was in December 1941 that Bell raised the question of refugees, with special references to the interned persons in Canada and Australia, in the House of Lords; see his speech in Hansard, HL Deb., Vol. 121, cols. 336–47 (17 December 1941).

[3] Alexander Dunlop, or more famously A.D., Lindsay (1879–1952), philosopher and Master of Balliol College, Oxford from 1924 to 1949 and Vice-Chancellor of the University of Oxford, 1935–8. Active in public life and politics, and sympathetic to church circles, he became Baron Lindsay of Birker in 1945.

[4] When J.H. Oldham had set up the *Christian News-Letter* movement in 1940 to discuss current affairs and their significance in a moral perspective, Lindsay and Milford initiated an Oxford branch of the movement.

Leibholz to Bell, 8 May 1941, Bell Papers 40, fol. 27 (typewritten); BA, N 1334 (copy)

My Lordbishop,

This is just to enclose a copy of a letter from Sir Cecil Hurst[1] who thinks it may perhaps be better not to publish the essay. As he does not give any reason I hesitate to ask him for a more detailed explanation. In my view, it may be that he does not consider expedient a discussion of the questions put forward in the paper either because of the general political situation or because of the stage in which the whole refugee question finds itself today or because of my being a refugee or of not being able to advocate a publication so long as he, as Chairman of the Tribunals, holds a responsible position within the Home Office. You, my Lord Bishop, are certainly able to judge the backgrounds better than I and to advise me to what extent I must take into account the letter.

On the other hand, I realize that if the United States entered the war the problem would become of much more importance because the whole situation is much more difficult in the Unites States than in this country. Also from this point of view a publication of the essay seems to me to be not quite unjustified.

The second paragraph of the enclosed letter refers to the letter of Sir John Hope Simpson the copy of which I enclosed in my last letter. In that letter Sir J. Hope [sic] mentioned the possibility of publishing the legal part of the essay in the Journal of the Grotius Society[2]. But I did not take any steps in this direction.

Yours ever,
G. Leibholz

ªP.S. I just got a letter from the Society. I enclose a copy of it.[3] It refers to the Rockefeller Foundation.ª

[1] Sir Cecil James Barrington Hurst (1870–1963) worked in 1929–45 as a judge to the Permanent Court of International Justice in The Hague serving from 1934 to 1936 as president of the court. See Hurst (Home Office, Interned Enemy Aliens Tribunal [Germans and Austrians], Royal Courts of Justice) to Leibholz, 7 May 1941, Bell Papers 40, fol. 28.
[2] Named after the famous Dutch jurist, Hugo Grotius (1583–1645) and founded in Britain in 1915, the Grotius Society existed to 'advance the study of international law', particularly with reference to issues of war and peace. The journal was called *Transactions*. The Society was dissolved in 1958.
[3] See Esther Simpson to Leibholz, 7 May 1941, Bell Papers 40, fol. 29; Bell to Esther Simpson, 7 May 1941, Bell Papers 40, fol. 26. Esther Simpson (1903–96) had been working with the World Alliance of YMCAs in Geneva and became in 1933 secretary of the Society for the Protection of Science and Learning. Devoted to a life of public service, she became a figure of crucial importance in the lives of many exiled academics.

Bell to Leibholz, 16 May 1941, BA, N 1334 (typewritten and carbon); Bell Papers 40, fol. 28ᵛ (carbon)

My dear Leibholz,

Many thanks for your letter and copies of letters from Sir Cecil Hurst and Miss Simpson. I don't know why Sir Cecil Hurst thinks it better not to publish your essay now. But I think we will wait to hear from Sir Humphrey Milford of the Oxford University Press, to see what he thinks of the possibility of publishing your essay in the series of *Oxford Pamphlets*.[1]

There is a discussion next Wednesday by the Grotius Society on a paper on the Status of the Refugee, by Dr Loewenfeld,[2] at 2, King's Bench Walk, E.C. I am a member of the Grotius Society, having just been elected, but I fear it is possible that I may not be able to go.

Yours sincerely,

ᵃP.S. Letter just come to say the Press is unable to publish – as outside scope of series.ᵃ

[1] The *Oxford Pamphlets* were published throughout the war, presenting brief discussions of current affairs by various public authorities; the pamphlets were often international in character.
[2] Loewenfeld = Carl Loewenstein.

Leibholz to Bell, 17 May 1941, Bell Papers 40, fol. 30; BA, N 1334 (copy)

My Lordbishop,

Many thanks for your letter.

I am not surprised that the Oxford Press is not prepared to publish the essay in the series of its pamphlets. For it is not only outside their scope but also hitherto all their pamphlets have been written by British Nationals. It may also be too long.

It is another question whether to follow up the question of publication. For except from Sir Cecil all other people who read the Ms. warmly advocated its publication. Prof. Barker[1] advised me to write to Mr Stanley Unwin[2] and to refer to his advice (Mrs Buxton[3] gave the same advice), Sir John Hope Simpson wrote me I should consult the Master of Balliol and Mr Lafitte[4] advised me to approach the

Hogarth Press, which also publishes a well known series of pamphlets on current problems.⁵ It may also perhaps be that Sir Humphrey Milford has mentioned in his letter another publisher who may be interested in the subject. I did so far not approach a publisher because you, my Lordbishop, were kind enough to take up the matter. I think as Sir Cecil has not given any reasons for the conclusion he has come to I cannot weigh the reasons and therefore hardly take them into account. I should be grateful if you, my Lordbishop, kindly let me know how you think. Should you take the view it would be better to publish the essay in the United States I could do so without difficulties.

I hope to see the paper of Dr Loewenstein soon. As far as I know we approach the problem from quite different points of view and deal also with rather different questions. But I should not think this matters if the basic attitude of mind is the same.

Yours very sincerely,

---

[1] Sir Ernest Barker (1874–1960), principal of King's College London from 1920 to 1927, became professor of political science in the University of Cambridge in 1928, being the first holder of the chair endowed by the Rockefeller Foundation.

[2] Sir Stanley Unwin (1884–1968) was a British publisher, founder of the George Allen and Unwin House in 1914, which published *The Hibbert Journal*.

[3] Dorothy Frances Buxton (1881–1963) was from 1933 active in protesting against the policies of the Nazi state, and particularly against the treatment of Christians in Germany. Well connected in society (her sister was Eglantyne Jebb, the founder of Save the Children, her husband the politician, Charles Roden Buxton, and her brother-in-law the Bishop of Gibraltar), she maintained sporadic contact with Bell but found her essential constituencies elsewhere, particularly in the Kulturkampf Association, publishing documents of the Church Struggle. During the Second World War she campaigned for refugees from Germany, as well as for the welfare of German Prisoners of War.

[4] François Lafitte (1913–2002) was a research officer and translator for the Miners' International Federation, 1936–7, before he joined the research staff of Political and Economic Planning (PEP), 1938–43. Until 1959 he was on the editorial staff of *The Times* as social policy correspondent. In 1959 he was appointed as professor of Social Policy and Administration and Head of the Department of Social Administration at the University of Birmingham, serving as dean of the Faculty of Commerce and Social Science, 1965–8. See Lafitte, *The Internment of Aliens* (Penguin Special 57), (Harmondsworth, 1940).

[5] The Hogarth Press was a publisher mostly of literature (not least by members of the Bloomsbury Group) but in wartime also the publisher of a succession of diverse studies of political affairs, including, in 1939, Herbert Rosinski's *The German Army* and, in 1941, Julian Huxley's *Democracy Marches* and Norman Leys' *The Colour Bar in East Africa*. Here Bell probably refers to the *Day-to-Day* pamphlets series, which predated the outbreak of war in 1939.

H. P. van Dusen to Bell, 21 May 1941, Bell Papers 40, fol. 31 (copy)

My dear Bishop,

Thank you warmly for your letter of April 29th. I am today cabling you:

UNION SEMINARY SUPPLEMENTING CAMBRIDGE APPOINTMENT WITH ADDITIONAL INVITATION LEIBHOLZ TWO-YEAR LECTURESHIP ONE THOUSAND DOLLARS PAPERS FOLLOW AIR MAIL[1]

Three copies of the formal invitation are enclosed. We all trust that this invitation, supplementing the one already in hand from Dean Dun, will clear away the final obstacles for Leibholz.

Let me explain the exact situation as regards finances. The Episcopal Theological School call, carrying a stipend of $1,000 a year for a two-year period, still holds; this you already have in hand. You will note that our invitation provides for 'a stipend of $1,000', and that it is not specified that this shall be for each of the two years. This is partly because we actually have in hand at this moment only $1,000. It is partly because we still hope to secure aid from the Rockefeller Foundation. We assume that you and Paton are pressing your request to the Foundation representative in London for a grant of $1,000–$1,500 a year. In the meantime Dr. Coffin[2], who has rather favourable contacts with the Foundation here, has also written them asking for a grant of $1,000–$1,500. In view of this additional call from Union Seminary, we hope that you and Paton will try to press the Foundation representative in London to a definite affirmative decision. Unquestionably he will consult New York, and Dr. Coffin's appeal at this end should help toward the securing of a grant in Leibholz's favour either through London or through New York. In the event that we are refused by the Foundation, the Directors of our Seminary have every intention of making certain that Leibholz will not fail of funds during this two-year period. While at this moment we are not in position to offer formally more than $1,000 for the two years, you and Leibholz can be assured that matters will be arranged so that he will have not less than a total of $2,000 a year for each of the two years. In brief, the present offer is framed with the intention of satisfying the American Consul and of assuring Leibholz of the requisite support.

I am pressing the Episcopal Theological Seminary at Alexandria, Virginia, of which Dr. A. C. Zabriskie is the Dean,[3] to take over the Berkeley invitation to Ehrenberg. Their Board of Trustees meets on June 6th when we will know their decision.

With cordial regards,

---

[1] Communicated by Bell to William Paton, 24 May 1941, Bell Papers 40, fol. 32.
[2] Henry Sloane Coffin (1877–1954) became pastor of Madison Avenue Presbyterian Church in New York City in 1910 and was president of the Union Theological Seminary, 1926–45.
[3] Alexander C. ('Zab') Zabriskie (1898–1956) taught Church History during the 1920s and 1930s at the Virginia Theological Seminary and was Dean from 1940 to 1951.

Bell to Leibholz, 24 May 1941, BA, N 1334 (typewritten)

My dear Leibholz,

I think you would be well advised to write to Stanley Unwin, and to say that Professor Barker has advised to do so. The Oxford University Press said that they thought that your work would be suitable for publication in such other series of pamphlets as the Macmillan Series or the *Christian News-Letter* Series. I doubt, myself, whether the Macmillan Series would consider it. *The Christian News-Letter* Series might do so, but here again I am not very sure. If you would like to try you could write to

Dr J.H. Oldham, Arlosh Hall, Mansfield College, Oxford
saying that you had been advised by me to ask him whether they would publish it. But I think that Stanley Unwin is really the best. Failing Stanley Unwin, the Hogarth Series might be usefully approached.

I should certainly, if I were you, peg away at English publishers, though with the consolation that if England fails, America may be still available.

Mrs Bell will have, I hope, shown you the cable from Van Dusen. This does seem to me much more like business. I will, of course, send you the airmail letters as soon as they arrive.

With all best wishes,
Yours sincerely,

Bell to Leibholz, 3 June 1941, Bell Papers 40, fol. 34 (carbon)

My dear Leibholz,

I have today received a letter from Dean van Dusen, enclosing 3 copies of a formal invitation for the Union Seminary. I think I had better send you a copy of his letter to me, so that you may have all the facts before you, but I have no doubt from the way in which van Dusen has taken the matter up and is pushing it through that you can rely completely on what he says. If you are agreeable, I think it would be well that we sent a cable on your behalf accepting. I am sending a copy of his letter and van Dusen's letter to Dr. Paton.[1]

Yours very sincerely,

[1] See Bell to Paton, 3 June 1941, Bell Papers 40, fol. 35, and Paton's answer of 10 June 1941, Bell Papers 40, fol. 3.

Bell to Leibholz, 10 June 1941, BA, N 1334 (typewritten); Bell Papers 40, fol. 38 (carbon)

My dear Leibholz,

Many thanks for your two letters. I have written to Allen and Unwin, as you have requested. I also return your manuscript to you, bearing in mind the fact that you will be kindly willing to let me see it again if the need arose.

I am sending a telegram to Van Dusen, saying that you accept the offer in the Union Seminary[1] and I am seeing what I can do about approaching the representative of the Rockefeller Foundation in London. I don't like to act in that matter without Dr Paton's approval.

With all best wishes,
Yours ever,
(without signature)

[1] The cable: LETTERS RECEIVED LEIBHOLZ GRATEFULLY ACCEPTS UNION POST CHICHESTER is found in Bell's letter to Helen Roberts, 10 June 1941, Bell Papers 40, fol. 39 (carbon).

Bell to G. Allen and Unwin, 10 June 1941, Bell Papers 40, fol. 34 (carbon)

Dear Sirs,
Professor G. Leibholz, of 100 Banbury Road, Oxford, tells me that you are considering a manuscript on The Issue of Internment Policy and the Refugee Problem. I write to say what a very high opinion I have of Dr. Leibholz and his work. He was one of the foremost scholars in Germany in political science, and particularly in matters relating to international law. I have read his manuscript, which interested me profoundly. And I cannot help thinking that the publication of such a reasoned argument would be a real contribution to learning, and also to better understanding of the issues raised. It is scholarly, and well argued and documented and constructive, in a field where constructive work is, in my judgment, very much required.

Yours faithfully,

Paton to Bell, 13 June 1941, Bell Papers 40, fol. 40 (typewritten)

My dear George,
Two points – first, I think it might be quite a good thing for you to write and back up the Rockefeller application on behalf of Leibholz. He is quite curiously difficult about his American business. The letter from H. S. Coffin says that it is a two-year appointment (Union Seminary job) and that 'the stipend is $100'. I should undoubtedly take this to mean that the stipend is $1000 a year not, as Leibholz seems to think, $1000 spread over two years. However, it will do no harm I think for you to press the Rockefeller application, especially as you had some previous touch with them on the subject.

I agree with you that we should now press for Diehl[1] and his wife to be in the mixed camp but not press for Diehl to minister to the women's camp. I shall take this up.

Yours ever,

P.S. You will like to see the enclosed letter to William Ebor.[2]
Dictated but not signed personally owing to absence from the office.

---

[1] Heinrich Johannes Diehl (1908–2002) was German pastor of the Evangelical Seamen's Mission at South Shields and other parishes 1935–9. Interned on the Isle of Man he was exchanged for British civilian prisoners in 1944. After the Second World War he committed himself to international and humanitarian work, becoming director of the department of ecumenical social welfare work of the Evangelical Church in Germany.
[2] Paton to William Temple, 13 June 1941, Bell Papers 40, fol. 41.

Leibholz to Paton, 14 June 1941, Bell Papers 40, fol. 44 (carbon)

Dear Dr. Paton,
I thank you for your letter. I am afraid that I am not wrong in assuming that the stipend Dr. H. S. Coffin has mentioned in his letter is meant to be spread over two years.

To make this clear I may perhaps refer to the letter of Dr. van Dusen to the Bishop, which runs as follows as far as this point is concerned:

> You will note that our invitation provides for 'a stipend of $1,000', and that it is not specified that this shall be for each of the two years. This is partly because we actually have in hand at this moment only $1,000. It is partly because we still hope to secure aid from the Rockefeller Foundation. We assume that you and Paton are pressing your request to the Foundation representative in London for a grant of $1,000–$1,500 a year. In the meantime, Dr. Coffin, who has rather favourable contacts with the Foundation here, has also written them asking for a grant of $1,000–$1,500. In view of this additional call from Union Seminary, we hope that you and Paton will try to press the Foundation representative in London to a definite affirmative decision. Unquestionably he will consult New York, and Dr. Coffin's appeal at this end should help toward the securing of a grant in Leibholz's favour either through London or through New York.[1]

This is why I ventured to ask you and the Bishop very much not to cease to attack the Rockefeller people and I thank you warmly that you have, as you tell me, done all you can with these people. I trust that your kind endeavours will be successful and hoping this I have followed your and the Bishop's advice and accepted the offer.

Yours very truly,

[1] H. P. van Dusen to Bell, 21 May 1941.

Leibholz to Bell, 14 June 1941, Bell Papers 40, fol. 43 (typewritten)

My Lordbishop,

I thank you warmly for your line, the Ms. and, above all, the letter to Allen and Unwin. Please kindly let me know if for any reasons you want to have the Ms. back later on. I will be careful to send you, my Lordbishop, in this case the same copy you had in hands. If it is possible to publish the Ms. as a separate essay I shall ask you later on to allow me to dedicate it to you, my Lordbishop, as a very small token of my great indebtedness to you.

Many thanks also for the telegram.[1] I noticed, in the meantime, that the invitation from the Union Theological Seminary has not been sworn in. Therefore, I cannot hand it into the American Consulate and must ask for a new invitation.

I hope Dr. Paton will not mind my request to you, my Lordbishop, for a supporting letter to the Rockefeller Foundation representative in London or Dr. Kittredge in New York. I feel that Dr. Paton perhaps does not fully realize the importance of the Rockefeller grant with regard to securing the amount of $1000 from the Union Theological Seminary. I have written, therefore, to Dr. Paton the enclosed letter referring to the passages in question of Dr. van Dusen's letter to you, my Lordbishop, a copy of which you have kindly sent him before. I think Dr. van Dusen's letter is quite clear: he hopes that it will be possible to secure a grant of $1000–1500 a year in order to use this aid for making a grant of $1000 a year from the Union Theological Seminary.

Yours ever,

P.S. I have just received the line from your secretary together with the enclosures from Allen and Unwin. I thank you once again for your great kindness and think to write to you, my Lordbishop, again as soon as I shall have received an answer from the publisher.

---

[1] H. P. van Dusen to Bell, 13 June 1941, Bell Papers 40, fol. 42 (telegram) quoted by H. P. van Dusen to Bell, 18 June 1941.

Leibholz to Bell, 17 June 1941, Bell Papers 40, fol. 45 (handwritten)

My dear Lordbishop,
This is really grand.[1] I am overjoyed that this question has been settled so favourably and quickly. Many hearty thanks for all your kindness. I gratefully realize every day how much I owe to your friendship and indefatigable helpfulness and I may assure you that I shall never forget all this you have done on my behalf.

As to the shipping question I may say that, as a matter of precaution, I have been already registered with all shipping companies in question for some months past. Moreover, I shall now immediately get in touch with Miss Roberts and then report to you again. The shipping conditions are very difficult for the time being and as far as I can judge the situation I am afraid it will in no case be possible to be in New York before the opening of the lectures in September 1941. Perhaps one can give this date as the probable date of arrival to Dr van Dusen, although, under the present circumstances, a firm assurance seems to me to be not possible.

In the meantime, I have written by Air Mail to Dr Coffin and Dean Dun and accepted the invitations with my warmest thanks.

I am very much looking forward to seeing you here in course of the next week.

With all my good wishes
Yours ever,

---

[1] Bell's (lost) letter probably informed Leibholz about the new conditions of a grant; see van Dusen's letter below.

H. P. van Dusen to Bell, 18 June 1941, Bell Papers 40, fol. 46 (typewritten)

My dear Bishop:
On June 12th I received your welcome cable: LETTERS RECEIVED LEIBHOLZ GRATEFULLY ACCEPTS UNION POST. On the following day, June 13, I cabled you: DELIGHTED LEIBHOLZ ACCEPTANCE. ROCKEFELLER FOUNDATION GRANTING THOUSAND DOLLARS A YEAR FOR TWO YEARS. PLEASE NOTIFY US PROBABLE DATE ARRIVAL.

This grant from the Rockefeller Foundation is to be made available over a two-year period, and was in direct response to an appeal from Dr. Coffin, which I reported to you [in] my last letter of May 21st. In making this grant, the Rockefeller Foundation laid down only one condition – that Professor Leibholz should have reached this country and be prepared to undertake his lectureship under the grant not later than November 1st, 1941. In the correspondence leading up to the grant, the Foundation expressed some doubt as to whether it would be possible for him to secure passage across the Atlantic. We explained that you were taking a personal interest in his case and that we felt confident that you could arrange it.[1]

You will understand, of course, that the academic term both at the Episcopal Theological School and at Union Seminary opens about September 20th. If Dr. Leibholz is to fulfil the appointments for which the grants from these two schools are made, he ought to be here not later than September 15th. I am sure you fully appreciate this fact and will take every step within your power to assure his arrival by that date.

I am happy that, after such long and difficult negotiation, it now seems reasonably certain that Leibholz will be with us. On behalf of all who have interested themselves in his coming you can assure him a very warm welcome. Dean Dun and I have not yet worked out details for division of time between Cambridge and New York.

I have not yet had any report from Alexandria in response to my request that they consider a call to Ehrenberg, but I am not hopeful.

With cordial good wishes, I am
Faithfully yours,

---

[1] The paragraph is marked by a black line in the margin.

Paton to Leibholz, 8 July 1941, BA, N 1334 (typewritten)

My dear Dr Leibholz,

I am willing to do all I can to help you to get a passage to America, especially in view of the fact that the Rockefeller grant is conditional upon your reaching America so as to take up your lectureship by November 1st. You ought really to be there by September 15th, for the term at the Episcopal Theological School and the Union Seminary.

The difficulties are two: (a) the new consular regulations issued by the American Government[1]; and (b) the shortage of shipping.

Will you tell me by return of post just what you have done already under these two heads? I should be very willing both to write to the consular authorities (so will the Bishop of Chichester) on your behalf and also to do what I can with the shipping authorities, but I need to know what steps exactly you have taken already.

Yours sincerely,

---

[1] The effect of this new immigration policy was that during the period of American involvement in the war, 90 per cent of the quota places available to immigrants from countries under German and Italian control were never filled.

Paton to Bell, 8 July 1941, Bell Papers 40, fol. 47 (typewritten)

My dear George,

The enclosed copy of a letter from Van Dusen dated June 12th will interest you.[1]

I think that I am justified in exerting the strongest possible pressure upon the Ministry of Shipping about a berth for Leibholz. I am afraid, however, that the difficulties are going to be extremely great and it is no good minimising them. In the first place, as Emerson's letter to me, of which you have a copy,[2] shows, only very strong pressure will get him past the American Consulate. That we might perhaps manage. The other trouble is shipping and here it is not simply pressure of other people but sheer scarcity of boats. I have gone into this matter lately with the officials and the situation they have to face is quite extraordinarily difficult. However, we have as good as case with Leibholz as we are likely to have with any refugee and I will see what I can do.

Yours ever,

[1] The copy has not been traced.
[2] The copy has not been traced. Sir Herbert William Emerson (1881–1962) had become League of Nations' High Commissioner for Refugees, and director of the Inter-Governmental Committee on Refugees in 1938.

Leibholz to Paton, 10 July 1941, BA, N 1334 (carbon); Bell Papers 40, fol. 48 (copy)

My dear Dr. Paton,

Many thanks for your letter. I greatly appreciate the help you will kindly give me to overcome the present difficulties. I think I shall badly need it.

May I briefly report to you how things stand today:

First as to the visas I may say that I had a letter from the American Consul before the new regulations saying that he will be pleased to issue the visas for my wife, the children and myself as soon as I have been able to book the necessary accommodation. I have still to hand in to the Consul the invitation from the Union Theological Seminary and a certificate about the grant from the Rockefeller Foundation. As the invitation I have received from New York did not comply with the regulations (it was not sworn in before a public notary) I have asked Dr. Coffin by Air Mail Letter for a new one and I hope to get it soon. As to the grant from the Rockefeller Foundation I only know so far about it by the cable from Dr. van Dusen. Should you have received, in the meantime, a more detailed answer I should be very grateful to you if you could kindly let me have a certified copy of it, which I can forward to the Consulate.

As to the new regulations issued by the American Government I had recently a good talk with Miss Roberts about them. She told me that she was informed that the new regulations have more an advisory character and are not a strictly binding rule so that I hope that by a letter kindly written by you and the Bishop these difficulties can be overcome. I for myself have no near relatives on the European Continent as my brother and his wife at the Hague took their lives after the occupation of this place by the German troops.[1] My wife, on the other hand, has her relatives still in Germany. I think, you know her twin-brother Dietrich Bonhoeffer.

With regard to the shipping question I may say that I have done all in my power to settle this question in a quick and satisfactory way.[2] Already a few months before my closing with the American offer I was registered, as a matter of precaution, with all steamship companies in question (Cunard Line, Canadian Pacific Line & the Furness Withy Line) through the tourist agency of this place, Bell's Travel Service, Oxford, which has the reputation of being very efficient. But so far as I hear in the last six months no ordinary passenger ship has been running from this country to America and many thousands of people are placed on the waiting lists of the various steamship companies. Only people whose journey is of immediate national importance have the chance of getting away for the time being. But people and I hope that conditions will improve again if more ships will arrive in this country.

There is a weak chance of going to the United States in course of the next few months via Uruguay (Montevideo) and Argentine. But I am afraid I shall not be able to follow up this opportunity as the minimum expenses of this journey are £200 per adult and a further banker guarantee is required at the same rate. This would mean that we should have to pay £700 for our crossing and to give an additional banker guarantee of £800. I need not tell you that I do not see any way of paying even a part of this sum.

I have also made inquiries about the possibility of going to America via Lisbon and we are also placed on the waiting list to Lisbon by Thos. Cook, London. But the passport office in London wrote to me on 28th of May that 'it is not possible to grant exit permits to enable German refugees to proceed to the United States of America via Lisbon'.

May I finally say that I am still keeping a close correspondence with Miss Roberts who has kindly offered to help me. I shall, therefore, automatically be informed about all possibilities of leaving this country, which come to the knowledge of Bloomsbury House.

If under these circumstances you should be in a position to give me additional advice what more to do in this case I should be only too pleased to follow it up.

Yours very sincerely,

---

[1] Hans Leibholz (1899–1940), the elder brother of Gerhard, was judge at the district court in Berlin and immigrated to the Netherlands because of the Nuremberg laws of September 1935. He had many connections with supporters of the German resistance in the Netherlands but in May 1940 he was interned. During the German invasion he and his wife committed suicide; see Christine Koenigs, 'Unterstützung des deutschen Widerstands: Franz Koenings und Hans Leibholz', in: Detlef Blesgen (ed.), *Financiers, Finanzen und Finanzierungsformen des Widerstandes* (Berlin 2006), pp. 137–64, esp. pp. 139–42.

[2] See the many letters of travel agencies preserved in BA, N 1334.

Leibholz to Bell, 10 July 1941 Bell Papers 40, fol. 49 (typewritten)

My Lordbishop,

The Society for Protection of Science and Learning has written to me that they have approached Magdalen College, Oxford because the grant of 100 L. a year Magdalen

College awarded me two years ago will soon expire and that they hope that there is a chance of this grant from the College being renewed. I do not know whether you, my Lordbishop, remember that you had kindly written to Magdalen College on my behalf two years ago and that it is to you I owe that I was able to keep the grant in addition to the World Council stipend. Dr. Opie who, unfortunately, is now in America wrote at that time:

'The Committee has decided to continue the grant of 100 L. a year, despite the Fellowship from the International Churches Council in view of the heavy expenses of this family'. 'I hope that this will make it possible for you to work in more favourable conditions'.

I need not say that the reasons which prompted Magdalen College to make the generous decision in 1939 continue to exist to a growing extent at a time when the rate of living has so considerably increased and the future sources of income (as far as this country is concerned) are not secured in the same way as they were in 1939.

Of course, the whole question would not be acute if there were an actual chance of getting over and taking up the posts in the United States in the near future. I had a good talk not only with my tourist agency but also with Miss Roberts about this matter and I am also in correspondence with Dr. Paton about it. (I may perhaps enclose a copy of the report I have just given Dr. Paton about the situation.) If I am not completely misinformed I must take into account the probability of having to stay in this country for some time until it will be possible to overcome the present difficulties. This is also why the Society has made their approach [to] Magdalen College. For I told them that I have accepted the American offer, in the meantime.

I venture, therefore, to trouble you once again and to ask you whether you would be perhaps kindly prepared to write in the same way as you, my Lordbishop, did two years ago a supporting letter to the Committee of Refugee Scholars, Magdalen College in addition to the application made by the Society. I should think that such a letter would carry again great weight and secure the chance of getting the grant if there is any chance of renewing the grant at all. There would also be no risk if I should leave the country in course of the next few months as the grant is paid by the month at the rate of £8.6. through the Society and as in this case the Society could use the money in another way on behalf of other people.

You will certainly forgive me the trouble I am causing you and understand that I must look a little ahead as I am afraid there is no possibility of leaving this country for the time being. I am sure that the Society would warmly welcome your support, my Lordbishop, although it may perhaps be wiser not to mention to them the fact that I have asked you for help in this matter.

To justify my request to Magdalen College it may perhaps be worthwhile to mention that I am about to write a book on Christianity and the future international order, which is to contain, at the same time, a condensed analysis of the whole political and sociological situation of the totalitarian and Western countries and in which I am trying to make a positive constructive contribution to the new problems we have today to face from an attitude which wishes to take into account the conflicting claims of

Christianity and the political reality.[1] As things stand I hope to be able to finish this study still in this country – provided I have in the same way as hitherto the means of meeting the essential needs of living. And this is the reason why I venture to submit to you, my Lordbishop, my request.

With many thanks and kindest regards from all of us
Yours ever,

[1] An incomplete work not published.

Bell to Leibholz, 11 July 1941, Bell Papers 40, fol. 50 (carbon)

My dear Leibholz,

I have a letter dated June 18th from Van Dusen to the effect that they are delighted at your acceptance and adding that the Rockefeller Foundation Scholarship for two years is conditional on your undertaking the Lectureship not later than November 1st. Van Dusen also says that he wants you to get to U.S.A. by September 15th if in any way possible.

Mr. Paton has seen the letter and is going to exert the strongest possible pressure upon the Ministry about a berth for you. He thinks that with very strong pressure he may get you past the American consulate. He will do his best.

Yours ever,

Leibholz to Bell, 12 July 1941, Bell Papers 40, fol. 51 (typewritten)

My Lordbishop,
Many thanks for your letter.

I have just learned that the American Government has issued new regulations with regard to the emigration to the United States and I have asked Miss Roberts to send a copy of them to me. The main point seems to me to be that the State Department in Washington and not the American Consul in London has now to examine and decide the whole question and that two American citizens have to vouch for the would-be immigrants and to hand in all the necessary forms (curriculum vitae, statement about near relatives on the Continent, invitations and so forth). I cannot imagine that some time will not elapse till it will be possible to settle all these questions especially as an extensive correspondence from this country to America will prove necessary. I think, therefore, that I have been right in having written to you, my Lordbishop, my last letter.

I regret this new development all the more as I had already prepared everything with the American Consul in London and I have a letter from the Consul in my hands (written, of course, before the new regulations) saying that he would be prepared to issue the visas for all of us if I would be able to book the necessary accommodation.

I greatly appreciate the help Dr. Paton will kindly give me and I gratefully gather from your letter that Dr. Paton is going to exert a strong pressure upon the Ministry in this direction. I suppose that these efforts refer to my wife and the children as well as to myself. For I may perhaps make it quite clear as early as now that I would not be prepared to separate my fate from that of my family, under the present circumstances. Our and especially my position is very different from that of English people and I feel the strongest possible responsibilities for my family and I have no choice but in this case to take the possibility of an invasion into account. I should very much like to give you, my Lordbishop, the special reasons for having made up my mind in this direction if you wish to have them. I do not doubt that these would convince you, my Lordbishop, of their preponderance.

As to the fact that the Rockefeller Foundation Scholarship for two years is conditional on my undertaking the Lectureship no later than November 1st I may say that I hope to be in a position to comply with these terms. But, at the same time, I may perhaps point out that I know alone four people who have received an offer from the Rockefeller Foundation and that all these people have so far not been able to take up their posts because of present circumstances. Three of these people have been offered their posts a long time ago. But in no case the Rockefeller Foundation has cancelled the offer.

I am sending a copy of this letter to Dr. Paton.

Yours ever,

Paton to Leibholz, 15 July 1941, Bell Papers 40, fol. 53 (typewritten)

My dear Dr. Leibholz,

Thank you for your letter to me dated 10th July. I saw the Bishop of Chichester yesterday and had a word with him about this and your letter of 12th July together with your letter to him.

I had a talk the other day with Sir Herbert Emerson who told me that the impression he had first had that all visas were to be reviewed was wrong and that all existing visas for America will remain untouched, provided the holders can leave for America within the period of the visa. Should the visa expire before the traveller can make his journey, the question of revision then arises. I am afraid, therefore, that the principal problem is that of shipping and I fear that the trouble there is very serious and is not one to be got round by pressure on the Ministry of Shipping. The plain fact is that there are all too few ships available at all passenger transport to the U.S.A. [sic].

I think therefore that at the moment it might be well for you to verify with the American Consul the fact that the new regulations do not affect your existing visa and that the problem only arises if you have to overstay the period for which the visa is valid. You should also press on with the shipping arrangements.

As to the continuance of the Rockefeller grant, we would see, of course, what we could do by representations to the Rockefeller Committee.

Yours very sincerely,

Bell to George Gordon, The President of Magdalen College, Oxford, 15 July 1941, Bell Papers 40, fol. 52 (copy)

My dear Gordon,

I am writing about a German refugee, former Professor at Göttingen, Dr. GERHARD LEIBHOLZ (100, Banbury Road, Oxford). Two years ago Magdalen very kindly gave a grant of £100 a year to Dr. Leibholz, who is a married man with two children. The grant comes to an end and shortly as it was made for two years only in the first instance. He is one of the four scholars who are doing research work for the World Council of the Churches, receiving a modest stipend of £250 a year.

The Society for the Protection of Science and Learning have approached you for a renewal of the grant. I am writing to support this application as I know Dr. Leibholz very well indeed. We are in constant touch with one another, and he is quite first class. He has been offered a post in the U.S.A., together with a grant from the Rockefeller Foundation if he is able to commence his teaching in America in November. Dr. Paton and my Committee at Bloomsbury House are doing their level best to get over the immense difficulties, partly visa, and, still more, shipping, in order to enable him and his family to get to the United States. There is just a possibility of the difficulties being overcome, in which case, of course, we would not want the grant from Magdalen. But if you could renew the grant, in the event of his not being able to get a passage to the U.S.A., that would be a very great boon.

It may be worth adding that Dr. Leibholz is engaged in writing a book on Christianity and the future International Order, which will contain a condensed analysis of the whole political and sociological situation of the totalitarian states and the Western countries. He is hoping, thereby, to make a positive contribution to the new problems, which have to be faced in the light of the conflicting claims of Christianity and the political reality.

Hoping you are flourishing,
Yours ever,

Leibholz to Bell, 18 July 1941, Bell Papers 40, fol. 54 (typewritten)

My Lordbishop,

I warmly thank you for the letter to the President of Magdalen College backing up the application of the Society. Provided the financial secure funds are still available the Magdalen College will now certainly renew the grant after having received your letter, my Lordbishop. I will write to you again as soon as I have heard from them.

As to the America question I am just writing to Dean van Dusen and Dean Dun asking them whether they would kindly be prepared to act as my sponsors with the immigration authorities as the American Consul in London has only promised to issue the visas but has not yet actually (and this is unfortunately the decisive point) issued the visas themselves.

The whole matter is now more complicated than ever before and some further delay is inevitable. I am in touch with Dr. Paton and Miss Roberts and I hope I shall not need to trouble you with this matter. Only in a case of urgency I will ask you, my Lordbishop, for help.

Before pressing on with the shipping arrangements I think it wiser, under the circumstances, to wait until we hear from America that the State Department in Washington is prepared to admit us into the United States and to instruct the American Consul that the case has been tentatively approved. The special difficulty seems to me to be that my wife still has her near relatives in Germany but the wording of the regulations apparently admits exceptions to the rule that the issue of visas shall be withheld in these cases.

With renewed thanks and all good wishes
Yours ever,

Bell to H. P. van Dusen, 25 July 1941, Bell Papers 40, fol. 56 (carbon)

My dear van Dusen,
I was very grateful for your letter of June 18th and for the intimation which it contained confirming your telegram of June 13th with regard to the Rockefeller Foundation grant for Dr. Leibholz. Immediately I got your letter I informed Paton and Leibholz and your own office in Bloomsbury House. Everything possible is being done to secure a passage for the Leibholz[es]. Leibholz has himself I know written to America certain essential documents, and there is no doubt at all that everyone of us appreciates the urgent need of the maximum speed in getting Leibholz to America. But as Paton says, it is going to be a Herculean task to get the actual berths. Paton thinks that the Visa difficulty may be overcome, as Leibholz's is a very exceptional case, but berths are more difficult even than visas. However, you need not doubt that every possible step will be taken to get the family to America by September 15th, and we must hope and work for the best.

You have indeed done most splendidly on the scholarship side and there everything is happily settled, if only he can be got across in time.

With all best wishes,
Yours very sincerely,

H. P. van Dusen to Bell, 28 July 1941, Bell Papers 40, fol. 57 (typewritten)

My dear Bishop,
Thank you warmly for your letter of 2nd July. In today's mail, I also have a very fine letter from Leibholz.

I am today cabling you, asking you to cable if you experience difficulty in the matter of [a] visa from the American authorities. It happens that the Assistant Secretary of State who has responsibility in this area, Mr. Breckenridge Long,[1] is a personal friend who has already proven very helpful in the matter of the theological refugees, so we are assured of the best cooperation in Washington.

We are looking forward very eagerly to having the Leibholz family with us.

With cordial personal regards, I am
Faithfully yours,

---

[1] Samuel Miller Breckenridge Long (1881–1958), American diplomat and politician, appointed Assistant Secretary of State in January 1940.

H. P. van Dusen to Bell, 29 July 1941, Bell Papers 40, fol. 58 (cablegram)
IF LEIBHOLZ FACING VISA DIFFICULTIES PLEASE CABLE PARTICULARS IMMEDIATELY SO I CAN CONFER PERSONALLY WITH STATE DEPARTMENT NEXT WEEK
HENRY VAN DUSEN

Leibholz to Bell, 1 August 1941, Bell Papers 40, fol. 59 (typewritten)

My Lordbishop,
Many thanks for your lines, which I have just received. May I say that about nine days ago I wrote by Airmail letter to Dean van Dusen and Dean Dun about all questions arising out of the new regulations of the American Government. I expressed [to] Dean van Dusen my sincerest thanks for all that he has so far kindly done for me and asked him and Dean Dun – if possible – kindly to act as my sponsors with the immigration authorities. As various forms have to be filled up by the sponsors I provided them with all particulars and enclosed various documents. As about 15 questions (concerning my wife and myself) have to be answered in detail I am afraid that it will be too long for a cable.

If you, my Lordbishop, do not mind I would, therefore, suggest to cable that letters containing all particulars and a report about the situation are underway and that we hope that these letters will be there in the course of next week.

If the approval of the State Department is secured, they will authorise the U.S. Consul in London to grant us a preliminary interview for a visa. If this interview is satisfactory I have to inform my agency. It is, unfortunately, not possible to follow up the shipping question before the other questions are satisfactorily settled.

With all good wishes,
Yours ever,

Bell to the Editor of *The Times*, 16 August 1941, BA, N 1334 (copy)

Sir,
The Joint Declaration of President Roosevelt and Mr Churchill is a Charter of liberty. It sounds a trumpet call to the free peoples, and to all those in the occupied and enemy countries who long for deliverance from tyranny.

The Declaration is a political document, with the authority of Government behind it. It possesses therefore a political significance far beyond the reach of a churchman's manifesto. But there is one point, which the Church has a duty to press. What the President and the Prime Minister describe as 'certain common principles in national policies in their respective countries' are not for cold storage. In a famous letter to *The Times* on an agreed Christian order the English Primates, the Cardinal, and the Moderator of the Free Church Council wrote thus: 'No permanent peace is possible in Europe unless the principles of the Christian religion are made the foundation of national policy and of all social life'. (*The Times*, 21 December 1940).

If we are sincere, we must recognise that 'fullest collaboration between all nations in the economic field', and 'access on equal terms to the trade and to the raw materials of the world', and the lightening of the 'crushing burden of armaments', will involve great sacrifices. The Christian religion teaches that covetousness is idolatry, and that the love of money is the root of all evil. Never was there greater need that men and nations should listen to that teaching. This means a Reformation of a new kind, with visible results. Without it, the Joint Declaration would be only another example of wishful thinking: with it, the beginning indeed of a New World Order.

Yours, etc. GEORGE CICESTR.
The Palace, Chichester. August 16.

Leibholz to Bell, 19 August 1941, Bell Papers 40, fol. 60 (typewritten); BA, N 1334 (two copies with minor differences)

My Lordbishop,
I have read with great interest this morning your letter to the Editor of the *Times* in which you call attention to the main weak point of the joint declaration. I am in complete agreement with you and I think it cannot be stressed strongly enough that on freedom alone no new international Order can be built up. Above all, there must be a basis for freedom, ᵃforᵃ its intrinsic value and significance, its goal and its limit. I think, therefore, it is excellent that you, my Lordbishop, have quoted in this connection the famous letter to the *Times* of December 21, 1940.[1] Indeed there is no other foundation on which actually a better World Order can be solidly constructed in times to come.

The following reflections also show up the weak point you have mentioned:

The third point of the declaration says that the Anglo-Saxon countries will respect the right of all peoples to choose the form of Government under which they will live. This right is obviously to be enjoyed ᵃalsoᵃ by the totalitarian states. ᵃButᵃ in fact, this is not possible as the main war aim is directed to overcome the Nazi regime. In Point Eight of the declaration the 'final destruction of Nazi tyranny' is also expressly mentioned as the presupposition for any peace talk[s].

Further, the same Point says that 'pending the establishment of a wider and permanent system of a general security' the disarmament of the aggressor nations is essential. Actually, this goes farther than the Versailles Treaty in so far as in it a promise of general disarmament was, ~~in any case~~, held out. Herewith not only a Nazi regime but also any regime of military or conservative kind or tincture will be ruled out for Germany in future. If this is so one cannot say that the peoples can choose their own governments. The different statements proceed from different points of view. This is not surprising because, in my view, the principle of self-determination cannot longer claim validity in its traditional form. In truth, the freedom of peoples to choose their governments is limited today. A system of government can only be chosen within the framework of certain principles on which the new order shall be based. And I need not say that I have in mind the principles you have mentioned in your letter.

Also the promise of 'fullest collaboration between all nations in the economic field' and 'access on equal terms to the trade and to the raw materials and so on' has its weak point. For Point four says that the existing obligations of the nations, which make the declaration shall not be affected. That means that, for instance, the resolutions of the Ottawa Conference,[2] which have driven many countries – frequently against their own will – into the hands of the totalitarian Powers will apparently not be altered in any way. It seems to me as if I had heard the same principles after the last war and also in the last decades. As these principles failed so sadly in the past and did not bring about a true peace nor hinder the outbreak of the present war how shall they do better now? Reading these and other phrases of the statements it sounds to me like a tale from old times.

I think one of the most important tasks of any declaration of war aims is to appeal to the peoples of the totalitarian states in some way which would appeal to their better judgement. For I for my part believe that this war can only be won with the help of the German people. Sporadic risings in the occupied countries will fail unless they are supported by the Germans themselves in any form. And when I examine the declaration from this special aspect I must openly confess that it seems to me (except for the giving up of the plan of the disarmament of Germany) rather disappointing and without a really constructive lead. The declaration in its present form cannot appeal to the German people because the so-called new principles are, in truth, the old slogans.

As far as I can see a change of the political system in Germany can only come from above by a coup d'État of army leaders or from below. The joint declaration makes it impossible for the army – should an occasion arise later on – to take the first way. Should, however, the resolution come from below and the declaration retain its relevance for all peace negotiations in times to come,[3] then, I am afraid, the course of events will take a quite different direction from that which responsible people in this country imagine. For it is not true that National Socialism is the same as Communism and there is another possibility for people who are now in despair to find out a way after the present regime in Germany has been overthrown, all the more as the present alliance between Britain and Russia is only directed to destroy 'Hitlerite Germany'.

With all good wishes,
Yours ever,

---

[1] *The Times* 21 December 1940, p. 5, col. c; a joint letter written by the Archbishops of Canterbury and York, Cardinal Hinsley and W.H. Armstrong, Moderator of the Free Church Federal Council, to endorse the Five Peace Points of Pope Pius XII, attaching them to the Five Economic Standards adopted at the 1937 Oxford Conference on Church, Community and State.

[2] The British Empire Economic Conference held in Ottawa 1932 worked to establish a zone of limited tariffs within the Empire, but with high tariffs with the rest of the world. This was called 'Imperial preference' or 'Empire Free-Trade' based on the principle of 'home producers first, empire producers second, and foreign producers last'.

[3] 'Are to be conducted' corrected to 'in times to come'.

Bell to Leibholz, 22 August 1941, BA, N 1334 (typewritten); Bell Papers 40, fol. 61 (carbon)

My dear Leibholz,

I was very glad indeed to get your letter of 19th August, commenting on my letter to *The Times*. I very much appreciate what you say, and I am delighted with the fact that you are not only in agreement with me, but that you have further points, which seem to me to be of the greatest importance. I should like to show your letter, if I may, to the Secretary for the Dominions,¹ whom I know fairly well. May I do so?

I have just had a letter from Dietrich ªJune 17ª through Zurich. He is well and asks me to give his love to your wife.²

I have just received the enclosed letter from Dean van Dusen, which you may like to see.

Yours ever,

---

¹ Robert Arthur James Gascoyne-Cecil (1893–1972), Conservative politician, since 1941 Baron Cecil, Viscount Cranborne from 1903 to 1947 (and, thereafter, 5th Marquess of Salisbury). Cranborne was Secretary of State for the Dominions from 3 October 1940 to 19 February 1942, Lord Privy Seal 1942–43 (and later in 1951–2), and Leader of the House of Lords, first in 1942–5 and later in 1951–7.
² See Dietrich Bonhoeffer to Bell, 12 or 17 June 1941, in: *DBW* 16, p. 185.

Leibholz to Bell, 25 August 1941, Bell Papers 40, fol. 64 (typewritten); BA, N 1334 (copy)

My Lordbishop,

Very many thanks for your letter. Certainly please do whatever you like with my last letter.

I may perhaps say in this connection that in the last *Christian News-Letter* Dr Oldham reports quite fully on a recent issue of 'Planning', which deals with the political future of Germany after the present government has been overthrown and which you will probably have seen.¹ The authors of the broadsheet mentioned come to the conclusion that after the defeat of Nazi Germany it will hardly be possible to find an alternative government to Nazism and that the victorious powers, therefore, would have to assume control and temporary responsibility for dealing with the post-war problems. I think this solution is neither desirable because it could not lead to a pacification of the world and a true New Order nor – and this seems to me to be still more important – a solution which puts the political realities to good account. A defeated Nazi Germany is, of necessity, in a stage of revolution and disintegration. The chance of getting a non-communist Government is already rather remote, all the more as the official policy of this country is practically directed in a way, which seems to me to make such a government more and more impossible. And what are the chances of a Communist Germany? The communist forces in Germany are not weakened in the same way as those of the former ruling classes and parties. Above all, a defeated Nazi Germany presupposes a weakened but victorious Russia, which is free from her alliance with this country. And Russia is nearer to Germany than the Anglo-Saxon countries – geographically as well as politically and spiritually. She is better able to conceive the mentality and feeling of the lower classes and masses in Germany than the Western countries. If Germany should not get from the victorious powers terms which fulfil the demands of the ideological character of the present war why should she not join Russia after the Hitler Regime has been overthrown [?] A second Versailles or a Super-Versailles (including occupation, education and so on) is as far as I can judge it wishful thinking. It is a dangerous dream of people who do not realize that the traditional political standards are not applicable to the present time. A defeated Germany offers the world a much more probable alternative: either a peace made on equal terms the possibility of which – as things are going – seems to be rather improbable or a Communist Europe against the Anglo-Saxon countries. I am afraid that people in this country do not realize this alternative quite clearly because so far the Nazi defeat, especially in the East, is still remote and, therefore, the precondition for a realistic peace talk is not given.[2]

Many thanks also for the letter from Dean van Dusen. I was very glad indeed to have had the letter, which I return herewith.

As Dr Paton was on holiday I got in touch with the American Consulate who replied that further action cannot be taken in my case with any prospect of success in London before the State Department at Washington has given its approval. I must therefore now wait till Washington has informed London. Not until this has happened can I get in touch again with the various shipping companies. In order not to trouble you with my personal affairs more than I have already done I have informed Miss Roberts asking her to report to Dean van Dusen about the state of affairs after having consulted Dr Paton. In any case I feel sure I shall have to stay here for some time so that I can see Dean van Dusen in case he should make his projected trip to this country. Then I can also tell him of the present shipping difficulties, which the Americans obviously do not fully realize.

My wife was extremely glad to hear from you about Dietrich and asks me to convey to you, my Lordbishop, her heartfelt thanks,

Yours ever,

---

[1] J. H. Oldham, in the *Christian News-Letter*, No. 95, 20 August 1941.
[2] In 1939 Bell had feared that a war to the bitter end would involve 'a much stronger and a much more dangerous Russia' and the victory of 'the powers of atheism and Communism'. *Hansard*, H.L. Deb., Vol. 115, col. 253 (13 December 1939), reprinted as 'Peace Meditation', in Bell, *The Church and Humanity*, pp. 32–7.

Bell to Leibholz, Chichester, 27 August 1941, BA, N 1334 (typewritten); Bell Papers 40, fol. 63 (carbon)

My dear Leibholz,

I am deeply interested in your letter and your views of Oldham's summary of the broadsheet on the future of Germany. I have a copy of that broadsheet, which I send herewith. Perhaps you would return it to me later on. If I can find a spare copy, you shall have it.[a] (Don't return this copy after all unless I ask for it.)[a]

I do not know whether you have read Paton's new book on *The Church and the New Order*.[1] It takes a rather similar line, and Dr Paton* is very definitely working and trying to influence opinion along these lines through the Commission of the Churches and other bodies. Your criticism of the *Christian News-Letter* summary makes me very anxious to get from you a statement of some constructive solution of this problem.

I think it is only too likely that most British people are hopelessly unrealistic in their conception of the possibilities resulting from this War. The defeat of Germany in any such form as could lead to an imposed peace seems to me to be a long way off, as far as one can judge from the ordinary sources of information and one's own sense of realities.

I have been asked by Siegmund Schultze[2] a few weeks ago whether I could put him on to any statement in British official circles, which was at all in the line with the sentiment expressed in my *Penguin* and particularly the contents of my chapter 8. He did not actually quote in words of mine in his letter, but I take it that what he and so many people really want is a kind of new world order in which a free German people could take their due place. I was challenged the other day by a group who were reading my *Penguin*, who asked whether any steps had actually been taken on the lines of my suggestion on Page 105 that Christians in one belligerent country should seek such opportunities as may be opened to discover 'from fellow-Christians in another belligerent country what terms of peace would be likely to create a lasting peace and not lead to a further poisoning of international relationships'.[3] I wonder what you would think such terms of peace might be? Our present official Government policy tends to the fixing of the old plan of separate alliances with the certainty of a new war in the end and probably the division of Europe, as you suggest, into a Communist camp versus an Anglo-Saxon one. I myself cannot help thinking that it might be the Churches' special task to keep the idea of the family of nations very much alive, and to give it concrete expression as against the idea of separate alliances.

The point which Dr Paton makes in his book *The Church and the New Order* is that nothing can be done without 'power' and that the only possessors of power holding the right views of the relationship of nations will be after the War England and the United States; but it is a long way yet to the War's end and many things may happen that none of us expect.

I entirely understand what you say about the position with regard to yourself and the American Consulate.

Yours ever,

[*][a]P.S. I have just received a confidential draft from Dr Paton,[4] please treat it as such, and return it to me with any comments arising out of the particular points relative to the remarks in my letter and on pp. 5 f.[a]

---

[1] William Paton, *The Church and the New Order* (London, Student Christian Movement Press, 1941).
[2] Friedrich Siegmund-Schultze's request was very likely connected with his own secret activities as intermediary between the German resistance and the British Government; see Stefan Grotefeld, *Friedrich Siegmund-Schultze*, pp. 307–9.
[3] See Bell, *Christianity and World Order*, p. 106.
[4] This would surely have been the memorandum of that summer which Visser 't Hooft devised under the title, 'The Church and the New Order in Europe'. Here he sought to represent, and integrate, the distinct views of Paton and Bonhoeffer. It was no mean feat. See Klemperer, *German Resistance Against Hitler*, pp. 272–3 and Visser 't Hooft, *Memoirs*, pp. 153–5.

Leibholz to Bell, 2 September 1941, Bell Papers 40, fols. 64–5 (typewritten); BA, N 1334 (carbon)

My Lordbishop,
Very many thanks for your letter and the enclosures you have kindly sent me. I have read them with great interest. May I add in this connection a few remarks to my last letter:

The problematic factor which must be taken into account in all the new 'Plans' seems to me to be the political condition in which Germany will find herself at the end of this war after the defeat of the Hitler regime. It depends on answering satisfactorily this decisive question whether there will be a chance of realising the various plans recently drawn up.

A defeated Nazi Germany will certainly be in a state of despair, starvation and demoralisation and in a stage of civil war, which will take a more violent character than the coup d'État from below in 1918. It is true that the authors of the broadsheet 'Planning' do not foresee such a revolutionary development within Germany even after a military defeat and say that the happenings of 1918 when Communism was at its fullest virulence will not come to pass again. 'We need no longer as in 1919 fear that Germany will go Bolshevik'. I think such a conclusion can only be the result of the largely spread opinion held today in this country that the German people stand united behind the Nazi regime. Everyone who is really acquainted with the political situation in Germany will voice another opinion. They know that in 1918 the number of Communists was extremely small (in the German National Assembly of 1919 there was not a single Communist MP) as contrasted with the situation in 1932 (there were more than six millions communists) and today (there are still more millions, especially the former liberal-minded socialists who will express communist sympathies after a Hitler defeat). The authors of the broadsheet say: 'A defeated Germany is likely to be like a Pétain Government'. But a Pétain Government is the model of a government for a country which is defeated by the Nazis and not a type of Government of a defeated fascist country.

Out of an Anti-Nazi revolution will come a Communist or Non-Communist government. In any case a government in a disintegrated Germany cannot stabilize its position unless it can rely very largely on support from outside. A Non-Communist government needs the help of the Anglo-Saxon countries, a Communist Germany, that of Russia. The chances of the Anti-Nazi government trying to evade the communist implications (no matter how the government itself may be composed) seem to me weaker than those of a Communist Germany, first because the former ruling classes which can possibly support such a government have no longer the old strength and secondly because such a government would presumably not get the help it needs from the Western countries for its existence. As a result of the strain of the war and of publications like Vansittart's[1] (cf. also the able but no less one-sided and therefore dangerous book *The Roots of National Socialism 1783–1933* by R. d'O. Butler[2]) the present war is being waged to a growing extent as a national and not an ideological war. From this point of view a policy which wants to finish the war in terms of power-politics seems to be only consequent [sic]. Even more humanitarian reconstruction plans, which do not want to impose on a defeated Germany a Versailles or Super-Versailles are not free from resorting to the old means of power-policy. Above all, this applies to the plans recently much advocated to occupy Germany and to assume governmental powers in Germany by the Allies until it will be possible to re-establish normal political activities in Germany. An occupation of a country like Germany after the cessation of hostilities (together with education of the German nation) will always be in its practical effect an instrument of revenge and will lay the seed for hatred and new wars even if these measures are meant well.

I for my part do not believe in the possibility of such a kind of peace as a defeated Nazi-Germany will still be in the position to take another choice. Germany can switch over from the West to the East. A Communist Germany can offer the German people immediate gains of considerable significance. Russia is not fighting the German nation as a whole and certainly not a Communist Germany. On the contrary a communist Germany would receive all possible political, military and economic help from Russia. She would not insist on occupation, education, moral disqualifications, reparations and even disarmament. The bonds of the same creed and the same feeling are stronger than all the various safeguards which the Western countries are devising today in an understandable distrust against a post-Nazi Germany who, as far as she is non-communist, is compelled to stand for the same principles and values as the West. A communist Germany could evade national humiliations, especially an occupation, as this country and the Americans will probably not be prepared to send an occupation army to a communist Germany.

It may, therefore, happen again what has happened once before. [sic] One denied some rights of living to a Liberal Germany in order to give them [to] a national socialist Germany without reservations. It may happen again that a new Anti-Nazi government may be offered a dictated peace to the effect that Germany will eventually get communist. One has labelled the utopian appeasement policy as realism and will still more label as realism the old-fashioned national power policy hoping that in this way the German danger may be banned for ever and a permanent peace may be secured.

I come therefore to the conclusion that it may be wise to treat an Anti-Nazi government, which may come out of an Anti-Nazi revolution and has not a communist character, in the same way as Russia would treat a communist Germany. I need not explain what I mean by this. I should give such a government all possible help (on request even military help) so that they may be able to consolidate their position. The re-establishment of order in Germany should be the first stage in the making of peace, which should finally be negotiated as a peace between equals. A new international order worthy of this name presupposes a certain amount of common ideals and binding values, which holds the members of the community together. If this homogeneity does not exist, a true international order cannot develop. Such a common ethos is more important than the use of power, safeguards based on force and schemes, constitutions and blue prints. In my view the League of Nations collapsed finally because it was not able to withdraw itself from the political basis given to it by Versailles and because it served essentially to legitimise the existing political status quo. I myself cannot help thinking that the idea of the family of nations (against the old fashioned idea of separate alliances) and the principles to which we are attached (cf. the letter to *The Times* of Dec. 21st, 1940, your proposals and those of Dr Paton in his draft, pp. 1–4) have a chance of being realized only in a world which is not torn between a communist continent and a liberal democratic Anglo-Saxon world.

I am quite sure that my fellow-Christians in Germany would fully agree to such a procedure as it would provide the world with the basis which 'would be likely to create a lasting peace and not lead to a further poisoning of international relationships'. Should it be possible to secure such a basis then I think it would not be too difficult to set forth in a more precise and systematic form concrete terms of peace as the invaluable preliminary work put forward by the various Christian Churches, especially in this country, would be wholeheartedly acceptable for all true Christians in Germany to a large extent.

From this basic attitude of mind, it would also be possible to push forward a propaganda policy, which could claim more convincing power on the masses in Germany. Above all, communism in Europe could possibly be avoided in this way. For instance, I cannot see how France can evade becoming communist if we presuppose a victorious Russia, if we realize the impossibility of re-establishing the old liberal parliamentary system together with the strength of the communist movement in France and see the great communist neighbour in the East.

Of course, I know that many people see the alliance between Russia and this country from another aspect. They think that Russia will not come 'out of the war as she went into it' and will do everything in her power to avoid a conflict with the West and will eventually be won back to the West. This may be perhaps right if the Russians will collapse and yet a final and total victory is won. Otherwise I am afraid there is much wishful thinking in it. If Nazi Germany is defeated by help of Russia her strength over Europe and especially Central Europe will be increased enormously and I do not see any reason why in this case the winner on the Continent needs revising its principles [sic]. The old antagonism between Russia and the Anglo-Saxon countries would revive as soon ᵃasᵃ the purpose of the alliance, the destruction of Hitlerite Germany, has been accomplished.

I think all this is rather difficult to say in this stage of the war and does not be [sic] in keeping with the general lines, which are mostly taken in this country today. But as you, my Lordbishop, ask me to tell you what I think I do so quite openly without subduing some apprehensions that the public opinion in this country is partly misled about the real issues of the war and the peace to come, especially as the result of the growing nationalist tendencies.

I have so far not read Dr Paton's book *The Church and the New Order* but I am about to read it. If I have to make a special comment on it arising out of the particular point discussed in this letter I will write to you, my Lordbishop, again.

Yours ever,

ᵃP.S. I return herewith Dr Paton's draft with many thanks.ᵃ

---

[1] Robert Gilbert Vansittart (1881–1957), since 1941 1st Baron Vansittart. Vansittart had opposed British Appeasement before the outbreak of war and now, during the Second World War, supported a vehemently anti-German line, arguing that no distinction could credibly be drawn between Germans at large and Nazis in particular. For Vansittart the National Socialist State was no aberration, but the consequence of the traits of the German people at large as history itself had revealed them. See his widely read polemic *Black Record. German Past and Present* (London 1941).

[2] Rohan d'Olier Butler (1917–96), *The Roots of National Socialism 1783–1933* (London, 1941); see too Leibholz, 'Nationality in History and Politics', reprinted in Leibholz, *Politics and Law*, p. 74.

Bell to Leibholz, 20 September 1941, BA, N 1334 (handwritten)

What is Pastor Sutz's address?[1]

My dear Leibholz,
I was delighted to get the message from D.[2] It is a boon in itself, and very comforting in its contents. I hope, by the way, I thanked you for your earlier full and most instructive letter in commenting on the Broadsheet.[3] I am vy. glad to hear your view of King-Hall's book,[4] which I will try and get hold of. You will no doubt see van Dusen in Oxford shortly. I expect to be in Oxford for a few days (conferences) from September 30–October 5 or 6; and shall hope to arrange a time for a talk with you.
    All best wishes & remembrances to your wife and the girls.

Yours ever,

When we meet let us talk about the future, and your ideas of a possible new way for Germany (and Europe) as much as about yourselves.

[1] In his letter to Bell on 25 September 1941 Bonhoeffer thanked Bell for his letter (now lost); *DBW* 16, p. 210.
[2] This message is lost. Bonhoeffer's second visit to Switzerland lasted from 29 August to 26 September 1941.
[3] See Leibholz to Bell, 2 September 1941.
[4] Stephen King-Hall, *Total Victory* (London, 1941). Leibholz's letter is lost.

Bell to Leibholz, 26 September 1941, BA, N 1334 (typewritten)

My dear Leibholz,
Very many thanks for both your letters,[1] and particularly for the beautiful book Dietrich gave to his sister and you, which is double appreciation for the double connection. It is a lovely book, and I am most grateful.
    I am very much interested in what you tell me about the visit of the Dutch friend.
    I am hoping to see you next week, but I am afraid it is not very likely that I shall actually be able to get out to your house.

With all best wishes, and many thanks,
Yours ªveryª sincerely,

[1] The second letter is lost and the mentioned Dutch friend, perhaps a contact of Leibholz's brother, Paul, is unknown.

Bell to Leibholz, 30 October 1941, BA, N 1334 (typewritten)

My dear Leibholz,
Very many thanks for your letter.[1] I do hope that Magdalen College will come to a favourable decision.
    I entirely agree with your view on the comments from Geneva to Dr Paton's book.[2] I remember your letter to me after the Atlantic Charter very well.[3] I am also entirely

with you in what you say endorsing the comments and have written to Paton strongly in that sense myself. Thank you also for the cutting from the Swedish paper, and the comments on the Bishop of Münster.[4]

I am much interested to hear about your course of lectures on Christianity and Politics, and I do hope that you will give this course. Is it not possible that the lectures might be printed afterwards?[5] In any event it would be most healthy and helpful that you should give them.

I had a letter from Dietrich the other day: he wrote very cordially from Zurich, and is full of courage and hope.[6] I trust that you and your wife are cheered both by his reports from Germany and by his confidence, which I share, in a happy future for you and your wife and children. These months of waiting are difficult and trying, but I most earnestly hope and believe that the valley through which we are passing at the moment, and through which you are also passing, will not be a long or an endless one, but will lead to the day.

Yours very sincerely,

[1] This letter is lost.
[2] That is from the offices of the World Council of Churches (in process of formation) in Geneva.
[3] See Leibholz to Bell, 19 August 1941.
[4] Leibholz must have written here of the three courageous sermons of Clemens August von Galen, bishop of Münster, in July and August 1941. These received widespread international attention and were subsequently published in Britain as a pamphlet with an introduction by the Roman Catholic Archbishop of Liverpool, Richard Downey.
[5] The lectures are reprinted in *Politics and Law*, pp. 91–132.
[6] See Bonhoeffer to Bell, 25 September 1941, in *DBW* 16, pp. 210–11.

Leibholz to Bell, 18 November 1941, Bell Papers 40, fols. 66-7 (typewritten); BA, N 1334 (copy)

My Lordbishop,

I was just about to write to thank you, my Lordbishop, for your very kind letter of October 30th when yesterday your letter of November 15th reached me with the message from Dr van Dusen.[1] I have thought over all that you, my Lordbishop, have kindly written to me and I think you are right in all you say. As things stand I believe I ought to take the opportunity which opens to me for more constructive work and take the natural risks involved in such a step, under the present circumstances (especially the danger of the passage for the children). I also trust with you that Dr van Dusen will help me to see the things through, both to satisfactory work and to a settlement of the financial questions.

I hope to see the consul in London in the course of next week. From a communication I have just received from him I gather that the State Department at Washington has tentatively approved the issuance of non-quota visas to my family and myself. Therefore I need not reckon with any difficulty in this respect. But according to the American regulations my wife and I need 'a statement in writing, in duplicate, from someone in authority or of good standing who has known applicant for a number of years, establishing applicant's character'. I should be very grateful to you, my Lordbishop, if you would kindly let my wife and me have such a short statement, in duplicate. Please forgive me for troubling you with this matter.

As to the financial arrangements Dr van Dusen told me that the Rockefeller stipend was limited to the 1st of November last. But I hope very much that he will find out a way of having it renewed. I suppose Dr van Dusen will have written to you, my Lordbishop, on this question and I think we need not write to him until we have more details [as to] how things now stand in this respect.

In any case it would not be easy, under the present circumstances, to leave this country where we have met with so much kindness and above all to lose you, my Lordbishop. You have cheered us up so often and have given us again and again not only help and protection whenever we needed them (and I needed them continuously) but also new hope and courage. But I trust you will keep up your friendship with us even when we are overseas. How true it is that all life is a pilgrimage.

My wife and I were delighted to hear the good news you had from Dietrich. I need not tell you how much we hope that the confidence with which he faces the future is well founded. Other people from whom we heard lately obviously seem to take a similar view. In any case I think you, my Lordbishop, did very well in endorsing the comments written from Geneva. There are so few outstanding people who see the happenings on the continent in a clear light and from a sober and realistic attitude. And it is on these men that our hope for the future is based.

In the meantime, I am still going on with my preparations for the lectures on *Christianity and Politics*[2] next term although I do not know whether I will give the course. I will try to prepare them in such a way that they could be submitted to a publisher later on. Dr Hodgson[3] told me that he will do whatever is within his power to help me in this matter.

I wrote to you, my Lordbishop, recently that I think that Nazism is waging its war against Christianity indirectly by attacking Judaism, which has first enshrined the spiritual doctrine, which according to the demonical radicalism of Nazism must be destroyed. Yesterday I read an article by J. Maritain on Christianity and Anti-Semitism, which takes the same line – only much more stressed the issue at stake.[4] The article impressed me so strongly (much more than the rather disappointing supplement to the *Christian News-Letter* a few weeks ago) that I dare to enclose it in this letter – presuming you might be interested in reading it. I should be grateful to you, my Lordbishop, if I could have it back later on.

In connection with our talk on propaganda I also enclose an extract of a typical Goebbels statement [of] 'what defeated Germany would face' (I read it in *The Times*), which in this or another form is rubbed into the German people every day. This form of propaganda should be counteracted by every means possible in every broadcast stating that the whole misery in Germany of today is the work of the present regime and that when the conquests will be disgorged and the Nazis will be overthrown, there remains a decent future for the German people as well.

With all good wishes and renewed thanks
Yours ever,

1   This letter is lost.
2   The printed programme is preserved in the Bell Papers, Vol. 40, fol. 105 (print); N 1334 (photocopy):
    REGIUS PROFESSOR OF MORAL AND PASTORAL THEOLOGY (L. HODGSON, D. D.)A course of four lectures on 'Christianity and Politics' will be delivered for the Professor by Dr G. Leibholz, formerly Professor der Rechte in the University of Göttingen, in the Chapter House, Christ Church, on Saturdays at 11 a.m., as follows:

    24th January. Christianity, Politics and the Political Claims of the Church.
    31st January. Political Totalitarianism and its Religious Implications. The Process of De-Christianization.
    7th February. The Issue at Stake: Paganism or Christianity.
    14th February. The Christian Hope and the Tasks of the Church for the World of Tomorrow.
    Dr. J. K. Mozley's Lectures on 'The Use of the Bible' will be postponed until Trinity Term.

3   Leonard Hodgson (1889–1969), in 1938 elected Regius Professor of Moral and Pastoral Theology and Canon of Christ Church, Oxford, and between 1944 and 1958 Regius Professor of Divinity. During the 1930s he had become an active ecumenist in the Faith and Order movement (he was secretary-general of the Edinburgh World Conference on Faith and Order in 1937). Hodgson also served on the Archbishop of Canterbury's Council on Foreign Relations.
4   Jacques Maritain, 'On Anti-Semitism', in *Christianity and Crisis*, 4 October 1941, now to be found in *Oeuvres Complètes*, Vol. 8 (Fribourg 1989), pp. 562–4. The opinion that anti-Semitism was a disguise of Christophobia was essential to Maritain's thinking. The philosopher Jacques Maritain (1882–1973) had in 1906 converted to Roman Catholicism. It was through his study of Thomas Aquinas's *Summa* that he became a leading Catholic professor of Metaphysics and, from the middle of the 1930s, of practical philosophy (in, for example, his *Humanisme Integral*, 1936).

Bell to Leibholz, 21 November 1941, BA, N 1334 (typewritten); Bell Papers 40, fol. 68ᵛ (carbon)

My dear Leibholz,

Very many thanks for your most interesting and useful letter, and for the extremely valuable article which struck me greatly. I have sent a reply to Lord Vansittart's attack, and shall be interested to see whether the *Sunday Times* will print it.[1]

Thank you for the quotation from Goebbels. I return *Christianity and Crisis*.

I do feel very much for you with regard to the future and the making of plans. It will be a real loss to me personally that you and your wife and children should be leaving England. I regard our friendship as something very deep and important, and it must be a lasting friendship, for wherever you are I shall count you as a brother and a friend; and your wife has a very special place in my affection, for her own sake and for Dietrich's. You must let me know how plans develop.

In the meantime, I gladly send you herewith a note for the consul.

Yours always,

ᵃEnclosed: not to handᵃ

1   By now Bell and Vansittart were jousting regularly in the House of Lords and in the press, where Bell had determined that his adversary should never go unanswered. See the *Sunday Times*, 23 November 1941, now to be found in Besier, *Intimately Associated for Many Years*, pp. 226–7.

The Bishop of Chichester, 21 November, 1941, BA, N 1334 (photocopy and copy); Bell Papers 40, fol. 68 (carbon)

This is to testify that I know Dr G. Leibholz and his wife and two children very well. Dr Leibholz and Mrs Leibholz are people of the highest standing and personal integrity.

Dr Leibholz is a scholar of European reputation and a man of highest capacity and character.

Bell to Leibholz, 8 corrected into 12 December 1941, BA, N 1334 (typewritten)

My dear Leibholz,

Many thanks for your letter, and for letting me know of your forthcoming appointment at the American Consulate* I shall be very much interested to know what happens. Please tell me what your address will be in London.

I am very sorry not to have returned Maritain's article, which I read with the deepest interest. It has been reprinted, I am glad to see, in *Time and Tide*.[1]

Yours ever,

[*] ªSince then[2] the whole world is changed: and I expect [crossed out: you will hardly think] all American plans effecting you are all changed too!ª

[1] On 7 December the Japanese air forces attacked the American fleet in Pearl Harbor. On the following day the United States declared war on Japan. On 11 December Germany and Italy declared war on the United States.
[2] *Time and Tide*, first published in 1920, was an influential, though not widely read, British weekly review offering an impressive body of broadly leftwing and feminist writing on political and literary affairs.

Leibholz to Bell, 19 December 1941, Bell Papers, 40, fol. 69 (typewritten)

My dear Lordbishop,

I was very sorry indeed not to have met you in London the day before yesterday. I rang Miss Roberts up several times but, unfortunately, in vain as you had been kept in the House of Lords.

As Miss Roberts will have told you, my Lordbishop, the appointment with the American Consul took a satisfactory course and the Consul told me that we all shall get non-quota visas if shipping accommodation should be available. This does, however, not exclude the future possibility of the visas being cancelled. Then the American government would proceed in the same way as the British government did at the outbreak of the present war.

But apart from this the situation seems to me changed now in some other directions. First so far the 'enemy aliens' in America have not had much to suffer. But a repetition of the Pearl Harbor events by reason of which even naturalized people of alien extraction have been interned would change the whole picture all the more as in America (unlike in this country) a fifth column problem of great weight certainly exists. I think that if I should go to America, under the present changed circumstances, in the long run, there would only be the choice between being interned or being prepared to take the first papers in order to become an American subject as soon as possible. This would mean that I would be immediately liable to military duty. And although I doubt whether I am fit (because of my heart) the position of my family would cause me great anxieties in this case, especially as there are no means upon which they could live. Moreover, the chance of perhaps a possible return to Germany after the war would be much aggravated as a result of taking the papers with all its implications in the present time. – Further I do not know how the war as a whole will affect my suggested position there. Especially I doubt whether the Rockefeller Foundation, which has bound itself only until the 1st of November, will now be prepared to extend the stipend as Dr. van Dusen had definitely hoped.

For all these reasons I would frankly not mind if we could postpone our crossing until we have from van Dusen a satisfactory answer to the questions which have now arisen and considerably affect the whole matter. I fully realize my great indebtedness to Dr. van Dusen for all he has kindly done on my behalf and I am the last who would wish to disappoint him in any way. I also fully appreciate the great opportunity which the new post in the United States offers me for more constructive work, especially also possibly after the war.

Of course, I do not like to interfere with your plans, my Lordbishop, but if you allow me to tell you what I now think then I should suggest that it would be very helpful if you would kindly write a letter to van Dusen stressing the points mentioned and ask him for his advice with regard to all the new circumstances. If it would save you, my Lordbishop, any trouble I should gladly draft the letter myself and send it to you (or Miss Roberts) for correction. In this letter I should try to put the alternative between postponement for a short time or coming over (and not between withdrawal and coming over) and add as was suggested in the cable that if van Dusen deems it expedient for me to wait a while that I could continue my work here for the time being until the present difficulties have been overcome.

As to the suggested cable I think van Dusen cannot do otherwise than cable 'Everything all right' as he has not withdrawn the invitation either to the State Department in Washington or to me and he can probably not fully realize all the implications of the matter in question without his attention having been drawn to them. If we should cable in order to show van Dusen that I am doing all in my power in spite of the changed situation I should suggest 'Leibholz had satisfactory interview with Consul. Letter following'.

I admit that a new matter will cause some delay. But I think this delay is justifiable in view of the new and great risks at stake and it may be that in some directions we shall see clearer in a few weeks' time. I could also employ this time in furthering as far as possible the shipping question, which seems to me also more aggravated now than it was before.

I have thought the matter over for a long time and I do not know whether I am right. In any case I feel I must let you know the results of my reflections. I have asked Miss Roberts to keep the projected cable until you have received this letter.

Please forgive me this letter. But I do not know how to help myself otherwise. Our Christmas greetings follow in another letter.

Yours ever,

Bell to Leibholz, 26 December 1941, BA, N 1334 (handwritten)

My dear Leibholz,

I was much touched by your Christmas letter, your kind words and all the friendship they breathed. Believe me your & your wife's friendship has been a great encouragement to me, and a precious possession, which must not perish. I regard our friendship as threefold, embracing you & your wife (& children) and Dietrich – all together. And I feel the nearer to each of you, when actually in touch with one.

I don't suppose you listen to the English broadcasts in German often. But you may like to know that a broadcast message from me (spoken in German by Hildebrandt[1]) was sent over the air on Christmas Eve at 9 p.m. to the oppressed Christians in Germany. I hope some of our friends there were listening, and may have been encouraged – I will have a copy made and sent to you. I hope your Christmas went peacefully and with gladness for the children. And I hope that 1943 may be happier than 1942. You may care to have the enclosed photo.

With hopes also that the way for yourself & family in the immediate future may be clear soon, and warmest greetings

Yours very sincerely,

---

[1] Franz Hildebrandt had collaborated closely with Bell on this broadcast. The text of the sermon was reprinted in Bell, *The Church and Humanity*, pp. 67–9; see too their correspondence in the Bell Papers, Vol. 346, fols. 39–41; for the many difficulties attending such a broadcast to Germany see Holger Roggelin, *Franz Hildebrandt*, pp. 218–20.

1942

5 January	A major counter-offensive by Soviet forces begins.
14 January	The first conference of the Allied nations concludes in Washington.
15 January	The first deportations from the Lodz ghetto.
20 January	The Wannsee conference sets out the policy of a 'final solution to the Jewish Problem'.
30 January	Hitler's speech at the Sportpalast.
15 February	Singapore falls.
25 February	Japanese-American internment begins in the United States.
13 March	Essen raid by RAF Bomber Command.
28 March	RAF Bomber Command attacks Lűbeck.
23 April	German Baedeker Raids over Britain until 6 June.
24–7 April	RAF Bomber Command attack Rostock on four successive nights.
20 May	Burma falls; Molotov arrives in London; an Anglo-Soviet Treaty is signed six days later undertaking that no separate peace will be signed with the enemy powers. On the same day German forces begin a new offensive in North Africa.
29 May	French Jews are ordered to wear a Star of David, two days after the same order is given in Belgium.
30 May	The first One Thousand Bomber raid on Cologne..
9 June	The village of Lidice is destroyed and its inhabitants murdered in retaliation for the assassination of Reinhard Heydrich by Czech agents.
21 June	Tobruk falls.
25 June	One Thousand bomber raid on Bremen.
22 July	The first deportations from the Warsaw ghetto.
3 September	German forces attack Stalingrad.
3 November	German forces are defeated at El Alamein.
8 November	Operation Torch: Allied forces invade Vichy Morocco and Algeria.
13 November	British forces re-take Tobruk.
18 November	RAF Bomber Command raid on Berlin.
17 December	British government statement on the mass murder of the Jews of occupied Europe.

Bell to Leibholz, 6 corrected to 8 January 1942, BA, N 1334 (typewritten and copy); Bell Papers 40, fol. 70 (carbon).

My dear Leibholz,

Many thanks for your letter. This is just to send you a copy of my Christmas broadcast. I am very glad you liked it.

I am much interested in reading what you say about John Armitage's request for an article on *Germany and the East*.[1] Have you seen the latest P.E.P. Memorandum?[2] I enclose a copy – please keep it.

I am afraid you are right in saying that the Vansittart frame of mind is getting rather influential. Harold Butler's book, *The Lost Peace* is not so bad as his son's book must be, though it is disappointing in many ways.[3] It is interesting and suggestive, however, on the more positive side. If one takes his criticisms of the British policy as much to heart as the Vansittart-ites take Vansittart's criticisms of German policy, some good might be done. I am much struck by your opinion as to what might happen in case of a German collapse.

Many thanks for your note about Darmstaedter.[4] He wrote to me without telling me anything very much about himself, and I sent the letter on to Miss Roberts. I don't think there is a great deal of chance of work of that kind at the present moment. The plan for teaching German to the English clergy is still in a very preliminary condition. I am dreadfully sorry that he is put to such unsuitable work. I will tell Miss Roberts what you say.

I am much interested in the impression, which you have of the development of Hitler's 'madness'.

Please let me know any further news you have from the American Consul.

Yours very sincerely,

[a]There is a good chance of a Service on January 14. 7 p.m. in S. Martin's in the Fields, to commemorate Niemollers's 50th birthday: if so so like broadcast to Germany [sic].[a5]

---

[1] John Armitage (1910–80), editor of *The Fortnightly Review*, 1939–54. See Leibholz, 'Germany between West and East', in *The Fortnightly Review*, October 1942, reprinted in Leibholz, *Politics and Law*, pp. 174–81.

[2] Political and Economic Planning, a British policy think tank, formed in 1931 and later influential in post-war planning and the formation of the National Health Service in 1947–8.

[3] Harold B. Butler, *The Lost Peace. A Personal Impression* (London, 1941). Bell quoted this book in his speech 'A single Christian Front', 2 December 1941, reprinted in Bell, *The Church and Humanity*, pp. 58–66 (here p. 60). Sir Harold Beresford Butler (1883–1951) played an important role in the International Labour Office after the First World War. In 1938 he became Warden of Nuffield College, Oxford. His son was Rohan d'Olier Butler, whose book *The Roots of National Socialism* so concerned Leibholz.

[4] Friedrich Darmstaedter (1883–1957) enquired after opportunities to teach German in Leeds; see Helen Roberts to Bell, 8 January 1942, Bell Papers Vol. 31, fol. 380. Darmstaedter was a judge at the District Court in Mannheim and qualified as a professor of law philosophy at the Heidelberg University in 1930. Deprived of his office in 1935 he migrated first to Italy and then, in 1939, to Britain. He taught German political history and theory at Cambridge and, in 1942–53, at the London School of Economics. Darmstaedter first returned to Germany in 1951 and became professor at the University of Heidelberg, though without holding a formal university Chair.

[5] Hildebrandt could only read a message of Bell; see Roggelin, *Franz Hildebrandt*, p. 230.

Leibholz to Bell, 11 January 1942, Bell Papers 40, fols. 71–2 (typewritten); BA, N 1334 (copy)

My dear Lordbishop,
Very many thanks for your letter. I am so glad to have your broadcast talk (I am going to read it once again to my wife and the children) and to know that you are going to have a talk with Miss Roberts about Darmstaedter.

I have read with great interest your remarks on Butler's book and I now hope to read the book itself as soon as I have made some more progress in the preparations for the lectures. I would not like to say that his son's book is really bad. I do not doubt his abilities. But I fear his attitude is fundamentally wrong and his book is very dangerous.

It was extremely kind of you to send me the new P.E.P. broadsheet. I had so far only read a summary and I am now very glad to have it in full and to be allowed to keep it. I have already read those pages which are of special interest to me and I think it is a very valuable contribution to the urgent problems we have to face today and a great aid to clear thought about the future. The main contention of the broadsheeters that there will be a common interest between Soviet Russia and the Western Powers upon which a common policy can be built up and that this common interest consists in creating a security against renewed attack by Germany is ᵃin my viewᵃ fully acceptable. But the decisive question is: how is it possible to guarantee this security? The Western Powers (and also the broadsheeters) refer to the Atlantic Charter with its provision for the unilateral disarmament of Germany. I for my part think that a genuine security between the nations can only be guaranteed if there are common moral and religious convictions, which bind the nations together. I do not, of course, deny the element of power in politics. But I do not believe that by power alone (i.e. unilateral disarmament in the sense of the Atlantic Charter) the new order can be really secured.

The Western powers will gain security only if the Germans will accept of their own accord the fundamental principles of the West and I think that, after a Hitler collapse, there will be a great (perhaps the last) chance for Germany to join the West. But at the same time I fear that this chance will be missed again by the Western powers.[1]

On the other hand, from a communistic point of view, Russia's security will be fully secured only if Germany becomes communist. And I think that the Russians know this and are much more interested in getting Germany communist than in the provisionary disarmament of Germany. Yesterday I read some recent Russian passages. For instance, on the last anniversary of the Russian revolution (1941) the Soviets sent 'Greetings to the German people groaning under the yoke of Hitler's Blackguards bands'. Or in his speech on November 6th Stalin himself said: 'Only Hitlerite fools do not understand that it is not only the European rear, but also the German rear, of the German fascist army, which is [a] volcano, ready for eruption and ready to bury Hitler's adventurers'. I think these and other utterances of the same kind are very illuminating and symptomatic. The real problem, therefore, starts at the very point where the broadsheeters cease discussing it. And the reason why I cannot see a satisfactory solution of the security problem in Europe is the continuous reference to the power clause in the Atlantic Charter.

I do not know whether you listened in to the broadcast made by Mr Eden[2] after his return from Russia. Amongst other things he said there: 'What matters in foreign affairs is not the form of internal government of any nation but its international behaviour.

The trouble with Hitler, for instance, was not that he was a Nazi at home. The trouble with him was that he would not stay at home …'. The thesis, however, that the internal government of a country has no necessary bearing on international policy is, to my view, old-fashioned and out of date. This passage might have been necessary with regard to the particular context. But at the same time it proves that the old fundamental differences between the two countries have not been bridged. If that is so as I think it is, then one should face the consequences and carry on a policy, which aims at winning a post-war anti-Nazi Germany and not at pushing her into the arms of Russia. The lack of courage and responsibility on the part of the German army to strike at the right time is not an excuse for risking and probably losing the whole European continent – especially if one bears in one's mind that Hitlerism would not have attained its formidable power if the foreign policy of the Western countries had not enabled Hitler to break the resistance of the German army (think f[or] e[example] of the Rhineland occupation).³ I have sometimes the feeling that the light of reason becomes dimmer and dimmer and at the end all will be swallowed up by the earthquake of which we are witnesses today.

Yesterday I had a letter from the American Consul saying that he cannot decide the question whether non-quota visas will be affected by the telegraphic instructions 'until further information is received from the Department of State regarding German applicants'. He will communicate with me immediately upon receipt of additional information from the Department. I had presumed this and I am afraid I must now wait until I hear from the Consul again.

Yours ever,

---

¹ See Leibholz, 'The Future of Germany', Bell Papers, Vol. 40, fols. 82–4.
² Anthony Eden (1897–1977), conservative politician and British Foreign Secretary, 1935–8, 1940–5 and 1951–5; prime minister 1955–7; in 1961 1st Earl of Avon. In December 1941 Eden had travelled by ship to Russia where he met with Stalin and surveyed the battlefields upon which the Soviet forces had successfully defended Moscow from German attack.
³ The occupation by German forces of the Rhineland in March 1936. The success of this move had further undermined criticism by now evident, and growing, within the German army.

Leibholz to Bell, 19 January 1942, Bell Papers 40, fol. 73 (handwritten)

My dear Lordbishop,

Thank you for the line I have just received.

May I suggest to send a cable on about the following lines:

'Leibholz had favourable appointment Consul December 15. Now awaiting Consul's answer concerning inquiry Washington whether new authorisation necessary according visa regulations December 20. Keeping you informed'.

You were kind enough, my Lordbishop, to tell me that you would forward a letter I should draft for you to Dr van Dusen concerning the questions following the entry of the United States into the war. But if you do not mind I think it better to write this letter not before the visa question is satisfactorily cleared up in order to save you, my Lordbishop, and Dr van Dusen a possibly double trouble. If you do not agree please kindly let me know. For I should only like to act in full accordance with you.

Yours ever,

Leibholz to Bell, 27 January 1942, Bell Papers, 40, fol. 76 (typewritten)

My dear Lordbishop,

Please kindly excuse me for not having written to you before to thank you for the cable you kindly sent to Dr. van Dusen on my behalf. But just as I was going to write to you and to thank you I had a third letter from the American Consulate in the visa matter saying that new telegraphic instructions from Washington had been received requiring the reapproval of our case by the Department of State and that, therefore, the former communication could no longer be held valid. As, however, the Consul himself offered to telegraph for me to the Department of State I have asked him (after consultation with Miss Roberts) to do so as then we need not to cable again to Dean van Dusen in this matter. I think that the Department of State will soon cable the reapproval.

Today I am enclosing the draft of a letter to Dean van Dusen[1] and I ask you kindly to have a look at it. I hope you will find something in it, which you can make use of in the letter to van Dusen for which I have begged you.

I have tried to express my feelings in it as well as I could. On the one hand I should like to go to America (especially with regard to the future after the war); on the other hand, I fully realize the risks and uncertainties as the result of the incalculable consequences of the new situation. These carry all the more weight, as at present I am very glad to work here. I have, therefore, some doubts and scruples as to the wisdom of going just now – as long as the new situation has not cleared up to some extent. I know that some of my colleagues who are in exactly the same position as myself think also on these lines.

In any case I think it is very important to have the opinion of van Dusen on the new situation and the particular questions I have broached in the enclosed letter. I think I can then easier act without being so burdened with doubts and scruples as I am today.

May I ask you once again, my Lordbishop, to forgive me all the trouble I am causing you.

I am enclosing a copy of the announcement of the lectures I am just delivering. Perhaps you would like to see it.

Yours ever,

---

[1] Preserved in the Bell Papers, Vol. 40, fols. 77–9 (typewritten).

Bell to Leibholz, 28 January 1942, Bell Papers, 40, fol. 79 (carbon)

My dear Leibholz,

The enclosed cable has just come from Van Dusen. I think it clears the air, and has the advantage of having the difficulty raised from the American end rather than this end. I think Dr Paton wants to see you before he goes to America on February 12th. I am sending him a copy of the cable.

Yours sincerely,

H. P. van Dusen to Bell, 28 January 1942, Bell Papers, 40, fol. 86 (cablegram)
IN VIEW LATE DATE IMPOSSIBLE UTILIZE LEIBHOLZ PRESENT ACADEMIC YEAR SUGGEST DEFERRING FURTHER PLANS UNTIL CONFERENCE WITH PATON

Van Dusen to Bell, 29 January 1942, Bell Papers, 40, fol. 86 (cablegram)
THANKS SUGGEST NOT FORWARD LETTER VAN DUSEN = LEIBHOLZ

Gerhard and Sabine Leibholz to Bell, 3 February 1942, Bell Papers 40, fol. 85 (handwritten); BA, N 1334 (copy)

My dear Lordbishop,
Tomorrow is your birthday and you know that our warmest wishes for many happy returns of the day accompany you on this very day. Our thoughts also go out to Dietrich who would join our united wishes for your welfare if he knew of your birthday. In spite of recent events I do not give up the hope of meeting again sometime this year and of seeing the collapse of the Nazi regime.

Your birthday reminds my wife and me again of all we owe to you for all the help you have given us in the last year. It is your great kindness alone, which enables us again and again to trouble you with our personal concerns of greater and smaller significance, knowing that you will forgive us although there is no hope of even being able to redeem our debt.

As to the cable of van Dusen I am not so much concerned about it, under the present circumstances. In my last letter to you, my Lordbishop, I wrote quite frankly about everything that was troubling me in the matter. But I think with you that now after van Dusen (probably for the same or similar reasons) has raised some difficulties it is better to keep the letter back and to write to him on rather different lines later on. I hope I shall see Dr Paton and have a talk with him about the whole matter and we shall then hear from Dr Paton after he has seen van Dusen. On the whole, I still attach the greatest weight for the future to van Dusen's offer although it may not materialise until a later date.

I am enclosing a copy of the comments on the P.E.P. broadsheet *Germany and Europe*.[1] A good deal of it will be familiar to you.

With all good wishes and °my° very kind regards, also to Mrs Bell,

Yours ever,

---

[1] See Leibholz, 'The Future of Germany', Bell Papers, Vol. 40, fols. 82–4.

Bell to Leibholz, 6 February 1942, BA 1334 (handwritten)

My dear Leibholz,
It was very good of you to think of my birthday as well as Dietrich's on Wednesday; and I greatly value your and your wife's thoughts and best wishes. It is such a special link to have Dietrich born the same day and month, though many years later; and your own wife too. Please give her my affectionate greetings and best wishes, and the hope that it

will not be very long before the Nazi regime is defeated, and she can spend her birthday free from care in Germany.

Thank you very much also for the article on *The Future of Germany*, which I shall read before we meet next week. Best greetings to you and your wife & children.

Yours very sincerely,

Bell to Leibholz, 6 February 1942, Bell Papers 40, fol. 86 (carbon)

My dear Leibholz,

I had a talk with Dr Paton today, and I know you are going to see him on Monday in Oxford. I told him what I thought generally on the subject and he will tell you. In the circumstances, seeing that it would take a long time for a letter to reach America, Paton does not think it necessary for me to write to Van Dusen, for he will explain everything to him by word of mouth. But I think you had better keep a copy of this letter yourself. I have thought it wise to put in writing the substance of what I said in conversation, so that Dr Paton can show the letter to Van Dusen if he wishes.

Yours ever,

Bell to Paton, 6 February 1942, Bell Papers 40, fol. 87 (carbon)

My dear Bill,

Leibholz

This follows our conversation this morning. I gather from Van Dusen's cable that in any case the original offer of the two American posts would not now stand, as the academic year has advanced so far. The difficulties of visa could not be solved any earlier so as to enable Leibholz to take advantage of Van Dusen's most kind and hospitable offer. Clearly this non-availability of the offer for the current year changes the situation from the point of view of these two posts, for if Leibholz were to cross the ocean now, the posts would not be open to him.

The situation has also changed in another way. When Van Dusen secured the offer, America was neutral, and it was because of this that one welcomed the readiness of the Colleges concerned to help a belligerent power in placing a distinguished refugee and his family. Now that both Britain and the U.S.A. are belligerent, that argument no longer applies.

But apart from this, and supposing the academic posts were to be available for Leibholz later on – what will be [the] attitude in America on the part of uninstructed people to German refugees as the war grows more and more intense? Leibholz has already been through the mill in England, owing to the state of alarms caused after the collapse of France. He and his family are safe here, and have friends who know them well, and have been through their tests and trials. Should one really encourage them to go to America, with the possibility (for you never can tell how people will react as the war goes on) of new trials and tests in an unknown land? I am divided in two myself:

on the one hand I am so grateful to Van Dusen for all the trouble he has taken; and I want to forward any plan of his to the best of my ability. On the other hand, bearing Leibholz in mind and his experiences in the last few years, I cannot help feeling that he might be better advised to stay where he is.

Yours ever,

Leibholz to Bell, 17 February 1942, Bell Papers 40, fol. 88 (handwritten); BA, N 1334 (copy)

My dear Lordbishop,

I myself should like to tell you how very sorry I was not to have been able to come to the pastors meeting[1] last week and, therefore, to have missed the pleasure of seeing you. But I was very glad to hear from Kramm[2] that it took a very satisfactory course.

Unfortunately, the lectures, which are just now finished, pressed me a little. As Dr Hodgson and Dr Quick[3] and some other outstanding people attended the lecture-course I had the feeling that I must prepare them a little more thoroughly than I otherwise should have done. Now, Dr Hodgson thinks they should be published. I am going to look them through and then to send them to Dr Vidler[4] (*Christian News-Letter Books*) for consideration.

What I especially appreciated and for which I am so grateful was that Dr Hodgson himself took the initiative in this matter. The general tendency – this is at least my feeling – is here in Oxford rather the other way round. On the whole it seems to me that on this point as well the Church is a much more vital force than the university.

As to the book the pastors dedicated to you, my Lordbishop, we had just a letter from Hildebrandt saying that he had completely forgotten to ask me (obviously because I am not a pastor) and that he is very sorry about it.[5] It is really a pity. You know, my Lordbishop, that if H. had asked me to contribute I should have considered it a special privilege. I am all the more sorry, as I have made some contributions of similar kind to colleagues of mine, with whom I am not in so close a touch of friendship as with you. How much rather would I have done it for you, my Lordbishop!

I also have still to thank you warmly for your last letter. I think your letter to Dr Paton has clearly and splendidly summed up the whole position and I can only say that I feel exactly like you and that I am very much divided in my mind. Dr Paton will kindly ask van Dusen whether there is a chance of keeping the position open in some way (as is the [practice] in some similar cases of which I know). If not I will do my best to comply with the wishes of v. Dusen although I for my part do not think that there is a chance of getting shipping accommodation for a family of four, under the present circumstances. I think therefore to stay here still for a considerable time and to be quite, quite frank I am quite happy in this thought for the time being.

With all good wishes from all of us to Mrs Bell and you

Yours ever,

1. A meeting of the Conference of the Lutheran Pastors of German Speaking Congregations.
2. Hans Herbert Kramm (1910-55) participated in Bonhoeffer's student circle at Berlin University 1932/33 and also at the youth conference at Fanø in 1934 but his engagement in the Church struggle took its toll: his position was in the eyes of the authorities compromised and his health was impaired. In consequence the Council of Brethren of the Confessing Church gave Kramm the opportunity to develop his academic studies abroad. In 1936 he came as a liaison officer for the Confessing Church to Britain where the principal of the Congregationalist Mansfield College in Oxford, Nathaniel Micklem, invited him to study for a doctorate. He served the German Lutheran Church at Oxford and London until his return to Germany in 1953.
3. Oliver Chase Quick (1885-1944), Regius Professor of Divinity at the University of Oxford, 1939-44.
4. Alexander Roper, or 'Alec', Vidler (1899-1991), Anglican priest, theologian and church historian. In 1938 he had become editor of the Anglican journal, *Theology*, and in 1939 Warden of St. Deiniol's Residential Library (the library of William Gladstone) at Hawarden.
5. Franz Hildebrandt (ed.), *'And other Pastors of Thy Flock': A German Tribute to the Bishop of Chichester* (Cambridge, 1942), presented as the Christian Fellowship's 'humble and sincere gift of our deep gratitude and affection' on his sixtieth birthday; see too Bell to the German British Christian Fellowship, 4 February 1943, BA, N 1334 (copy); also Roggelin, *Franz Hildebrandt*, pp. 206-7.

Bell to Leibholz, 2 March 1942, BA, N 1334 (typewritten); Bell Papers 40, fol. 89 (carbon)

My dear Leibholz,

Very many thanks for your letter of the 17th February. I got laid up with laryngitis just after the Pastors Conference, and I am afraid my correspondence fell into arrears in consequence. The Conference went very well.

First of all, let me say how delighted I am that you had such a good support from Dr Hodgson and Dr Quick at your lectures. I am delighted that Dr Hodgson wants them published. I should be thankful if this were to prove possible. Tell me what Vidler says. If by any chance he says he cannot, I would gladly have to try with the Oxford Press, through Sir Humphrey Milford if that would help, though of course we did not have much luck with them when I wanted them to publish an Oxford pamphlet by you. But it is most encouraging that Dr Hodgson is taking the initiative.

It is very nice of you to speak as you do about the book dedicated to me by the Pastors. I should have loved to have had a contribution of you; it would have added to the value of the book, and I should have valued it very much from the personal point of view as well. But still it can't be helped now.

I am very glad you had a good talk with Dr Paton and I hope all goes well.

Yours ªveryª sincerely,

Leibholz to Bell, 5 March 1942, Bell Papers 40, fol. 90 (typewritten); BA, N 1334 (copy)

My dear Lordbishop,

My wife and I are very sorry indeed to hear that you have been laid up with laryngitis. If I had heard about it before I should have written to you sooner sending you all our best wishes for a speedy recovery. From the fact that you write to me again I gather that you are now much better. But forgive me for asking you to take care of yourself in order to avoid any kind of relapse and to make a more speedy recovery, as the attack will probably have affected you more or less seriously.

Very many thanks also for your letter and kind willingness to help me with the publication of the lectures. Dr Quick has also just written to me that he wants the lectures published before long and I feel sure that we can count upon his support – if necessary. I have just looked through the lectures and am going to send the Ms. to Dr Vidler. As soon as I hear from him I will write to you once again.

By the way, I have recently had a long talk with Dr H. Butler (Nuffield College). After having sent him my comments on the P.E.P. broadsheet he wanted to see me and I was rather struck (for I had expected to the contrary) by his strong sense to see the political issues and alternatives.[1] Most of the Oxford people whom I have had the opportunity of meeting take, I am afraid, a rather different line. I was, therefore, all the more pleasantly surprised to meet him. I was able to speak quite openly and to tell him how remote from reality, in my view, the attitude even of many influential circles in this country is towards Germany today and that there is the possibility of losing peace for a second time if a revision of this attitude does not take place in time. And I had the impression that Dr Butler, at bottom of his heart, shares this view. If one compares, for instance, the last statement of Mr Eden concerning Germany and Stalin's recent order of the day[2] I cannot help feeling that there is a considerable difference in statesmanlike realistic conception of the political situation. And, I am afraid, the Germans will also feel this.

With all good wishes, also from my wife,
Yours sincerely,

---

[1] See Bell's commentary in his letter to Leibholz, 8 January 1942; also Leibholz to H. Butler, 27 March 1942.
[2] Stalin's Order of the Day No. 55 issued in his capacity as People's Commissar for Defence on 23 February 1942, published in English by the Soviet embassy in London, in *Soviet War News* No. 193, 24 February 1942; see too Bell Papers Vol. 51, fols. 10–11.

Leibholz to Bell, 20 March 1942, Bell Papers 40, fol. 91 (handwritten)

My dear Lordbishop,

Just a line to tell you that the Editorial Board of the *Christian News-Letter Books* is gladly prepared to publish the lectures. I am delighted about it, as I thought that, under the present circumstances, difficulties might arise. I am enclosing a copy of the letter of Dr Vidler and a copy of my letter to Professor Hodgson. It would be very kind of you if you would consider especially the questions I broached in the letter to Dr Hodgson with regard to Dietrich (and the other relatives of my wife) and the possible consequences for the Confessional Church. The question troubles me a little. You know I do so greatly value all you say, as no one understands the difficulties involved in this question better than you, my Lordbishop.

I very much hope that you are quite well again and think to write to you soon in another matter.

Yours ever,

A. Vidler to Leibholz, 18 March 1942, Bell Papers 40, fol. 92 (copy); BA, N 1334 (copy)

Dear Prof. Leibholz,

I am glad to say that the Editorial Board of the *Christian-News Letter* has warmly approved the publication of your lectures in the C.N.L. series of books. The publishers will in due course communicate with you about terms: I think the usual arrangement has been a ten per cent royalty to the author.

We should like you to consider whether a more distinctive title is possible. 'Christianity and Politics' is rather general and colourless: but we do not press this point if no alternative occurs to you. We also think it would be a good plan if you would ask Canon Hodgson to write a brief foreword explaining a) how the lectures came to be delivered, b) who you are, and c) his estimate of their value in this country. Not more than two or three pages would be needed.

I understand you to say that another copy of the typescript was being emended as regards its English by one of your friends, and that you should be able to send this on to me as the copy actually to go to the printers. We felt that while your frequent quotations from English writers showed your familiarity with what has lately been written in this country on the subject, yet that perhaps the formula 'As Mr X says ...' is a little overdone.

Yours sincerely,

Leibholz to L. Hodgson, Oxford, 20 March 1942, Bell Papers 40, fol. 93 (copy); BA, N 1334 (copy)

Dear Professor Hodgson,

I have just received the answer from Dr Vidler and I am enclosing the original. I am delighted that the Editorial Board of the *Christian News-Letter Books* have approved the publication of the lectures in their series and as I know that is, above all, owing to your kind intervention I should like to thank you once again warmly for the kind help you have given me in this matter.

I wonder what you think about Dr Vidler's wish with regard to a more distinctive title of the booklet. What would you say to 'Christianity and Politics and the issue at stake today' or 'The political implications of Christianity at the present time'. I think the former would perhaps be better.

Further may I venture to ask you whether you would perhaps be prepared to write a brief foreword as Dr Vidler suggests. It would be too kind but I do not know whether it is asking too much from you. I for my part should like to ask Dr Vidler to allow me to write a brief foreword after yours (provided you were willing to do so) in which I would point out the necessarily fragmentary character of the lectures and would like to say a few words of thanks.

Then I am afraid there is still another point to be raised and I should also be grateful for your advice in this respect. Unfortunately, I have the doubtful privilege of being rather well known in Germany and I have no doubt that the booklet will also not escape the attention of the authorities there. I for my part have no longer any near relatives on the Continent as my brother and his wife died at the Hague on the day when the German armies occupied the town (15th May 1940). The Swiss Legation in London has informed me that both (who, by the way, were entirely unpolitical) were shot on that day. Another version is that they met their death in another way. I myself have not been able up to now to lift the veil of this mystery. Although I do not think that my own activities can be connected in any way with their death the burden of their tragedy weighs heavily upon my heart. As to my wife she still has in Germany a number of near relatives. Apart from her parents and sisters there is her twin brother who plays a rather important part in the Confessional Church in Germany. He is personally very well known to the Bishop of Chichester and I think you also met him in Oxford shortly before the outbreak of war. And there is a brother-in-law who was pastor in Berlin-Dahlem and who, we think, is now in prison as most of the pastors who had held illegal examinations in the Confessional Church (and he did so) have recently [been] imprisoned.[1] And finally there is the Confessional Church herself. I do not know whether the book if it be published under my name might not perhaps aggravate her position still more than it is already today. On the other hand, from my personal point of view, I realize that it would be much more advantageous to publish the lectures in this country under my own name. But I must openly confess that after all the experiences we have gone through I feel strongly that I must take into account the possible serious implications mentioned, which would be avoidable if the book could be published under a pseudonym. I think – also in this case – it would be possible to comply with Dr Vidler's wishes as to the personal remarks (b) – even if one should have to put them in rather more general terms. I should therefore be grateful to you if you would kindly let me know how you think about the question.

As to paragraph 3 I may say that Mrs D. F. Buxton kindly emends the Ms. once again and that I hope to receive it today or tomorrow so that it could go to the printer in the course of next week.

With renewed thanks
Yours sincerely,

---

[1] Walter Dress (1904–79) was not imprisoned. Dress had married Susanne Bonhoeffer, the youngest sister of Dietrich, in 1929. In 1937 he was struck off the register of lecturers at Berlin University and succeeded the imprisoned Martin Niemöller as Pastor in Berlin-Dahlem. He also gave lectures on Church History at the theological college of the Confessing Church until it was closed in 1941. After the war Dress lectured at Humboldt University in Berlin and after 1962 as professor at the Kirchliche Hochschule.

Leibholz to Bell, 22 March 1942, Bell Papers 40, fol. 94 (handwritten); BA, N 1334 (copy)

My Lordbishop,

I have just received the answer from Dr Hodgson and am enclosing a copy of his letter and the foreword he has kindly written. I am divided into two but I think I must give my scruples with regard to Dietrich etc. precedence over all personal wishes and advantages. What would you think, my Lordbishop? I should be very grateful to you for your advice, which is always so helpful. And I should not like to act without it.

Yours ever,

L. Hodgson to Leibholz, 21 March 1942, Bell Papers 40, fol. 95 (copy)

Dear Dr. Leibholz,
Congratulations. I am very glad indeed that Vidler and his associates have had the good judgment to undertake to publish your lectures.

I am terribly sorry that you feel as you do about the desirability of the book being anonymous. I am sorry because I had hoped that this publication might do something to make you better known in this country and help towards securing to you that standing in the public mind to which your own academic distinction in Germany entitles you. But I do entirely understand the reasons against it. Only you and your wife can judge what ought to be done, and if you decide that the risk of publishing your name is one which, for the sake of other people ought not to be taken, we must abide by that decision.

This has put me in some little difficulty with regard to the foreword. Vidler's letter asks for a foreword saying who you are and how the lectures came to be given. Is the Nazi espionage system such that an attempt is likely to be made to turn up backnumbers of the Oxford University Gazette and thus identify you? That is the question I have had in mind. I enclose what I have written. I have tried to be sufficiently definite to give the English reading public the information they need, and at the same time sufficiently vague to avoid any such identification. Do you think I have succeeded?

As for the Title, I would suggest
CHRISTIANITY AND POLITICS
The issue at Stake today

I think that to make 'the Issue at Stake today' the subtitle is just as arresting and less cumbersome than in the form you suggested.

Yours sincerely,

Bell to Leibholz, 24 March 1942, BA, N 1334 (typewritten); Bell Papers 40, fol. 99 (carbon)

My dear Leibholz,
I am deeply interested in getting your two letters, and to know that your lectures have been accepted for publication by S.P.C.K. in the *Christian News-Letter* series. This is a great encouragement and will be of great interest to the readers.

I respect and appreciate your hesitations with regard to letting your name appear on the title page; you and your wife are naturally very careful not to do anything which would hurt any members of your or your wife's family, but particularly Dietrich, who is in an exposed position. I take it from what you say that the lectures show a very clear antagonism to the National Socialist State. That is to say that what you have written for this book will be much more antagonistic and outspoken than any articles or essays, which you have hitherto published in this country. It may, on the other hand, be the case that this book says in a more extended form what you have already said. What I mean is that to my mind so much depends on the amount of additional antagonism and strong criticism which your book will convey, over and above what your essays have conveyed. If your book is simply an enlarged edition of criticisms you have previously made, or in accord with criticisms you have previously made, then I do not think you should worry over much about your name appearing on the title page of the book; for the Nazis would assuredly have seen your essays, and no one in Germany, so far as you know, has suffered on that account. I know that a book is a much bigger affair than an essay, and it must be the case of course that more attention is focussed on a book than on an essay. Nevertheless, it does seem to me to be a question rather depending on the strength of your criticisms, and how far the book is what might be called a strong attack on the Nazi system rather than a piece of research work, with an approach which, while of course practical, is in the main academic.

Suppose however that you feel that the book is, and would be taken by the Nazis to be, a strong attack on the Nazi State, then you know more about the Nazi reaction and how that would be likely to affect Dietrich and others, than many people here can know. Naturally you would wish to avoid hurting Dietrich. If, knowing the Nazis as you do, you feel that there is a very grave risk to his safety as a result of the publication of your book in England, then I think people here would thoroughly appreciate your unwillingness to let your name appear on the cover.

There is always, of course, the possibility that the Nazis would unearth the author's identity, even though he did his best to disguise it. But I do not think one ought to consider that risk as a very serious one. I take it that some German refugees who write on purely political subjects in this country have some experience as to the effect on their relatives in Germany of what they have written and published. There may be such refugees in Oxford who could tell you personally about this, and you might find their experience very valuable.

I expect the Editors of the series would be rather disappointed at not having your name if you decide, in view of the risk, not to publish it. But in that case, I should be inclined to adopt a pseudonym. Don't make the book entirely anonymous, but adopt a name. That is much better than anonymity, and presents the writer as a personality to English readers. I believe Sebastian Haffner, for example, is a pseudonym.[1] Why should you not have a pseudonym of your own?

It looks to me as though Hodgson's preface, which is excellent, would not need much if any change, as no University is mentioned, if you adopt a pseudonym.

Yours very sincerely,

---

[1] 'Sebastian Haffner' was Raimund Pretzel (1907–99). He had reached London in 1938 where, after a period of great struggle, he was adopted by the editor of the Sunday newspaper, The Observer, David Astor. His pseudonym combined the names of Johann Sebastian Bach and the 'Haffner' Symphony of Mozart.

Leibholz to Bell, 2 April 1942, Bell Papers 40, fol. 99 (typewritten); BA, N 1334 (copy)

My dear Lordbishop,

It was extremely kind of you to advise me in such detail about the matter in which I consulted you. I greatly appreciate all you say. I had almost made up my mind to publish the book under a pseudonym. Now after having received your letter I am rather tending again to publish it under my own name. Dr Vidler himself told me that he would not mind publishing the lectures under a pseudonym. I have just had a letter from him saying the book should either appear with my name and Dr Hodgson's preface or that, if a pseudonym is used, also Dr Hodgson should not appear as it would be too obvious a clue. The lectures imply a strong antagonism to the secular totalitarian regime and especially to that of National Socialism although I hope that the research character of the study as a whole is not affected by this. On the other hand I do not think that Nazism recognizes such a differentiation. But perhaps I can find a solution by cancelling a few sentences, which I am afraid might possibly do harm to Dietrich and others and then publish the whole in the way you I feel advocate, my Lordbishop. Then I could also retain Dr Hodgson's foreword, which I should be very sorry to miss.

I am enclosing a copy of a letter I wrote a few days ago to Dr H. Butler. Perhaps you might be interested in having a look at it.[1] I have tried to put forward what I for my part feel with regard to the British policy towards the Axis, from a more continental point of view. As it is the only copy I have I should be glad if you would kindly let me have the copy back at your convenience.

        With all good wishes, also from my wife, to Mrs Bell and yourself.

                                      Yours ever,

[1] On 15 May 1943, Bell discussed Leibholz's letter at Stockholm with Knut Bernhard Westman and Anton Johnson Fridrichsen, who 'agreed generally'; Bell, Diary Notes, published in *DBW* 16, p. 281.

Leibholz to H. Butler, 27 March 1942, Bell Papers 40, fols. 100–4 (copy); BA, N 1334 (copy)

COPY

Dear Mr Warden,

In our last talk[1] you put the question to me what kind of policy should be advocated towards Germany, as the present one is obviously unsatisfactory. I have pondered over the question and I should like to make a few additional remarks to what I already said about a week ago.

I think the whole dilemma and the discrepancy between the Russian policy and that of the Western countries towards Germany is due to the fact that the countries try by different means to obtain 'security', which safeguards them against a repetition of the happenings of today.

On the whole, the leading Western politicians (even those who do not agree with the Vansittartism in its various shades) hope to reach this goal by unilateral complete disarmament possibly together with an occupation and re-education of Germany.

The disarmament seems to be – as the Atlantic Charter shows – a preliminary condition of any kind of peace talk even with a new anti-Nazi government, which might have come to power as a result of a revolution or a military coup d'état in Germany. Not until then would the West be prepared to negotiate with Germany and concede to her economic equal partnership and try to reconstruct a 'New Order'.

Russia, on the other hand, endeavours to solve the same problem in a quite different way. In the British-Russian pact of July 12th it is declared that this is a joint war against 'Hitlerite Germany'. This phrase has been repeated again and again in a number of public speeches, broadcast[s], etc. – even when the German armies were almost at the gates of Moscow. And Stalin's last Order of the Day most clearly shows that Russia is prepared to make peace as soon as the Russian soil is 'liberated from the invader' implicitly assuming that such a decisive defeat of Hitler would lead to an overthrow of the 'Hitler clique' and that of the whole present regime and would result in the outbreak of a revolution which – as things stand today – would probably take on a communist character. For those forces in Germany, which look rather to the East than to the West are greatly strengthened by the present policy of the Anglo-Saxon countries. Those forces can point out that a communist Germany would be able to offer the German people immediate gains of the greatest significance and that a communist Germany could make a much more honourable peace with the East than she could obtain from the West. And the Russians could accept such a peace, from their point of view, because they realize that the security of their country against a renewed attack by Germany is more strengthened by a communist Germany and a new international order based on the communist creed than on the belief of the innate wickedness of one nation alone and in the various safeguards based on force and power.

I for my part am afraid that the Russians if they win the war on the Continent will rather succeed with their policy unless a drastic change of that policy of the Anglo-Saxon countries takes place in time. For their present policy towards Germany – as far as I can judge – is, at bottom a policy in the old terms of national power politics, which was perhaps suitable for the last war but is certainly not for the present one. For if this war is – as I think it is – a revolutionary and international war the policy bent on liquidating such a war cannot be run on nineteenth-century ideas. It is a policy of 'veterans', which must have the effect that those forces in Germany who look to the West for salvation feel themselves betrayed in the same way as at the time of the appeasement policy in which the Western countries practically helped again and again Hitler against those who opposed him. Even these forces will put up rather with a communist Germany than will a humiliated anti-Nazi Germany. The last act of this tragedy would be that strange as it may sound today, Stalin would save Germany from the West and secure for her in a New Europe the proper place, which she otherwise cannot find. In my opinion, a not very pleasant prospect although I feel this is more true to life than the many illusions which are held in various ways today.

If this policy [is] to be changed, first of all, one must appeal to the Germans in the same immediate way as Stalin has done since the outbreak of the German-Russian war. Why, for instance, not agree with the sentences of Stalin's Order of the Day: 'It is not our aim to exterminate the German people and to destroy the German State. We have not such idiotic aims. We should welcome the ousting or destruction of Hitler's clique. But it would be ridiculous to identify Hitler's clique with the German people and the

German State. The experience of history shows that Hitlers come and go whereas the German people and the German State remain'.

A few days ago a leading article of *The Times* proceeding from the assumption that this war can only be won if the Allies are united complained of the lack of unity in the war aims and propaganda policy between Russia and this country. But such a unity could be relatively quickly established. If the government could only make up their mind to accept the realistic lines of the Russian policy and would clearly state that they were prepared to make peace with any German government the true anti-Nazi character of which would be beyond doubt a decisive battle were won. One would not only have secured a common policy with Russia and have created a sound basis for the propaganda policy towards Germany but would also have reached at least a starting-point from which a constructive peace policy which appeals to the Germans could be conducted.

I admit that such a policy would imply the stopping of all talk about unilateral disarmament as a preliminary condition for a future peace, about only economical equal partnership and so on. In fact, I think the disarmament is a matter which must be settled later on. A defeated Nazi-Germany who has gone through a revolution will only be too willing to sign a reasonable agreement concerning this matter – even if only to prove her good will and changed attitude.

On the other hand, such a policy would not imply an indifference to the form of the future regime in Germany. This is not possible because the old maxim that the international regime of a state does not concern third states is no longer true. The structure of a regime is no longer a matter of domestic policy. The truth lays much more the other way round today. In the twentieth century foreign policy grows from the internal structure a state takes on. For instance, National Socialism and liberal Democracy cannot live side by side and if the state adopts fascist or national socialist totalitarian policy it is, at bottom, the modern equivalent of a declaration of war on Democracy. When, therefore, for instance Mr Eden stated after the return from his visit in Russia 'What matters in foreign policy is not the form of the internal government of any nation but its international behaviour. The trouble with Hitler was that he would not stay at home'[2] I should say that such a kind of statement is no longer valid. Today the democratic countries must revise their tradition[al] non-interventional policy and direct their foreign policy in the same active way as the totalitarian states have always done in correspondence with the altered ideological situation. Also for this reason I am afraid the Atlantic Charter is no longer up to date. But in spite of the fact that the structure of the future political system in Germany is of the greatest importance for the democracies I think this question cannot be broached now. For the proposed agreement and necessary co-ordination with Russia on the basis of the fundamental proclamation of her war aims in the Order of the day would hereby be upset since as a natural result of the present political situation each country has different aims in mind about the future regime in Germany. But such an agreement would at least give this country for the first time the chance of gaining a leadership in the post-war reconstruction as far as Germany is concerned and of opening a way to the Germans to choose a post-war world which is more in harmony with the basic principles and values of the West than those of the East.

I fully realize the great difficulties in the way of this policy under the present circumstances. But if the issue is clear a political leader should be able to overcome these difficulties before it is 'too late'. Especially I realize that behind the present policy there is a great mistrust that the Germans without changing their temper or outlook might make a spurious revolution and deceive the West for the second time. But this argument is more of [a] theoretical character. Such a deception is only possible if the policy, which is made (as, for instance, the appeasement policy) is bad i.e. not based on the political realities and if there are politicians who let themselves be deceived. For this, however, there is no proved remedy.

Moreover a revolution cannot conceal its true character, especially an anti-Nazi revolution. There is even a formal criterion which will allow a reliable judgement of what kind and character a future German government will be. I think of the attitude towards the Christian Churches and the Jews. Today the degree of the dependence of the Continental States on Nazi Germany can almost be measured by their attitude towards these questions. The more perfect the imitation of the Nazi model is in this respect the greater is the vassalage of the states concerned. The less the Nazi principles and methods have been adopted in these matters the more the states maintained their independence.

Of course, all that I am writing to you is very inadequate and provisional and needs working out in many directions and details. But I think that the basic attitude I have been trying to sketch out is not wrong provided one wishes to make at least an attempt to avoid a communist Europe and not only to win the war but also the peace. I am afraid this is only possible if one revises the present policy, joins the Russian war-aims and propaganda policy and helps the Germans to get rid of the Nazis and offers them a fair and honest alternative which appeals to them.

Yours sincerely,

---

[1] See Leibholz to Bell, 5 March 1942.
[2] See Leibholz to Bell, 11 January 1942.

Bell's secretary (Mary Balmer) to Leibholz, 14 April 1942, Bell Papers 40 (I), fol. 106 (carbon)

Dear Dr. Leibholz,

The Bishop asks me to return the letter to the Warden of Nuffield College, which you kindly sent him. He has ventured to take a copy of it.[1]

The Bishop will be at Wadham College to-morrow, Wednesday, and would be very glad to see you if you could call in at any time in the afternoon.

Yours faithfully,

---

[1] Bell discussed the position of this letter at Stockholm with the Norwegian-Swedish professors Knut Bernhard Westmann (1881–1967) and Anton Friedrichsen (1888–1953) who promised to send Leibholz's message to Bonhoeffer; see Bell's Diary Notes, in *DBW* 16, p. 281.

H. P. van Dusen to Bell, 17 April 1942, Bell Papers 40, fols. 108–9 (typewritten)

My dear Bishop:

I must apologize for not replying earlier to your cable of late January regarding a final decision in the Leibholz matter.

On February 5th President Coffin of Union Seminary received a communication from the Chief of the Visa Division of the State Department indicating that Leibholz's application for admission to this country had been reconsidered and an unfavourable decision reached, and offering us the opportunity to appear at a hearing in support of his application. I then entered into correspondence with Mr. Warren,[1] the Chief of the Visa Division, quoting to him your cable reporting Leibholz's favourable appointment with the American Consul in London on December 15th and the subsequent confirmation that his case was not affected by the new visa regulations. In reply, Mr. Warren wrote me on February 21st the enclosed letter.[2] In view of the whole situation Dr. Coffin and I did not think it wise to press Dr. Leibholz's case and we therefore did not ask for a special hearing before the board of appeals. On the contrary, we waited until Paton's arrival when we could explore the whole matter fully with him.

The sum of the matter is that our judgment completely coincides with yours and Paton's. There is no change in the readiness, indeed eagerness, of both the Episcopal Theological School and Union Seminary to welcome Dr. Leibholz. But these appointments were for a period of only two years when a more permanent appointment in this country might present real difficulties. Furthermore, while the present attitude of the American government toward alien enemies closely parallels that of the British government, there is always the possibility that a crisis might arise analogous to that which Britain faced in the summer of 1940 and that in consequence much more drastic measures of restraint might be instituted. Since the Leibholzes have passed through this experience in Britain, it would seem quite unfair to subject them unnecessarily to a similar possibility here. Therefore it does seem wisest for them to continue in the present very happy relationships that you have been able to arrange for them in Great Britain.

I trust you will convey the substance of this information as opportunity offers to Dr. Leibholz. Paton will be able to report our situation here more fully. If after further consultation and consideration it should seem wise to raise again the possibility of a call to Leibholz, we should be glad to take the matter up sympathetically and energetically. But our present judgment would be definitely unfavourable.

Let me thank you most heartily for your letter of March 17th with regard to the material on peace aims. I have discussed this with Paton and he is taking back with him copies of all of the important material, which has thus far been brought out on this side.

With cordial personal greetings, I am
Faithfully yours,

---

[1] Avra M. Warren (1893–1957) served as the chief of the Visa Division of the US State Department enforcing stringent immigration controls and delaying, where they could not deny, acceptance of refugees from Nazi persecution.

[2] See too A. M. Warren to H. P. van Dusen, 21 February 1942, Bell Papers 40, fol. 110.

Bell to Leibholz, 30 April 1942, Bell Papers 40, fol. 112 (carbon)

My dear Leibholz,

I have just received a letter from Dr. Van Dusen. I think the simplest way of giving you the substance of it is to send it to you just as it stands.

I have seen Paton since his return last Sunday (?) from America and he and I are quite clear that the whole idea of your going to America should be left over.[1] I am thankful myself that things have turned out as they have turned out and that the difficulties had come from the American end owing to 'the changed conditions'.

Yours very sincerely,

[1] See Paton to Bell, 30 April 1942, Bell Papers 40, fol. 111.

Leibholz to Bell, 2 May 1942, Bell Papers 40, fol. 113 (handwritten)

My dear Lordbishop,

Many thanks for your letter and the enclosures. As things stand today I fully agree with you that it is wise to leave the idea of our going to America for future consideration. Although I do not quite see the reason why our American friends have not made use of the opportunity to settle the visa question I think that, even in this case, practically the effect would have been the same as no shipping across and return would probably have been available. I myself am not so sorry about this solution, under the present circumstances, all the more as the contact made with Union Theological Seminary has not been broken off and the difficulties have arisen on the other side. I only deeply regret to have caused you, my Lordbishop, so many troubles in this matter but openly I am thankful now for now being enabled longer to stay with you in this country.

In the meantime, we have moved into a small house and we all, especially the children, are much happier in it than in the boarding house. We only regret to have not taken the step earlier. But I did not venture to do it – as long as the America question was not cleared up in some way.

We have received via America a photo from Dietrich who looks rather thin and aged. He contracted a pneumonia on his return from Geneva last year. But we have gained the impression from the letter we have also got from our friends that he has completely recovered at the end of last year.

Carr's book[1] to which you kindly called my attention when I saw you last, my Lordbishop, is deeply impressing me. As far as I can see it seems to me to be the best book which is written in this country on the subject in question. I have not yet finished it and I hope to come back to it later on.

With all good wishes, also from my wife and the children, to Mrs Bell and yourself

Yours ever,

[1] E.H. Carr, *Conditions of Peace* (London, 1942). Edward Hallett Carr (1892–1982) was an assistant editor at *The Times* (1941–6), where he was noted for his leading articles urging an Anglo-Soviet alliance as basis of a post-war order. Carr argued against a Carthaginian peace with Germany and for a post-war reconstruction of Germany along socialist lines. Later he became an eminent historian of the Soviet Union.

Bell to Leibholz, 6 May 1942, BA 1334 (handwritten)

My dear Leibholz,

I am deeply grateful for Dietrich's affectionate message,[1] and your letter, and the very remarkable news.

I am myself going to Sweden for 3 weeks on May 10, to visit the Church of Sweden. I wish I could see Dietrich there. But I shall certainly hear his news.[2]

My address should be c/o British Legation, Stockholm

I have had a warm welcoming telegram from Eidem[3] and letter from Rodhe.[4] I look forward eagerly as you can imagine. Your letter is destroyed.

In haste. If you have any message – write *here* by return.

Yours ever,

Please let me have van Dusen's letter back. I have no other copy of it though unsigned!

[1] Bonhoeffer's letter from Stockholm to the Leibholz family, 17 April 1942, in *DBW* 16, pp. 262–3.
[2] For Bell's visit to Sweden from 13 May to 11 June 1942 see Bell Papers, Vol. 276 (partly published in *DBW* 16, pp. 280–99); Bell's Memorandum of Conversations is published in *DBW* 16, pp. 315–20; while his public report may be found in the *Christian News-Letter*, 24 June 1942, nr. 139. Later papers may be found in Dietrich Bonhoeffer, *Gesammelte Schriften*, Vol. 1, pp. 390–413; Bethge, *Dietrich Bonhoeffer*, pp. 850–8; Klemens von Klemperer, *German Resistance against Hitler. The Search for Allies Abroad 1938–1945* (Oxford, 1992), pp. 247–53. Bonhoeffer wrote again from Stockholm to the Leibholz family on 1 June 1942, published in *DBW* Vol 16, pp. 306–7.
[3] Erling Eidem (1880–1972), Swedish pastor, theologian and, from 1932–50, archbishop of Uppsala. Bell and Eidem knew each other well in the context of the Life and Work movement.
[4] Edvard Magnus Rodhe (1878–1954), Swedish theologian and Bishop of Lund, 1925–48.

Leibholz to Bell, 16 June 1942, Bell Papers 40, fol. 114 (handwritten); BA, N 1334 (copy)

My Lordbishop,

I have just learned that you are safely back in this country and I should only like to tell you how delighted we are to know that we have you back again. I am so thankful for it. Our thoughts have frequently gone out to you during your stay in Sweden and our best wishes have always accompanied you. I feel sure that you will have had a very interesting and impressive time and I am anxious to know how you are and what you will have to tell us.

I assume that you will not have met Dietrich. For he wrote to us from Zurich[1] (where he was for a 'short holiday') about four weeks ago on the same lines as in his last letter emphasising again that your last lines a few months ago gave him very much encouragement and saying that he wanted to write personally to you before leaving Switzerland.[2] I hope[3] you will have received his letter, in the meantime.

I am enclosing a few critical notes on Butler's book *The Roots of National Socialism* in which you might perhaps be interested.

Once again, I am so very glad to have you back. With kind regards, also to Mrs Bell, from us all

Yours ever,

[1] Copy: Munich. See Bonhoeffer to the Leibholz family, Zürich, 13 May and 21 May 1942, in: *DBW* 16, pp. 265–6, 273–6. Bonhoeffer's third trip to Switzerland lasted from 11 to 26 May.
[2] See Bonhoeffer to Bell, 23 May 1942, in *DBW* 16, pp. 276–7, in which Bonhoeffer offers his thanks 'for giving time and encouragement to my brother-in-law'.
[3] Copy: Perhaps.

Bell to Leibholz, 20 June 1942, BA, N 1334 (typewritten and copy); Bell Papers 40, fol. 115 (carbon)[1]

ªPrivateª

My dear Leibholz,

Very many thanks for your letter and its welcome back.

To my great surprise I saw Dietrich at the end of my stay.[2] He had come over especially as a courier[3] with a 48 hours visa in order to see me. We talked very much on very important matters. I told him your news, of which he was very glad. He was very well. He said that Hitler's health was unfortunately very good; the uncle of whom he spoke in his letter was the war, not Hitler.[4] His Seminary had been closed twice, and he had been forbidden by the Gestapo to preach or speak. He is at work now on a book and in connection with the Brethren's Council and at nights on political work.[5]

I told him about your book, and your question as to publishing it anonymously.[6] He wanted to know what was its exact subject, and whether there were things in the contents of the book which in themselves might cause difficulties for relations. We might get a word about this when we meet at Cambridge.[7] He asked me to say he ªHansª was very well and continuing his work on the right side.[8] Of course he sent his sister and you and the girls his warmest love. It was a real delight to see him, as you can imagine. His coming was entirely unexpected. I had heard of his passing through Sweden on his way to Norway before I arrived (also as a courier), but Archbishop Eidem[9] thought he had gone through as a soldier, and I could not find any way of communicating with him in any case. But he heard that I was in Stockholm, and so arrived.

Yours ever,

[1] Published in *DBW* 16, pp. 323–4.
[2] See Bell to Leibholz, 6 May 1942, note 2.
[3] See Bonhoeffer's courier-card in *DBW*, 16, pp. 299–300.
[4] Reference to Bonhoeffer's letter, 17 April 1942, speaking about 'Uncle Rudy'; *DBW* 16, p. 263. The code is a reference to lieutenant general Rüdiger Graf von der Goltz (1845–1946), brother-in-law of Paula Bonhoeffer, the mother of Dietrich and Sabine.
[5] See Bethge, *Dietrich Bonhoeffer*, pp. 659–60, 765–6.
[6] See Bell's Diary Notes in *DBW* 16, p. 304.
[7] Bell was able to tell Gerhard and Sabine Leibholz of his meeting with Bonhoeffer during a conference of the Christian Brotherhood in Wartime in Cambridge; see S. Leibholz-Bonhoeffer, *Vergangen*, pp. 192–3.
[8] Hans von Dohnanyi (1902–45), son of Ernst (Ernö) von Dohnány and Elisabeth, née Kunwald, was married to Christine Bonhoeffer (1923–65). In 1934–8 he was the head of Franz Gürtner's office at the Ministry of Justice and after 1938 judge at the German Supreme Court. At the beginning of the Second World War he was conscripted into the Office of Military Defence where he became a

collaborator of Hans Oster, one of the most committed and active resisters of the Hitler regime. On 5 April 1943 the Gestapo arrested Dohnanyi, his wife and Dietrich Bonhoeffer. Although the investigations were concluded by March 1944, a trial was postponed because Dohnanyi was ill and confined to the sickbay. He extended his illness by infecting himself with diphtheria. After the failure of the plot of 20 July 1944 he was sentenced to death by a drumhead court of the SS on 6 April 1945 in the Sachsenhausen concentration camp. He was murdered there on 9 April 1945.

[9] See Bonhoeffer to Eidem, 11 April 1942, in *DBW* 16, pp. 259–60.

Leibholz to Bell, 21 June 1942, BA, N 1334 (copy)

My Lordbishop,

Today I am enclosing a letter I have just written to Dr Oldham – in case you may be interested to have a look at it.

A few days ago we had another letter from D[ietrich] from Stockholm dated June 1st.[1] We are deeply moved by the news and we feel with him the 'indescribable joy' to have seen you. He writes that it still seems to him a miracle.[2] And you, my Lordbishop, can certainly imagine how anxious we are to hear from you the full story. As a matter of course, we shall keep the news to ourselves and not speak of them – even to our common friends.

Yours ever,

[1] See Bonhoeffer to Leibholz family, 1 June 1942, in *DBW* 16, pp. 306–7.
[2] See Bonhoeffer to Bell, 1 June 1942, Bell Papers, Vol. 42, fol. 72.

Leibholz to J. H. Oldham, 19 June 1942, Bell Papers 40, fol. 114 (copy); BA, N 1334 (copy)

Dear Dr Oldham,

After having carefully read the new Anglo-Russian treaty I venture to ask you whether it is not time now to raise the question what kind of regime in Germany the Anglo-Saxon countries would be prepared to accept after a collapse of 'Hitlerite Germany'. This question seems to be all the more acute as not only members of the government appeal to the German people urging them to take an active part in the overthrow of the present regime but also because obviously many forces in the Germany of today are actually working in this direction hoping that after the overthrow of the present regime and the destruction of all that the regime stands for it will be possible to get a tolerable peace. But I am afraid that – as things stand today – that is not so. For if I am not mistaken this country will not come to terms with these forces as these cannot establish a new regime of law and order without the help of the Western-minded oppositional forces in the Army. And the disarmament of even these forces is a preliminary condition of any kind of peace talks according to the Atlantic Charter. Now as there is almost a general understanding that in a post-war Germany a mere restoration of the old liberal political and economic system is not possible and another Western-minded regime without the support of the army and some kind of authoritarianism cannot be established – what kind of regime is practically left but a national-communist one like that of Russia and this without the need of the Soviet-Union to interfere in German inner-politics? And I cannot imagine how such a development could be efficiently prevented by the Anglo-Saxon countries, all the more as these are probably not willing to send an occupation army into a communist Europe. And the question I should like to raise is whether the establishment of such a regime is actually the last aim for which the democracies are standing today. Must this prospect not inevitably lead to deeper helplessness and despair to those people who are oppressed in Germany (I learn that Swedish papers report that on the average ten Germans are executed daily) and look for salvation and liberation and guidance to the West in order to be disappointed again and who for reasons of mere self-existence are forced to accept a regime they deeply hate? If this is so as I think it is then is it not really time to put forward a more constructive peace policy towards Germany and to show those people a realistic and tolerable alternative, which would give them at least a chance of choosing a post-war political system, which is in harmony with the main Western principles and values and which would not make a kind of Russian communism on a national basis an inescapable necessity for Germany and herewith for the whole of Continental Europe?

Yours very sincerely,

Leibholz to Bell, 23 June 1942, Bell Papers 40, fol. 118 (typewritten)

My Lordbishop,
Very many thanks for your letter and the interesting and good news. If possible – I should *very* much like to have a talk with you, my Lordbishop, when we next meet at Cambridge on some of the topics you have mentioned in your letter. I should be very glad indeed.

May I put forward today a personal request in regard to a matter in which you, my Lordbishop, have given me your help sometimes before. It is the question of the additional grant of £100 I am receiving from Magdalen College. The present grant expires on the 1st of October but as far as I know the Committee for the assistance of Refugee scholars has to decide now how the existing funds shall be allocated next term. Therefore, I myself have made an application to Magdalen College asking for a further extension of the grant – if possible for the duration of the war. In this connection I have stressed the following points:

First I referred to my application of November 1941 in which I expressed the hope that before long I should be able to take up a post which had been offered to me by the President of Union Theological Seminary and by the Episcopal School at Cambridge. I remarked that the entry of the United States into the war frustrated these plans but that van Dusen wrote that 'There is no change in the readiness, indeed eagerness, of both the Episcopal Theological School and the Union Seminary to welcome' me later on and that they would 'be glad to take the matter up sympathetically and energetically ..., if it should seem wise to raise again the possibility of a call'.

Secondly, I referred especially to the series of lectures which I gave during Hilary term in Christ Church at the instigation of Dr. Hodgson and to the book on *Christianity, Politics and Power*, which is just being published in the series of the *Christian*

News-Letter Books. I mentioned also a few other articles published this year and some other lecture work I hope to do in the course of the next few weeks and months.

Thirdly, I remarked that the World Council of Churches has continued its stipend but that considering the fact that I have to provide for a family of four, that we are compelled in live in furnished rooms and that the increasing cost of living presses rather hard on us I should be most grateful for the extension of the grant. I referred, in this connection, to a letter written by Dr Opie[1] in 1939 saying that the grant was made by Magdalen College 'in view of the heavy living expenses of this family' and added that this is much more true *now* than it was already at that time.

As I know that it would be really a great help if you would support this application. I venture to trouble you again in this matter and I should be most grateful to you, my Lordbishop, if you would kindly lend me your help once again. The Presidency of Magdalen College is still vacant. Vice-president is now – as far as I know – either K.B. McFarlane[2] or C. S. Lewis.[3]

My wife and I are very much looking forward to seeing you at Cambridge soon

Yours ever,

[1] Redvers Opie (1900–84), the Bursar of Magdalen College, had in 1939 become the UK Treasury representative in Washington, D.C., and Counsellor and economic adviser at the British Embassy there in 1939, a position which he held until 1946.
[2] Kenneth Bruce McFarlane (1903–66), since 1927 a Fellow of Magdalen College, Oxford, was one of the most influential British historians of late medieval England.
[3] Clive Staples Lewis (1898–1963), the prolific British novelist, poet, medievalist, literary critic, essayist, lay theologian, broadcaster, lecturer and Christian apologist. Lewis held academic positions at the University of Oxford (he was a Fellow of Magdalen College), 1925–54, and later at the University of Cambridge, 1954–63 (where he was a Fellow of Magdalene College).

Bell to Leibholz, 26 June 1942, Bell Papers 40, fol. 119 (carbon)

My dear Leibholz,

I was very glad to get your first letter and now your second. I should much like to have a talk with you both about personal and general matters.

I am writing at once to Magdalen with regard to the application for a grant. Of the two men you name as possible Vice-President, C.S. Lewis is the one I know, so I will write to him.[1]

Yours very sincerely,

[1] Bell wrote to C.S. Lewis on 26 June 1942. See Bell Papers, Vol. 40, fol. 120.

Leibholz to Bell, 8 July 1942, Bell Papers 40, fol. 121 (typewritten); BA N 1334 (copy)

My Lordbishop,

First I wish to thank you very much for your masterly report,[1] which has greatly impressed me and strengthened my conviction that the success of all planning about the rebuilding of new Christian relationships after the war in a better world depends from a realistic point of view, on the right use of the great chances which are opening up today. I think if I may say so that the highly political character of the whole question does not relieve Christians in any way from doing all in their power to find a positive solution out of the difficult situation as I cannot imagine how otherwise in times to come a Christian way of life can be actually secured in the political sphere. I venture to say this although I for my part have but little hope that these efforts will succeed. People who are in the swim of the always changeable public opinion do not like to face unpleasant facts. They are so confident that they are always right and the others wrong that one can only hope that future events will not disprove them again.

By the way, as to Winant[2] I heard he is a man who is very anxious to have the kind of news, which you, my Lordbishop, have to offer. And as he is obviously a man of initiative and imagination and gifted with a sense of realism the idea of approaching him might perhaps prove helpful. If you should think it inadvisable to approach him officially one could perhaps, if you think it well, let him know the essentials in another rather unofficial way. There are many possibilities of doing so.

As to the book about which we spoke I am enclosing a copy of the contents. I very much hope that the decision to publish it under my name is not wrong. Dr Clarke[3] wrote me that it will probably not come out before August. As they print several thousand copies binding difficulties prevent an earlier publication. In the Preface after having thanked Dr Hodgson, Quick and Vidler I have included a paragraph which runs as follows:

'I wish to express the debt of gratitude I owe to the Bishop of Chichester, who, always guiding, advising and supporting me, has given me countless proofs of his personal friendship. The greatness of my indebtedness to him precludes specification'.[4]

I should be very grateful to you if you would allow me to express my gratitude to you, my Lordbishop, in this, I admit, quite inadequate way.

Yours ever,

P.S. May I ask you kindly to return the enclosure.

---

[1] See Bell, Memorandum of Conversations, 19 June 1942, published in *DBW* 16, pp. 315–17.
[2] John Gilbert Winant (1889–1947) was ambassador of the U.S.A. to Great Britain, 1941–6.
[3] Unidentified.
[4] Leibholz, Preface to *Christianity, Politics and Power*, p. ix.

Bell to Leibholz, Hove, 10 July 1942, BA, N 1334 (typewritten)

My dear Leibholz,

Ever so many thanks for your kind letter of 8th July. I am very much pleased and very glad that you thought that my report on my experiences in Sweden was so useful and realist.[1] I entirely agree with you that the high political character of the whole question by no means relieves Christians from doing what they can to find [a] positive solution. I have heard nothing from Mr Eden since my interview with him on June 30th. I hope that he is giving careful consideration to the matters I laid before him. I hope indeed that other members of the Cabinet may also have been informed of what I told him.

I should very much like to see Mr Winant, but I am not quite sure what would be the best way of setting about it. I feel that I do not want to get things tangled and should be much happier if I had heard something from Mr Eden. But I will see what can be done and I realize that one has to act fairly quickly.

Many thanks for sending me the table of contents with the foreword. It is an extraordinarily interesting table of contents and deals with the very things that we most ought to be considering in relation to Christianity and politics. There does not seem to me, from the table of contents, the least sort of reason why the book should not be published under your own name. I am sure that Dietrich would be of the same opinion. I do very greatly appreciate the words, which you have inserted in your preface about myself though I feel very unworthy of what you so kindly say.

I shall be in Oxford on Thursday [16 July] at Balliol for a Conference on what are called Peace Aims,[2] in which the Archbishop of Canterbury will be taking part, and if there is a moment of free time in which to get hold of you – I am afraid it is rather doubtful – I will do so.

All warmest greetings to your wife and the children.

Yours ever,

---

[1] See Bell, Diary Notes, in *DBW* 16, pp. 327–8; Foreign Office notes, ibid., pp. 330–1; see too Boyens, *Kirchenkampf und Ökumene*, pp. 212–13; also Klemperer, *German Resistance*, pp. 287–8.

[2] Peace Aims Conference in Oxford meeting under the aegis of A.D. Lindsay at Balliol College.

Leibholz to Bell, 15 July 1942, Bell Papers 40, fol. 122 (typewritten); BA N 1334 (copy)

My Lordbishop,

I am so glad to have your extremely kind letter and thank you warmly for it. If I could have done as I wanted to I should have dedicated the whole book to you instead of only expressing in inadequate terms the great indebtedness I owe to you. But I hope another opportunity of doing so will arise in times to come.

I am addressing this letter to Balliol because I understand you are attending a meeting there on Peace aims. And I should like to say a few words in this connection.

A few days ago it struck me that the Archbishop of Canterbury in a speech delivered to the Foreign Press accepted the thesis of the necessity of the elimination of what is called Prussianism and included this as one of the peace aims. I do not know whether this question will arise at your meeting to-morrow. But if so I should like to point out a few facts, which may perhaps be of interest in this connection.

First, the leading Nazis and the ideologists of National Socialism are not Prussians (as e.g. the Austrian Anti-Semites and Hitler, Hess (born in Egypt),[1] Darré (born in Argentine),[2] the Baltic author Rosenberg,[3] the Frenchman Gobineau,[4] the English renegade Chamberlain[5]). – Secondly, the Nazi movement has grown and been developed in Austria and South Germany and not in Prussia. – Thirdly, the Confessional Church has or at least had its strongest roots in specific Prussian provinces (and not e.g. in Thuringia, Hannover, Mecklenburg). – Fourthly, those circles, which are today characterised as Prussian had in the 19th century and have partly today a more Christian tradition than other strata of society. In the 19th century those conservative forces were the pillars of the so-called idea of the Christian state. And it was those who propagated the 'alliance of throne and altar'. I think this fact should be borne in mind even if this kind of Christianity seems to us today to be based on some misunderstandings of the Christian conception of life. In any case, even today these forces are still operative in some way in the Army, and I know that the confessional Church and the Catholic Church in Germany have or at least think they have some of the most faithful and reliable allies in the army without whose help they will never be in a position to act against the regime. Under these circumstances, it is not surprising to see that the political conservative and Prussian organisations have been actually treated in the same way as all other political groups.

As to the structure of the army of today I think we should not forget that the army is no longer a homogeneous body. There are, of course, Nazis, there are the Eastern-minded elements which favour a collaboration with Russia against the West (and many disillusioned Nazis will join them), and there are the Western-minded forces, sometimes of so-called Prussian origin, some of whose names are mentioned in your admirable statement, which has so deeply impressed me. It is true that the army is still today a gigantic instrument of eminent significance and immense power. But this should not lead us to overlook the fact that, at bottom, its unity is undermined and that the army has no longer a spiritual or political driving power of its own and can develop its machinery only if there is an independent scheme of good or devilish values which lay hold on the soul of the masses. To put it in another way, if I may say so, as things stand today, the army is placed more in a position of a servant than of a master.

Now, if today the destruction of Prussianism i.e. of the Army as a whole is put in the stead of the complete destruction of Nazism I am afraid that behind this transformation of the war aims policy the political line becomes visible, which desires in some way the destruction of Germany as a whole and makes a Western-minded Germany practically impossible. I am afraid that those who do not want this but accept the anti-Prussian thesis are in some way ill advised and do not overlook the far-reaching implications of this thesis. I venture to say this because I myself strongly dislike the so-called Prussianism and the 'Prussian spirit'. –

I realize how fully your time will be taken on Thursday and you know, my Lordbishop, that I do not like at all to trouble you in any way. But I thought I must write this to you and hope your meeting will be an interesting and helpful one.

With all good wishes

Yours ever,

---

[1] Rudolf Hess (1894–1987), appointed Deputy Leader to Adolf Hitler in 1933. He served in this position until 1941, when he flew solo to Scotland in an attempt to negotiate peace with the United Kingdom. He was promptly taken prisoner. At the Nuremberg Trials in 1946 he received a life sentence which he served at the Allied military prison at Spandau.

[2] Richard Walther Darré (1895–1953) studied agriculture with a main emphasis on stock breeding and heredity, and in this light turned to the promotion of race theories. In his books *Das Bauerntum als Lebensquell der nordischen Rasse* (1929) and *Neuadel aus Blut und Boden* (1930) he propagated

the idea of the peasantry as the racial heart of the German people. In 1930 he became leader of the agricultural department of the NSDAP Reichsleitung and one year later of the SS Rasse- und Siedlungshauptamt (the main office for race and settlement). As the leading 'blood and soil' ideologists he served as Reichsminister of Food and Agriculture from 1933 to 1942.
3   Alfred Rosenberg (1892–1946) was considered by many the leading ideologist of Nazi antisemitism. In 1930 his published his main work *Der Mythus des 20. Jahrhunderts*. He was later tried and sentenced to death at the Nuremberg Trials.
4   Arthur de Gobineau (1816–82), most widely known for his *Essai sur l'inégalité des races humaines*, 1853–55.
5   Houston Stewart Chamberlain (1855–1927), racial theorist and author of *Die Grundlagen des neunzehnten Jahrhunderts* (1899) and *Arische Weltanschauung* (1905).

Bell to Leibholz, 24 July 1942, BA, N 1334 (typewritten); Bell Papers 40, fol. 123 (carbon)

My dear Leibholz,

Many thanks for your two letters. I have tried to find the reference to Goebbels in the *Daily Telegraph*, but unfortunately I could not find it. I will have another look later on. I very much appreciate what you say about Prussia; it was very useful to have this at the back of my mind when I was attending the Peace Aims Conference in Oxford. It was a very good conference indeed.

I am sorry to say that I have had a reply from Mr Eden, which, though it shows a real interest in what I told him, and in the memoranda I left with him, and throws no doubt on the trustworthiness of the source, takes the line that it would not be in the national interest to make any reply.[1] This is a disappointment.

With all best wishes,
Yours very sincerely,

1   Anthony Eden to Bell, 17 July 1942, in *DBW* 16, p. 343; see the private correspondence, 25 July–17 August 1942, ibid., pp. 345–8. See too the reaction of the Foreign Office to the memorandum of Adam von Trott zu Solz, of April 1942, in Boyens, *Kirchenkampf und Ökumene*, pp. 211–12. Churchill took this line in his letter to Eden, 20 January 1941: 'Our attitude towards all such inquiries or suggestions should be absolute silence. It may well be that a new peace offensive will open up as an alternative to threats of invasion and poison gas'. Paton wrote to Visser 't Hooft, 12 December 1941: 'In this country there is a quite clear and unanimous conviction that the only "war aim", which is worth talking about it is to win and I think that that is fairly well understood outside this country'. Boyens, *Kirchenkampf und Ökumene*, pp. 203–4; see ibid., p. 208: Churchill to Eden, 10 September 1941.

Leibholz to Bell, 28 July 1942, Bell Papers 40, fol. 124 (typewritten); BA N 1334 (copy)

My Lordbishop,

Thank you ever so much for your letter and the enclosed copy of your letter to Mr Eden.[1] Your reply is indeed an admirable statement and is put in such a masterly fashion that I cannot imagine how the case could have been brought forward more strongly. Your letter proves again that a Christian can have a much deeper insight into the actual political situation and happenings than the appointed political leaders of a nation.

The answer itself to which you, my Lordbishop, refer has in so far not disappointed me as I had not expected anything different. People do not like to see the real social and spiritual background of the present struggle and the true issues at stake. Their eyes are riveted on the Army as if this gigantic machine were the decisive factor and a homogeneous body and as if its elimination would secure permanent peace in time to come. To put the question of disarmament as the main war aim (I could hardly discover a word about the destruction of the Nazi regime) as was done in the Nottingham speech, seems to me rather disastrous. It would then have been better not to have made mention of this point at all. For the demand for complete disarmament as a presupposition for opening peace talks makes actually an action of the opposition in Germany impossible as the Army is the only power factor which can act against the regime. As you so cogently and convincingly have made it clear to everyone who is still accessible to reason, this kind of policy leads to no other end than to that of Vansittartism. I am afraid that if the Nazis should succeed in the East, also from a military point of view, the Nazi regime cannot be destroyed without the help of the Germans themselves i.e. without the assistance of the German army. But I very much hope I am wrong and the responsible circles have a better-founded view. Be that as it may, this negative attitude seems to me to be harmful not only for the opposition which wages its war in Germany against the regime but no less for this country and the Allies who, I am afraid, will never be able to get a better peace, and I think if the truth would squarely be put before the whole nation in such an illuminating way as your letter does the answer would be quite a different one.

You probably know, my Lordbishop, that Miss Rathbone[2] has recently put a question to Mr Eden in the House of Commons pointing out that throughout the whole of Germany Vansittart's Black Record has been distributed in a German translation,[3] and asking whether the Foreign Minister would be prepared to make a statement to the effect whether Vansittart's policy is that of H. M. government or not? Would it perhaps not be expedient that the few who in this country see the true and grave issues which are at stake today should unite in concerted action? You wrote to me that the Peace Aims Conference in Oxford was a very good one. Are there not like-minded people who would join such an action?

With all good wishes and renewed thanks for all you have done in the interest of your country and beyond that in the interest of a better future for all nations.

Yours ever,

---

[1] Bell to Eden, 25 July 1942, in *DBW* 16, pp. 345–6.
[2] i.e. Eleanor Rathbone.
[3] Robert Vansittart, *Black Record: German Past and Present* (London, 1941); but a German translation of the whole text is unknown. Very possibly extracts were translated for propaganda leaflets.

Bell to Leibholz, 14 October 1942, BA N 1334 (handwritten)

My dear Leibholz,

Very many thanks for your letter, and for *The Fortnightly*.[1] I have read the article with great interest and approval and should very much like to see its views promoted among and accepted by leaders of opinion in this country. I take in *The Fortnightly* myself, and (naturally) had not realized Gerard was a pseudonym for yourself.[1] I wonder if you have sent it to Butler, or Carr? I will send it shortly to Winant.

I am vy sorry to have left you without news for so long. Time flies; and I spent August in Scotland, in charge of a little parish but also getting a complete change.

I took your advice and wrote to Winant, with the result that I had a vy useful and encouraging interview with him in July. I told him of my Swedish experiences, and sent him some papers afterwards. He was clearly attentive, and (I thought) more alive to the importance of my conversations and their provenance than the 2 English statesmen. He was very kind. And when I wrote to him (with the papers) he replied that he was reporting the whole matter to Washington. I also heard from an American (YMCA secretary)[2] who was out from Geneva, though we could not meet, as I was in Scotland: that his colleagues in Geneva (in touch with Dietrich) were disappointed that nothing had come of the proposals, and that he thought nothing further was likely while Russia was in the foreground.

I hope to be in Oxford on November 1 at Corpus: but my time is in other's hands, so that, while I hope we may meet, I can't be certain.

All best greetings to your wife & the girls

Yours ever,

---

[1] Gerhard (= G. Leibholz), 'Germany between West and East', reprinted in *Politics and Law*, pp. 174–81.

[2] This was Tracy Strong (1887–1968), Secretary-General of the YMCA World Committee, 1926–38, and then director of YMCA's 'War Prisoner' Aid until 1953.

Leibholz to Bell, 20 October 1942, Bell Papers 40, fols. 125–6 (typewritten); BA N 1334 (copy)

My dear Lordbishop,

Ever so many thanks for your last kind letter. It was a great joy for me to hear from you again. I am so glad to know that the proposals you brought home from Sweden have not altogether been put upon the shelf. I think that they are really worth[y] of being followed up in one way or other as I can hardly imagine how a better peace will ever be available. The other chance – as I see it – is a Europe in anarchy and under mob-rule or, strange as it may sound today, a united Europe (including Russia) on a communist basis against the Anglo-Saxon countries. All the other plans projected in this country seem to me implicitly to presuppose a helpless, if not a collapsed Russia – but take it for granted that notwithstanding even then there is a possibility of winning the war, from a military point of view, against a united Germany. I hope that this will not prove another illusion.

I greatly appreciated what you kindly said about the article. It is good to know that you, my Lordbishop, and a few other thoughtful minds see the whole situation in a similar light. It is interesting to note that these are just those who know the Continent in one way or other. I do not know whether you have seen the speech delivered by Sir Samuel Hoare[1] a few weeks ago. I think what he said covered our own views in many points. I should also wish that some of the books of the Americans who left Germany about ten months ago (especially Smith's book *The Last Train*[2]) would be read more by the men who makes politics today. On the other hand, there were some reports in *The Times* and other newspapers about a stiffening of the German morale. I think one cannot wonder at this reaction in face of the present official policy, which in its effect must be of great value for Goebbels' propaganda policy.

I am very glad that you will kindly pass on a copy of the article to Dr Winant (I am enclosing a reprint for this purpose). I have also sent copies to Butler and Carr. If you think, my Lordbishop, that there are in the Church or the House of Lords members who are sympathetic to our basic attitude of mind and are possibly interested in reading the article without prejudice please kindly give me their names. I preferred to publish the article under a pseudonym among other reasons in order to avoid any discussion on being accused of interfering in politics.

Unfortunately, I have to address a meeting in Queens's College on Sunday November 1st at 11. I cannot alter the date, which was fixed some months ago. But I heard from Kramm that you are preaching also at Corpus at 7 o'clock. If it is permissible we should greatly look forward to hearing you then.

My wife and the children send you and Mrs Bell their love. Marianne who is now 15 took her certificate in July with matric off [sic] and she is now in the 6th form specialising herself in science.

Yours ever,

---

[1] Sir Samuel Hoare (1880–1959), since 1944 1st Viscount Templewood, Conservative politician who was Foreign Secretary in 1935 and Home Secretary from 1937 to 1939. Hoare was one of the foremost Chamberlain loyalists. He was British ambassador to Spain from 1940 to 1944.
[2] Howard K. Smith, *Last Train from Berlin. An Eye-Witness Account of Germany at War* (London, 1942).

Bell to Leibholz, 26 corrected to 28 October 1942, BA N 1334 (typewritten)

My dear Leibholz,

I have sent the reprint to Mr Winant. If you have half-a-dozen more copies I would send them to some friends who would I know be interested. Like you, I wish that books such as *The Last Train from Berlin* could be read by those engaged in making politics.

I hope I may see something of you at Oxford during next weekend. I think it should be possible for you to get into the Corpus service if you would like. I should advise your writing to the President.

Mrs Bell and I join in sending you and your wife our love. I am so glad Marianne has taken her Certificate.

Yours ever,

[a]P.S. Since dictating I have received enclosed from Dietrich[1] – *with* the note re. Censorship![2][a]

---

[1] Bonhoeffer to Bell, 28 August 1942, in *DBW* 16, p. 353.
[2] Note stating the British regulations for receiving letters from correspondents in enemy countries.

Leibholz to Bell, 30 October 1942, Bell Papers 40, fol. 130 (typewritten); BA, N 1334 (copy)

My Lordbishop,

I thank you warmly for your letter, Dietrich's letter and for kindly sending the reprint to Mr Winant.

We were delighted to have the good news from Dietrich and I think the contents of the letter, especially the sentence that 'things are going as I expected them to go' is rather encouraging. It is a great pity that you cannot get into touch with him – all the more, as he will anxiously be awaiting your reply. By the way, the Censor, in my view, was wrong in attaching the usual note you enclosed. For the regulation referred to does not apply to people of 'Enemy nationality' who are staying in neutral countries. For these people are not in 'enemy or enemy occupied countries'. As far as I know this is the practice for a long time and I have acted accordingly.

I am enclosing four reprints of the article and hope to send you two more soon. It is very good of you to pass them on to some of your friends. I had also a letter from Dr Paton in this matter with some comments. I enclose a copy of this letter together with a copy of my reply.

I also wrote to the President of Corpus[1] and am very much looking forward to seeing you somehow or other on Sunday.

With our best wishes to Mrs Bell and you, my Lordbishop.

Yours ever,

[1] Sir Richard Winn Livingstone (1880–1960), Oxford classicist and educationalist and Vice-Chancellor of Oxford University, 1944–7. He was the brother of Henrietta Bell.

Paton to Leibholz, 26 October 1942, BA. N 1334 (copy); Bell Papers 40, fol. 127 (copy)

My dear Leibholz,

I have read your paper with very great interest and shall look forward to seeing your book.[1] I am interested in the thesis you advance, which you will remember you made in a memorandum[2] which you sent me last January and which you further elaborated in your speech at the Cambridge Conference. I think that the argument for the Western Powers giving every chance to the constructive democratic western forces in Germany is a very important argument. Frankly I do not think it is strengthened by the effort to show that the alternative would be a communist Germany by choice. My reasons for thinking this are two: in the first place it a little looks as if the danger of communist Germany were being used especially in dealing with rather conservative English Circles, as a kind of bogy or threat. In the second place, and more important, I gravely doubt your analysis of the Russo-German relationship. There is every evidence that in Germany there is an overwhelming fear of what Russia would do if she got a free hand in any part of Germany, and on the Russian side the behaviour of the German troops has nurtured a ferocity of hatred, which will not speedily be banished.

These two facts make it, in my judgement, exceedingly doubtful whether the kind of voluntary acceptance of Russian Communism in Germany, resulting in a cordial friendship between the two powers as against the West, is all likely.

As I say, I think that the argument for strengthening the pro-western democratic elements in Germany is strong enough without the rather doubtful argument, or so at least it seems to me.

Yours very sincerely,

[1] That is Leibholz, *Christianity, Politics and Power*.
[2] That is Leibholz, 'Germany, the West and the Possibility of a New International Order', reprinted in *Politics and Law*, pp. 154–73.

Leibholz to Paton, 30 October 1942, BA. N 1334 (copy); Bell Papers 40, fols. 128–9. (copy)

My dear Dr Paton,

Very many thanks for the comments on the article in *The Fortnightly*. I very much value them and am especially delighted to see that you also advocate a policy directed to strengthen the pro-western elements in Germany.

Perhaps you will be surprised if I say that I quite agree with the facts you state. I think you are quite right in noting that in Germany there is an immense fear of what may happen if Russia got any free hand in Germany. But I think we must not forget that this fear is sustained by those strata and circles with which we are in contact i.e. the Church, the remainder of the Western minded bourgeoisie, the trade-unionists and so on. It is those who think – and I think rightly so – that a collapse of the Nazis would also mean their end – provided Russia be the decisive factor after the war on the Continent. But I am afraid there are also the more than six million Communists of 1933 who will not have disappeared, but on the contrary will have gained in strength by the support of former liberal-minded workers and other disillusioned strata of society, including also National Socialists. If I have spoken in the article of a choice Germany would have between the West and the East I did not mean by this that the Western-minded strata could also accept an Eastern solution. I think you are quite right in saying that such a solution would never be accepted by a Russia who has gone through the awful experience of this war. But another matter is whether Russia would not be prepared to make peace with those strata, which would be a safe guarantee for a true communist Germany. It is this possibility which 'our' people fear deadly. Actually, if this should occur it would be the end of the hope of ever getting a Western-minded Germany.

Your other argument is no less important. The attitude of the circles to which you refer seems to me so dangerous because they only see the alternative between Communism and National Socialism and because they are prepared to prefer in a given case the latter solution in order to evade Communism. But the unfortunate thing is that, I am afraid, there is a half-truth in the statement as far as Communism is concerned, and that – I ask you to forgive me for being quite open – the official policy implicitly furthers this attitude by not offering Germany an opportunity, which could save the world from final destruction.

In this connection I feel strongly that the official campaign against Prussianism is a serious obstacle for seeing things clearly. It overshadows the true issues and prevents, as it seems to me, the United Nations from pursuing a really constructive peace policy for the post war period. The point seems to me to be that in truth the army in Germany is no homogeneous body. There are quite heterogeneous elements in the army and among them also important elements which we simply cannot afford to ignore if we do not give up all hope of support from inside Germany. I think one cannot stress enough the point that the army is the only power factor, which – when the time comes – can act against the regime and I cannot see any plausible reason why as a result of the campaign against what is called Prussia these forces should be welded (for simple reasons of self-preservation) to a regime the overthrow of which they themselves want.

I should be very grateful if you would kindly consider these points, from your point of view. As our aim is the same I should be only too glad if we could also come to a complete agreement as to the means of securing it. This seems to me all the more important as I know that you have the possibility of influencing those who make politics in the right direction while I can only do my best by talking and writing.

Yours very sincerely,

Bell to Leibholz, 3 November 1942, BA, N 1334 (handwritten)

My dear Leibholz,

I am so sorry I had to be so rushed from chapel to Hall, and so had no moment for a word with you or even a hand with your wife! But it was very nice to get a glimpse of you both – and on *such* a wet day!

Thank you also for copies of your correspondence with Paton. He is a correspondent (and speaker and writer!) on *this* subject very difficult to shake. It will be interesting to see whether he takes the points of your last letter. Would you remind me, next time you write, of the address Dietrich stays at, and the pastor's name, in Switzerland.[1] I think he must have heard of my reply by cable and letter many weeks ago to 't Hooft. I am glad you got a favourable impression from his words.

Yours ever,

---

[1] This time Bonhoeffer did not stay with his friend Erwin Sutz in Switzerland but in Munich.

Bell to Leibholz, 6 November 1942, BA, N 1334 (typewritten)

My dear Leibholz,

I am delighted to have the book,[1] which you have so kindly sent me and I shall read it with avidity and I am sure with great admiration too. It is a real token to me of our close personal friendship and the delight I have in my association with you and your wife and children.

Yours ever sincerely,

ᵃYou may like the enclosed – Don't trouble to acknowledge.ᵃ [2]

[1] That is Leibholz, *Christianity, Politics and Power*.
[2] This enclosure is now lost.

Bell to Leibholz, 4 December 1942, BA, N 1334 (typewritten); Bell Papers 40, fol. 131 (carbon)

My dear Leibholz,

Very many thanks for the *Christian News-Letter*,[1] which I am delighted to have, and also for your former letter of the 8th November. I am reading the *Christian News-Letter* during the weekend and will let you have any thoughts that it arouses.

I am very glad to have the message from Dietrich. I have written to Pastor Sutz. I have also written much more fully, in the hope that the news will get round to Dietrich, to Harry Johansson at Sigtuna.[2] I am glad to say that Bishop Brilioth[3] spent a good many hours with me at Chichester when he was over from Sweden, and I gave him a careful account of the important talks I had, of which you know. I very much hope that he may see some of our friends in Sweden, so that they may know what I have tried to do.

I wonder whether you have seen Fraenkel's book, *The Other Germany*,[4] which is just out? It contains in summary form seven *Questions and Answers*, which were broadcast early in July in the *B.B.C. German News Service*, giving far more definite and satisfactory answers about the Government policy to a Germany in which Hitler has been overthrown than have ever been made public in this country. I have been able to get the original text of these *Questions and Answers*, and am seeing Lord Cranborne about them in the hope of being able to ask a question in the House of Lords to see whether they are a correct representation of the policy of His Majesty's Government.

Please give my best remembrances to your wife.

Yours very sincerely,

[1] *Christian News-Letter Supplement* No. 162, 2 December 1942: Leibholz, 'Christianity, Justice and Modern Society', reprinted as 'The Foundation of Justice and Law in the Light of the Present European Crisis', in Leibholz, *Politics and Law* pp. 253–70. Originally Leibholz delivered the paper at a conference on 'National Law', no doubt encouraged by Alec Vidler, the Warden at St. Deiniol's Library, Hawarden.
[2] Harry Johansson (1900–83) was Nils Ehrenstrom's assistant director (and later director) of the Nordic Ecumenical Institute, founded in 1940 at Sigtuna. It was here that Bell had met Bonhoeffer and Hans Schönfeld. See Bell to Erwin Sutz, 3 December 1942, in *DBW* 16, pp. 375–6.
[3] Yngve Brilioth (1891–1959) was Lutheran Bishop of Växjö 1938–50 and Archbishop of Uppsala 1950–8. See Bell to Harry Johansson, 3 December 1942, in *DBW* 16, p. 377.
[4] Heinrich Fraenkel, *The Other Germany* (London, 1942). See Bell to H. Fraenkel, 3 December 1942, Bell Papers 51, fol. 25 (carbon): 'I have just finished reading *The Other Germany*, and I should like to congratulate you most heartily on the book. It seems to me to be of quite extraordinary

importance, is admirably clear, and by the accumulation of facts and pieces of evidence it has a most persuasive effect, which far outstrips the force of any number of rhetorical arguments or any amount of expression'. Heinrich Fraenkel (1897–1986) had left Berlin on the night of the burning of the Reichstag (27/28 February 1933) to evade imprisonment and emigrated to Britain. Now he worked for the German service of the BBC.

Leibholz to Bell, 9 December 1942, Bell Papers 40, fol. 132 (typewritten); BA, N 1334 (copy)

My Lordbishop,

Thank you very much for your last letter. I am so glad to know that you have written to Pastor Sutz and Harry Johansson and that you had a good long talk with Bishop Brilioth. I saw the latter only for a few minutes and it was, therefore, not possible to have real talk with him. I hope that in any case, in one of these ways Dietrich will learn of the great endeavours you are making here.

Up to now I have not read Fraenkel's book *The Other Germany* but after what you have told me about it I will try to get hold of it. The broadcast to which you refer, my Lordbishop, seems to have been extraordinar[il]y important indeed and I think it is a good idea to raise the matter in the House of Lords. Of course, I agree with Fraenkel's main thesis that there is an Other Germany (in truth, it is not a thesis, but a fact) but I think at the same time we must bear in mind that Fraenkel and his friends want a communist Germany in the Russian sense, even if they speak of a socialist Germany.[1] They are 'Marxists' and want, therefore, like the Russians not only the destruction of Hitlerite Germany but also of those strata of society out of which according to their view the Nazi-regime has grown. From their basic point of view, this is not surprising. For they have no religious ties. From my point of view, however, those strata of society also include the most valuable elements for a future Western-minded policy. I also think that a defeated Nazi Germany must be socialist. But the point seems to me to be the spiritual basis of this socialism. If we want a Western solution we need the help of those who according to radical Marxism must be destroyed. And this is why I think we must be careful in order not to be used by those circles which want communism on the whole Continent. I admit they have the better chances and our task is the more difficult one.

By the way, I had a letter from the National Peace Council[2] saying that they intend to hold a meeting in January on the question as to what policy ought to be pursued towards Germany after the war. Do you think, my Lordbishop, that it is worthwhile going up to London? I cannot judge it. I should be grateful to you for your advice.

Please give our best remembrances to Mrs Bell.

Yours ever,

---

[1] In 1943 Fraenkel was one of the founding members of the Freie Deutsche Bewegung (FDB) in Great Britain with many communists. But in 1944 he left this group supporting the NCFG because of the position of the USSR and the Communist Party of Germany (KPD) on the question of the future of Germany.
[2] The National Peace Council, founded in 1908 by Quakers, acted as the co-ordinating body for almost 200 groups across Britain.

Bell to Leibholz, 11 December 1942, BA, N 1334 (typewritten); Bell Papers 40, fols. 133–4 (carbon)

My dear Leibholz,

I was very glad to get your *News-Letter Supplement*. I took it, and *Christianity, Politics and Power* away with me to read on a journey to Birmingham yesterday, and I have now read both the Supplement and the book. I am immensely impressed with both, but of course with the book particularly, as a full and clear statement of the position. I am a learner from you, but I agree whole-heartedly with you. I am sure that the position, which you put before your readers is one which ought to be put forth on a large scale by the Churches just now wherever they can find an opportunity. There are two points on which I should very much like you, if you have time, to expand a little.

First, it would be extremely important to define in a clear way a statement of principles on which Christians could agree and could issue. On page 63 you speak about the continuous contribution of Christian thought, with special concern for the order of social life, etc.[1] On page 64 you deal with the relations which should exist between the nations. You give certain illustrations of the points on which agreement could be found and stated, and you deal with the point at the beginning of the chapter on the final issue at stake. What I feel that we badly need is a platform on which Christians of different Churches should unite, and on which they could collaborate with others sympathetic to the Christian tradition, comparable for force and clarity with the Fascist Decalogue given on page 180 of Oakshott's *Social and Political Doctrines of Contemporary Europe* (Cambridge Press),[2] and Hitler's *Twenty-Five Points* given on page 190 of the same book. There are probably similar brief statements of the Communist position. The *Ten Points* of Christmas, 1940[3] – the Pope's and the Oxford Conference – give something of what I mean.[4] But I think they want to be put a little more sharply on the one hand, and possibly (though here collaboration with non-Christians raises a difficulty) in a rather more religious framework. Long ago Archbishop Söderblom pressed for a moral creed on which the Christian Churches could unite. But nobody has really tackled this. I mentioned it once in a letter to Madariaga,[5] after reading a letter of his to the *Times*. He was sympathetic but really non-committal. I think Professor Vincent Smith[6] of Oxford would be more sympathetic to this. I wonder if you know him?

The kind of combination which I would like to see would be that of the statement of the Principles of Natural Law given by Catholic Bishops in Germany earlier (I think) this year, in their protest to the State,[7] and reproduced either in one of the *Spiritual Issues* bulletins of the M.O.I.[8] or in the C.N.L.,[9] and the *Ten Points* of Christmas 1940. Does this wake any spark in your mind?

The second point concerns your brief analysis of power in your second chapter. I wonder whether there are ways in which the element of spiritual power, used I agree for political purposes, could be further drawn out for creative work in connection with the task, Christianity and politics?

I am writing a longer letter than I intended. But there is one other matter of which I want to tell you, for I am sure it will interest you. I enclose a copy of a leaflet scattered by the R.A.F. at the beginning of last July, and widely disseminated on the B.B.C. German News. I was able to get hold of it through Heinrich Fraenkel, who gives a brief summary in his new book published by Lindsay Drummond and called *The Other Germany*.[10] When I came to this chapter (at the end) in which the *Questions and Answers* are summarised, I at once saw how very important they were, and asked him if he could get me the original text in full. He did, and I got them translated. I have given notice two weeks running to ask a question in the House of Lords as to whether the Answers to these Questions are a correct representation of the policy of His Majesty's Government. I postponed asking the question, at Lord Cranborne's request, pending a talk with him. I had this talk, and it was arranged that I should ask the question last Wednesday [9 December]. But he rang me up again to ask for postponement, and I am to see Mr Eden. There is great reluctance to give any publicity to these *Questions and Answers* in this country. This makes me very anxious. The Answers seem to me to give a far clearer and more satisfactory description of what our war aims should be than any we have yet heard. I am hoping to see Mr Eden in the next three or four days.

I am so glad you have heard from Dietrich. With all warmest remembrances for your wife and yourself,

Yours very sincerely,

ᵃP.S. I appreciate what you say in your letter received today about Fraenkel and his Communism etc.ᵃ

---

[1] Reprinted in Leibholz, *Politics and Law*, pp. 91–132; here p. 130.

[2] Michael Oakeshott, *The social and political doctrines of contemporary Europe* (Cambridge, 1939). Michael Oakeshott (1901–90), later an influential political philosopher, and at this time actively seeking war work.

[3] 'Foundations of Peace. A Christian basis. Agreement among the Churches', letter to the *Times* (published 21 December 1940, p. 5 col. c); this paper accepted then cited 'The Pope's Five Peace Points'; see Boyens, *Kirchenkampf und Ökumene, 1939–1945*, vol. II, pp. 356–6; also pp. 202–3. See too Bell's speech of 19 May 1941, 'The Pope's Five Peace Points', reprinted in *The Church and Humanity*, pp. 48–57.

[4] i.e. The Oxford Conference on Church, Community and State, July 1937. See Bell to William Temple, 6 November 1942, Bell Papers, Vol. 216, fols. 34seq. Here Bell proposed to invite the Pope and other leaders of Christian communions to a gathering with a view to 'setting up an international commission on a Christian basis in order to consider what are the most effective steps that can be taken through the co-operation of Christians in all countries concerned to prevent further bloodshed arising from the spirit of revenge after hostilities have creased and to deal with the grave problems caused by starvation and disease'.

[5] Salvador de Madariaga y Rojo (1886–1978) was Spanish Ambassador at Paris from 1932 to 1934 and in 1931–6 member of the embassy at the League of Nations. After the victory of General Franco in 1936 he emigrated to Britain and gave lectures in Spanish literature at the University of Oxford.

[6] Bell here has in mind Herbert Arthur Smith (1885–1961); see his letter to Leibholz, 19 December 1942.

[7] See 'Hirtenwort der deutschen Bischöfe zur Lage der Kirche', 22 March 1942, reprinted in Ludwig Volk (ed.), *Akten deutscher Bischöfe über die Lage der Kirche*, Vol. V (Mainz 1983), pp. 700–4.

[8] The Ministry of Information of the British government.

[9] i.e. *The Christian News-Letter*.

[10] Hermann Fraenkel, *The Other Germany* (London, 1942).

Seven Questions and Answers Dropped by Leaflet early in July and widely disseminated by the B.B.C. German News between 3 and 7 July [1942], Bell Papers 51, fols. 18–20 (copy); BA, N 1334 (copy)

CAN HITLER'S GERMANY COUNT ON A COMPROMISE PEACE?

No. In the London Agreement[1] England and Russia, with the consent of the United States of America, declared once more that they would never negotiate with the Hitler regime, or any other German Government, which does not unequivocally renounce all aggressive intentions.

DOES HITLER'S DEFEAT MEAN GERMANY'S DESTRUCTION?

No. Again and again the British Government declared, first in September 1939, finally on the 21st May 1942 that it has two aims: to destroy the Hitler Tyranny and after the war to enable all the peoples of Europe, *including Germany*, to reconstruct a state which would ensure to every individual impartial Justice, Freedom of Speech and of Association and Protection against Unemployment and economic Exploitation. Therefore Hitler's defeat does not mean the destruction of Germany, but on the contrary the salvation of Germany from destruction.

WILL ENGLAND HAND OVER THE GERMAN PEOPLE TO BOLSHEVISM?

The British and Russian Governments have in Article V of the London Agreement[2] pledged themselves not to interfere with the internal affairs of other states, after Hitler's War Machine has been destroyed, and a recurrence of aggression has been made impossible. The U.S.A. take up the same attitude. The 'Bolshevik Danger' has therefore been revealed to be what it always was: 'a Propagandist Myth'.

DOES HITLER'S DEFEAT MEAN UNEMPLOYMENT AND INFLATION FOR GERMANY?

In the world of today the prosperity of every country depends on the prosperity of all other countries. There can be no lasting peace and no prosperity, as long as one nation tries to make itself the 'Herrenvolk'. In the Roosevelt-Churchill Declaration[3] England and the U.S.A. pledged themselves, in their own interests, not to allow the vanquished countries to be handicapped by economic disabilities. The Roosevelt-Churchill Declaration was accepted by the Russian Government as the basis of their own policy, and was reaffirmed in the London Agreement. After Hitler's downfall, Germany can therefore become prosperous along with other countries in a lasting peace.

WOULD HITLER'S DOWNFALL INVOLVE A SUPER VERSAILLES?

The assertion that the United Nations want to impose a Super Versailles on Germany is a definite lie. Such a Super Versailles does actually exist: Hitler has imposed it on Europe.

The United Nations are determined to avoid three mistakes of Versailles.

The Allies' first mistake was the fact that German Militarists were too leniently treated. The United Nations are determined this time to finish with them once and for all.

The second mistake of the Versailles Treaty was that it did not make provision for the economic prosperity and reconstruction of Europe. The United Nations are determined in their own interests to make such provision this time.

The third mistake was that neither Russia nor America took part in the peace settlement, nor in the pacification of Europe. The United Nations are determined not to allow this mistake to occur again.

DOES ENGLAND EXPECT THAT THE GERMAN PEOPLE WILL TAKE PART IN THE DESTRUCTION OF THE HITLER REGIME?

England recognises the difficult position of Germans of all classes who are opposed to Hitler. To these Germans we say: The United Nations will destroy Hitler's war machine. If the German people accelerate Hitler's downfall, that will mean the saving of millions of human lives. We know that revolt against Hitler will involve sacrifices, but the scale of such sacrifices would only be a fraction of that which Hitler offers up every day in the vain effort to escape his own downfall. The roots of German Militarism must be destroyed by the German people themselves. And the sooner the better. So long as the German people have not freed themselves of German Militarism, so long will England and her Allies remain armed in order to prevent a third World War.

WHAT IS THE RESULT OF ALL THIS FOR GERMANY?

The real enemies of Germany are the war-mongers. Germany could have peace tomorrow if she would free herself of Hitler and militarism – a peace in freedom and justice.

---

[1] A Twenty-Year Mutual Assistance Agreement Between the United Kingdom and the Union of Soviet Socialist Republics was signed in London, 26 May 1942.
[2] 'The high contracting parties [. . .] will act in accordance with the two principles of not seeking territorial aggrandizement for themselves and of non-interference in the internal affairs of other States'.
[3] The Atlantic Charter, issued on 14 August 1941.

Bell to Leibholz, 11 December [?] 1942 (postmark), BA, N 1334 (postcard handwritten)

I forgot to answer your query about Peace Aims Conference, I should know for this [sic] if you would tell me where it is, and who are the speakers. I said (when asked) I would not speak.

Leibholz to Bell, 16 December 1942, Bell Papers 40, fol. 135 (typewritten); BA, N 1334 (copy)

My Lordbishop,

I am very greatly pleased to have your appreciative letter and am delighted to know that you agree with the basic tendencies of the publications.

The comments you have made on them have much impressed me and I agree wholeheartedly with you in the urgent need for further expansion of many of the points I have tried to raise. I think it is hardly possible to exaggerate the religious, moral and political importance of the suggestion you have made. Will you allow me to think over the whole matter quietly? I will then write to you in greater detail on it. I have yet now to finish an article *before Christmas* for Christopher Dawson[1] who wishes to publish on the issue raised in the Supplement of the *Chr. News-Letter* a more detailed article and I hope it will be possible to publish the article in the next issue (January) of *The Dublin Review*.[2] I think the idea, which struck you should be most energetically followed up and if possible pressed home. It seems to me to be of *eminent* significance. – Unfortunately, I do not know Professor Vincent Smith.

In the meantime I have seen Fraenkel's book and have carefully read the copy of the questions and answers, which you kindly sent me. As to Fraenkel I think my assumption is right and you know, my Lordbishop, that I for my part have great doubts as to whether it will be possible to combine those values to which we are committed with a kind of Russian communism, which after the present war promises to become more cruel and savage than even in Russia. But I admit these people have the better chances. I think Mr Eden will have tried to make you desist from publicly raising the question you intended to put forward – probably pointing out that national interests do not allow such a discussion or that propaganda has only a tactical significance. In any case I fully agree with you that this attitude gives cause for very serious anxiety.

The answers themselves if seriously taken would bring us an important step forward but I am afraid that the frequent mentioning of the complete destruction of German militarism considerably diminishes the practical value of the statement. Not that I also do not wish the destruction of this militarism in the end. But the point which from my point of view cannot be stressed enough seems to me to be that the army is the only power factor which can possibly act against the regime and it is wishful thinking to sustain the thesis that the German people can revolt against both the regime and the army. I do not know whether you read the day before yesterday in *The Times* the article *Hitler and the Wehrmacht*. It is said there that the Waffen S.S. (Himmler's army), which originally had only symbolic significance is today over 1.000.000 men. They are prepared to obey any order of Hitler as they know and rightly know that their lives depend on the Nazi regime. And now the German people are called upon not only to destroy the Hitler regime but also the army, which is the only force to struggle against this New army. I think these facts are so clear and cogent that I wonder how it is possible that responsible circles see themselves in the position to ignore them. My only hope is that in the course of time the force of circumstances will compel these circles to revise their present policy, especially as the Americans seem to be more realistic. Let us hope that it will then not be too late.

In the first letter concerning the meeting of the Peace Aims conference, which is projected to be held in London on January 29th and 30th, 1943 the following names were given as probable speakers: P. Gordon Walker,[3] Mr H. N. Brailsford,[4] Colonel T. H. Minshall,[5] Mr R. W. B. Clarke,[6] E. F. Schumacher[7] and F. Hildebrandt. Apart from Hildebrandt I only know Schumacher. He is a young and gifted German Marxist [a]of the radical type[a]. But he would not cause me to go up to London as I know beforehand what he will have to say. I do not know, however, the Englishmen. The subject of the conference is to consider 'the political, economic, spiritual policies, which ought to be directed towards Germany to ensure a general peace and security and her re-entry into a peaceful international system'. I should very much appreciate your advice in this matter.

Yours ever,

1. Christopher Dawson (1889–1970) converted to Roman Catholicism in 1914 and became one of the leading Catholic thinkers and writers of the mid-twentieth century. From 1940 to 1956 he was editor of the *Dublin Review*, the essential periodical for contemporary Roman Catholic thought.
2. See Leibholz, 'The Foundation of Justice and Law in the Light of the Present European Crisis', reprinted in *Politics and Law*, pp. 253–70. The *Dublin Review* (1836–1969) had long been established as the most widely read periodical for Roman Catholic opinion and argument.
3. Patrick Gordon Walker (1907–80), Labour Party politician and later Member of Parliament for Smethwick. In 1942 he was working for the BBC European Service, with particular responsibility for the now-daily broadcasts to Germany.
4. Henry Noel Brailsford (1873–1958), perhaps the most prolific British left-wing journalist of the first half of the twentieth century; member of the Fabian Society. During the Second World War he wrote a weekly column in the left-wing *Reynold's News* and continued to write books, not least *Our Settlement with Germany* (London, 1944).
5. Colonel Thomas Herbert Minshall (1873–1972), a widely known consultant electrical engineer and newspaper proprietor; now active in the Peace Aims group and author of *What to Do with Germany* (London, 1941) and *Future Germany* (London, 1943).
6. Richard W. B. Clarke (1910–75), at this time working for the Ministries of Information, Economic Warfare, and Supply and Production.
7. Ernst Friedrich 'Fritz' Schumacher (1911–77) emigrated to Britain before the outbreak of war in 1939. In exile he became a close collaborator with the economist John Maynard Keynes and, later, one of the fathers of the Bretton Woods system of monetary management.

Leibholz to Bell, 16 December 1942, Bell Papers 40, fol. 136 (handwritten)

My Lordbishop,

I will not let my letter go today without sending you and Mrs Bell our best wishes for a good and happy Christmas. I have again to thank you most warmly for all you have so very kindly done for us in the last year. You know how I think and how unable I am to express the greatness of my indebtedness towards you in adequate terms. On the whole, from a military point of view, the situation seems to be more favourable than the last few years. Let us hope that the other year will also bring us a better political understanding so that we may have peace again and our real work can start.

The two little candlesticks, which my wife has painted, are for Mrs Bell and you as a special Christmas greeting from my wife.*

She and the children join with me in sending you and Mrs Bell our love.

Yours ever,

---

* She sends them separately.

Bell to Leibholz, 17 December 1942, BA, N 1334 (typewritten); Bell Papers 40, fol. 137 (carbon)

ªPrivateª

My dear Leibholz,

I saw Mr Eden on Tuesday [15 December] about the R.A.F. leaflet. He said that he was now in charge of political warfare, and that the leaflets were distributed according to a plan, and that he had made it an absolute condition that the contents of the leaflets should not be canvassed in Parliament or elsewhere. A debate on the contents of a particular leaflet would be in his judgement most mischievous from the point of view of the general political warfare campaign. I replied that what had pleased me about the answers to these Questions was the clear distinction between Hitlerite Germany and the other Germany, a distinction which was not anything like so evident in his or the Prime Minister's public statements; that I was not wedded to the contents of this leaflet, but that I did very much want to get a statement made, which showed that His Majesty's Government was acting on that policy and was ready to tell Germany so officially.

He did not object to my raising a debate on this subject in the House of Lords, and when I said that one way of doing it might be to call attention to the remarks made by Stalin on Russia's war aims at the end of his speech of November 6th, and to ask whether the intention to destroy the Hitlerite State but not Germany, the Hitlerite army but not the German army was also the policy of His Majesty's Government, he said that he thought he could probably say yes to that, and liked the idea.[1] I said that I would like to do that. He told me to take the matter up with Lord Cranborne, who would consult him. My idea would be to ask the Question towards the end of January, as the House only resumes sittings about January 17th.

I have drafted a Question as follows: 'To call attention to the passages in M. Stalin's speech of November 6th in which he drew a distinction between Germany and the Hitlerite State, the German army[2] and the Hitlerite army, and said that Russia did not contemplate the destruction of Germany and the German army,[3] but the destruction of the Hitlerite state and the Hitlerite army (and their leaders), and to ask whether His Majesty's Government made the same distinction in their war aims; and to move for papers'.

However, before writing to Lord Cranborne, I want to ask you whether the form in which the Question is put could and would be twisted by Goebbels so as to make it appear that I or the Church of England had turned Communist. In my speech I should make my attitude absolutely clear to a quite different effect. But the advantage of using Stalin's remarks as a peg on which to hang a question is that it is very difficult for His Majesty's Government to refuse to make the same distinction. If I were to make my question broader, without reference to Russia's war aims, it would be easier to give a vaguer reply. And even if I did put a more general question, without mentioning Stalin, I expect I should have to mention the distinction drawn by him as an illustration in my speech. One of the main points, however, in my speech would be to express the advantage of *Britain* showing that there is another alternative besides a Communist revolution to National Socialism. I should stress the character of the opposition which is based on[4] the Churches, and the bureaucracy, and certain quarters in the army etc.

Let me have your candid opinion. If you care to amend my Question, or suggest an alternative, all the better.

With all best wishes to you and your wife and children for Christmas,

Yours very sincerely,

---

[1] See Bell Papers, Vol. 51, fols. 34–6: Stalin's Speech Delivered at the Celebration Meeting of the Moscow Soviet of Working People's Deputies and Party and Public Organisations of Moscow on

6 November 1942, published in *Soviet War News*, No. 408, 9 November 1942, pp. 1–4; marked p. 4: 'We have no such aim to destroy Germany, for it is impossible to destroy Germany, just as it is impossible to destroy Russia. But the Hitlerite State can and should be destroyed, and our first task, in fact, is to destroy the Hitlerite State and its inspirers'. Bell Papers, Vol. 51, fol. 15v.
2   In the margin, handwritten by Leibholz: 'armed forces'.
3   In the margin, handwritten by Leibholz: 'of all armed forces in G[ermany]'.
4   'based on' instead of 'much more in touch with'.

Bell to Leibholz, 19 December 1942, BA, N 1334 (handwritten)

Private

My dear Leibholz,

Very many thanks for both your very kind letters. I am delighted to hear you are at work on an article for Dawson.¹ Also that you think my suggestion sound. The Professor Smith in mind is (Vincent Smith's² son)

Professor H. A. Smith
Burcote Grange
Abingdon
Professor of International Law, University of London.

You would find him very sympathetic. I could try and bring you together.

I don't think the Conference on the future of Germany is worth bothering about. From [a] British point of view unimportant with exception perhaps of Brailsford.

I have been thinking more of the form of my Question in the Lords. (Don't let it interrupt your article.) There *is* an advantage in linking up with Russia from the point of view of getting a satisfying answer from Eden. But I do not want to risk confusion of Xty or Church with alliance with Stalin – if that risk is real.

Another way of approaching the matter occurs to me – as January 30 is the 10th anniversary of Hitler.

'To call attention to the 10th anniversary of commencement of the Hitler tyranny in Germany (with its devastating results for all the countries which it has occupied, commencing with Germany,) (and the ruin it has brought to the greater parts of Europe including Germany) and to ask His Majesty's Government whether in declaring that its first war aim is to destroy the Hitlerite tyranny (and that its enemy is Hitlerite Germany,) it draws a clear distinction between the leaders of the Hitlerite state (with their associates) and the people of Germany and does not design the destruction of a German government & people, which unequivocally renounced all aggressive intentions'.

This is very rough – and wants careful relating to documents as well as a better formulation of the *point* of the question.

Yours ever,

---

1   See Leibholz, 'The Foundation of Justice and Law in the Light of the Present European Crisis', reprinted in *Politics and Law*, pp. 253–70.
2   Vincent Arthur Smith (1848–1920), the leading British historian of India and author of the standard *Oxford History of India* (Oxford, 1919).

Leibholz to Bell, 20 December 1942, Bell Papers 40, fols. 138–40 (typewritten); BA, N 1334 (copy and fragments of carbon)

My Lordbishop,
I have read your letter of December 17 with the utmost interest and I thank you very much for it. I thought Mr Eden would ask you not to raise the whole matter and, therefore, I was afraid that possibly nothing would come of your good intentions. It is indeed very good news that Mr Eden's attitude seems to be sympathetic to your question. Let us hope that he will not revise his opinion before January and that he will express his sympathy in a forcible way.

As to the draft of the question, my Lordbishop, I think it is excellent. The only thing I should like to say is the following and I only do so because you have allowed me to be quite candid.

I am wondering whether it would not perhaps be better from the psychological point of view, to use the vaguer and more ambiguous expression 'German armed forces' instead of German army. It seems to me to have possibly some advantages. First, the opposition in this country, which today wants the complete destruction of the whole German army would perhaps not take such a strong stand against the question as they perhaps would if they thought you were trying to shield the 'German army'. Secondly, the use of this expression would be an agreement with that exactly used by Stalin himself (who I suppose used it deliberately) and this would again perhaps restrain opposition and government from taking up a stand against the question. Thirdly, there is a German inner political consideration. I for my part think we need not so much to be afraid of what Goebbels will make out of the debate. He can make everything out of it and it is very difficult to protect the Church against all these possible misrepresentations and lies. I think people to whom the appeal is directed are aware of this. More important seems to me that by using this rather vague expression we make it perhaps easier for those to whom we appeal. From all we have learned in the last few months we know that the position of these circles in Germany has become very difficult because Hitler knows the only danger he has to face. In a report from a (it seems me reliable) Diplomatic Correspondent in a British newspaper we can read:

'The professional Prussian clique has been cleared out. The result is that the great Prussian army, which the world has known since the 18th century is no more. That remarkable fighting machine, a combination of tradition, morale and military Science, has been replaced by a fanatical Nazi army owing loyalty to the Führer alone'. I think those who see in the whole war simply a war against Prussianism and the Prussian spirit will perhaps be surprised to see one day that Hitler has done the job for them. In the interest of the people concerned I think it may perhaps be better to use the vague expression.

Then I do not know whether it would not perhaps be better to leave out the words: 'and their leaders'. For Mr Stalin the inclusion of the leaders of the Army has its good meaning because he wants a Red Army and wishes, therefore, to get rid of all its present leaders – no matter whether they are Nazis (e.g. Rommel[1]) or come from the Prussian and those 'class circles', out of which according to Communist-Marxism Nazism has grown. I think there is still after the Anti-Prussian purge a lot of higher officers on whom we can count if it comes to the clash. And I feel no necessity, in this connection, expressly to mention this point.

The draft of the question would then run as follows: 'To call attention to the passage in Mr Stalin's speech of November 6th in which he drew a distinction between Germany and the Hitlerite State, the German armed force and the Hitlerite army, and said that Russia did not contemplate the destruction of Germany and of all armed forces in Germany, but the destruction of the Hitlerite State and the Hitlerite Army, and to ask whether His M. Government made the same distinction in their aims: and to move for papers'.

Further, I have drafted in I admit very clumsy way an amendment to the question. It runs as follows:

2) 'to call attention to reliable reports, which have reached this country and have found their expression in the article "Hitler and the Wehrmacht" in *The Times* of December 14, according to which the "Waffen S.S." represents an independent and very powerful army within the German war machine and to ask whether in face of this new development His Majesty's Government would be prepared to look sympathetically at all attempts, from whatever sources they may arise, to destroy the Hitlerite regime and the special Hitlerite army'.

(or whether in face of the new development the projected destruction of German militarism also refers to those elements, which at the risk of their life and existence would possibly be prepared to destroy the Hitlerite regime and the special Hitlerite army).

I do not know whether the material to which I have referred justifies the drafted question. My experience is too limited. You, my Lordbishop, can judge this much better than I. Perhaps it is also sufficient to refer to the point only in the speech you plan to deliver.

I see the advantages of this question in the following:

First, it would call attention to the new development in Germany, which shows quite clearly who is the real enemy. ᵃ*The Times* correspondent says that the S.S. army is over 1 million.ᵃ Secondly, this development might help the government to start a new more constructive policy towards Germany without disavowing its former policy against German militarism. Thirdly, the Germans who are waiting for this appeal would understand it without being more endangered than they are already and Goebbels would have greater difficulties to twist the story as in this question there would be no reference to Mr Stalin's speech.

Perhaps it is as well that the discussion will not take place before the end of January. At the moment as the result of the Nazi-organised mass murder of the Jewish people the feeling that the whole German people are responsible for these crimes committed by the Nazis seems to me to have become still stronger than before. If one is prepared to accept the thesis of the collective responsibility would it then not be better to affirm the collective responsibility of the S.S. instead of that of the whole German people [which is] what Hitler wants to be the policy of this country. In any case the commitment to such a policy would not deteriorate the political situation in Germany [sic] and would correspond to a widely spread feeling in all countries concerned, including Germany.

Then a last point: I think for the sake of argument it would be good to mention in the projected speech also the Trade unions as a prop for new 'Western-minded' Germany. It would perhaps help to reconcile the Vansittart group of the Labour party with the question and would make it more difficult for the Nazis to act against a special section of the population.²

I do not know, my Lordbishop, whether the points I have tried, I admit, quite inadequately to raise will appeal to you. But those are the ideas which have strongly struck me when thinking over the question you have raised. There is no doubt that it is hardly possible to exaggerate the importance of the question if it were possible to extract a favourable answer from Mr Eden.

Once again with all best wishes to you, my Lordbishop, and Mrs Bell from us all.

Yours ever,

---

¹ Erwin Rommel (1891-1944), general in the German Army, known in Britain as the 'desert fox' in light of his role as commander of the Tank Group Africa in the Libyan desert, 1941/42. His victory over the British Army in the recent battle of Tobruk was followed by his appointment as Field Marshal on 21 June 1942. As supreme commander of Army Group B Rommel later stood against the Allied Invasion in Italy and then in France. By then Rommel had some contacts with members of the German Resistance, but his attitude to Nazi ideology and his views of action against Hitler remained unsettled. Even so, implicated in the 20 July 1944 plot in the following October he was forced to commit suicide. Mourned as a national hero he received a state funeral.
² This paragraph is marked by a black line in the margin.

Bell to Leibholz, 22 December 1942, BA, N 1334 (typewritten); Bell Papers 40, fol. 142 (carbon)

My dear Leibholz,

I am extremely grateful for your letter. It was a great help. It answered fully my question as to the fear of mixing up the Church with Communist propaganda. In view of what you said and the way in which you put your suggestions, etc., and also in view of the need for haste and striking while the iron is hot, I decided not to wait for a reply to my letter written to you on Sunday about another way of asking the question, viz. by reference to the tenth anniversary of the Hitler regime. I do not think really that reference to the *Times* article about the Wehrmacht would carry the same sort of weight, or be likely to elicit the same sort of reply as a question referring to Stalin's speech. At the same time, the point which that form of the question makes, is a point which I hope to make when speaking on the subject, for it is obviously of great importance. I have accordingly gratefully accepted your amendments and have sent a question in this ᵃexactᵃ form to Lord Cranborne and the Clerk to the House of Lords, and will let you know what happens.¹ I am very grateful for the points you make about the armed forces and the leaders.

I agree about the unfortunate tendency in British circles to let the responsibility for these ᵃterribleᵃ massacres embrace the whole German people without distinction. This is a point which I shall have to meet incidentally in my speech. I had already written to Wilfrid Israel² and to another friend asking for ammunition. If during the next fortnight you have thoughts on this subject, I shall of course gratefully welcome them.

I am not quite sure whether I ever sent you a copy of my ªpre-warª Oxford University sermon *God Above the Nation*³. In it I quoted a letter from Professor H. A. Smith to *The Times*. Anyhow, it can do no harm to send you a copy.

With renewed thanks and best wishes for Christmas,

Yours ªveryª sincerely,

---

1. See Bell to Cranborne, 22 December 1942, Bell Papers, Vol. 51, fol. 24.
2. Wilfrid Israel (1899–1943), Anglo-German businessman and philanthropist. Protected by a British passport he was active in the rescue of Jews from Nazi Germany. In 1938 he emigrated to Britain where he worked in a number of Jewish refugee organizations, joining the Foreign Research and Press Service of Lionel Curtis's Royal Institute of International Affairs. A friend of Adam von Trott, Israel had a number of connections with the German resistance movement. See Naomi Shepherd, *Wilfrid Israel: German Jewry's Secret Ambassador* (London, 1984).
3. Bell, 'God Above the Nation' (a sermon to the University of Oxford, 18 June 1939), reprinted in *The Church and Humanity*, pp. 201–10.

Leibholz to Bell, 22 December 1942, Bell Papers 40, fol. 141 (typewritten); BA, N 1334 (copy)

My Lordbishop,

Very many thanks for your letter. I am carefully thinking over all you write concerning the form of your question in the House of Lords. The only thing I am afraid of is that Mr Eden will give an evasive answer to the question if he does not see a reason for being precise. On the whole, the statements made by Mr Eden recently have been, in my view, very disappointing indeed and I am not sure whether the 10th anniversary of the Hitler regime alone will cause him to change his stiff attitude in this respect.

On the other hand I fully understand the point you make, my Lordbishop, as to whether it is expedient to link up the question with Stalin's statement. As I wrote in my last letter a few days ago I for my part think that we need perhaps not take the German propaganda machine so seriously, which in any case will try to make the worst of the debate and to misrepresent your question. But another point, of course, is in how far you think a confusion might arise in this country and America of the linking up of the question with Stalin's statement. You can judge this much better than I. I had much more the German repercussions in mind when I wrote you last.

What do you think about a combination of both your proposals, my Lordbishop, perhaps in the following way:

'To call attention to the 10th anniversary of the commencement of the Hitlerite tyranny ... and to ask His Majesty's Government whether in consideration of the fact that Mr Stalin in his speech of the 6th of November drew a distinction between Germany and the Hitlerite State and said that Russia did not contemplate the destruction of Germany and all armed forces in Germany they would be prepared to declare that their first war aim is the destruction of the Hitlerite tyranny and not of the German people as a whole and especially not of those who (from whatever walk of life they come) would help to destroy Hitlerite Germany and all that it stands for and who unequivocally unswear all aggressive intentions'.

I do not know how this suggestion strikes you. I think it perhaps makes it more difficult for the government to give an evasive answer: on the other hand, the reference to Stalin's statement is not so conspicuous and central as in the first draft so that perhaps the danger of confusion may be lessened. But, of course, I do not know how strongly you assess this danger. On this everything depends.

Thank you very much for your kind suggestion to bring me together with Professor Smith later on. I hope this will be a great help.

I have been told that 58 internees were drowned a few weeks ago on a ship which was sailing from Australia to this country. Is this true?

With all our good wishes

Yours ever,

Henrietta Bell to Sabine Leibholz, 26 December 1942, BA, N 1334 (handwritten)

Dear Mrs Leibholz,

Thank you so much for those beautiful and artistic candlesticks, which arrived most beautifully packed, and which I much appreciate. This will be a very attractive reminder of you and yours.

We had a very quiet and peaceful festival, my mother-in-law was not well enough to be with us as usual. And my sister was on A.R.P.[1] duty in London. So our party was of lonely people serving in the forces round here. I hope you and yours were together, and I am sure the little girls created the right Christmas atmosphere of joyousness and giving, which adorns and harmonises the deeper thoughts that Christmas brings. In the evening my husband read us that wonderful poem of Browning's, *Christmas Eve*,[2] do you know it?

We both send you & the Professor and the girls our best wishes for the new year – may it brings us all peace, & courage for the future.

Very sincerely yours,

---

[1] Air Raid Precautions. Created in 1924 this organization was dedicated to the protection of civilians from the danger of air raids.
[2] Robert Browning, 'Christmas Eve and Easter Day' (1850) in *The Poetical Works of Robert Browning, 1833 to 1868* (Oxford, 1940), pp. 396–409.

Leibholz to Bell, 29 December 1942, Bell Papers 40, fol. 143 (typewritten); BA, N 1334 (copy)

My Lordbishop,

Very many thanks for your last kind and appreciative letter. I am delighted to have your most impressive sermon *God above the nation*, which up to now has completely escaped me. I read it on Christmas day (it was a real Christmas joy) and I think it is a masterly and prophetic piece of work, which has a special appeal to me just now and to which I feel sure I shall frequently recur [sic].

As to the projected speech, my Lordbishop, may I confine myself to stressing only one point (in addition to those, which I tried to put forward in the article in the *Fortnightly*[1] and the last letters) and this is the following:

I think that Hitler's plan to exterminate all people of Jewish origin in Europe is connected with a special political purpose. Of course, above all, these terrible massacres serve to satisfy his blind racial hatred and sadistic lust of cruelty. But at the same time I think he combines with this lunacy (as far as I know this is frequently the case with lunatics) a highly remarkable instinct for political realities. And I suppose the specific political aim of these massacres is to rouse in a flagrant manner public opinion, especially of the Western countries and to cause them to make the whole German people responsible for these unprecedented outrages. Then by presenting the cries of vengeance he hopes to be able to consolidate the breaking German morale and to show the German people the correctness of Goebbels' alternative: victory or final destruction. If, therefore, public opinion in the Western countries reacts in this way as it seems likely to do this political aim is attained. I am afraid that in this connection certain refugees (especially those who are associated with Vansittart etc.) in view of the personal experiences which they have gone through have lost their clear political judgement and discernment and play a rather unfortunate part in this development.[2]

That the whole German people are not responsible for these Nazi massacres can, in my view, clearly be shown by the fact that it is necessary – in spite of war and great transport difficulties – to bring the victims to Poland. This seems to me to prove that these mass-murders are not much less hated in Germany than in other countries.

By the way, I do not know whether you think it possible, my Lordbishop, that the opposition in the Lords will try to prevent the government from giving a positive answer to your question or whether the government will possibly make use of the opposition in order to evade a precise answer. If you think, my Lordbishop, that such a possibility exists would it not perhaps be worthwhile considering the question whether it would not be well to inform of your plans one or two friends in the Lords who would be prepared in this case to support you in pressing home the matter. Probably a very stupid idea, which struck me. In this case forgive me, my Lordbishop. I am frankly writing you all that crosses my mind, even if it has no weight at all.

Yours ever,

[a]P.S. My wife was delighted to hear that Mrs Bell likes the candlesticks, which she has painted.[a]

---

[1] See Leibholz, 'Germany between West and East', in *The Fortnightly Review*, October 1942, reprinted in *Politics and Law*, pp. 174–81.
[2] This and the next paragraph is marked by a black line in the margin.

1943

14–24 January	Casablanca Conference of the Allied Powers ends with the announcement of the united demand for 'Unconditional Surrender'.
31 January	The German Sixth Army surrenders at Stalingrad.
5 February	RAF Bomber Command begins a four-month bombing campaign against the Ruhr valley with an attack on Essen.
18 February	Goebbels calls for 'Total War' by the people of Germany.
22 February	Execution of members of the White Rose group in Munich.
19–30 April	The Bermuda Conference of British and American leaders to discuss the mass-murder of European Jews.
12 May	Roosevelt and Churchill meet in Washington DC.
13 May	Allied forces achieve victory in North Africa.
19 May	Churchill addresses both Houses of Congress.
10 July	Allied forces land in Sicily.
24 July	'Operation Gomorrah': the obliteration bombing of Hamburg.
25 July	Mussolini is arrested.
17 August	Allied forces take Sicily.
9 September	Allied forces land at Salerno.
10 September	German forces occupy Rome.
13 October	The new Italian government declares war on Germany.
18 October	The Third Moscow conference begins at which the Allies begin to discuss a post-war order.
22 November	Roosevelt, Churchill and Chiang Kai-Shek meet in Cairo.
28 November	The Tehran Conference of the Allied leaders.

Bell to Leibholz, 2 January 1943, BA, N 1334 (typewritten); Bell Papers 40, fol. 144 (carbon)

ªI have mislaid my *Times* article on the Wehrmacht (? Dec 14). I suppose you have not a cutting you could lend me?ª

Private

My dear Leibholz,
Very many thanks for your letter. I agree very much with what you say both about the motives of Hitler and the reply, which should be made; and also about the great desirability ªof finding stepsª of getting others to support me in case of attack. ªI am taking steps.ª

After a lot of reflection, and after examining the full text of Stalin's speech, I have reworded my question, and enclose a copy. ªIt will be on January 27, all being well.ª

Yours ever,

ª*The Times* of today (purge by Gestapo + Hitler's New Years messages) shows how sad it is that the Allies tarry so long in appealing to the Opposition.ª

HOUSE OF LORDS, Second Sitting after the 24 January

The Bishop of Chichester. To call attention to the passage in M. Stalin's speech of November 6th, 1942 in which he said that it was not Russia's aim either 'to destroy Germany, for it is impossible to destroy Germany' ... but that 'the Hitlerite State can and should be destroyed'; or 'to destroy all organised military force in Germany for ... it is not only impossible ... but is also inexpedient from the point of view of the future', but that 'Hitler's army can and should be destroyed': and to ask whether His Majesty's Government in their war aims make the same distinction between Germany and the Hitlerite State, and between all organised military force in Germany and Hitler's army; and to move for papers.

Bell to Leibholz, 4 January 1943, BA, N 1334 (typewritten); Bell Papers 40, fol. 145 (carbon)

My dear Leibholz,
I don't want to be continually troubling you with questions. But when you next have occasion to write, as I am naturally thinking a good deal about my speech, I should be grateful for any reflections you would care to give me on the question of the *expediency* (to use Stalin's word) of retaining an organised military force in Germany.

I had a talk with the Archbishop of Canterbury[1] yesterday, and am glad to say that he is noting the date for the House of Lords debate and will do his best to come and also to speak. He was interested in Stalin's remark about the army. He thought that one argument was that a State Army was a protection against private armies, which this or that General might somehow get on his own. Were there in fact at the end of the last war any private armies, which it was difficult to disband? I think there were private armies in Russia and Stalin may have been thinking of this! But when did private armies begin in Germany, and what were they? I take it that Hitler had one, but I don't quite know when it started; and then there were other private armies competing with his, but I don't know when, nor do I remember their names.

Yours ever,

[1] William Temple (1881–1944) had become Archbishop of Canterbury on 23 April 1942.

Leibholz to Bell, 6 January 1943, Bell Papers 40, fols. 146–7 (typewritten); BA, N 1334 (copy)

My Lordbishop,

Thank you very much for your letter. I am only too pleased if I can in any way be of use to you. If there is time and you have no objection I should very much like to read the draft of your paper. I should send it back by return.

I am very glad indeed to know that in case of attack you have secured the support of the Archbishop of Canterbury. I very much hope that he will take the same line.

As to the interpretation of the 'inexpediency' to destroy all organised military forces in Germany, from the point of view of the future, I think that Stalin had in mind a future Red Army in Germany with which, from a Communist point of view, he thinks he could deal with (without disarmament, occupation etc.). The trouble seems to me to be that it is hardly possible at the present time to give expression to this thought, especially as, unfortunately, the public opinion of today is most sensitive in this matter. I think that the spirit behind the Army is the most important matter and I hold the view that if the Nazi spirit is broken there will only be room for the Communist spirit, which is sympathetic to Stalin or the Western spirit, which should be encouraged in every possible way. May I perhaps quote in this connection the few pertinent sentences of my article in *The Fortnightly* in case it is not at your disposal:

'In order to appreciate rightly the function the army can exercise at the present time we must realize that in the highly industrialised states a purely military authoritarianism is no longer possible since it is incompatible with the whole structure of modern mass society. ... From a sociological and political point of view, the army is today irrevocably placed in the position of a servant and not of a master. The happenings in Russia, Germany and Italy confirm this. In all these states the army is at the disposal of totalitarian leaders. Where the attempt has been made to interfere with the political claims of the totalitarian regime it has met with complete disaster ... The only excuse the German army can make for its subservience to the originally detested Nazi regime is the fact that there was actually behind the specific military ideology no political, social and spiritual conception of life which could attract the minds of the masses and permeate them with a new spirit. At bottom, the army of today is only a gigantic technical instrument. In so far, it is true, its significance is eminent and its power immense. But the point is, it cannot itself provide the basis for a new order ... It has no longer a spiritual or political driving power of its own.'[1]

I think that I am in disagreement with 90 % of all Englishmen on this particular point, but in spite of this I think this analysis still holds good.

In your case, my Lordbishop, I do not think I should specify the special function the armed forces would have to fulfil later on. For from our point of view, the main point seems to me to be that the army should be encouraged to take up the fight against the S.S. Army instead of being continuously threatened with complete destruction. Should it come to such a conflict and the regime collapse, the men behind the new regime – as far as this will have a Western character – will offer on their own initiative a disarmament and be fully satisfied with a small army for the maintenance of order and security.

As to the argument that a State army was a protection against private armies I may say that there were indeed after the last war some parts of the army, above all those which had fought in the Baltikum (especially the Ehrhardt Brigade, which made a 'Putsch' in 1921), which were difficult to disband and were not disbanded before 1921.[2] But the much greater danger for the republic came later on from the militant party organisations, which one might call private armies. The main organisations were the 'Rote Frontkämpferbund' (communistic), the 'Reichsbanner' (democratic) and the national socialist Storm Troopers (S.A.). The existence of such half-military organisations in a liberal democracy is a sure sign of its disintegration and the expression that parties which are totalitarian in their character, are aiming at getting the power in their own hands. The first military organisation of this kind was of communist character, then the Nazi S.A. was formed (it can be traced back to 1922) and the democratic Reichsbanner was not formed until communists and national socialists together were struggling against democracy. All these half-military organisations did not become a real public danger before the rise of Nazism i.e. 1930. I do not think that after the war the question of such private military armies will be very acute. For if it be possible to avoid Communism I think we must expect a socialist authoritarian regime, as the idea of a liberal regime in the English fashion on a Continent ravaged by war is to my mind an illusion. And the task we have is to give this regime a Christian basis and this is what our fellow-Christians in Germany also actually want.

I am enclosing the cutting from *The Times*.[3] I think the article is so important because it so clearly shows the dualistic character of the German war machine of today designed to keep down the army and the population and well suited to demonstrate to all who have eyes to see how things stand from a realistic point of view. If you, my Lordbishop, would kindly let me have it back later on I should be very glad.

I quite agree with what you say about the Gestapo purge and Hitler's New Year message.[4] Among the arrested who are mentioned in *The Times* is a friend of ours. Let us hope that this is not a bad omen.

With all good wishes

Yours ever,

---

[1] See Leibholz, 'Germany between West and East', reprinted in *Politics and Law*, p. 180.
[2] See Robert Thoms and Stefan Pochanke, *Handbuch zur Geschichte der deutschen Freikorps* (Bad Soden-Salmünster, 2001).
[3] This report referred to the arrests of members of the 'Rote Kapelle' (Red Orchestra); the friend to whom Leibholz refers is probably the diplomat Rudolf von Scheliha (1897–1942) who in September 1939 had become the head of the Department of Information in the Foreign Office where he

collected materials of Nazi crimes and passed them to contacts in the Polish underground and in Switzerland. Imprisoned, he was later murdered on the pretext that he was a member of the so-called Red Orchestra. This arrest marked a growing danger to other active resisters like Adam von Trott, who worked in the same government department.
4   On 1 January 1943 Hitler gave his fourth new year message to Party members and a further message to the armed forces.

Bell to Leibholz, 8 January 1943, BA, N 1334 (typewritten)

My dear Leibholz,

Very many thanks for your extremely valuable letter, and for all the good information and advice you give about the army question. I am also very grateful to you for lending me the *Times* article, which I let you have back.

You may like to see, but please don't bother to acknowledge, my current diocesan Gazette.[1]

Yours ever,

[1] Bishop's letter, *Chichester Diocesan Gazette*, January 1943, p. 1.

Bell to Leibholz, 22 January 1943, BA, N 1334 (handwritten)

Private

My dear Leibholz,

My question[1] has been postponed to February 10, at the request of the Foreign Office. They were most anxious to wait till after January 30, when Hitler if he follows precedent would speak to the German people. The argument is that he will have the most difficult speech of the war to make – and they don't want him to ride off on a House of Lords debate, making capital out of Vansittart (who is speaking) and ridiculing the rest of us. I think it has point.

I have secured Addison,[2] Noel Buxton,[3] Cecil,[4] Perth (formerly Eric Drummond)[5] & the Archbishop[6] to speak for me: with sympathy from Keynes[7] and Hankey,[8] though not speaking.

Yours ever,

[1] The final submission of Bell's question may be found in the Bell Papers, Vol. 51, fol. 101: 'The Lord Bishop of Chichester – To call attention to the passage in M. Stalin's speech of 6 November 1942, in which he said that it was not Russia's aim either "to destroy Germany for it is impossible to destroy Germany" ... but that "the Hitlerite State can and should be destroyed"; or "to destroy all organised military force in Germany; for ... it is not only impossible ... but is also inexpedient from the point of view of the future," but that "Hitler's Army can and should be destroyed"; and to ask whether His Majesty's Government in their war aims make the same distinction between Germany and the Hitlerite State, and between the organised military force in Germany and Hitler's Army; and to move for Papers. In the published version the addition a ... a is omitted'.
[2] See Bell to Addison, 22 January 1943, Bell Papers, Vol. 51, fol. 92. But Addison did not speak on this occasion. Lord Christopher Addison (1869–1951), since 1937 1st Viscount Addison; professor of medicine and politician. He had served as Minister of Munitions during the First World War

and later as Minister of Health in the 1918–22 coalition under Lloyd George. After 1945 he would become Leader of the House of Lords.
3   Noel Edward Noel-Buxton (1869–1948), since 1930 1st Baron Noel-Buxton; Liberal and later Labour politician; he too did not speak in the debate.
4   Robert Cecil (Edgar Algernon Robert Gascoyne-Cecil), (1864–1958), since 1929 1st Viscount Cecil of Chelwood. Cecil was one of the architects of the League of Nations and a figure much admired by British church leaders. He was a particularly close friend of Archbishop Lang. See his speech in the House of Lords in *Hansard*, H.L. Deb, Vol. 126, cols. 561–7 (10 March 1943).
5   Sir James Eric Drummond (1876–1951), since 1937 7th Earl of Perth; the first secretary-general of the League of Nations (1920–33) and Ambassador to Rome (1933–39). In 1939–40 he had been chief advisor on foreign publicity in the Ministry of Information (1939–40). In 1946 he would become deputy leader of the Liberal Party in the House of Lords. See his speech in the House of Lords on 10 March 1943 in ibid., cols. 571–3.
6   Archbishop Temple did not take part in the debate.
7   John Maynard Keynes (1883–1946), since 1942 Baron Keynes; one of the most influential economists of the twentieth century and the founder of modern macroeconomics.
8   Maurice Hankey (1877–1963), since 1939 1st Baron Hankey; made the rare transition from the civil service to ministerial office; Minister without portfolio and a member of Chamberlain's War Cabinet, 1939–40. After the end of hostilities in 1945 he became a leading public critic of war crimes trials.

Leibholz to Bell, 26 January 1943, Bell Papers 40, fol. 148 (typewritten); BA, N 1334 (copy)

My Lordbishop,

Thank you very much for kindly letting me know how things stand. The reasons why a postponement of the debate was desired seem to me quite plausible and convincing.

I feel that under the present circumstances the forthcoming debate in the Lords may even gain greater weight than I originally ventured to hope. For now when the Nazis are ventilating their alternative: 'Victory or perish Germany and Europe under Communism' in all imaginable keys, a constructive and imaginative post-war policy, which opens at least the possibility for a non-Communist solution on a Christian basis must I think strike all who have retained their political balance and judgement.

Today I read in the last issue of the German Newspaper *Die Zeitung*[1] an interview given by the last American correspondent of the Associated Press L. Lochner who left Germany six months after the outbreak of the American-German war.[2] Like all other American correspondents who were in Germany he stresses the strength and determination of the opposition against the present regime but also points out that these people, for pure reasons of self-preservation, would fight to the end if only confronted by the Western powers with the alternative 'complete and unconditional surrender', which must mean in their eyes 'destruction'.[3] Even if this aim could be reached with the decisive help of Russia I am afraid the struggle will still last a rather long time and, above all, I am afraid, Europe would be lost for the cause for which the Anglo-Saxon countries are fighting this war. Perhaps it is worthwhile thinking over, my Lordbishop, whether it is desirable to refer to the series of new American publications in this connection, because they contain the latest and generally accessible reports of reliable and trustworthy people who were inside Germany and who so splendidly support our case.

I am so glad to know that you have secured the support of a few more friends. For Vansittart and his friends will not let the opportunity escape them to attack. I deem it possible that he will try to invoke the Russians in justification of his position, as some of his adherents have done (e.g. Mr Rowse[4] who calls himself a Vansittartist). Therefore it may perhaps be well to have at disposal the text of Stalin's manifesto to the Red Army of February 23rd, 1942 apart from his last statement in November. Today I listened in to the new *Order of the Day* in which Stalin seems to have limited the task of the Red Army to liberating the motherland from the invader (no occupation). But one must read it.

Thank you, my Lordbishop, also for your advice concerning the National Peace Council. I have followed it and written them that I shall not be coming to speak at their meeting to be held in these days.

You wrote me in one of the last letters of Wilfrid Israel. When you write me next, my Lordbishop, it would be kind if you would give me his address. I was at school with him in Germany and should be pleased to meet him here, should such an opportunity arise.

With all good wishes

Yours ever,

---

1   *Die Zeitung* was a German opposition newspaper published in London, 1941–45.
2   The foreign correspondent of the Associated Press in Berlin (1928–42) was Louis P. Lochner (in reality Ludwig Paul Lochner). Lochner was interned after the declaration of war between Germany and the United States and released in May 1942 as part of a prisoner exchange for interned German diplomats and correspondents.
3   The second half of the sentence is marked by a black line in the margin.
4   Alfred Leslie Rowse (1903–97), British academic elected a Fellow of All Souls College, Oxford in 1925. A literary critic and prolific writer, Rowse became an authority on Elizabethan England. In the 1930s he had twice tried unsuccessfully to become a Labour MP. Rowse had known, and admired, Adam von Trott at Oxford.

Leibholz to Bell, 2 February 1943, Bell Papers 40, fols. 149–50 (handwritten); BA, N 1334 (copy)

My Lordbishop,

May I send you today my sincerest wishes for your 60th birthday. May God keep you under His special protection in the new decade in the same way as He has done hitherto, for your own sake as well as for the sake of all those who are connected with you by strong bonds of personal friendship. I think we all shall need your help after the war more than even before.

I wonder what you think about the formula, which the English and American statesmen have issued in Casablanca (unconditional surrender).¹ To me it seems to be rather unfortunate. Actually it is the same as the Vansittartists want and I regret that as a result of the long duration of the war also the Americans now follow this line. In practice as long as Stalin not sincerely accepts this line (and I do not think he will accept) this pronouncement will result first in a stiffening of the German resistance as the Nazi propaganda machine will not find it difficult persuasively to show the German people that unconditional surrender means virtually total destruction and secondly in an increased probability that we shall have to face Communism on the Continent in future. No one on the Continent will discuss the Nazi propaganda with regard to Communism as a *mere* bogy. The secrecy [secret] of the Nazi Propaganda seems to me to be that there is always a kernel of truth in it, which then is more or less falsified. But to think of Communism in Europe as a fantasy only to scare the peoples is to my mind quite far from the truth. Unfortunately, I cannot trace an attempt to avoid this 'solution' in the official policy of the Western countries and I am afraid that even if Mr Eden would prefer not to give an evasive answer to the question put before him he will not now be in a position to do so after the Casablanca Conference.

I am enclosing today the article about which I wrote to you and which has just come out.[2] I am considering whether it would not perhaps be worthwhile to enlarge the article in some directions and then perhaps to publish it separately in booklet form, as articles, on the whole, are not taken seriously. Especially I thought to draw the international aspect of the question into the analysis and in this connection to take up in greater detail also the most important question you raised in your letter some weeks ago. I wonder what you think about this plan, my Lordbishop.

By the way, should you know prominent lawyers who are at the same time convinced Christians I should be glad to have their names as I should like to send them a copy of the article. I am connected with N. Birkett. I think to remember you having once mentioned Gutteridge.

On the 4th we shall think of you. Once again all good wishes

Yours ever,

---

[1] On the conference in Casablanca President Franklin D. Roosevelt announced the war aim of 'Unconditional surrender' on 24 January 1943.
[2] This was 'The Foundation of Justice and Law in the Light of the Present European Crisis', reprinted in *Politics and Law*, pp. 253–70.

Leibholz to Bell, (2 February 1943), Bell Papers, 40, fol. 151 (handwritten)

My dear Lordbishop,

I wholeheartedly join in the wishes of my husband for your birthday and wish you many happy returns of the day. I am sure if Dietrich knew it was your birthday he would very much like me to express his heartfelt wishes for your personal welfare.

Of the few things we have saved of our home in Germany I have looked out a little glass picture of the Christ child, which is very old. We hope it will give you as much pleasure as it has done us.

With kind regards to Mrs Bell
I am, my Lordbishop,

Yours very sincerely,

Bell to Sabine Leibholz, 2 February 1943, BA, N 1334 (handwritten)

My dear Mrs Leibholz,

This is just a line which will I hope reach you on your and Dietrich's birthday to offer you and him my affectionate greetings, and best wishes. I have chanced a telegram of greetings to Pastor Lutz [Sutz], hoping he may understand. It is such a happy link that you and Dietrich and I should have our birthday on the same day. How I hope that as this year grows, we may get steadily nearer peace and order and a reunion of families and friends.

Please tell your husband my debate will now be *first* business on March 10. It seems a long way off. But there have been many obstacles.

I shall be in Oxford on February 9, and trust I may somehow have the chance of a word with him.

My love to the children

Yours most sincerely,

Leibholz to Bell, 5 February 1943, Bell Papers 40, fol. 151 (handwritten)

My Lordbishop,
Just a line to thank you for your most kind letter to my wife who was charmed with your good wishes and to tell you that I am delighted to know that you will be in Oxford on the 9th of February. Unfortunately, a good while ago we accepted an invitation to Dawson's[1] for Tuesday and this will take us from Oxford from about 3 until 6 o'clock in the afternoon. At any other time on Tuesday and Wednesday I should be at your full disposal. My wife asked me whether you would perhaps like to have lunch with us here on the 9th or 10th of February. You know it would give us quite a *special* pleasure, but, of course, I do not know whether your time will allow it.

Yours ever,

[1] Presumably Christopher Dawson.

Bell to Leibholz, 8 February 1943, BA, N 1334 (telegram)

VERY SORRY ILLNESS PREVENTS COMING TOMORROW = BISHOP CHICHESTER

Leibholz to Bell, 9 February 1943, Bell Papers 40, fol. 152 (handwritten)

My Lordbishop,
My wife and I were extremely sorry to hear that you are not well and, therefore, were prevented from coming to Oxford. We were already greatly looking forward to seeing you here. Our only hope is that it is not more than a slight indisposition. If it is not asking too much I should be very grateful to you if your secretary would let us know how you are. I should be delighted to know that you are better again.

All our good wishes for a speedy recovery and our most affectionate greetings

Yours ever,

Bell to Leibholz, 12 February 1943, BA, N 1334 (handwritten)

My dear Leibholz,
First of all I want to thank you and your wife from my heart for your good wishes, and letters, and the gift of the picture which you made me. I value the thought behind the gift very much: and think it extraordinarily good of you to part with it, feeling a

real wonder whether it is right for you to part with it. But I do want to say how greatly I value it, and thank you for it.

My flu-like cold kept me a prisoner in bed – hence absence from Oxford: and though I went to Town on Wednesday for prayers in the Lords and spoke yesterday.[1] I have not by any means got rid of it. I will send you a copy of my speech, which was very well received.[2] I will write also about *lawyers*.

Yours very sincerely,

I hope you and Dawson[3] got on well together.

---

[1] Bell's speech in the debate of the House of Lords about German atrocities – in opposition to Vansittart – in Hansard, HL Deb, Vol. 125, cols. 1076–82 (11 February 1943); also in Bell, *The Church and Humanity*, pp. 86–94.
[2] See some reactions in the Bell Papers, Vol. 51, fols. 166–8.
[3] Bell's correspondence with Christopher Dawson may be found in the Bell Papers, Vol. 206, fols. 216–18.

Bell to Leibholz, 13 February 1943, BA, N 1334 (handwritten)

My dear Leibholz,
Here is *Hansard*. At your leisure I shd. like comments especially on passages against which I have put a mark

Yours ever,

I don't want it back.

Bell to Leibholz, 15 February 1943, BA, N 1334 (typewritten)

My dear Leibholz,
I am sure you will be interested to see the enclosed copy of a letter from Bishop Brilioth, which I have no doubt refers to Dietrich and Schönfeld. I think Bishop Brilioth is rather over-cautious and pessimistic but he obviously got a very deep impression of the ª(alleged)ª friendliness in this country to Bolshevism.

Yours ever,

Y. Brilioth to Bell, 12 January 1943, BA, N 1334 (copy)

COPY:

My dear George,
Already six weeks have passed since I left England.[1] I look back with great thankfulness on my visit, as well for the many interesting experiences I made as for the personal kindness that met me everywhere – not least in Chichester.

After my return I had – about a month ago – a most interesting visit from two Germans well known to you.[2] They wanted to hear of my impressions, above all what might be the attitude of England to a Germany that had changed its government and its policy. I don't think that what I had to tell was very reassuring to them. I tried to make them understand how difficult it is for people in England to form a true estimate of the strength and the reliability of an opposition of which so far they knew little. But I also said that public opinion in England probably would be much impressed if something really happened in Germany – although they could hardly hope for much encouragement before some decisive steps were taken. This makes the situation so very complicated. Yet it is much to be wished in my opinion that some sort of encouragement could be given. On the other hand it is very difficult to make them understand that public opinion in England cannot easily exonerate the German people from all responsibility for the acts of its government – although, as *we* know, there is very little possibility for the German people to influence the policy of its Government – also because they are largely ignorant of much that has happened. They on the other hand strongly insisted on the grave danger that a possible, perhaps a likely, development towards some form of communism would mean to the whole of Western Civilisation. The inability of large groups in England to realize the real nature of communism, above all in its Bolshevistic form, in my opinion constitutes a very grave danger for the future. But there is no need to enlighten *you* in this matter. In a few talks which I have had opportunity to give here I have felt bound to stress this danger. I cannot say that I was much reassured by my short conversation with Sir Stafford Cripps.[3] But I hope that other English statesmen may see things in a clearer light.

We are all well. Please give our warm greetings to Henrietta.

Yours affectionately,

---

[1] Invited by Archbishop Temple, Bishop Brillioth stayed between 4 and 27 November in Britain; see Klemperer, *German Resistance against Hitler*, p. 291.

[2] In December Brillioth met Hans Schönfeld and Eugen Gerstenmaier as delegates of the Kreisau Circle, the group of men and women which had gathered around Helmuth James von Moltke and Peter Yorck von Wartenburg to discuss the future of a Germany free from the Nazi state; see Bethge, *Dietrich Bonhoeffer*, pp. 865–6.; Klemperer, *German Resistance against Hitler*, pp. 290–1. Bell had met Schönfeld in Sweden on 26 and 29 May 1942, and he also knew Gerstenmaier through his church connections.

[3] Sir Richard Stafford Cripps (1889–1952), Labour politician, had also been a leading figure in the World Alliance for International Friendship through the Churches in the 1920s. He had joined the Labour Party in 1930 and was MP, 1931–50. Cripps had been expelled from the Labour Party for his advocacy of a Popular Front with the Communist Party in 1939. As Ambassador to the USSR he became a key figure in forming an alliance between the Western powers and the USSR in 1941. After his return in 1942 he became a member of the War Cabinet, with the jobs of Lord Privy Seal and Leader of the House of Commons, later becoming Minister of Aircraft Production.

Bell to Leibholz (and to all members of the German British Christian Fellowship in Wartime), 16 February 1943, BA, N 1334 (typewritten)[1]

Dear Professor Leibholz,

I was glad to hear at the Christian Fellowship in Wartime meeting held last month it was felt the time had come for the pastors to meet once more for Retreat and discussion.

Arrangements have therefore been made for us to meet together at Gilmore House, Clapham Common, London S.W. 4 on Monday, April 5th – Thursday, April 8th. I feel strongly the necessity of such a meeting and would like to urge you to take advantage of this opportunity.

In particular I feel you will wish to deepen your fellowship together and your representation of the Confessional Church in this country. Those of you who go about speaking for the Fellowship feel, I know, that now the facts of the Church Struggle in Germany have been presented, it is time to discuss the further message which your group has to give to this country. The future of the Fellowship itself is another subject, which needs your careful thought.

I shall be with you on the first day but unfortunately have to leave at lunch time on Tuesday. Most of the rest of the time will be spent in Retreat, which will, I feel sure, do much to deepen your fellowship.

I would put it to you as a special obligation that you should make every possible effort to attend this meeting. There is a great deal on which we have to think together, you and I, and on which the pastors as a company have to think. I should like to ask you for your prayers that God's blessing may attend the meeting.

A definite programme will be sent to you in a few days' time.

Yours sincerely,

[1] This letter is an invitation sent not from the Bishop's Palace, Chichester, but from Bloomsbury House. For further reference to the group see Leibholz to Bell, 17 February 1942.

Leibholz to Bell, 18 February 1943, Bell Papers 40, fols. 153–5 (typewritten); BA, N 1334 (copy)

My Lordbishop,

First of all, our very warm thanks for your letter of February 12. It is really a great joy to us to know that you like the small glass-picture.

In the meantime, I have read your speech in the Lords and the ensuing debate. I greatly admire the excellent way in which you put your, or if I may say so, our case, in the tensed atmosphere of today. I think it is a statesmanlike achievement to put things as you did and I am so glad to know that the speech was very well received. Especially I think it was [a] good thing to remind the House of the fact that the Germans themselves are not aware of the extent of the atrocities committed by the Nazis, and further to remind them of the time in which you with only a few supporters took the same attitude as today with regard to the atrocities committed in Germany itself between 1933 and 1938, while the Government and many people here were inclined to overlook them in order to avoid embarrassment between the countries. I also think that the letter in *The Manchester Guardian* to which you referred is very important. The whole problem could hardly be put in better terms than in the words quoted by you and I feel sure that these will not have failed to impress the House.

With regard to the two marks you made in the margin I may say the following:

1. It is true that Nazism (like Bolshevism) legally came to power. But the Nazis had never exceeded more than 40% of the given votes. That they came to power was

due to certain conservative circles, which supported the Nazis hoping to get rid of them later on, while the development just took the opposite course. But, to my mind, this proves only that Nazism is a mass-movement (of the lower middle classes) and a part of a social (and spiritual) revolutionary process as a result of the destruction of the economic and social basis of Liberalism. The only point on which I agree with Vansittart is that Nazism is not a matter of the upper classes as Left-wing circles and many refugees say. In fact, Nazism is a much more complicated phenomenon. To simplify it by ignoring the social and spiritual causes of the rise of Nazism and reducing it to a purely national matter seems to be misleading to the utmost. I do not know whether you have seen the two new books by Drucker[1] and Dawson,[2] especially the first chapters. I think that if those who are in charge of the Foreign Politics in this country would find time to read such books they would not consider Vansittart the expert on Germany in the House of Lords.

2. The Statement that 'more men of the Left were killed under Weimar than during the six years from 1933 to 1939, and that all those murders took place ... at the instigation of German Army'[3] is after all I know entirely irreconcilable with the true facts. As Vansittart repeats this statement in *The Times* of yesterday in a reply to Wedgwood and maintains that his statement is based on facts would it not be advisable to ask him to make the facts known publicly?[4]

First, he can argue that during the revolutionary unrest between 1918 and 1920, among others, many communists were killed as a result of the clashes between the military forces in the service of the Republic and the communists who at that time tried to establish a communist regime. If he should have these events in mind it would be an obvious misleading statement. Secondly, he can refer to the clashes between the Left-wing organisations (Communists and Socialists) and the Nazis in the last years before the Nazis came to power. But the army had never had anything to do with them. Thirdly, he can refer to the so-called *Fememorde* in the twenties.[5] But there were not many and as far as I know they were due to radical organisations which can be looked upon as the forerunners of the Nazi-organisations. Perhaps there were here and there some connections with the Army in these cases. But I have heard nothing to this effect and if there were some guilty men there is I think hardly a doubt that these circles had been eliminated in the Republic immediately after the facts had become known. This is why I think Vansittart should be requested to verify his statement. Then we would be in a better position to refute it.

It was very kind indeed of you, my Lordbishop, to let me see a copy of the letter from Bishop Brilioth, and I was very much interested in reading it. You know that I share to some extent the anxiety of Bishop Brilioth and think that the impression he received during his stay in this country about the attitude towards Bolshevism is not quite unfounded. Today this danger is actually too easily dismissed as a bogy.

I have also received a letter from Bloomsbury House signed by you with regard to the Retreat Conference at the beginning of April.[6] Unfortunately just for the week from 3rd to 10th of April we have through Dawson's [sic] the opportunity of going to Berkshire and we made our arrangements accordingly. I thought I had to take advantage of this opportunity as my wife and the children had no holiday at all during the four years we have been in this country and as especially my wife is in *urgent* need of a holiday as she has the care of us since we have been in Oxford and she has no help at all. When I heard about the date of the conference I tried to change the day of our stay, but in vain. Unfortunately, I cannot choose my own time for a holiday, but am dependent on others. The question, therefore, arises whether we have to cancel our plans altogether. You know, my Lordbishop, how greatly I appreciate any possibility of meeting you and seeing the pastors. Perhaps if you would like me to come up to London for a day (Monday or Tuesday) I could certainly arrange it. In any case I very much want to be guided by you in this matter. If you think it better to cancel our plans please kindly let me know.

At your instigation Sir Hubert Young[7] sent me his paper *Aiming at the year 2000*, which he read to Chatham House and which you have certainly seen too. I wrote him in detail. The main point on which I do not quite agree with him is that I feel that the fixation of such a long date in advance takes away the stimulus to action. I do not think that the man in the street would like to work for such a distant aim. In addition, if one realizes that events are moving with great rapidity today and that the last decades have probably changed human life more completely than any other period in history, then I think it is also possible that a counter movement in the opposite direction can develop with the same rapidity. This is our hope and I wonder how you think about this point.

A Mrs Reiter sent me a copy of a letter she wrote to you with regard to her relatives in Spain. In this letter she mentioned me. May I say that I only know Mr Reiter whose acquaintance I made when I was interned. He seems to me a decent and honest man and this was why I put his name on a special list, which passed on to you at that time. This was all I did.

I am very glad that the Dawsons are living so near. He is one of the best men I have met in this country. He is a profound thinker with a really wide outlook. I am so glad that we have so many interests in common and I hope that we shall often meet. I have to learn very much from him.

I very much hope that, in the meantime, you have completely got rid of the influenza. With all good wishes and our warm greetings to you and Mrs Bell

Yours ever,

---

[1] Peter Ferdinand Drucker (1909–2005) emigrated from Frankfurt/M. to Britain in 1933. In 1937 he went to the United States to become Professor of Philosophy and Politics at the Bennington College in Vermont. See P. F. Drucker, *The end of economic man: a study of the new totalitarianism* (London, 1939; new ed. 1943); also *The future of industrial man: a conservative approach* (London, 1943).

[2] See Christopher Dawson, *The Judgement of the Nations* (New York, 1942; London, 1943).

[3] Bell's comment referred to a speech of the Earl of Selborne in the House of Lords, in which he had remarked that the Germans could not be exonerated with respect to their descent from democracy to Nazism. See Hansard, H.L. Deb., Vol. 125, col. 1089 (11 February 1943).

[4] See Lord Vansittart's reply to Bell in ibid., col. 1091.

[5] A succession of political murders carried out by right-wing vigilantes in the first years of the Weimar Republic. These resulted in few prosecutions and a general amnesty for those who were convicted followed in 1930. The role of the army in all of this was, at best, dubious: a number of the murders were of individuals suspected of informing the Allied Commission of infringements

of the provisions of the Versailles treaty. Those whose investigations criticized the Reichswehr were liable to be prosecuted for slander. See Bernhard Sauer, *Schwarze Reichswehr und Fememorde. Eine Milieustudie zum Rechtsradikalismus in der Weimarer Republik* (Berlin 2004).
6   See Bell to Leibholz, 16 February 1943.
7   Sir Hubert Winthrop Young (1885–1950) was a soldier, Liberal Party politician, diplomat, colonial governor and celebrated mountaineer. In May 1934 he had taken a memorial protesting against concentration camps, the work of senior British lawyers and church leaders, to Berlin with the soldier Sir Wyndham Deedes. After 1942 he organized European relief work.

Bell to Leibholz, 20 February 1943, BA, N 1334 (typewritten); Bell Papers 40, fol. 156 (carbon)

My dear Leibholz,
Very many thanks for your letter of the 18th February. This is only a brief note, for I am unfortunately still in bed with a kind of influenza – nothing serious. I greatly appreciate what you say about my speech in the Lords. It is a real encouragement. On the other points:

1. I am very glad to read what you say about the rise of Nazism and the folly of reducing it to a purely national matter. I am trying to get Drucker's book. I am so glad you and Dawson have made such a good contact.
2. Vansittart in today's letter to *The Times* very much reduces what he said in the Lords; but it would be a very good thing if he could be still further shown up. What would you say if you were writing[?] Though I am not very anxious to write, if nobody else does during the next few days I might have a shot.
3. I am very glad you liked Bishop Brilioth's letter, and to know your impressions.
4. Please do not put yourself out to attend the Retreat Conference at the beginning of April. You should make no alteration in your plans. Honestly I was not expecting you. I thought that those who would be asked would be the Pastors pure and simple. There are certain complications, which call for a better understanding. I need not go into this further; but I regard it really as a conference of clergy – some of them clergy before they came to England, and the rest just ordained or about to be ordained in England.

With all best regards to your wife,

Yours ever,

ᵃ*Re Vansittart* I wonder whether there is a first-class English historian who could be quoted as saying before the war the Nazi atrocities were unparalleled (or something like it).ᵃ

Leibholz to Bell, 23 February 1943, Bell Papers 51, fol. 155 (typewritten)

My Lordbishop,
Very many thanks for your letter. I am very sorry to hear that you are still confined to bed but I very much hope you will be already better when this letter reaches you. I think influenza is an insidious matter [sic] and you should be very careful.

I am enclosing a draft of a letter to the Editor of *The Times* and I wonder what you think about it. I am afraid that the letter might lose its weight in the special case if published under a German name. Therefore I am thinking of signing it 'Gerard' as I did in *The Fortnightly*: but I do not know whether *The Times* publishes letters under a pseudonym. If you think it better to write the letter yourself or have it written by another Englishman please make use of the draft if it seems to be useful.

I am so glad to learn from you that the projected meeting in April is only thought of as a meeting of the clergy and that I do not need to alter our plans. Miss Murray[1] wrote three times in this matter and the last letter was rather urgent so that I thought you wanted to see me there.

Sir Hubert Young is thinking of coming up to Oxford and discussing his plans and suggestions here. I think, therefore, I shall meet him tomorrow.

With our best wishes to you and Mrs Bell

Yours ever,

Draft – To the Editor of *The Times*.

Sir,

In his letter of February 19 Lord Vansittart bases his statement that 'more men of the Left were killed under Weimar than during the six years from 1933 to 1939' on 'all that happened in Munich, Bremen, Brunswick, Mechterstaedt, Lichtenberg, Berlin, the Ruhr, and Mittel Deutschland'. He overlooks the fact that from 1918 to 1920 numerous revolts at the establishment of a communist-bolshevist regime in Germany [occurred] and that the German Left Government of that time, consisting of Socialists, Liberals and Catholics, was forced to make use of the army in order to maintain their liberal-democratic regime. The numerous victims of these uprisings, therefore, can hardly be imputed to the Army, which only acted as the executive arm of the most liberal regime Germany has ever had in its history.

As to the relatively few[2] Black Feme murders one should bear in mind that they were committed by right-radical organisations, which – if not national-socialist in character – were at least spiritually their immediate forerunners. Whether and in how far [sic] certain circles of the German army were involved in these cases has up-to-now not been proved. In any case, it cannot be said, that 'all those murders took place not only with the connivance but at the instigation of the German Army'. 24th February 1943

---

[1] i.e. Barbara Murray.
[2] 'relatively' here is crossed out.

Leibholz to Archbishop Temple, 23 February 1943, London, Lambeth Palace Library, Temple Papers Vol. 51 fol. 90

Your Grace,

Pastor Kramm told me that when accompanying Your Grace to Queen's College last Sunday afternoon he spoke of my brother-in-law Bonhoeffer who is one of the leading pastors in the Confessional Church in Germany. He thought it would perhaps be of interest to Your Grace to learn that my brother-in-law visited Bishop Brilioth after his return from this country in order to hear of his impressions which he had gained with regard to the attitude of this country to a Germany that had completely and radically changed its government and its policy. Bonhoeffer although a deadly opponent of the Nazi regime and of all that it stands for strongly insisted on the grave danger that a possible, perhaps a likely, development towards some form of communism would mean to the whole of Western civilisation. [sic] I know that Bishop Brilioth himself fully shares this view and thinks too that communism in its bolshevist form constitutes a great danger for the future of the European Continent. I think I sent Your Grace my article on 'Germany between West and East' published in the *Fortnightly*. If not it would be a great pleasure to me to send a copy to Your Grace. I tried there to point out how, from a Continental point of view, the political situation presents itself today. I think it would be worthwhile encouraging a constructive policy which would try to solve the post-war problems on a Western basis before it is too late.

May I thank Your Grace once again warmly for having given us the honour of your visit and for the most impressive sermon which will be unforgettable to the whole congregation.

Yours sincerely,

P.S May I ask Your Grace to treat confidentially what I said about Bishop Brilioth and my brother-in-law.

Bell to Leibholz, 27 February 1943, BA, N 1334 (handwritten)

My dear Leibholz,

I think you might try your letter, signed Gerard, to the *Times* [sic]: explaining in a covering letter your real name. It is a good reply; though Vansittart will probably find means of retort! I am trying to get hold of Dr Gumbel's book[1] (via Schütz[2]) to which he referred last letter.

I might use a little of the facts in my speech on March 10. It depends how things work out.

Yours ever,

---

[1] Probably Emil Julius Gumbel, *Vier Jahre politischer Morde*, with a preface by Albert Einstein (Berlin, 1922), or possibly *Lasst Köpfe rollen! Faschistische Morde 1924–1931* (Berlin: Deutsche Liga für Menschenrechte, 1932). But for these Bell would have required the services of a translator.

[2] Wilhelm Wolfgang Schütz (1911–2002) emigrated to Britain in 1935 and worked as a free correspondent of some German-language newspapers. He returned to Germany after the war where he supported Jakob Kaiser at the Ministry for All-German Affairs, 1951–57. Kaiser was one of the survivors of the German resistance against Hitler and, indeed, one of those named by Bonhoeffer and Schönfeld to Bell in Sweden in May 1942.

Leibholz to Bell, 1 March 1943, Bell Papers 40, fol. 157 (typewritten); BA, N 1334 (copy)

My Lordbishop,

Thank you very much for your letter. I am making a try in the direction you suggest and am going to send the letter to *The Times* under Gerard. I have deliberately not mentioned Gumbel's book as up-to-now I have not seen and checked it. I once met him in Berlin and may say that the book to which Vansittart refers has always been the subject of much lively controversy, even in Left wing circles, with regard to its reliability in the matter of question.

One may admit that after 1918 all Germans wanted to get rid of Versailles. But the point, which is completely overlooked by V. and his adherents seems to me to be the way in which this aim was to be reached. In 1918/19 there hardly existed the Nazis. The overwhelming majority wanted originally to attain equality in a liberal-democratic or perhaps conservative way.[1] That this was not possible and the masses supported eventually the Nazis who not only promised them equality but also the rulership, at least over the Continent and perhaps over the world, was, to my mind, not least due to the policy of the Western countries, which refused to support the liberal democracy at a time when it was still possible,[2] ªand thereby to avoid the war.ª Instead of that they tried to come to an arrangement with the Nazis hoping that it would be possible to satisfy the German claims, which were in reality Nazi-claims and could, therefore, not be given satisfaction in any way whatever.

Yours ever,

[1] This sentence is marked by a black line in the margin.
[2] The second part of the sentence is marked by a black line in the margin. This would certainly have supported Bell's own view.

Leibholz to Bell, 4 March 1943, Bell Papers 40, fol. 158 (handwritten)

My Lordbishop,

I am afraid I have not yet thanked you for having sent me the *Penguin Book* to which you also contributed.[1] It was very good of you. Your contribution is enlightening and impressive as all you write and say. I think it was very good to remind people that you made a stand against Nazism from the very first. I think we should lay stress on this in order to show that the voices which make themselves heard today (and sometimes very loudly) vary greatly in weight.

I sent the letter to *The Times*. But I think they will *not* publish it as it is against the constantly practised tradition to this newspaper to publish letters under a pseudonym.

Yours ever,

[1] William Temple (ed.), *Is Christ Divided?* (Harmondsworth, 1943). To this Bell contributed two pieces: 'Unity in spite of War' (pp. 54–64) and his Christmas 1941 broadcast to Germany (pp. 122–5). Other contributors included William Paton, Franz Hildebrandt, Karl Barth and Emil Brunner.

Bell to Leibholz, 11 March (1943), BA, N 1334 (handwritten)

My dear Leibholz,

Here is *Hansard*, which please keep.[1] I shall be very much interested to hear what you think of the debate, and particularly the *reply*. And I am most grateful for all your help.

Yours ever,

[1] The number of Hansard containing the 1943 debate in the House of Lords: see Hansard, H.L. Deb., Vol. 126, cols. 535–45 (10 March 1943); Bell's final statement follows on 581–2. Bell's speech is reprinted in Bell, *The Church and Humanity*, pp. 95–109; see too Peter Raina, *Bishop George Bell: House of Lords speeches*, pp. 32–9.

Leibholz to Bell, 12 March 1943, Bell Papers 51, fol. 180 (handwritten)

My Lordbishop,

My warmest congratulations on what you achieved in the Lords on Wednesday. From what I heard on the wireless and read in *The Times* I conclude it must have been a great success and I very much hope that you are also satisfied. I think you have pressed the government more forward in stating a more constructive policy than any other speaker or statesman in the last two or three years and I feel that if the government is in earnest and acts in accordance with their statement i.e. bases their future policy on it and uses their power to make the statement widely known in Germany (by all means of propaganda) far-reaching consequences may perhaps be expected in future. I was also very glad to see that after Vansittart's attack other speakers supported your case so vigorously. I only missed Dr Temple who recently wrote me that the present government policy towards Germany appeared to him 'disastrous'.[1]

Your valiant and moving speech and the support you received from Dr Lang[2] seems to me to prove that Christians are in a much better position today to [judge?] bad peoples in Politics than the pure secularists who by no mere chance do not see the actual driving forces behind the actual happenings.

By the way, I do not know whether you have seen the important passage in Mr Wallace's[3] speech saying that without 'understanding between Russia and the United States there is grave probability of Russia and Germany sooner or later making common cause'. Should it not be possible to prevent this development by finding means to win Germany back to the West after the destruction of the present regime? In any case, I think you have laid a foundation-stone in this direction by your brilliant action in the Lords. I greatly admire you.

Yours ever,

P.S. Just as I am writing this the post brings me your letter and *Hansard*. Very many thanks for it. I will make once more comments soon after having carefully read the verbatim report.

[1] A letter not found in the Temple Papers in Lambeth Palace Library.
[2] The speech of Lord Lang of Lambeth in Hansard, H.L. Deb., Vol. 126, cols. 556–61 (10 March 1943).
[3] Henry A. Wallace (1888–1965), American politician and Vice President of the United States, 1941–5.

Leibholz to Bell, 14 March 1943, Bell Papers 51, fols. 186–7. (typewritten)

My Lordbishop,

The verbatim report confirmed and strengthened the impression I gained from what I had heard and read before. I think you put the case in a masterly way and I can hardly imagine how it could have ᵃbeenᵃ better put forward. I think it was a great success and I feel that the House and the government were very sympathetic to what you, my Lordbishop, had to say and that Vansittart was in a rather isolated position. Considering the whole situation an amazing result, which you have achieved ᵃand whichᵃ is alone your personal merit.

The most important point seems to me to be that just now the government has stressed again the distinction between Hitlerite Regime and Germany and has emphasized the fact that the destruction of the present regime does not imply the doom of the German people as a whole.[1] This must, no doubt, be very encouraging to all oppositional forces in Germany. Frankly, I cannot say that the reply of the government is fully satisfactory. Briefly, Lord Simon says that the government is prepared to support all Germans who want to destroy the present regime and bids them to do so as otherwise they would also become responsible for the crimes, which the Nazi-regime is committing in their name.[2] But at the same time he deprives them of the means of doing so by stressing the urgency of the complete deconstruction of all armed forces, which – please forgive me for repeating myself – represent actually the only power which can possibly take action against the regime. I admit, the Germans would be stupid if they did not see the falsity of Goebbels propaganda. But of what avail is this insight if those who want to support the opposition in Germany take at the same time away the only weapons of any possible use to the opposition in Germany. I do not see why on the part of the government it was necessary to broach this question – all the more as I think that the government has asked you beforehand to drop that part of your question which dealt with the army. Thus you were not in a position to put forward the reasons why without some armed forces a revolution in Germany is a complete impossibility. I know you do not misunderstand me. I fully realize that, under the present circumstances as a result of the identification of Hitlerism and Prussianism, it is simply impossible (I think nearly all the speeches made in the discussion stressed this point) to say anything that seems like an appeal to the oppositional forces in the army. But what I do not quite understand is that this question had to be broached. As far as I know Mr Stalin has not done so. And I think he knows why.

As to the other speeches I should only like to say a few words:

You quote, my Lordbishop, in column 541 Bishop Galen's utterance of the fight against the enemy outside and within. It is perhaps worthwhile mentioning that Galen speaks of this country only as the 'Gegner' i.e. the opponent and not as the enemy as he does with regard to the Nazi S.S.[3]

I welcome the utterance made by Lord Faringdon with regard to those refugees 'who seeks now to curry favour with us in this country by abusing his own country men' [sic] although their own records 'cannot bear close inspection'.[4] These are the people who back Vansittart today.

One of the few Vansittart sentences with which I agree is ᵃthe statementᵃ that if one accepts General Smut's thesis of 'Germany's second thirty years war'[5] much of his case is conceded. I only draw the conclusion from this that his statement, although attractive, is ᶜin so far fundamentallyᶜ wrong as it seems to prove that he sees the present war in exactly the same terms as the last war.

As to the frequently made statement that militarism and Prussianism stand behind Nazism I should like to say that I agree with your cautious statement that 'certain powerful antidemocratic forces, partly in military circles, partly in industrial circles, betrayed their own country for their selfish ends'.⁶ But there hardly seems to be a doubt that, on the whole, Nazism appeals to other strata of society i.e. to the suburban masses, to those who are not integrated into society, to the lower middle-classes. This explains why, on the whole, the upper classes were more opposed to Nazism than the strata just mentioned. This is also why I cannot agree with the basic attitude of English Left-wing circles, according to which Nazism is simply a matter of the Junkers, capitalists and militarists. Yes, it seems to me that this attitude gives Vansittart a good opportunity of attacking those circles. To my mind, the national-socialist phenomenon cannot be explained in Marxist terms. It seems to me that the Vansittart attitude can only be overcome by showing its complete inadequacy in the spiritual and general sociological field – in a way in which you have frequently given us an example.

I also think, one point the Earl of Onslow made is important: Germany is the source of unrest and war in the last century because it was the last great power which came on the scene at a time when all other great powers had already satisfied their national ambitions and had their Empires.⁷ But unlike the speaker I think Prussianism is already dying and will be extinguished even if the Nazis would win the war. It is being destroyed by the Nazis themselves. I admit nobody will be prepared to accept this thesis today. But the future will show who is right. I think that Prussianism is effective ᵃtodayᵃ only as an instrument but it is no longer a creative, dynamic force.

Also what the Earl of Perth said about the desire of peace in the German people (in contrast to the Nazis and some other circles)⁸ agrees with all I have heard until the outbreak of the war.

I could expatiate upon some other points broached in the debate. But I am afraid I have already to apologize for undue length of the letter.

In any case I think it would be very important indeed to make the debate widely known among our friends. And I think it would ᵃperhapsᵃ not be a bad idea to send a few copies as soon as possible to your Swedish friends, especially Bishop Brilioth. As far as I know, a special permit is necessary for doing so. To send other copies to Switzerland is perhaps rather risky for the people who receive the letters with regard to the fact that all post from and to Switzerland is now controlled by German censor.

Once again very many thanks for all you have so selflessly done in the interest of a better future of all ᵃnationsᵃ.

Yours ever,

---

1   In his answer the Lord Chancellor (Viscount Simon) said: 'I now say in plain terms on behalf of His Majesty's Government, that we agree with Premier Stalin, first, that the Hitlerite State should be destroyed, and secondly, that the whole German people is not (as Dr. Goebbels has been trying to persuade them) thereby doomed to destruction.' Hansard, Vol. 126, col. 575 (10 March 1943).
2   Ibid., col. 579.
3   Here Leibholz is mistaken. On 13 July 1941 Galen spoke in the quoted sermon of the 'äußere Feind und Kriegsgegner' (external enemy and war opponents), but on 20 July he emphasized presented the two in parallel, speaking of 'Angriffe der Kriegsgegner ... Angriffe unserer Gegner im Inneren des Landes' (attacks of war opponents and the opponents inside). See Peter Löffler (ed.): Bischof Clemens August Graf von Galen – Akten, Briefe und Predigten 1933–46 Vol. 2 (2nd ed., Paderborn, 1996), pp. 844, 855.
4   Hansard, HL Deb, Vol. 126, col. 548 (10 March 1943); the last quotation reflects 'records, which we now know would not bear close inspection'.

[5] Quoted by Vansittart, ibid., col. 552.
[6] See ibid., col. 537: 'I dare not acquit the Germans as a whole of some guilt for accepting the Nazi régime, but the chief blame in Germany for letting the Nazis seize control lies with certain powerful anti-democratic forces, partly in military and partly in industrial circles, who betrayed their own county for their selfish ends.'
[7] See ibid., col. 568. Richard William Alan Onslow (1876–1945), 5th Earl of Onslow styled Viscount Cranley until 1911, was a diplomat, parliamentary secretary and government minister; Chairman of the Committees and Deputy Speaker of the House of Lords, 1931–44.
[8] See ibid., cols. 571–2.

Bell to Leibholz, 16 March 1943, BA, N 1334 (typewritten); Bell Papers 51, fol. 192 (carbon)

My dear Leibholz,

Very many thanks for your two letters about the debate and the speeches made. I am very glad you agree with my presentation of the case. I think it is quite true that the sympathy of the House was more with my side of the case than with Lord Vansittart's statement, that is to say so far as the speeches went. There are of course people who applaud Vansittart more vehemently than they would a speaker who takes the opposite line.

When I heard, just before the debate began, that Lord Simon was to answer for the Government, I was a little fearful lest a general affirmative might be so much hedged about with reservations as to deprive it of all value. So the clearness of the answer on the precise point which I raised was a real satisfaction. It is all the more gratifying since I have good reason to know that the answer drafted in January for Lord Cranborne, as Leader of the House (he was then to make the reply) was of a much vaguer kind and would not have carried one any distance. I think it more than probable that the omission of the reference to the Hitlerite Army helped to secure a more satisfactory reply. But I also think that the delay of six weeks or so after Hitler's speech on January 30th[1] has contributed to show the importance of speaking to the German people in this way.

I appreciate what you say about the impossibility of revolution in Germany without some armed forces. It seems to me that Lord Simon's remarks with regard to unconditional surrender[2] showed a wish on his part to water it down just a little bit. I agree that the Government has not at present shown signs of appreciating the impossibility of a rising without arms. I am much interested in all the points you make about the different speeches. I note also the description by Bishop von Galen of our country as only 'Gegner'.

I am in touch with the Ministry of Information about the possibilities of getting a few copies of *Hansard* over to Sweden.

Yours very sincerely,

ᵃThe press has been very good on the debate. And I know dispatches have come to Sweden and Switzerland.ᵃ

[1] See Max Domarus (ed.), *Hitler, Reden und Proklamationen, 1933–1945* (Wiesbaden, 1973), Vol. 2/2, pp. 1976–80. The proclamation was not made by Hitler in person, as in previous years, but read by Goebbels.
[2] See Hansard, Vol. 126, cols. 575–6 (10 March 1943).

Leibholz to Bell, 19 March 1943, Bell Papers 40, fol. 159 (typewritten); BA, N 1334 (copy)

My Lordbishop,

Very many thanks for your letter. I wholeheartedly agree with you that considering the fact that Lord Simon replied for the government the success in getting such a satisfactory answer on the decisive point makes its value all the higher and I think you are perfectly right in saying that such a satisfactory reply would not have been possible if you, my Lordbishop, had combined the question with the 'armed forces' problem. I also felt in accordance with you that Lord Simon tended in some way to weaken a little bit the unhappy unconditional surrender clause of Casablanca.

As to the manifesto and circular I have some doubts as to whether it is expedient to express your approval. I think it depends on the reliability of the people who have approached you. I do not know them and, therefore, cannot myself form an opinion. But it seems to me that the *Tribüne* is the organ of the Free German League of Culture, which – as far as I know – is known for its communist character.[1] Nor do I think that a publication of the manifesto, if it is to be a serious action, can lie in the interest of those who adopted it. I cannot quite help feeling that other motives (such as Propaganda etc) stand behind the action, which, to my mind, – if in earnest – would presuppose secrecy and a personal approach. I should regret a possible misuse of your name by some irresponsible people all the more as your help and guidance is today more urgently needed than ever before in all decisive questions and issues at stake. Apart from that your attitude to those forces in the name of which the manifesto pretends to speak is so widely known also in Germany and will become wider known after the recent debate in the Lords that I see no reason why to say more.

Yours ever,

P.S. I am also delighted to see that the Press has been so good on the debate.

I think you will have received the last volume of the *Transactions* of the Grotius Society. On page 160seq. a memorandum of mine on structural changes of nationality (in connection with the refugee question) has been published there.[2] It may perhaps interest you. I have no copy myself and, therefore, I am not able to send you one.

---

[1] Constituted on 1 March 1939 the Free German League of Culture in Great Britain had close relations with the small group of German Communists in London. Its strategy mirrored communist tactics during the Popular Front period of the 1930s. Bell was invited to be a member of a special honorary Committee of an exhibition; see German League to Bell, 19 June 1942, Bell Papers, Vol. 47, fol. 13. The newspaper of the League was called *Freie Tribüne*. See Charmian Brinson and Richard Dove, *Politics by Other Means: The Free German League of Culture in London 1939–1946* (Edgware, 2010).

[2] G. Leibholz, 'Nationality in International Law', reprinted in *Politics and Law*, pp. 320–3.

Bell to Leibholz, 23 March 1943, BA, N 1334 (typewritten); Bell Papers 40, fol. 160 (carbon; without P.S.)

My dear Leibholz,

Very many thanks for your letter and your advice. I agree with it, and will not give my name. I am glad you called my attention to your memorandum on structural changes of nationality in the transactions of the Grotius Society, and I hope to read it. I enclose a copy of my article in *The fortnightly*.[1] Don't bother to reply.

Yours ever,

P.S. I have just received a telegram from Siegmund-Schultze, a copy of which I enclose. Any comments you care to send me would be gratefully received. I am in touch with the Foreign Office ªI see Richard Law[2] tomorrow (25th)ª about it, and am told by a very high official at the Ministry of Information who deals with all these questions that my speech was given immense publicity abroad.

[1] G. Bell, 'The Church and the Future of Europe', reprinted in *The Church and Humanity*, pp. 110–22.
[2] Richard Kidston Law (1901–80), from 1954 1st Baron Coleraine, Conservative MP 1931–45. In 1940 he was appointed Financial Secretary to the War Office and then transferred to the post of Parliamentary Under-Secretary of State for Foreign Affairs. From 1943 to 1945 he was Minister of State at the Foreign Office. It was Law who had received a succession of Christian and Jewish delegations to the Foreign Office pressing for a formal acknowledgement by the British government of the mass murder of the Jews of occupied Europe.

TELEGRAM RECEIVED BY THE BISHOP OF CHICHESTER ON MARCH 23, 1943, FROM DR SI[E]GMUND SCHULTZE, ZURICH.

'Church friends deeply grateful for your differentiation but official declaration regarded as only aiming disunity. If not such free peace negotiations are accorded as asked through Archbishop two years ago. The refusal of answering that demand rejected differentiation and prevented concerned from using opportunity. Present destruction of civilian life also contradicts official differentiation.[1] Consequences regarding European civilisation apparent not so much danger of conquest by Bolshevistic forces but of communist development in middle Europe. Outcome of nationalistic warfare instead of overcoming evil forces by common efforts of good may be continental anti-Christian bloc. The more excellent way still now would reach majority, which never consented with un-Christian regime. God has not ordained us administrators of punitive measures of states but ambassadors of reconciliation of Christ. Gratefully acknowledging communion of spirit.'

[1] i.e. by the 'obliteration' bombing campaign of RAF Bomber Command.

Leibholz to Bell, 26 March 1943, Bell Papers 40, fol. 161 (typewritten); BA, N 1334 (copy)

My Lordbishop,

I hasten to thank you for your letter and for kindly letting me see the copy of the telegram from Siegmund Schultze, which greatly interested me and touched me.

I am delighted to know that your speech has been given such immense publicity abroad but I do not wonder at it. I can imagine how warmly and eagerly our friends in Germany and beyond in neutral and even occupied countries welcomed this voice of Christian reason for which they have so long been yearning. I feel sure that your speech will have given them great encouragement and will help them to get away from the feeling of political hopelessness, which, to my mind, must have befallen them after all the disappointments they have experienced.

As to the telegram I entirely agree with the following sentences: 'Consequences regard. European civilisation apparent not so much danger of conquest by Bolshevist forces but of communist development in middle Europe. Outcome of nationalistic warfare instead of overcoming evil forces by common efforts of good may be continental anti-Christian bloc.' You know, my Lordbishop, that this is the thesis I have long held in face of the fact that the official politicians of the Western countries ª(excepting Lord Simon in his last statement)ª are intentionally doing their utmost to destroy the only power, which could help them in winning Germany back to the West and in putting the future reconstruction work on a firm basis.

I do not know whether you read yesterday in *The Times* the report on an American plan published in the *American Mercury* regarding the future of Germany.[1] This plan, which seems to reflect official views in America is fantastic and I wonder whether Mr Eden is actually discussing such plans with the Americans just now. What they want is obviously a kind of Super-Versailles with all its implications. The consequences of these plans seem to me to be, first, the impossibility of an 'activisation' of the German opposition and secondly the possibility of winning this war *only* by a complete military defeat of the Axis everywhere which, I am afraid, will prolong the war for a considerable time without gaining anything. Thirdly, even if this aim were reached the chance of getting an anti-Western and anti-Christian Continent (probably under active assistance of Russia) seems, ªas Schultze says,ª to be greater than the attainment of the nationalistic post-war aims proclaimed in such kind of plans.

I do not quite know to which speech of the Archbishop the telegram refers. Obviously, Schultze and his friends think that the lack of an official statement, according to which the United Nations were prepared to conclude a fair peace with a radically changed Germany, is responsible for the inactivity of the German opposition. All this seems to me like a cat and mouse game. The Germans maintain – and I think, with justice – that they cannot act before the government in this country says that they are prepared to deal fairly with a completely changed Germany and the government holds the view that they cannot make a statement before a revolutionary change in Germany itself has taken place.

What I think about the official statement made by Lord Simon in the Lords I tried to say in the last letter I wrote to you, my Lordbishop. I feel that my people on the Continent do not fully realize the status of public opinion in this country and cannot understand it. This is, to my mind, the reason why they cannot fully appreciate the great gains contained in this statement. On the other hand, I do not think that they regard this statement as wholly unsatisfactory as they refer in a later sentence to the differentiation made in it in a positive sense ('Present destruction of civilian life also contradicts official differentiation').

A most encouraging point seems to me to be that they say that even now the possibility still exists of organising a majority 'which never consented to an un-Christian regime', I think this should give us fresh hope to continue with renewed courage in the way you are leading us.

Many thanks also for the off-print of your article in *The Fortnightly*. I had already read it with wholehearted agreement and the utmost interest. I am delighted now to have it. I hope to come back to the whole matter in the next few weeks and will then write to you in greater detail on it.

I am *greatly* perturbed at a report published in the *Daily Telegraph* two days ago saying that a group of Foreign Office officials in Germany have been arrested and that two of them with whom I was well acquainted ªv. Scheliha and v. Harnack, a son of the great German theologian and a relative of ours,ª have already been executed.[2] I feel sure you understand me and I need not tell you more ªon possible further implications with regard to others.ª

Yours ever,

---

[1] *The Times* 25 March 1943, 'American plan for future of Germany'.
[2] Arvid Harnack, a leading member of the 'Red Orchestra' resistance group and a cousin of Ernst von Harnack, and Rudolf von Scheliha, an active resister but not a member of that group, had been tried, sentenced and hanged in December 1942 after a special order from Hitler.

Leibholz to Bell, 2 April 1943, Bell Papers 40, fol. 162 (typewritten); BA, N 1334 (copy)

My Lord Bishop,

From the news I am getting I gather that the movement about which Dietrich informed you has been discovered and dealt with in the typical Nazi way. From the last news I read in the newspapers there have been 50 executions and about 200 arrests.[1] But I am afraid the number will still increase. Why the army has not acted – whether it could or would not – I do not know. I am afraid, this inactivity is connected in some way with the policy of the Anglo-Saxon countries towards the army as a *whole*. If Mr Eden again and again confirms that the *main* war aim is the total and permanent destruction of the armed forces of the Axis I am afraid they cannot act without at the same time committing suicide. What seems to me worse is that this policy will, I fear, result in the liquidation of that stratum in Germany, which alone would have been able to build up a new Germany on Western lines.

Under these circumstances, we are naturally greatly concerned about Dietrich and I have just sent a telegram to Pastor Sutz asking him to let me know how things stand. I am also thinking whether it would not perhaps be wise to get into touch by telegram resp. cable with Eidem or Visser 't Hooft – in case they may be able to help him in getting out, if this should still be possible. I think one could perhaps approach Visser 't Hooft if one calls Dietrich by his Christian name.

I wonder whether you saw Richard Law in the Foreign Office, my Lord Bishop, and you took any action with regard to Siegmund Schultze. I am afraid it is hardly possible to do anything, under the present circumstances.

Yours ever,

1. These reports probably referred to the executions of members of the 'Red Orchestra' and also to executions of members of the student White Rose group in Munich. At the end of 1942 139 members of the former had been arrested and between December 1942 and July 1943 30 men and 19 women were sentenced to death. Later five others were killed and 29 received jail sentences. There were only some casual personal contacts between members of the Red Orchestra and Dietrich Bonhoeffer and Hans von Dohnanyi, both of whom had been arrested on 5 April.

Bell to Leibholz, 7 April 1943, BA, N 1334 (typewritten); Bell Papers 40, fol. 163 (carbon)

Confidential.

My dear Leibholz,

I was very glad to get your letter of the 2nd April, though distressed by the news it contained, which I have since seen at greater length, though without names, in *Zeitung*. I was rushed, and could not write to you at once. But I telegraphed to Visser 't Hooft at Geneva, and said that I was anxious about Dietrich and ask[ed] him to help. I am sure he would understand what I meant. I will let you know, of course, if I get any reply, and I am sure you will do the same.

I saw Mr Law twice. On the first occasion, when I gave him a copy of the telegram, he was in rather a hurry. He wrote afterwards, finding the telegram difficult to understand. I saw him again on Monday. In my first conversation I had suggested that one might ask what was meant by 'free peace negotiations', and with whom; but he said he was quite certain the Foreign Office would not recommend any reply. I had however brought with me a draft, which I showed him, and he said there would be no objection to that, as it did not bring them in. I have therefore sent the telegram, a copy of which I enclose. Actually the last sentence was added after I had seen Mr Law, as I told him I should add some religious words.

He seemed rather distressed by the state of the world, and was obviously a religious minded man. I impressed upon him the importance of recognising the existence of sound forces in the army and of trying to find phrases when talking about disarmament which would make it plain that the whole army was not brought under complete condemnation; I pointed out that it would only be with the help of armed forces that any overthrow from within could take place. He saw and appreciated this point.

I heard last week that a Red Cross representative from Geneva[1] who was in Berlin lately found the attitude of the Berliners very different from what it had been. They were all saying it was not our fault. They were obviously very much upset by the bombing, and kept saying it is not our fault, which again implies a strong criticism of Hitler.

Please keep all I have said confidential.

Yours ever,

1. Bethge and Jasper, in *An der Schwelle*, p. 108, suspect that this was Jaques Courvoisier (1900–88), who since 1939 had held the Chair of church history at Geneva University.

Bell to F. Siegmund-Schultze, 7 April 1943, Bell Papers 51, fol. 215 (copy of telegram); BA, N 1334 (copy)

OFFICIAL DECLARATION MOST DELIBERATE AND POSITIVE YET MADE ON DIFFERENTIATION BETWEEN NAZI REGIME AND GERMAN PEOPLE STOP DECLARATION ALSO REAFFIRMED REFUSAL NEGOTIATE WITH HITLER OR ANY NAZI REPRESENTATIVES STOP BUT SHOULD HITLER AND NAZIS BE OVERTHROWN WITHIN GERMANY AM PERSONALLY CONVINCED WHOLE SITUATION TRANSFORMED STOP DEEPLY APPRECIATE YOUR COMMUNION OF SPIRIT AND YOUR EMPHASIS ON CHURCH'S RECONCILING FUNCTION STOP. BELL.

Leibholz to Bell, 12 April 1943, Bell Papers 40, fol. 164 (typewritten); BA, N 1334 (copy)

My Lordbishop,

I am very glad indeed to have the news of your last letter of the 7th April and I thank you very warmly, also on behalf of my wife, for having sent the telegram to Visser 't Hooft. Yesterday I had a letter from Paton giving me the following message from R. C. Mackie[1]:

'Inform Leibholz that Dietrich Bonhoeffer is well and working actively for new future, and that he (presumably I) should perhaps write and tell Harry[2] how he is getting on.'

We are greatly relieved by this message, which Mackie received from Schönfeld[3] and we hope that Visser 't Hooft or Sutz will confirm this. I will write to Johansson[4] and in case you wish me to give him a message please let me know.

I pressed upon the people in *Die Zeitung* only to give a general account and to leave out all details and names, which might possibly be of use to the Nazi-authorities. I thought I must do so, under the special circumstances, because I remembered how strongly we felt in Germany each time when people (especially the press) showed a lack of responsibility for those who are in their daily work in permanent danger of their lives.

I do not know whether you, my Lordbishop, have read the latest Reuter message from Zürich saying that 'two student demonstrations have occurred in Munich since the last raid. Sixteen students, including two girls were shot. Three days after the execution a big poster appeared on their mass grave with the inscription: 'And you nevertheless conquered'.[5] I only mention this to show that, on the whole, the situation in Germany does not seem to me to be very different from that in the occupied countries. It is a pity that only a few papers (*The Times* not among them) publish news concerning the underground movement in Germany itself.

I was deeply impressed by your telegram to Siegmund Schultze and greatly interested in what you wrote me on your talk to Mr Law. It is very good of you to let me know the details and I will keep all you have said strictly confidential. I think it is quite a special merit on your part to have made clear the urgent need of handling the whole question of disarmament in a more diplomatic and differentiating manner if one wants to overthrow the Hitler regime from within. I think what we have to say in this direction is so cogent, simple and convincing to a man who is familiar with the real situation in the totalitarian states that I cannot quite conceive of that [sic] a politician can evade the evidence of this argument and I am very glad that Mr Law appreciated the point you made. I think there are people who do not want an inner collapse of the Nazi regime, even if this should considerably shorten the war. I think of those who want to finish the present conflict in pure terms of power-politics (a kind of Super-Versailles) and who feel that they cannot attain their aim if the Nazis collapse from within.

I was also very much interested in what you said about the impression of the Red Cross representative. I was afraid that the bombing would possibly embitter even the Anti-Nazis and perhaps have a unifying effect and I am very glad that this is not the case.

With all good wishes from us all and renewed thanks

Yours ever,

---

[1] Robert C. Mackie (1899–1984) led the Scottish, then the British, Student Christian Movement. He had been appointed secretary-general of the World's Student Christian Federation in 1938 and later became Associate Secretary-General of the WCC in 1948.
[2] i.e. Harry Johansson.
[3] Hans Schönfeld (1900–54) had studied theology and economics. Delegated by the German Evangelical Church Federation in 1931 he became Director of the Research Department of the Life and Work movement and later of the World Council of Churches (in the process of formation). In 1948–50 he worked in the office of foreign affairs of the Evangelical Church of Germany at Frankfurt/M.
[4] See Jørgen Glenthøj, *Dokumente zur Bonhoeffer-Forschung 1928–1945* (Munich, 1963), pp. 318–9.
[5] This imperfect account relates to the activities of the *Weiße Rose* group, a students' resistance circle built around a brother and sister, Hans and Sophie Scholl, in Munich. On 18 February the Scholls were taken into custody after distributing leaflets in the main hall of Munich University. The Scholls and their friend Christoph Probst were sentenced to death on 22 February. On 19 April a second trial of 14 young men and women followed, 3 of whom were sentenced to death. There were no demonstrations in support of these resisters in Munich.

Bell to Leibholz, Easter 1943 (24 April 1943), BA, N 1334 (handwritten)

My dear Leibholz,

I have been asked to go to a Conference in USA in July and write a paper on the Future of Germany.[1] The conference is an important one – you have probably seen its last utterance in [*The*] *Times* and *Christian News-Letter*. I can't go to USA, but I propose to send a paper, as it might be useful to exchange and clarify ideas. I should be most grateful if *you* could let me have any suggestions in the next fortnight. I am sure we want to get our American (& English) friends to see *Germany's* place in a realist way in Europe: the problem being partly economic (and political) and partly the integration of a due military contribution to a European security plan or force.

Yours ever,

I have heard nothing from 't Hooft.

---

[1] A conference at Princeton University, 8–11 July 1943.

Leibholz to Bell, 29 April 1943, Bell Papers 40, fol. 165 (typewritten); BA, N 1334 (copy)

My Lordbishop,

Thank you ever so much for your letter, which I received yesterday. I will gladly comply with your request and hope to send you within a fortnight a few suggestions in the connection. I am very glad that it is just you who has been entrusted by the Americans with this most important task and that you are willing to fulfil their wishes. It is a pity that you are not personally able to express your views from but, frankly, I am glad that you are not going to America as – even for a short time – I do not like to miss you here in my thoughts.

I think the Polish-Russian tension,[1] regrettable as it is, has perhaps also one good side. It will help to rouse some people from wishful thinking. For this 'misunderstanding' seems to me to be more than a mere misunderstanding. I admit, it involves a great danger, which however, in my view, can only be overcome by a policy towards Germany in the sense you advocate. I hope to write you more on this question soon.

If it is all the same to you I will return the letter of the Americans together with my notes.

We too have heard nothing from Sutz. If we had not had the message Mackie-Schönfeld (via Sweden) about which I wrote to you, my Lordbishop, we should be very alarmed. I have written to Johansson, in the meantime.

Yours ever,

---

[1] The Polish government in exile, based in London, had broken off relations with the Soviet Union on 25 April 1943 after the discovery by German forces of mass graves in the Katyn forest in the east of the country, an area occupied in 1939–40 by Soviet forces. By now the Polish government was also deeply, and rightly, suspicious that the Soviet government would not free Poland from German occupation but instead brush it aside and impose its own authority there.

Leibholz to Bell, 13 May 1943, Bell Papers 40, fol. 165 (typewritten); BA, N 1334 (copy)

My Lordbishop,

Today I am enclosing an exposé in which I have tried to broach some questions with which you will probably deal in your paper. I feel it is unsatisfactory in many respects and yet I hope there is something in it with which you will agree. In any case I should be very glad if it were of any use to you.

I have been quite frank and have tried to analyse the situation in accordance with the lines you, my Bishop, and I have already pursued. The Americans write they wish that the question should be dealt with, from a non-German view. In so far I think I have certainly failed. But provided the analysis is a true one and we have the same aims in mind it should not matter from what standpoint the paper is written. As Christians I think Americans, Englishmen and Germans should come to the same conclusions.

I have refrained from quoting the literature in question. The material seems to me too vast and apart from a few exceptions is more confusing than clearing. I think that our common friends in Germany etc. would, on the whole, take the same lines I have tried to sketch. But they may disagree with the remark on page 16 where I say that if

Nazism or communism were actually the only alternative in Europe left we should prefer communism. I feel I must take for this the responsibility on myself as I feel strongly that many of our friends on the Continent may say that great and devilish as Nazism be it is more tolerable than Bolshevism.

With all good wishes
Yours ever,

Leibholz, Exposé, Bell Papers 40, fols. 167–84 (typewritten)[1]

If the Church has the right and the duty to act politically it is not enough to formulate some basic principles as has been done by the Pope and the Churches in this country and the United States. In addition, the Church has to see to it that these principles are applied in practice in a realistic way, compatible with the spirit behind these principles.

I think that a Christian politician, from the spiritual background he has, is in a better position to pursue a realistic policy than the secular politician who had badly failed in the past. For let us not forget that if the secular politician had comprehended political events on the Continent more realistically and had seen the social and spiritual driving forces behind them, – in more concrete terms, if he had supported the liberal regime in Central Europe and had not appeased National Socialism and Fascism, the present war would probably have been avoided.

Under these circumstances, the Churches bear an increased responsibility today. They must ask themselves again and again whether the policy advocated by them is a truly Christian policy, which does justice to the political realities. If they fail to do so either by backing a policy, which is not Christian, although perhaps compatible with the literal interpretation of the stated general principles[a] or by advocating a policy, which is not based on political realities they run the risk of being excluded from taking part in the future reconstruction work and of being exposed to the reproach of having wrongly interfered in politics.

I think there is a large amount of agreement on these presuppositions among Christian and secular politicians today. Today one is inclined to make the pre-war utopian Liberalism, Pacifism and Idealism responsible for the collapse of the post-war policy of the Western countries.[b] It is argued that the necessity of using power as a means of politics was wrongly overlooked and that, therefore, in future power must be used and organised realistically. This explains why in the whole post-war discussion the power problem has become the decisive one and the public opinion in the Western countries demands the drastic application of power-politics to the Axis in the future peace.[b] This is, for instance, why the question of the disarmament of the Axis, of the occupation of the Axis-countries, of the establishment of not only military but also economic controls stand in the foreground of the discussion, why measures are demanded, which shall secure this disarmament and control for an unlimited period, why projects are discussed directed to the breaking up of German unity and dividing Germany into two or more separate states. 'Unconditional surrender' of Germany and Italy as proclaimed at Casablanca is the latest expression of this policy.

The decisive question, however, is whether this policy is as realistic as its adherents think it is.

Of course, no politician will deny that politics can be thought of without the background of power. The Christian, if he be a realist, will have to acknowledge that power plays an eminent part in the political sphere. He may also agree that there is nothing unethical or unchristian about the nature of power itself. But he will also stress the fact that power is only a tool and all depends on how power and force are used.[d] It is not Christian utopianism but sound Christian realism to demand that power and Politics must be put into the service of God. In more secular terms, from a Christian point of view, power and force must be subservient to ethical purposes, fundamental beliefs and universal values. It must be used as a means to good and ethical ends.[d]

It will be said that in the present situation the traditional means of power-policy will be used in the interest of higher ends, namely of the preservation of peace and the prevention of renewed aggression. To support this argument one may point out that – in spite of the unconditional surrender policy of Casablanca[2] – their leading statesmen have stressed again and again that it is not their purpose to destroy the German nation as a whole, that the Atlantic Charter – unlike the Versailles Treaty – does not differentiate between victors and vanquished in the economic sphere, but proclaims a general equality among all nations in the economic field after the war, that plans are being elaborated for a re-education of Germany of today, so that when the time comes a completely changed Germany may be received again into the community of nations.

I think, however that this connection of power policy with certain general principles against which, from a Christian point of view, no objection can be raised, is not enough to change the fundamental character of this policy. This becomes quite clear if we realize that the Axis, from their point of view, could also accept these principles. Even under Axis leadership peace and an external order could be maintained and aggression prevented.[c] In addition, the Axis could easily associate the demands for unconditional surrender (including disarmament) of the United Nations with general statements like those that the United Nations (apart from the Jews) should not be destroyed or economically disqualified, but only be re-educated in the Nazi-spirit etc.

This shows [c]quite clearly[c] that this policy without being specified in greater detail is mere power policy.[c] This leads us to the further conclusion that it runs counter to the character of the present war. For such a [a]power[a] policy presupposes that the present conflict was like the last war essentially a war between national sovereign states in which only national power is at stake.[c] No further argument is needed, in the connection before us, to show why this is not the case. It has often been stated with good reasons why – without denying that the present conflict is also a life and death struggle for the United Nations – this war is, at bottom, a spiritual conflict, a war between two attitudes towards the world. As is known, this character of the present conflict was also recognized in the first years of the war by the leading statesmen of the United Nations and found its expression in statements like the following: 'We have no quarrel with the German people as a whole but only with Hitler and his regime'. Even today this differentiation is from time to time recognized by speakers of the government as e.g. in the recent impressive debate in the House of Lords dated March 10, 1943. Further, the existence of the refugee problem and the treatment of the refugees from enemy countries as friends of the United Nations show that the consciousness of the special character of the present war has not been lost. In addition, the existence of the Fifth column in all countries proves that the present war implies a clash between two irreconcilable conceptions of life and is more than a purely imperialist war.

From this it seems to me to follow that the Churches should not identify themselves with the Unconditional Surrender policy of Casablanca, which – as it looks to me – is mere power politics and not in harmony with the decisive character of the present conflict.

Further – and this is more important – I doubt whether this policy can be justly called realistic. A realistic power policy would presuppose an agreement among the great Allied powers on the conduct of the war and on post-war policy. All these powers must univocally pursue the same political line towards the vanquished. It is true the treaty of Alliance, collaboration und mutual assistance between this country and Soviet Russia serves this purpose. Its aim is also to determine a common line of action for the allied countries in the post-war period. Indeed it is greatly to be hoped that the present conflict will produce the desired modifications in the outlook of the Allies and thus lay the foundations for a new world. We must earnestly hope that the Russia which emerges from the war will be quite different from the Russia that entered the war and that Russia will eventually be won back to the West.

On the other hand, if we wish to remain political realists we must also bear in mind the following facts: First there are the deep ideological differences which existed between the pre-war Russia and the liberal democracies and which made the Soviet system in practice more akin in its whole structure and methods to the Nazi system than to the liberal democracies. Hence the acts of aggression against Finland, Poland, Romania and the other smaller states, hence the former friendship pact with Nazi-Germany. Secondly, we must bear in mind that the Alliance of today is the result of the unprovoked aggression by Nazi-Germany and not of an agreement freely made beforehand. Thirdly, we must put forward the question why the presupposed winner of the war on the Continent should need in future to revise its political and ideological conceptions of life. Such a change would to some extent contradict historical experience, which proves that it is the vanquished and not the conqueror who has to change its principles or to undergo a revolution. The facts which lie behind the Russian Polish 'misunderstanding' show that we cannot, with justice, take for granted that a fundamental internal change has really taken place in the Russia of today.

Therefore, the thesis that the ideological cleavage between the West and the East is a pure bogey invented by the Nazis in order to split the United Nations does not seem to me well founded. This admission does not exclude the fact that the United Nations have a common vital interest which transcends the ideological divisions and is strong enough to maintain the alliance for the present time. Neither the liberal democracies nor the Soviet Union can live as long as the Nazi threat is not eliminated.[d]

Beyond that, however, their post-war aims seem to me quite different ones. This is not surprising if we keep in mind that today the old maxim, according to which the international sphere of a state does not concern third states, is no longer valid.[e] The international structure of a regime is no longer [a] matter of mere domestic policy. The traditional Non-Intervention policy of the liberal democracies, which still found its expression in the Atlantic Charter and also underlies the treaty of Alliance belongs to the old world.ᶜ In an ideological age foreign policy grows from the internal structure of a State. Nazi-, Communist-, Western Foreign Policy have different goals in view. This fundamental change in the basis of Foreign policy corresponds to the international character of the present conflict.

It follows from this that – in the same way as in the case of a victory of the Axis countries the world would become national socialist in its basic character – in the case of the victory of the United Nations the Anglo-Saxon countries, on the one hand, and Soviet-Russia, on the other hand, must pursue different political lines.ᶠ The liberal democracies must favour both in the German-occupied countries and in Central Europe a regime built on the same Christian or Christian-secularized foundations as the West itself; Russia, on the other hand, must be interested in the formation of a new communist civilisation and, therefore, favour a regime based on radical-Marxist and anti-Western lines.ᶜ

(In passing, when I use, in this connection, the conception West and Western regime I do not mean herewith, by implication, a democratic-parliamentarian regime. Also an Authoritarian regime can possibly be a Western regime. To the Western group whose regimes are built on authoritarian lines there belong, for example, Yugoslavia, Greece, Portugal, Turkey, the South-American States. It is the ideological foundations of a regime which determine its character and not the constitutional organisation.ᵈ

So, for instance, no prophetic gift is needed to predict that after a victory of the United Nations the regime in Central Europe will take on an authoritarian character. It will not be possible for Germany and the other Central-European States to return to the liberal status quo. No other regime will be able to secure normal conditions of life there. The decisive question is only whether it will be possible to maintain behind such a regime a Christian and Western spirit).ᵍ

The interesting point, in the connection before us, is that the Western countries have not drawn the conclusions from this state of affairs. As we have seen, they conduct, on the whole their post-war policy today on the traditional lines of national power politics. This is, above all, due to the fact that people widely think that the ideology and practice of National Socialism are based on specific German thought and inherent traits of the German soul and that, therefore, National Socialism is a typical phenomenon that could not have grown on other soil.ᵈ

The Russians, on the other hand, have adapted their post-war policy to the ideological character of the present war.ʰ Their whole policy against Germany is based on the fundamental differentiation between Hitlerite-Germany and Germany. In all leading proclamations, especially in the most important statements made by Stalin himself, it has been made perfectly clear that it 'is ridiculous to identify the Hitler clique with the German people or the German State'. This line has been followed up by Stalin ever since the beginning of the German Russian war (see the quotations in *The Fortnightly* 1942, p. 257, and *Parl. Debates* House of Lords, vol. 126, col. 535seq.). The latest order of the day by Stalin dated May 1, 1943 has caused many circles to believe that Stalin made the Casablanca formula his own. 'Is it not quite clear,' says Stalin, 'that only the full rout of the Hitlerite Army and the unconditional surrender of Hitlerite Germany can bring peace to Europe?' In fact, if one puts this passage in the full text of the

Order of the day, which continually refers to the 'Hitlerite Fascist Camp', the 'German Fascists', the 'Hitlerite Germany' etc. one notices that the formula used fits in well. There is no change in the traditional Soviet Policy. Whether one speaks of the complete destruction of Hitlerite-Germany or of its unconditional surrender it does not matter. The point is that in Casablanca the leaders of the liberal Democracies did not qualify their statement in the same way as Stalin did. They had the unconditional surrender of Germany herself in mind. Just this makes all the difference.[j]

From this it follows that the Russians would come to an understanding with Germany which had gone through a Red revolution. It is this basic attitude which also explains why the Russians have not pledged themselves to pursue a policy of repression or national humiliation towards Germany. The Russian policy does not make it necessary to impose on the enemy moral disqualifications, controls over German territory and industry, unilateral disarmament etc., to occupy Germany and to establish special bodies appointed to govern Germany after the collapse. They use power and force consciously as means for securing their ideology. They realize that a common faith and common standards and convictions are more important than all the various safeguards based on force and power.[k] They know that they would be protected from a new attack by Germany if Germany became truly communist in her outlook and a new international order based on common feeling of the communist creed were created. One must admit that this policy reveals a great realism, which is all the more amazing as the Soviet Union has had to bear greater burdens and sacrifices than the liberal democracies. I call this policy realistic because it is adapted to the ideological age in which we live and to the special international character of the war in which this age has found its expression. ᶜAnd I venture to say thatᶜ The liberal democracies have not reached in the same degree such a realistically minded attitude; for a mere power policy can only claim to be realistic in the age of the national State where the power of the sovereign state is the supreme law in international life.

If this analysis is correct then we must assume that the Russian post-war policy has greater chances of being realized than that of the West, unless the liberal Democracies are prepared to change their official policy in time and to take those lines which were advocated at greater length by the Bishop of Chichester and others in the memorable debate in the House of Lords already mentioned.

That even in this case the position of the Western countries will more difficult than that of the Russians can be seen from the fact that the dynamic of the political situation in Germany will automatically favour an Eastern development. And this for following reasons:

In what position will Germany find herself after the destruction of her present regime? No matter, whether Germany will be occupied or not, whether a defeated Nazi-Germany will be shattered by a revolution (as I suppose it will) or not, it seems certain that, in any case, no future regime in Germany will be able to stand without support from outside. A defeated Nazi-Germany will have no other choice than that between the East and West. Only the principles and values of either of these worlds can provide the political ethos for the future Germany. A Western regime in a post-war Germany, no matter whether this be authoritarian or parliamentarian, or conservative, liberal or socialist, would only be able to establish itself if this regime could get the help of the Anglo-Saxon countries, and a communist Germany must appeal to the Soviet Union for help.

Now, we must not forget that before the Nazi regime there were more than six millions communists in Germany. Further, those millions who are organized today in the Nazi party and its various auxiliary organisations will not easily find their way back to a way of life which is familiar in the Western. Their despair and disillusionment will probably lead them to express communist sympathies, unless the revised Christian faith appeals to them.[1]

In addition, we must not forget that those strata of society who are looking to the West are politically in a more difficult position than the Communists. For those strata are greatly weakened, physically and spiritually, by their indirect responsibility for having not prevented the Nazis from seizing power. For this reason e.g. the former liberal-minded workers who were organized in the Socialist party (that was the organisation which in its whole structure corresponded to the English Labour party) will certainly not be prepared to revive their experience under the Weimar Constitution. They will take the radical-Marxist lines unless it will be possible to create new religious bonds with the working people. The communists, on the other hand, can claim never to have formed a government in the Reich and justly disclaim, therefore, the responsibility for the crimes of the Nazis.[j]

These difficulties of consolidating a Western regime in Germany are increased by the fact that the Marxist Left wing circles in the Anglo-Saxon countries hold the view that Nazism is but the expression of capitalist class-rule, which uses the military cast to carry out its imperialist and expansionist plans at the expense of the Lower classes. They think, therefore, that if the capitalists, squires, the Junkers and the military cast could be eliminated a democratic-socialist regime on a liberal basis could be established. But this is an illusion For National Socialism is anti-capitalistic in its basic structure.[k] It has not maintained the capitalist system in its traditional form but has abolished private initiative and the free enterprise system as thoroughly as Communism although for technical reasons it has maintained private property and profits for the time being. It is, therefore, wrong to see in National Socialism an exclusive product of the upper classes. In truth, National Socialism is a mass-movement (especially of the lower middle classes) and part of a general social revolution. (In passing, this does not justify Vansittart's thesis of the specific German character of the national socialist revolution, as in other countries the same revolutionary events have led to similar results).[l]

Finally, as a result of the Russian ideological post-war policy we must bear in mind that a future communist regime in Germany can offer the German people considerable political gains. By becoming communist Germany would evade the worst national humiliations (such as occupation, dismemberment, possibly even disarmament). In other words, Germany could get a better peace from Russia than from the Anglo-Saxon countries. It is true that Art. 11 par. 2 of the Alliance forbids separate peace talks with any German government that does not clearly renounce all aggressive intentions. But a communist regime, once established in Germany, will not entertain aggressive intentions, from the Russian point of view.[c] And what will happen if the Democracies hold another view in this matter is not settled in the Treaty.

For all the reasons stated Russia has no need to interfere in German internal affairs because – as things stand – the natural trend of development will favour the formation of an anti-Christian and anti-Western block in Central Europe. Nor will the direction of this development be materially affected by the fact that at the end of this war the balance of power may stand in favour of the liberal democracies which may be in a position of a giving power and not of a receiving power like Russia and the Continental States. For in an ideological age mere power politics cannot finally determine the prevailing ideological outlook on the Continent.

As the Churches must do everything in their power to prevent this development and, therefore, to win Germany back to the West they must (in addition to what I have tried to point out above) help the liberal democracies to realize that even after the complete destruction of the Hitlerite regime – as long as the ideological differences between West and East are not truly bridged – Germany will have to play an important task on the European Continent, as its fate will decisively determine the solution of the European problem.

It is, therefore, the task of the Churches to make clear that the Alliance with Russia does not relieve the democracies from their responsibility of pursuing a constructive policy towards Germany, i.e. a policy which is based on the fact that we live in a decisively ideological age and that, therefore, mere power politics no longer counts in the same way as in former times.[c] Such a constructive policy presupposes that the differentiation between the Nazi regime and the German people should not only occasionally be made for certain political purposes but should become the basis of the official policy of the liberal democracies. The Churches should urge that the liberal democracies take the same lines towards Germany as Soviet Russia (complete destruction of Hitlerite Germany, and of the Hitlerite Army, unconditional surrender of Hitlerite Germany etc.) and to treat those in Germany who look for salvation, liberation and guidance to the West in the same way as Russia would treat a communist Germany.[b] They should give those Western-minded forces the chance of getting a more or less tolerable peace i.e. a peace which must not imply destruction or Eastern communism and beyond that gives them all possible help in re-establishing order and preventing anarchy and mob-rule in Germany.[b] Only if these forces are given a politically realistic and tolerable alternative will it be possible to avoid that the anti-Nazi strata in Germany (especially in the Churches that in truth are the 5th column of the liberal Democracies in Germany) will be forged – against their will – for pure reasons of existence into a regime which they detest. Even such a regime must seem to them better than unconditional surrender in the sense of Casablanca, which – considering the Nazi propaganda and the ambiguity of proclaimed general principles – they must think is equivalent to destruction. Only thus will it be possible to await revolutionary events in Germany and to prevent a senseless prolongation of the war and all its sufferings.[l]

I think the Churches have a special right to take this political line. We have spoken of the improbability of restoring the former liberal political, economic, and cultural system in Germany. There is actually only one hope. After all we know about the courageous stand of the Catholic and Confessional Church in Germany (and the other evangelical Churches in German occupied Europe) the Nazi regime and the present war have resulted in an awakening of the consciences and a revival of the Christian faith on the Continent.ᶜ It may be difficult to judge, from this country, how deep the change in the fundamental outlook is. But, on the whole, we may consider the situation not without a certain amount of optimism. Even people who have dissociated themselves from the many divisions of the bourgeois society and even from organized Church life may find their way back to the only power which has withstood tyranny, can provide a firm spiritual basis for a new international order, can vitalize the humanitarian values of Liberalism which without the fire of Christianity has lost its ground today and can at the same time overcome the danger from the East.ᶜ

Finally, a word must be said on the German army. For it is the German army which has to a growing extent caused the liberal democracies to think that this war must be finished in the traditional terms of power politics.ᶜ The thesis is that the army is the root of all evil and the trouble-maker in the last hundred years. It is argued that the army is also responsible for the doings of the national socialist regime as without the help of the army the regime could not have established itself and [that] the spiritual equipment of the army is not basically different from the Nazi-ideology. Therefore, it is said, the most important aim of the United Nations must be to enforce a complete disarmament of the Axis Powers, especially Germany, as that security which will safeguard the world from the repetition of the happenings of today cannot be obtained in any other way.

From a Christian point of view, nobody will raise his voice against the disarmament of nations and especially of nations which are responsible for the present state of affairs. But the Churches will also be realistic enough to bear in mind that history has taught us that a permanent unilateral disarmament will never guarantee that peace the world needs and reconcile the nations with each other.ᶜ The Churches should, therefore, point out that, in the long run, the question of disarmament can be satisfactorily settled only if, as the Pope said, a 'mutually agreed, organic and progressive disarmament, spiritual as well as material' can be secured in future and that such a disarmament presupposes an underlying common spirit. The Churches, therefore, should try to include the whole question in a wider program which, in the course of time, would to a certain extent give security to all nations.ᶜ

Apart from these long-term considerations there are others which should be borne in mind now. An army even if it has like the German army a special character and spirit cannot exercise the same functions in an ideological age as in the age of the national State. The wars, which were conducted by Germany and Italy in the 19th and beginning of the 20th century were national wars. They resulted from the fact that these countries arrived very late on the world stage as world powers and did not find their national unity until the middle of the last century, that is to say at a time when the Western powers had not only consolidated their national unity but had also satisfied their claims as Great Powers.ᶜ At that time the army could play a decisive part also in the political sphere. But this is no longer possible in an ideological age. Today in modern mass society the army is irrevocably placed in the position of a servant and not of a master.ᶜ The happenings in Russia, Nazi-Germany and Italy confirm this fully. In all these states the army is no longer an independent political and spiritual factor.ʰ It is at the disposal of totalitarian leaders. Where the attempt has been made to interfere with the political claim of the totalitarian regime it has met with complete disaster as, for instance, is shown by the fate of the Generals von Schleicher, von Bredow and Fritsch.[3]

The only excuse the German Army can make for its subservice to the Nazi regime is the fact that there was actually behind the specific military ideology no political, social and spiritual conception of life which could attract the minds of the masses and permeate them with a new spirit. At bottom, the army is only a gigantic technical instrument. In so far, it is true, its significance is eminent and its power immense. But the point is, it cannot of itself provide the basis for a new order of a planned society. It has no longer a spiritual or political driving power of its own.[k]

Therefore, when the liberal democracies lay the responsibility for the happenings of today on the shoulders of the army they miscalculate the proper function an army can exercise, und the present circumstances, [a]in modern mass society in an ideological age.[a]

In addition, if the destruction of the German army is put so strongly in the foreground of the discussion as is the case today in the Anglo-Saxon countries a collapse of the Hitler regime from within cannot be expected.[c] For the German Wehrmacht is the only power factor which is not fully Nazified and includes strong anti-Nazi forces. That even the Nazis do not consider the Wehrmacht reliable follows from the strengthened position which the Waffen S.S. has recently received. Originally this troop had only symbolic significance, but six months ago it was announced that they had reached a numerical strength of over 1 million men (cf. Hitler and the Wehrmacht, in: *The Times*, dated December, 14, 1942). It is probable that this number has considerably increased in the meantime. These men as is generally known form the backbone of the Nazi-regime. They will stand by Hitler and his regime fighting with the tenacity of the best German troops and defending the system to the death.

It is obvious that, under these circumstances, it is only the Wehrmacht which can act against the regime. But how is this possible if the Western countries again and again proclaim as their first war-aim the destruction of the army and its unconditional surrender? Is it logical, from the point of view of the Western countries, on the one hand, to call the German people to rise against their oppressors and, on the other hand, to take away from them the arms without which they cannot act?[g]

The Russians pursue also in this matter a more realistic policy. If they speak of the destruction, the annihilation and unconditional surrender of the army they always add the epithet 'Hitlerite'. If the Hitlerite Army were substituted by the Red Army I do not doubt that the Russians would not raise any objection against these 'armed forces'. Implicitly this is proved by Mr Stalin's speech of November 6, 1942 in which he said that it was not Russia's aim to destroy all German armed forces but that the Hitlerite army should and would be destroyed.

The situation becomes still more complicated by the fact that, from the Russian point of view, the destruction of the Hitlerite Army must imply not only the destruction of the 'Hitlerites' but also of those Western-minded army circles, from which, according to the Marxist-Soviet view, Nazism, has grown.[e] It seems, therefore, as if in so far a full agreement exists between the Western powers and the Soviet Union. But the point is that this policy is logical only from the Eastern and not the Western point of view. For the Russians – unlike the Western countries – have probably no 'Allies' in the higher ranks of the Army.[c] Therefore, it seems to be plausible that the Russians demand the destruction of the 'clique' as a whole. But the position of the Western countries is a quite different one. They cannot be interested as the Russians are in the destruction of those probably powerful elements in the army which want a regime in harmony with Western and Christian principles and values. I think the West can do without them only if the hope of overthrowing the Nazi regime from within is given up and the war be finished as a national war and not an ideological one.[c] To avoid this the Churches should say that they include among the 'Allies' also those armed forces which would be prepared to fight side by side with the liberal democracies to overcome the present regime in Germany (including the Hitlerite Army) and all that the regime stands for. Such a differentiating policy seems to be more realistic and also diplomatic as it will not be difficult after the collapse of the Nazis to secure in practice the desired full disarmament – all the more, as probably the Germans themselves will be willing to disarm – even if only to prove their good will and changed attitude.[m]

It may be objected [c]against this analysis[c] that by stressing this ideological antagonism between West and East the Nazis may draw advantage from it. We know how strongly the Nazis endeavour to make capital out of it. But I think this point can hardly invalidate our argument, especially if we add that if Communism and National Socialism were actually the only alternative before we should prefer Communism. But this cannot prevent us from stating that the secular totalitarianism on the communist basis in its present form is reconcilable neither with the Western way of life nor with Christianity. National Socialism seems to be wrong not so much stressing the ideological cleavage between West and East as in stressing that National Socialism is the only alternative to Bolshevism. Today it is generally said that Bolshevism is a Nazi bogey. The truth lays just the other way round. Not Bolshevism but the statement that Nazism is the only alternative to Bolshevism is the bogey the Nazis have invented to split the United Nations, to maintain the Nazi regime and to come to a compromised peace. If the Churches press the liberal democracies to do everything in their power to pursue that constructive policy [which] we have inadequately tried to sketch the incorrectness of the second part of the Nazi statement will be proved.

The reasons why up-to-now the liberal democracies have not taken this line are manifold: They are partly due to the duration of the war and the strain it implies, partly to a miscalculation of the social and spiritual driving forces behind Nazism and of the functions an army has exercised in a totalitarian mass society, partly to certain forces which are operative in the Anglo-Saxon countries themselves. To illustrate this last point; It may be, for instance, that the actual and potential fascist or national socialist circles in the Anglo-Saxon countries are so strong that it seems inexpedient to admit by implication the possibility of a Red Continent.[h] These circles may then press the government – in order to avoid this possibility – to conclude a compromised peace with the Nazis and thus to lose the war. Or it may be that the nationalist circles may be unwilling to face the 'other Germany' with which the Anglo-Saxon countries could possibly act together in order to be able to finish this war in terms of mere national power politics, even although by such a policy the war may be senselessly prolonged.[h]

If the Churches wish to justify their claim to political leadership they will have all this in mind. They will also have to differentiate carefully between the advice offered them by people who are well informed about the inside-position in Germany, especially the refugees. Although these are all united in the desire to overthrow the Nazi regime their individual aims are quite different.ʰ There are among them many who after their experiences wholeheartedly agree with those who see in the present war the expression of innate German wickedness and want to finish the present conflict in a spirit of hatred and revenge and to apply the specific means of national power policy. Further there are others – and their number is also considerable – who stress with good reasons the necessity to differentiate between Nazi-Germany and the German people but want a radical Marxist Germany realizing that in a defeated Nazi Germany no room will remain for the traditional liberal system of the West, which they themselves dislike. They welcome the present-day policy of the Western countries because they think that, in the long run, this policy will not succeed and favour, therefore, that political development they have in mind. And finally there is that numerically limited group, which realizes that whatever the shape the new regime in Germany may assume it is the spirit behind it which is decisive and that this spirit must be Christian in its basic character if destruction and anarchy and the danger of a formation of an anti-Christian and anti-Western block on the Continent be avoided.ᵉ They advocate a policy, which – although different from that officially pursued today in the Western countries – seems to me constructive and realistic in character.

Not until Germany (in connection with Russia) is finally prevented from forming the nucleus of an anti-Western block can the task of the re-Christianisation of a victorious Russia be undertaken with any chance of success.ᶜ In recent times it has been frequently stated that the technical civilisation of today has created among the nations an independence which inextricably binds them together and that the irresistible trend of history points also to a spiritual unification of the world. This is indeed true. As President Roosevelt recently said: 'The whole world in one neighbourhood'. That the attempt could be made to unify Europe and the world by mobilizing the evil and bestial instincts and forces in man and society is, at bottom, due to our own failure. As has been remarked: 'Because we failed to unite Europe by reason Hitler is uniting it by force and power'. Indeed there seems to me no doubt: if humanity is to survive Europe and the world must become a unity also in a spiritual sense. Not until this spiritual unity is established is a true international order possible, can international security be guaranteed and can the ideal of a United States of Europe be realized. International institutions based on mere power and without a spiritual vision will never pacify the world. Therefore, in the end the question whether modern secular totalitarianism or Christian totalitarianism, East or West will determine the political shape of the world must be decided. Without a decision in this respect the world cannot find the spiritual unity it urgently needs. From this point of view, the struggle for the soul of Germany is the first step towards a political re-Christianisation of Europe and the world.ᶜ

¹ Bell evidently studied the following exposé very intensively as the marks in the margin demonstrate:
   ᵃ This alternative is marked by a black line in the margin.
   ᵇ The first half of the sentence is marked by a black line in the margin.
   ᶜ The sentence is marked by a black line in the margin.
   ᵈ The last two sentences are marked, in part, by two black lines in the margin.
   ᵉ The second half of the sentence is marked by a black line in the margin.
   ᶠ The second half of the sentence is marked by a black line and a black cross in the margin.

g The whole paragraph is marked by a black line and two black crosses in the margin.
h The sentence is marked by a black cross in the margin.
k The last four sentences are marked by a black line in the margin.
l The last three sentences are marked by a black line in the margin.
m The last two sentences are marked by a black line in the margin.
n The first half of the sentence is marked by a double black line in the margin.

2 Handwritten: instead of the United Nations.
3 Kurt von Schleicher (1882–1934), infantry general and politician, and Ferdinand Eduard von Bredow (1884–1934), major general and deputy defence minister in Schleicher's cabinet, December 1932 to January 1933, were murdered by SS men during the so-called Night of the Long Knives on 30 June 1934. On 5 February 1938 Senior General Werner Freiherr von Fritsch (1880–1939) had been relieved of his duties as supreme commander of the army (1936–8) in light of a campaign of slander by the Gestapo leaving Hitler free to appoint a new, supportive leadership.

Bell to Leibholz, 17 May 1943, BA, N 1334 (typewritten); Bell Papers 40, fol. 185 (carbon)

My dear Leibholz,

I am extremely grateful to you for your exposé, which reached Chichester on Friday. I have read it with the keenest interest, and shall study it very carefully. The point you make about the distinction between Hitlerite Germany and the other Germany must be pressed home, with all its implications. And at the same time, somehow or other security must be taken that neither Germany nor any other European power has the chance, so far as human foresight can secure it, of provoking another world war.

I do not think what you describe as the unconditional surrender policy of Casablanca meant more than the unconditional surrender of the army, from the military point of view; in other words, the ᵃAlliedᵃ Generals would make no terms as to the conditions of the ᵃEnemyᵃ army's surrender. They must simply lay down arms and leave themselves prisoners, from the military point of view, in the hands of the Allied Forces. I do not think there is any further implication of a political kind.

This is just a preliminary note to express my very great gratitude.

Yours ever,

Leibholz to Bell, 20 May 1943, Bell Papers 40, fol. 185 (typewritten); BA, N 1334 (copy)

My Lordbishop,

Many thanks for your letter. I am very glad that you think that we have not to take the unconditional surrender policy of Casablanca too seriously and that its significance is limited to the military issues. If I had gained another impression it was because the political (and not military) leaders of the liberal Democracies have repeatedly demanded since Casablanca the unconditional surrender of Germany (and not like Stalin of Hitlerite Germany). Even at the time of the debate in the Lords Mr Eden had pressed home this policy with all vigour in the United States and had not mitigated this statement by the reservations made by the speaker of the government in the Lords. If 'Casablanca' is not to be interpreted in political terms I do not quite see why this point, which seems to me, from a military point of view, a matter of course, plays such a great part in the official policy of today. Especially I am afraid the Germans, Italians etc. will understand 'Casablanca' in political terms as they will and perhaps must (in view of the Goebbels propaganda) combine 'Casablanca' with that trend of public opinion which tends strongly to favour a pure power policy (cfol. the last statement signed by Members of the Commons and Lords published in *The Times* of the 17th of May). How inadequate the Casablanca formula is can, in my view, be seen today at the hand of its implications with regard to Italy.[1] Today people begin to feel that politically something more must be done than to demand unconditional surrender in order to make this formula more attractive to the Italian people. Is it not strange to see how much time it has taken to discover this?

I quite agree that there must be some guarantees against a renewed attack by Germany. But I think that such a security can only be firmly built on a common spiritual basis. If this is lacking all kind of organised power, whatever its special form, I am afraid will fail in the end. If we agree that power cannot provide a substitute for the Spirit even in the Political sphere that means that our common efforts can only then be successful if either Russia or Germany will be won back to the West. And as I personally think that a victorious Russia has no need to revise its ideological foundations the attempt at least should be made with a defeated Anti-Nazi-Germany. This seems to me to be the point. As I think security can be attained only under this condition I feel in some way that the task of sketching a security scheme of which we have so many should not be made until at least an agreement on the spiritual basis of the future security system has been reached and this basis has actually been secured. Otherwise I feel our whole work hangs in the air.

Yours ever,

[1] On 13 May the German and Italian forces had capitulated in Tunisia. On 10 July Allied forces would land in Sicily.

Leibholz to Bell, 10 June 1943, Bell Papers 40, fol. 187 (typewritten); BA, N 1334 (copy)

p.c. sent. 15.6.43. How many words?

My Lordbishop,

Please forgive me for approaching you in the following matter:

I do not know whether you remember, my Lordbishop, that I tried to deal with the question of the relationship between Christianity and Justice and Law in an article published in the *Dublin Review* a few months ago.[1] I have been asked on various occasions whether it would not be possible to publish the article separately in order to give it a wider circulation. I have thought this suggestion over for some time and have come to the conclusion that it might perhaps be a good idea to enlarge the essay in various directions and then to publish it in a book-form.

Just at the present time it seems to me important to make the attempt to bridge the gap which exists today between Theology and Jurisprudence and to make clear why the basic position secular Jurisprudence has taken up in the last century must be abandoned. If I am not mistaken, lawyers, on the whole, are not aware of the urgency of the task of basing the whole framework of Jurisprudence again on religion. From the theological point of view, much of value has already been said, if I think of your book and of what Quick and Niebuhr have written.[2] On the other hand, I think it may perhaps be worthwhile to supplement these expositions, from other points of view. Especially I think in this connection to take into consideration the relationship between the fundamental principles of Christian Natural Law, on the one hand, and Justice, Law and Politics, on the other hand. I think that such a more detailed analysis would be also of practical weight in the national and international field, especially if it were possible at the same time to bring into a more systematic cohesion the various statements made by the Pope and the various Churches here and on the Continent during the last few years.

I have already made some preparatory work in this direction and think I could finish what I have in mind in a short time. On the other hand, I think it is sensible to go on with this work now only if in spite of the present difficulties a publisher were, on principle, prepared to bring it out. I learn that the S.C.M. Press made an arrangement with another writer for a brief work on the subject of Natural Law some time ago and that they cannot take further obligations.[3] Nor do I know whether it would be wise to publish the book there as I think it should appeal to a wider circle of readers. I have thought of the Centenary Press (in connection with the *Christian Challenge* Series) or of the Oxford Press as a suitable publisher. But I do not know what you, my Lordbishop, think about the whole idea. If it should be sympathetic to you I should be most grateful to you if you would be kind enough to write to a publisher who you trust would be possibly interested in such an undertaking. I know this would carry much greater weight than if I try to approach a publisher directly. It would be a great help.

I wonder if, in the meantime, you, my Lordbishop, have sent on your paper to America.

I am greatly touched by the tragic death of Israel.[4] He was a school-fellow of mine for 10 years. Unfortunately, I never met him in this country. We are also alarmed that we have not received a reply from Switzerland. I hope that technical difficulties explain the silence of Visser 't Hooft and Sutz. Perhaps our telegram has not reached them.

With all good wishes to you and Mrs Bell

Yours ever,

P.S. I am enclosing a copy of my article in case you would like to refer to it when writing.

---

[1] See Leibholz to Bell, 16 December 1942; Leibholz, 'The Foundation of Justice and Law in the Light of the Present European Crisis', reprinted in *Politics and Law*, pp. 253–70.
[2] See Bell, *Christianity and World Order*; Oliver Quick, *Christianity and Justice* (London, 1940); Reinhold Niebuhr, *The Nature and Destiny of Man. A Christian Interpretation* (London, 1941).
[3] Untraced.
[4] In April 1943 Wilfrid Israel investigated the situation of Jews in Portugal and Spain. He also distributed certificates of entry to British-ruled Palestine and planned the rescue of Jewish children from Vichy France. Flying back from Lisbon to London his airplane was shot down by a German air force squadron on 1 June.

Bell to Leibholz, 12 June 1943, BA, N 1334 (handwritten)

Israel's death is a great blow. I knew him well – and was in touch with him re. Lisbon and refugees.

My dear Leibholz,

Very many thanks. I shall write to Sir Humphrey Milford and see if I can interest him and the Oxford Press in such a book.[1]

I have completed my memo. for USA, and enclose a copy. Your thoughts and exposé were a great help. I hope my reflections will commend themselves to you. I worked hard at them! and I wonder *how* they will be received at the Dulles conference in Princeton. I fear not all my friends in this country would approve.

I have heard nothing from 't Hooft – but I hope no news is good news, so far as Dietrich is concerned.

F. A. Voigt[2] told me very great stories of Russia's dealing with Poles this week. You should read his article in June *Nineteenth Century*.

Yours ever with all remembrances to your wife & the girls

Your,

---

[1] See Bell to Milford, 17 July 1943, Bell Papers 40, fol. 195.
[2] Frederick Augustus (Frank) Voigt (1892–1957), British journalist and author of German descent; foreign correspondent of the *Manchester Guardian* in Berlin 1920–33. Back in London he became the newspaper's diplomatic correspondent. In 1938–46 Voigt was editor of the periodical *The Nineteenth Century and After*. His assessment of the totalitarian dictatorships, *Unto Caesar*, was published in 1938 and this book marked a shift in Voigt's political thinking. In 1940 he joined the Department of Propaganda in Enemy Countries, where he worked as German advisor to the British psychological warfare department.

Bell, Memorandum on the future in Europe, BA, N 1334 (carbon)

Private:

For the International Round Table at Princeton Inn, U.S.A.
July 8 – 11, 1943
(Commission to study the Bases of a Just and Durable Peace)
THE FUTURE IN EUROPE
GERMANY
Memorandum by the Bishop of Chichester

There are three types of view which command varying degrees of support as to the right policy to be adopted by the United Nations towards a defeated Germany.

1. The view of those who, from fear of Russia, or desire of profit through trade, favour a settlement which would leave Germany still moderately strong both in armed power and in economic resources. (*The policy of appeasement*)
2. The view of those who insist on the complete humiliation and repression of Germany, including permanent unilateral disarmament, occupation for an infinite period, dismemberment, and control of education, wireless, printing, etc. (*The policy of repression*)

3. The view of those who, while whole-hearted in their determination to end the whole Hitlerite system and military machine, distinguish between those who direct the Hitlerite system, with the Hitlerite army, and those in Germany who are the victims or its adversaries. (*The policy of discrimination*)

The Policy of Appeasement.

With regard to those holding the first of these views, it is right to recognise that many of them are certainly impressed with the necessity of seeing Europe as a whole, a point of cardinal importance for the future: though Europe must be viewed also in relation to other continents. But, apart from other considerations, the lack of security both as to the character of the future government and as to the control of armaments is a fatal objection to any policy proceeding on these lines.

The Policy of Repression.

This policy is pressed with great vigour by certain Continental powers amongst the United Nations, as well as by a strong group in other countries, such as the Post-war Policy group of members of both Houses of Parliament, of which Sir John Wardlaw-Milne[1] is Chairman. It is perfectly intelligible that those who, like the Poles, the Czechs, the Serbs and many more, have suffered such cruelty from the Nazis, should desire the Nazis to suffer most severely in return. But a determination to exact vengeance can only lead to an equal determination on the enemy's part to repay in a similar kind, however long it may be necessary to wait for the opportunity. In this way new Hitlers would be created. There must be safeguards against further aggression by a foe that has proved himself so ruthless. But long as the process of moral and spiritual conversion may be, it has got somehow to be attempted; for it is a change of spirit that is the decisive factor. In any case, a policy of repression can only deal with the surface of the whole problem. What is really required is a better order in Europe. A system which aims at securing just relationships, difficult as it is, can be the only sure foundation of peace. Should it not therefore be our principal aim to find out, and if possible establish, the conditions of such a true European (and world) order? It seems also relevant to ask whether in any case a policy of repression, with its various consequences of large allied occupying armies, etc., can be permanently supported by the United Nations, and particularly by U.S.A. and Great Britain.

The Policy of Discrimination.

If both the policy of appeasement and the policy of repression for different reasons would fail to give the long-range peace security in Europe, which is our aim, what can be said of the policy of discrimination?

I do not think it can be stated too emphatically that the war in which we are engaged is an ideological war – with all its consequences. It is not primarily a war of the United Nations against the Axis Nations, as antagonistic armed powers. It is a war of Democracy against Fascism. The policy of appeasement ignores this fact, and is really concerned with the balance of powers. The policy of repression similarly ignores it, and harks back the old conception of power politics. After all, in the case of economic resources, the real question is not whether particular nations or parties are to have the dominating control, but how these resources can be best used for the service of the community of nations. Even with regard to the armed forces, the real question is, to what use are they put? For the United Nations to make the primary aim of a peace settlement after victory over Germany the complete suppression of German commerce in the interests of the United Nations, and the dismemberment of the German Reich in the same interests, would mean the emergence on the Allied side of the very power politics which are the god of the Nazis.

Under the Nazi regime Germany has been a terrific military power. The threat which such a gigantic military power offers to the peace of the world cannot be tolerated. Every practicable step must therefore be taken to secure that the renewal of such a situation is impossible, so far as man can achieve this. For such a purpose the policy of discrimination must be applied in different fields, (1) military, and (2) economic and political.

1. *Military*. On November 6th, 1942 Stalin made an important distinction when he said that 'It is not our aim to destroy all organised military forces in Germany ... but Hitler's army can and should be destroyed.' The whole of the Hitlerite S.S. and S.A., and other satellites, who have now permeated all ranks of the German army, must be brought to an end. It is almost certain that after Germany's defeat big forces of this 'Hitler's army' will be fighting for their lives in different parts of Germany against the Allies, and against anti-Nazi Germans. But apart from 'Hitler's army' (in this sense), there is the considerable body of 'organised military forces' with which the Allies would have to reckon. Here there are, I suggest, two stages to be considered:

(i) *The Immediate Future*.

Following the surrender of the Nazis, in view of the chaotic conditions likely to obtain both in Germany and in the occupied countries, it would be justifiable in my opinion to make it plain that while a large part of the total German army must be completely disarmed, the Allies are willing to use those armed forces of the German Reich which are prepared to side with the Allied democratic powers, as a part of the forces required for maintaining order in Europe in the immediate crisis of the interim period – *always provided that those forces are under Allied command, and that any German officers used by the Allied command satisfy that command of their reliability.*

(ii) *The Treaty of Peace*.

In a large country situated as Germany is situated psychological factors at least will require that Germany has adequate protection against an attack upon itself – an attack, which it may be all the more likely to fear in view of the terrible cruelties which other countries have suffered from the Nazis. It is impossible to contemplate in any near future the toleration of an *independent* German army, even for defensive purposes inside Germany. But in my judgement some form of international protection will be required; and for this purpose a small 'organised military force', forming part of an international military force, might properly be permitted. If such a plan were carried out, I believe that, subject to whole-hearted efforts being made to grapple with the general economic problem of Europe, other nations would be more adequately secured from future aggression by Germany than by a complete and permanent prohibition of any German army, navy, air force, civil aviation or aircraft industry. The whole question of international control of civil aviation and the aircraft industry in all countries, as well as of transport and roads in all countries, has in this connection to be most carefully considered. I also believe that in the long run the question of disarmament can only be satisfactorily settled if, as the Pope has said, 'a mutually agreed, organic and progressive disarmament, spiritual was well as material' can be secured in future, and that such a disarmament presupposes an underlying common spirit.

2. *Economic and Political*. It is impossible to condemn too severely the fearfulness of the cruelties wrought on the suffering occupied countries and upon the Jews by the Nazis. All the territories and possessions that can be restored must be restored to their rightful owners, both nations and individuals. The dead cannot be restored to life, nor can those who have lost all receive it back again; nothing can repair the unspeakable injury done. The Nazi horrors and brutalities cry out to heaven, and no earthly compensation or comfort can avail for the victims. Whichever way we look we are conscious that men have been brought down to the very depths; and it is only out of the depths (*de profundis*) that we can turn to the future. Yet we must turn to the future, and try to see how a beginning in renewal can be made. The German nation as a whole has been caught by the terrible evil of Hitlerism. Although Hitler and his partners are the main criminals, Germans generally have to bear responsibility for their surrender to the evil. There are other factors outside Germany operating in different ways and at different times – things done, and things left undone by the victorious powers during this 20-years crisis among them –, which must be taken into account when the full history of these 30 years is written. But Hitler and Himmler and the rest, who are not the only portents but also figures of demonic and anti-theistic power, must at all costs be deprived of all possibility of doing further injury to mankind. There still remains, nevertheless, whatever the volume of their responsibility, the great bulk of the Germans. Here again Stalin made the distinction, in the speech of November 6th, 1942 already referred to, when he said 'We have no such aim as to destroy Germany ... but the Hitlerite State can and should be destroyed.'

Stalin is a realist. It will be essential for him to find a *modus vivendi* with a defeated Germany, and such a *modus vivendi* cannot consist of trying to treat the sixty or seventy million Germans in the heart of Europe as outcasts. It is equally necessary for the other United Nations to be realists. It would be wise statesmanship not to try to keep Germany suppressed, because that would lead to an accumulation of bottled-up pressure; but to help her maintain a high standard of living through the use of her domestic resources, and international trade. This means a combination of all United Nations, especially America, Russia and Britain, for the purpose of giving a defeated Germany a stake in the peace; and with that end in view, the working out in a common partnership between the United Nations of a genuine plan for the establishment of a family of nations, in which Germany has neither more nor less than her share, and all the other nations, including those with a lower standard of living at the present time, have neither more nor less than theirs, as required for giving individuals in all the countries of the world enough food to eat, enough shelter to live under, enough warmth to heat themselves, and enough work to do.

All this has a very important bearing on our attitude to certain proposals for a rigorous treatment of all Germans. Thus, while Germany must be required to abandon all the territory which it has seized, the dismemberment of Germany must be ruled out by the considerations stated above. And while boundaries might be reconsidered, any large political reorganisation of the whole German Reich for example on a federal basis can only be satisfactorily accomplished by consent. Again, while those guilty of war crimes should be brought before properly appointed tribunals, and loot should in all possible cases be restored, or compensation given where restoration is not possible, it would not be consistent with the considerations advanced above that large scale reparations or indemnities should be imposed on the nation as a whole. Further, while every precaution should be taken to secure that the training of youth should be entrusted to reliable teachers throughout the educational system, the responsibility for the working out of re-education should be definitely entrusted to German authorities.

That there is a faith more powerful than the Nazi faith, the strong stand taken against the Nazis before and during the war by the Confessional Church and the Catholic Church in Germany makes plain. There are also teachers and professors, dismissed by the Nazis from Universities and schools, who are ready to give their aid. Beyond all doubt it is the help of such teachers and professors, and of the leaders of the Confessional Church and of the Catholic Church, which should be invoked and encouraged by the liberators of Germany in the vital task of the moral and spiritual renewal of the German nation, and especially of German youth.

SUMMARY

To sum up, the view here set out of the 'Future in Europe, particularly in relation to Germany' is based on a policy of *discrimination*. The writer urges that the war is essentially an ideological war between Democracy and Fascism. He presses the great importance of drawing a sharp distinction between the Hitlerite State and the German people. He insists on the restoration of all territory and possessions which have been seized by the Nazis, and on compensation where restoration is impossible. He also affirms the necessity of the trial and punishment of all war criminals from the highest to the lowest, and of making it impossible for the principal Nazi leaders, their followers and accomplices in all ranks, to do more injury to mankind. He insist further on the complete elimination of 'Hitler's army', as well as the 'Hitlerite State and its conspirers'. He also recognises the necessity of safeguards against aggression. But he believes that these safeguards will be most effective if they are secured in co-operation between the United Nations and Germany. Thus, with regard to the immediate *military situation*, after the disarming of a large part of the German army, he advocates the occupation of Germany by allied military forces, with the assistance under allied command of such German 'organised military forces' as is prepared to side with the democratic powers, and is found reliable for that purpose. For the long-range military situation, he contemplates an international military authority controlling all armed forces, civil aviation, aircraft industry and transport within and under which a proportionate German 'organised military force' can take its place for defensive purposes. With regard to the *economic and political situation*, the writer urges that instead of any attempt to keep Germany suppressed or dismembered, there should be a combination of all the United Nations, especially U.S.A., Russia, and the British Empire, with a view to giving a defeated Germany a stake in the peace; and also a combination of the victorious and vanished powers in the task of raising the standard of life in the poorer countries of Europe, so that all may have enough food to eat. He also urges that underlying the whole huge task of establishing order and just relations, and of securing healthy economic and political conditions among the different nations, a task likely to last many years, there is the fundamental problem of religious faith; and that while it will take a long time for the curative forces of the spirit to gain say over the German and over other peoples, the crux of the whole matter lies in the spiritual and moral realm.

[1] Sir John Wardlaw-Milne (1879–1967), Conservative Party politician and MP 1922–45. In June–July 1942 he was involved in an attempt to force Churchill out of power with a vote of no confidence in the House of Commons.

Leibholz to Bell, 16 June 1943, Bell Papers 40, fol. 188 (typewritten); BA, N 1334 (copy)

My Lordbishop,

Very many thanks for your letter and your kindly offering to write to Sir Humphrey Milford. This will be a great help and I should be delighted if it were possible to interest him in the planned book.

I have read very carefully and with the greatest interest your thoughtful and very courageous and well-weighed memorandum. When reading it the immense task that lies ahead before the United Nations has clearly risen in my mind. I hardly need to tell you how wholeheartedly I agree with almost everything you say and how I admire the way in which you put forward the most difficult questions so convincingly and impressively. If you allow me to say an additional word, from my point of view, to this statesmanlike statement, which I am certain will deeply impress the Americans, it is the following:

The policy of discrimination as you, my Lordbishop, happily call the policy we advocate and you put forward in greater detail, seems to me to be based on one fundamental presupposition, namely that unity exists between the Anglo-Saxon countries and Russia with regard to their post-war policy. You know, my Lordbishop, I hope this unity will be really at hand although I have my serious doubts. If this unity should not exist I am afraid the Russians would be prepared to make far-reaching concessions to a Red Germany, for instance, allow her to have a Red Army force under German command and to have a force for defensive-purposes in Germany. I also doubt whether they would insist on an occupation of the whole of Germany. If this were so it may have serious consequences for the future of Europe (Central-E), ᵃand lead Germany to embrace Communism in some form.ᵃ In face of such a possible Eastern development of Germany and of the Continent I for my part favour a differentiation between those who, from fear of Russia, would compound with the Nazis (I agree this is fatal, would make security impossible and actually mean having lost the war. This is the old appeasement policy) and those who fundamentally agree with the policy of discrimination you put forward so lucidly but – in face of the Eastern threat – try to combine this policy with one which leaves Germany some moderate strength under certain conditions, after the complete destruction of the Hitlerite Army and the present regime. I fully realize the fundamental objection which can also be raised against this attitude from the point of view of security. But I think with you, my Lordbishop, that the last and only true basis of security is the spirit i.e. all depends on the spirit, which will develop in Germany after the collapse of its present regime. If this spirit is 'Western-minded' then I fear that all suggestions which go beyond Versailles will stifle again the development of such a spirit and history may take quite a different course.

How refreshing and sensible was Roosevelt's last appeal to Italy.[1] One would only have wished it would have come earlier and have taken the place of the disastrous Casablanca-formula of the unconditional surrender, which – even if openly meant as a matter of military importance – must have and has actually most serious political consequences as can be gathered from almost all statements made in Germany in the last few months (cf. the last statement by Kauffmann[2] published in *The Times* on Monday last). And I think it would be wise to pursue the same policy towards Germany and to drive home the fact that the United Nations came as liberators and not as oppressors of the German people.

Many thanks also for calling my attention to Voigt's article. I will certainly read it.

With all good wishes in which my wife and the children join to you and Mrs Bell ᵃand with renewed thanks.ᵃ

Yours ever,

---

[1] On 17 July 1943 Roosevelt and Churchill had made a joint appeal to the people of Italy to sue for peace. The text was dropped by aeroplanes over Rome two days later.
[2] Kurt Kauffmann, a lawyer, later went on to act as counsel for Ernst Kaltenbrunner at the Nuremberg Trials in 1946.

Leibholz to Bell, 16 June 1943, Bell Papers 40, fol. 189 (handwritten)

My Lordbishop,

I [had] just sent off my letter to you when your card arrived. I thought of only about 20,000 words but I could adapt the length of the Ms. to the wishes of the Oxford Press, i.e. I should be prepared to enlarge or abbreviate it according to what the publisher thinks most suitable.

With renewed thanks

Yours ever,

Bell to Leibholz, 26 June 1943, BA, N 1334 (typewritten); Bell Papers 40, fol. 191 (carbon)

My Lordbishop,

I have been away in town this week – hence the delay in replying to your letter enclosing a copy of yours to Dr Paton. I thought this admirable and I do not anticipate any difficulty whatever. I should certainly hope that the Church of England Committee's grant towards your rent can be renewed. I suppose it will have to be considered at the meeting of the Committee at the end of July; but so far as I know there is no need for anxiety.

I saw Pastor Söderberg[1] yesterday. He had just had a message from Pastor Forell[2] in Sweden. I asked him if he could find out from Forell any news of Dietrich. Forell is expecting to go to Berlin shortly. It may take a little time, but I will let you know anything I hear.

I shall hope to write to you soon about the project of the book.

Yours ever,

[1] Herman E. Söderberg, pastor of the Swedish church in London.
[2] Birger Forell (1892–1958), minister of the Swedish church in Berlin, 1929–42. A regular, and significant, correspondent of Bell, Forell was a strong supporter of the Confessing Church and of victims of Nazi persecution. Under pressure from the German state he left Germany in 1942 and became minister in Borås, where he remained until 1951. In 1943 the WCC sent him to Britain to look after German prisoners of war.

Leibholz to Bell, 26 June 1943, Bell Papers 40, fol. 196 (typewritten); BA, N 1334 (copy)

My Lordbishop,

I am enclosing today the answer to the questions you put before me. I have answered these questions as frankly and precisely as possible. I think, on some points you will take another line but I feel sure that we are in substantial agreement on all the main issues. If possible I should like to see a copy of the periodical in which your contribution will appear because I think I have much to learn from you also in this respect.

What do you say, my Lordbishop, to the recognition of the 'Free Germans' in Russia and to the fact that they broadcast to the German people three times daily from there?[1] I think this fact eloquently proves the correctness of our basic thesis and the insufficiency of the policy of the leaders of the Liberal Democracies. I wonder what Vansittart and his adherents will say to this. He and many others have maintained, especially in the last few months, that Stalin has been converted and pursues today the same policy towards Germany as the liberal democracies and Vansittart himself. Now the cat is out of the bag. I think the *New York Herald Tribune* is right in writing: 'If Britain and the United States enter Germany at one end with AMGOT,[2] and Russia enters the country at the other with the new committee, the situation will be embarrassing, to say the least.'

I think it is hardly to be doubted that facing this alternative the Germans will choose a free communist Germany and not an occupation in Vansittart-style as projected by the liberal democracies. I have the greatest respect for this amazing realism after all the terrible suffering the Russians have been undergoing. In fact, the act of recognition is more far-reaching than anything we have ever asked for. Our aim was only to induce the government to state a policy acceptable to a new anti-Nazi government on Western-Christian lines. I feel the moment is now ripe to raise this question again and to ask the government what the government thinks about the latest development and whether it would not be suitable to state a similar policy now.

There was in the *Observer* of yesterday an article, which seems to me extremely interessant [sic] and almost sensational.[3] It takes emphatically that view which we have long held. I think one could underline every word. If you have not already read the article or could get hold of it I will try to get one and to send it to you. I hope this article will also wake up other circles.

As to the book on *Christianity, Justice and Law* I think the procedure you suggested seems to me much better than that I had thought of. If you do not mind and you, my Lordbishop, do not think I am asking too much I should suggest writing to E. Barker[4] (17 Canmor Road) and telling him that you know I am working on the above book, which will have about a size which would fit in his series *Current Problems*. Perhaps he would be prepared to publish this book if you kindly approached him. When the article was published in the *Dublin Review* I sent him a copy so that he will probably know (if he has read it) the basic lines on which the book is being written. Should he be prepared to accept it I could get into touch with him later on and arrange all further details. If this should not be possible then I should venture to ask you to write to the theological publisher you had in mind when we spoke to each other on Wednesday last. I know you forgive me all the trouble I am causing you.

Yours ever,

---

[1] The 'National Committee for a "Free Germany"' (NCFG, Nationalkomitee 'Freies Deutschland', NKFD) was founded on 22 June 1943 by German prisoners of war and communist refugees from Germany living in the USSR.
[2] Allied Military Government.
[3] This is puzzling. *The Observer* was published not on 25 July but on 27 July 1943. This edition contained two articles, one on the propaganda of Goebbels and German public opinion ('Voice of the Axis: An Echo stirs German Memories', p. 7, cols. 2–3) and 'The Battle of the Ruhr' (p. 4, cols. 3–5).
[4] i.e. Sir Ernest Barker. The address is unclear and may be a mistake (possibly Cranmer Road?).

Question I: What is Vansittartism?

Answer: Vansittartism is that view which identifies Nazism and Germany and sees in Nazism a specific German phenomenon which could never flourish on any other soil. Vansittartism, therefore, regards Nazism as the genuine expression of the German soul and mentality, which has plunged the world again and again into war. In the same way as Hitlerism believes that every crime and outrage committed in the past is traceable to the Jews the trend of Vansittart-thought tends to do the same with regard to the Germans in the last hundred-and-fifty years. This explains why

Vansittartist-thinking has been called racial. According to this view the overwhelming bulk of the German nation has stood united behind Hitler since the beginning of the regime and, therefore, the German nation as a whole must be held fully responsible for the crimes and atrocities of the Nazis and must be dealt with accordingly after the war is won.

Question II: How would you define your attitude to the German people when they have accepted the terms of armistice?

Answer: Realising that the present war is a primarily ideological one which has deep-rooted spiritual and sociological causes I am strongly in favour of a view which differentiates between Hitlerite-Germany and the Germans in the same way as, for instance, Mr Stalin does. Since the outbreak of the Russian-German war he has never been weary of basing the Russian policy towards Germany on this fundamental distinction. It has found its most striking expression in the recent official recognition of the 'Free Germans' by the Russian government. This differentiation is also recognised in the Treaty of Alliance between this country and the Soviet Union and has frequently found its expression in the speeches by the leading statesmen of the liberal Democracies (recently in the House of Lords by the speaker of the Government in March, 1943[1]). What we have failed to do so far is to draw the practical consequences from this differentiation. Of course, force is required to restrain Germany's aggressiveness. But at the same time we must bear in mind that a policy based exclusively on the use of power and force and the imposition of special disabilities on Germany can never secure that peace for which mankind is longing today. It is mere illusion to think that such a policy can ever succeed in changing the outlook of the German people.

Peace can only be secured if it is backed by development of a co-operative mentality which appeals to the spirit of a new Germany. This means we must use force and power cautiously in a way which does not kill at the same time that spirit which we need for that purpose. This is why I wish to see the problem of security in its right perspective and why we should make up our mind to help those forces in Germany who have been opposed to the Nazi-regime and driven either underground or fought against the regime as heroically as the anti-Nazi forces in enemy-occupied countries and which after a lost war would be prepared to build a new Germany on those Christian and Western lines which are underlying modern civilisation.

Question III: Do you favour an allied occupying force in Germany, or a non-British?

Answer: Frankly, beyond what is necessary, from a military point of view, in order to win the war, I am in favour of an occupation of Germany only under certain conditions. For an occupation of a country is one of the most drastic means of power and force that is possible. If we use this means we must always ask ourselves whether we use power as an end in itself or as a means to a higher end. As I have stated under II. we must strengthen by all means those people in Germany who want to rebuild a new Germany on Western lines. An occupation without having this aim constantly in mind would fail in its further purposes. It could, above all, not have an educational effect. It can only bring forth hatred. Therefore, I am in favour of an armed occupation of Germany, beyond the military necessities, only in so far as it is also desired by those German strata which we must support. The recent events in Italy show (after twenty years of Fascism) that we are welcomed there as friends and not as enemies. The same might happen in Germany if our policy does not make such a welcome impossible. I think a desire for occupation may be confidentially expected by those Germans who (after the collapse of the present regime) look for salvation rather to the West than to the East. They will be in favour of a temporary occupation in order to avoid mob-rule and anarchy. Only if the civil war would break out I should recommend an occupation of Germany without being asked, in order to restore order in Germany and herewith to lay the foundation stone, on which later on a Western regime could be based.

Question IV: Do you favour German labour being sent to help the reconstruction of ravaged European countries for some years?

Answer: I am not in favour of German labour being sent to help the reconstruction of ravaged European territories. It is true the Germans are doing this on a large scale at the present time and people may think it would be a good thing to teach the Germans the same lesson. On the other hand, at present we are at war but then arms will have been laid down. It is true we are compelled to use some of the brutal methods of war the enemy has used against us. But we have done so only in order to shorten the war and to avoid unnecessary suffering going on. Using a means of war as forced labour undoubtedly is in times in which hostilities have come to an end a perpetuation of war, as was the case when in the last war the blockade was continued after the armistice [sic]. Such a means cannot have any beneficial effect on those labour forces which cannot find occupation in Germany after the war would be given an opportunity of possibly being employed in devastated areas.

Question V: How can we teach the German youth that war does not pay?

Answer: Let us not forget that after Germany has lost the second world war millions of Germans will have died in vain, that other millions of the German youth will be crippled for life, that all the sufferings of the civilian population will be in vain, that German economic life will lie on the brink of ruin and the Mark will have lost again its value, that many districts of the Reich will be ravaged and laid waste. More important than to give the German youth an additional special lesson that war does not pay seems to me that we must do something more constructive in order to avoid German youth falling again into despair and seeking to create an anti-Western and anti-Christian block on the Continent (in connection with Russia). Let us not forget that spiritual and economic despair was one of the causes which has led to National Socialism and to the present war.

Question VI: Should we restore diplomatic relations with Germany after the armistice and if not after what period?

Answer: I am in favour of restoration the diplomatic relations with Germany after the armistice. For such a restoration would be of great value for the tasks of reconstruction we have to fulfil after the war.

Question VII: Do you favour the mixing of British and German youth after the war to hope that the latter to become more civilised? [sic]

Answer: I am in favour of mixing of British and German youth after the present war on as great a scale as possible as I see in this mixing a valuable means of making German youth familiar with the British way of life and the fundamental principles and values on which this way of life is based.

Question VIII: What should Vansittartism begin? [sic]

Answer: I think Lord Vansittart would answer this question better than I can do. I should say that from the fundamental point of view Vansittartism takes this would logically have to come to decide upon the destruction of the German nation as a whole. From the point of view of Vansittartism, there seems to me no other way of giving security to Europe and the world in order to eliminate this source of danger once and forever. But I know that even Lord Vansittart does not come to this logical conclusion of this policy. Vansittartism limits itself to the demand for a Super-Versailles. But we have seen whither Versailles had led us. We need not picture to ourselves whither a Super-Versailles must lead. A Cathago would be necessary to secure a peace from this point of view. But such a peace would not eliminate the real and deeper lying spiritual and social causes of the present war. In addition, the imposition of such a peace presupposes among the United Nations concerned an agreement which does not seem to me to exist as the liberal democracies on the one hand, and Russia on the other hand, do not form an ideological unity.

[1] See Vansittart in the debate of the House of Lords in Hansard, H.L. Deb., Vol. 126, cols. 549–50 (10 March 1943).

Bell to Leibholz, 3 August 1943, BA, N 1334 (handwritten)

Private

My dear Leibholz,

I am extremely grateful to you for your careful and illuminating answers to the 8 Questions. They have been a great help in composing my answers, which as you will see follow you in spirit and very often in actual words. I have found it difficult to fulfil my task in 800 words, but I think I have just managed. I enclose a copy. I believe the issue of the *Illustrated*[1] with these Answers will appear in a month's time. I will send you a copy.

I have not seen the *Observer* of the Sunday before last. I hope to get hold of a copy in the Club[2] tomorrow – though I am not sure.

The Moscow National Committee seems to me of great importance, and a warning to the other Allies to look sharp – for their own sakes if for no other reason. With some trepidation I have composed a Memo on the Committee's manifesto and sent it to Eden.[3] I saw Duff Cooper[4] on Friday and asked him (I did not know him previously) what he thought of this Committee, and he did not seem to have given it any thought – looking upon it as a *German* manoeuvre, and not apparently scenting Soviet policy. Later that day I saw Schutz, Müller-Sturmheim,[5] Hertz[6] and a Pole of the Polish Research Office, and asked each in turn their opinions. They were all, in different degrees, very sensible of the importance of the event. Schutz was especially illuminating. You may like to see my memo. I have not heard anything yet from Eden.

All best wishes to you and the family

Yours vy sincerely,

P.S. *August 4*

Letter from Eden's secretary, saying Eden has my letter, and will send considered reply.

---

[1] *The Illustrated London News*, founded in 1842 this famous national weekly closed down in 1971.
[2] The Athenaeum, a private members' club on the Strand in central London, of which Bell was for many years a member.
[3] Bell, Memorandum on the 'National Committee of Free Germany', 30 July 1943, AWCC, IMC26.11.47/4. Later Bell became a patron and vice-president of the 'Allies Inside Germany' Council, which was founded to support the NCFG in Great Britain in cooperation with the Free German League of Culture; see Bell Papers, Vol. 47, fols. 16–18.
[4] Alfred Duff Cooper (1890–1954), Conservative politician and MP and Secretary of War 1935–7. Cooper had resigned from the government in 1938 over Neville Chamberlain's appeasement policy. He served as Minister for Information during the war and became ambassador to France 1944–7. In 1947 he became 1st Viscount Norwich.
[5] Emil Müller-Sturmheim (1886–1952) had emigrated from Austria to Britain in 1938. He became the first secretary-general of the Free Austrian Movement in London in 1941. Under communist influence he and other Socialists later founded the Austrian Democratic Union. In 1943 Müller-Sturmheim was involved in the foundation of the Austrian section in exile of the New Commonwealth Society of Justice and Peace.
[6] Friedrich (Otto) Hertz (1878–1964), professor of world economy and sociology at Halle University in 1933 had emigrated to Vienna and in 1938 arrived in London, where he became a leading figure in a number of Austrian refugee organizations.

'Vansittartism' – by the Bishop of Chichester and Lord Vansittart

Carbon with many corrections by Bell, BA, N 1334; printed in: *The Illustrated London News*, 11 September 1943

1. WHAT IS VANSITTARTISM?

A disease which causes those who suffer from it to identify Nazism with Germany, and to see in Nazism a specific German phenomenon which could never flourish on any other soil. The gravity of the disease varies ᵃin different individualsᵃ. Those who suffer from it in its extreme form regard all Germans as butcher-birds, just as the Nazis regard all Jews as sub-men.

2. HOW WOULD YOU DEFINE YOUR ATTITUDE TO THE GERMAN PEOPLE WHEN THEY HAVE ACCEPTED THE TERMS OF AN ARMISTICE?

The question is not clear; for there might be no formal armistice, or there might be more armistices than one, concluded at different dates for different areas. But, speaking generally, I would define my attitude to a defeated Germany as follows.

This war is primarily an ideological war, with far-reaching economic and social implications. Agreeing with the ᶜradicalᶜ distinction drawn by Stalin on November 6th, 1942, between the Hitlerite State and Germany¹ (accepted by the British Government on March 10th 1943), I wish the United Nations to follow a policy in accordance with that distinction. This means *on the one hand* the destruction of the Hitlerite State; the punishment after trial of all war criminals, Nazi leaders, accomplices and agents; ᵃthe destruction of 'Hitler's army'ᵃ; the withdrawal of all organised military forces from occupied territory; the renunciation of all ᵃHitler'sᵃ conquests; the surrender of all stolen property with ᶜfullᶜ compensation where restoration is impossible. It means *on the other hand* the ᶜimmediateᶜ release of all Nazi victims; the repeal of all Nazi laws based on racial or national hatred; the restoration of freedom of speech, religion, the press and assembly; the encouragement of the anti-Nazi forces in Germany to form a free, democratic government; and a full collaboration by the United Nations with such a government in establishing a just economic and political order in Europe.

3. DO YOU FAVOUR AN ALLIED OCCUPYING FORCE IN GERMANY, OR A NON-BRITISH?

Occupation² may have three objects,

1. To prove to all Germans that the United Nations have defeated Germany beyond ᶜallᶜ possibility of doubt.
2. To prevent ᶜmob rule andᶜ civil war, and the re-emergence of military, aggressive forces ᶜon German soilᶜ.
3. To hold down a vanquished nation and prevent its recovery.

I am in favour of occupation for (i) and (ii), but not for (iii). ᵃIn spite of all Russia's sufferingsᵃ Stalin stated on November 6th, 1942 that he had 'no such aim as to destroy Germany'; and the ᵃMoscowᵃ 'National Committee of Free Germany' declared ᶜin Moscowᶜ in July that its aim was the creation of a 'strong democratic power'. Britain and America should be no less clear in putting forward a constructive programme for the recovery of Germany ᶜon liberal and democratic linesᶜ, in keeping with the ᶜgreatᶜ ᵃliberalᵃ European tradition. There must be fullest guarantees of international security, ᶜwhich involvesᶜ making it impossible for Germany to possess a striking force for offensive purposes. But a repressive occupation would ᶜengender hatred, andᶜ in the ᶜlong runᶜ, ᵃendᵃ produce a third World War. Occupation should be by Allied forces. It should be for a limited period, sufficient to ᶜrestore order andᶜ make possible the beginning of a freely elected, liberal, democratic regime.

4. DO YOU FAVOUR GERMAN LABOUR BEING SENT TO HELP THE RECONSTRUCTION OF RAVAGED EUROPEAN COUNTRIES FOR SOME YEARS?

[First version:] If the Germans, after liberation from Hitlerism, as a sign of repentance for the unspeakable wrongs done to so many other European nations, freely offered their labour for the recovery of the ravaged countries, I should welcome their action. Further, it should be the aim of international policy in Europe to allocate to all nations in Europe their shares in the economic rebuilding of Europe. I am not in favour of German labour being compulsorily sent in the way proposed. Such compulsion (like the Nazis' forced labour in the war) would only intensify bitterness and delay recovery. The only exception to this general principle might be found in the temporary use of Nazi accomplices for whom life would be impossible in a free Germany, thereby assisting in the solution of the problem raised by the large number of those accomplices.

[Final version:] It should be the aim of international policy in Europe to allocate to all nations in Europe, ªand Germany as one of theseª, [printed version: them] their ªrespectiveª shares in the ªreconstructionª of ravaged territories and in the economic rebuilding of Europe. ªCompulsory sending of German labourª would only intensify bitterness and delay recovery. ªNeverthelessª if the Germans as a sign of repentance for the unspeakable wrongs done ªin Germany's nameª to other European nations, freely offered their labour, I should welcome their action.

5. HOW CAN WE TEACH THE GERMAN YOUTH THAT WAR DOES NOT PAY?

German youth will be taught that 'war does not pay' ᶜby the heavy defeat of their country andᶜ by seeing that millions of Germans have died or been maimed for life in vain, ªandª that German economic life lies on the brink of ruin ᶜand that Hitler has made the name of Germany abominable in Europe. But a more positive remedy is also neededᶜ. ªButª It should ªalsoª be one great task of the leaders of Europe to help European youth, including German youth, to find a place in the rebuilding of European life, and ᶜto be enlistedᶜ in the campaign to give everybody³ enough food, enough shelter, enough warmth, enough work. We must not forget that spiritual and economic despair was one of the causes which gave rise to National Socialism and the present war.⁴

6. SHOULD WE RESTORE DIPLOMATIC RELATIONS WITH GERMANY AFTER THE ARMISTICE AND IF NOT AFTER WHAT PERIOD?

As soon as there is a settled, free, democratic Government in Germany, ᶜand internal order is secured,ᶜ diplomatic relations should be restored.

7. DO YOU FAVOUR THE MIXING OF BRITISH AND GERMAN YOUTH AFTER THE WAR IN THE HOPE THAT THE LATTER MAY BECOME MORE CIVILISED?

The ᶜspiritual impulse of theᶜ awaking of a religious faith is an indispensable factor in the education of all European youth, including both British and German. ªI also consider that youth of all countries should mix with one another.⁵ªWith these principles well in view, I am in favour of mixing British and German youth after the war, as I see in this mixing a valuable means of making German youth familiar with the British way of life and the fundamental principles ᶜand valuesᶜ on which the way of life is based.

8. WHEN SHOULD VANSITTARTISM BEGIN?

Never.

---

¹ Crossed out: the German people.
² Instead of: The occupation of Germany.
³ Added by the printed version: everywhere.
⁴ This sentence is omitted in the printed version.
⁵ Printed version: with each other.

Leibholz to Bell, 8 August 1943, BA, N 1334 (copy)

My Lordbishop,

Very many thanks for your kind letter. I am so glad to know that my remarks were of some use to you. It is very good of you to offer to send me a copy of *Illustrated* later on. I did not realize that you had to limit the answers to 800 words. Otherwise I would have shortened my paper.

I have read your Memorandum with the greatest care and deepest interest and I think it is a really brilliant statement. It gives an outline of the policy in which we are so greatly in need and which, from a Western point of view, is the only policy which deserves the name realistic. As I wholeheartedly agree with all you say, my Lordbishop, I have no comments to make on it. I can only underline every word you have said in it.

Excellent as your Memo. is I feel sure that the considered answer Eden has promised to give will be disappointing. I am afraid it cannot otherwise as the government is bound by its unconditional 'surrender policy'. As long as this policy is not revised they can only give an evasive answer. When you prepared your report for the American Churches two months ago and I sent you a few remarks for it we corresponded on the question whether the 'unconditional surrender' has only military significance or also a political one. I am afraid the recent policy towards Italy has shown that, in fact, the Casablanca policy is a policy which is not limited to military issues. It seems to me to be a pure power policy which in the end will be detrimental to the liberal democracies themselves. In a letter to Oldham I tried to make clear how, to my mind, the unconditional surrender policy changes the whole character of the present war and I am enclosing a copy of this letter together with a copy of a letter to Noel Buxton to whom I wrote in reply to a letter from which I gathered that he was interested in the matter.

I only mention this because I fear that the hope of getting a favourable answer is small. But should we not think over what is to be done if the answer is negative? In this connection, the article in *The Observer* dated July 5 seems to me important. I hope you were able to get hold [of] a copy in the club. Otherwise I will try to get one here. Yesterday I read a very impressive article 'What to do with Germany' by Sir Andrew McFadyean[1] in the last issue of *The Contemporary Review*. It will interest you I think.

It would be kind of you, my Lordbishop, to let me have the enclosures back later on as I am thinking of writing an article on the implications of the unconditional surrender policy in *The Fortnightly* (under 'Gerard').[2] But I do not know whether this is an undesirable interference in Politics.

What do you think, my Lordbishop, of my suggestion of perhaps writing to Barker[3] in the book matter? I wonder whether you think it a good one.

With all good wishes to you and Mrs Bell.

Yours ever,

P.S. The remarks on the copy are written by Noel Buxton.

P.S. Just received telegram from Sutz saying that 'everybody well, looking forward confidently'. We are thankful and greatly relieved.

[1] Sir Andrew McFadyean (1887–1974), private secretary at the Treasury and after 1918 its main authority on war reparations. A Liberal, he sat on the council of Lionel Curtis's Royal Institute of International Affairs and became a leading advocate of European unity.
[2] See Leibholz to Bell, 31 August 1943, note 1.
[3] i.e. Sir Ernest Barker.

Bell to Leibholz, 11 August 1943, BA, N 1334 (typewritten)

Private[a]

My dear Leibholz,

Very many thanks for your letter and for the enclosures, which I return, having read them with deep interest. I quite agree about the unpromising prospects opened out by a combination of the Atlantic Charter and the Casablanca formula. The trouble is that the P.M.[1] will not think about these things or the conclusions to which they point. I saw Duff Cooper on Saturday. He opened the conversation by saying that he was very much interested in my memorandum, and was obviously impressed. He wondered what Eden had said. He was quite clear that the prospect opened out was a gloomy one, and I felt that he was much more alive to future prospects than some of his recent utterances had led one to suppose.

I have just had a letter from Ernest Barker saying that he is very sorry indeed that he cannot hold out hopes about taking your book into his series.[2] He says that Wood's book, *Christianity and Civilisation*[3] to some extent deals with that field, and there is another, which has been accepted. He speaks very warmly about you. He wonders whether the Mannheim series[4] would be useful – but that is not really what you want. Should I try the *Christian Challenge* series – Eyre & Spottiswoode?[5]

I am *delighted at the news about Dietrich*.[6] I also very glad you are writing in the *Fortnightly*.

Yours ever,

[a]I have got hold of the *Observer* for July 25, and very much struck by the article.
I have written a letter to the *Times* today on 'Taking Stock' – but they may not print it.[a]

[1] i.e. Prime Minister
[2] See Barker to Bell, 9 August 1943, Bell Papers 40, fols. 200–1.
[3] Herbert George (H.G.) Wood, *Christianity and Civilisation* (Current Problems Series, Number 19), (Cambridge, 1943).
[4] Karl Mannheim (1893–1947), Hungarian-born sociologist, exiled to Germany shortly after the end of the First World War where he worked with Alfred Weber in Heidelberg. From 1929 to 1933 Mannheim was professor at the University of Frankfurt am Main, where he collaborated with Norbert Elias, but he left for Britain after losing his position there. He found a place at the London School of Economics and contributed to new, international circles of constructive thought, like the Moot of J.H. Oldham, while successfully developing what became an influential series of sociological books for the publisher Routledge.
[5] A series of popular polemical books committed to contemporary religious issues. The publisher was not Eyre & Spottiswoode but the Centenary Press.
[6] Sutz's telegram (see Leibholz to Bell, 8 August 1943) concerned only the Bonhoeffer family in Berlin, and gave no information about Dietrich Bonhoeffer.

Leibholz to Bell, 18 August 1943, BA, N 1334 (copy)

My Lordbishop,

Very many thanks for your letter. I quite agree that the root of the whole trouble is that the political leaders persistently refuse to face the real issues and, therefore, back a policy which in the end will prove detrimental not only to the Continent but even to this country. The repeated plea of *The Times* for a concerted policy strikes one [as] rather strange as things stand. For such a concerted policy, desirable as it is, seems to me to be only possible by ignoring the primacy of the ideological issues in this war. It is obviously very difficult to break away from the traditional political methods [and] the conventional forms of political thought. I wonder how they will react to your letter.

In the meantime, I have read once again your admirable Memorandum and frankly if I may say I think it is the best political statement I have seen in this country on this subject and I only wish that all political circles would have an opportunity of taking it to heart. By the way, I think that Vernon Barlett[1] and Lord Astor[2] who addressed a question to Mr Eden on this subject in the House of Commons a fortnight ago would be interested in seeing the Mem. [sic] I think they take the same line as you, my Lordbishop.

I am sorry to have troubled you again in vain. Judging from my experiences with E. Barker it seems that he obviously always reacts in the same way. I have really a very bad conscience towards you for all the trouble I am causing you. I should think that the *Christian Challenge* series would now be the right place. But please kindly write to them only if it does not take up too much of your time just now and if you fully agree. I do not know whether you perhaps have a better suggestion than I. In any case, I do not think that the Mannheim series, which Barker suggests is just the suitable series of the kind of book I have in mind.

With all good wishes and renewed thanks

Yours ever,

---

[1] Vernon Barlett (1894–1983), writer who served as a 'libertarian socialist' MP 1938–50.
[2] John Jacob Astor V (1886–1971), American-born English Conservative politician (and MP 1922–45), proprietor of *The Times*, 1922–59. In 1956 he became 1st Baron Astor of Hever.

Bell to Leibholz, 22 August 1943, BA, N 1334 (handwritten)

ᵃtill August 30 May Place Hotel, Malvern Wellsᵃ

My dear Leibholz,

Many thanks for yours. *The Times* 'carefully considered' my letter, but decided against. So I sent a revised version to *Man[chester] Guard[ian]*, which printed at once. I enclose my only copy, *so please return*. I don't like Brendan Bracken's *dreadful* effusions – and am sure you don't.[1] I am glad you think so well of my Memo. I had a letter from R[ichard] Law, in Eden's absence, to say

'The questions to wh. you draw attention in your mem. are very much in our minds, but I do not think there is any thing I can usefully say at the present stage.'

I will write to *Chr[istian] Challenge* about the book.

Yours ever,

[1] Brendan Bracken (1901–58), a successful magazine publisher and newspaper editor who became Conservative MP in 1929. Bracken was Minister of Information in the wartime government, 1941–5. In 1952 he became 1st Viscount Bracken. Bracken was ardent in his support for the RAF's bombing policy.

Leibholz to Bell, 24 August 1943, BA, N 1334 (copy)

My Lordbishop,
Thank you very much for your letter and for kindly letting me see the cutting from *The Manchester Guardian*, which I have read with deep interest. I have made a copy of this letter for my own purposes and am returning the cutting herewith with many thanks.

That *The Times* did not venture to publish your letter seems to me to be an indication of the weakness and the unreal policy it is advocating today. I think your letter is *most* interesting and just meeting the exigencies of the time.

What you say about 'unconditional surrender' was new to me although I ought to have known it. I formerly thought that unconditional surrender was a unilateral act unlike honourable capitulation. That presupposes an agreement containing the terms of surrender. I was re-affirmed in my belief by the *Oxford Dictionary* but then again in doubt by the official statement (after the fall of Mussolini) that there is no difference between unconditional surrender and honourable capitulation.[1] Now I very much hope that the government will draw the consequences from the reminder as I feel that they have given 'unconditional surrender' a political meaning (see the policy towards Italy) and will say something 'useful' before it is too late.

By the way, I had a sympathetic letter from Sir Andrew McFadyean in connection with his article on Germany in *The Contemporary Review* and I think he would be very much interested in seeing your Memorandum. I do not know how you think about it, my Lordbishop. I always feel it would be a good thing if the few people who in this country seem to us to see the crucial political issues in the right perspective would get in touch with each other.

It is very kind of you that you have in mind to write to the *Christian Challenge* people because of the projected book. But please do not do it while you are on holiday.

I am just learning that Himmler has been appointed Minister of the Interior. This seems to me to prove that the crisis is approaching its climax.[2]

With all good wishes to you and Mrs Bell.

Yours ever,

[1] After Mussolini's fall on 25 July a delegate of Marshall Badoglio had from 3 August been negotiating with the Allies in Lisbon. One month later authorized representatives signed an armistice in Cassibile (Sicily). For the time being it remained secret because it only formally corresponded to the idea of an unconditional surrender.
[2] Himmler had been appointed Minister of the Interior on 25 August 1943.

Bell to Leibholz, 25 August 1943, BA, N 1334 (handwritten)

My dear Leibholz,
Coming to Dr Paton's (too lamentable) funeral[1] I saw Tracy Strong in the club, just back from 2 weeks in Sweden. He arrived here on Monday and flies to USA next Monday.

He had news of Dietrich – but, he thinks, *earlier* than yours. A message from Geneva, written *before July 20*, came via Jo Hanno[,] one of the chief YMCA men in Geneva, specially for Strong (also YMCA – once visiting Sweden about prisoners).

The message was that Dietrich has been arrested, but certain people very influential were doing anything possible to secure his release, and were pretty confident of success. *The confidence in success was insisted on.*

I told Strong that your wire from Sutz was, I felt pretty sure, subsequent to July 20. But you will test this by looking at date.

If so, the fact that Sutz telegraphed when he did explains why he did so.

In haste – only I felt you and your wife ought to know at once –

Yours ever,

[1] William Paton had died suddenly on 21 August 1943.

Leibholz to Bell, 27 August 1943, Bell Papers 40, fol. 207 (handwritten); BA, N 1334 (copy)

My Lordbishop,

It was very kind of you to let me have the news about Dietrich. They explain very much and confirm what we instinctively have been feeling for the last few months. So far I have not told my wife of your letter because I know the news will very much upset her and she herself is not quite well just now. We know what such an arrest means, not only for Dietrich but for the whole family of my wife, especially her old parents, and for his friends. The wire was received here on the 8th of August and hesitating to conclude from it his release I very much hope that at least no deterioration of his position has taken place. I am sure that in Germany everything possible will be done on his behalf and that every possible pressure from many quarters will be brought to bear upon the authorities. But I do not know how strong this pressure can be under the present circumstances (especially after the appointment of Himmler).

I am afraid Visser 't Hooft and his friends can not do very much in addition to what has already been done unless it be possible to get him away to Sweden or Switzerland.

I feel deeply the loss the Church and Dr Paton's numerous friends have sustained through his sudden death. It is a heavy blow and a scarcely replaceable loss.

Yours ever,

P.S. Was the Swedish news about Dietrich different from that coming from Switzerland, my Lordbishop?

Bell to Leibholz, 31 August 1943, BA, N 1334 (handwritten)

My dear Leibholz,

Very many thanks for your article sent on 22 August, and for your letter received today telling me of the *Times*' unwillingness.

I liked the article very much, and found it full of meat, and should greatly wish to see it in print for the enlightenment of English newspaper readers. I think the next step is to try *The Man[chester] Guardian*; and (to some friend) I accordingly send a covering letter, though as I don't *personally* know the Editor as I know the *Times* Editor, I can't write in quite the same way.

One point I shd. like to suggest for your consideration. The article is in some respects not quite easy enough for the ordinary reader, and is not in completely flowing English – I mean in certain idiomatic phrasing. This is unimportant in a long monthly article, but might make an Editor with many demands on his space unwilling. I *suggest* that you might in your covering letter say something like this –

'If you would find the article easier to use in a slightly altered or abbreviated form I have no objection to your making any verbal changes, that would seem adapted to make the text of the article more suitable to English readers, provided the changes do not alter the sense.'

I don't say these should be the exact words. But if you can give the Editor a little liberty – it would improve the chances.

Failing M.G. I would try the *News Chronicle*. Did you see Vansittart's letter in *yesterday's* N/C about Goerdeler[1] and Schacht[2]? It refers to an article in N/C of August 22, which I have not seen.

Yours ever,

I am here till Sept. 8
Very glad you gave Moore a copy for F.O.[3] I don't know Southern.[4]

---

[1] Carl Goerdeler (1884–1945) became Lord Mayer of Leipzig in 1930, also acting as Reich Commissioner of Price Control. After 1935 he was increasingly at odds with the Nazi party, and he resigned over the removal of the city's monument to the composer Felix Mendelssohn Bartholdy in November 1937. Goerdeler became an advisor to the industrialist, Robert Bosch and under this aegis travelled abroad to search for allies against Hitler and forces ready to rally against a new war. From 1938 he was in many ways the effective head of the civil resistance in Germany, actively planning the future of Germany after Hitler. If the plot of 20 July had succeeded he might have become Reich Chancellor. He was imprisoned and sentenced to death by the People's Tribunal on 8 September 1944 but his execution did not take place until 2 February 1945.

[2] Hjalmar Schacht (1877–1970) served as President of the Reich Bank in 1923–30 and again in 1933–9. He was also German Minister of Economics in 1934–7. Dismissed because of his criticisms of financial and rearmament policies he made contact with resisters like Carl Goerdeler and Ulrich von Hassell. Schacht was arrested after the 20 July 1944 but survived the war. He was acquitted by the Nuremberg Trials.

[3] William Moore, Oxford academic and Congregationalist who travelled with the Dean of Chichester, A.S. Duncan-Jones, to see the trial of Martin Niemöller in Berlin in 1938. F.O. = Foreign Office.

[4] Richard William Southern (1912–2001), noted medieval historian at Oxford University. During the Second World War he served in the army, after 1943 as a major in the Intelligence Department of the Foreign Office.

Leibholz to Bell, 31 August 1943, Bell Papers 40, fol. 208 (typewritten); BA, N 1334 (copy)

My Lordbishop,

Today I am enclosing a copy of the article *Unconditional Surrender and Central Europe*.[1]

It takes the same basic line as you favour and contains I think nothing that is new to you, my Lordbishop. On the contrary, you will see from it what I have learned from you and your recent work. I felt that I must write the article although I do not know whether, under the present circumstances, anyone will be courageous enough to publish it. I have just sent a copy to Armitage for *The Fortnightly* as he published the article on *Germany between West and East* to which this article, which deals with some of the most important events of the last year, can be considered in some way as its sequel [sic].

In the meantime, I have told my wife of your letter and have tried to comfort her by saying that you, my Lordbishop, and I think that Dietrich is free again and I think that this considerably mitigated the shock.

Yours ever,

---

[1] 'S. H. Gerard' (G. Leibholz), 'Unconditional Surrender and Central Europe', Bell Papers, Vol. 40, fols. 209–19 (typewritten). The article was finally published as 'Ideology in the Post-War Policy of Russia and the Western Powers', in *The Hibbert Journal* in 1944; reprinted in Leibholz, *Politics and Law*, pp. 182–93.

Bell to Leibholz, 1 September 1943, BA, N 1334 (handwritten)

My dear Leibholz,
Many thanks for your letter. I can indeed understand your concern for Dietrich in view of all that is happening. I wrote at once to T. Strong,[1] and caught him just on his way to fly back to America. He says he has no further knowledge – nothing in Sweden itself, only what he told me had come to him from Geneva. If I hear anything, of course, you shall have it. I go back home on Tuesday from The Hop Pole, Bromyard, Worcester,[2] where Mrs Bell and I spend the weekend.

Yours with much sympathy,

---

[1] i.e. Dr. Tracy Strong.
[2] An old hotel, still in existence.

Bell to Leibholz, 15 October 1943, BA, N 1334 (typewritten)

My dear Leibholz,
Many thanks for your letter. We are both well, and I hope you and your wife and two girls are well also. Alas, I have had no news from Geneva: you can rely on my giving you at once any information I get. I am glad to hear of your publishing your *Unconditional Surrender*. I am writing to Dr Leiper[1] about you.

Yours ever,

[1] Henry Smith Leiper (1891–1975), American Congregationalist minister and since 1930 Executive of the Commission of Relations with Churches Abroad of the Federal Council of Churches of Christ in America. From 1938 to 1952 he was Associate Secretary-General of the WCC.

Bell to Leibholz, 21 November 1943, BA, N 1334 (handwritten)

My dear Leibholz,

I send a copy of a letter just received for me at Edinburgh House[1] from Visser 't Hooft.[2] It gives news of Dietrich – though I wish indeed he were free[.] We can take comfort that there is no reason for 'special anxiety'. Yet I know well that these weeks must be full of care for you and your wife, and for all who are dear to you in Germany.

I shall be much interested to hear your views of the Moscow Conference.[3] There are *grandes silences* though a beginning to co-operate is something.

I have written a letter to the *Times* about Italy[4] (I was asked to make the point I do make by certain persons right in the midst of Italian affairs, who are troubled by the inaction of Government and the passivity of the public). But I do not know if they will print it. In the enclosed letter Martin is Niemöller. Henry is Leiper. Marc is Boegner.[5]

All affectionate remembrances

Yours always,

[1] The Head office of the British Council of Churches.
[2] W.A. Visser 't Hooft to Bell, 22 October 1943, now published in Besier, *Intimately Associated for Many Years*, p. 234.
[3] The conference of the three Ministers of Foreign Affairs from 19 October to 1 November discussed what steps would be taken against a defeated Germany, including occupation, the creation of an Allied Control Commission and demilitarization.
[4] Untraced and evidently unpublished.
[5] The French Reformed pastor and theologian Marc Boegner (1881–1970), first President of the Protestant Church Federation in France (1929–61) and in 1948–54 one of the presidents of the WCC.

Leibholz to Bell, 25 November (1943), Bell Papers 40, fol. 220 (handwritten)

My Lordbishop,

Many thanks for your kind letter. Unfortunately, I was not able to write to you by return, because I have been in bed with bronchitis for the last few days. My wife also is not well. Together with all the other news of the last few weeks things look rather gloomy and depressing. As soon as I am up again (I hope in a few day's time) I will write to you in greater length and come back to all you wrote me.

I hope you and Mrs Bell are well.

With all good wishes
Yours ever,

P.S. I cannot write about Dietrich today. – As to Moscow I do not think that the issue at stake has been affected by the Conference. – But what I fear is that the Power Policy of the Western countries has politically blinded a number of their leaders (see the speech of Mr Bracken of yesterday).

Bell to Leibholz, 7 December 1943, BA, N 1334 (typewritten)

My dear Leibholz,

I was so very sorry to hear that you and your wife were ill. I do most earnestly hope that you are well again now. I shall be eager to get news, and also your views on the present situation, when you have time.

I enclose a confidential memorandum, which I have prepared for the Peace Aims Group, of which the Archbishop of Canterbury, Toynbee,[1] Zimmern,[2] Hope-Simpson, Cockburn,[3] Routh[4] and others are members.

Yours ever,

[1] Arnold J. Toynbee (1889–1975), British historian and philosopher of history. In 1925 he had become Professor of international history at the London School of Economics and Director of Studies at the Royal Institute of International Affairs in London. His main work remains *A Study of History* (12 vols., 1934–61).
[2] Sir Alfred Zimmern (1879–1957), classical scholar, historian and political scientist; Montague Burton Professor of International Relations at Oxford University from 1930 to 1944. He had been an active participant in the Oxford Conference on Church, Community and State in 1937 and later played a significant role in the WCC.
[3] James Hutchinson Cockburn (1882–1973), Church of Scotland Minister and then Senior Minister at Dunblane Cathedral (1918–45); Moderator of the General Assembly of the Church of Scotland (1941) and later Director of the WCC Department of Inter-Church Aid (1945–48).
[4] Probably the economist Guy Routh (1916–93), most of whose academic career was later spent at the new University of Sussex.

Bell, Memorandum for the Peace Aims Group, 2 December 1943, Bell Papers 26, fols. 209–10; BA, N 1334 (copy)

Private & Confidential.

<u>PEACE AIMS GROUP</u>
A Note for the Members
from
The Bishop of Chichester
Meeting to be held at Presbyterian Church House,
86 Tavistock Place, London, W.C.1. from 11 – 3.30
Friday, December 10, 1943

Bill Paton's circular letter of August 3rd noted American appreciation of our joint statement, and asked advice about the future work of the Group. The replies received agreed with Bill's keen desire to focus attention on topics of moral significance involving Anglo-American co-operation and of some urgency for the future. While the *Colonial question* was accepted as requiring early treatment, more emphasis appeared to be laid, for the purposes of immediate discussion, on the *treatment of vanished enemy nations*. Writing to me on August 11 on the problem of *Russia* and the 'terrific hatred of

Germany in Russia', Bill says, 'Certainly the Group must work at this – it is a plain duty.' The facts since our own tragic bereavement, notably the co-belligerent status of Italy, the Moscow Conference, and the intensity of the bombing of enemy cities, have served to make both *Russia* and the *treatment of vanquished enemy nations* peculiarly urgent. The foundation of principles has been laid in *A Christian Basis for Reconstruction*,[1] but now we ought to try and see what practical conclusions follow on specific points. Perhaps this is all the more desirable in view of the tendency to hug the general and avoid the particular, which is still so conspicuous in the pronouncements of the United Nations. Events indeed are moving so fast that the preparation of something in the nature of a Christian judgement on concrete problems would appear to be a pressing duty.

The extreme political as well as and because of the military importance of *Russia* has become even more obvious than it was when we met in the summer. Our conception of Russian Policy, and of the proper attitude to be adopted by us towards Russia, can hardly fail to colour our thoughts about everything else. It has become more and more imperative that, if Europe (and the world) are to recover within a reasonable period, there must be a united policy to which Russia, America, and Britain (and China) all make their proper contributions. And in order that the proper contributions of all the partners may be given, it is of primary importance that we should frankly consider *Europe* as a whole. It is also, I suggest, essential that we should keep in the very forefront of our thinking the Atlantic Charter of 1941, framed when we were in a far less powerful position than we are today, but none the less binding. The Atlantic Charter was first signed by Roosevelt and Churchill, and then accepted by Soviet Russia and other Allied Governments. The document is perhaps a tentative and incomplete statement. It is in some respects too vague, and may be criticised as raising too large hopes on the economic side to desperate and destitute masses; and as looking at the world and armaments and sovereign rights in too static a fashion. But it is the spirit, which is important, and churchmen are on strong moral ground when they call for a thoroughly loyal adherence to that spirit in the positive provisions which the Charter contains. It is to be noted that the Atlantic Charter has lately dropped into background, and there is no reference to it in the Declaration of the Moscow Conference. If reference is made to it by the Four Nations before the meeting of the Peace Aims Group on December 10 it would be extremely welcome. But even so, some of the dangers and, for frankness' sake, criticisms, set out below, may still be remedied. For it is on the position of Russia, without any diminution of the profound admiration and gratitude which we owe it, that our mind has to be clear. Russia should and could be a partner of immense value for the future history of Europe. But the best kind of partnership is not likely to be obtained if we fail to look at the danger points.

A. *Europe*: The immediate position.
Informed opinion is agreed about the chaos impending – if no steps are taken by the United Nations to prevent it. At present Russia is defending its own soil; and at the same time Stalin is discriminating between the Hitlerite State and Germany. Note must be taken of the Manifesto of the National Committee of Free Germany issued in Moscow at the end of July, which asks for a genuine German National Government to [be] set up, which will overthrow Hitler and disarm him and his patrons and accomplices,

and states that this government must 'immediately cease military hostilities, withdraw German troops from the frontiers, and enter into negotiations for peace, relinquishing all conquered territory'; which also offers the German people as a whole 'a Free Germany', viz. 'a strong, democratic power, which will have nothing in common with the overthrown regime'; and involves 'a just and merciless trial of those guilty of the war'; together with an amnesty 'for all those adherents of Hitler who recant in time'; and further appeals to German soldiers on all fronts to return to their fatherland with 'their arms in their hands'. Russia is thereby claiming friends in Germany.

Britain and America at the same time are giving no signs of any similar discrimination. They offer no alternative programme either to Hitler or to Stalin. They simply call for unconditional surrender. And by the systematic bombing of great German towns, they are in danger of arousing the opposition of the whole German people to Britain and America, and rallying all Germans behind Hitler. There seem to be few signs of a sense of Europe as Europe here, and too many indications of a giving way to the predominance of Russia in Germany and so in Europe.

B. *Post-Armistice.*
There is an undoubted dread in Northern Europe of Russian *Communist* occupation. But whether that is justified or not on the economic side, the history of the war years gives ground for the fear that Soviet occupation, like Nazi occupation, would be ruthless. In any case, the evolution towards a militaristic state is very marked. Evolution into an imperialistic expansionist state is apt to be a natural sequel. There are ominous signs of Russia's intention to absorb the Baltic States and a large part of Poland, at the least. The process of extending frontiers for greater security easily develops a habit of further extensions for greater power, as history reminds us. The re-establishment of the Patriarchate, associated with Czarist Russian ambitions in the Near East, may again have a political significance in the same quarter. If Germany collapses, her defeat will probably be due in the main to Russia's efforts. The immediate consequence of victory will probably be the Red Army's occupation of the whole of central Europe and a large part of Germany. Russia alone would have the strength to place an effective army of occupation in these countries. At the same time, the British and American armies might occupy the countries of Southern Europe and some part of Germany. What if in the countries occupied by the British and American armies there were an acute struggle between the Right and the Left? What if the Left appealed for help to Stalin? What if the Left gained such power that they applied to join the U.S.S.R.? What if Stalin requested the British and American occupying forces to depart?

Once again, it has to be remembered that Stalin draws a sharp distinction between the Hitlerite State and the German people. The Allies apparently not. The Allies, further, by their silence, not only encourage the Left elements in Germany, but arouse feelings of something like despair amongst the ordinary anti-Nazis who oppose Hitler on liberal and democratic or religious grounds.

Danger points for the Peace Aims Group to bear in mind.
The danger of European chaos.
The danger of so waging the war in Europe as to cause irretrievable destruction and lasting bitterness.

The danger of an overwhelming Russian predominance in Europe, unless Britain, U.S.A., and Soviet Russia have a common mind, to which British and American ideals are really giving their historic contribution.

The complete silence of the Moscow Conference about the Atlantic Charter.

The danger of acquiescing in a victory in which Poland, after having suffered untold agony, is handed over to Russia by a Britain which first went to war to save Poland from Germany.

The particular position of the Baltic States as a test case, and the relevance of the principles of the Atlantic Charter.

Positive points for the Peace Aims Group to emphasise.
The necessity of the Four Nations stating the <u>basis</u> on which they are to collaborate for security, etc.

The necessity of the Four Nations holding firm to the Atlantic Charter, especially

Point 2.	No territorial changes that do not accord with the freely expressed wishes of people concerned.
3.	Restoration of sovereign rights and self-government to those who have been forcibly deprived of them.
4 & 5.	Fullest possible economic collaboration between all nations great or small, victor or vanquished.
6, 7 & 8.	Security, including the disarmament of such nations as threaten aggression outside their own frontiers.

The necessity of discriminating between 'Nazi tyranny' and its victims.
Treatment of vanquished enemy nations
This Memorandum is already long enough. Incidentally it carries certain consequences in our attitude to the vanquished enemy nations, and I would suggest here too that the Atlantic Charter is a very good guide to the spirit in which we should approach them. The Charter does point to a better future in which the vanquished nations share after the final destruction of the Nazi Tyranny. Insistence on it may be a better way of shortening the war than the demand for 'unconditional surrender', which while presumably a military term, is widely represented as probably including political extinction. Indeed, it requires the restoration of sovereign rights and self-government to those who have been forcibly deprived of them, as well as the disarmament of aggressor nations. At the same time, while insisting on security, and acknowledging the right of all peoples to choose the form of government under which they will live, it holds out a hope to the vanquished, whether in Italy or Germany or elsewhere, that a means for their moral recovery must in the end be found within a particular nation and cannot be imposed from without.

2.12.43.

---

[1] 'A Christian Basis for Reconstruction' (final form), 22 July 1943, Bell Papers, Vol. 26, fols. 206–8.

Leibholz to Bell, 10 December 1943, Bell Papers 40, fols. 221–2 (typewritten); BA, N 1334 (copy)

My Lordbishop,

I must apologise for not having written to you earlier. But just as I was recovering my wife and the children fell ill with a rather bad attack of flu and as we have no domestic help I had to see to them all. Now, although still confined to bed, they are better and the first letter I am writing is to thank you for all your kindness.

The news about Dietrich has filled me with great sorrow.[1] We had always confidently hoped that, in the meantime, he had been set free again, but now our hopes are dashed to the ground. I could not bring myself to tell my wife the sad news because (apart from the flu) she is not well at all and, no doubt, she would worry terribly if she knew the content of Visser 't Hooft's letter. She knows that these news [sic] have bad implications for her old parents, brothers and sisters. The passage that there is no need for special anxiety is rather vague and not very encouraging.

By the way, Niebuhr has just asked me how Dietrich is. I feel you will allow me to pass on the news I have received from you.

I wonder what you think about the bombing. I quite agree with what you say in your last memorandum and think that it will have a unifying effect. In addition, as far as I can judge, it seems to me to exceed what is strictly necessary to attain military ends, unless one calls the indiscriminate destruction of the whole population in the cities a military end. The fact that the Nazis have invented this method of waging war does not seem to me to justify the present procedure. If I am not mistaken, the Churches stated in former years that they would raise their voices if the bombing would exceed what is necessary, from a military point of view. I think it is hardly possible to leave to the military authorities the last decisive word in these matters.

As to Moscow-Teheran[2] I doubt whether with regard to central Europe the Russians have changed their basic attitude. If I am mistaken, the Central Europe would be ruled in times to come by the help of the traditional means of power politics. But I think that if any lesson is to be learned from history it is that all the various attempts hitherto made to pacify the world in this way have not succeeded. In the connection before us: if Versailles was not able to bring peace to the world how can a policy which must inevitably lead to a policy of unending repression pacify the world? How can a Central Europe settlement, which deals with Central Europe as a pure object, avoid an alignment of Central (or even Western) Europe against the Three Great Powers? In addition, I should not think that such a harmony among the 'Three Big' would last long. For the planned introduction of 'Democracy' in Central Europe should not deceive us on the fact that the Western Powers and Russia understand by it a different thing. And as you know, my Lord Bishop, I am afraid that in face of the lamentable policy of the Western Powers the political dynamics in the Central European countries favour a development which in the end will lead these countries to embrace some form of Eastern totalitarian democracy. If this is the case then I feel sure the ideological line of Russian policy would make its reappearance and break up the Three Powers' 'unity'. Therefore, even if the Soviet Union should accede to the Western security policy the decisive Central European problem would hereby not be solved. It would only be veiled in a new form. And in the end the Western powers would be the losers of this ideological struggle.

Now, I have read with the greatest interest and wholehearted agreement your new Memorandum. I am so grateful to you for having broached these questions. Your arguments seem to me realistic, full of lively imagination and courageous. I think your time will come. The question seems to me to be only whether the fateful 'too Late' will again play its disastrous part. From my point of view, I welcome, above all, what you say about the non-European character of the Western policy of today and the implications of this policy. The questions you broach on page 4 are quite similar to those I have in mind myself. That the Atlantic Charter has been lately dropped in the background seems to me to be also largely due to the fact that the war loses more and more its ideological character. I wonder how the meeting went off yesterday and whether you found support from any of the members of the group.

By the way, I re-wrote the article on *Unconditional Surrender* in the light of the Moscow Conference.[3] It will come out in the next issue of *The Hibbert Journal* and I will send you a copy of it.

As to Italy I cannot judge the situation. But, on the whole, I think the development will take there the same line as in Central Europe. Your arguments in the last *Times* letter seem to me to carry such a great weight that the policy ought to be clear. But even in this respect I doubt whether the right way will be taken. I think that Sforza[4] and Croce[5] represent no political forces of weight which will hold good in the Italy of tomorrow. Badoglio,[6] the Liberals and the other Western forces I fear are all compromised by the implications of the Unconditional Surrender policy.

Thank you very much for the pamphlet on the Barmen Declaration.[7] I am very glad that you have written the foreword to it and I hope it will impress those whom it concerns. I am enclosing a political pamphlet of my own. Please do not bother to read it. I send it to you only as a token. – In the last issue of the Bulletin of the Fellowship I have tried to explain in greater detail what you, my Lord Bishop, said on the refugee problem in one of the sessions in the House of Lords.[8]

With all good wishes to you and Mrs Bell, also from my wife and the children,

Yours ever,

---

[1] See Bell to Leibholz, 21 November 1943.
[2] Conference of the 'Big Three' (Churchill, Roosevelt, Stalin) at Teheran from 28 November to 1 December.
[3] See Leibholz to Bell, 31 August 1943 (note 1).
[4] Carlo Graf Sforza (1866–1952), Italian Minister of Foreign Affairs in 1920–1. In 1927 he emigrated to France, Britain and Switzerland, moved in 1940 to the United States. In October 1943 Sforza had returned to Italy and in the following April joined the provisional antifascist government. After the war, between 1947 and 1951, he again became Minister of Foreign Affairs.
[5] Benedetto Croce (1866–1952), idealistic philosopher and occasional Liberal politician. In April 1944 this 'icon of liberal anti-fascism' became minister without portfolio in the cabinets of Badoglio and then Bonomi, but only for three months.
[6] Pietro Badoglio (1871–1956), since 1936 1st Duca di Addis Abeba; an Italian general during both world wars, named prime minister by King Victor Emanuel III on 25 July 1943. On 3 September 1943, General Giuseppe Castellano signed the Italian armistice with the Allies in Cassibile on behalf of Badoglio, who hesitated to announce the treaty formally, wary of a hostile German response. On

13 October Badoglio and the Kingdom of Italy officially declared war on Nazi Germany. Badoglio continued to head the government for another nine months until 8 June 1944.
[7] G. Bell and J. O Cobham (eds.), *The Significance of the Barmen Declaration for the Ecumenical Church* (*Theology. Occasional Papers*, NS 5), (London, 1943).
[8] See Bell's speech of 28 July 1943, reprinted in *The Church and Humanity*, pp. 123–8.

Mary Balmer[1] to Leibholz, 15 December 1943 (typewritten), BA, N 1334; Bell Papers 40, fol. 223 (carbon)

Dear Doctor Leibholz,

The Bishop is confined to bed with influenza; but he asks me to thank you for your letter, and to say how sorry he is to hear that your wife and family have been ill. He very much hopes that the worst is now over.

He also asks me to tell you that there was a good discussion on his Memorandum at the meeting of the Peace Aims Group last week. The group is to meet again to consider a concrete document on January 7th. The Archbishop of Canterbury is speaking in the House of Lords on Thursday,[2] and the Bishop hopes that what he says will be influenced by the discussion.

Yours sincerely,

[1] Bell's secretary of many years.
[2] William Temple spoke in the debate about Allied Conferences; Hansard, H.L. Deb., Vol. 130, cols. 400–5 (16 December 1943).

Leibholz to Bell, 17 December 1943, Bell Papers 40, fol. 224 (handwritten)

My Lordbishop,

My wife and I are so very sorry to hear from your secretary that you are also confined to bed with influenza. We very much hope that you have caught it in a rather slight form and that the worst is over when this letter reaches you. But please forgive me for asking you to take care of yourself. After our experiences I feel this influenza is rather insidious. After we had thought we had got over it the temperature came back again and even after it had finally gone none of us has felt fit again quite a good tune. [sic]

I am very glad that there was a good discussion on your memorandum at the meeting of the Peace Aims Group last week and I hope to read the Archbishop of Canterbury's speech in *Hansard* tomorrow. As soon as you are better again I hope to write to you more about it.

It would be very kind if your secretary would drop a line to tell us how you are. For I shall be very eager to have better news.

Our thoughts will again be this Christmas with you and Mrs Bell in renewed deep gratitude for all you have done for us in the course of the last few years. May you and Mrs Bell enjoy a blessed Christmas – in spite of the dark days we are living through.

Once again our very best wishes in which the children also join go out to you for a speedy recovery.

Yours ever,

Bell to Leibholz, 20 December 1943, BA, N 1334 (handwritten)

My dear Leibholz,
Very many thanks for your tender inquiries, which I much appreciate. I am recovered! and have recommenced work today. Fortunately I have nothing much on this week in the public or out of doors line: so I *can* (and will) go slow!

I do hope you are all out of the wood yourselves: and will have a peaceful Christmas. I understand well how it can['t] be free from anxiety. And I constantly think of Dietrich and our other friends in Germany. The bombing is terrible to think of; amongst so much else.

You will now have read the Archbishop's speech in the Lords. But while of course it contained good stuff, to me it was a bit disappointing, for it failed to make the point I was so anxious he should make that we must put the *case of Europe as a whole* in the vy. foreground of our thinking, and must give continental countries, including Germany, the conviction that we (*British* + USA) should stand for a liberal and Christian order in Europe, and this means freedom, and room everywhere for the human personality to develop: that we also want a Europe in which a recovered Germany plays its full part.

It may be that the document now being drafted for the Peace Aims Group by a young European-minded member very well informed and in much sympathy with myself will be able to say this.[1] At present I am too conscious of a trend *away* from our former affirmations in favour of a recovered Germany either to the vague and general or to what is worse[:] the Great Power Protection theory.

I enclose the Foreword and opening chapter of my new Pamphlet[2] to be published shortly by Gollancz (ch. iv is the Memo. for the Princeton USA Round Table of July 1943, which you have). I am awaiting the proofs. What I say will be unpopular. But I want it to be as effective for *Europe* as I can make it. Please criticise and correct with that aim in view. Your comments and improvements will be invaluable.

Yours always,

---

[1] This is most likely to refer to pamphlet 'The Future of Germany', published as Number 19 in the *Peace Aims Pamphlet* series in 1943. The pamphlet presented a succession of contributions by the journalist H.N. Brailsford, the Labour politician Patrick Gordon Walker, Colonel T.H. Minshall, the Quaker H.G. Wood and the Methodist Henry Carter. The 'young European-minded member' might well be Patrick Gordon Walker, who was still in his mid-thirties.
[2] George Bell, *Germany and the Hitlerite State* (London, 1943).

Leibholz to Bell, 28 December 1943, Bell Papers 40, fols. 225–6 (typewritten); BA, N 1334 (copy)

My Lord Bishop,
How thankful I am to hear that you have made a good recovery and I hope you will really be able to go slow for a time.

What a brilliant idea to bring out the two important speeches in the Lords together with the Memorandum for the Americans in a separate book. Thus the speeches will have in the public that effect they ought to have had from the beginning and I hope they will powerfully contribute to counterbalance the main political trend of today.

I read the foreword and the introductory chapter immediately with ardour and was immensely interested. I wholeheartedly agree with what you say so courageously. As the truth is unpalatable today as at all times I think one should be prepared for a possibly not very friendly reception of the book by some sections of the political press. I think the book will be recognised in its real significance only in later times just as was the case with Keynes' book.[1]

The passage from Mr Churchill[2] was unknown to me. It is most striking and it is a very good idea to begin the book with it.

If the lesson were learnt from what you say at the end of the introductory chapter one might be inclined to argue: When the Ruhr occupation[3] had the consequences Söderblom rightly predicted what much more far-reaching consequences must result from the occupation of the whole of Germany, yes of Central Europe for an unlimited period?[4] Instead of coming to this conclusion people argue (see Mr Roosevelt's last speech): as Versailles with all its implications (e.g. the Ruhr occupation) was not able to crush Germany's militarist spirit we must impose on her a Super-Versailles. They entirely forget that they themselves have greatly contributed with their power policy (after Versailles) to re-vitalising German militarism and to weakening all democratic and liberal forces there.

I think your book, my Lordbishop, will be a most valuable supplement to the Archbishop of Canterbury's policy, which, to my mind, lacks in some essential points the inner coherence. I have read his last speech in the Lords. I think he rightly stresses that the new German generation must not grow up with the feeling that it is relegated to a position of permanent inferiority. Otherwise, the Archbishop argues, 'there will be a source of irritation and an increasing feeling of soreness, which will bode ill for future peace'.[5] Quite so. But at the same time the Archbishop advocates a policy which makes a good neighbour policy hardly possible. The deeper-rooted reason for this is that – as you have fully made clear – the power policy, which the Western countries are pursuing today, excludes a constructive Western Policy, which is the presupposition of a good neighbour policy. This is the great dilemma into which the policy of the Western countries has fallen today. To my mind, it is a fatal mistake to think as people generally do today that the creation and organisation of overwhelming power will secure future peace, and that ideological considerations can be relegated to the wings. Such a policy would have a chance of success only if the Allies would aim at the destruction of Germany. But these are not only Mr Stalin's but also Mr Churchill's and Roosevelt's statements, which point quite clearly and unmistakably to the contrary. If so, then the policy favoured today by the Western countries must lead to a policy of unending repression, which in the end will cause Europe finally to break away from the West and also to break up, by implication, the unity seemingly established today among the three Great Powers.

My point is, first, that real security can only be established on common ideological grounds and that power must be used *ab initio* as a means in the service of this purpose, and secondly, that the present policy of the Western countries is non-European in its basic character because it is directed to the undermining of a future ideological community between the West and Central Europe and is leading hereby to ruin and perpetuation of war. All the ideological pretences of Western policy cannot deceive us today as to the fact that Western policy points to the quite illusory idea (especially in the 20th century) that nothing is real but power. One of the regrettable consequences of this policy is that it must unify (and has already probably unified) the Germans in their struggle of pure existence and stifles all attempts of the opposition to get rid of the present regime in Germany from within.

Your book has made me fully realize the rather tragic political situation of today: if one tries to analyse the various political groups in this country with regard to their policy toward Central Europe I think one can distinguish between the following groups:

First there are the Communists and their sympathisers who aim at a Communist totalitarian Continent in the Russian fashion.

Secondly there are the fascist groups, which to avoid this result favour a compromised [sic] peace with Hitler and wish to erect a fascist regime in this country.

Thirdly, there are those who form the overwhelming bulk of the population who are faithful to the ideas of Western tradition as developed in this country. They seem to me to fall in two large groups. First, there is the Left, which is inclined to distinguish between Nazism and Germany but, as it seems to me, is not able – because of its dogmatic Marxist ties – to come to realistic conclusions with regard to the future of Germany and Central Europe. These circles favour a socialist-communist Germany hoping that this new Germany will respect religious freedom and leave room for the development of the human personality in the Western sense. Although many Christians in this country share this view, I think it is hopelessly un-realistic (The reasoning for this argument would lead me too far in this connection).

The other group, however, which wants a new Germany on a democratic basis, the Conservatives, roughly speaking, (as far as they have not fascist sympathies) favour more or less a Vansittartist power policy, which drives Central Europe still further from the West than it ever was and is in its effects non-European as it plays into the hands of the Russians. As far as I can see, you and a few other personalities alone pursue – what I should call – a realistic and constructive policy from the Western point of view. I feel this situation is tragic because, in the long run, on the success of this latter policy the fate of Europe depends.

By the way, General Smuts in his last speech favoured a close union of Great Britain with the smaller Western democracies, which have the same way of life and outlook as Great Britain.[6] I agree. But why not pursue this policy on a much larger basis and do all in one's power to win over the enemies of today. The situation in Italy should be a forcible reminder. Your suggestions point to the right direction, if I may say so, my Lordbishop. It is this policy, which in the end can alone finally secure peace.

I am enclosing the copy of an essay at, which you may like to have a look. It has come out in the last issue of *Blackfriars*.[7]

Once again with all good wishes for the New Year to you and Mrs Bell, also from my wife and the children

Yours ever,

---

[1] Almost certainly a reference to John Maynard Keynes, *The Economic Consequences of the Peace* (London, 1919).

2   See Bell, *Germany and the Hitlerite State*, p. 4.
3   The French Ruhr occupation – and German passive resistance – lasted from January 1923 to July 1925.
4   See Nathan Söderblom to Gottfried Billing, 27 January 1923, and also the enclosure to Gustav Johansson, 2 February 1923 ('An Appeal from all of Sweden's bishops to our fellow Christians in all countries and to the responsible statesmen'), in Dietz Lange (ed.), Nathan Söderblom, *Brev – Lettres – Briefe – Letters. A. Selection from His Correspondence* (Göttingen 2006), no. 200–1.
5   Hansard, H.L. Deb., Vol. 130, col. 403 (16 December 1943)
6   A controversial speech on future relations between the British Empire and the Soviet Union and the United States, made at a private meeting of the Empire Parliamentary Association at the House of Commons and reported by the British press on 3 December 1943. Jan Christian Smuts (1870–1950), Prime Minister of the Union of South Africa, 1919–24 and 1939–48. Smuts had joined the wartime Imperial War Cabinet and was widely respected for his views. On this occasion there was anxiety as to whether these opinions represented government policy.
7   'The Essence of Politics', in *Blackfriars: A Monthly Review Edited by the English Dominicans*, December 1943, Vol. XXIV, No. 285, pp. 453–9, reprinted in Leibholz, *Politics and Law*, pp. 13–19.

1944

4 January	Soviet forces enter Poland.
20 January	Heavy bombing of Berlin by RAF Bomber Command.
22 January	Allied forces land at Anzio.
20–5 February	American and British bombing forces launch the 'Big Week' of attacks against German aircraft manufacturers, attacking night and day.
20 March	Bomber Command attacks Nuremberg.
4 June	Allied forces enter Rome.
6 June	'D Day': Allied forces invade France.
20 July	The attempted coup d'état in Germany fails to kill Hitler and remove the National Socialist state.
24 July	Majdanek concentration camp is liberated by Soviet forces.
1 August	The Warsaw Uprising begins.
7 August	The first trials of members of the German resistance begin at the People's Court in Berlin; the first executions follow the next day.
21 August	The Dumbarton Oaks conference begins to frame a post-war order and look towards the creation of a United Nations Organization.
25 August	Paris is liberated.
31 August	Soviet troops enter Bucharest.
3 September	Brussels is liberated and, two days later, Antwerp.
16 September	Soviet forces enter Sofia.
21 September	The second Dumbarton Oaks conference.
2 October 1944	The Warsaw Uprising is defeated.
9 October	Churchill and Stalin meet in Moscow to discuss the post-war settlement in the Balkans.
14 October	British troops enter Athens.
6 November	President Roosevelt wins a fourth term in office.
16 December	German forces counter-attack in the Ardennes.

Bell to Leibholz, 3 January 1944, BA, N 1334 (typewritten); Bell Papers 40, fol. 227 (carbon)

My dear Leibholz,

Very many thanks for your most interesting letter of the 28th December. I am glad you are in agreement with my Foreword and introductory chapter. I have made one or two verbal amendments in the proof. You shall of course have some copies of the pamphlet when published. I agree with you that it is likely to be criticised, and I may get a certain amount of scolding. But I write with care and deliberately after having thought carefully about the wisdom of thus writing and speaking.

What you say about the tragedy of the political situation today is only too true, and I agree with your diagnosis. I also agree with your comment on General Smuts' speech, and the possibility of pursuing his policy on a much larger basis, and doing all in one's power to win over the enemies of today.

Thank you very much for your essay in *Blackfriars*. I am going away for a week's holiday shortly, and shall hope to read it, and your earlier article and write again.

By the way, I am rather concerned about the programme to be followed in connection with the Centre for which a house in North Street, Westminster has been found.[1] Emmerich[2] is the leader of the little theological group there. But there must be a great widening of the appeal. I myself want to see some lectures given there by Germans on current problems, and amongst the lecturers I naturally want to see you. I should be very glad if you would give your mind to the idea of the programme, and make suggestions as to speakers and subjects. I personally want the house to be a kind [of] forum for the discussion of and interchange of views upon the present international situation; and also for the enlightenment of both German and British friends on religious, sociological and political trends in Germany.

I do hope you are all well again now.

With best wishes for the New Year,

Yours ever,

---

[1] In 1942 the exiled German theologians discussed plans to create a training centre for those drawn to ministerial work after the war. This became the German Confessional Institute. Wolfgang Büsing served as secretary under C.G. Schweitzer. In the first term (November/December 1942) 37 men and women studied theology or missionary/social work there. Leibholz lectured on Church and State. Soon difficulties arose and a new prospect opened outside London, in a house in Wistow, near Leicester. In July 1943 the Wistow Training Centre for Post-War Christian Service was opened. Under Schweitzer's leadership 12 students were instructed in pastoral work. The German Confessional Institute remained in London, set aside for theological courses, but it could not be opened before June 1944. See Friedeborg L. Müller, *The History of German Lutheran Congregations in England, 1900-1950* (Frankfurt am Main, 1987), pp. 152-64; see too Eberhard Röhm and Jörg Thierfelder, *Juden - Christen - Deutsche*, Vol 4/1, Stuttgart 1995, pp. 560-1; Bell Papers, Vols. 35 (fols. 195-6) and 37.

[2] Kurt Emmerich (1903-76), a lawyer until 1933 when he lost his job because of his Jewish descent. In 1935 he emigrated to Paris where he was baptized by Pierre Maury. He studied theology in Basle in 1936-9 and, with Bell's help, immigrated to Britain in August 1939. Emmerich taught at Bishop Wilson Theological College on the Isle of Man, 1940-3, and at Wistow Training Centre, 1943-6. He returned to Germany in 1947, becoming a lawyer at the district court at Karlsruhe and, in 1961, head of the court.

Leibholz to Bell, 7 January 1944, Bell Papers 40, fol. 228 (typewritten)

My Lordbishop,

Very many thanks for your letter.

I have carefully thought over what you have written me about the new Centre. May I ask you to allow me to submit [to] you a few remarks on this matter for consideration.

I fully share your concern and think with you that it would be desirable to enlarge the functions of the centre in the direction you have in mind. What I am not quite sure about is whether there would be a real need and interest in additional lectures.[1] I remember the German Confessional Institute organized about a dozen courses of lectures on various religious, political and social questions in 1942 and as far as I know these lectures, as far as they were delivered in German, were not attended by more than six people on an average. And I doubt whether this number could be raised under the present circumstances as the German 'Freie Hochschule'[2] and the 'Kulturbund'[3] deal also with the same subjects and lays hold on those refugees who have time and are interested in these subjects.[4] Of course, I know there are serious doubts about the 'Hochschule', first because of its political aims and, secondly, because, on the whole, they have at their disposal second-rate lecturers. On the other hand, however, they have a working organisation, have funds at their disposal and seem to me to satisfy the existing needs on [the] part of the refugees. And yet I would hardly say that their work proves a real success. For instance, last term the 'Hochschule' opened here a branch backed by the university and was also able to secure some able scholars for a few lectures which, however, had also only a poor attendance. Even if the number of the audience in London should be higher, what can we expect if we try to organize in certain fields a kind of parallel running enterprise? I am afraid those whom we approach – as far as they are qualified – would tell us that they feel there is no real need on the part of the refugees and the audience would probably [be] too small. I do not know whether these fragmentary and inadequate remarks, which need further elaboration, are in any way convincing to you. But I think I should tell you what I feel in this matter.

On the other hand I think it is a brilliant idea to develop the house as you say, my Lordbishop, 'into a kind of forum for the discussion of and interchange of views upon, the present international situation'. Would it not be possible to attain this aim by forming a Study Group consisting of both British and German friends interested in political, sociological and religious problems as far as Germany and Central Europe is concerned? Within such a Study Group lectures on special subjects as you suggest, my Lordbishop, could be delivered and discussed, reports be made and its works perhaps published by you in a special series on behalf of this institute. I think that such a Study Group perhaps in connection with other groups of similar aims (e.g. in Chatham House, P.E.P)[5] under your guidance could fulfil valuable functions, especially after the war has come to an end. What I do not know is whether there is a real interest on the English side to work together with Germans in this way.[6] You can judge this much better. I am a little sceptical, although I have just heard that e.g. Chatham House is no longer disinterested [sic] in working together with Germans as some time ago. It is true, organisations like the National Peace Council pursue similar aims. But I think the difference lies in the fact that we would have only to deal with matters within Germany or Central Europe.

I do not know whether what I have tried to say appeals to you in any way. Should such a plan be about in accordance with what you have in mind I should be very glad and I could then try to suggest a few subjects or current subjects, problems to be discussed later on and name you some able people who should perhaps be considered members of this group.

In any case I wish to comply with your wishes and I should be grateful to you if you would let me know them after having read this letter.

I am enclosing *The Hibbert Journal*[7] about, which I wrote to you, my Lordbishop, in a former letter. The article may perhaps interest you.

I do hope you had a refreshing holiday and have now fully recovered.

With all good wishes from all of us

Yours ever,

---

[1] Indeed the German Confessional Institute did not flourish; students could only study once the working day was done and in January 1945 only four students came for the evening classes. On 1 January 1946 the Institute was closed; see Müller, *German Lutheran Congregations in England*, pp. 152–64; also Röhm and Tierfelder, *Juden*, 4/I, pp. 580–1.

[2] The 'Freie Deutsche Hochschule' was founded by the 'Freie Deutsche Bewegung' in Great Britain. For Leibholz's criticisms, see his letter to Laura Livingstone, 18 June 1943, Bell Papers, Vol. 40, fols. 143–4.

[3] The 'Freie Deutsche Kulturbund in England' (the Free German League of Culture) was a forerunner of the Kulturbund in the GDR.

[4] This sentence is marked by a black line in the margin.

[5] Like the influential Royal Institute of International Affairs at Chatham House, Political and Economic Planning was a policy think tank, founded in 1931.

[6] The last two sentences are marked by a black line.

[7] See Leibholz, 'Ideology in the Post-War Policy of Russia and the Western Powers', reprinted in Leibholz, *Politics and Law*, pp. 182–93; see too Leibholz to Bell, 31 August 1943.

Bell to Leibholz, 17 January 1944, BA, N 1334 (typewritten); Bell Papers 40, fol. 229 (carbon)

My dear Leibholz,

Very many thanks for your letter, which was as usual full of wisdom and encouragement. I think your idea of joint discussion in groups or study circles is excellent, and I will see what can be done in that direction at our Committee meeting on Tuesday. I am very grateful for your own readiness to help.

I have read your article in *The Hibbert* with the greatest interest and agreement. It is, of course, extremely well set out and documented; but in addition to that it is most wise and persuasive. I am very glad that *The Hibbert* gave you the hospitality of its columns for such an able and clear, but not hard or unfriendly, criticism of the present trend of British and American policy. I do very much wish that many members of our own government and leaders of thought would read it.

I am sure you are following with close attention the proceedings with regard to Poland.[1] F.A. Voigt, with whom I am in touch from time to time, is terribly unhappy about what he regards as an impending second Munich. There is no need, he says, for Britain to make war on Russia because of a Polish dismemberment; but it is not bound to acquiesce in the policy in any sort of way. Is it perhaps possible that Benesch (this is not what he has said) takes the role of Mussolini?[2] And if Russia is allowed to get what it wants now with regard to Poland, can you not hear an echo of the old promise – positively the last territorial demand? And can you not see how, if once there is acquiescence with regard to Poland, the Baltic States[3] go, and one after another territory is absorbed? I am not saying that the ªexactª boundaries claimed by Poland are right; but it is the principle that matters.

I have also read your two reprints from *Blackfriars* and the *Dublin Review* with much pleasure. I am particularly interested in your criticism of the proportional system.

I received a letter recently through the Estonian Minister, dated October 26th, the writer being Klaus Scheel.[4] When I was in Sweden in 1942 I had a long talk with him about Estonia and the Baltic States, and he has once or twice sent me material to keep me up to date. On this recent occasion, thanking me for a letter which I had written to him, he sent me two very interesting typescripts, *Have the Baltic Countries voluntarily renounced their Freedom?* and a criticism of Ambassador Davies' book about the Moscow Embassy.[5] At the close of his letter to me he writes as follows:

'I have been asked to let you know that the position of Mr Dohnanyi, a brother-in-law of Friedrich Bonhoeffer, is now viewed more optimistically and that Mrs Dohnanyi has already been set free.[6] This information reached me incidentally in the early days of August but I heard a few days ago that the lawyer who had their case in hand has now been imprisoned himself.[7] Personally I do not know any of the people mentioned above.'

I pass this on to you, thinking that probably you will know to whom it refers.

Once more, ever so many thanks,

Yours very sincerely,

---

[1] According to the Teheran Conference the eastern border of Poland should be the Curzon line while the Oder should mark the western border.
[2] Edvard Beneš concluded on 12 December 1943 a Czechoslovak–Soviet mutual assistance pact to cover the time after the war. Stalin accepted Beneš' plan of the expulsion of Germans and Hungarians. In consequence of this Beneš became a supporter of Soviet expansion towards the west, particularly in the case of Poland.
[3] After the German occupation of the Baltic States in 1944 Socialist Soviet Republics, named as they had been under the terms of the 1939 Molotov-Ribbentrop Treaty.
[4] Klaus Scheel (1890–1961), an Estonian banker, had since 1939 been head of the bank G. Scheel & Co. After the Soviet occupation he migrated to Brazil and, in 1954, to Germany.
[5] Joseph Edward Davies (1876–1958), United States ambassador to Moscow, 1936–8; he was the author of *Mission to Moscow* (New York, 1941).
[6] Christine von Dohnanyi was arrested on 5 April 1943 but detained only until 30 April 1943.
[7] See Bethge and Jasper, *An der Schwelle*, p. 138. Bethge suspected that Dr. Carl Langbehn had been arrested in October 1943. Langbehn was not Dohnanyi's defence lawyer, but he had intervened on his behalf with Himmler and the Gestapo.

Leibholz to Bell, 17 January 1944, Bell Papers 40, fol. 230 (typewritten)

My Lordbishop,

I have just read Visser 't Hooft's most illuminating and striking *Christian News-Letter* on *The Future of Europe*.[1] I think he confirms exactly what we think and what you have so forcibly and admirably voiced at various occasions. Should not the new Centre about which we have recently corresponded be made a centre for furthering just this policy, i.e. a centre with the aim of reminding the West again and again of its European responsibility and of pressing for a more concrete and consistent Western policy in order to avoid (as Visser 't Hooft says) the Russian way-out becoming the only way-out for Europe and thus committing suicide? Should you be, my Lordbishop, on the whole, in favour of such a plan do you not think that in this case the main task of the Institute should be to influence the English in the direction mentioned, which would entail the refugees only being used in so far as they can really help in attaining this aim in one way or another. To further such an aim seems to me of the utmost and urgent importance. Thus we should have a clear line of demarcation over against all the other various organisations which today deal with post-war relief, post-war training, education of refugees, the so called Free German 'Hochschule' etc. I wonder what you think about this.

Yours ever,

---

[1] Willem Adolph Visser 't Hooft, 'The Future of Europe', in: *Christian News-Letter – Supplement*, December 1943.

Leibholz to Bell, 20 January 1944, Bell papers 40, fol. 231 (typewritten); BA, N 1334 (copy)

My Lordbishop,

Very many thanks for your extremely interesting and encouraging letter. I am so glad that you find my suggestion useful and I wonder how the Committee meeting went off on Tuesday. The more I think about the whole matter the more important seems to me the task which such a discussion group or study circle under your guidance could fulfil in future. I can imagine that something bigger might develop out of it in course of time.

I was grateful to Dr Jacks[1] for having given me hospitality in his periodical for the essay and in addition I was glad to gather from the correspondence with him that he himself is obviously in agreement with the basic lines of the article. By the way, I am also indebted to you in this connection as without your initiative and without what I have learned from you I should not have been able to write the article. It grew out [of] the Memorandum I wrote for you in connection with your work for the American Round Table Conference.[2]

You are right, my Lordbishop, I am closely following the proceedings with regard to Poland. I think the whole Polish-Russian tension lends much force to our plea for a more far-sighted ideological policy. Frankly, I should not have thought probable that this tension would become acute so soon after the Moscow and Teheran Conferences. If one thinks of the enthusiasm with which these Conferences were hailed here and in the United States and bears in mind how these conferences were celebrated as epoch-making victories by the Press (e.g. *The Times*) one cannot help thinking that the leaders of political thought have again miscalculated the political and social driving forces ªof this warª. I wholeheartedly agree with all you write in this respect, my Lordbishop. I for my part have very little doubt that Russia will absorb not only the greater part of Poland, but also the Baltic States, Lithuania and a part of Finland and Rumania. I think this is the least the Western powers will have to swallow.

The news you very kindly passed on to me has filled me with great anxiety: It is the question of my wife's sister and her husband, Dr v. Dohnanyi (a son of the great Hungarian musician) who obviously together with Dietrich were arrested. And the lawyer is either another brother of my wife or a great friend of mine on whom I have always put my special trust.³ I have not passed on the depressing news to my wife since – as I wrote to you before – my wife is not well (she will possibly undergo an operation before long) and I think I should spare her this extra anxiety at least for the time being.

Once again, very many thanks for all your kindness,

Yours ever,

---

[1] Lawrence Pearsall Jacks (1860–1955) was professor of philosophy and theology at Manchester College, Oxford, and the first, and longest-serving, editor of *The Hibbert Journal* from 1902 until 1948.
[2] Enclosure to the letter of Leibholz to Bell, 13 May 1943.
[3] Klaus Bonhoeffer or Kurt Wergin. Klaus Bonhoeffer (1901–45) was chief lawyer of Lufthansa 1937–44 and from 1940 heavily involved with the resistance movement. He would be arrested on 1 October 1944 and later sentenced to death by the People's Tribunal on 2 February 1945. A SS-commando squad murdered him, his brother-in-law Rüdiger Schleicher and others on the night of 22/23 April. The lawyer Kurt Wergin was a friend of Klaus Bonhoeffer who had lost his position as legal adviser to the Berlin transport services in 1934 because of his refusal to become a member of the NSDAP. In the following years Wergin helped a number of victims of persecution; on 16 September 1943 he became counsel for Dietrich Bonhoeffer.

Mary Balmer to Leibholz, 24 January 1944, BA, N 1334 (typewritten); Bell Papers 40, fol. 232 (carbon)

Dear Doctor Leibholz,

The Bishop asks me to let you know that he is passing through Oxford to-morrow, Tuesday, on his way to a funeral at Moreton-in-the-Marsh. The train leaves Paddington at 9.45 and reaches Oxford at 11.30. He has nothing special to say to you; but he will look out of the carriage window (third class) in case you were free and could walk down to the station to see him.

He asks me to say also that he has just received a letter from Dr Visser 't Hooft dated 23 December, which contains the following sentence: 'The situation of D. is unchanged neither better nor worse'.¹ The letter goes on to deal with other matters, and nothing more is said about D.²

Yours sincerely,

---

[1] W. A. Visser 't Hooft to Bell, 23 December 1944, published in Besier, *Intimately Associated for Many Years*, p. 239.
[2] This paragraph is crossed out.

Leibholz to Bell, 27 January 1944, Bell Papers 40, fol. 233 (typewritten)

My Lordbishop,

We were very glad indeed to have the opportunity of seeing you on your way to Moreton-in-the-Marsh, even if it was only for a few minutes.

It was a great shock to me when I heard of Quick's sudden death.[1] For when I saw him last in the Acland[2] before Christmas I found him better. I remember he told me that he did not mind retiring at all and that he was looking forward to resuming his work on Christian dogmatics in his new home.[3] He was not only a great theologian but an unusually attractive personality whose charm and goodness captivated one completely. How wonderful that you accompanied him in his life for such a long time. I shall greatly miss him here.

What you told me on Visser 't Hooft's comments on your *Fortnightly* article[4] interested me very much. It seems to me that the Continental Bible interpretation and the Catholic-Anglican Natural Law ideas and conceptions must be connected with each other. I think we can only speak of a specific Christian Natural Law if we can base it on the Bible in one way or another. Our occasional meetings in Hawarden on Natural Law[5] deal just with this question and I personally hope to follow up the matter more close[ly] as soon as I have finished another work.

If it were possible to see a copy of Visser 't Hooft's letter I should be glad. The time at the station was so short that I could not easily grasp what he wrote on the situation on the Continent.

I am greatly looking forward to your new article and the book. I feel sure that the latter will have a great repercussion on the Continent and especially in Germany. I for my part think that your position on the Continent is unique and I only wished that more men of leading political thought in this country would take to heart what you have to tell them. I think the new Centre in London could possibly play its special part in this connection and exercise a great influence if it were possible to organize it properly and to get the right people together.

With all good wishes
Yours ever,

[1] Oliver Quick had died on 21 January 1944.
[2] i.e. the Acland Hospital in Oxford.
[3] See Oliver Chase Quick, *The Gospel of the New World. A Study in the Christian Doctrine of Atonement*; with a prefatory memoir by the Archbishop of Canterbury (London, 1944) (posthumous publication).
[4] Almost certainly Bell, 'The Church and the Future of Europe', the paper which Bell had read to the Austrian Democratic Union in London on 20 January 1943, to be found in Bell, *The Church and Humanity*, pp. 110–22. See too W. A. Visser 't Hooft to Bell, 23 December, in Besier, *Intimately Associated for Many Years*, pp. 239–40.
[5] Hawarden being the location of St Deiniol's Library, where Vidler was Warden. See the Preface in A. Vidler and W. A. Whitehouse (eds.), *Natural Law. A Christian Re-consideration*, (London, 1946), pp. 7–8.

Bell to Leibholz, 29 January 1944, BA, N 1334 (typewritten); Bell Papers 40, fol. 234 (carbon)

My dear Leibholz,

Very many thanks for your letter. I enclose a copy of Visser 't Hooft's letter to me, which you can keep. I will send you a copy of my article in the *Fortnightly* as soon as possible. It was a real pleasure to see you.

By the way, I think you may be interested in the enclosed letter from Emmerich,[1] in reply to mine. I am afraid that our German Pastors are not very receptive. I am proposing to answer quite briefly, and let things be worked out in conversation.

Yours ever,

[1] Now lost.

Leibholz to Bell, 3 February 1944, Bell Papers 40, fol. 235 (handwritten)

My Lordbishop,

Tomorrow our thoughts will go out to you and Dietrich in special remembrances. We pray that the coming year will bring deliverance to him and to our other common friends from their sufferings and agony and that you will give us that help and guidance which we so hardly need if the spiritual reconciliation of the nations is really to be attained and the war not to have been fought in vain again. Personally we all wish you many happy returns of the day thanking you again for all you have so very kindly done for us in the last year. You know, my indebtedness to you preludes specification. It has forged a band which cannot be broken. This link is the most valuable I have gained in this country and which has immensely enriched my whole life.

I have still to thank you for your last letter and the enclosures. I was especially interested in Visser 't Hooft's letter. What I do not quite understand is that what is contained in Revelation about the life of nation and society should not be used as a basis for Natural Law. But we shall perhaps see more clearly on this point when we have V.H.'s report on this matter in hand.

I think you, my Lordbishop, should follow up the plan about which we corresponded, even if our common friends should not be receptive. I think it is too important to be lightly put in the margin. With renewed good wishes, especially also from my wife and the children

Yours ever,

Bell to Leibholz, 5 February 1944, BA, N 1334 (typewritten); Bell Papers 40, fol. 236 (carbon)

My dear Leibholz,

Very many thanks for your letter. I thought much of Dietrich and your wife on our joint day. I realize fully how heavy her heart must often be as she thinks of her twin brother. But I do most earnestly trust that he may be preserved and fortified in his tribulation. I do value his friendship very deeply, and look forward to the day when we shall all be reunited.

I enclose herewith a copy of the *Fortnightly* with my article. Please keep it.

Yours ever,

Leibholz to Bell, 14 February 1944, Bell Papers 40, fol. 237 (typewritten); BA, N 1334 (copy)

My Lordbishop,

I have just read in *Hansard* the speech you made in the Lords on February 9[1] and must tell you that I have greatly again admired you. Not only that I think that you are right in all you have said. There is indeed not a single sentence to which I should not give my wholehearted consent. In addition, it is such a wise and persuasive statement and so far superior in its arguments and conclusions compared with the reply of the government that I should only wish everybody could have the opportunity of reading it. I regret it that such a truly statesmanlike statement is published in the press in a rather inadequate form.

I really think you are the living Christian conscience of this country and I only feel it a little painful that the other acting Archbishops and Bishops have not taken the opportunity of openly supporting you in a matter which concerns them too. In any case, at a time when the political leaders are obviously not able to see the implications of their policy it is a comfort to know that there are in this country personalities who have the courage to stand up against public opinion and to warn the nation in a truly prophetic way of the dangerous road they are taking.

I wonder what the general impression was in the House. I have had the impression – but I may be wrong – that the hearts of the audience must have been touched by what you had to tell them. That the government's reply[2] was negative and disappointing I think was no surprise: probably nobody expected another attitude.

By the way, your remark on col. 740 that 'there must be a fair balance between the means employed and the purpose achieved' is in full agreement with a generally recognised principle of law in the national and international field. I myself wrote a treatise on *Das Verbot der Willkür und des Ermessensmissbrauches im Völkerrecht*[3] about 15 years ago and I am still thinking sometimes whether it would not be worthwhile translating and amplifying it. The present war has provided us with new impressive instances in this respect, the most striking among them (in this country) seem to me the infringement of international law as a result of the internment and bombing policy. If you should possibly care to see the study (in connection with your own work) please kindly let me know.

Your speech seems to me to prove, in addition, something else, namely, that the application of Christian principles in Politics leads to more reasonable results in the political sphere than the attempt to base Politics on ʿotherʿ purely secular foundations. I think you have shown us, my Lord Bishop, at hand of an impressive example [sic] that power is only justified in so far as it is subjected to reason defined in its more concrete content by Christian principles. At bottom, the decisive point in question seems to me to be: what are the implications of the present bombing policy? Does the present policy lead to a pacification of the world or to a perpetuation of war? I quite agree with you that it does not shorten but prolong the war and make the future much more miserable. It seems to me an implication of a policy which sees the whole conflict in a wrong perspective.

Many thanks also for your article in *The Fortnightly*, which I have also read with the greatest interest.[4] Your refutation of Oldham's criticism seems to me quite convincing and I think the implications of your argumentation very far-reaching. I feel I myself must think over the whole question and will also read in this connection Maritain's article you have quoted. Then I hope to write you again.

Yours ever,

---

[1] Hansard, HL Deb., Vol. 130, cols. 737-46 (9 February 1944); published as 'Obliteration Bombing' in Bell, *The Church and Humanity*, pp. 129-41; Raina, *Bishop George Bell: House of Lords Speeches*, pp. 52-62, 71-2; see Jasper, *George Bell*, pp. 276-7; Andrew Chandler, 'The Church of England and Obliteration Bombing of Germany in the Second World War', in *English Historical Review* 108, no. 429, 1993, pp. 920-46.
[2] See Raina, *Bishop George Bell: House of Lords Speeches*, pp. 66-71.
[3] Leibholz, 'Das Verbot der Willkür und des Ermessensmißbrauchs im völkerrechtlichen Verkehr der Staaten', in *Zeitschrift für ausländisches öffentliches Recht und Völkerrecht*, Vol. 1, 1929, pp. 77-125.
[4] George Bell, 'Religions and World Recovery', in *The Fortnightly Review*, 1944, pp. 96-100.

To Miss Barbara Murray, London, Genève, le 18.2.44, BA, N 1334 (typewritten)

Für Prof. LEIBHOLZ Nachricht vom 4.2.1944:

'Alles gesund, Wohnungen noch bewohnbar, Dietr. u. Hans noch nicht zu Hause[1]; sind zuversichtlich. Kinder in Friedrichsbrunn. Renate[2] gestern einen Jungen bekommen, beide gut im Stande. Gedenken herzlichst Deines heutigen Festtages mit unseren Wünschen.'

---

[1] Dietrich Bonhoeffer and Hans von Dohnanyi had been arrested: Bonhoeffer was now in Tegel prison while Dohnanyi was a patient in the prison-hospital in Buch, near Berlin.
[2] Renate Schleicher, Bonhoeffer's niece, born 1925. She married Eberhard Bethge in May 1943; their first son, Dietrich, was born on 3 February 1944.

Leibholz to Bell, 5 April 1944, Bell Papers 40, fol. 141 (typewritten); BA, N 1334 (copy)

My Lord Bishop,

I have not heard from you for a rather long time, but I hope you and Mrs Bell are well and my last letter about two months ago has reached you.

In the meantime, we have had a notice from Freudenberg[1] via Kullmann[2] that the position of Dietrich and my brother-in-law Dohnanyi is, unfortunately, unchanged.

I am glad that the modifications, or better the cancellation of the Atlantic Charter with regard to Germany, has at least resulted in some protest-actions and that the question will be raised again in the House of Lords after its postponement yesterday. I have recently attended a meeting here where Lady Snowden[3] made a really splendid speech, just as courageous as wise in its arguments. I feel that the weaker the policy of the Western countries come[s] to be, the more impressive and realistic does that of the Soviet Union become. I do not know whether you have noticed, in this connection, the militant address of the communist leader in Italy, Ercole.[4] He strongly appeals to the Italian Army and Navy and the recognition of the Badoglio regime by the Russians seems to me to have its special significance just in this respect. As you know, my Lordbishop, I am afraid that the present policy of this country furthers the same development in Germany and that we have to face one day an alliance of the Russians with the 'armed forces' in Germany.[5] Then 'Prussianism' will become a really formidable danger to the West. Do you think that if Mr Eden leaves the Foreign Office a real change in the policy of this country will take place?

On the other hand, I think it is interesting to note how, under the pressure of events, the voices of reason and cool judgement are getting stronger. For instance, there is the excellent leader on 'Unconditional Surrender' in the last issue of the *Observer*. If you have not seen it I think you should try to get hold of it, my Lordbishop. It expresses nearly to the last letter what we think and have tried to explain. I wonder who the author is. Do you not think it would be worthwhile getting into touch with him? Further, there is the Editor of the *Nineteenth Century* who obviously begins to change his attitude again. From the last *Editorial* (April) I gained the impression that Europe and Germany seem no longer to him a necessary contradiction and that Germany can even possibly fulfil a European mission. I think this is interesting because it is typical of the development, which all those must undergo who want that peace, which Mr Voigt calls Pax Britannica[6] and face at the same time the possibility of an Eastern development on the Continent. I always felt that this development must come because the historical realities are stronger than passions and a misled public opinion. But what I am really afraid of is whether it will not be again too late for a reversal of the present policy.

By the way, have you seen Mrs Buller's book *Darkness over Germany*[7]? I think it gives no new facts that are not already known to those who are familiar with the German situation. But it seems to me of great value that it has been written because it catches the ear of the English audience and makes the immense difficulties plausible, which the vast majority of Germans who are not Nazis have to face ªin Germanyª.

Has your new pamphlet come out, in the meantime? I think I saw it advertised. And what about your plans, my Lordbishop, to arrange a joint discussion and study group in connection with the new Institute?[8]

About six weeks ago we moved to 7, Linton Road. The landlord told us that his brother-in-law (a chaplain) was together with you with the former Archbishop of Canterbury and that you married him. But I forgot his name.

With all good wishes to you and Mrs Bell, also from my wife and the children,

Yours ever,

---

[1] Adolf Freudenberg (1894–1977) resigned from his position in the German Foreign Office in 1935 because of the Jewish descent of his wife. He studied theology but the Confessing Church could not employ him. In 1938 the WCC in Process of Formation appointed him Secretary for refugee aid in London but because of the outbreak of war he remained in Switzerland, setting up a department of ecumenical refugee aid for the WCC in Geneva itself.
[2] Gustave Kullmann (1894–1961), a distinguished Swiss lawyer who played a leading role in the YMCA's work among Russians and worked for many years with the League of Nations. His final appointment was as Deputy High Commissioner for Refugees.
[3] Ethel Snowden (1881–1951), since 1931 Viscountess Snowden, was member of the Fabian Society and the Labour Party, campaigner, pacifist and feminist.
[4] Ercole Ercoli: a pseudonym of Palmiro Togliatti.
[5] The last three sentences are marked by a black line in the margin.
[6] See Frederick Augustus Voigt, *Pax Britannica* (London, 1949).

7   Edith Amy Buller, *Darkness over Germany*. With a Foreword by A.D. Lindsay (London, 1943).
8   Bell argued that the German Confessional Institute should be 'a good centre for humane and Christian contacts between those engaged in problems of reconstruction and the future of Europe' (Bell to W. Schutz, 27 October 1944, Bell Papers Vol. 24/II; see too ibid., Vol.37; also Roggelin, *Franz Hildebrandt*, pp. 211–12.

Bell to Leibholz, 7 April 1944, BA, N 1334 (handwritten)

My dear Leibholz,

Many thanks for your very interesting letter. I will write later. Meantime here is my pamphlet.[1] I quite thought I had instructed that it should reach you on publication. I am *very* sorry Dietrich's position is unchanged.

But remembrances and wishes to your wife & children.

Yours ever,

1   i.e. George Bell, *Germany and the Hitlerite State* (London, 1943).

Bell to Leibholz, 10 April 1944, BA, N 1334 (handwritten)

I have *not* seen Ercole's militant address. Thank you for telling me.

My dear Leibholz,

I am very sorry if I appeared forgetful: but it was not my intention to neglect a cherished friend and valuable correspondent. Two months ago, and for some time after I was bombarded with letters about the debate in the House of Lords,[1] and while I fear I answered very few of them the subject matter added to the general pressure. I was intensely surprised at the *commotion* my speech made: not thinking it would be considered very suitable to respond and discuss so fully! But I think it was good that it did: and I got appreciation messages from Sweden and Switzerland: while my supporters (so far as *letters* to me went) were 3 to 1 against my foes. The most gratifying published article was by Cyril Falls[2] (the military correspondent of the *Times*) in the *Illustrated London News* at the end of which (of his serious discussion) he concluded that I was justified in raising the question: and expressed the opinion that both the ethical issue and the military value of this policy were open questions: which for such a writer is going a long way towards approval!

I am much interested in hearing of Lady Snowden's speech. She wrote to me *very* warmly after my speech. I hear however she is a pacifist – did this strike you when you heard her? I am greatly worried about our foreign policy. I do *not* think there would be any real change if Cranborne succeeded Eden. More likely (though with the Prime Minister really on top of everything it is not very probable) if Law succeeded: for Law is serious and independent. I saw him a fortnight ago and had an informal talk with him in my diocese. I know Voigt, and will get hold of the *Nineteenth Century* April number. I also have had the impression that his animus against Germany has been considerably modified: and that he sees that the corrollary of his strong anti-Soviet policy is a better attitude to Germany.

I have read Miss Buller's *Darkness over Germany*: which I think very good. She gave it to me: and told me the other day that the Queen had sent for her and talked for one hour about the book.

The new Institute has just started: there is a committee at the end of April. I hope something may be planned as a result for a joint discussion and study group. I hope you like the new house. Perhaps the landlord's brother was Canon *MacMichael*, who was my fellow chaplain at Lambeth.[3]

All kindest remembrances to Mrs Leibholz and the girls from us both. We are off for 6 days rest to Talbot Arms, Stow on the Wold, Glos.

Yours ever,

---

[1] i.e. the House of Lords debate on 9 February 1944 on British Bombing Policy.
[2] Cyril Bentham Falls (1888–1971), military historian. An authority on the First World War, he later became Chichele Professor of Military History at All Souls, Oxford, 1946–53.
[3] Canon Arthur William MacMichael, Rural Dean of Thanet, 1938–44, Vicar of Goudhurst, 1944–55; Rural Dean of West Charing, 1947–52.

Bell to Leibholz, 19 April 1944, BA, N 1334 (handwritten)

Vansittart attacked me in last Sunday's *Sunday Dispatch*. I have written an answer for next Sunday's issue.[1]

My dear Leibholz,

I have just received a letter from Visser 't Hooft of 29 February from Geneva. It contains the following–

'I have now a little more news about D. He is still in the same place, but he has there at least an opportunity to follow his calling and is ministering to the others. This shows you how paradoxical the situation of some of our friends there is.'[2]

I hope your wife will feel that this is on the good side, and shows that Dietrich's situation has not got worse, which is ground for encouragement. I am constantly thinking of him.

It was a great pleasure to see and talk with you and Mrs Leibholz on Saturday. All best wishes to you both and the girls

Yours ever,

---

[1] The telegram requesting a one thousand word response by Bell was sent 18 April. The article was sent the following day and published on 23 April 1944. See Bell Papers Vol. 51, fols. 258–61.
[2] W. A. Visser 't Hooft to Bell, 29 February, to be found in Besier, *Intimately Associated for Many Years*, pp. 244–6, here p. 244; see also Bethge, *Dietrich Bonhoeffer*, pp. 949–50.

Leibholz to Bell, 27 April 1944, Bell Papers 40, fol. 142 (typewritten); BA, N 1334 (copy)

My Lordbishop,

My wife and I thank you very warmly for letting us have the message from Visser 't Hooft concerning Dietrich. We also think that, on the whole, its content is on the good side and that the possibility of exercising his calling alleviates his suffering. I hope that Forell will be able to give us a more detailed account and I am just asking him to call on us if he should come to Oxford. It is very good of you also to have Dietrich constantly in mind. We know that Dietrich relies on this and I feel sure that this is ground for encouragement to him in these stressing days and helps him to bear his trial.

By the way, I wonder whether it would not be a good thing to have Dietrich's book *Nachfolge* (I do not know whether you know it) translated into English.[1] I think it is more actual than ever today. I remember that Micklem[2] spoke to me two years ago of such a plan and if I am not mistaken the Christian Student Movement considered this plan at that time. Why it has not been carried out I do not know. But it should perhaps be taken up again.

I am very sorry indeed to hear that Vansittart has attacked you again in the *Sunday Despatch*. I have not seen the paper. Is it an organ of weight? If you have still a copy of the paper in which *your* answer has appeared I should very much like to see it.

I am enclosing a cutting from the last *Observer* 'Free German Army may enter Reich' in case you have not seen it. If this were true it seems to prove that in spite of the Moscow and Teheran Conferences the Russian policy has not changed in its fundamentals.

I wonder whether Emmerich has replied to the Pinov [sic] criticism you mentioned in our last talk. As you know I wholeheartedly agree with the line you have taken and I think that under the pressure of present events Protestants on the Continent would also be inclined to accept the Anglican attitude to Politics. In any case, they have hardly ever come nearer to it than at the present time. Dietrich's attitude seems to me to be symptomatic in this respect and I fear that our common friends in this country represent a kind of Lutheranism, which prevailed in the ªpre-warª Confessional Church but is no longer held ªthereª today.

I have tried to find out which Smith wrote to you, my Lordbishop, in the matter of the grant from Magdalen College – but so far without success. There is no fellow who bears this name in Balliol or Magdalen. If I could possibly get the initials it might perhaps help to find the right one. As the grant expires in a few months' time I think I should make a new application before long.

We were delighted to meet you and Mrs Bell at Stow on the Wold. I was grateful thus to have the opportunity of discussing with you at least a few questions, although I had a bad conscience to have broken into your so greatly needed rest. How did you find Christopher Dawson when you saw him here?

With all good wishes to you and Mrs Bell from us all,

Yours ever,

---

[1] Dietrich Bonhoeffer, *Nachfolge* (Munich, 1937). This would be translated and published in English as *The Cost of Discipleship* in 1948.
[2] Nathaniel Micklem (1888–1976), Congregationalist minister and theologian. Micklem was a natural ally of Bell. From 1932 he worked at Mansfield College in Oxford, first as vice-principal and then, until 1953, as principal. An author of many books, he was widely regarded as an authority on the German Church, publishing an important study of *National Socialism and the Roman Catholic Church, 1933–1938* (Oxford, 1939). In 1944 he was chairman of the Congregational Union.

Bell to Leibholz, 1 May 1944, BA, N 1334 (typewritten); Bell Papers 40, fol. 143 (carbon)

My dear Leibholz,

Many thanks for your letter and for the cutting from the *Observer*. I am very glad to have this cutting. I did read it in a borrowed *Observer*, and was much struck with the statements made. I will, if I may, keep it. It is all the more useful as it is now being said that Stalin has altered his policy about differentiation. The Association for International Understanding[1] wrote to me to that effect after reading my article in the *Sunday Dispatch*, of which I enclose a copy,[2] which you can keep. The *Sunday Dispatch* is one of the Northcliffe papers, and has a very large circulation.[3]

I do not know Dietrich's book *Nachfolge*. Why not take it up with Micklem, and see if it can be translated?

No, Emmerich has not replied to the Pinoff criticism, but I will let you know as soon as he does. We had quite a good meeting of the Committee last week, and are hoping to have a sort of formal opening in about six week's time.

The man who wrote to me about the grant from Magdalen College was not Smith, but R.P. Bell, Balliol College, Oxford.[4] It was stupid of me to have confused you.

With all best wishes,

Yours ever,

---

[1] The British Association for International Understanding in the Dominions and Colonies, a body which sought to cultivate a view of the world based not on 'popular sentiment and prejudice' but 'an honest appreciation of facts'. The Association was the publisher of the series *British Surveys*, the first number of which appeared in April 1939 (with a circulation of 340 copies). By 1943 the surveys were reaching as many as 60,000 readers, many of them in the armed forces and in school staff rooms. See G.M. Young, 'The British Association for International Understanding in the Dominions and Colonies', in the *Journal of the Royal Society of the Arts*, December 1943, pp. 56–7. The Society ceased to exist in 1993.
[2] 'The Stop Bombing Bishop Challenges Lord Vansittart', in the *Sunday Dispatch*, 23 April 1944, p. 4, cols. 6–8; for a German translation see Bethge and Jasper, 'An der Schwelle des gespaltenen Europa', pp. 309–11.
[3] The *Sunday Dispatch* existed between 1801 and 1961 (when it was absorbed with the *Sunday Express*).
[4] Ronald Percy Bell (1907–96) was a leading physical chemist. At Balliol College he was Tutor for Admissions, Senior Tutor and Vice-Master. See R.P. Bell to Bell, 3 and 14 March 1944 ('I think it most likely that we shall be able to continue the grant of L100 from Magdalen or from other sources.'); For this, and Bell's reply of 10 March, see Bell Papers, Vol. 40, fols. 238–40.

Leibholz to Bell, 4 May 1944, Bell Papers 40, fol. 244 (typewritten); BA, N 1334 (copy)

My Lordbishop,

Many thanks for your letter and for kindly sending me a copy of your article in the *Sunday Dispatch*. I think it is really excellent. The points you have made are highly impressive and convincing. I am very glad to be allowed to keep this copy.

I presume that you have seen in *The Times* of today the report according to which, with the support of a group of American Liberals, a 'Council for a democratic Germany' has been formed in the United States.[1] I think this is important and as Tillich[2] is the provisional chairman and Niebuhr the supporting leader of the Americans, the right men (the most important thing in this matter) seem to me to be at the top of this movement. I wonder what you think about this and I should like to know whether you would possibly favour the formation of a similar organisation in this country. I think it is very remarkable that Theologians have taken the lead and I still entertain the hope that your new institute may play a part in furthering similar plans in future in one way or another. On the other hand, I realize that the whole situation is more complicated in this country than in the United States and the present time is not very suitable to materialise such plans. But I think they should be kept in mind even if their realisation is not possible at the moment.

When I next write to Micklem I will take up with him the question of the translation of Dietrich's book.

Thank you also for giving me the name of Mr Bell who wrote you about the grant from Magdalen College.

With all good wishes,

Yours ever,

---

[1] The Council for a Democratic Germany had been founded on 17 June 1944 by non-communists in American exile as a response to the National Committee Free Germany.

[2] Paul Tillich (1886–1965), Protestant theologian and Christian socialist, emigrated to the United States in 1933 and found a new academic home at Union Theological Seminary in New York. It was instead of Thomas Mann that Tillich became chairman of the Council for a Democratic Germany in 1944. In 1955 he went on to become Professor at Harvard University.

Bell to Leibholz, 9 May 1944, BA, N 1334 (typewritten)

My dear Leibholz,

Many thanks for your letter of the 4th of May. I have looked diligently through *The Times* of the 4th of May (and the 3rd of May) and can't find any reference to a 'Council for a democratic Germany', which you mention. It may be in an earlier edition, and have slipped out in mine. But any reference you can give me will be most interesting. I enclose an Order Paper of the House of Lords, as you will be interested in the items down for May 16th, and Vansittart's motions for May 17th and after Whitsun. I don't want it again.

Yours ever,

Leibholz to Bell, 10 May 1944, Bell Papers 40, fol. 245 (typewritten)

My Lordbishop,

Many thanks for your letter of yesterday. I am enclosing the cutting from *The Times* dated 4th of February, which I referred to in my last letter and, which I think will interest you.

Thank you also for the Order Paper of the House of Lords. I was interested in reading various items and motions laid down for the next few weeks when the House of Lords meets. Indeed Vansittart understands well his job but I hope that the more he overstresses his point the more will people become aware of the disastrous consequences this policy implies.

Yours ever,

Bell to Leibholz, 31 May 1944, BA, N 1334 (typewritten); Bell Papers 40, fol. 247 (carbon)

My dear Leibholz,

I ought to have written before to thank you for the cutting from the *Times*; but there has been so much on. I have written to Niebuhr to ask him for information, and will let you know what he replies in due course. In the meantime, I wonder what you thought of the Prime Minister's last speech?[1]

Yours very sincerely,

[1] For Churchill's speech in the House of Commons see *Hansard*, HC Deb., vol. 400, cols. 762–86 (24 May 1944).

Leibholz to Bell, 2 June 1944, Bell Papers 40, fol. 248 (typewritten); BA, N 1334 (copy)

My Lordbishop,

I am glad that you have written to Niebuhr in the matter of the new German council in America and thank you for your intention of letting me know his reply in due course.

As to the Prime Minister's speech a week ago I should say that as far as it deals with the policy of this country towards the Axis it stresses the old line in a rather accentuated form. This is – although not surprising – very disappointing and the prospects for the future seem rather dark to me. For I cannot imagine that a mere power politics towards Central Europe will be able to pacify the Continent.

Mr Churchill's statement that this war has become less ideological in its character seems true to me. But he forgets to add that this tragedy is due not least to the policy of the Western countries. If an ideological conflict is waged by one of the belligerents as a national war with the aim at destroying the national enemy, then I am afraid, this enemy must fight to the last man for pure reasons of existence, as the Hitler tyranny must seem – even to those who hate Hitler most – relatively better than chaos and destruction. I think no nation could or would act differently.

In my opinion, this is a tragedy because even if the war is waged and finished as a national war this country will have nothing to win from it. For it will win the war at the cost of a ruined Europe, which will also have disastrous consequences for this country. For the truth seems to me to be that this country is a part of Europe and inextricably involved in its fate. I think that the last *Christian News-Letter* has rightly stressed just this point again. Therefore, I can only subscribe to the view expressed in the debate by Wing Com. James that the present policy 'was going to cost us tens of thousands of lives in the coming offensive because our propaganda told the Germans they had no hope'.[1]

Further, as I do not think that the existing antagonism between West and East can be overcome by an alliance or something like that (unless the West is prepared to accept the Eastern conception of life) I fear that the present policy will enormously weaken the position of this country on the Continent. As Mr McGovern said 'this country is in danger of surrendering politically to Soviet Russia ... People talk about the armed might of Germany but they never talked about the armed might of Russia. Were we going to disarm Germany and allow Russia to maintain her strength? If that was so Stalin would be able to march from one end of Europe to the other'.[2] This seems perfectly true to me.

By the way, I do not think that even Mr Churchill was very consequent from his basic thesis of the national character of the present conflict as he at the same time stresses the necessity of eliminating future Fascism and Nat. Socialism in Central Europe. True this must be done very thoroughly. But I think this necessity can only be justified from an ideological conception of this war and Mr Churchill's differentiation between an aggressive Fascism in Central Europe and a non-aggressive Fascism, which must be respected in Spain, does not seem to me to carry convincing power. This argument is a makeshift resulting from the present war situation but not more.

From the Prime Minister's point of view the statement of a Labour member that the German people would have to suffer the consequences of the actions taken in their name, the innocent as well as the guilty, seems quite consequent to me.[3] The House even accepted it with 'cheers'. But then I am afraid one must also discard the principle of justice for which the Western countries are supposed to stand in this war. There is no justice without differentiation. If it is a stated political principle that there is to be no differentiation between the guilty and the innocent the fundamentals of the principle of justice have gone. Then every kind of national war or class- or race war (in the Nazi sense) – can be justified. Such a war has nothing more to do with that justice, which is based on the traditional values of Western civilisation.

Please accept my apologies for these frank and rather fragmentary and inadequate remarks.

Yours ever,

---

[1] Hansard, HC Deb., Vol. 400, cols. 863–8 (24 May 1944), here: col. 865. Sir Archibald William Henry James (1893–1980), Conservative politician who served in various government departments, not least the India Office.
[2] John McGovern (1876–1968), Scottish socialist and Independent Labour MP 1930–59. Ibid., cols. 847–55, here: cols. 851–2.
[3] Ibid., cols. 812–20, here: col. 815–6. Frederick Pethick-Lawrence (1871–1961), Labour politician and MP who became 1st Baron Pethick-Lawrence in 1945.

Bell to Leibholz, 6 June 1944, BA, N 1334 (handwritten).

My dear Leibholz,

Very many thanks for your letter, which I found most interesting, and with which I agreed. Vansittart's question in the Lords comes up on June 14 'whether the occupation of Germany will be undertaken by all the Allied Powers and not merely by the three Great Powers'.[1]

I am asking Liddell Hart[2] for his views. Have you any?

Yours ever,

[1] Vansittart's motion was postponed; see Bell to Leibholz, 27 July 1944.
[2] Sir Basil Henry Liddell Hart (1895–1970) was military historian and theorist who had corresponded supportively with Bell over the strategy of obliteration bombing.

Leibholz to Bell, 7 June 1944, Bell, Papers 40, 249 (typewritten); BA, N 1334 (copy)

My Lord Bishop,
Thank you for your letter. Up to now I had not formed a judgement on the subject of Vansittart's question. But if you ask me for my personal view now and if we take the occupation of the whole of Germany as a settled matter, I should say that the more the Anglo-Saxon countries occupy Germany the better. Those who favour a future communist Germany will be inclined to favour an occupation by Russia as far as technically possible. As to the other Allies Vansittart obviously wants them to have their part in it in order to give the occupation a penal character and to let revenge have its way. I should argue that the occupation ought to have a constructive purpose and prepare the future collaboration with those forces which need the support of the Western countries. And I think that in spite of the rampant Vansittartism of today an occupation by the Anglo-Saxon countries would cause the least harm because I still entertain the hope that the published opinion gives a wrong picture of Public Opinion.

I hope to write to you soon in another matter concerning the happenings in the 'Freie Deutsche Bewegung', which seems now to stand under purely communist influence.

Yours ever,

Leibholz to Bell, 18 June 1944, Bell, Papers 40, 250 (typewritten); BA, N 1334 (copy)

My Lord Bishop,
I do not know whether you have seen the enclosed cutting published in *The Times* of June 15th.[1] If not, you may be interested in reading it. I think it is a good thing that ªjustª the correspondent of *The Times* has sent in this report since even this paper holds the view today that Communism in Central Europe is a bogey invented by the Nazis to intimidate and to blind the Western Countries. I feel that this report is perfectly true and that we shall find a similar situation in Germany.

By the way, I had quite an interesting correspondence with Hankey. It seems to me that he does not favour 'UNCONDITIONAL SURRENDER'. Does he support our policy? I wonder.

Yours ever,

P.S. Have you seen, my Lord Bishop, the article *Germany's Foreign Legions* in *The Observer* of today? It is interesting and worth reading because it contains a convincing answer to the Prime Minister's recent statement that 'this war has become less ideological in its character'. Indeed the fact that the foreign troops have fought hardly inferior than the Germans seems to me very telling.

[1] Newspaper cutting attached to the letter: 'Italian trend to Communism. Russian Example'; shortened German translation in Bethge and Jasper, 'An der Schwelle des gespaltenen Europa', pp. 311–12.

Bell to Leibholz, 23 June 1944, BA, N 1334 (typewritten)

My dear Leibholz,

Very many thanks for your letter of June 18. I had noticed with a good deal of interest the news from the special correspondent in Rome. It is very significant. I am so glad to hear you are in correspondence with Hankey. I saw him 18 months ago, before my motion in the House of Lords. And at that time he was obviously sympathetic, but said he had not studied the problem sufficiently to justify speaking. I should be much interested to see his letters, if you could let me have a look at them; and I would send them back.

Yours ever,

Leibholz to Bell, 25 June 1944, Bell Papers 40, fol. 252 (typewritten)

My Lordbishop,

Many thanks for your letter of June 23. I am enclosing Hankey's letter to which I referred. There was still another letter, which, however, I cannot discover. But it was not important and added nothing to the enclosed.

I have just found out that in the next issue of the *Hibbert Journal* an article by Jacks himself will come out under the title *Peace by compulsion or?* I gather from the correspondence with him that he will probably take our line in it. As I contributed to the same number an article *Re-education in Germany* I think I shall get a copy so that I shall be able to send it to you.[1]

With all our best wishes

Yours ever,

[1] Lawrence P. Jacks, 'Peace by Compulsion or Otherwise?', in *The Hibbert Journal*, No. 42, p. 289; Leibholz, 'Education in Post-War Germany', ibid., pp. 136–42, reprinted in Leibholz, *Politics and Law*, pp. 194–200.

Bell to Leibholz, [postmark: 14 July 1944], BA, N1334 (handwritten)

Very many thanks for inquiry. It was a mistake (fortunately, of *Daily Mail* & *Mirror*). The Bishop concerned was *Maidstone*.[1] I am very well. I am asking Hugh Rees to send you Hansard of yesterday's debate in the Lords.

GC

[1] The *Daily Mail* and *Mirror* were concerned not with the Bishop of Chichester but with the terminally ill Bishop of Maidstone, Leslie Owen.

Leibholz to Bell, 15 July 1944, Bell Papers 40, fol. 253 (typewritten); BA, N 1334 (copy)

My Lordbishop,

I am greatly relieved to hear from you that the Press reports were wrong and I am delighted to know that you are well.

In the meantime, I have read in *The Times* the last debate in the Lords and have greatly admired again your courage to stand up at these difficult times to your convictions, which – although unpopular – will prove to be true in times to come.[1] I think the more the war perturbs the minds and sound judgement of people the more unique becomes your position in this country. You seem to me to be the only personality who reflects the Christian conscience in the political field today.

By the way, I remember to have read in a paper that the Gestapo when taking over the prisoner of war camp concerned shot all those who were in charge of this camp and held responsible for the escape of the prisoners. Therefore, I am afraid, Vansittart will hardly be able to put his plans into practice as far as they are concerned. I also wonder whether Winster[2] would have protested if he happened to be born in Germany. No doubt, if he had done so he would have been done away with in time.

The whole tragic circle of the government policy can clearly be seen in Lord Cranborne's reply.[3] He said that the German people were today fighting with fanatical zeal to see the regime maintained. But why do they fight so? In my opinion because the policy of the Western countries compels them to do so. Owing to this policy they cannot bring about the end of the Nazi regime. Therefore, Cranborne argues again, the German people must share the responsibility for the crimes committed in their name.[4]

I do not know whether you have noticed the debate in the House of Commons on Wednesday last. From it follows that Mr Stokes[5] will raise on the Adjournment the question of the treatment, which the German people may expect to receive from the United Nations provided the Germans themselves overthrow the Nazi regime.[6] He adds that no encouragement has so far been given them.

Yours ever,

[1] In the debate about the massacre of fifty Allied officers at Stalag Luft III Bell contradicted Vansittart's proposal; *Hansard*, HL Deb., Vol. 132, cols. 923–8 (13 July 1944).
[2] Ibid., cols. 928–9. Reginald Thomas Herbert Fletcher (1885–1961), Labour politician and MP, 1935–42. In 1942 he had become 1st Baron Winster.
[3] Ibid., cols. 930–4, here: col. 391
[4] This paragraph is marked by a pencil-line in the margin.
[5] Major Richard Stokes (1897–1957) was independently-minded Labour politician, and, from 1938, MP. With a second Labour MP, Alfred Salter, Stokes spoke out against obliteration bombing in the House of commons. In 1950–1 he became Minister of Works, also in that year appointed Lord Privy Seal and Minister of Materials.
[6] See Hansard, HL Deb., Vol. 401, cols. 1713–33 (12 July 1944).

Leibholz to Bell, 21 July 1944, Bell Papers 47, fol. 77 (typewritten)

My Lordbishop,

I think the news of today that an attempt on Hitler's life was made by (as Hitler said in his broadcast) 'a clique of ambitious, irresponsible and at the same time senseless and criminally stupid officers' are a splendid proof for what you said in the Lords a week ago. How unfair Public Opinion has become today seems to me to follow from the fact that even *The Times* hardly mentions the fact. Of course if Hitler and Nazism are the incarnation of Prussianism it does not put well in the picture that so-called Prussian officers try to eliminate him. If Frenchmen or others had done the same reaction would certainly have been quite different.

I am just hearing about the further development in Germany. I know Stauffenberg very well. I have worked together with him in the same institute for three years before he joined the army.[1] He was no real warrior. It is a tragedy that he did not succeed. The tragedy for all decent men in Germany would become disastrous if the whole 'Prussian' revolt would fail.

I am enclosing the current issue of *The Hibbert Journal*. Perhaps you may like to have a look at it. – Jack's article seems to me a little diffuse but in its basic attitude very sympathetic. If I am not mistaken you told me at Stow that you are in close contact with a committee which deals with the re-education of Germany. It would be most kind of you if you would perhaps pass on the enclosed copy to this Committee later on as they may possibly be interested in the article on the *Education in Post-War Germany* and I myself have no further copy for circulation.

Yours ever,

---

[1] Here Leibholz means Berthold Schenk Graf von Stauffenberg, the brother of Claus, between 1929 and 1931. He was an assistant at the Kaiser Wilhelm Institute for Foreign Public and Public International Law where Leibholz had worked between 1926 and 1928. In 1931 Berthold von Stauffenberg did not join the army, but went to the Permanent Court of International Justice as secrétaire-rédacteur. After Germany left the League of Nations he returned to the Institute. See Peter Hoffmann, *Stauffenberg. A Family History: 1905–1944* (2nd ed., Montreal, 2003).

Bell to Leibholz, 24 July 1944, BA, N 1334 (handwritten)

My dear Leibholz,

In these grave times I am, as you will readily believe, constantly thinking of Dietrich (and of other friends). I do hope and pray he may be kept safe. I feel much for your wife in her anxiety. The whole situation seems very obscure – and one longs for more light. How indeed I wish that the Allies had given a sign two years ago and thereby perhaps saved the world much suffering.

Yours always,

P.S. I had closed the envelope and was about to post, when your letter of 21st arrived with the *Hibbert*. What you say is most interesting. And a striking sidelight on Stauffenberg. What a tragedy he did not succeed. But I do most earnestly hope that the revolt itself may triumph. The price paid by the brave starters is a heavy one. But it is surely true that the start having been made nothing can be the same again in the 3rd Reich and it is a question of time.

Bell to Leibholz, 27 July 1944, BA, N 1334 (typewritten); Bell Papers 47, fol. 83 (carbon)

My dear Leibholz,

I have read your article in the *Hibbert* with the greatest interest. I thought it was a very effective reply to a not very well considered article on the other side.[1]

Vansittart, I am glad to say, has postponed his question about the occupation of Germany. I have sent a notice for the Order Paper for Wednesday, August 2nd, to the following effect:

'The Bishop of Chichester: to ask His Majesty's Government whether they have any information about the use of political warfare at the present time, particularly in relation to Germany; and to move for papers.'[2]

I shall be most grateful for any ammunition you can give me. How would you define 'political warfare'? And any hints as to the line I should take at this juncture would be of the greatest value. Would it be a useful thing to remind the Government of the effect, which it had in 1918, or would this be a mistake from the German angle? I have an idea that the Memoirs of some German statesmen or Generals have made a statement about the effectiveness of this. I don't know whether you have any quotation handy. One could of course point out the great difference between this and that war, and say, *a fortiori* now.

Of course any reflections you care to make on the present situation and the recent statements made by Hitler, Goebbels or others; or your interpretation of the present crisis in Germany would be enormously helpful.

Yours very sincerely,

[1] See the commentary of 'Janua' in *The Spectator*, 4 August 1944, p. 96.
[2] This motion was not accepted, as Bell's letter of 30 July 1944 makes clear.

Leibholz to Bell, 30 July 1944, Bell Papers 40, fols. 254–5 (typewritten); BA, N 1334 (copy)

My Lord Bishop,

It was too good of you to write to us in these grave days. It is a great comfort to us that you have been in your thoughts with Dietrich and our common friends. It is a tragedy that they did not succeed and the consequences are incalculable.

Your second letter of July 27 did, unfortunately, not reach me until today as I was away for a few days. I hasten to answer instantly as I understand that your question will be discussed as early as August 2nd.

I should define 'political warfare' as a warfare by which a favourable conclusion of the war is to be attained without the use of armed forces. I admit this is a rather negative definition. But it seems to me that the word 'political' can hardly be described in a more positive sense in this connection. It is obvious that this kind of warfare plays a much more eminent part in an ideological war than in a purely national conflict. In spite of this I think it played its part in 1918. I admit this would not have been the case if the German army had succeeded at that time. But as it was beaten the Allied propaganda weakened its power of resistance and accelerated its collapse. Vansittart's statement in *The Times* that the German army had fought to the bitter end in 1918 seems to me to be utterly incompatible with the historical truth.

If today political warfare has become a blunt instrument it is due to the fact that the political leaders of the Western countries have done everything in their power to turn the present conflict into a national war. Today political warfare does not even play the part it played in the First World War. This seems to me due to the unconditional surrender policy. It is argued that this policy alone provides an efficient protection against the repetition of the legend that the German army was not defeated in the last war but 'stabbed in the back'. I never understood how such an argument could become the 'Leitmotiv' of the policy of this country. For it will be easy for a clever propaganda to invent another story in order to show that it was by accident that this war was lost (e.g. by Treachery of Germany's confederates, the air terror raids, the conspiration of the generals, etc. etc.). The point seems to me to be that the Germans are credulous enough to believe in these stories. This credulity should be fought against with the help of political weapons – even if the present conflict is wrongly waged as a national war. But the sterile 'unconditional surrender policy' makes this impossible.

Whether I should mention the actual effect the Allied propaganda had in 1918 I do not know. Probably not. For what happened in 1918 is so closely connected with Versailles etc. that I cannot see how, from a German standpoint, the mentioning of these events can stimulate or further a revolutionary movement in Germany.

As to the recent events in Germany I must confess that I feel the deepest admiration for the brave men and patriots. For I even think that their fate is more tragic than that of other people who died for their country. For these men – whether they fell at the front or in the occupied countries as members of the resistance movement – died for a cause which will prevail in the end and is at once the cause of their country. But the 'conspirators' in Germany are put to death by their own countrymen and are despised and dishonoured in their own homeland. They were prepared to take action against a regime the overthrow of which would include 'unconditional surrender' with all its implications. They are suspected, laughed at and resented in the Allied countries by those who ought to help them and – whether they understand or not – have the same cause with them. I feel the people here only see in them the militarists who to avoid the worst want to save what can be saved in Germany and only wish to prepare for a new world war.[1] They do not see that the only power group which can take action against the regime was the army. First it has been argued that, unlike Badoglio, the army leaders in Germany are militarists and not patriots and therefore not prepared to act against the regime. Now that they have acted they remain militarists and the enemies of freedom and of the Allies (and what about freedom and militarism in Russia) although all men definitely known to have been connected with the Putsch had more or less a conservative or liberal Western outlook. I have not the slightest doubt that all men who have still a Western outlook in Germany would have gladly joined 'the militarist regime' – first of all, the Churches, simply because without the setting up of such a regime a new Western democratic order could not have been established.

Now that the attempt has failed I fear the army is driven into submission and I think the replacement of the ordinary military salute by the Hitler salute is of symbolic significance in this connection. I remember that this demand was already raised by

Röhm in 1930 and was since repeated again and again. Now they have succeeded and this means that the army has played up his game as far as the setting up of a regime on Western lines is concerned. The purge will be so thorough and relentless as the purge of 1934[2] and stop at nothing. The recent reports of shootings and arrests of a large number of officers confirm this. It has been said that the Putsch has been a rather amateurish affair and can only be considered an isolated incident at the top of the German army. I do not think that this is true. Under the present circumstances it is impossible to give such a planned undertaking publicity beforehand without endangering it *ab initio*. If the attempt on Hitler's life had not failed the whole plan would have succeeded.

The purge now in progress will also include the typical Prussian elements. I have always entertained the view that the Nazis will eagerly support the Western Allies in eliminating Prussianism as a political force in Germany. Actually they do it now. The Allies, therefore, have every reason to be satisfied, from their point of view, although they do not know what they do. All that will remain is a Nazified army, which will be militaristic, but not Prussian in its specific outlook.

The open question which remains is: What might happen in Germany if the military situation goes on deteriorating? I fear that in this case the attempt will be made to engineer a second Putsch, either by the Nazis themselves or some generals by making a communist revolution – perhaps together with a capitulation to Russia. I gather from the newspapers (including *The Times*) that the German leaders are actually debating whether, after defeat, German policy should lean eastward or westward and that Himmler, of all, is supposed to favour a 'Ostlösung'. I do not know whether you have seen, in this connection, the alarming leaflet printed in *The Times* of July 14th under the title *Himmler prepares a bolshevist coup*, where we can read, among others:

> Himmler is getting ready for a great treachery. When the time is ripe Himmler wants to sell us lock, stock and barrel to the Soviets, he counts on the home army being powerless to resist …

This may sound farcical and I am optimistic enough to think that the strength of the Allied solidarity is strong enough to stand this test. But the fact that *The Times* speaks in this connection of 'reminders of the cunning as well as brutal force with which the Allies are faced' seems to me to show that the Alliance is built on rather 'very' weak foundations. But even if the Russians should decline to negotiate with a communist Germany under Himmler's leadership the possibility or better probability remains that some German generals will make their appearance and try to link up with the Germans officers' league in Moscow. I think that Stalin may be prepared to deal with them, especially if no agreement with Poland is reached in time and the Allies do not make more substantial progress in the West. Here is *in nuce* the German-Russian alliance. The recent debate in the House of Commons seems to me to show the complete helplessness of the government in this respect. In fact, everything depends on Russia. If they were to deal with the Germans in one way or other then Central Europe and possibly the Continent will be lost to the Anglo-Saxon countries. But it seems to me that now that the Western 'conspiration' has failed (and the Western countries are co-responsible for its miscarriage) the Eastern Putsch will be staged sooner or later – and I fear with more success.

All that I have tried to say is very inadequate. But the time is too short to elaborate the arguments in greater detail.

Again many thanks for your goodness.

Yours ever,

---

[1] See Churchill's often-quoted jibe in the House of Commons: 'The highest personalities in the German Reich are murdering one another, or trying to, while the avenging Armies of the Allies close upon the doomed and ever-narrowing circle of their power.' Hansard, H.C. Deb., Vol. 402, col. 1487 (2 August 1944).
[2] The so-called Röhm-Putsch, or Night of the Long Knives, of 30 June 1934.

Bell to Leibholz, 30 July 1944, BA, N 1334 (handwritten)

Private

My dear Leibholz,

I am sorry to say that the Government are opposed to my bringing forward the question of political warfare in the House of Lords. Subject too delicate! I am asked to put any points I wish to make in a memo. and Cranborne will put them to the Government.[1]

What disappoints me is not the failure to bring off this particular motion, but the blindness and negation of our outlook.

I shall nevertheless be grateful for any points you could *jot down* for such a memo.

Yours ever,

---

[1] Cranborne to Bell, 28 July 1944, Bell Papers, Vol. 47, fol. 86; Bell to Cranborne, 1 August 1944, ibid., fol. 89; Bell to Eden, 27 July 1944 and Eden's answer, 8 August 1944, BA, N 1334.

Leibholz to Bell, 1 August 1944, Bell Papers 47, fol. 92 (typewritten)

My Lordbishop,

How disappointing it is that the Government are not inclined to take the opportunity of fixing a day for the discussion of your most important and timely motion. Frankly, I am not surprised at this as this attitude is in harmony with all the statements the government has made in recent times. One feels inclined to shrug one's shoulders if the fate of Western civilisation were not at stake.

I wrote to you on Sunday in greater detail but I do not know whether my remarks will be of any use to you. As things stand the main point seems to me to be the point I tried to explain on page III. The 'Western' revolution if I may [say] so has miscarried and after all one can hear on the wireless I fear it has taken much greater proportions than is generally realized. You probably remember that Beck,[1] Halder,[2] Gördeler* were all on Dietrich's list and, therefore, our anxiety is very great. I am sick to death when I think of all this (including the disastrous suicidal policy of this country).

I cannot understand how it is possible for this country to give up its traditional political principles. In former times the political leaders pursued a constructive policy directed in the end to win over the enemy of the time being. I think Smuts is a living example of such a policy. Further, I thought it belongs to the traditional line of English policy to make a stand against that military power which sets out to dominate the Continent – simply because of the vital implications of such a domination for this country. England has made a stand against France. It has made a stand against Germany. But it seems to submit to ªRussiaª.³

Now I think the time will come sooner or later when the 'Eastern' revolution will be staged in Germany and the Russians will decide its fate. They have always two irons in the fire and they will use the one that best suits their purposes. Even if the Western powers should be prepared to revise their policy (I fear there is no indication for such a change) there is in Germany hardly anybody left who would still be able to take up the challenge. In spite of this – I wholeheartedly agree with you that every attempt should be made to give the policy of this country a more constructive *European* shape, even if it often seems to be a rather hopeless undertaking.

I gather from your last letter that you are thinking of writing the memo. for which the government has asked you. Would it perhaps not be ªa good idea to send meª⁴, my Lordbishop, a rough sketch of it, so that in case I have to make some additional suggestions I could submit them to you for consideration. You know I should be only too glad to do so.

By the way, Niebuhr recently wrote me that he was sending two copies of the documents connected with the Council for a Democratic Germany⁵, one of which I was to send you. But up-to-now they have not arrived. He adds that it would be a great help if a similar organisation started in England. I wonder what you think about it. It seems to me that the time for the formation of such an organisation in this country is not favourable. In America the situation is obviously not so tense.

Yours ever,

* ªAll Conservative-liberal in their attitude.ª

---

[1] Ludwig Beck (1880–1944), since 1938 senior general, had been Chief of the General Staff, 1936–8. He had become the acknowledged military head of the resistance. He died in the Bendlerblock, the headquarters of the army in Berlin, on 20 July 1944.
[2] Franz Halder (1884–1972), since 1940 senior general, had followed Beck as Chief of the General Staff, holding that office from 1938 to 1942. Involved in the attempted coup of 1938, Halder played little role in the wartime resistance, though he was kept in touch with developments. After 20 July 1944 he was interned but later freed by the U.S. Army in May 1945.
[3] A line added in the margin from 'English policy' till the end.
[4] Instead of 'the best if you would send me'.
[5] See Leibholz to Bell, 4 May 1944.

Bell to Leibholz, 3 August 1944, BA, N 1334 (handwritten)

My dear Leibholz,

Very many thanks for your full and most helpful letter. I wish I could have used its good advice in a speech in the Lords. But, as my latest line told you, the Government objected.

I heard Churchill yesterday – it was all 'battle', and its reference to ideology and 'internal disease', most depressing.[1] I get more and more worried about the official attitude. I have written to Eden reminding him of the information I gave him two years ago from Stockholm and that the attempt of July 20 was made in far worse circumstances than were possible in 1942 when the same persons were leaders – Beck and Goerdeler – the same plan and organization etc: if only he had acted then! I have urged him at least to do what is possible to help those who can escape to escape, for I suppose we have ways and means of assisting prisoners of war to escape. And I have also asked him to say a word even now to those in Germany who are seeking to destroy the regime.[2]

Yours ever,

P.S. I shall hope to speak on Vansittart's motion just put down for the first day after recess (26 September). At your leisure thoughts on the *general* position be welcome.

---

[1] Churchill had spoken in the House of Commons about the war situation at large: Hansard, H.C. Deb., Vol. 402, cols. 1459–87 (2 August 1944).

[2] See Bell to Eden, 3 August 1944, Bell Papers, Vol. 47, fols. 99–100; see too Eden to Bell, 17 August 1944, ibid., fol. 111, in which Eden writes that he 'cannot admit that we have any obligations to help those concerned in the recent plot, who had their own reasons for acting as they did and were certainly not moved primarily by a desire to help our cause.'

Bell to Leibholz, 5 August 1944, BA, N 1334 (handwritten)

My dear Leibholz,

Very many thanks for yours of 1 Aug, which crossed mine. I had drafted a letter to Cranborne setting out a series of considerations for 'political warfare'; but on the publication of Goerdeler's name as the prime mover wanted by Himmler I decided to write direct to Eden pointing out how closely the information I brought from Stockholm in 1942 fitted in with the facts of July 20 1944, reminding him of other names beside Beck and Goerdeler and including Witzleben[1] (before of course the new denunciation of him in today's press). I asked Eden whether he could not (1) take steps to help rescue any of the leaders of the Revolt not yet killed – by such steps (formidable as the task is) as might be taken to help our prisoners of war escape; and (2) even at this late hour make a strong public appeal over the heads of Hitler and Himmler to anti-Nazis in Germany and give them hope of a life of security for a Germany which has overthrown the Nazis. By the same post I wrote to Cranborne telling him what I had done and why.

I had already written to Eden last week asking him whether he would care to do anything (via Stockholm e.g.) to help the clergy in Germany now in still greater peril, through the area opened up in the summer of 1942. I have had no reply to this letter. He should have had my latest letter yesterday. I will tell you any news I receive.

In these circumstances I wonder whether it is worthwhile preparing a Memo. on policy for Cranborne to consider and pass to the F.O? I am quite ready – if you like to draft one to use it in some suitable form and send it to Eden or Cranborne. So please draft such if you feel able to do so, and think there is a chance of our Government being persuaded to see light.

I heard Churchill – as I think I told you – but he is living in a world of battles only, and seems to me to have the mind of a child with regard to deep policy – for home affairs as well as the far graver matters of Europe. And disaster gets nearer and nearer. One feels so powerless.

Christopher Dawson is to spend a few days with me here at the end of the coming week. I hear from Schutz that there is an article in the *New Statesman* referring to opposition students and a foreign bishop (supposed by him and the Editor to be me).

I cannot tell you how deeply I share your and your wife's anxieties for Dietrich. May God spare him for the service of the Church and Germany and the world.

Yours always,

I am writing to Winant remind him of what I brought from Stockholm in 1942.

I rather agree with you that the time for founding a Council for a Democratic Germany here is not favourable. I have known nothing from Niebuhr.

[1] Erwin von Witzleben (1881–1944), field marshal since 1940, participated in all of the resistance groups which emerged in the German military, 1938–44. If the 20 July 1944 conspiracy had succeeded it was agreed that Witlzleben should became supreme commander of the armed forces. After its failure he was sentenced to death by the People's Tribunal and hanged on 8 August 1944.

Leibholz to Bell, 8 August 1944, Bell Papers 47, fol. 107–8. (typewritten)

My Lordbishop,

Very many thanks indeed for your last two letters and for kindly letting me know your decisions. I agree one feels so powerless but you have done all that is possible under the circumstances and I think it was very wise of you to write directly to Eden and to remind him of the memo. you brought from Stockholm in 1942 and of his responsibility for not having taken up the matter at that time when the 'conspiracy' would have had a so much greater chance of success.

I cannot quite get rid of the suspicion that Himmler himself had a hand in the plot. I think there can hardly be a doubt that the existence of the 'conspiracy', which goes back to 1941, was well known to Himmler and his circles. In the same way as the officers etc. have certainly had their special agents in the Gestapo so had Himmler his agents in the 'Wehrmacht'. Further that Himmler wanted to have an opportunity to crush the opposition and to become 'leader' of the Wehrmacht is I think also an established fact.[1] Now there are three points, which seem to me mysterious: 1) the miraculous way in which Hitler escaped, 2) the fact that the news of Hitler's death was made known in Berlin and other centres before the result of the attempt on Hitler's life was accurately known, 3) the part of the Major Remer[2] in the plot. If the leading Generals of the Wehrmacht in Berlin were involved in the plot (which has been proved) than it is hard to understand how just this man who was a devoted and loyal adherent to the 'Führer' was ordered to occupy the government offices etc. I also think that Himmler would also not shrink from staging a real attempt, even at the cost of a few Nazi officers if it suited his purpose and I fear that if Stauffenberg actually put the mine in Hitler's room he was deceived by a man who was playing Himmler's game. Otherwise it seems to me unintelligible that this well prepared plot was nipped in the bud. The prompt actions that followed the attempt (e.g. Himmler's appointment as supreme commander, replacement of the military salute by the Nazi salute etc.) all fit well into the picture.

I do not venture to think that Eden if even he could, would do anything for those involved in the conspiracy. I think what Mr Churchill said last Saturday: If it (the killing of each other in Germany) goes on it will save us a lot of trouble is characteristic of the mentality in official circles. How short-sighted not to see that the killing of the remaining decent men in Germany will enormously increase the difficulties the Western powers will have to face in Germany. I fear that when the letter will reach you these men will no longer be alive.

To our dismay, two or probably three of the men named in the list published are connected with the family of my wife and, therefore, also with Dietrich and my other brother-in-law who was arrested a year ago. The maiden name of my wife's mother is von Hase and the General v. Hase is her first cousin.³ They are both grandchildren of the Church-historian von Hase who was imprisoned 1848 (because of his liberal activities).⁴ Then we are distantly related with York of Wartenburg⁵ (who is a descendent of the Yorks who signed the treaty with the Russians against Napoleon (and his ally the Prussian King) in 1812) and v. Hansen.⁶ We ªstronglyª hope that Dietrich and our other brother-in-law were arrested a year ago may save them now [sic].

The only comforting sign in all the misery seems to me to be that Goerdeler has so far not been found.⁷ Rundstedt's motives are very obscure.⁸ I am still hoping that he is not quite as bad as he seems to be. However that may be I feel sure that the tragic death of all these brave patriots is at once the unglorious end of what is usually called 'Prussianism' in this country. The Prussian spirit will never be able to recover from such a blow.

I also doubt whether Eden will comply with your second request. One would sooner be able to melt a stone than to cause the government to change their policy. Therefore, I fully understand that you do not find it worthwhile putting a new memo. before Cranborne and the government. And I also very much doubt whether under these circumstances a memo. drawn up by me would be helpful in any way.

What ªhasª crossed my mind is whether it would not perhaps be possible to enlist the interest of a leading newspaper (*The Times* or *The Manchester Guardian* or *The Round Table*) urging them to bring a full article on the German plot, its background and consequences.⁹ I know that *The Times* publishes also ªleadingª articles written by refugees (on economic matters) ᶜas leaders or as written by a special correspondentᶜ. Carr wrote me in another matter some weeks ago. Therefore, he knows of me and perhaps ªheª would be inclined to bring such an article if one could approach him. I think such an article in one of these papers might have a more ªfar-reachingª effect than a memo. for two or three people who would probably shelve it. I wonder what you think about it.

I also found Mr Churchill's speech discouraging and disappointing from a political point of view. All that has happened in the last decades seems to me to have been approached from a rather naïve aspect and from the old-fashioned national angle of the 19th century, although even there the Holy Alliance strongly insisted on an ideological unity and solidarity in Europe. I do not know whether you intend to deal with Mr Churchill's speech in the House of Lords on Sept. 26. But if so I should submit to you for consideration that passage in which Mr Churchill speaks of 'the new brotherhood among men based not on ideologies but on the broad, simple and homely ideals of peace, justice and freedom'.¹⁰ But how to define these principles and values? These abstract conceptions can in their real meaning be used ªonlyª if the world is ideologically unified. But today justice, freedom etc. will be defined in quite a different way according to the views one takes of them from a communist, fascist or Western point of view. To act so as if these differences do not exist is an ostrich policy the hollowness of which will come to light at the moment when one tries to establish the new world on these abstract ideals.

I am glad Christopher Dawson will stay with you this weekend. In this connection I think it worthwhile considering whether we should not all try to put under the cover of the European mission of this country what we have in mind and thus to explain our aims more clearly. I think this 'European' slogan would awake public opinion to a certain extent (especially as far as it is not expressed in the press) as I think that neither the Left nor the Right are in favour of a domination of the Continent by Russia. I admit, of course, that many different things can be understood by such a European policy. But two things seem to me ªnecessaryª characteristic of such a European policy: 1) the exclusion of Russia from the Continent proper 2) a creative Central European policy, which in the end must lead to a revision of the present official policy. Even Voigt who seeks to combine the exclusion of Russia from the Continent with a power politics towards Germany is compelled to modify his policy towards Germany. I think nobody can evade this conclusion as Germany belongs to Europe. By the way, Voigt seems to have got into some trouble as can be gathered from the statement published on page 1 of the August issue of his periodical.¹¹

I am enclosing the material connected with the Council for a Democratic Germany. I see a number of questions from a point of view different from that expressed in the *Statement* and the subsequent *Declaration*. On the other hand, there is much in it that seems to me very good. Please keep the copy.

Please excuse my typewriting but I think it saves your time.

Thanking you once again for all your goodness

Yours ever,

---

1. Himmler became commander-in-chief of the Replacement Army, not of the armed forces.
2. Instead of following the resisters' orders Major Otto Ernst Remer requested, and carried out, orders from Hitler himself to suppress the revolt in Berlin on 20 July 1944. See Peter Hoffmann, *Widerstand, Staatsstreich, Attentat: Der Kampf der Opposition gegen Hitler* (3rd ed., Munich, 1979), pp. 528-9.
3. Paul von Hase (1885-1944) was married to Margarethe Baronesse von Funck (1898-1968). As lieutenant general and city commandant of Berlin von Hase took part in both the planned coup of 1938 and the attempt of 20 July 1944. He was sentenced to death by the People's Tribunal and hanged on 8 August 1944.
4. Karl Hase, from 1883 von Hase (1800-90), held a chair of Church history and Dogmatics at Jena University 1836-83, during which time he also served a number of terms as vice chancellor.
5. Peter Graf Yorck von Wartenburg (1904-44) had worked in the office of the price commissioner (Kommissars für Preisbildung) since 1936. From 1940 he and his friend Helmuth James von Moltke had drawn together a circle of resistance to discuss plans for the future of Germany after the end of National Socialism. Many members of the circle, not least Moltke himself, were opposed to a violent revolt, but after the arrest of Moltke in January 1944 Yorck supported an uprising against the regime. On 20 July 1944 he was arrested at the centre of the plot in the Supreme Command of the Army. On 8 August 1944 he was sentenced to death by the People's Tribunal and hanged.
6. Probably a misspelling of Georg Alexander Hansen, or even Albrecht von Hagen, but no relationship with either of these is known.

7   On 18 July Goerdeler had learnt that the Gestapo intended to arrest him and hid himself in Berlin and its environs. On 8 August he fled to Marienwerder, his former hometown in Western Prussia. By now he was on the wanted list with a reward of one million Marks. On 12 August he was arrested and brought to Berlin.
8   Gerd von Rundstedt (1875–1953), since 1940 field marshal, was Commander West from 1941 to July 1944. A career-minded soldier, Rundstedt had turned down invitations to join the resistance. He accepted Hitler's appointment to the court of honour (Ehrenhof) after the 20 July 1944.
9   Leibholz's article, 'The Opposition Movement in Germany', was, after some revisions, published anonymously in *The New English Weekly* in October 1944. The final version was reprinted in Leibholz, *Politics and Law*, pp. 210–3. A fragment of an earlier version may be found in the Bell Papers, Vol. 40, fols. 500–6.
10 See Hansard, HC Deb., Vol. 402, col. 1479 (2 August 1944).
11 Frank Voigt 'Statement', in *The Nineteenth Century and After*, Vol. CXXXVI, No. 810 (August 1944), pp. 49–61; but see too 'Notes on the situation in Germany', pp. 61–4.

Bell to Leibholz, 11 August 1944, BA, N 1334 (typewritten)

My dear Leibholz,
I am very grateful for your letter and for all you say in it. I will write again next week, when I have had time to look into things with Christopher Dawson. But I want to let you know at once that I have just heard from 't Hooft, Geneva, dated July 3. He speaks of Dietrich and Niemöller in the following terms: 'You ask for news of Dietrich. His situation is unchanged. There is no reason to have special fears about him. As to M. he seems to be keeping on rather well as far as his health is concerned.' I am afraid that one cannot avoid being very anxious with the situation in Germany as it is, alas. One prays most earnestly that being in prison ªD. (and M.)ª may be kept protected.

Yours ever,

Bell to Leibholz, 17 August 1944, BA, N 1334 (typewritten); Bell Papers 40, fol. 258 (carbon)

My dear Leibholz,
I am sorry to say that Christopher Dawson got a temperature and could not come. His visit is therefore postponed. I wanted to discuss with him your point about Europe, which is of course of great importance. ªI am also for a statement about Europe.ª

But I think it would be very unwise to put out a statement at the present time, which deliberately excluded Russia from Europe. I think that America, Great Britain and Russia must be on reasonably good terms with one another, and must not be in antagonism though the price of not being in antagonism should be a clear recognition by Russia of interests other than its own. To drive a wedge between Russia and Britain and America would, I feel sure, be asking for trouble.

I wrote, as you know, to the *Times*, suggesting an article, and the Editor liked the idea and has written to you.¹ I do very much hope something may come of this.

I am terribly stricken today to read in the *Daily Telegraph* that Goerdeler has been arrested. Your wife and Dietrich and you are constantly in my thoughts.

Yours very sincerely,

ªI go for a fortnight to Somerset on Monday. Any letters shall be noted to leave forward.ª

[1] See Bell to Robert Barrington-Ward, 12 August 1944, and Barrington-Ward's answer, 14 August 1944, Bell Papers 40, fols. 256–7 (typewritten); BA, N 1334 (copy). Robert McGowan Barrington-Ward (1891–1948), barrister and journalist, editor of *The Times*, 1941–8.

Leibholz to Bell, 18 August 1944, Bell Papers 40, fol. 259 (typewritten); BA, N 1334 (copy)

My Lord Bishop,

Many thanks for your last letter and the news from Visser 't Hooft about Dietrich and Niemöller. We are very glad to have them and only hope that the recent events will not have affected his situation unfavourably.

Thank your also for the letter to the Editor of *The Times*. John Webb[1] wrote me that the Editor would be much interested to see a paper on the recent events in Germany without, however, committing himself to publish it. I fully appreciate that it will be difficult to judge the possibility of the publication of an article until the Editor has seen it. In any case, I am preparing an article and hope to send you a copy of it soon.

The National Peace Council hopes to reprint the 're-education' article in *The Hibbert Journal* as a pamphlet. Today I am enclosing a copy of a recent article in *The Fortnightly* on PUBLIC OPINION!!![2]

Yours ever,

[1] Presumably a staff member at the *Times*.
[2] See Leibholz, 'Public Opinion', reprinted in *Politics and Law*, pp. 81–7.

Bell to Leibholz, 21 August 1944, BA, N 1334 (typewritten); Bell Papers 40, fol. 260 (carbon)

My dear Leibholz,

Very many thanks for your letter of the 18th August. I shall be very much interested to hear what happens about the article for *The Times*. The Editor wrote a very nice letter to me about possibilities, though of course he could not commit himself. I do hope it may be published, whether in whole or in part. Anyhow, I hope you will let me see it. My address for the next few days is:

c/o The Rev. E.T.G. Hunter,
The Rectory,
South Perrott,
Misterton, Somerset

Very many thanks for the return of your article in the *Fortnightly*, which I have read with great agreement.

Yours sincerely,

Leibholz to Bell, 22 August 1944, Bell Papers 40, fol. 261 (typewritten)

My Lordbishop,

Today I am enclosing a copy of the paper which I am just sending to The Editor of *The Times* for consideration. Whether it will suit the purposes of *The Times* I do not know. The difficulty seems to me to be that all the facts known to us are not suitable for publication in order not to give the Gestapo further clues and to expose those who are involved in the 'plot' to still greater perils. Therefore, ᵃe.g.ᶜ I have not spoken of the Churches at all in the present connection. What I personally think of the situation in Germany I have tried to express in a cautious way on page 6 and 7. I am afraid that the conclusions to which I have come do not fully conform with the line taken by *The Times* in its leaders hitherto. I wonder what you think about the paper.

Many thank for your letter of August 17th. I am afraid I must have expressed myself badly in my last letter when broaching the question of a more constructive European policy. I did not think of a statement at the present time, which deliberately excludes Russia from Europe. I also think as you say that the three great powers must be on reasonable good terms. What I wanted to express was that, to my mind, the European issue is whether the Continent, politically, socially and culturally, will be organized on Western or Eastern lines. I am personally so deeply convinced of the ideological character of the age (in spite of its present nationalistic façade) that I think there is ultimately room only for this alternative: either the Continent takes on a more or less Eastern character – in this case the Continent will tend to the East and the Western countries will have no say there – or it assumes a Western character and then in the end Russia will be excluded from the Continent proper. Personally I am afraid that the Russians might win the game – for many reasons. But I think this should not prevent us from doing all in our power to try to hinder this development and to pursue a creative Western European policy.

I hope that you and Mrs. Bell will have a refreshing time in Somerset.

With all our good wishes

Yours ever,

ᵃP.S. Very many thanks for your kind letter of yesterday. It has just arrived.ᵃ

Leibholz to Bell, 29 August 1944, Bell Papers 40, fol. 262 (typewritten); BA, N 1334 (copy)

My Lordbishop,

May I let you know that, in the meantime, I have heard from the Editor of *The Times* that he finds the article 'very interesting': but he thinks it is not suitable for publication in *The Times*. I was not surprised at this decision as even in the cautious form I have tried to formulate the conclusions they seem hardly to be compatible with the general political line *The Times* has so far taken in the matter in question. On the other hand, I thought it was not well possible to give further facts away without exposing those who are involved in the plot to still greater perils. I felt I had already gone quite far enough.

In this connection, I may mention that I happened to meet Dr W.H. Moore[1] a few days ago. He is the Dean of St. John's College and now a government official in the Foreign Office (Department Germany). I showed him the paper and he was obviously very keen to get it for the Foreign Office for circulation among those concerned. I complied with his request and I very much hope that this will meet with your approval.

I have also thought of other ways of making further use of it. One could, of course, make a short article out of it and send it to the *Contemporary* or *The Fortnightly*. But I am afraid at a time when things are moving so rapidly the recent events in Germany are not interesting enough from the British point of view – moreover, such an article could not be published before October and this is rather late. I am still thinking of *The Manchester Guardian*, which I think is politically more liberal-minded than *The Times* but you can certainly advise me best in this matter. It would be easy to make the necessary slight changes and I could send you or *The Manchester Guardian* the paper without delay.

By the way, do you know, my Lordbishop, Mr R.W. Southern who seems to be in charge of a government department in the Foreign Office.[2] It obviously deals with personal matters concerning post-war Germany. He has asked me for some help in his department.

As to the news from France, I am glad that the F.F.I.[3] are able to play so important a part in the campaign. But I conclude from this that the former reports according to which the Nazis have drafted the French manpower into Germany (either as prisoners of war or as slave labour) were not correct.

Yours ever,

---

[1] See Bell to Leibholz, 31 August 1943, note 4.
[2] See Bell to Leibholz, 31 August 1943, note 5.
[3] Forces Françaises de l'Intérieur, originally the French resistance forces, were now being formally organized into light infantry units to supplement regular Free French forces.

Leibholz to Bell, 4 September 1944, Bell Papers 40, fol. 263 (typewritten); BA, N 1334 (copy)

My Lord Bishop,

Very many thanks for your kind letter and introductory letter to the Editor of *The Manchester Guardian*. I think you are completely right in what you say about the lack of flowing English. I felt the same about the paper and, therefore, I was not pleased with it at all. I have re-written it and I feel it may now have become a little more easily readable. And yet I have added to my letter to the Editor a clause as suggested by you. I will let you know his answer. On the whole, the interest in the recent happenings in Germany does not seem to me very great – in face of the general German collapse on all fronts.

In the meantime, I have seen the article in the *News Chronicle* to which you referred in your letter. It is indeed very interesting. The author of the article gives full particulars of former visits by Schacht and Goerdeler to this country in 1938 and 1939,[1] which (with regard to Goerdeler) was unknown to me hitherto. G. and Sch. had obviously tried to warn people here of the actual situation in Germany, of the threat of Hitler and the fatal errors of the appeasement policy. The quotations given from Sch. and G. seem to me genuine. I could only have a look at the paper: otherwise I would have sent it to you. I only fear that such publications are very dangerous for the persons concerned. I think one should not publish such things until it is known for certain that these persons are no longer alive. But journalists have other interests and their conscience is rather elastic.

I have also seen the article in the *New Statesman* referred to by you in a former letter.[2] I think the Editor and Schütz are right – you are certainly the 'foreign Bishop'. I wonder what is behind this story.

I have just had another letter from Southern (Foreign Office): They seek information in order to be able to compile lists of persons in Germany who may usefully occupy responsible positions after the defeat of the Nazis. In this connection I should like to ask you whether you can possibly spare a copy of the memo. which you wrote in July 1942 when you came back from Sweden.[3] If this be the case I should be glad to have one.

I hope you and Mrs Bell are having a refreshing time.

With all good wishes,

Yours ever,

[1] See Klemperer, *German Resistance against Hitler*, pp. 86–8.
[2] See Bell's letter to Leibholz, 5 August 1944.
[3] See Bell's 'Memorandum of Conversations', in *DBW* Vol. 16, pp. 315–20.

Bell to Leibholz, 9 September 1944, LPL, BA, N 1334 (typewritten); Bell Papers 40, fol. 264 (carbon)

My dear Leibholz,

I had not got the memorandum of my Swedish experiences with me; and it is kept, for obvious reasons, rather secret. But I gladly send it to you now I have returned. I hope *The Manchester Guardian* will print your article.

Yours ever,

Leibholz to Bell, 11 September 1944, Bell Papers 40, fol. 265 (typewritten); BA, N 1334 (copy)

My Lordbishop,

Just coming back from Hawarden I hear the distressing news about the new executions in Germany and I need not tell you how my wife and I feel. You know it was Adam von Trott[1] who always gave Dietrich the possibility of going abroad and also of meeting you in Sweden. I met him last in August 1939 shortly before the outbreak of the war.[2] His family is closely befriended with that of my wife and is strongly Christian. His father was a former minister of education.[3] I think he (Adam) is also quite well known in this country. He was a Rhodes Scholar and Balliol man. Unfortunately, I also know Wirmer[4] who was a young and strong Catholic. He was formerly a secretary with a leader of the German Zentrum's party (I think with Prälat Kaas or Lammers).[5] It is too sad to see that so many of our people with whom we are bound by so many ties and who could have played a leading part in a Western Germany involved in this 'ill-omened' plot. May God give [grant] that all the others, above all Dietrich, are safe and well. How terrible not to be able to help them in their ordeal.

Thank you also for your letter and the copy of the memo. I gather from the latter that Witzleben and Leuschner were also mentioned there and Leuschner was called a leader of the movement, together with Beck and Goerdeler. I do not know him personally. But if Dietrich said he was of a strong Christian character I think there is no doubt he was.[6] All this seems to me to show that the final conclusion of my paper is not unfounded.

I have so far not heard from the Editor of *The Manchester Guardian*. I wonder whether they have written to you. I think the matter has now become a little more actual again.

Yours ever,

---

[1] Adam von Trott zu Solz (1907–44) spent Hilary term of 1929 in Oxford studying theology at Mansfield College and again returned to Oxford in 1931 on a Rhodes Scholarship to study at Balliol College where he became a close friend of David Astor. It was at Oxford in 1937 that he met Helmuth James von Moltke. On a Rhodes Scholarship he went on to study in Peking in 1937-8: as an early opponent of the Nazis he did not want to work as a lawyer for the civil service. In June 1939 Trott was still searching for British allies in a quest to prevent war, meeting Sir Stafford Cripps and, with Astor's support, speaking with Lord Halifax and Prime Minister Chamberlain. In 1940 he entered the Department of Information of the German Foreign Office, there making contact with the resistance group of Hans von Dohnanyi and that of Helmuth von Moltke. As an acknowledged specialist in foreign affairs he made further travels in 1941–3 in the name of the Kreisau Circle. After the failure of the 20 July conspiracy he was sentenced to death by the People's Tribunal on 15 August and hanged that day.

[2] Trott had travelled to Britain in February 1939, and twice in June 1939, staying in Oxford. But he did not visit the country in August.

[3] August von Trott zu Solz (1855–1938) was Prussian State Minister of Education 1909-17.

[4] Josef Wirmer (1901–44) belonged to the left wing of the Centre Party. In 1936 he joined a group of former trade unionists in opposition to the Nazi regime and also made contact with active resisters. From 1941 he co-operated with Carl Goerdeler, in whose post-Nazi government he would have been minister of justice. After 20 July 1944 he was sentenced to death by the People's Tribunal and hanged on 8 September 1944.

[5] Wirmer was not a follower of Ludwig Kaas but of Heinrich Brüning. The reference to Hans Heinrich Lammers is erroneous: he was a National Socialist, a minister without portfolio and chief of the office of the Chancellor.

[6] Wilhelm Leuschner was not a member of a Church, but of a Masonic Lodge.

Bell to Leibholz, 12 September 1944, BA, N 1334 (typewritten)

My dear Leibholz,

Here is the reply from *The Manchester Guardian*. I am very sorry they feel as they do.

Yours ever,

[a]I have read the revised version, which is excellent. I think it will wait while trying the *Contemporary*.[a]

Bell to Leibholz, 12 September 1944, BA, N 1334 (handwritten)

My dear friend,

I had packed up the enclosed, when your letter arrived by the afternoon post. The news it contains – whose full implications I had *not* understood from the press – fills me anew with deepest sympathy for you and your wife and thoughts and prayer for Dietrich: and all your friends. Are you sure that Trott zu Solz (*Times* printing) is Adam von Trott? I should very much like to know this. He had so many friends in England – not least of them Stafford Cripps and Lionel Curtis.[1]

One of the most trying parts of this bitter experience is, as you say, the knowledge that one can do nothing, save pray.

May God keep D. and all.

Yours affectionately,

---

[1] Lionel George Curtis (1872–1955) was the founder of the Royal Institute of International Affairs. In his book *Civitas Dei: The Commonwealth of God* (1938) Curtis argued that the United States must rejoin the British Commonwealth, which had the potential to evolve into a world government. He was a close friend of Helmuth James von Moltke, but no friendship with Trott is known. As a trustee of the Rhodes Trust he would certainly have known of Trott.

Leibholz to Bell, 13 September 1944, Bell Papers 40, fol. 266 (handwritten); BA, N 1334 (copy)

My Lordbishop,

Very many thanks for all your goodness. There is, unfortunately, no doubt that Trott zu Solz is Adam von Trott. I myself listened to the wireless when the first news were given in the European broadcast where the Christian name Adam was mentioned and said that he was a Balliol man from 1930 to 1933. He used to call himself Adam von Trott but his full name was Trott zu Solz. I also know that he was a 'Legationsrat' in the Foreign Office and that you mentioned his name, in connection with Dietrich, when you came back from Sweden. ªIn the announcement over the wireless it was said that Trott was in contact with foreign agents in Sweden (last in 1943).ª [1]

I am just sending the Ms. to Gooch[2] with reference to you, as I know you will agree. I personally doubt whether it will be suitable for the *Contemporary* as the October number must already have gone into print and I am afraid it will not be actual enough for publication in November. But if so I think I can use the Ms. in another connection.

On the whole, I feel strongly that the recent happenings in Germany are hushed up in the press as they do not fit in with the general trend of policy. Even if one makes some allowances in this respect, I think it is not fair only to report on the atrocities and not to give the other side of the picture.

Yours ever,

P.S. I am enclosing a cutting from *The Times* of today.[3]

---

[1] See Klemperer, *German Resistance Against Hitler*, pp. 333–5.
[2] George Peabody Gooch (1873–1968) was British journalist, Liberal and historian, particularly of diplomacy. He was co-editor of the *Cambridge History of British Foreign Policy: 1783–1919*

(3 vols, 1922–23) and the series *British Documents on the Origins of the War*: 1898–1914 (11 vols, 1926–38). Gooch was for many years Editor of *The Contemporary Review*.
[3] Not preserved.

Bell to Leibholz, 14 September 1944, BA, N 1334 (typewritten); Bell Papers 40, fol. 267 (carbon)

My dear Leibholz,

Many thanks for your letter, and for what you say in sad confirmation of the death of Adam von Trott. I am writing to Sir Stafford Cripps and to Lionel Curtis, to be sure they know.[1] I agree with you in the miserable playing down of the significance of the Hitler plot. It is tragic to think what might have been prevented had the Foreign Office only believed what they were told, and acted on it, in 1942.

I hope Gooch will print your article.

The House of Lords resumes on September 26th. There will be a debate on the aims and manner of the occupation. Vansittart is starting it and I, with the goodwill of the Foreign Office, have put down another motion on the same subject, and have told Vansittart, who agrees. The debate will range, therefore, over the general theme. I enclose copies of the two motions.[2] I shall of course be grateful for any reflections with which you can fortify me.

You will be interested to know that I have been invited to the first Union Society debate in Oxford on October 19th, which is on the subject of the treatment of Germany. There are four undergraduate speakers and two guest speakers. I don't know who takes the opposite point of view to my own. I hope to have a chance of seeing you then.

Yours [a]very[a] sincerely,

[a]P.S. Since dictating the above, I have had a talk with Tracy Strong (USA – YMCA) just back from Sweden. He saw Ehrenström[3] and others. He had no news of Dietrich.

But Gerstenmaier[4] has been arrested

Hanns Lilje interrogated (twice)[5]

Heckel's assistant – Boorman (?)[6] – arrested.

And a general closing in on church circles.

Bishop Wurm[7] is more than ever the centre of Christian resistance: and arrangements have been made because of the immense value of his person, to spirit him to Switzerland if he is known to be in great danger.[a]

---

[1] See Bell to Sir Stafford (Cripps), 14 September 1944, Bell Papers, Vol. 47, fol. 124 (carbon).
[2] *The Bishop of Chichester* – To call the attention of His Majesty's Government, in connection with the coming occupation of Germany, to the distinction between Germany and the Hitlerite State drawn by M. Stalin on 6 November 1942, and endorsed by His Majesty's Government on 10 March 1943, and also to the difference between Italy and the Fascist totalitarian system into the clutches of which she had let herself fall, recognized by the Prime Minister at Rome in his message to the Italian People of 28 August 1944; and to move for papers. BA, N 1334 (carbon).
[3] Nils Ehrenström (1903–84) was sent by Archbishop Söderblom to study social ethics at Geneva in 1930. He served as co-director of the Study Department of the WCC, 1938–54, and as director of the Nordic Ecumenical Institute at Sigtuna, 1940–3.
[4] Eugen Gerstenmaier (1906–86) worked between 1936 and 1944 in the office of foreign affairs of the German Protestant Church under Bishop Theodor Heckel. In this capacity he was involved in

preparations for the conference in Oxford in 1937. From 1942 he belonged to the Kreisau Circle. On 20 July 1944 Gerstenmaier was at the centre of the plot, in the Supreme Command of the Army, but the People's Tribunal did not sentence him to death. Freed by the US Army he founded the main relief organisation of the Protestant church in 1945. Between 1949 and 1969 he was a member of the Bundestag, becoming President of the German Parliament in 1954–69.

5   Johannes 'Hanns' Lilje (1899–1977) was a pioneer of the ecumenical movement, as a member (since 1928) and then as Vice-President (in 1932–5) of the executive committee of the World Student Christian Federation. He was also Secretary-General of the Lutheran World Convention (1935–46). Before the 20 July 1944 Lilje had been repeatedly interrogated by the Gestapo and forbidden to speak and travel. Arrested on 19 August 1944 and detained until April 1945 in the Gestapo prison on the Lehrter Straße in Berlin, he was sentenced by the People's Tribunal to four years imprisonment on 18 January 1945. Between 1947 and 1971 he was bishop of the Lutheran Church of Hannover.

6   This was in fact Dr. Wilhelm Bachmann, a university friend and later a colleague of Eugen Gerstenmaier in the foreign office of the German Church. He was arrested in June 1944 and in 'Schutzhaft' until February 1945.

7   Theophil Wurm (1868–1953), bishop of the Lutheran Church of Wurttemberg (1929–48). In wartime Wurm became the leading personality of the Protestant Church in Germany. His 'Einigungswerk' ('Unity Work', or 'Work of Uniting') became the basis of the Church's reconstruction after the war.

Leibholz to Bell, 19 September 1944, Bell Papers 40, fol. 268 (typewritten); BA, N 1334 (copy)

My Lordbishop,

Very many thanks for your last letter.

How sad it is that now also other members of the Churches have been affected by the new terror drive of Himmler. I think you have noted in the last number of the *Observer* the article *Himmler rounds up Germans who might help Allies*, which also confirms the closing in of [the] Gestapo on the Churches. The article itself, if true, is distressing and heartrending – especially as far as it is concerned with the actual or planned massacres in the concentration camps. I think the more the facts become known the more your memo. proves to be correct even in its details.

Today it would be easily possible to prove the existence of the 'other Germany' with which the Western countries could deal but what I fear is that if we stress this point too much the Nazis would only be encouraged to eliminate more quickly and radically the active remainder of the Western-minded strata. This is the dilemma in which we find ourselves today. The Editor of *The Manchester Guardian*[1] who has written me in the meantime also takes the view that a public discussion of the recent events in Germany just now might endanger others. On the one hand, the playing down of the significance and implications of the conspiracy is misleading, short-sighted and miserable; on the other hand if we speak the truth the position of our people in Germany may become still worse and more hopeless.

Nevertheless, I am constantly thinking of what can possibly be done. If this war is ideological in its character as I think it is (in spite of Mr Churchill) one could possibly argue that political massacres against Germans just as those acts committed against other people in the occupied countries are crimes and that the perpetrators and abetters of these crimes will be held responsible as war criminals just as other war criminals too. But those who consider the present conflict a national war will, of course, instantly raise the objection that there is no right of interference in the internal affairs of a state, from the international legal point of view. I admit this is the prevailing view although I think it is wrong.

May I also call your attention to the statement made by the new French Foreign Minister and the head of the French resistance movement, George Bidault[2], after the liberation of Paris: 'German soldiers! I am the chief of the French resistance movement. I come to wish you a good recovery. May you find yourselves, tomorrow, in a Germany and a Europe equally freed.' The spirit of this statement has impressed me. If this is possible after a four year's occupation I ask myself why things in this country have gone just the other way. (Cf. in this connection the letter to *The Times*, 'The German People', published yesterday by Eden's brother[3].)

Gooch wrote to me that he would have very much liked to publish the article in the *Contemporary* if he had received it earlier, but now the earliest possible date would be November and he fears that the article might then be 'ancient history'. I understand this and I think I shall leave it now and will see whether I can use the article or a part of it in another connection.

I am very glad you are coming to Oxford to speak to the Oxford Union[4]. You know only too well how delighted we should be if you could find time to have lunch or tea with us. I will also see to get tickets for the Union.

Yours ever,

---

[1] A.P. Wadsworth became the new Editor of the *Manchester Guardian* in 1944.
[2] George Bidault (1899–1983) was active in the French Resistance. After the imprisonment of Jean Moulin in June 1943 Bidault became president of the Conseil National de la Résistance (CNR), publishing the post-war programme 'Charte de la Résistance' in 1944. After the Second World War he founded the *Mouvement républicain populaire* (MRP). He served the Fourth Republic as prime minister in 1949/50 and several times as minister.
[3] This was Sir Timothy Eden (1893–1963).
[4] The Oxford Union was founded in 1823 as a forum for the discussion and debate of controversial issues. In this period to become President of the Oxford Union was seen as a firm indication of promise in public and political life.

Leibholz to Bell, 24 September 1944, Bell Papers 40, fol. 269 (typewritten); BA, N 1334 (copy)

My Lordbishop,

I am enclosing an unimportant cutting but the marked sentence shows the line of the German propaganda machine, which explains the stiff[en]ing of the German resistance. On the whole, I think the Germans realize the hopelessness of the military situation as well as the Allies. If they go on struggling as they obviously do – it seems to me it is because the Western powers have more or less embraced Vansittartism. I think that the sacrifices which the Western countries have *now* to make for the execution of this policy will prove to be in vain later on, from a Western-European point of view. For when they have ultimately attained their aims they will note that their position will be worse than if they had strengthened the Western elements in Germany and had pursued a constructive Western policy, which you have always strongly advocated with such great courage and convincing power. But war darkens reason.

Yours ever,

Bell to Leibholz, 27 September 1944, BA, N 1334 (handwritten)

My dear Leibholz,

Here is *Hansard*. The House was very full, and gave me a much more sympathetic hearing, listening to my speech, than I expected.[1] I particularly valued Lord Perth's agreement.[2] But there was (that very rare experience for me!) applause of a moderate kind when I sat down. But Cranborne's reply (which he seemed to make from a typed MS) was vy. disappointing. How blind the govt. is.

I also enclose a letter from Lady (Stafford) Cripps[3] with an extract from a Swedish paper about von Trott[4] – very sad and disquieting. *Please return it to me.*

Yours ever,

Your quotation fr. Bidault came in very handy!

---

[1] See Hansard, H.L. Deb., Vol. 133, cols. 119–68 (26 September 1944); Bell's speech, 'Occupation of Germany', is reprinted in *The Church and Humanity*, pp. 142–50.
[2] Ibid., cols. 141–2.
[3] Isobel Cripps (1891–1979). She had married Stafford Cripps in 1911. At this time she was much involved in international aid work, particularly in China.
[4] 'Opposition Groups in Germany', in *Dagens Nyheter*, 12 September 1944, preserved in the Bell Papers, Vol. 42, fols. 138–9.

Leibholz to Bell, 2 October 1944, Bell Papers 40, fol. 270 (typewritten); BA, N 1334 (copy)

My Lordbishop,

How delighted I am to hear that you had a sympathetic hearing in the Lords and such cordial applause. Of course, I have read *Hansard* and, above all, your speech with immense interest and from that I do not wonder that you had so great a success. It is a really statesmanlike and constructive statement – the best I have ever read on the problem in question. Such a statement ought to have come from a really wise government: but I am afraid we cannot expect anything like it as things stand today. Under these circumstances, the reaction of the House is perhaps more important than that of the government.

May I make one point, which I think would provide an additional weight to your argument? I am thinking of the German occupation in the Allied countries. Should one not learn from the experiences made there and from the German methods employed? If, on the whole, one uses the same means can one expect anything else but a Quisling government, which may be a convenient instrument of the Allies for a while but which will be hated by the Germans as the Quislings governments [sic] were hated by their peoples?

Then there is another point: Cranborne ªsaidª that he agreed with Cecil that there is only one solution of the German problem – RECONVERSION.[1] Quite, this is just what we want[2] and I think that just from this aspect your speech is masterly. If it were only possible to make clear to the government or to enlighten Public opinion that the power policy of today (the hard facts of which Cranborne spoke) is the most unsuitable method in order to convert a nation. It will and must have ᶜjustᶜ the opposite effect.

And I think that there is nothing especially German in it. Every nation, big or small, would act in the same way. The Germans did so in 1919 and no doubt they will do so against a Super-Versailles.

Mr Eden spoke of the planned Guerrilla warfare. I am convinced that such plans exist. I even think that these desperados can finally only be overcome with the help of the Germans themselves. If as a result of the oppressive policy the 80% [of] Germans who are today anti-Nazis will be caused to join these 10, 15, or 20% Nazis, then I am afraid there will never be peace in Germany, even after the war has come to an end. I think this argument also supports your wise expositions.

I have read with deep emotion and great anxiety the copy of the article[3] the content of which was referred to in *The Observer* about a fortnight ago. I think it largely coincides with what you put in the Memo. before the Foreign Office. Trott and Dietrich and their friends were obviously troubled with the same questions as we are (unconditional surrender and its implications). I personally associate myself fully with the questions, which were raised by Trott in Stockholm.[4] There is also the 'interesting' remark that Allied circles suspected him of being an agent of the Hitler regime.

I am enclosing the copy of the article and Lady I. Cripps' letter. I could provide her with some material concerning Trott's person (he was a student in Göttingen when I was there and took there his degree[5] and the Trott's family is in close contact with Bonhoeffers for about 20 years) but I do not know more facts as far as the plot itself is concerned.

Yours ever,

P.S. By the way, Lindsay wrote me in connection with Trott that 'at first they were asking what was impossible'. I wonder whether you know what he has in mind.[6]

Bevan in the Commons[7] and the *Observer*'s leader of yesterday also stressed the point that Germany's stiffening resistance is due to fear i.e. to the unconditional surrender policy.

The Times' Leader of today, *Terms of peace*, is a little more encouraging. The 'Buchenwald' letter by Murray[8] and others raises the point I mentioned in one of my last two letters.

ᵃIf we may see you for lunch or tea on October 19th would you please kindly let me know. I should be delighted to have a talk with you. I have just seen C. Dawson who has sketched a draft concerning the foundation of a society for Europe and European culture. If you would encourage him here I think this would be of great value.ᵃ

[1] See *Hansard*, HL Deb, Vol. 133, col. 165 (26 September 1944).
[2] See Bell, 'Christianity and Reconstruction', in the *Fortnightly Review*, Vol. 148 (1940), pp. 558–64; see too Philip Coupland, 'George Bell, the Question of Germany and the Cause of European Unity', in Chandler (ed.) *The Church and Humanity*, pp. 118–20. Leibholz wrote to J.H. Oldham, 'I quite agree with you that security and reconversion of Germany, which have to be attained by meting out justice (distributive and creative) are aims of a specifically Christian concern and that Christianity itself offers no guidance about the way of preventing Germany from again plunging the world into war.' 16 October 1944, Bell Papers Vol. 40 (I), fols. 271–3 (copy).
[3] See Bell to Leibholz, 27 September 1944.
[4] Trott's three visits to Sweden are discussed by Klemens von Klemperer in *German Resistance Against Hitler*, pp. 289–90, 333–5 and 335–8. It is unclear to which documents Leibholz refers.

5   Trott studied at Göttingen University from the winter semester of 1927/28 to the following winter semester of 1928/29, and again in the summer of 1930. His doctorate became a study of *Hegels Staatsphilosophie und das internationale Recht*, published in 1931.
6   This probably refers to Trott's idealistic vision of a united Europe; see Malone, *Adam von Trott*, p. 65.
7   To be found in the debate about the war and international situation, in Hansard, HC Deb., Vol. 403, cols. 627-36 (29 September 1944). Aneurin Bevan (1897-1960), Labour MP 1929-51 and one of the chief spokesmen for the Labour party's left wing; subsequently the reforming Minister for Health in the 1945-51 Labour governments.
8   Gilbert Murray (1866-1957) was an outstanding scholar of the language and culture of Ancient Greece, a humanist and a great advocate of the League of Nations (and after the war the United Nations organization); Regius Professor of Greek at Oxford University between 1908 and 1936, he wrote and broadcast extensively on religious questions. Politically a liberal he supported Bell's rejection of obliteration bombing.

Bell to Leibholz, 13 October 1944, BA, N 1334 (typewritten)

My dear Leibholz,

I should much like to come and have tea with you on Thursday, say at 4.30. But with a view to showing me the way, do you think you could fetch me from the President's Lodging at Corpus, at four o'clock? I am hoping to see Christopher Dawson there beforehand. But please don't give me much for tea, as I must be rather ascetic and eat very little before the Union debate. I shall only arrive after lunch, and shall return first thing on Friday morning.

Yours ever,

Bell to Leibholz, 20 October 1944, BA, N 1334 (typewritten)

My dear Leibholz,

This is just to thank you and Mrs Leibholz for the very happy and enjoyable tea which you gave me yesterday in your home. It was a real pleasure to be with you, and to see your younger daughter. I hope one of these days soon I shall see your elder daughter too.

I don't know what was the result of the voting in the debate last night. It was an interesting occasion. The Proctors saw the President before the debate and said they did not wish the result of the voting to be published; so I do not myself know what the result was. But I expect I shall hear from the President tomorrow.

I enclose a copy of *Hansard* for October 10th.[1]

Yours ever,

ᵃAlso a *spare* copy of Walter Layton's pamphlet.[2] I have not read it.ᵃ

1   Hansard, HL Deb., Vol. 133, cols. 409-34 (10 October 1944); for Bell's speech see cols. 419-24; the speech was reprinted in Bell, *The Church and Humanity*, pp. 151-64.
2   *Probably* Sir Walter Thomas Layton, *The British Commonwealth and World Order* (Barnett House Papers 27), (London, 1944). Walter Layton (1884-1966), knighted in 1930, became 1st Baron Layton in 1947. An economist, editor, newspaper proprietor and Liberal Party politician, he was editor of *The Economist* from 1922 to 1938 and between 1930 and 1940 editorial director of the *News Chronicle*, to which he returned after the war. In 1944-63 he was also Chairman of *The Economist*.

Leibholz to Bell, 21 October 1944, Bell Papers 40, fol. 274 (typewritten)

My Lordbishop,

I was just going to write to you when your kind letter arrived. Very many thanks for it. It was too good of you to have taken the trouble to come and see us here. It was really a great joy to us. Unfortunately, Marianne had at the same time her first tutorial and she was not allowed to miss it. She was very sorry but I hope she may see you soon. ᵃIf we could have done, as we should have very much liked to do, we should have asked you to stay with us. But unfortunately apart from the sitting room you saw we have only two other bedrooms.ᵃ

I found the debate on Thursday was stimulating and I need not tell you how wholeheartedly I agree with all you said. The applause you got was very cordial and I should also very much like to know the number of votes which were given against the motion. – Frankly I was disappointed at Rowse's speech.[1] He reminded me of some 'Deutsch-nationale' German professors who could easily have made a similar speech. I thought these types would not exist here and it is rather a pity to think that these men have to teach the students history here. How demagogic and misleading were his arguments. And his personal way of arguing disgusted me. I feel he is more a clever politician than a good historian.

Yesterday I saw Dawson and I mentioned your suggestion – if possible – to connect the planned study group with a college. I also mentioned that it would perhaps be easier to bring the whole group together by planning a book, say, EUROPE, to which (on the basis of Dawson's paper) the people in question would have to make their contributions from the specific point of view from which they see the problem. It seemed to me that Dawson was sympathetic but he hopes to discuss all this with you in greater detail at Chichester next week.

Oldham wrote me in reply to my letter[2] that he will now re-write his paper and change it 'considerably'.

Many thanks for *Hansard*[3] and Layton's pamphlet. I am very glad to have both and I am especially looking forward to reading the new *Hansard* and your speech.

In the meantime I have also seen *The Call of Peace – a Christian Germany* by U. Bentinck and W. Richthofen.[4]

With all my good wishes to you and Mrs Bell ᵃand renewed thanksᵃ.

Yours ever,

---

[1] i.e. Alfred Leslie Rowse.
[2] See Leibholz to J. Oldham, 16 October 1944, Bell Papers Vol. 40, fols. 271–3.
[3] Hansard, H.L. Deb., Vol. 133, cols. 419–24 (10 October 1944): Bell's speech is reprinted in Bell, *The Church and Humanity*, pp. 151–7.
[4] This particular book is untraced but since the 1920s Wilhelm, Baron von Richthofen, had been an acknowledged authority on British-German relations in Germany, publishing *Brito-Germania: die Erlösung Europas* in Berlin in 1926.

Bell to Leibholz, 3 November 1944, BA, N 1334 (typewritten)

My dear Leibholz,

Very many thanks for the *New English Weekly*. I was delighted to have it, and thought your article read ever so much better in the revised form.¹

Yours ever,

ᵃI have had a vy happy visit from Dawson.ᵃ

---

¹ 'The Opposition Movement in Germany', in *The New English Weekly and the New Age*, 19 October 1944, Vol. 26, pp. 5–6, reprinted in Leibholz, *Politics and Law*, pp. 210–3; see too Leibholz to Bell, 8 August 1944 (note 9).

Bell to Leibholz, 14 November 1944, BA, N 1334 (handwritten)

My dear Leibholz,

I am very sorry you and your wife should have this worry of a move and very sorry for the difficulties that have caused it. I do hope you will be happy and comfortable in the new quarters.

I asked 't Hooft¹ about Dietrich, and he was so far as he went reassuring. He has no reason to think he has come to any harm, and believes him to be safe, so far as he knows. The fact that he had been in prison for so long before July 20 was (he says) very much to his advantage, for he could not well be incriminated.

't Hooft did not mean that there was no danger – that is inevitable: but no special cause for alarm now.

Yours ever,

---

¹ Visser 't Hooft had visited Britain in the autumn of 1944, participating in a meeting of the provisional committee of the WCC on 6 November and attending a meeting of the Peace Aims Group on 7 November, at which he spoke about the plot of 20 July; see Boyens, *Kirchenkampf und Ökumene*, Vol. II, pp. 226–7.

Leibholz to Bell, 16 November 1944, Bell Papers 40, fol. 276 (typewritten); BA, N 1334 (copy)

My Lordbishop,

Very many thanks for your kind letter.

I was just going to write to you when your letter arrived and to ask you whether Visser 't Hooft could give you any more detailed news about Dietrich. Now we are thankful (although still very anxious) for the rather reassuring news which you were so kind to convey to us. We hope and trust that the fact that he was imprisoned before July 20th will save him. All our attempts to get further news about him (and his and our nearest relatives), unfortunately, have failed in the last five months.

Yesterday there was an interesting report in *The Daily Telegraph* (based on the statement of somebody who was involved in the 'plot' and escaped from Germany¹) saying that Hitler's double was killed when caused by Himmler to attend the meeting of the Generals. The report sounds very trustworthy and as far as I know the same version of the failure was given by Visser 't Hooft. This explanation would confirm the conclusions to which I came in my little article, namely that Himmler set the conspiracy in motion in order to get rid of the disloyal elements in time.

By the way, in the debate in the Commons on November 10th Mrs Rathbone referred in detail to the article in the *New English Weekly*.[2] Her speech has again deeply impressed me by her political wisdom, fairness and courage. I wonder whether you would not also think it a good idea to let her have confidentially for her information a copy of the Memorandum you wrote after your return from Sweden. I think she would be greatly fortified in her stand in the Commons if she knew a little more of the details even if she cannot make use of them in Parliament. I feel that your Memorandum could thus well have some good effects just now.

I have also had a letter from Lady S[tafford]. Cripps saying that her husband sent the copy of the *New English Weekly* to Mr Eden. Although I do not entertain any illusions about all this the article has perhaps thus fulfilled its purpose and I may thank you once again in this connection for all the help you have given me in this special matter. The article will be reprinted in *Raven's Bulletin* and will also be published in an enlarged form in the *Bulletin of the Fellowship*.[3]

In the meantime, we have settled down and although the house is not situated in a nice district (it is not far from the station) the flat is comfortable and above all we are again on our own and have our peace so that I can go on with my work.

With all my good wishes

Yours ever,

P.S. Have you seen Michael Foot's letter[4] (reply to Vansittart) in *The Times* of today? I think it is excellent.

---

[1] This was probably Otto John, who was at the effective headquarters of the plot, in the Bendlerblock, in Berlin when Stauffenberg returned from Rastenburg convinced that he had killed Hitler.
[2] See Hansard, H.C. Deb., Vol. 404, cols. 1725–31 (10 November 1944); here col. 1727.
[3] These journals have not been traced.
[4] Michael Foot (1913–2010), Labour Party politician, influential journalist and author; later MP and leader of the party, 1980–3.

Bell to Leibholz, 5 December 1944, BA, N 1334 (handwritten)

My dear Leibholz,

Very many thanks for your article on *Unity of Europe*.[1] I am particularly glad to have it, and will study it carefully, bearing in mind a debate in the Lords on December 19 on the unifying forces in Europe. I enclose [the] Order Paper.

I read Huizinga's article[2] with much interest. It is very relevant. I also liked Barth in CNL.[3]

Yours ever,

1 Leibholz, 'The Unity of Europe', in *Blackfriars* Vol. 25, December 1944, pp. 445-3, reprinted in *Politics and Law*, pp. 241-9.
2 Johan Huizinga (1872-1945), eminent Dutch historian particularly of medieval and Renaissance culture. Alarmed by the rise of National Socialism in Germany, Huizinga had written several works of cultural criticism. Many points of comparison may be found between his analysis and that of contemporary critics such as Ortega y Gasset and Oswald Spengler. Huizinga argued that the spirit of technical and mechanical organization had replaced spontaneous and organic order in cultural, as well as political, life.
3 *The Christian News-Letter* published only Karl Barth's Second Letter to the French Protestants: 'A Question and Request to French Protestants', *CNL* Supplement to No. 66, 21 January 1941. But here Leibholz was probably referring to The Christian News-Letter Book series: K. Barth, *A Letter to Great Britain from Switzerland*, with an Introduction by A. Vidler (London, 1941), pp. 1-29, a volume which was greatly appreciated by Bell; see Diether Koch (ed.), *Karl Barth, Offene Briefe 1935-1942* (Zürich, 2001), p. 273. By now Barth's reputation was immense. At the founding conference of the WCC at Amsterdam in 1948 he would be the principal speaker.

Leibholz to Bell, 11 December 1944, Bell Papers 40, fol. 278 (typewritten); BA, N 1334 (copy)

My Lordbishop,
Many thanks for your last letter.

As to the debate projected in the Lords on December 19th I think that Europe must become a unity in spite of all opposing forces if it is to survive at all. But I feel that such a unification depends first on the existence of a common ideology and secondly, from the organisational technical point of view, on the abandonment of the traditional dogma of sovereignty. It seems to me that both these presuppositions are closely related to each other and that only those states which are ideologically united with each other will be prepared to relinquish their sovereignty in favour of federations and unions in course of time.

If this basic thesis is correct it seems to me to follow that a European federation can only work if it is based either on the Eastern or Western conception of life. This is why I myself very much doubt whether it will be possible to create a workable European federation which would last, among states which are so different as, say, Great Britain and the Soviet Union. States which are not united by a common ideology can conclude an Alliance and pool their power in the traditional terms of power politics. Dumbarton Oaks[1] shows this quite clearly and I am afraid that such a concerted power will never secure the peace in the world.

In my view, the decisive ideological issue is today: Is the world to be organised according to secular totalitarian lines or on the basis of the Western conception of life. In this connection it seems to me misleading to use the term 'Democracy' as a totalitarian regime can possibly just as well claim to be democratic as the traditional Western regime. As Bryce once said: 'Democracy really means nothing more nor less than the rule of the whole people expressing their sovereign will by their votes.'[2] The more concrete content of democracy cannot be defined in greater detail. Sir Samuel Hoare seems to me to aim at the strengthening of the Western-minded forces in Europe. But this has nothing to do with democracy.

Of course, I am pessimistic about the possibility of realising the various plans for a unification of Europe. The situation in Greece, the other Balkan countries and Poland all point in the direction that the ideological issues are decisive today and that, therefore, the Great Powers seek to secure spheres of influence and regimes which are akin to them. I hope that they will not be the strategical positions for the next war. I fully agree with what *The Observer* said yesterday in its article 'Russia silent on our policy in Greece'. All this is (as things stand today) perhaps inevitable but what I cannot understand is how under these circumstances the Prime Minister could state that ideological issues matter less; and further, how it is possible to pursue a mere power politics towards Central Europe irrespective of its ideological consequences. I think Vansittartism in all its various shades makes a European unification on a Western basis an inner impossibility because it drives Central Europe towards the East. – I realize that Curtis, Catlin,[3] Smuts and others advocate a European unification of this country with the Western powers. But the point seems to me to be that Central Europe is an integral part of Europe and cannot be eliminated without destroying Europe itself. I think that those who will be able to win Central Europe over will in the end also win the West. The price the Western countries are paying[4] for the appeasement policy is this war, the price of Vansittartism will be the loss of Europe. What this means you know, my Lordbishop, better than I.

Yours ever,

---

[1] The conference of the Allied powers at Dumbarton Oaks in the United States, on 7 October 1944, planned the foundation of the United Nations and discussed the economic consequences of the earlier conference at Bretton Woods.
[2] James Bryce, *Modern Democracy* (vol. I, London, 1921), p. viii. James Bryce (1838–1922), British internationalist and historian, most famously of the Holy Roman Empire and 'The American Commonwealth'.
[3] Sir George Edward Gordon Catlin (1896–1979), English political scientist and professor at Cornell University and other universities in the United States and Canada. Politically on the Left, he served on the executive committee of the Fabian Society. A strong proponent of Anglo-American cooperation, and even of an organic union between the two countries, he was a founder of the Movement for Atlantic Union, which was later established in 1958.
[4] The copy alters the original version: 'have to pay'.

Leibholz to Bell, 21 December 1944, Bell Papers 40, fol. 279 (handwritten)

My Lordbishop,

My wife, the girls and I myself send you and Mrs Bell again this year our best wishes for a blessed Christmas with the hope that this year at least may bring peace to us all – a peace, which will last and not contain the seeds for future wars.

I have found the enclosed picture of Christ Church Cathedral where you frequently were as a student. I should be glad if it would give some pleasure to you.

Many thoughts weigh heavily on our hearts this year. But we fully realize that we have still to be very thankful for many things we have and we know that we may enjoy them by what you have done for us again this year. I think Christmas is the day when I may tell you again how deeply indebted I am to you for your friendship, which belongs to the most precious possessions of my whole life.

God bless you and Mrs Bell also in the New Year.

Yours ever,

Bell to Leibholz, 23 December 1944, BA, N 1334 (handwritten)

My dear Leibholz,

I am late, I fear, in sending you and Mrs Leibholz and the daughters my best wishes for Christmas, and affectionate greetings. And as I write your own kind letter and beautiful Xmas card of Ch[rist]. Ch[urch]. comes, which I am delighted to have.

I greatly value your personal friendship, which I have found during these nearly 6 years so enriching in various ways, and whenever I think of your wife I think of Dietrich. God grant that this coming year may bring the end of hostility, and the beginning of a just peace. Indeed the whole international situation is in a grievous state, and gets worse rather than better. I enclose *Hansard* of December 19. I prepared my speech carefully as a statement (in that context) of the Oecumenical movement.[1] I am told that some report of it was sent to Swiss & Swedish papers. I liked your *Blackfriars* article very much, and told Lord Huntingdon[2] about it – he was going to get it.

Once again my best wishes for Christmas to you all

Yours very sincerely,

[1] 'The Unifying forces of Europe', *Hansard*, H.L. Deb., Vol. 134 cols. 373–417 (19 December 1944); Bell's speech, cols. 403–7, was reprinted in Bell, *The Church and Humanity*, pp. 158–64.
[2] Francis Hastings (1909–90) was artist and Labour party politician who in 1939 had become the 16th Earl of Huntingdon.

Leibholz to Bell, 28 December 1944, Bell Papers 40, fol. 280 (typewritten); BA, N 1334 (copy)

My Lordbishop,

Our heartfelt thanks for your kind letter and Christmas wishes. Your letter came just in time and I greatly valued it as a special Christmas gift.

I think the German offensive[1] shows what a unifying effect despair can have with a people who have to face political destruction. Sometimes it seems to me as if it were a warning to the United Nations not to abuse their victory by self-righteousness and lack of humility. I am enclosing the copy of a letter which I think will be published in the *New English Weekly* under the headline *The Rehabilitation of Power*. There was an article in it under this title dealing with Jacob Burckhardt's dictum that power is evil.[2]

I had already read *Hansard* before receiving the copy you kindly sent me but I am very glad to have it. I think your speech dealt with the crux of the whole problem at the deepest level. As to Templewood's speech itself[3] I was disappointed (in spite of much agreement in other respects) in so far as he has also fallen into the error of identifying Germany and Nazism and further in so far as he seems to believe that the Russians would even be prepared to put the Constitution of 1936 in operation and to interpret this document in Western terms. In face of the fact that Communism is victorious in the East and possibly even in Central Europe I very much doubt whether such a view can be maintained, and will not prove mere wishful thinking. On the other hand, Lord Lang of Lambeth[4] seems to me now to approach the line you have advocated and even Lord Rankeillour[5] was obviously not too bad.

I am glad you liked the article in *Blackfriars*. It deals perhaps too much with technical details. For the whole problem of sovereignty is, from an ideological point of view, a technicality, even if an important one.

With all good wishes for the New Year to you and Mrs Bell.

Yours ever,

---

[1] The last German offensive in the west, in the Ardennes, began on 16 December 1944 and was decisively defeated by a counter-attack on 3 February 1945. By 27 February Allied forces had reached the Rhine.
[2] See Burckhardt's essay 'The Three Powers', in which he discussed Louis XIV and Napoleon. Jacob Burckhardt, *Reflections on History* (transl. 'M.D.H.', London, 1943), p. 38.
[3] Hansard, HL Deb., Vol. 134, cols. 374–85 (19 December 1944).
[4] Ibid., cols. 397–402.
[5] Ibid., cols. 444–9. James Hope (1870–1949), Conservative politician who had in 1932 become 1st Baron Rankeillour.

Leibholz to the Editor of *The New English Weekly*, 28 December 1944, Bell Papers 40, fol. 281 (copy); BA, N 1334 (copy)

Sir,

Re: The Rehabilitation of Power

I fear that anyone, who has followed the trend Politics have taken since the Unconditional Surrender formula was accepted at Casablanca cannot help feeling that it seems as if the time has not yet come to refute Jacob Burckhardt's dictum about the evil nature of power. Mr Churchill's statement made at the beginning of the war that 'we fight against evil things' must lose much of its significance if we bear in mind that the character of the present conflict is becoming increasingly more nationalistic and less ideological. This development has found its recent expression, not only in the laying in the margin of the Atlantic Charter and in the various plans for carving up Germany and enlarging the territory of her neighbours at her expense, but also in Mr Churchill's last statement in which we can read that as the war enters its final phase 'it is becoming and will become increasingly less ideological'.

This fundamental change in the whole outlook may well result in losing the ideological war. For nationalism, because of its close links with power politics, is, in its essence, tainted with concomitant evil. Of course, it will be argued that this time power and force will only be used to obtain security and, therefore, is only employed as a means to an end but not as an end in itself. But if there is one lesson which history taught us for certain it is that security based on mere power and force can only guarantee peace for a transient period. If this is already true of the national age in which in spite of the antagonism of the national states the nations were still bound to each other by a common ideology how much more must it be true of an age in which the world is torn by ideologies which are by no means dead and will make their re-appearance when the present stage of the war with its savagery in thought and deed has come to a close. The events in Greece and Poland prove this fully. It is because of this development that there is disappointment and both here and abroad talk of another war in future. If a system of security is to work it must be founded on justice, without which there can only be a technical and formal security of no permanent effects.

You note elsewhere in your issue that the worst in today's thinking is the growing of the idea that politics have nothing to do with principles and you add that if this idea prevails Western civilisation may easily be found to be beyond repair. This is perfectly true. It is this terrible possibility, which needs challenge. To obviate this danger power must be closely linked with justice in the sense in which this idea has been shaped by the spiritual traditions underlying Western civilisation. It is upon this relationship that the 'rehabilitation of power' depends.

[a]Yours faithfully[a],

1945

17 January	Soviet forces enter Warsaw.
27 January	Auschwitz is liberated by Soviet forces.
31 January	Soviet forces cross the Oder river.
4 February	The Yalta conference begins, concluding on 11 February.
13/14 February	Dresden is bombed.
20 March	American forces take Mainz.
29 March	Soviet forces enter Austria.
9 April 1945	The death of Dietrich Bonhoeffer in Flossenbűrg concentration camp.
10 April	Buchenwald concentration camp is liberated by American forces.
12 April	Death of President Roosevelt.
29 April	Dachau concentration camp is liberated by American forces.
30 April	Hitler commits suicide.
2 May	The Battle for Berlin ends.
7 May	German forces surrender to the Allies at Rheims.
8 May	Victory in Europe Day.
9 May	Soviet forces enter Prague.
26 June	The United Nations Charter is signed in San Francisco.
17 July–2 August	The Potsdam Conference of the Allied Powers.
6 August	The first atomic bomb is dropped on Hiroshima.
8 August	The Soviet Union declares war on Japan; the London Charter, an agreement between the Allied Powers, sets down the basis for trials for war crimes before an International Military Tribunal.
9 August	The second atomic bomb is dropped on Nagasaki.
15 August	Japan surrenders.
21 November	The Nuremberg Trials begin with twenty-two defendants, all of them leading figures in the National Socialist state.
20 December	The Allied Control Council issues Control Council Law Number 10. This grants individual Allied governments the power to try suspected war criminals in their own zones of occupation after the conclusion of the International Military Tribunal at Nuremberg.

Bell to Leibholz, 8 January 1945, BA, N 1334 (handwritten)

My dear Leibholz,

Very many thanks. I hope I shall have a revise ready to the weekend. Anyhow could you meet me for a talk at the Athenaeum *Tuesday* 15th at 12? & lunch.

Yours ever,

Leibholz to Bell, 9 January 1945, Bell Papers 40, fol. 282 (typewritten); BA, N 1334 (copy)

My Lordbishop,

Just a line to call your attention to Voigt's article 'Germany' in the January issue of *The 19th Century*. In this article he also deals in greater detail with the conspiracy of July 20th. I had contacted him and provided him with the necessary data. Although I am just as critical of the editorials of this periodical as you the article seems to me the best that has so far been published in this country by an Englishman. He points out that the conspiracy was an event of European significance and that the men involved in the plot died as patriots in the best sense for Europe as well as for Germany. I was very glad to read this tribute to those men who have been treated as traitors and criminals in Germany and as enemies by the Western powers. The details are rather vaguely described so that the article can hardly do any harm.

Have you noticed Stafford Cripps' address to the Baptist Board?[1] I think it is the first speech of a member of the government not couched in the traditional terms of power politics. I have just written to Lady Cripps and told her a story which I have just heard from a British medical student who has just gone to the Western front. He together with five other Englishmen came to blows with some Germans and one of the German soldiers (a boy of 18) was mortally wounded. The British tended the dying German and they said a few words to each other. The last words of the German were: 'We do not hate you. We are looking to you as liberators'. Our friend writes: 'We felt as if one of our comrades was dying'. The story has impressed me and I wish I could give it a wider publicity.

I hope that the disastrous consequences of the policy of the Western countries towards Central Europe and especially Germany will become more and more evident to wider circles. I was glad, for instance, to read in the *Observer* of December 31 and in the *New Statesman* of a fortnight ago that a country which has not been offered an alternative but only unconditional surrender and more or less political destruction cannot be blamed for putting up a desperate resistance. The tragedy is only that British and American soldiers have to pay with their lives for this non-constructive policy.

Yours ever,

---

[1] Sir Stafford Cripps speech to the Baptist Board, 'A Time for Greatness in International Relations', 3 January 1945. See *The Times*, 4 January 1945, p. 2 col. d.

Bell to Leibholz, 11 January 1945, BA, N 1334 (typewritten); Bell Papers 40, fol. 283

My dear Leibholz,

Many thanks for your letter. Voigt had sent me this month's *Nineteenth Century*, and I had read his article. Like you, I was very much struck with it, and thought it quite admirable. I very much liked the way in which the conspiracy was dealt with, and the insistence on the conspirators as patriots, both for Europe and for Germany. The whole tone of the article seemed to me to breathe a different note (as well as being much more constructive) from anything of Voigt's that I had seen before. I am writing to tell him how pleased I am.

I saw Gilbert Murray yesterday in town, and he told me that there was a very good article in the *Hibbert* on the punishment of Germany; but I have not seen it yet.

I had already cut out Stafford Cripps' address to the Baptist Board because I liked it so much. I am dining with him on Tuesday, and shall tell him how much I liked it. I am glad you have told Lady Cripps of the dying German's words. I am taking the opportunity of passing them on to the Religious Division of MOI.[1]

Did you read last Saturday's *Economist*? There was an admirable leading article there on this very question of the policy of the 'Western countries'.

I enclose a copy of the *Christian News-Letter*, with a slightly abbreviated version of my speech which is also being printed in the form of an article in the *Contemporary Review* for March.

Yours ever,

[1] i.e. the Ministry of Information.

Leibholz to Bell, 14 January 1945, Bell Papers 40, fol. 284 (typewritten); BA, N 1334 (copy)

My Lordbishop,

Very many thanks for your letter. I am delighted to see that by the reprint in the *Ch.-N-Letter* (and in the forthcoming issue of the *Contemporary Review*) of your contribution to the last debate in the Lords this admirable address will be given a wider publicity.

By the way, I was also glad to see Oldham's criticism of Mr Churchill's policy.[1] Today the main question seems to me to be whether in order to maintain the agreement among the three Great Powers this country (and America) are prepared to pay any price and to return to a mere power politics with its probable implication to lose Europe for good.

Indeed, Voigt's article is impressive and, like you, I was very much struck by it. Voigt's development seems to me typical for those who are European-minded enough to see that Europe and Vansittartism are not compatible with each other and are prepared to draw the consequences courageously. All the people who are thinking today in mere terms of power politics are I am afraid no good Europeans.

This was why I so much welcomed Stafford Cripps's speech, which seems to me more constructive than most of the addresses we usually hear from the government. Lady Cripps sent me a verbatim copy of the address and I think it is worthwhile reading the address as a whole. The Press reports are rather scanty. ªIf you want to have it please kindly let me know.ª

In a few days' time I will send you a copy of the last *Hibbert Journal*.² I have just lent it to a friend of mine who will return it to me. Ewing's³ article on *The Ethics of Punishing Germany* is very good. Two other articles published in the same issue take the same basic line and I find that *The Hibbert Journal* is a periodical which fulfils a noteworthy political function just in this respect.

Unfortunately, our landlord died a few weeks ago and his Executors want the house back so that we have to vacate the house again. It is a great pity as for the first time we felt at home here and we had just settled down. Now the whole trouble with all its implications starts again. You were so very good to let me have three years ago a letter of recommendation, which ran as follows:

'This is to testify that I know Dr G. Leibholz and his wife and two children very well. Dr Leibholz and Mrs Leibholz are people of the highest standing and personal integrity.

Dr Leibholz is a scholar of European reputation and a man of the highest capacity and character'.

It would be very kind of you to let me have a letter of a similar kind* because I think it would help me to find a new accommodation in the course of the next few months.

I am enclosing a copy of a pamphlet, which has just come out and contains the reprint of an article formerly published in *The Hibbert Journal*.

Yours ever,

*P.S. Marianne is now a student here and Christiane is 14 years old.

I have so far not seen last Saturday's *Economist*. But I will see to get a hold of it to-morrow.

---

¹ *The Christian News-Letter*, January 1945.
² The number which contained Leibholz's own article, 'Nationality in History and Politics', is reprinted in *Politics and Law*, pp. 72–80.
³ Alfred Cyril Ewing (1899–1973), lecturer in Moral Science at Cambridge and a distinguished participant in public debates about crime and punishment.

Leibholz to Bell, 16 January 1945, Bell Papers 40, fol. 285 (typewritten)

My Lordbishop,

It was a great joy for me to see you yesterday and it was so very nice to have lunch with you. Please accept the best thanks for all your kindness.

The paragraph I had in mind yesterday when we talked about Niemöller's letter runs as follows (in an interview with Chaplain Ben L. Rose¹):

Will you give a reason for your offer to serve in the German Navy?

'It was certainly not for the reason that I wanted to fight Hitler's war for him, and most assuredly not with any idea of trying to redeem myself with the Nazis. I was thinking only of my people and my country. At that time I saw three possibilities ahead for Germany: 1. total defeat, which would be bitter for Germany; 2. total victory for the

Nazis, which would be even bitterer for Germany, and 3. to fight on in the hope that the Nazis might be thrown out of government and a negotiated peace reached. If the latter occurred, and I had good hopes that it might, I did not want to be in prison but wished to be free in order that I might do my part for the future of my country. I was also moved to this offer by the fact that my three sons were being drafted into the Army and I felt that the place of a father is by the side of his sons".[2]

The second reason seems to me more plausible than the first one under 3).

I am also enclosing the copy of Dietrich's letter mentioned yesterday.[3] What Dietrich says on God being in this world and on God's suffering from this world seems to me very profound. I am not a theologian: but does this idea not represent something new in the traditional theological thinking? In any case, it is an idea which often occupied his mind and I myself am thinking on similar lines. Is not his suffering a part of God's suffering in this world? What he says about the French pastor seems to me to apply to him. I think it would be worthwhile having this passage translated into ᶜgoodᶜ English. Rupp[4] would certainly do it. If so, it would be very good of you to let me have a copy. The enclosed one is the only one left us. But it will be published in the book which is going to be published in Switzerland. ᵃIt will come out this month.ᵃ[5]

I am enclosing the remainder of what was left for you on the table yesterday.

Once again, many thanks

Yours affectionately,

ᵃP.S. By the way, I wrote the letter (not Sabine) referred to in the News-Special containing Dietrich's poem. Its reproduction is not fully correct, there is one mistake.ᵃ

[1] That is Ben Lacy Rose.
[2] Ben Lacy Rose, 'As Niemoeller Sees Germany's Future', in: *The Christian Century*, vol. 62, 1945, cols. 1155-7, here col. 1156. See James Bentley, *Martin Niemöller* (Oxford, 1984), p. 147.
[3] See Gerhard Ringshausen, 'Dietrich Bonhoeffer und der 20. Juli 1944', in the *Bonhoeffer Jarhbuch*, Vol. 6, 2017 (in print).
[4] Ernest Gordon Rupp (1910-86) was Methodist minister, historian and Luther scholar. During the Second World War he was Theological Secretary of Christian Fellowship in Wartime. In 1947, he was appointed assistant professor at Richmond College, the Methodist theological college in London, before becoming Professor of Church History at the University of Manchester, 1958-67, and then Dixie Professor of Ecclesiastical History at the University of Cambridge, 1968-77.
[5] The pamphlet appeared only after Bonhoeffer's death as *Das Zeugnis eines Boten. Zum Gedächtnis von Dietrich Bonhoeffer*, published by the Abteilung für Wiederaufbau und Kirchliche Hilfsaktionen des Oekumenischen Rates der Kirchen (Geneva, 1945). Here the shortened letter of 21 July 1944 (pp. 56-7) is the only letter to have been written by Bonhoeffer from prison.

Leibholz to Bell, 21 January 1945, Bell Papers 40, fol. 286 (typewritten)

My Lordbishop,

I am enclosing the last issue of *The Hibbert Journal*, which I referred to in my last letter and in which you will find Ewing's article *The Ethics of Punishing Germany*. In another article which I myself contributed to the same issue I dealt (in Chapter II.)

with Butler's book (*The Roots of National Socialism*)¹ in which the same views are held as were expressed by Rowse* at the meeting of the Oxford Union last October.

I should be grateful to you if you would kindly return the copy later on: it is the only copy which I have received and there are no off-prints.

Yours ever,

a*Butler's cleric friend[a2]

[1] See Leibholz to Bell, 2 September 1941.
[2] But Rowse was not ordained.

Bell to Leibholz, 31 January 1945, BA, N 1334 (typewritten); Bell Papers 40 fol. 287 (carbon)

My dear Leibholz,

I return the *Hibbert*; I like your article very much, and I am much interested in what you say about Hertz's book.¹ Is he an Austrian? And was he chairman of a Free Austrian Committee at one time before Left politics played rather too much of a part? If so, I know him. I am also very glad of your criticism of Butler.

I thought Ewing's essay on *The Ethics of Punishing Germany* first-rate. I am going to take in the *Hibbert* this year, and see what happens.

Yours ever,

[1] Probably Friedrich Hertz, *Nationality in History and Politics* (London, 1944). Friedrich (Otto) Hertz (1878-1964) changed his name to Frederick Hertz in 1946. Born in Vienna, he was deprived of his Chair in world economy and sociology at Halle University in 1933. Thereafter he was attacked by the Nazi regime as a 'Jew, Freemason and pacifist' for his publications on issues of race and nationality. He fled to Vienna and in 1938 to London where he was actively working with Austrian refugee organizations.

Bell to Sabine Leibholz, 2 February 1945, BA, N 1334 (handwritten)

My dear Mrs Leibholz,

I cannot help thinking very much of Dietrich and you in these days of momentous happenings in Germany. And I take the opportunity of our common birthday to express once again with all the sincerity I possess my affection for and deep trust in Dietrich as well as my ardent hopes and prayers for his deliverance. I can judge how anxious you must be as the war in all its violence approaches Berlin. Would God that the whole Hitler castle might be brought down in ruin, even now, and so the means granted for the surrender of the German forces and the saving of that true German soul which is yet so precious a care to those silent, suppressed and persecuted multitudes of true patriots like Dietrich, for the gradual if costly rebuilding of the nation. We must pray that God may bring the War to an end, with the breaking of the Hitler spell, and save Europe from even more pitiless destruction. And may the lives of those most needed, as we humans see it, for recovery and illumination be saved. And may God of His mercy guide the three Allied Leaders to such a common policy as may give hope for unity and charity in Europe, and space and freedom for the European family of nations to breathe again the spirit of the Christian tradition and faith.

We are now at the very climax – God grant wisdom, mercy and peace. With love to you all, and especially words of love to Dietrich.

Yours affectionately,

Leibholz to Bell, 3 February 1945, Bell Papers 40, fols. 290–1 (handwritten)

My dear Lordbishop,

Tomorrow our thoughts will go again to your and Dietrich's common birthday and we should like you to know that our prayers will embrace above all you on that day.

I have not the slightest doubt that the time will come (even if it be too late) when the policy which you have advocated with such an admirable steadfastness and courage and with so great political wisdom in the last few years will one day be recognised as the only truly European policy. But how difficult will it be to carry out such a policy at a time when more and more European countries come under the Russian influence? Benesch's [sic] recent recognition of Lublin,[1] the executions in Bulgaria,[2] which have shocked me, because these men (which were mostly non-Nazis) merely surrendered to Nazi pressure, the happenings in Germany, the Polish dilemma and so on seem to me all to prove the ascendancy of Russian power over that of this country. I still remember a talk with Paton a few years ago in which he dismissed the apprehension of Russia dominating Europe with the argument that Russia would be too weak after this war and economically too dependent on the Anglo-Saxon countries.[3] I fear that the actual development does not point in this direction.

We are constantly thinking of all our dear ones and friends in Germany and sometimes it seems to be hardly bearable. On the other hand, God has been gracious enough to push again and again a veil on the happenings in Germany, thus giving us the strength to carry on.

I myself do not think [it] possible that the Germans themselves can do anything effectual to end this war. Fear of Hitler and Himmler, fear of the Russians and fear of the unconditional surrender policy (in spite of Churchill's recent slight modification) will make them go on with their struggle. I only hope that the loss of 'Silesia'[4] with its industry, the deterioration of the food situation, the confusion due to the fact that millions are on the move and that the problems resulting from it cannot be solved, will lead to an automatic collapse so that the whole of Germany will not be destroyed. Even if this be the case I fear that the consequences of this 'migration' will be tremendous for the future shape of Europe.

Unfortunately, this is not the birthday letter I wanted to write to you. But I am writing this just today in order to assure you that I have not abandoned hope for a truly European settlement as long as men like you can raise their voices – men whom I earnestly hope and trust will guide the nation one day.

In deep affection

Yours ever,

P.S. Yes, Hertz is an Austrian and was as far as I know the Chairman of the Austrian [authority] here.

---

1. Lublin was until 17 January 1945 the domicile of the Polish Committee of National Liberation (*Polski Komitet Wyzwolenia Narodowego*), founded in Moscow in July 1944 by the Soviets as the basis of a communist Poland after the war. Edvard Beneš (1884–1948) supported Stalin's policy. Beneš had been president of Czechoslovakia in 1935-8 and had emigrated to England where in 1940 he founded the Czechoslovakian Government in Exile under his presidency. From 1943 he had intensive contact with Stalin and it was in Moscow that he planned a future National Front government, together with the communists, but without the other parties of the pre-war First Republic, under Klemens Gottwald. In May 1945 he again became president of Czechoslovakia.
2. The Red Army occupied Bulgaria in September 1944, although the country was not actually at war with the Soviet Union. From December to February 1945 the communists prosecuted the former authorities and more than 2,700 men and women were sentenced to death and murdered.
3. See Paton to Leibholz, 26 October 1942, and Leibholz's answer, 30 October 1942.
4. The Yalta or Crimea Conference (4–11 February 1945) was the second meeting of the Big Three and determined the Oder-Neiße-Line as the western border of Poland, inclusive of Silesia.

Sabine Leibholz to Bell, 25 February 1945, Bell Papers 40 fols. 293-4 (handwritten); BA, N 1334 (copy)

My dear Lordbishop,

I can hardly tell you how much I valued your birthday letter. It was very, very good of you to think of Dietrich in this way just now, and to write to me. I only deplore that I cannot pass it on to Dietrich who would be greatly strengthened if he had only the opportunity of reading it. I find great comfort in the book which Dietrich wrote in 1937 and which I read again and again. It is called 'Nachfolge'. There he writes 'der Nachfolger soll das ihm verordnete Mass von Leiden und Verworfensein tragen. Es ist für jeden ein anderes Mass. Den einen würdigt Gott grosser Leiden, er schenkt ihm die Gnade des Martyriums, den anderen lässt er nicht über seine Kraft versucht werden. Doch ist es das eine Kreuz. – Wer in die Nachfolge eintritt, gibt sich in den Tod Jesu, er setzt sein Leben ins Sterben. Das Kreuz ist nicht das schreckliche Ende eines frommen, glücklichen Lebens, sondern es steht am Anfang der Gemeinschaft mit Jesus Christus. – Nicht die Menschen sind zu fürchten, ihre Macht hört mit dem leiblichen Tode auf. Todesfurcht sollen die Jünger überwinden durch Gottesfurcht. Wer Gott fürchtet, der fürchtet die Menschen nicht mehr. – Nachfolge ist Bindung an den leidenden Christus. Darum ist das Leiden der Christen nichts Befremdliches. Es ist vielmehr lauter Gnade und Freude'.[1] – We feel sometimes that it is good that there is a veil over what is happening in Germany today. We are full of anxiety as apart from Dietrich my parents, three married sisters and brothers with their children used to live in Berlin, with whom we are united by love and understanding. I hope that at least this stage of the war will not last for long.

My husband does not share the optimism generally held in this country about the Yalta decision. He fears that the methods envisaged there will not secure peace and [will] make Germany an ulcer in Central Europe. We cannot imagine how a super-Versailles can pacify Europe when Versailles itself failed to do so – especially if the Big Three are not united by a common ideology. I do not understand all this but I trust that in the end God will grant us mercy and peace.

With renewed thanks

Yours very sincerely,

---

[1] See Dietrich Bonhoeffer, *Nachfolge* (*DBW* 4), pp. 80–1, 81, 208, 83; or, as rendered in the new English edition: '[The disciples] must bear the suffering and rejection measured out to each of them. Everyone gets a different amount. God honours some with great suffering and grants them the grace of martyrdom, while others are not tempted above their strength. But in every case it is the one Cross ... Those who enter into discipleship enter into Jesus's death. They turn their living into dying ... The Cross is not the terrible end of a pious, happy life. Instead, it stands at the beginning of community with Jesus Christ ... Human beings should not be feared. They cannot do much to the disciples of Jesus. Their power stops with the physical death of the disciple. The disciple is to overcome the fear of death wth the fear of God ... Anyone who fears God is no longer afraid of people ... Discipleship is being bound to the suffering of Christ. That is why Christian suffering is not disconcerting. Instead, it is nothing but grace and joy.' *Discipleship* (*DBW* 4), pp. 87, 87, 196, 89.

Bell to Leibholz, 27 February 1945, BA 1334 (typewritten)

Private

My dear Leibholz,

I was most grateful for and touched by your wife's letter. Please thank her for it.

I am writing at once to you, for I badly want to know what you think of the Crimea Conference. When I first read the report it seemed to me a very hard Conference, with few gleams of light. And I was surprised to see the *New Statesman*'s attitude, which was on the whole approving. The fundamental defect is the failure to distinguish. But that seems a chronic failure, and does make it as it were permanently hard. But I should be very thankful for any comments and criticisms that you cared to send me. I am the more anxious to have them (though this is private) because I am going to Paris on March 9th for three or four days, to stay with Boegner, and I shall have plenty of opportunities, in conferences and conversations, for finding out French views.[1] The future of Germany is not precisely defined, but I suppose the general reports have something in them with regard to the Rhineland and Upper Silesia.

I expect also to be going to America towards the end of April, for five or six weeks.[2]

Yours ever,

(Dictated but not personally signed)

P.S. I should be rather glad if you would have a look at the enclosed letter from Ruth Gaevernitz,[3] together with the article on the Re-education of the German people.

---

[1] Bell visited France on 10–14 March 1945.
[2] See Bell to Visser 't Hooft , 31 January 1945, published in Besier, *Intimately Associated for Many Years*, Vol. II, pp. 265–7; here p. 265.
[3] Ruth Gaevernitz (1898–1993), the daughter of Gerhard von Schulze-Gaevernitz, professor of economics at Freiburg University. A student of religious studies she had become head of the Socialist Students Youth in Berlin. It was because of this that she fled early in 1933 to France and again, in 1940, to London. After teaching at adult education centres she settled into a position at the British Museum.

Leibholz to Bell, 3 March 1945, Bell Papers 40, fols. 295–7 (typewritten); BA, N 1334 (copy)

Personal

My Lordbishop,
Very many thanks for your letter.

You have asked me what I think about Yalta and I must openly confess that I see the results of this conference from a very different point of view than public opinion does. Generally, people think that by Yalta a secure foundation for world peace has been formed which makes it possible to erect an enduring structure on it. I think that Yalta forms part of an appeasement policy which has taken gigantic proportions. The whole mentality and phraseology reminds me very much for the former appeasement policy towards Nazism. The necessity of making sacrifices and of coming to a compromise in order to ensure peace also justified the appeasement policy towards Hitler. I think that all 'compromises' are only tactical means in the hands of the leaders of totalitarian states who will use or abandon them 'according to circumstances'. They are against the very nature of [the] totalitarian state. Therefore, I do not think that Eastern – and Central – Europe – in so far as it comes under Russian influence – will be 'free' and 'independent' in the sense in which these terms are used in the West. Under these circumstances, it is not surprising that the Poles in this country will refuse to go back to their country. In fact, I have heard that among the Polish teachers and students here there is none who is prepared to go back to Poland. I feel sure that we shall make the same experience with the other countries under Russian influence. This is why I think that Yalta is anti-European in its basic character. It brings East- and a part of Central-Europe under the anti-European political, economic and spiritual system.

Of course, I fully realize that a good case can be made for the attitude the Western countries have taken in Yalta. They think that peace can only be preserved by 'concessions' (quite apart from the urgently needed Russian help in the Pacific). But the price paid seems to me rather high – and too high if future events should show (as I think they will) that Allied unity is not built on a firm foundation. In any case, I think a statesman who looks ahead should at least have considered the possibility of such a development. In this respect, however, I fear that the Conference has failed in a disastrous way.

True, Hitler set out to conquer Europe and to establish a system of power. But what is planned now ᶜis not only the same butᶜ seems to me rather worse. For I do not think that Hitler would have imposed such a peace on the Western countries (apart from the Jewish case) as they now want to impose on Germany. It seems to me a Super-Versailles based on *mere* power and force without any constructive idea at all. People think that the policy announced in Yalta is the only hope of saving the world from another and worse catastrophe. I am deeply convinced of the contrary. The major operation from which the Allies expect the future health of Europe and the world can – at least spiritually – not eradicate German militarism and I think there is nothing peculiar[ly] German in it. Even the British would become a militarist nation under such a 'peace-system'.

I think there is a deep tragedy in all this, because millions of Germans want the complete extirpation of Nazism and would only be too glad to render German militarism harmless and to give the world that feeling of security without which the world cannot recover. But the method planned to attain this aim defeats its own purpose. *How* shall it be possible to pacify a people who will have been more punished by the war than any other people involved in it (apart from the Jews) and who, in addition, will be exposed to an occupation with all its implications in the political, military and economic field (for 50 years according to Mr Roosevelt) and subjected to big territorial losses and reparations – and all this although their country will be ravaged by war and their towns will be bombed in ruins. It seems to me madness. The effect of this policy will be either a collapsing Germany falling into complete chaos – then the problem will not be the prevention of German military resurgence but rather of general European disintegration – or if this be not the case continuous war will be waged in Germany. Human beings have a short memory. I fear that even people who hated Nazism will forget this in future if they are oppressed politically, economically, culturally for an unlimited period. As I see it, Versailles essentially contributed to the present conflict and I fear that a Super-Versailles will have more far-reaching implications and sow the seeds of further disaster. It is a vicious circle by which every war leads to another by creating its political and psychological presuppositions.

What I so deeply deplore is that the first victims of this policy are those Germans who are deeply convinced that Germany has to make good the crimes of Nazism and has to make a new start in order to become again a Christian and European country. They are sacrificed once again by those who should help them in their own interest. I see no way how, under these circumstances mentioned, the help of those forces can be won without at the same time degrading them to Quislings. As things stand I personally welcome that the Allies themselves have to form a government in Germany because thus at least those Christian and European-minded Germans (so far as they have survived the Nazi terror) will be spared a Quisling fate. Therefore, I do not think that the future holds much good in store for Europe. In any case, I think that events will take another course than that envisaged by the statesmen of today and I feel sure that in 50 years the world will not look like as Mr Roosevelt thinks it will. [sic]

In his last speech Mr Roosevelt spoke of the incompatibility of German militarism with Christian ethics. I quite agree. But I wished he would also have seen the German cities which were destroyed by American bombers just at the time when they were overcrowded by hundred thousands of refugees. I wonder whether this way of warfare is compatible with Christian ethics. I was glad to see that at least some people appealed to Christians asking them to raise their voices against what had happened in Berlin and Dresden.

I am returning the paper about re-education. I had already seen it and I think it is a very good one although I do not fully agree with all its statements and conclusions. I think the author is very well informed and I wish the article would be given a wide publicity.

I wonder what you will hear from Boegner and his friends. I shall miss you badly when you are in America in May and I am already looking forward to the day when you are back again.

Yours ever,

ᵃP.S. Have you noticed Lord Ailwyn's speech in the Lords?¹ He pleaded for the wholesale internment of all Germans resident in this country now. Who is this gentleman?

G. L.

ᵃWould you please kindly let me know the impressions you will collect in France? I should be grateful to you.ᵃ

---

[1] See Hansard, H.L. Deb., Vol. 136, cols. 102–16 (2 May 1945). Eric Fellowes (1887–1976) became 3rd Baron Ailwyn in 1936. He was a Royal Navy officer and, in 1942, a member of the British Parliamentary Mission to China and then from 1943 to 1948 President of the China Association.

Leibholz to Bell, 25 March 1945, Bell Papers 40, fol. 198 (typewritten); BA, N 1334 (copy)

My Lordbishop,

I wonder what impressions you have gained in France during your stay there.

I hope that you were not too much disappointed with my last letter dealing with the result of the Crimean Conference. By the way, Voigt takes a similar line in the current issue of his periodical.¹ He also thinks that the Yalta Conference is anti-European in substance and, therefore, detrimental to the true interests of this country. He also does not seem to favour a reduction of Germany to the state of an enslaved nation, which, in spite of the fair words used, will certainly be the result of the present policy. I feel that, in the end, things will take a very different course from that envisaged at Yalta. The development in Rumania, Bulgaria, Poland and the hostile attitude towards Turkey seem to me to confirm this. I think that all depends on the interpretation of the term democracy and as the Western conception of democracy is entirely different from that of the East I fear that as a result of this fundamental misunderstanding the whole edifice built up there will collapse one day.

Yours ever,

---

[1] See Frank Voigt, 'Yalta', in *The Nineteenth Century and After*, Vol. CXXXVII, No. 817 (March 1945), pp. 97–107.

Bell to Leibholz, 27 March 1945, BA, N 1334 (typewritten)

My dear Leibholz,

I ought to have replied to your letter about the Crimea Conference, which I valued very much. Please do not think I was disappointed in any way. It was very salutary counsel. I have read Voigt's article – he sent it me – and the more of the proceedings and the probable sequel, the greater seem the difficulties looming ahead.

I enclose a report of my visit to Paris, and you shall have a copy of my *Diocesan Gazette* in a day or two.¹ I was much struck by the fear of the French with regard to Germany still, and their anxiety about the Rhineland. I did not think they were enthusiastic about Russia in a personal way; but they believed they were adopting a realistic attitude in depending on Russia before depending on anybody else. They regard Russia as priority No. 1 because that is the only Power, they think, which gave them security in Europe. The British Empire is priority No. 2, as British Imperial interests have a usefulness for their Empire; while the international organisation comes last, as their world interests, so to speak, also come last.

I am hoping to speak in the House of Lords to-morrow on San Francisco,[2] though I have not got a great deal to say, and there will be many others speaking.[3]

I don't know whether you read what seemed to me an unfortunate speech of the Archbishop of York's about war crimes?[4] He was the only speaker who seemed to disregard law, leaving punishment to the somewhat haphazard process of being satisfied as to identity, and then shooting. None of the legal speakers took that line, and I was sorry that a churchman did. But it is so often said that the German people repeatedly voted for Hitler, or confirmed him in his rule. Apart from the overwhelming argument concerning the force behind the totalitarian regime, could you briefly remind me of the voting situation just before, during, and after, 1933? I know I have got it in two or three books but I don't quite know at the moment where to lay my hands on it.

With all best wishes for Easter,

Yours very sincerely,

---

[1] A shortened German translation of Bell's report in Bethge and Jasper, *An der Schwelle*, pp. 313–15; see too *Chichester Diocesan Gazette*, April 1945.

[2] The United Nations Conference on International Organization at San Francisco (25 April–26 June 1945) effectively rewrote the Dumbarton Oaks agreements and resulted in the creation of the United Nations Charter.

[3] See Bell's speech in the debate on World Organisation for Peace in Hansard, H.L. Deb., Vol. 135, cols. 1135–8 17 April 1945); also found in Peter Raina, *Bishop George Bell: House of Lords Speeches*, pp. 88–90.

[4] See 135 HL Deb., 5s, col. 671 (20 March 1945): 'Whenever I speak of war criminals, however moderately I may frame my words, I receive afterwards a number of letters from people telling me that it is unchristian and wrong to demand the punishment of these people. ... They forget that retribution is a stern side of the Christian faith.' The Archbishop of York was Cyrid Forster Garbett.

Leibholz to Bell, 29 March 1945, Bell Papers 40, fol. 299 (typewritten); BA, N 1334 (copy)

My Lordbishop,

Very many thanks for your letter and for kindly letting me have your extremely interesting notes on your visit to France. Of course, after all that France and the world have suffered the security argument is quite plausible. But I think that one of the few lessons history has taught us is that security cannot be based on power *alone*. And it is just this which is going to happen today. Such a power politics may perhaps postpone a new war for a while but, in the end, makes its outbreak inevitable, because power in itself, without a constructive idea behind it, is an evil. The French conception of security has always been static: it has led them to disaster but obviously they are trying to play the same game again. This policy will make them dependent on Russia and will contribute to making Russia (and communism) the dominant factor on the Continent. From a Western point of view, this development is very disappointing.

As to the question concerning the voting force behind the Nazis may I give you the following facts?

In 1932 when the presidential elections took place 19,360.000 votes were cast for Hindenburg and 13,418.000 votes for Hitler. On the 5th of March 1933, the last free election after the Nazis came to power 647 Members were elected, of whom Nazis were *288* (= 43,9%) and Conservatives 52 (= 8%). The latter formed a coalition with the Nazis and both the Nazis and Conservatives had thus a majority of 51.9%. From this it follows that the Nazis of their own accord were never able to secure a majority.

After the destruction of the liberal-democratic foundations of the Weimar Constitution in 1933 the Nazis got over 90% in the subsequent plebiscites, which were frequently called elections. But these elections were not free and elections under the pressure of a totalitarian regime prove nothing. The same results were obtained under Napoleon, under Mussolini, Franco, Stalin etc. and could easily be obtained in other countries, so far as they are subjected to the same terror.

You may perhaps also like to know how, in comparison to these figures, the Germans voted when they elected the National Assembly in 1919: Nazis none, Conservatives 44, Catholics 91, Right-wing Liberals 19, Left-wing Liberals 75, Labour 163, Independent Labour 22, Communists none. I think that this election has shown that democracy is not (or perhaps better was not) impossible in Germany.

I only read the Archbishop's of York speech in *The Times* and, therefore, I was not able to form a judgement on it. I myself think that the dealing with the war criminals is primarily a political matter (see the shootings in Bulgaria and other countries) and it would be better for the sake of Justice and law to deal with them from a political point of view. Of course, I myself firmly believe in the eternal Christian principles of Natural Law, which ought to be respected even in the political sphere. But the trouble is that as a result of the relativisation of all these principles the prevailing opinion in all countries (including this country) holds, in fact, the opposite line.

If the war comes to an end soon I ᶜshouldᶜ think it would be better to have you here. ᶜI thinkᶜ We shall need you then urgently.

With all good wishes to you and Mrs Bell for a happy Easter, from my wife and the children.

Yours ever,

P.S. I saw Hodgson today. He is, fortunately, much better again and hopes to go for a holiday soon.

Leibholz to Bell, 8 April 1945, Bell Papers 40, fol. 300 (typewritten)

My Lordbishop,

Just a line to call your attention to *The Observer* of today in which the two articles written by the *Observer* War Correspondent on the attitude of the German civil population and on the extent of ruin in Germany seem to me highly remarkable. They seem to me to confirm what I tried to explain in former letters. The conclusion that in spite of bombing and suffering a large section of the population welcomes the invading army as liberators seems to me especially important. What I only fear is that this spirit will be killed by the sterile policy of the Western powers.

By the way, last Friday I lunched with G. Clutton Brock[1] who is a member of the newly appointed Allied Control Commission and especially responsible for education and religion.[2] I had a very good impression of him and I wonder whether you know him. If not I think it would be worthwhile getting in touch with him before he leaves for Berlin. He seems to me a man of imagination and initiative and full of the best intentions. But I do not know whether your plan of going to America will allow you to spare the time.

I wonder when you actually are thinking of leaving this country and when may we expect you back?

With all good wishes

Yours ever,

---

[1] Guy Clutton Brock (1906–95), eminent as a social worker and a committed 'practical Christian'. He became Head of the Religious Affairs Section of the British Control Commission that year, but resigned in 1946 to work for Christian Reconstruction in Europe. Also an agriculturist, he later went on to play a significant part in the creation of Rhodesia's African National Congress and the struggle against the segregationist state in that country. He was expelled in 1971.

[2] After the Conference of Teheran (28 November–1 December 1943), the British War Office established a Control Commission for Germany/British Element (CCG/BE). Under the Control Office for Germany and Austria in London (COGA) it began to work in Berlin under the aegis of the Military Government Staff of the British Army of the Rhine (BAOR) from July 1945. The CCG/BE was structured in 12 Divisions with some Branches. The Education and Religious Affairs Branch was a part of the Internal Affairs and Communication Division and located in Bünde. But the magnitude of problems, and the degree of interest taken by the Church of England, and by Bell in particular, led to a division of the branch. In January 1946 the Religious Affairs Branch under Controller-General Russell Luke Sedgwick was established.

Bell to Leibholz, 10 April 1945, BA, N 1334 (typewritten); Bell Papers 40, fol. 301 (carbon)

My dear Leibholz,

Many thanks for your letter. I have seen the *Observer*, and cut out the article, which made a real impression on me and I hope on all other readers. It does make what you rightly describe as the sterile policy of the Western Powers a melancholy affair.

I am glad you have been in touch with Clutton-Brock. He was to have stayed here for a night the week before last, but was laid up with 'flu. I am very anxious to see him, and am hoping to get hold of him before I go to America,[1] which will be on or after April 28th.

Yours ever,

---

[1] Bell's visit to the United States lasted from the end of April to the middle of June 1945.

Leibholz to Bell, 21 April 1945, Bell Papers 40, fol. 302 (typewritten); BA, N 1334 (copy)

My Lordbishop,

Thank you very much for your last Lord's debate concerning St. Francisco.[1] I found your criticism on the Dumbarton Oaks proposals very good indeed. I was especially glad to see that Cranborne accepted your view that the Great Powers must not use their power just as Powers but as the servants of law but he seems to me to have forgotten to add that law that deserves the name must be connected with some fundamental principles of justice and that the Dumbarton Oaks alliance of the Great Powers does not provide this.

I had not seen Stalin's address referred to in your speech before. Esp. No. 5 is interesting.[2] By the way, I wonder whether you have noted the conflict between *Red Star* and *Pravda* reported in *The Observer* last week. It seems to me very important, just from our point of view, because it shows that Stalin's former differentiation between Hitlerite Germany and Germany has not been abandoned. I feel sure that without Stalin's authorisation the Communist propaganda minister would not have ventured to call attention to Stalin's former statements. Vansittart will not be glad about this.

On the other hand, the reactions on the horrible disclosures in Buchenwald[3] and the other concentration camps are rather disappointing. Instead of coming to the conclusion that there are two Germanies (the Hitlerite Germany and the Germany who has been murdered and tortured in these camps) there is rather a new outcry against Germany as a whole. I feel that this is partly due to the propaganda of the B.B.C., which causes the average Englishman to think as if Buchenwald and the other concentration camps were primarily foreigner camps, while, in point of fact, just the opposite is true. Until 1940 they even were exclusively German. I think it would be worthwhile considering to ask for a more detailed statement concerning the national status of the prisoners so that people may see for themselves whether more Germans have perished in the concentration camps inside Germany or more nationals of other countries. We can hardly tell you how terribly worried we are about the fate of Dietrich (and those of our close relatives and friends who are still in these camps). Knowing what is going on without being able to help makes one feel sick and miserable.

I think you expect to leave this country for the United States soon and my best wishes accompany you and your work there. I myself am most anxious to have you back as soon as possible. The time is approaching when we all shall need you most urgently here.

God be with you

Yours ever,

P.S. I wonder whether you have seen Clutton Brock in the meantime. I hope you have.

---

[1] Hansard, 135 H.L. Deb., 5s., cols. 1135–8 (17 April 1945).
[2] This is strangely obscure.
[3] The Buchenwald concentration camp was liberated on 11–13 April 1945 by prisoners of the camp itself and by soldiers of the US Army.

Bell to Leibholz, 24 April 1945, BA, N 1334 (handwritten)

My dear Leibholz,

I have just seen Visser 't Hooft, who has given me news of Dietrich.[1] It is troubling, but not hopeless. Dietrich was tried for sharing in the plot, by the people's tribunal, and his judge was the same as that of those tried last year – (Freisler? or Kreisler?[2]). He was condemned to death.[3] But before the sentence of execution was signed by the judge, the judge was killed by a bomb. No one will take the responsibility of carrying out the execution, as a consequence – no actual order having been signed by the competent authority. A 'new trial' has been ordered, but, says 't Hooft, it will never be carried out. So Dietrich has been mercifully saved on the very brink. That he is in danger still of some kind – like all people living in besieged Berlin – is beyond doubt. And the danger from the regime to him, as to all others opposed to it, is clear. But thanks be to God for *this* mercy, at least. And I pray with you and your wife that he may be spared, having been saved so far by the hand of God, for the work, the heavy work, of rebuilding stricken Germany. God be with him, and with you both.

I am at this club till Friday morning: and shall be seeing 't Hooft again.

I expect to fly to USA on April 29 or 30.

Yours affectionately,

---

[1] Bell met Visser 't Hooft at the meeting of the European members of the WCC on 26 April.
[2] Roland Freisler (1893–1945) was Nazi jurist, President of the People's Court and the presiding judge at the trials which took place after 20 July 1944. Hitler referred to him as 'our Vyshinsky', recalling the judge who oversaw the show trials of the Stalin state. Freisler indeed admired Vyshinsky and sought to emulate him. He was killed as he made his way to the air-raid shelter of the court during a raid by the U.S. Air Force on 3 February 1945.
[3] This is incorrect and probably shows a confusion with Klaus Bonhoeffer, who was sentenced to death by the People's Tribunal under Freisler on 2 February 1945. On 31 May Rieger came from London to Oxford to bring the Leibholzes the news of Dietrich Bonhoeffer's death, after receiving information from Adolf Freudenberg in Geneva. See Leibholz-Bonhoeffer, *Vergangen*, pp. 215–16; A. Freudenberg to G. Leibholz, 14 June 1945, BA, N 1334. For Bonhoeffer's end see Bethge, *Dietrich Bonhoeffer*, pp. 1026–8.

Bell to Gerhard and Sabine Leibholz, 22 June (erroneous: July) 1945, BA, N 1334 (photograph of handwritten original)

My dear friends,

I cannot express to you how sad I am for and with you both at Dietrich's death, with Klaus. I had a cable in New York, but did not know how to reach you immediately: and indeed believed that a letter posted in Chichester on my return would reach you as soon as anything I could write in USA. Alas!

Dietrich and Klaus had already been murdered when 't Hooft told us of the death sentence being impossible to carry out – at least so I suppose. For you, my dear Sabine, the agony of thus losing your dearest brother, so close to you, and Klaus with him, is sharp indeed: nothing can fill the gap, though your husband and your daughters will become all the greater comfort! I feel for you both – and your whole family – with all my heart. And for the Church in Germany, the loss is as heavy a loss as can be imagined: for Dietrich, had God willed, could have done so mighty a work in the long and troubled process of recovery and revival. But the work he has done for the Confessional Church, and so both for Germany and for the Oecumenical Church, is of a value beyond measure. He was unflinching and clear sighted and devoted in faith and loyalty to his Master. And he never thought of himself. He was a martyr for Christ – and for the Germany he loved and in which, in God's purpose for which, he so truly believed. I should like somewhere, in place and time most suitable to you, to have a service of remembrance for him – to thank God for this brave, steadfast and suffering soul, and to pray that the life he gave for others may be blessed and fruitful. Perhaps at the time of the Christian Fellowship meetings in London (July 26)?

May God comfort you both, my dear friends – to whom Dietrich brought me – and to whom I shall always for his and your own sake cling. With my love and prayers, in which Mrs Bell unites.

Your affectionate,

Bell to Leibholz, 26 June 1945, BA, N 1334

My dear Leibholz,
This is just a line, following my earlier letter, in case by any chance that earlier letter failed to reach you – though it was only written on Friday. It was addressed, I fear, to your former address, and not to Lincoln Road.

I still *think* and *think* about Dietrich and Klaus, ªand feel deeply for you both.ª

Yours ever,

Bell to Leibholz, 6 July (1945), BA, N 1334 (handwritten)

My dear Leibholz,
Thank you very much for your letters. They – especially the long one you wrote first – moved me deeply. I cannot tell you how I feel for you and your wife. I saw Rieger yesterday in London and he spoke of you both and his visit to you.

The Bonhoeffer family has indeed suffered supremely and incalculably – it is very hard to take it all in. I will write again.

God bless you all

Your affectionate,

Bell to Leibholz, 8 July (1945), BA, N 1334 (handwritten)

My dear Leibholz,
For some while I have been thinking that I ought to publish the facts about Dietrich's visit to Stockholm and my communications with Eden in 1942. Not in order to discredit Eden or the Foreign Office (though it would be bound to be a criticism by implication) – but to show the strength of the Opposition to Hitler long before

July 1944. But I should only do harm if I *timed* my publication badly, apart from the need of taking care about the *form* and manner. It is important to say it with the maximum of wise publicity, if at all. I don't know how I could make an excuse to speak about it in the *Lords*: and though in some ways I should think that good, I am not quite sure of it being the best course.

It would take more space than the *Times* would allow for a letter. I should be very grateful for your advice both on the desirability of publishing; and on the *time* (and the form).

Kurt Hahn[1] has just telegraphed that he wishes to see me – and is lunching here on Tuesday.

Remembrances to your wife

Yours affectionate,

I enclose a letter from E. G. Rupp.

P.S. The enclosed has just come – and I know you would wish to see it. Any comments I shall welcome.[2]

---

[1] Kurt Hahn (1886–1974), educationalist and teacher, who founded the Salem boarding school in 1919. After his emigration, as a Jew, to Britain in 1933 he founded the British Salem School at Gordonstoun (in Scotland) and, in 1941, the first Outward Bound school in Aberdovey (in Wales).
[2] Not preserved.

Leibholz to Bell, 11 July 1945, Bell Papers Vol. 42, fols. 89–90 (handwritten).

My dear Friend,

Thank you very much for your letters and the enclosures.

I have carefully thought over what you have asked me and I think what you say about the active opposition movement and its origins in 1940 and 1941 should definitely be brought into the open – all the more as even Christian periodicals like e.g. the *Christian News-Letter* and the *Guardian* say and say again that 'undoubtedly the Germans cheered and praised Nazism in 1940 & 1941'. What I do not quite know is whether it may perhaps not be better to wait until a good opportunity of broaching this matter arises. You can much better judge than I whether 'Foreign Affairs', treatment of Germany, Vansittart's activities, will not provide you with such an opportunity in the Lords in the course of the next few months. (By the way, when I talked in the July issue of *Strand*[1] of the 'plotters' [as] upholders of the European tradition Vansittart replied that no wise man will agree with that. 'They were militarists who tardily saw that Hitler made a mess of their profession. His sin in their ways was not that he had made war, but that he was losing it.'

I remember here a letter by Lady Cripps last year in which she said that they were thinking of doing something after the war (with special regard to Adam von Trott). If this was not meant merely personally it may perhaps be helpful to connect your action with that of Cripps and his circle.

I already thought of your writing a letter to *The Times*. We had in mind to announce Dietrich's and Klaus's death in the *Times* as soon as plans and time of the memorial service were fixed. Would this perhaps not give you an opportunity of writing an appreciation? To the general public Dietrich's name is not known simply because he was the martyr of the 'silent church'.² You know Dietrich did not like what possibly smelt of propaganda. I think in such an appreciation Dietrich's political actitivities ªwith their implications for the Confessional Churchª could be mentioned and the [execration] of your plan would not be anticipated.

I saw Rieger yesterday and he told me of his talk with you. Of course, we thankfully agree with all that you have discussed. The only thing I should like to submit to you is this: I do not quite know whether you had Rieger's church in mind when you wrote to me of a memorial service for Dietrich. I could imagine that a memorial service in an English Church would have its significance in itself in this time and would honour Dietrich and the Confessional Church quite in a special way. Please do not misunderstand me. I do not wish to press this point. Only if – *you* had originally this in mind I should plead for a service in an English Church. Please kindly tell Rieger as *you* feel. What *you* say is what we should prefer.

I think a statement in Rupp's booklet would certainly be a great help in the present situation. Do you think it a bad suggestion to publish either the letter to *The Times* (provided you decide to write one) on the article in *The Observer* (I have just heard about it) in Rupp's booklet?

In the meantime we have heard through Goerdeler's son[3] that Dietrich was in the Gestapo prison in the Prinz-Albrechtstrasse in Berlin in the last few months (during the air raids) and that he was moved from there (end of March) to the prison in Passau, Regensburg and so on until he was taken to the concentration camp in Flossenbűrg near Weiden. We have also heard that the only surviving brother of my wife does not yet know what has happened to Dietrich & to his brother (unfortunately, he had now come under Russian control) and that Dietrich's (and ours) parents, Dietrich's fiancée, my wife's three sisters and sisters-in-law (with their ten children) stayed in Berlin when the Battle of Berlin started because they thought Dietrich and their husbands (who were all condemned to death) were imprisoned in Berlin.

My wife gives you her special love. She will write to you later when she is able to do so. She is still reading Dietrich's books. They comfort her as far as this is possible under the circumstances.

Yours affectionately,

P.S. Did K. Hahn who knew Dietrich make any suggestion which impressed you?

---

[1] i.e. *The Strand Magazine* (a London periodical, established in 1891, which would close down in 1950).
[2] A reference to Rieger's book, *The Silent Church: The Problem of the German Confessional Witness* (London, 1944).
[3] Reinhard Goerdeler (1922–96), who had been liberated at Dachau by American troops on 5 May 1945.

Bell to Leibholz, 16 July 1945, BA, N 1334 (typewritten)

My dear Leibholz,

I enclose a letter from Dr Welch,[1] which explains itself. I wrote at once to Rieger and Prebendary Williams Ashman,[2] suggesting Holy Trinity, Kingsway.[3] I have not heard from Rieger: but I have had a very nice letter from Williams Ashman saying that he would be delighted to have the service in his church, and will let Rieger draw it up. I may hear from Rieger by the second post today.

I should be very ready to write something about Dietrich in the *Times* if you send a notice of his death and that of Klaus. It would be a good thing to time the notice so as to appear at the beginning of next week, in order that people may know of the Memorial Service. Of course it is impossible to say whether the *Times* would print what I send them: but I will write personally and make a special request, ªwhen you tell me.ª

Yours ever,

---

[1] William Neville Welch, Anglican priest and Rural Dean of Barking, 1946–53.
[2] Edward Harold Williams Ashman, Vicar of Holy Trinity, Kingsway with St John the Evangelist, Drury Lane, London, 1939–59.
[3] For the Memorial Service for Dietrich and Klaus Bonhoeffer see Leibholz-Bonhoeffer, *Vergangen*, pp. 220–1; Roggelin, *Franz Hildebrandt*, pp. 244–5.

Bell to Leibholz, 19 July 1945, BA, N 1334 (handwritten)

My dear Leibholz,

Rieger telegraphs – Holy Trinity Kingsway, Friday July 27 *6 p.m.*

Yrs affly,

Bell to Leibholz, 20 July 1945, BA, N 1334 (telegram)

PLEASE SEND BRIEF DETAILS DIETRICHS CAREER =
BISHOP CHICHESTER

Bell to Leibholz, 20 July 1945, BA, N 1334 (handwritten)

No special reaction to my *Observer* article. Schutz said his journalist friends were impressed by the evidence of the plot so far back.

My dear Leibholz,

I have written to Fenn[1] about 'Nachfolge'.

Forgive my wire this morning – it was to fortify me about facts, curriculum vitae.

I have written personally to the Editor of the *Times*, seeing his Berlin correspondent's reference to the underground religious war today: and asked if he will print an article about Dietrich's visit to me at Stockholm: failing that a letter supporting the Churches as powerful for good in this crisis.

Yours affly,

I am moved by your words about D. as a hostage – and the gt. debt we owe him and those others.

---

[1] Eric Fenn, at this time an editorial assistant of Hugh Martin at the S.C.M. Press.

Sabine Leibholz to Bell, 23 July 1945, Bell Papers 40, fols. 303–4 (handwritten); BA, N 1334[1] (copy)

My dear Lordbishop,

I feel I must thank you for all you have been to Dietrich during all these years. I know how much your friendship and the fellowship of your Church meant to him during this long time of his struggle and trial.

Now God has set an end to his brave suffering and both my brothers Dietrich and Klaus, who fought the good fight with him, are at rest. But the gap they leave will never be filled. – May God send His peace and strength on the hearts of my parents and all those who mourn, and so sadly miss them.

I am sending you a photo of Dietrich. It is only an enlarged copy of a small passport-photo, but it is very dear to me. His eyes reflect his sincerity and kindness, and I find that the expression of the mouth shows that he had decided to stand against evil – and was also prepared to suffer for it.

Yours affectionately,

[1] Eberhard Bethge erroneously gives the date as June.

Bell to Sabine Leibholz, 25 July 1945, BA, N 1334 (photocopy of typewritten); Bell Papers 40, fol. 305 (carbon)

My dear Sabine,

(If I may thus call you). I am deeply grateful for your letter. All you say, so undeserved, is a great comfort for me; and I am very happy to have Dietrich's photograph. You know something, I am sure, of what his friendship and love meant to me. My heart is full of sorrow for you, for alas, it is only too true that the gap he and Klaus leave can never be filled. I pray that God may give peace and strength to your parents, and to all who mourn, and bless them.

I am greatly looking forward to seeing you both on Friday. I do not know whether your daughters will be there; but my telegram just sent will of course include them.

I sent a brief tribute to the *Times*, with a note to the Editor, asking him to print it. There is a summary of it, without my name, and with certain parts omitted, in this morning's paper. I thought you might like to have the full text.

Yours very sincerely,

Sabine Leibholz to Bell, 29 July 1945, Bell Papers 40, fols. 306–7 (handwritten.); BA, N 1334 (copy)

My dear Lordbishop,

After I had just read your deeply moving and comforting address again, we received a telegram from Freudenberg saying that Rüdiger Schleicher[1] (aged 50) and Hans von Dohnanyi (aged 43) are both dead. Pastor Bethge (son-in-law of Schleicher and close friend of Dietrich) held a memorial service for Klaus and Schleicher in Berlin then still under Russian occupation. At that time they obviously did not know about Dietrich's and Dohnanyi's fate.

The last hope I held for my sisters that their husbands may be spared after we lost our brothers is gone. Before me I have the photos of my ten nieces and nephews, who are left without their fathers.

'What I do thou knowest not now, but thou shall know hereafter'.[2]

The wire says that they had in hand 'a courageous letter' from my father, which I hope to get soon. Both my sisters are very brave women, and I know they will carry on in the right spirit. My sister Christine v. Dohnanyi was imprisoned herself for two months when her husband and Dietrich were taken away.

It was very good to have seen you.

Yours affectionately,

P.S. We saw the man who was in the plot and escaped to England.[3] He is under certain restrictions and therefore not yet allowed to see us as he would have liked to. He gave us very detailed news about Dietrich – Klaus – Dohnanyi – Schleicher and many other friends. On April 1st 1943 Dietrich, H. v. Doh., and his wife were arrested in my parent's house.[4] After very bad months in Gestapo-prison Dietrich was taken to Tegel-Strafanstalt Berlin,[5] where he had a good guard and was able to go on with his book, to minister to his fellow-prisoners and to send and get letters. He even managed to have a wireless for some time, and to listen to the B.B.C. I am pretty relieved about these news. He was engaged to Maria von Wedemeyer[6] (relation to the Kleist's family who helped Dietrich in his difficult time of Finkenwalde against the Gestapo) shortly before he was arrested.

Dohnanyi fell very ill soon with some mysterious illness, which darkened his mind, and there was the suspicion that the Gestapo had infected him with some poison. He obviously has played a most leading and active part in organising the resistance movement already before war broke out. – As to Gerstenmaier, Dietrich seems to have had certain reservations, but all this only hold[s] good up to July 1944.[7]

---

[1] Rüdiger Schleicher (1895–1945) was married to Ursula Bonhoeffer. A lawyer, he worked in the Air Travel Ministry and, in addition to this, became in 1939 Honorary Professor at the Institute for Air Law at the University of Berlin. As a member of the resistance he was sentenced to death on 2 February 1945 and murdered, together with Klaus Bonhoeffer and others, by an SS commando in the night of 22/23 April 1945.
[2] John 13:7 (Authorized version).
[3] See Leibholz to Bell, 1 August 1945, note 1.
[4] On 5 April; for corrections and details see Bethge, *Dietrich Bonhoeffer*, pp. 883–5.
[5] Bonhoeffer was first arrested in Tegel and came to the Gestapo prison on Prinz-Albrecht-Straße in October 1944.
[6] Maria von Wedemeyer (1924–77), daughter of Hans Wedemeyer and Ruth née Kleist, had become Dietrich Bonhoeffer's fiancée on 17 January 1943. She studied mathematics at Göttingen University and – from 1948 – at Bryn Mawr College near Philadelphia in the United States, where she obtained her MA in 1950. A year before she had married Paul-Werner Schniewind, son of the famous theologian Julius Schniewind. The marriage ended in divorce in 1955.
[7] The sentence is crossed out in the copy. Gerstenmaier had been regarded, and suspected, as the instrument of Bishop Heckel.

Leibholz to Bell, 1 August 1945, Bell Papers 40, fol. 308 (typewritten); BA, N 1334 (copy)

My dear Lordbishop,

We have just received a letter written by our parents.[1] I am enclosing a copy. The letter speaks for itself. I think that the spirit of the family can hardly find its finer expression than in the common suffering of all those men with whom we were united by such close bonds of friendship.

The man (Christoph Jürgens[2]) to whom we talked on Saturday made on me a trustworthy and reliable impression. He obviously was a friend of Dietrich and the other members of the family. I do not think that he played a leading part in the plot, but he was an active participant in it and is obviously the only active conspirator who is in this country. He left Germany by airplane for Spain a few days after the attempt was made and he came to this country last November. When he was released from the camp he spent a few months in the country in order to recover from breakdown. Several months ago he asked the Foreign Office for permission to see you and me. But the answer was in the negative and he observed the restriction because of the particular circumstances of his case. Last week he attended the service. He told me that he has made a new application to the Foreign Office for getting the permission to see you. So far he has not received an answer.

He told us that Dietrich did not fully trust Gerstenmaier and Schönfeld. I have just seen a detailed report about the plot by Gerstenmaier in the *Züricher Zeitung*.[3] He describes in it his struggle against Nazism and maintains the view that his former attitude against the Confessional Church was only taken in order to conceal his true views about National Socialism. I feel that his statements with regard to his former activities should be carefully weighed.

Jürgens also made some hints that some important stories have still to be told. It even seems that the invasion was practically prevented by a false military report for which Dietrich or other members of the family were responsible or co-responsible. I felt that he will tell you the whole story. – By the way, Freudenberg cabled that he sent us some documents just received from [the] Bonhoeffers.

Eric Fenn wrote that the S.C.M. P[ress] have decided go ahead with the publication of Dietrich's book.[4] I am very glad about it and thank you once again, for your having written to them.

I was very much struck when I re-read your address yesterday. I will send a copy to Berlin. We listened in to the broadcast of the service and we very much hope that our family was able to join us. In his introduction to the broadcast Rieger mentioned the purpose of Dietrich's journey to Sweden in 1942: I felt that it did not fit in. I am very sorry that he broached the whole question in the press without having consulted you beforehand.

Once again many thanks for all you have done for Dietrich in the last few weeks. He is more alive to us now than ever before.

Yours ever,

[1] Karl and Paula Bonhoeffer to Gerhard and Sabine Leibholz, 23 July 1945, BA, N 1334; Bell Papers 40, fol. 309.
[2] Christoph Jürgens was the code name of Otto John who had escaped after the plot of the 20 July to Madrid and then from Lisbon to Britain, where he arrived in November 1944. After some weeks in an internment camp he worked as a member of the German department of Political Warfare Executive (PWE) for the Army Network Calais of the Foreign Office under Sefton Delmer. In June 1945 the PWE had been united with the Political Information Department (PID) of the Foreign Office.
[3] Eugen Gerstenmaier, 'Zur Geschichte des Umsturzversuches vom 20. Juli 1944', in *Neue Zürcher Zeitung*, 166, 1945, Nos. 979 and 983, 23 and 24 June 1945.
[4] An abridged translation of Bonhoeffer's *Nachfolge* would be published as *The Cost of Discipleship* by S.C.M. Press in London in October 1948.

Bell to Leibholz, 2 August 1945, BA, N 1334 (handwritten)

My dear Leibholz

Very many thanks for your letter, and the copy of your parents-in-law's wonderful letter to their children. It makes one terribly sad, to think of the waves of trouble growing over their heads, and their surviving children's heads. And I fear that the more one hears the greater the volume of sorrow in all Europe.

How strange that the FO[1] should *not* permit Jürgens to see me. Have they a right to refuse permission anyhow? Is he free *sub conditione*?[2]

I had the enclosed from 't Hooft today. *Please send it back by return.* It throws light on Gerstenmaier.[3] Also I have bad news of the Russian behaviour in Berlin – and 't Hooft guardedly confirms this, but my details are vy bad.

The Chaplain General[4] wants me to go and see Montgomery (and German churches) in Germany: and has approached Montgomery with that object. And I have written to him today emphasising my readiness to go.

Yours affectionately,

I see Dawson here on Monday.

[1] i.e. the Foreign Office.
[2] The 'Soldatensender Calais' was interested that Otto John as a member of the resistance movement was unknown to Germany during the war and so he did not speak on the wireless. In his time as an employee of the Control Commission he had also to hide his identity until the end of 1946; see Erik Gieseking, *Der Fall Otto John. Entführung oder freiwilliger Übertritt in die DDR* (Lauf/Pregnitz, 2005), pp. 47, 135.
[3] Bell probably enclosed Visser 't Hooft's letter of 24 July 1945, which gave a summary of Gerstenmaier's articles and the reactions of Karl Barth and Emil Brunner; see Besier, *Intimately Acquainted for Many Years*, pp. 275–80, here pp. 275–7.
[4] Llewelyn Hughes (1894–1967) served as Chaplain-General from 1944 to 1951, in which year he became Dean of Ripon (a position which he held until 1967).

Sabine Leibholz to Bell, 2 August 1945, Bell Papers 40, fol. 310 (handwritten); BA, N 1334 (copy)

My dear Lordbishop

Your letter is a great comfort. Thank you very much for it. Gerhard has written to you and sent you a copy of the first letter of my parents.*

I belief Jürgen Winterhager is identical with the man to whom we talked. He obviously gave us his Christian name for his surname. I do not know why, but I clearly remember that in 1939 my mother frequently spoke of Winterhager in connection with Dietrich's friends.¹ After what he told us he must have had – at least for some time – very close contact with Dietrich and Klaus.

I never heard anything about Peter Bielefeld.² It is a pity we never met Heinrich v. Trott.³ He is the youngest son and was born after old Trott's retirement – after their Berlin days.⁴ Gerhard sends his love and will write as soon as the Potsdam conference is over.

Yours affectionately,

* But Freudenberg sent a cable about 'the sure death' of H. Dohnanyi.

---

1. Jürgen Winterhager (1907–89), between 1931 and 1937, was Bonhoeffer's student and then assistant in ecumenical relations. After 1937 he had served as pastor in Hohennauen.
2. Almost certainly Peter Bielenberg (1911–2001), a German lawyer, married to the Anglo-Irish Christabel Burton in Hamburg in 1934. In the same year he had met Adam von Trott who became his closest friend and who involved him in resistance activities in Berlin. He had withdrawn from these by 1944 and was not informed about the plans leading to the plot of 20 July. Bielenberg was arrested and imprisoned in Ravensbrück, but after the intervention of his wife was released in February 1945. After the war the family emigrated to England and in 1947 Ireland. See Christabel Bielenberg, *The Past is Myself* (London, 1968).
3. Heinrich von Trott zu Solz (1918–2009), Adam's younger brother, served as officer during the Second World War and deserted on 1 August 1944, the day of his brother's death.
4. This sentence is crossed out in the copy.

Leibholz to Bell, 4 August 1945, Bell Papers 40, fol. 311 (typewritten); BA, N 1334 (copy)

My dear Bishop,

Very many thanks for your kind letter and for letting me see Visser 't Hooft's letter,¹ which I read with great interest. I also felt that Gerstenmaier presented his case in the *Neue Züricher Zeitung* in a very egocentric manner. I myself should not have minded using national socialist methods in order to fight National Socialism. But the point seems to me whether G. was not more or less Nazi-minded at the time when he was on the wrong side in the Church conflict in the pre-war period. This was about what Dietrich was obviously very much in doubt and I feel he would rather have taken the line of K[arl] Barth. As to Marahrens² and Heckel³ you know much better than I how compromised they are. It is surprising indeed to see from 't Hooft's letter that they have not yet disappeared and that the authorities have not replaced them by reliable personalities. This applies especially to Heckel who (as far as I know) made life for Dietrich and many others, to say it mildly, extremely difficult in the pre-war years.

If it is proved – as 't Hooft writes – that Dietrich and the others who were involved in the plot did not act for the Protestant Church as a whole or for one of its important groups (I thought Dietrich came to Sweden on behalf of the Church leaders) it is rather bad for the Confessional Church: I had hoped that there was within it a strong trend, which advocated the struggle with Hitler on political grounds. What a pity that the right insight and spirit was limited to a small number of Christians.

As Sabine wrote to you we think that Jürgens is identical with Winterhagen [sic]. I also doubt whether the F.O. has a right to give him such an 'advice'. His address is Oskar Jürgens, Esher/Surrey. If you contact him please kindly do not tell him that you got his address from us. I think he has to do some work for the F.O. (Bush House). I am enclosing a letter of his and I am just going to write to him whether he is identical with Winterhagen. By the way, we are not quite sure whether he has fully recovered from his breakdown. But I think that he has to tell you very important things.

I am writing to you about Potsdam separately. It is a phantastic and absurd document and the consequences of such a treatment of Germany will be disastrous not only for Germany but for the whole Continent. I hope my comments will reach you by Monday.

I hasten to return Visser 't Hooft's letter and I am also enclosing Rupp's letter, which you kindly sent me a fortnight ago.

Yours ever,

---

[1] Visser 't Hooft to Bell, 24 July 1945, in Besier, *Intimately Associated for Many Years*, pp. 275–80.
[2] August Marahrens (1875–1950) served as bishop of the Lutheran Church of Hannover, 1925–47. In accordance with his Lutheran theology he stressed the difference of the two kingdoms of church and state and led his church into a middle way between the Confessing Church and the 'German Christian' movement, but with some adaptations of National Socialist ideology. Since 1943 Visser 't Hooft had been convinced that Marahrens was a collaborator with the Nazi Regime and must be replaced; see Gerhard Besier, *'Selbstreinigung' unter britischer Besatzungsherrschaft. Die Evangelisch-lutherische Landeskirche Hannovers und ihr Landesbischof Marahrens 1945–1947* (Göttingen, 1986), p. 113.
[3] Theodor Heckel (1894–1967) served as the head of the office of foreign affairs of the German Protestant Church 1926–45, as bishop, from 1934, he hindered the activities of the Confessing Church and advocated the enforcement of the *Arierparagraphen* against Jews.

Leibholz to Bell, 5 August 1945, Bell Papers 40, fols. 312–14 (typewritten); BA, N 1334 (copy)

Private

My dear Lordbishop,

I have just read the report,[1] which has confirmed my belief in Lord Acton's saying that power corrupts and absolute power corrupts absolutely.[2] It seems to me that the necessary elimination of Hitlerism and militarism is used in order in point of fact (in spite of all reservations to the contrary) to destroy Germany as an independent national unit and to starve and enslave the population. In my view, it is an instrument of mere power politics (and even bad power politics) and dictated by hatred, envy (people wish to get rid of an old and dangerous economic competitor) and lust of booty. The practical acceptance of the Russian and Polish claims in the West (*The Times*, which up-to-now was not in favour of the Polish claims, in the manner typical of this paper, declared in the leader of yesterday that Poland is 'now assured of the Oder-Neisse line as the Western frontier') is especially monstrous. No moral reason, whatever, can be given for this territorial claim. This change implies that the 7 or 8 million Germans who are the legitimate inhabitants of these lands ᵃfor centuriesᵃ are all to be crammed up into [a] rump 'Germany', which cannot sustain its old population. In practice this means the annihilation of millions of Germans. Other provisions are no less shocking as, for instance, the provision that Germany is not allowed to have one sea-going ship or the provision that the productive capacity not needed for permitted production shall be removed in accordance with the reparation plan ... *or if not removed shall be destroyed.*

It is a historical experience that vanquished states frequently succeed in imposing something of their own will, methods and ideas upon their victors. I am thinking e.g. of the Congress of Vienna, which intended to put an end to Napoleon's tyranny and French ideas, but it was after the peace that France gradually imposed its spiritual energies upon her victors. Something of the similar kind had already happened during the war but many of the absurd things which are planned now (such as the mass expropriation of Germans, the mass-expulsion of millions of Germans, the mass starvation, the territorial changes) can only be justified with the argument that Hitler did the same or similar things. I think that what is planned now is even partly more rigorous and harder than what the Nazis did: at least the Western countries had been better treated by Nazi-Germany (apart from Jews, refugees, and political opponents) than a non-Nazi Germany by the Western powers. This seems to me due to the fact that Hitler was primarily a Nazi: he wanted a Nazi-France, a Nazi-England, a Nazi-Holland, but he did not want to destroy these countries in the sense in which this is now being tried with regard to Germany.

As to the reparation question I feel the question is now how best to loot Germany systematically. I do not know whether you, my Bishop, have heard the stories of looting by individuals, not only by the Russians but also by the Americans and British. I have read that the British were even given definite encouragement by orders to loot civilians. When Germans did the same or similar things there was an outcry about their behaviour.[3] Now the systematic robbery at the highest level (probably at the instigation of the Russians) has been legalised. Please do not misunderstand me. I do not complain that the Germans have to make due reparations. What I regret is the method, the systematic robbery and the acceptance of Russian standards by the guardians of Western civilisation.

What I wish to show by these instances is that the general political standards are lowered and adapted in many respects to the Nazi level by adopting Nazi lines of thought and principles which are very similar to those of the Russians and that the Western countries (frequently unconsciously) have abandoned their own standards.

To call the Potsdam report 'just' as *The Times* did yesterday shows only how far the perversion of the language has already gone even in the Western countries. The Potsdam report seems to me in many essential parts hardly more just than Hitler's New Order.

I need not tell you that I deeply regret that no constructive approach to the German problem has been made. But I cannot say that I am surprised. Potsdam is the logical conclusion of the Unconditional Surrender policy, which has falsified a primarily ideological conflict into a primarily national war – a change for which, in my view, Mr Roosevelt and Mr Churchill will bear the responsibility before the bar of history. True, it can be argued that at least the unity between the Great Powers has thus been secured. But I think that a unity based on mere power will not last for long: the ideological issues will come forward as soon as the common victim either has died of the treatment or is no longer of interest, from an economic point of view.

As to the consequences of this policy, first, I think Power politics cannot be localised. True, the Atlantic Charter has been accepted by all the United Nations. But you certainly remember, my Bishop, that Churchill stated last year in the House of Commons that the Atlantic Charter does not apply to Germany. It seems to me, however, an inner impossibility to localise the application of the Atlantic Charter to certain states. If it is not applied generally it will not be applied to other states and ultimately it will not be applied at all. When Hitler came to power people thought they were able to treat him like an ordinary being, although they knew that he was a criminal in certain respects. In the end they found out that one cannot be both, a criminal and at the same time a gentleman. I think Potsdam is the end of the Atlantic Charter and the talk about the Atlantic Charter need no longer to be taken seriously.

Secondly, I am thinking that, on the whole, nationalism is declining today in spite of many signs which point to the contrary. The ᶜonlyᶜ way of staying this process is a policy of oppression and enslavement as envisaged by Potsdam. No nation can be kept down in perpetuity unless it be destroyed. Perhaps Germany will be destroyed. I do not know. But if not, oppression and enslavement must rekindle nationalistic passions and people must start again believing in what Hitler told them again and again, namely that the United Nations did not want to destroy Hitlerite Germany, but Germany as a whole. I know what Versailles meant for the Germans. If the German nation has not completely changed its mentality and survives these years a Super-Versailles must have catastrophic effects on the German soul.

Thirdly, and this is the point which concerns you and all of us most and is closely connected with what I have just said: Potsdam excludes the hope of a re-education. One cannot simultaneously enslave a people and educate for freedom. This means that Potsdam is a deadly blow for the Churches in Germany. They will not be able to fulfil their functions if at the same time they are burdened with the responsibility for Potsdam. This is all the more tragic as (after all that I hear) wide strata of the population are prepared to suffer for, and to repent, the crimes the Nazis have committed in their name. But such an act of self-purification presupposes a behaviour on the part of the victor nations in accordance with the way of life for which they claim to have entered the war.

Frankly, if I were in Germany, I should not be able to associate myself with essential parts of the Potsdam report. What I fear is that the Great Powers have a greater need for Quislings than for Germans who believe with their whole heart in those values and standards which are the mark of Western civilisation. And I think that the Churches in Germany will have to face the same dilemma. How can they go on with their work if the Potsdam report becomes a political reality. If they accept it they will lose all contact with the nation they have gained as a result of the Hitler tyranny. ᵃEven if they refuse it (what, no doubt, they will and must do) the cause of freedom and Western civilisation⁴ will be compromised by the new spirit of Potsdam.ᵃ How the authors of the report think to be able to re-educate the German nation with the help of such methods is beyond my grasp.

I am afraid I must close because I wish you to have the letter to-morrow morning.

Please forgive my being frank: I have written the remarks under the impression of the document and I should have re-written and qualified them if I had to weigh every word. You certainly understand. What I have tried to say is I feel sure in agreement with what those who gave their lives for freedom within Germany would say today.⁵

Please give my love to ªMrs Bell and toª Christopher Dawson in case you see him to-morrow.

Yours ever,

ªP.S. K. Hahn who called on us yesterday evening (11 o'clock) said that he had seen Jacks and that Jacks would gladly be prepared to bring an article about your journey to Sweden and your meeting with Dietrich in the *Hibbert* – Hahn will write to you about this.

From to-morrow (Monday) until Wednesday our address will be S.C.M. Conference, The College, Cheltenham.ª

---

1 Report of the Potsdam Conference of Stalin, Harry S. Truman and Winston Churchill (later Clement Attlee), (17 July–2 August 1945) about the future of Germany.
2 John Dalberg-Acton (1834–1902), from 1869 1st Baron Acton, Catholic historian, politician, and writer. The famous statement is made in his letter to Mandell Creighton, bishop of London, 5 April 1887, published by J. N. Figgis and R. V. Laurence (eds.), *Historical Essays and Studies* (London, 1907).
3 Corrected, but not in copy: 'the behaviour of the Huns'.
4 Copy: 'ministerization'.
5 For an historical analysis of these debates see Anne Deighton, *The Impossible Peace: Britain, the Division of Germany and the Origins of the Cold War* (Oxford, 1990).

Bell to Leibholz, 9 August 1945, BA, N 1334 (typewritten); Bell Papers 40, fol. 315 (carbon)

My dear Leibholz,

Forgive my delay in replying to your letter, which actually reached me on Tuesday, so that I could not send my answer to the S.C.M. Conference at Cheltenham.

I was much moved by your criticism of the Berlin policy, and feel the force of what you say very strongly.¹

I will not write more now, because I am most anxious that you should get this without further delay, together with the cuttings enclosed, about the Memorial Service, which you may keep. I also enclose a letter from Madame von Hase, for you to look at. And I return the letter from ªChristophª Jurgens, with many thanks.

On Tuesday I saw Werner Koch,² and asked him if he knew Winterhager. He said he did. I asked him if he knew his handwriting, and showed him the letter. He said it was Winterhager's writing. This makes me all the more anxious to get in touch with Winterhager. Do you think the address you gave me – just Esher – is enough?

Yours ever,

ªI had a most interesting talk with [Heinrich] von Trott too.ª

---

1 See Bell's criticisms of the Potsdam Conference in the House of Lords on 22 August 1945, Hansard, H.L. Deb., Vol. 137, cols. 141–5.
2 Werner Koch (1910–94) was curate in Bonhoeffer's seminary at Finkenwalde and reported events in the Church Struggle to foreign newspapers. In 1936 he was involved in passing on the memorandum

to Hitler written on 28 May by the Second Provisional Government of the Confessing Church, to the foreign press. He was arrested and incarcerated in Sachsenhausen concentration camp. He was later released in December 1938. Conscripted into the army in 1939 Koch deserted in March 1945 and was held in a British prisoner-of-war camp at Ascot, where he served as pastor. He worked for the B.B.C. until 1947.

Leibholz to Bell, 10 August 1945, Bell Papers 40, fol. 316 (typewritten); BA, N 1334 (copy)

My dear Lordbishop,
Many thanks for your kind letter. I am very glad to see that you did not find my comments too explicit and frank. My conscience was a little bad. I think that the Russian declaration of war on Japan[1] explains why the Western powers have yielded to the Russian demands. As to the planned 'reparations' *The Times*' correspondent wrote on Monday last: These clauses 'have an air of unreality for the traveller who has seen something of this, the most devastated country in history. It would have been thought that the De-industrialisation of Germany and the dismantling of her war machine had already been largely achieved by air bombardment'. Somewhere else it is said in *The Times* that the Ruhr will need the whole of its damaged industrial capacity if Germany is to have the 'peace economy' for which the declaration of Potsdam provides. If this be so how can the 'reparation' plan be carried out?

I am sorry that the atomic bomb has been actually used against the Japanese.[2] A few months ago people protested here at the indiscriminate bombing by V1 and V2. But is not the new weapon [a] thousand times worse? Apart from that the secrecy cannot be kept and after all history has taught and we have experienced there is not much hope that the morality of man keeps pace with this technical revolution.

Unfortunately, I did not give you the full address of Winterhager. It runs as follows: Oskar Jürgens, 125 Emberlane, Esher/Surrey. I also heard from somebody else that his freedom is limited. I do not know how this is possible. I wonder what you have heard from Trott and Koch. Unfortunately, I do not know them personally.

In the meantime, we have had more news. The picture is as follows. Hans von Dohnanyi and Dietrich started their activities as early as in 1939 and 1940. (Therefore, Brunner's statement that Dietrich joined Gerstenmaier 'only some time later' is incorrect as well as the other statement that G. is the only Christian conspirator.[3]) In autumn 1944 Dietrich came to the Gestapo-prison in Berlin and since then it was not possible to contact him. Dietrich himself was obviously not condemned to death: his trial was postponed because it was connected with that [of] von Dohnanyi who was seriously ill. On the 7th of February Dietrich was taken with the so-called 'extra-group' (prominent anti-Nazis) first to Buchenwald, then to Dachau and finally to Flossenbűrg where he was murdered. Dohnanyi who played a leading part in the plot was arrested with Dietrich: but he was soon paralysed as a result of diphtheria, which he got in the prison camp. He was taken to Sachsenhausen in April. Here he has obviously been executed. Nobody has heard anything about him since. Klaus Bonhoeffer and R. Schleicher were both condemned on the 2nd of February. Klaus was cruelly tortured and both were chained. Schleicher himself was not an active conspirator but he knew about it. He was not able to lie and this led to his death. They were in the 'Zellengefängnis' (Lehrter Strasse) and were both shot in the night from April 22/23. Bethge (son-in-law of Schleicher) was also imprisoned with Klaus and Schleicher, but was released by the Russians.[4]

The surviving brother of my wife[5] writes about our parents:

'The parents knew the activity of them, approved of it and helped them. I think there were very few families in Germany during the last 12 years in which there was such a political unanimity and no doubt, this spirit confirmed all in their plans.

Their mental constancy and firmness is astonishing, but their physical strength has decreased rather rapidly during the last years and especially the last weeks. We hope that it will not take too much time that you will be allowed to come and see us. There is nothing that they would enjoy as much as that'.

Therefore, I am now thinking how it can be best arranged to see our parents. I think that the Home Office would give us permission to see them for a week or so, under the special circumstances, provided the military authorities do not object. But how to get the permission of the military authorities? Do you think, my Bishop, one could possibly approach the Chaplain General, simply point out the facts as they are, and to ask him to see whether, under the special circumstances, the authorities would make an exception to the rule and let us go for a short time. – Otherwise we should have to find a reason for our going. I have been thinking of writing to Clutton Brock and of asking him whether he could ask the authorities to allow us to come. Perhaps I could possibly be of some use to him. I think that you will probably not go to Berlin, and even if so you would most certainly need the support by a theologian. Our special difficulty is that we are two: my wife cannot go by herself and I should not like to leave her behind under the circumstances just now, all the more as it is especially she whom, after all, her parents want to see. In case you can give me an advice in the matter it would be very good of you.

Thank you for letting me have the cuttings. If you do not mind I shall send them to Berlin. I already sent a copy of our address. In fact, our family listened to the memorial service relayed to Germany and to the translation of your address. I am very glad about this and thank you once again for having written to the B.B.C. when I asked you for it. It was very good of you.

I am enclosing Mrs v. Hase's letter. There is obviously no postal connection between Westphalia and Berlin. Her husband was a cousin of my mother-in-law. We ourselves have hardly ever met this family. But Sabine says that they are good people with a religious tradition. Their bravery they have proved.

Yours ever,

---

[1] On 9 August 1945.
[2] The first atomic bomb was dropped over Hiroshima on 6 August and the second over Nagasaki on 9 August 1945.
[3] In theology Gerstenmaier was a disciple of Emil Brunner (1889–1966) who had followed Barth's Dialectical Theology in the 1920s, but broken off in a different direction in 1934. Subsequently, as professor of Systematic and Practical Theology at the University of Zurich, Brunner searched for a new *theologia naturalis*.
[4] See John W. de Gruchy, *Daring Trusting Spirit: Bonhoeffer's Friend Eberhard Bethge* (London, 2005), pp. 88–93.
[5] After securing his postdoctoral lecturing qualification in 1927 Karl-Friedrich Bonhoeffer (1899–1957) became a full professor at the University of Berlin. In 1930 he had been appointed Professor of Physical Chemistry at Frankfurt University. Four years later, he became Professor of Physical

Chemistry at the University of Leipzig, returning to Berlin as a professor of Physical Chemistry in 1947.

Leibholz to Bell, 13 August 1945, Bell Papers 40, fol. 317 (typewritten); BA, N 1334 (copy)

My dear Lordbishop,

I hasten to enclose Jürgen's letter from August 11 just received.[1] He hopes to get an answer soon whether and when he may see you. He is not identical with Winterhager, but he is not Jurgens: in point of fact, I do not know who he is. Somebody else wrote to us that we should be amused to hear his name. 'But at the moment he is not allowed to speak about himself and his present occupation'. I know that he is doing some work in Bush House (Foreign Office). The whole matter is rather mysterious to me although I have not the slightest doubt that he is a reliable man from whom we still have to hear interesting and perhaps important stories.

Yours ever,

[1] The letter in German (Bell Papers, Vol. 40, fol. 320) is to be found in Bethge and Jasper, *An der Schwelle*, p. 218.

Bell to Leibholz, 14 August 1945, Bell Papers 40, fol. 318 (carbon)

My dear Leibholz,

Very many thanks for your letters, which are extremely interesting and important. I will wait to hear from Oskar Jürgens. I am interested to hear that he is not after all Winterhager.

I thoroughly appreciate your wish, with Sabine to visit Germany and see her parents. Any help I can give in backing up a request, I will give. I don't really think the Chaplain-General would be the channel to approach, for he deals only, to the best of my belief, with applications for visits to the Churches. I have just received a statement from Boehm,[1] a copy of which I have sent to the *Spectator*. In this message, though I do not print this actual sentence, he stresses the importance of my going to Berlin. If I go to Germany, I have already arranged to take with me the Rev. E.G. Rupp, to act as British theologian interpreter. I am making an enquiry at the Foreign Office to see what the possibilities are of getting permission for you and Sabine to make such a visit, in the special circumstances.

You must have had some expenses in connection with the Service at Holy Trinity, Kingsway. The B.B.C. has sent me three guineas for my expenses, which were really nil: so I am venturing to ask you to pay your expenses with it.

Yours affectionately,

[1] Presumably Hans Böhm (1899–1962) was consultant in ecumenical relations to the second Provisional Leadership of the German Evangelical Church. He had met Bell in London in 1937, preparing the Oxford conference together with Dietrich Bonhoeffer. Between 1945 and 1959 he was provost of Berlin and member of the church assembly of Berlin-Brandenburg.

Leibholz to Bell, 17 August 1945, Bell Papers 40, fol. 319 (typewritten); BA, N 1334 (copy)

My dear Lordbishop,

Very many thanks for your letter.

It is very good indeed of you to make enquiries at the Foreign Office on our behalf. We hope that the answer will not be too much in the negative.

In the meantime, we have received the post from Geneva, which (apart from a letter of my father-in-law) includes Dietrich's poem, Klaus's last letters[1] and a detailed report of the events in the 'Zellengefängnis' in Berlin.[2] It follows from the latter that about 100 political prisoners were in the prison; about twenty were murdered, among them Klaus and R. Schleicher. There was obviously a struggle between the Gestapo and the S.D. on the one hand, and the ordinary authorities on the other. All prisoners were told that they were to be released. But the twenty prisoners when they were supposed to be released were led by the S.S. to a place near the prison and killed by a shot in the neck in the night from April 21/22 at one o'clock. That the details have become known is due to the fact that one of the prisoners shot at in this way was not mortally wounded and managed to escape.

Dietrich's poem is going to be published in Switzerland with an introduction by Visser 't Hooft.[3] It is to be published by the Oikumene itself. I am trying to get it published here. This poem and Klaus's letters have deeply moved us. The letter in which K. took farewell of his parents was signed 'Your thankful and *happy* Klaus'.

I am very glad to see that you are thinking of possibly going to Berlin. If so, you will certainly also see our parents (Marienburger Allee 43, Berlin Charlottenburg 9). They would be *very* happy to see you and to thank you personally for all you have done for Dietrich and us in all these years. They know that without your ever ready helpfulness and goodness we should not have been able to get through these difficult years in as good a way as we have done. We also think that your visit would give them new hope and comfort: especially they would certainly be happy to hear that you will back up our request to come and see them as quickly as possible. – By the way, there is also Bethge (son-in-law of Schleicher) who is now living there and is now working in ecumenical matters under Dibelius.[4] I think you met him here once.

I found out that Oscar Jürgens is, in truth, Otto John. As I see from the document just received from Geneva his brother Hans John was murdered in the same night as our relatives. O. John is in great anxiety about the fate of his brother but I hesitate to give him this very sad news. His brother was included in the memorial service held by Bethge for Klaus and Schleicher in Berlin in June.

You were so very good as to send me the cheque for our expenses. In point of fact, the travelling expenses were refunded to me. But if you allow me to keep the cheque to cover the other expenses incurred during our three days' stay in London I gladly accept it with many thanks for the very pleasant surprise.

Yours affectionately,

[a]P.S. I am enclosing a copy of the lecture delivered in Cheltenham. Perhaps you may like to have a look at it? Would you please return it? I think the *Economist* was excellent in its Comment on 'The German settlement'.[a]

[1] See Eberhard Bethge (ed.), *Dietrich and Klaus Bonhoeffer, Auf dem Wege zur Freiheit. Gedichte und Briefe aus der Haft* (Berlin, 1946).
[2] See Johannes Tuchel, '*... und ihrer aller wartete der Strick.' Das Zellengefängnis Lehrter Straße 3 nach dem 20. Juli 1944* (Berlin, 2014).
[3] See Leibholz to Bell, 16 January 1945, note 3.
[4] Otto Dibelius (1880–1967) was a leading figure in the German Church Struggle, became a member of the Brethren Council of Brandenburg in 1934 and after the war organized the Evangelical Church of Brandenburg as its bishop, 1945–66. As member of the council of the Evangelical Church in Germany he drew up the Stuttgart Confession of guilt together with Theophil Wurm in October 1945. From 1949 to 1961 he was chairman of the council of the Evangelical Church. At the first assembly of WCC in 1948 Dibelius became a member of the Central Committee, and from 1954 to 1961 he served as one of its six presidents.

Bell to Leibholz, 27 August 1945, BA 1334 (typewritten)

My dear Leibholz,

Very many thanks for letting me see your lecture at Cheltenham. I have read it with the greatest interest and sympathy, and return it herewith.

Today I have had a letter from Theodore Delbruck in Amsterdam, which speaks for itself. I have just sent him an acknowledgement, saying I am putting him in touch with you.

I am hoping to post you the first draft of my article for the *Contemporary* on Wednesday.[1] Please let me have it back as quickly as possible.

Yours ever,

[1] A longer version of Bell's article, 'The Background of the Hitler Plot', was subsequently published in the *Contemporary Review*, October 1945, reprinted in *The Church and Humanity*, pp. 165–76, and also to be found in Eberhard Bethge (ed.), *Dietrich Bonhoeffer, Gesammelte Schriften*, Vol. 1 (Munich, 1958), pp. 390–98.

Leibholz to Bell, 27 August 1945, Bell Papers 40, fol. 321 (typewritten); BA, N 1334 (copy)

My dear Lordbishop,

I see from the report just received about Dietrich's last days that he was taken from Buchenwald on April 3rd together, among others, with Major Folkener[1] who is an agent of the British Secret Service. Folkener is said to be in this country and I have been asked to contact him. Could you possibly advise me how this could be done?

Dietrich himself was taken to the prison of Schönberg near Passau on the 6th of April. On Sunday the 8th he still took the service: then he looked after Mrs Goerdeler and Mrs v. Hammerstein (the wife of the former chief of the General Staff). On the same day he was taken by himself in a police car to Flossenbürg. On the 10th of April a drunk man of the guard told fellow-prisoners that Dietrich and others were murdered the day before. I feel more and more that Dietrich had something of a saint [sic].

Things in Berlin must be terrible. The brother-in-law of Klaus who was released from prison when the Russians arrived was re-imprisoned eight weeks ago and he has not returned.² – It is a great comfort to us to know that Mr Clutton-Brock is in Berlin now. He has had tea with my wife's parents and some of the sisters and grandchildren and has written to us that 'they are wonderfully cheerful, composed and courageous' and that he 'loves them all'. Unfortunately, Mr Wingfield-Digby who is the Senior Chaplain to the 7th Armoured Division has to leave Berlin soon.³ Through him we have received the letters within two days' time. He wrote to us in the same sense as Mr Clutton-Brock and adds: 'If I leave Berlin the only regret will be in leaving your family'.

Today I have had a rather urgent enquiry from Switzerland (Barth, Ev. Press-Service) to provide them with further material concerning the relationship of Dietrich to Gerstenmaier. They feel deeply the dishonesty in G.'s report especially with regard to Dietrich and they deplore the egocentric way in which G. put himself into the limelight.⁴ – I also found it rather strange that Oldham did not mention Dietrich in his last *Christian News-Letter*.

You wrote to me some time ago that you were asked about Winterhager. If it is not confidential would you be good enough to let me know whether W. who is still in Germany wishes to come over to this country for a visit. My wife's sister (Mrs v. Dohnanyi) has asked us whether there is such a possibility, as she wishes us to tell some important things. This is why I should like to know whether there is a precedent. In this case I could advise her accordingly.

Many thanks for the last *Hansard*. I am grateful to you for having broached the terrible fate of those going to be deported in East Germany.⁵ I feel that the Western Powers cannot get rid of the responsibility for the fate of these 8 or nine million Germans. As you say, how can these mass deportations eliminate the war mind of the German people. I wonder whether other speakers took up the argument in the debate and whether the speaker of the government referred to it in his reply.

Yours affectionately,

ᵃP.S. Many thanks for your letter of yesterday. It has just arrived. I shall contact Delbrück in Amsterdam. Thank you for letting me have this letter. I am looking forward to the draft of your article.ᵃ

---

1. That is Major Hugh M. Falconer, but the agent of the British Secret Service was Captain Payne Best.
2. Justus Delbrück (1902–45), whose sister Emmi was married to Klaus Bonhoeffer, began to work in the Office of Military Defence in 1941. Here he worked in close contact with other resisters. Arrested after 20 July 1944 he was released in April 1945 but again arrested one month later by the Soviet NKVD. He died in a camp at Jamlitz on 23 October 1945.
3. Stephen Basil Wingfield-Digby (1910–96) served as Senior Chaplain to the British armed forces in the Second World War. Afterwards he returned to parochial ministry, in 1947 becoming vicar of Sherborne.
4. See Visser 't Hooft: 'Gerstenmaier presented himself as the outstanding resister in a most egocentric manner.' Besier, *Intimately Acquainted for Many Years*, p. 276.
5. In the debate on the Charter of the United Nations Bell spoke of his impressions of his visit to the United States, raising the question of the deportations from the former German eastern regions; see Hansard, H.L. Deb., Vol. 137, cols. 141–5 (22 August 1945).

Bell to Leibholz, 28 August (1945), BA, N 1334 (handwritten)

My dear Leibholz,

I enclose [the] first draft of my article. Please scrutinise with a *vigilant* eye. And suggest corrections and improvements of any kind. In particular look at the last paragraph. Is the reference to Bonhoeffer family correct & full? I should be vy. glad if I could have it back by Saturday first post.

Yours ever,

The article may have to be greatly shortened.
What year did *Hammerstein* die?
Do you know any details of Kaiser[1]?

---

[1] Jakob Kaiser (1888–1961). In the Weimar Republic Kaiser had been a leading representative of the Christian trade unions and an early opponent of the Nazis. After 1933 he gathered a circle of resisters and was from 1941 in touch with Carl Goerdeler. Kaiser was one of the resisters named to Bell by Bonhoeffer and Schönfeld in Sweden in 1942. After 20 July 1944 he went into hiding, surviving with the help of Elfriede Nebgen, later his wife. In 1945 he became a co-founder of the new Christian Democratic Union (CDU) Party in Berlin. He served as Federal Minister of All-German Affairs, 1949–57.

Leibholz to Bell, 30 August 1945, Bell Papers 40, fols. 322–3 (typewritten); BA, N 1334 (copy)

My dear Lordbishop,

Many thanks for kindly letting me see your very interesting and impressive article, which has very much moved us.

As you ask me to make suggestions may I raise the following points for consideration?

1. Page 2: You say that Sch[önfeld] came 'to inform me of strong movement in Germany against Hitler, in which the Churches were prominent'. I remember Visser 't Hooft's last letter (you sent it to me) in which he said that neither Gerstenmaier nor Dietrich acted either on behalf of the Confessional Church as a whole or of an important group within the Church.[1]
2. Page 6: Now that Schacht (together with Krupp, von Bohlen und Halbach[2]), absurd as it is, has been included in the list of major war criminals (probably a concession to the Russians: the whole thing seems to me to be spoiled by the inclusion of some of these people), I do not know whether it is wise, from a political point of view, to mention the name of Schacht in this connection.
3. Page 14: You say: 'My sole purpose ... is to call attention to the importance of the opposition to the Hitler regime, which lay behind the Hitler plot'. I think it is not a bad idea to make this clearer.

    In my view, your article proves two things of the utmost importance:

    First, it proves that the widely-spread view in this country (and voiced by Mr Churchill in the House of Commons last year) that the plot of July 1944 was a plot of the 'militarists' is not compatible with the established facts as shown in your article. The truth is that behind the plot stood the upholders of liberal and democratic (and Christian) European tradition in Germany who to attain their aim allied themselves with the Western-minded forces of the army (without which the regime could not conceivably be destroyed) and for tactical reasons with a group of opportunists, which wanted to get rid of the regime.

Secondly, your article proves that the no less widely-spread view is incorrect that the plot was simply the expression of a conspiracy of people who realized in 1944 that they were losing the war. As you say the plot was prepared at the latest (see page 3) in the winter 1941/1942 – i.e. at the time when Germany's chances to win the war were not bad at all. In point of fact, the foundations of the militant opposition movement were laid in 1940 and 1941 and further material in this respect will be provided in due course. E.g. Dietrich started his political activities together with v. Dohnanyi at the outbreak of war in 1939. John, of whom I wrote to you, told us in London of the despair in July and August 1940[3] of all those who were involved in these activities and who were partly even prepared to join the army in order to share v. Fritsch's fate (who had been seeking death in battle). Only Dietrich was firm: coming to the decisive meeting he said that, from a Christian point of view, Hitler was the Anti-Christ and that they had to go on with their work, whether Hitler be successful or not.

4. Page 15: I entirely agree with what you call 'The two strands in the opposition' and with their analysis. But what you say, my Lordbishop, with regard to 'the touch with the Secret Service' and the 'collaboration with Canaris' I should say in a little other way, if I should mention it at all. No doubt, there were these connections mentioned. But they were not limited to the opportunists. v. Dohnanyi obviously collaborated with Canaris[4] and as Dietrich closely collaborated with D[ohnanyi], he probably worked together with Canaris, Oster etc. too. It even seems that he was murdered together with them in Flossenbürg. As you say the German situation was highly complicated at that time and made these contacts necessary. But, of course, this has nothing to do with the basic differentiation concerning the motives of those who wanted to destroy the regime. I even think that this is an important point ᵃin your article.ᵃ

5. Page 16: There is a question-mark before Goerdeler. But what you say applies to Beck[5] as well as to Goerdeler.

6. Page 16: As to our people the facts now established are as follows:

Dietrich was *not* sentenced to death (because his case was connected with that of Dohnanyi ᵃwho was illᵃ), but was murdered in the concentration camp Flossenbürg on April 9 without any trial at all. His brother-in-law Dr H. von Dohnanyi was murdered in the concentration camp Sachsenhausen in April shortly before the Russians arrived. Dietrich and Dohnanyi closely worked together ᵃthroughᵃ all the years. Dietrich's brother Klaus and brother-in-law Dr R. Schleicher (I suggest to call him Dr and not Professor, because he was primarily a government official and only secondarily a professor, a Honorary Professor since 1942) were sentenced to death on February 2nd by the Volksgerichtshof in Berlin and murdered in Berlin in the night from April 22/23. As to the General v. Hase he was called an uncle: exactly, he was a first-cousin of Dietrich's mother. Before the war our contacts were rather loose and I am not

perfectly sure whether one should mention him in this special connection. He was a professional soldier and people here might wrongly call him a Prussian or militarist and this may lead to misunderstandings with regard to the whole family.
7. Schonfeld is spelt Schoenfeld or Schönfeld.

The surname of our brother-in-law is spelt v. Dohnanyi: he is the son of the famous Hungarian composer who is very well known in this country.

It is very good of you to mention the name of Dietrich's brother and brothers-in-law in your stimulating article and we thank you for it.

I do not know whether the suggestions appeal to you. Please kindly accept them as what they are meant – namely as ideas, which struck me when reading your paper and, which may be utterly irrelevant, from the point of view from which you are dealing with the matter.

Yours affectionately,

P.S. To the best of my belief, Hammerstein died in 1943. As to Kaiser I think there was something in the article in the *Neue Zürcher Zeitung* referred to in your article. I trust that John will know more about them. It may be that he will come to Oxford next Sunday. In this case I shall ask him and write to you – in case he has something to add.

Could I possibly get two off-prints of your article – if you get some. I should like to send one copy to Berlin.

P.S. Following the line in your article I submit to you for consideration the following version:

One of the latest victims was Dietrich Bonhoeffer. Although in prison on July 20, 1944, he was murdered in the concentration camp Flossenbűrg by the S.S. on the 9th of April after a protracted martyrdom of two years. In the same month his brother Klaus and his brothers-in-law Dr H. von Dohnanyi and Dr R. Schleicher were murdered in Berlin and Sachsenhausen for their share in the plot.

---

[1] See W.A. Visser 't Hooft to Bell, 24 July 1945, in Besier, *Intimately Associated for Many Years*, pp. 275–80, here p. 277.

[2] Alfried Krupp von Bohlen und Halbach (1907–67) was from 1931 a member of the SS and, as deputy of his father, chairman of the committee of the *Adolf-Hitler-Spende der deutschen Wirtschaft*.

[3] After the capitulation of France on 22 June 1940 Hitler, as the 'greatest commander of all times', had indeed triumphed over the warnings of critical generals and the hopes of the resistance movement at large. See Helmuth James von Moltke's reflection on the 'triumph of the evil' in his letter to Peter Count York von Wartenburg, 17 June 1940, in Ger van Roon, *Neuordnung im Widerstand: Der Kreisauer Kreis innerhalb der deutsche Widerstandsbewegung* (Munich, 1967), pp. 491–81.

[4] Wilhelm Canaris (1887–1945) was admiral and, from 1935, head of the 'Abwehr', the intelligence service of the Department of Military Defence. From 1938 to 1944 he was head of the Office of Military Defence (*Amt Ausland/Abwehr*) of the Supreme Command of the Armed Forces. From 1938 Canaris had supported the activities of the resistance group which his protégé Colonel Hans Oster had built up from his office. He was murdered in Flossenbűrg concentration camp on 9 April.

[5] Ludwig Beck (1880–1944) was Chief of the General Staff, 1936–8, and thereafter the acknowledged moral and practical head of the military resistance. A close ally of Carl Goerdeler and, later, Julius Leber, he died in the Bendlerblock on the night 20 July 1944.

Bell to Leibholz, 31 August 1945, BA, N 1334 (typewritten); Bell Papers 40, fols. 324–5 (carbon)

My dear Leibholz,

I am most grateful for your very valuable comments on my article. I send it back, as there are some points on which I should like elucidation and, if you are willing, some written corrections or improvements. Please mark the text in any way you like. If your friend John sees you during the weekend, please take any advantage you can of his knowledge: and if you can let me have the article back by the first post on Tuesday, I shall have it in time to make a corrected version for Dr Gooch.

I take your comments in particular:

1. *Prominence of the Churches*. As I read through my diary again, I was very much struck by the great prominence, which Schonfeld[1] gave to the activities of the Churches. He made this point very emphatically, while he talked to me. I know that 't Hooft takes a different view now, some three years later. But Schonfeld made a most vivid impression upon me in this particular. At the same time, looking at my own memorandum of the conversation, a copy of which you have, and which I gave to Mr Eden, I see that I do not put the Churches quite so prominently. What I wonder is whether I might not reword the latter part of page 2, in some such way as this:

'He told me that this opposition was made up of three principal elements, (i) Members of the State administration and the State police; (ii) large numbers of former Trade Union chiefs; (iii) high officers in the army. He said that the leaders of the Protestant and Catholic Churches were also closely in touch with the whole opposition movement; and he told me of the determined fight, etc. ... Bishop of Berlin. The purpose of this opposition was the destruction of the whole Hitler regime, including Himmler, Goering, Goebbels, and the central leaders of the Gestapo, S.S., and S.A. Extensive preparations, etc.'

2. *Page 6*: It may be well to omit Schacht. It may also be well to omit mention of the Field Marshals at the bottom of page 6 and top of page 7, with the exception of von Witzleben, as these Field Marshals may find their way into the list of War Criminals as having been commanders on the Russian front.
3. I will certainly look up what Churchill said in the House of Commons about the plot and the militarists and see how I can bring out that point. In my diary I find that Schönfeld made the point that the Germans at that time believed that their military prospects in the war were good; and of course that was a time when Germany held 1000 miles of Russian territory, and nearly all Europe was occupied. Could you develop a little what you say about the despair of those involved in these activities in July and August, 1940, and the willingness to share von Fritsch's fate?
4. *The two strands*. What I am anxious to meet is the criticism that some of the opposition was opposition intended to keep the militarists in authority, but eliminating Hitler. I wanted to show that there was what may be called an idealist

opposition, entirely uncompromising, represented by Dietrich, and the other opposition circles (see page 10 of my memorandum), which beforehand had no real contact with each other, and some of whom had mixed motives – yet with this opposition the idealists were associated, because it was only by joining all forces that there was any chance of overthrowing Hitler.

5. I am trying to find out from Schutz what is the most accurate statement I can make about Beck and Goerdeler's visit to England, and their warning of the government before the war. I knew Beck came over: the reason I put a query was: Did Goerdeler too?
6. I am very grateful for the settled facts with regard to Dietrich and all your friends. Perhaps it would be better to leave out General von Hase. Thank you also for the post-script and the suggested wording.

Do you think that my article would be more effective if I embodied more of the text of the memorandum I gave to Mr Eden? Have you any suggestions to make, in that case, as to how?

Then I have a major problem. I have had a talk with Schutz, and he questions very much the political wisdom *now* of publishing the text of the Schönfeld memorandum. He says that there are points in it which would be severely criticised, and would play into the hands of the Russians. It is altogether too much a memorandum of the Generals. He thinks there is a certain naiveté, to put it mildly, in the paragraphs on page 13 about the Russian problem. The reference to the Jewish part of the population is also very much exposed to criticism; and would really be doing less than justice to the Churches who, as is now much better known, had put up a strong fight against the anti-Jewish forces. There are other points in the memorandum which make the printing of the whole undesirable. At the same time there are portions which I could quote as coming out of the memorandum with which Schönfeld supplied me.

The more you can correct and improve the whole article, the more grateful shall I be.

Yours ever,

---

[1] i.e. Hans Schönfeld.

Leibholz to Bell, 3 September 1945, Bell Papers 40, fol. 326 (typewritten); BA, N 1334 (copy)

My dear Lordbishop,

Very many thanks for your letter of August 31st. I have carefully re-read your draft, Schönfeld's statement and your own memorandum left with Eden. I am ʻthusʼ very glad to have the opportunity of adding a few more words to my last letter.

1. May I start with the major problem?
   When re-reading Schönfeld's statement I felt very *strongly* that you and Schütz are perfectly right. It seems to me indeed impossible to produce it in full

(especially pages 12 and 13). The statement has an air of unreality today and as things have developed some of the suggestions made in 1942 would have a bad effect today and encourage criticism. Therefore, I also think it would be much better to omit the whole statement and only to quote those parts which can do no harm. I myself have made this attempt and have re-written page 2a and 2b taking into account Schönfeld's statement, your memo. and your letter (page 1 and 2).

2. As to your memo. I should not suggest its publication. There are in it some passages which seem to me it would be better not to publish today. I am thinking, e.g., of the passages on page 3 ('The opposition has full confidence in the strength of the German army, and is ready to go on with the war to the bitter end if the Allies were to refuse to treat with a new Government controlling a non-Hitlerite Germany, after the overthrow of the whole Hitler-regime.') or on page 7 ('The help of the Allied Armies as assistants in the maintenance of order would be necessary and welcome …').

   I feel that the content of your memo. has been reproduced by the article. I have included some more passages of your memo. in it. But I did not know where to put the passage on page 3: 'The establishment of a European Army for the control of Europe, of which the German Army would form a part, under Central authority'. I was not able to include it because I did not know whether Schönfeld or Dietrich made this remark.

3. I have made a number of suggestions in pencil in the draft. Perhaps you may like some of them. I had two aims in mind: a) to meet criticism b) to correct some facts. These latter corrections are partly due to what John told me yesterday: For instance, page 6:

   a) Beck was Chief of the General Staff before the Austrian crisis: b) Hammerstein was Supreme Commander of the army: by the way, John holds the view that Hammerstein was not a Prussian: on the contrary, he said, he made much fun of the Generals.

4. I quite agree with what you say about the Field Marshalls. Therefore, I have only mentioned von Kluge and Witzleben who are both dead.

5. What you say about the two strands is I think of great importance. What I have in mind in this connection I have re-written on page 14a). I have combined the content of my last letter with what you say on page 15 about the two strands. What I have put down there about the despair of those involved in subversive activities in July and August 1940 and about Dietrich is a story told me by John. No doubt, it is correct. But, of course, I do not know whether you like to mention it in the connection.

6. Page 16. I have re-written the worded suggestion of the post-script of my last letter concerning the settled facts of Dietrich and our family.

7. Goerdeler was in Great Britain in 1938 and 1939.[1] I remember a letter from Gooch (about a year ago) in which he told me of Goerdeler's visit to him and of Goerdeler's warning. Goerdeler told him that after the elimination of Hitler Himmler would seize power and play the role of Robespierre in Germany: but

that he, Goerdeler, would not survive this. Unfortunately, I cannot lay hands on this letter.
8. Would you not perhaps think it better to title the article: The Hitler Plot or The Origin of the Hitler Plot or The Background of the Hitler Plot. I feel that the title 'The Hitler Plot: 1942' may cause people to think either that there is a misprint or that there was a second plot not connected with the plot of 1944.

I think this is all that I should like to submit to you for consideration. I hope that some of the remarks may be helpful.

Yours ever,

---

[1] Goerdeler had visited Britain in March 1938 but his five secret meetings with the British businessman, A.P. Young, who had hosted a private dinner for him at the National Liberal Club in London in June 1937, took place under the silent auspices of Sir Robert Vansittart at the Foreign Office between August 1938 and March 1939. See A.P. Young, *The 'X' Documents: The Secret History of Foreign Office Contacts with the German Resistance 1937–1939* (London, 1974).

Bell to Leibholz, 4 September 1945, BA, N 1334 (handwritten)

You shall of course have offprints when I get them: say 10.

My dear Leibholz,

Very many thanks for the MS, with its extremely helpful suggestions and revisions, of which I am making very full use. My problem now is to keep it within my limit (Gooch's limit) of 3000 words. And I am working hard at reducing it, with justice to the proportions, now late at night.

Yesterday I saw an Englishman (of the War Office) who personally had many dealings with Goerdeler in London in 1938 and 1939. He confirmed that he saw F.O. people at the highest level (– Vansittart) though I cannot very well in so many words name V.

I will send you the final MS as soon as I can. But I am away in St. Leonards Wednesday – Friday.

You will like to know that after getting the support of the Abp of York,[1] M.E. Aubrey[2] and the Archbp. of Westminster,[3] I have today written to ask Attlee[4] to receive a deputation of the churches next week about conditions in East Germany.[*] I saw Sir A. Cadogan[5] yesterday at the FO. he in no way denied the gravity. I am in touch with Sir A. Salter[6] for briefing. You may see letters from Grűber[7] and Wurm to me in *Man. Guardian* this week.

Yours ever,

[*] I am of course in touch with Abp of Canterbury and hope he may come or [depute]. But I made sure of York.

---

[1] Cyril Forster Garbett (1875–1955) was bishop of Southwark 1919-32; bishop of Winchester 1932–42; Archbishop of York 1942-55.

² Melbourn Evans Aubrey (1885–1957) was General Secretary of the Baptist Union of Great Britain and Ireland, 1925–50. He would become a member of the Central Committee of the World Council of Churches, 1948–54.
³ Bernard William Griffin (1899–1956) was Archbishop of Westminster from 1943 until his death. He was elevated to the cardinalate in 1946 by Pope Pius XII.
⁴ Clement Attlee (1883–1967) was Leader of the Labour Party 1935–55 and Prime Minister 1945–51.
⁵ Sir Alexander Cadogan (1884–1968) was Permanent Under-Secretary for Foreign Affairs, 1938–46.
⁶ James Arthur Salter (1881–1975) was MP for Oxford University, Gladstone Professor of Political Theory and Institutions from 1937–50 and Fellow of All Souls. At this time Salter was Deputy Director-General of the United Nations Relief and Rehabilitation Administration. He would become Baron Salter in 1953.
⁷ Heinrich Grüber (1891–1975) was Reformed theologian, a prominent member of the Confessing Church and an opponent of the Hitler regime. In 1936 he had established a 'Relief Centre for Protestant Non-Aryans' in Berlin to support Christians of Jewish descent. This was named by the Gestapo 'Bureau Pfarrer Grüber'. In 1945 Grüber had re-opened his bureau, now serving survivors returning from the concentration camps, in the American sector of Berlin. On 18 May 1945 Berlin's provisional city council, newly installed by the Soviet occupational power, had appointed Grüber as advisor for ecclesiastical affairs. In the following years of the early Cold War he maintained a link between Eastern and the Western Germany, but in 1964 the government of the GDR denied him entry into East Berlin.

Leibholz to Bell, 7 September 1945, Bell Papers 40, fol. 327 (handwritten)

My dear Lordbishop,

Very many thanks for your letter. I am very glad to see that you think my remarks are helpful to you.

I am [excited] to hear that you will go with a deputation of the Churches to see Attlee and press your points with regard to what is happening in Eastern Germany today. I do not know whether you have seen the enclosed copy of an article published in the *News Chronicle* a fortnight ago. I am also enclosing a copy containing extracts from the *Catholic Herald*. They may interest you. Have you seen the article 'Potsdam and After' in the current issue of the *Contemporary*? It is worthwhile reading just as well as the article in *The Economist* two or three weeks ago. They are much more explicit than the comments I sent you after Potsdam, and they are extremely sharp, if not aggressive.

You may also like to know that Rev. S.B. Wingfield-Digby, SCF. has just returned from Berlin. His present address is: Brinsworthy, Parkstone, Dorset (Tel. Parkstone 155). He will be at this address until Sunday the 9th. He has to return to Germany in about 3 or 4 weeks time, but not to Berlin. He was very kind and helpful to us. You may perhaps like to see him.¹

Yours affectionately,

¹ See Bell to S.B. Wingfield-Digby, 8 September 1945, Bell Papers, Vol. 40, fol. 328.

Bell to Leibholz, 20 September 1945, BA, N 1334 (typewritten)

My dear Leibholz,

I enclose the general reply from the Foreign Office to a question which I asked about visits of people liberated from concentration camps, and exit permits to see relatives liberated. Mr Henderson adds that the military authorities have a very hard task, and are doing everything possible.[1]

Yours ever,

ªI have corrected the proof of my article. You shall have 10 offprints as soon as I get them.

I have just heard from a staff chaplain that Heckel was *denounced* at Treysa (Niemöller in his place)[2] and Marahrens effectively 'boycotted' though still holding office of Bishop of Hannover.

I will proceed to ask permission for you by name to visit your relatives. But please give me any addresses you may have; and also your registration number. I realise your parents-in-law have not been 'liberated from concentration camps'. It would of course help if you could give me the name of a relative who has been liberated – though the strongest claim morally is to see your parents-in-law.ª

[1] See I. L. Henderson to Bell, 11 September 1945 (extract), BA, N 1334.
[2] The first post-war conference of Protestant church leaders took place at Treysa on 27–31 August 1945. This led to the founding of a single Protestant Church in Germany (Evangelische Kirche in Deutschland, EKiD) and to the appointment of its first Council under Bishop Wurm. The first meeting of the newly established Council of the EKiD dismissed Heckel on 31 August 1945. The new head of the ecclesiastical foreign office (Kirchliches Außenamt) was Martin Niemöller.

Leibholz to Bell, 23 September 1945, Bell Papers 40, fols. 329–30 (typewritten)

My Lordbishop,

Very many thanks for your letter and the copy of the general reply from the Foreign Office.

In the meantime, we heard from a friend Mrs von Simson (whose late husband[1] was Secretary of State for Foreign Affaires in Germany in the first few years after 1918 and knew Sir A. Cadogan quite well) that she approached the Home Office and Sir A. Cadogan personally some time ago asking them to allow her daughter in Berlin to come to this country and to stay with her in the next few months. In order not to lose time I thought it might perhaps be wise to submit our case to the Home Office too (not, of course, to Sir A. Cadogan) stating simply the facts, which I thought speak for themselves.

Under the circumstances mentioned I asked first to allow my wife and myself to visit my parents-in-law for a fortnight or so. I added that the bodily strength of our parents had rapidly decreased in the last few months as a result of the terrible distress and all the other experiences they have gone through. I also mentioned that they have written to us that they would enjoy nothing [so much] as to see us once again. – Secondly, I asked for permission to take two members of our family (who had suffered most or could possibly give further valuable information) to this country as visitors for a limited period. I added that in case the Home Office would be inclined to consider favourably this application I should gladly submit the names and provide it with all necessary details. I also said that they could stay with us (or friends) during their visit here.

I posted the letter on August 28 (Ref.L.10258). So far I have not received a reply and I gather from this that the application is still under consideration. Now that you have received the reply from the Foreign Office it would be very good indeed of you if you kindly backed up the application I made to the Home Office. Then I think the application may have a chance of being considered favourably. Unfortunately, I forgot to mention place and address where we should like to go. The address of our parents (it was also Dietrich's address) is 43 Marienburger Allee, Berlin-Charlottenburg 9 (British Zone). The number of the Identity card is EIBN/75/2 (for my wife) and EIBN/75/1 (for myself). Liberated from prison were only my wife's sister Mrs von Dohnanyi (but as early as in 1943) and Pastor Bethge (son-in-law of Schleicher and friend of Dietrich) who is Secretary to Dibelius today: the latter was liberated by the Russians on April 25 (?), 1945.

I think Bethge will send us a report about Treysa in the next few days when Mr Clutton-Brock will again be back in this country. It seems as if – alas – Mr Clutton-Brock does not think to go back to Berlin for a longer time. It was, above all, he through whom we established the contacts with our people in Berlin and I am greatly indebted to him for all that he has done for our family there. Unfortunately all the parcels we were able to send to Berlin cannot be really effective as we have still 16 members of our family in Berlin (among them the parents, my wife's three sisters and ten children). I feel the responsibility for all of them very heavily on my shoulders. I hope that Hahn will take two or three of the boys to Salem so that they are able to finish their education. Niebuhr wrote to us that he would like to raise a special ecumenical fund in honour of Dietrich and for the sake of the children in America and that he wrote to Leiper in this matter. This would already be a great help as you know that my own financial position is unsettled and very weak.[2] I think the most urgent need is to get food to Berlin and I do everything in my power to mobilize all possible sources (Red Cross, Quakers, British friends and Americans).

We have also had the first letter from Dietrich's fiancée. It is very moving. We should very much like her to be included in any scheme made in honour of Dietrich. Dietrich somewhat foresaw his fate and did not want to burden her with it. Now, she fled from the Russians and, of course, lost everything. She now hopes to go to Göttingen[3] to read there (I think theology) and I am just going to write to the newly appointed rector there (who is, in point of fact, my successor) asking him to see after her. Perhaps there will be a possibility for her of going to this country or the United States for a year or so later on.

I am enclosing the stencilled copy of the Cheltenham address in case you like to have it. Oliver Tomkins[4] suggested that Oldham should embody it in a supplement. But I do not think that it suits this purpose.

I was very much glad to see the letter in the press concerning the food situation in Germany.[5] I very much hope that the action the Churches have taken at your initiative will strengthen the attitude of the government.

Yours ever,

---

[1] Ernst von Simson (1876–1941) married to Martha Oppenheim (1882–1971) and had to give up all his positions in 1937. He emigrated to Britain.

² This and the following sentence are marked by a black line in the margin.
³ Göttingen University was reopened on 3 September 1945.
⁴ Oliver Tomkins (1908–92), Anglican priest; Secretary of the WCC from 1945 to 1952; Bishop of Bristol, 1959–75.
⁵ The letter published to announce the creation of Christian Reconstruction in Europe: see *The Times*, 12 September 1945, p. 7, col. c. The 'Save Europe Now' campaign was now in full swing. See Matthew Frank, 'The new morality: Victor Gollancz, 'Save Europe Now' and the German Refugee Crisis, 1945–6', in *Twentieth Century British History*, 2006, Vol. 17 (2), pp. 230–56.

Leibholz to Bell, 24 September 1945, Bell Papers 40, fol. 331 (telegram)
PLEASE STOP LETTER HOME OFFICE NEWS RECEIVED BERLIN LETTER FOLLOWS = LEIBHOLZ

Leibholz to Bell, 27 September 1945, Bell Papers 40, fol. 332 (typewritten); BA, N 1334 (copy)

My Lordbishop,
Please forgive my troubling you with the telegram. But my father-in-law whose balanced judgement I very much value wrote to us in his last letter that things in Berlin are still rather chaotic as far as the entrance to Berlin through the Russian zone is concerned. This is why he advises us not to come just now, although he wants nothing as much as to see us as quickly as possible. The point is that we should have to pass the Russian zone as Germans coming from this country and this may, in fact, attract special Russian attention. I gather from other letters received that one of our nephews who recently crossed the Russian zone had been completely plundered, and another friend was even brought to a Russian prisoner of war camp. I am making further enquiries and as soon as I have received more encouraging news I will write to you again and ask you kindly to lend me your support and to back up my application to the Home Office. ᶜButᶜ I have not withdrawn it.

I am enclosing a letter of Bethge. He asked me to correct the English. But as the attempt to put the letter into purer English would affect the whole character of the letter I think it better to leave the letter as it stands and to ask you to excuse the obvious mistakes.

As to Treysa I have received the report of it and I should like to send it to you in case you should want to see it: it is written in German. On the whole, the constitutional and organisational questions stand in the foreground of the discussion. It is rather disturbing to see that in spite of the fact that the Churches have to perform so many important tasks these questions played such a big part in the debate. But this weakness is inherent in the German Protestant Church. A Council of the Evangelical Church in Germany has been constituted. The Council consists of 12 members. It is represented by Wurm, Niemöller, Meiser,¹ Dibelius, Lilje, Held² and Niesel.³ I feel that the younger generation is not duly represented. Apart from that the record of some of those who took part in Treysa is, unfortunately, not very clean.

Yours ever,

¹ Hans Meiser (1881–1956), in 1933–55, was the first bishop of the Evangelical Lutheran Church in Bavaria.

² Heinrich Held (1897–1957) was German pastor, member of the Confessing Church; from 1949 Präses (head) of the Protestant Rhenish Church and until 1954 Member of the Council of the Protestant Church in Germany.

³ Wilhelm Niesel (1903–88), Reformed theologian. He served as moderator of the Communion of the Reformed Churches in Germany (*Reformierter Bund*), 1946–73; he was a member of the Central Committee of the WCC, 1948–68, and President of the World Communion of Reformed Churches, 1964–70.

Bell to Leibholz, 2 October 1945, BA, N 1334 (typewritten); Bell Papers 40, fol. 333 (carbon)

My dear Leibholz,

I have been away in East Sussex during the last few days – hence my delay in replying to your two letters.

It does certainly seem from what your father-in-law says that it would be wiser for you to postpone your visit to Berlin, greatly as you and your parents-in-law long to meet. I will certainly support your application to the Home Office whenever you want it.

I am greatly touched by Bethge's letter. I will write to him myself, and I take it I may send my reply through you? What I should particularly like would be the original German of Dietrich's words quoted by Bethge. They are most moving.

I hope that the *Contemporary* will arrive in a day or two. You shall have twelve copies at once. I wonder who it is at Treysa whose record was not very clean? Pastor Forell told me that he had spoken some firm and plain words to Mahrarens who was there, though not invited.¹

Yours ever,

¹ Though German and British people intended the resignation of August Marahrens as bishop of Hannover he was indeed invited to Treysa 'but was to all intents and purposes boycotted by the other leaders. He was silent throughout the conference and was not invited to speak.' See Besier, *Selbstreinigiung*, p. 125; see too Bell to Leibholz, 20 September 1945. The records of the conference do not quote the conversation of Forell with Marahrens; for an historical overview and discussion see Gerhard Besier et al. (eds.), *Der Kompromiß von Treysa* (Weinheim 1995). Besides the information supplied by Bethge's memorandum, Bell learnt of the meeting from Martin Albertz; see Albertz to Bell, 17 September 1945, EZA Berlin 50/557/1.

Sabine Leibholz to Bell, 2 October 1945, Bell Papers Vol. 42, fols. 92–3 (handwritten)

My dear Lordbishop,

As you have written to us, that you would like to have the German translation of what Dietrich wrote to Bethge, I think you might also like to see some of the German poems Dietrich wrote in prison. I think you have already seen the first, long poem (I believe Rieger sent it) which Dr. Visser 't Hooft is going to publish in Switzerland. So I only enclose the three others.

Today I had a letter from Lt. Ford¹ saying that he has been to see my whole family in Berlin and had a good talk with them. He got all the information about the 20th of July 1944 for which he had been looking. I was very pleased to hear from him, that he was able to take to my relatives some American field ration cans, as they, especially the children, are going very hungry there. That is a constant worry for me. We are most grateful for your Appeal 'Save Europe Now'. My youngest sister, a clergyman's wife in Berlin, is very active in helping the refugees from the Eastern provinces.² She spends hours on the Wannsee station, where people still arrive in the most deplorable condition. There is a lack of everything, food, shoes, clothing, medicines, soap etc. Although having been bombed out totally, and living under most difficult conditions with her husband and two young children herself, she is sheltering, cleaning and feeding many children every night – the food being got together in the parish by voluntary contributions. On Sunday every worshipper brings one slice of bread to Church, which is collected and brought to the Stations.

Last week we have seen Mr. Clutton-Brock in London. He has been very kind and ready to help. I think he will be back in Berlin by now.

With kind regards
Yours affectionately,

---

[1] Franklin L. Ford (1920–2003) was an officer in the U.S. Strategic Services during the war. Afterwards he published one of the first articles on the German resistance in the United States ('The Twentieth of July in the History of the German Resistance', *American Historical Review*, Vol. 51, Issue 4, July 1946, pp. 609–26). It became his first important publication. Ford and Bell corresponded during this period. Ford would go on to become a distinguished and much admired historian at Harvard University.

[2] Susanne Bonhoeffer, who had married Walter Dress in 1929.

Leibholz to Bell, 3 October 1945, Bell Papers 40, fols. 334–5 (typewritten); BA, N 1334 (copy)

My Lordbishop,

Very many thanks for your letter and the October issue of *The Contemporary Review*, which I have received this morning. Thank you also for your kind intention to send me copies of your article. I shall be very glad to have them. I will send half of them to Germany and the remainder to people in this country, the United States and Switzerland. It will be very difficult to raise an objection to what you say: for the facts and the conclusions drawn from them cannot be disputed. I only hope that the article will find among the public the attention it deserves. In *The Times* of today your article was especially dealt with in the review of the monthly periodicals. – By the way, in the same issue in which your article appeared I read a good review on Wiener's pamphlet.¹

As to Treysa I feel somehow that the younger generation is not duly represented in the new Council. The gap left by Dietrich's death has not been filled. But it is probably not possible to fill it. When I spoke in my last letter of people whose record does not seem to me very clean I had in mind the two jurists who were there. First, Eric Wolf (Prof. of Jurisprudence) who was entrusted with the drawing up of the new constitution for the Evangelical Church, was ᶜfirstᶜ a Socialist under Weimar and ᶜthenᶜ a National Socialist in 1933.² I still remember having read in 1938 his memoranda for the Research Department of the World Council. In these memo. [sic] he tried to reconcile the whole stuff of Nazi ideology with the Christian dogma. I feel rather anxious to see him now. – Further, as to Smend, who is a member of the new council, it is true he was never a Nazi and that he is a very able man.³ He had become professor in Göttingen when I was dismissed and he has now been appointed rector of the university by the British. I do not mind the right-wing political views he had in former times.[4] What I much more deprecate is his weakness and his incapacity to make a real stand in a risky situation. Although my experience with him goes only as far as 1938 I feel sure that he would never have joined our people or would have actively supported them. He belongs to the large group of secret sympathisers ªand waverersª. I admit I may have become too hard in judging people. But there are too many who acted like Smend. I have now written to him to take care of Dietrich's fiancée Maria von Wedemeyer who wants to study in Göttingen and who has not been admitted for technical reasons. I wonder how he will react.

I am also very keen on getting the original German of Dietrich's words quoted by Bethge and I will ask him to send them to us. Of course, I will pass on any letter you may like to write to Bethge.

I am making further investigations about our possible going to Berlin and I will write to you again as soon as I get better news. In any case, it is a great comfort to us to know that you will back up our application to the Home Office as soon as circumstances allow.

Would you be kind enough to let me know when you are actually thinking of going to Berlin. Bethge wrote to me that there were rumours in Treysa that you would be coming to the conference.[5] If you go I should like to write to you again and ask you kindly to take a letter with you for our parents.

I wonder what you think about the recent political development. I should not have ventured to think that all that what we feared would become a political reality so soon. I still remember the *Times*' articles some time ago pointing out again and again that it were [sic] only German and other mischiefmakers who sowed seeds of discord among the United Nations and went on with Goebbels' work. I wonder whether Mr Carr traces back the present disunity to the same kind of mischiefmaking. The recent events seem to me to prove the complete failure of the policy of the Western countries as initiated and sponsored by Mr Roosevelt and Mr Churchill and supported by public opinion and the overwhelming majority of the population. They seem to me to prove again that an ideological issue was and is still underlying the present power conflict. Today people are complaining of the Russians being so reserved, suspicious and distrustful. I think this attitude is due to the difference in the basic ideological outlook between West and East. If we are frank I think we must admit that Mr Churchill's and Roosevelt's policy have led (at least this country) to a big political defeat. For the fact that this policy is ªnowª crowned with the division of Europe in different zones of influence means that half of Europe has been lost to Great Britain and to Europe herself. The nationalistic unconditional surrender policy was of the same kind as the appeasement policy towards the Nazis – a short-sighted policy without any imagination.

I even fear that the loss of half of Europe will not be the last page of the story. People in this country think that at least it will be possible to hold Western Europe including the Western part of Germany. But Western Europe cannot live without Central Europe, especially in an atomic age. This is why, from a Western or European point of view, I have always considered it a political crime to give up all the territories West of the Oder including Thuringia and Saxony. The only excuse for this disastrous decision at Yalta may have been the weakness of this country. But there are people of standing who say that Great Britain's position was not so weak and that the pressure brought upon her at Yalta could have been resisted.

Further, I doubt whether the Russians will acquiesce in the creation of a Western block. The Russians are against closer association of the Western countries and although they themselves claim special zones of influence they contest similar claims by the Western countries. As you know, my Lordbishop, the Russians have already appointed a new German (on the whole, communist) government in their zone. I think we shall not have to wait for long until the new German government backed by Russia will demand the national unification of the Reich. Then the Rhine will be the Russian borderline, especially if the Americans should leave the American zone before long. To judge from former experiences, I am afraid people in this country will wake up too late and will begin to revise their sterile and negative policy towards Germany when the Russians will have created a 'fait accompli'. I fear that the Western countries will again miss their opportunity.

The tragedy is that the people have always to pay for the political mistakes of their leaders whom they have backed without having been duly enlightened at the real issue at stake [sic]. Hitler's saying that phrases such as 'I have not thought of this' or 'I had no faith in it' can never excuse a policy, seems to me true: it applies to totalitarianism as well as to Western democracy.

In the October issue of *The Hibbert Journal* you will find an article about the two possible types of democracy.[6] The article, which contains a part of my work may interest you since the subject is just now controversial. Unfortunately, I shall receive no off-prints. But I think you wrote to me that you take the *Hibbert* in. Otherwise I will send you a copy of the whole issue.

John asked me to tell you that he would also like to come to Chichester if this should suit you better.

Yours ever,

---

[1] For the monthly review of journal articles see *The Times*, 3 October 1945, p. 6 col. 2. Peter Wiener, *Martin Luther: Hitler's Spiritual Ancestor* (London, 1944); a polemic arguing that the roots of National Socialism were to be found in the prophet of the German Reformation.

[2] Erik Wolf (1902–77), held a Chair in the history of jurisprudence and the philosophy of right at Freiburg University, 1930–67. At the beginning of the Third Reich he sympathized with the NSDAP and became Dean of the Law Faculty under Martin Heidegger, who was then Rector of the university. In 1937 he became a member of the NSDAP, but in the year before a member of the Confessing Church. In 1942 Wolf was a member of the Freiburg Circle, a group of academics which gathered around the historian Gerhard Ritter. Wolf wrote a section discussing the legal system in their memorandum 'Politische Gemeinschaftsordnung' ('The Political Order of the community'). The memorandum envisaged a Germany after Hitler and after the war it became the subject of an ecumenical discussion. In 1946–48 Wolf was chairman of the Constitution Committee of the Evangelical Church in Germany and in 1948 delegate to the WCC Conference at Amsterdam. He became one of the most widely respected authorities on Church Law in Germany, following the theological teaching of Karl Barth and, unlike Leibholz, repudiating Natural Law.

[3] Rudolf Smend (1882–1975) became Professor of public law in Tübingen in 1911, in Bonn in 1915 and then in Berlin in 1922. Under political pressure he moved to Göttingen in 1935, where he lectured until 1965. In 1945–55 Smend was a member of the Council of the Evangelical Church in Germany, while between 1945 and 1969 he ran the Institute of Church Law of the Evangelical Church in Germany at Göttingen. His main interest lay in Church-State relations.

[4] See Smend's 'Intergrationslehre' in Klaus Tanner, *Die fromme Verstaatlichung des Gewissens. Zur Auseinandersetzung um die Legitimität der Weimarer Reichsverfassung in Staatsrechtswissenschaft und Theologie der zwanziger Jahre* (Göttingen, 1989), esp. pp. 123–5. For the relationship of his thought to that of Leibholz about the end of the Weimar Republic see ibid., pp. 143–5.

[5] Bell was invited by Bishop Wurm but he received no Exit-permit from the British authorities; see Bell Papers, Vol. 9, fols. 378, 385. Only his address to the delegates could be read in Treysa.
[6] Gerhard Leibholz, 'Two Types of Democracy', reprinted in *Politics and Law*, pp. 37–48.

Bell to Leibholz, 5 October 1945, BA, N 1334 (typewritten); Bell Papers 40, fol. 336 (carbon)

My dear Leibholz,

Very many thanks to you and Sabine for your letters today. This is an immediate answer, to thank Sabine for the poems, and to say how glad I am that I can get the German translation of what Dietrich wrote to Bethge. I enclose a letter for Bethge, if you would kindly send it.

I think there is every hope now that I shall be able to go to Germany on October 17 or thereabouts.[1] The Archbishop of Canterbury has heard from the War Office generally approving a proposal for delegations. The British Council of Churches is to send a delegation: but this will take some time, and the Archbishop has agreed that I should go with the World Council instead.[2] I saw one of the principal Secretaries of the War Office yesterday, and he thought there would be no difficulty. I am taking the Rev. E. Gordon Rupp with me.[3] He is a young Methodist, Principal Flew's[4] assistant at Cambridge, and an extremely good German scholar. The Lutterworth Press are publishing a reply by him to Wiener.[5]

I am applying to go first to Stuttgart, for the meeting of the Reich Council[6]; thence into the French zone, Baden-Baden perhaps; to the British zone, Hannover, etc; and to Berlin; I am also trying for Breslau. The British, of course, can only deal with the British zone. What I shall be able to do in the way of visiting friends during my short visit I don't know; but of course I shall see your parents-in-law. I am making enquiries: but it seems as though I am not allowed to take food in. Do you know what the possibilities are?

I will of course investigate the wishes and possibilities in Berlin for a visit from yourself.

I feel much sympathy with what you say about the political and moral catastrophe in Europe. And I am also much interested in what you say about two members of the Reich Council.

Yours affectionately,

---

[1] Bell visited Germany on 18–30 October 1945.
[2] For the planning of the visit and the visit itself see the reports of Willem A. Visser 't Hooft, Alphons Koechlin, and Bell in Clemens Vollnhals (ed.), *Die evangelische Kirche nach dem Zusammenbruch. Berichte ausländischer Beobachter aus dem Jahr 1945* (Göttingen, 1988), pp. 194–233; see too Jasper, *George Bell*, pp. 293–5.
[3] See E. Gordon Rupp, *I Seek My Brethren. Bishop George Bell and the German Churches* (London, 1975), pp. 24–8.
[4] Robert Newton Flew (1886–1962) was Methodist minister, theologian and ecumenist; at this time Professor of New Testament Language and Literature at Wesley House, Cambridge. Newton Flew was Moderator of the Free Church Federal Council, 1945-6. He was also the first non-Anglican to be awarded a Doctorate in Divinity by the University of Oxford.
[5] This became *Martin Luther: Hitler's Cause – or Cure? A Reply to Peter Wiener* (London, 1945).
[6] The body newly established by the Treysa conference.

Leibholz to Bell, 12 October 1945, Bell Papers 40, fol. 337 (typewritten); BA, N 1334 (copy)

My Lordbishop,
Very many thanks for your letter of October 5. What good news that you will go to Germany (including Berlin and possibly even Breslau) on October 17.

Please give all our love to our parents and family in Berlin and tell them that we very much hope to be able with your help to go to Berlin before long. In the meantime, I have made further inquiries. We no longer need a special Exit-permit (but, of course, travelling papers and re-entry permit). The main difficulty still is to get the permit by the Allied Control Commission in Germany (Bad Oeynhausen). So far it seems as if for mere compassionate grounds a permit has not been granted. I have been advised that if I make such an application I should do it with a letter by you. Therefore, we should like to make this application unless our parents tell you that the situation in Berlin is still too chaotic. It also seems as if, at least in theory, we could go by airoplane if we can secure the permit of the British Control Commission.

In case you happen to see Smend (one of the 12 members of the Council) in Stuttgart would you perhaps be so very kind as to ask him whether he received my letters concerning Dietrich's fiancée, Maria von Wedemeyer whose application for reading mathematics in Göttingen was refused on the grounds that she is a woman and a newcomer. In the meantime, I have learned that there is a special regulation, according to which women are allowed to study if their husbands or parents have become victims of the Nazis. A proper interpretation of the rule, therefore, seems to justify her admission.

Then I should like to submit to you a second request in the interest of my parents-in-law:

Up-to-now Clutton-Brock has done something for them: but he will probably leave Berlin before long. I think it would give them some protection if you were kind enough to leave with them a letter simply stating the facts of the case and asking for special protection by the occupation authorities. You know that my father-in-law (about 78) is one of the leading German psychiatrists and neurologists and is an honorary fellow of the Royal Society for Medicine in London. It seems as if the society has taken some action with the Control Commission in Berlin to protect him. But I am not perfectly sure. In any case, we know that my parents-in-law would be very grateful to you for such a letter. They would then be able to produce the letter in case of need and this would certainly prove very helpful.

Please forgive my troubling you with these minor personal matters. But I feel we must do everything in our power to ease their external position. But I do not wish to trouble you with asking to take some food with you, all the more as you go first to other places. I met Rupp in London yesterday and he is prepared to take a small parcel with him.

I was very glad indeed to see in the *Times* of yesterday that your resolution concerning the expulsion of Germans was carried unanimously.[1] But the way in which *The Times* dealt with the matter did not seem to me very fair.

By the way, E. Wolf, about whom I wrote to you in my last letter and who is now playing rather an important part in the attempt to re-organise the Church is not a member of the Council. But he was Dean of the law faculty in Freiburg 1933 and 1934. I have also seen the names of the men who are invited by Wurm to come to a Conference at Boll. I can only say that the selection of the jurists (I know something about four of them) is not fortunate. If *former* national-socialists or nationalists are to play a *leading* part in the new organisation of the Church I fear things will not develop very satisfactory [sic]. At this Conference Visser 't Hooft, Schönfeld and Gerstenmaier were also present and delivered addresses.

With our best wishes for your journey from Sabine and myself

Yours affectionately,

---

[1] Bell's resolution deploring the expulsion of German families from Poland and Czechoslovakia where they had lived as minorities had been accompanied by a second resolution proposed by the Bishop of Sheffield, Leslie Hunter, at the York Convocation. See *Chronicle of Convocation of Canterbury*, sessions of 10, 11, 12 October 1945, pp. 160-7, 187-96; *York Journal of Convocation*, 10, 11, 12 October 1945, pp. 8, 54-8. The British Council of Churches had also passed a resolution on 4 October 1945 which called for the implementation of Article 12 of the Potsdam Protocol. See Matthew Frank, *Expelling the Germans: British Opinion and Post-1945 Population Transfer in Context* (Oxford, 2007), pp. 122-63.

Bell to Gerhard and Sabine Leibholz, 30 October 1945, BA, N 1334 (handwritten)

My dear friends,

I was with your parents and the family circle yesterday (Monday) afternoon for about half an hour between 4 and 5. Bethge conducted me to their house. It was a great joy to see them – and to speak of Dietrich. Your parents are well, but looked tired and grieving as you would indeed suppose. But they were happy that I came. And I saw the latest Dietrich[1] of 2 (?) years old – and his mother – a great-grandson. They showed me photos of D. We arranged about 'Ethic'[2] in principle with the hope it might be published in German & English with a small memoir with help from Pastor Dress (?) fellow student at Tübingen – and I am also hoping to start a memorial fund for D. in England. I will write later about attitude to visit by you to Germany – when I have it a little clearer (and of course all depends on possibility of F.O. permission). I got all those in the house to write their names on the enclosed sheet in my pocketbook. I had a *wonderful* time. I will write about it. Press Conference (probably) MOI on Thursday 11.30.

All affectionate greetings as you know from your home –
and

Your affectionate friend,

---

[1] Dietrich Bethge, born on 3 February 1944, was the son of Renate and Eberhard.
[2] Eberhard Bethge was now editing the manuscripts written between 1940 and 1943 in a systematic order. The first edition of Bonhoeffer's *Ethik* was published by Chr. Kaiser in Munich in 1949. Translated by Neville Horton Smith, *Ethics* was published by Macmillan in the United States (New York, 1955), and the SCM Press published a second impression in 1971.

Leibholz to Bell, 31 October 1945, Bell Papers 40, fol. 338 (handwritten); BA, N 1334 (copy)

My dear Lordbishop,

How extremely good of you to write to us immediately after the strain of your home-journey. This as well as what you say in your letter has deeply moved us.

I am delighted to hear that you had such a wonderful time in Germany. Our thoughts went out daily to you in those days and we often talked about your probable whereabouts in those two weeks. It would be very kind of you to let us have a copy of the paper in which you will write about your experiences and impressions. I am also looking forward to what you are going to say at the Press Conference on Thursday.

I wonder whether my wife's parents have talked to you on [sic] their new grief. The only remaining son (out of four) who is professor of Physical Chemistry in Leipzig has been taken away by the Russians and they (and his family in Leipzig) have not heard from him for a couple of weeks.[1] He is one of the leading scientists in atom research and refused to go on with it under the Nazis. Now, the Russians have got hold of him. When a couple of months ago it became known that the Russians would occupy Leipzig I wrote to the Research Department of Shaef[2] (to Major Blount[3] who was in contact with you) to call their attention to the facts mentioned and I asked them to consider the transfer of the family to the Western Zone. In fact, they considered it °but acted° so slowly that they were too late, and I now fear °that° the Russians will extort him. I am going to write to the Russian Embassy to find out the address of Kakkerin (= Kokorin), Molotow's nephew, with whom Dietrich spent a couple of weeks in Buchenwald and other prisons (learning Russian and trying to convert him).[4] He might perhaps intervene or at least find out his present whereabouts.

In the meantime, I have heard from Schütz that his wife (also a German who has her relatives in Germany) has managed to go to Germany. She obviously goes as a correspondent and Schütz told me that I should try to find a similar job for Sabine in case there should be an opportunity of my going to Germany. Now after the eldest and last son has been taken from Sabine's parents I feel that it will be their special wish to see Sabine. In addition, I may tell you this as my very trusted friend confidentially – after all Sabine has gone through and is still suffering she is psychically labil [unstable] and from this point of view, it would be very disquieting to leave her behind. Sabine's father who knows Sabine very well wrote in the letter you sent me that he would like to talk about this difficulty even with you but I do not know whether this was possible and he could make himself understood. Therefore, I am thinking of perhaps getting into touch with one of the religious papers (*Church Times*, or *Guardian*, or *New British Weekly*,[5] I know Mairet[6] quite well) with a view of arranging something in this respect, if you think I should. Or could she perhaps possibly do some welfare work for the Church of England during her stay in Germany?

Once again very many thanks

Yours affectionately,

There is a broadcast in memory of Dietrich (in German) on Friday evening between 9 and 9.30 p.m. on wave length 1200. – Some of his poems have been translated, in the meantime, by Leishman[7] into English. L. is – as far as I can see – the best available man for the translation of German poems in this country. Has also translated Hölderlin and Rilke. I will send you copies as soon as the translations have been copied.

1. Karl Friedrich Bonhoeffer (1899–1957) was the eldest brother of Sabine and, from 1934, Professor of physical chemistry at Leipzig University. His special field was the research of heavy hydrogen but he desisted from participating in the government-sponsored research on uranium in 1939. His abduction by the Soviet forces ended a short time later (see Leibholz to Bell, 5 November 1945) and he was allowed to travel to Berlin. In 1947 Klaus Bonhoeffer got a Chair in physical chemistry at Berlin University and was also appointed Director of the Kaiser Wilhelm Institute for physical- and electro-chemistry. In 1949 he became Director of the Max Planck Institute for Physical Chemistry in Göttingen.
2. Supreme Headquarters of the Allied Expeditionary Force.
3. Formerly Dean of St. Peter's Hall, Oxford, 1939–45, Blount served as a Major in the Army Intelligence Corps and then in the Control Commission in Germany and Austria.
4. See H.M. Falconer to Leibholz, 1 October 1945; see too Sigismund Payne Best, *The Venlo Incident* (London, 1950), pp. 171–3.
5. The *Church Times* represented Anglo-Catholic opinion in the Church of England while the *Guardian* was more broadly based and liberal. The *New British Weekly* was the voice of English and Welsh Congregationalism.
6. Philip Mairet (1886–1975) was designer, writer and journalist, also editor of the *New English Weekly*.
7. James Blair Leishman (1902–63) was leading translator of German poetry and from 1946 University Lecturer in English Literature at the University of Oxford.

Bell to Leibholz, 31 October 1945, BA, N 1334 (typewritten)

Confidential

My dear Leibholz,

I have been asked *confidentially* to give a list of German books which it would be useful to make available in fairly substantial numbers in the British Zone. I am most anxious to give as good an answer as I possibly can, for I have been able, I think, to make some powerful connections with the authorities, which will serve for later on. The books wanted are German classics, and I suppose some recent books written before Hitler. I should be very grateful if you could send me a list of 12 or 20, in the order of your choice, and let me have it by Saturday ᵃor Mondayᵃ.

I had a talk with Dr Smend at Stuttgart about Dietrich's fiancée, and he told me that the number of applicants for vacancies was immense. Of course he knew you, and when I told him about the Bonhoeffers, and her relationship to Dietrich, and spoke of the claim which the victims of Hitler had, he said that was so, and that he would see what he could do. At the request I gave him the name, and the faculty.

I was also glad to hear from the head of the Education Branch in the Control Commission that the Rectors of German Universities, on the initiative of Dr Smend (who is Rector of Göttingen), had passed a resolution welcoming the help of University Professors now in exile.[1] I will send you a copy of the resolution as soon as I can.

Yours ever,

1. 1st resolution of the conference of the university rectors in the British zone, 26/27 September 1945, published in Manfred Heinemann (ed.), *Hochschuloffiziere und Wiederaufbau des Hochschulwesens in Westdeutschland 1945-1952*, vol. 1: Die Britische Zone (Hildesheim 1990), pp. 70, 549. The initiative for the resolution did not come from Smend, but from the British Education Branch; see Anikó Szabó, *Vertreibung, Rückkehr, Wiedergutmachung. Göttinger Hochschullehrer im Schatten des Nationalsozialismus* (Göttingen, 2000), pp. 238–9.

Leibholz to Bell, 2 November 1945, Bell Papers 40, fols. 339–40 (typewritten); BA, N 1334 (copy)

My Lordbishop,

Very many thanks for your letter. I am delighted to hear that you have been able to make some powerful connections with the authorities in Germany.

I am enclosing a list of books, which I hope may serve your purpose. I hope I have been right in excluding religious and scientific books and writers in German who are not themselves of German origin like the Austrians and the Swiss. I am not perfectly sure as to whether the books wanted are to be collected or selected works of German classical authors. Therefore, I have put in brackets a concrete suggestion in case the publication of the collected works might prove impossible. The Oxford book of German verse and of German prose is an excellent selection of German lyric and prose and it seems to me to be a good idea to reprint these books in Germany in order to show (apart from other reasons) how much German lyric and prose has been appreciated in this country for a long time.

It was very good of you to think of Maria v. Wedemeyer, in spite of all you had in your mind during your journey. We thank you very much for it.

I should very much like to see the exact wording of the resolution you refer to in your letter. If it runs about as mentioned, I fear that the resolution has been passed to please the British authorities without having any real meaning. Smend is a clever diplomat of anti-liberal and nationalist leanings. In my view, the resolution should have stated that the German universities would do everything possible to make good the wrong the Nazis have done to scientists and that all university-professors, lecturers etc. deprived of their Chair would be fully reinstated in their former position if such a desire is expressed by the people concerned. I have seen from a letter by Smend to a friend of mine that e.g. in my former faculty vacancies have been filled, among others, of [sic] people who are in America and have thus had no possibility at all of considering to go back to Germany in future.[1]

I wonder whether you think it wise to approach the Head of the Educational Branch of the Control Commission and to ask him whether he would submit to the Law faculty in Göttingen as a test case the question whether – considering the resolution of the Rectors of the universities – they wish me to come back in case I should contemplate such a possibility.[2] Not that I am keen on considering this question under the special circumstances in which our family as a whole finds itself today in Germany. But I do not know how things will develop here. If they say 'no' the position is at least clear. If they say 'yes' then we may see together what decision seems to us to be best taking all other possibilities and plans into account. You know I feel very strongly the responsibility for the whole family in their distress and so far I have been able to do much more for them from here than if I had been in Germany. Perhaps there may also be a chance of doing something more important in future than holding a chair in Göttingen. I raise the question only because in a short time the vacancy may be filled and I do not know if I can afford this. In point of fact, my old faculty does not exist any longer (half of it has died, in the meantime, the other half was transferred resp. dismissed [sic]) and Smend will have to give the answer. As he has obviously not broached the question when he talked to you I feel he will take evasive action for reasons I may perhaps tell you some other time.

The facts concerning my person and work are well known in Göttingen. The British authorities can find them in the '*Deutsche Gelehrtenkalender*', the '*Wer ist's*', in '*Who's Who*' (Intern. Edit.), the *American Biographical Encyclopaedia of the World* (1945). Of course, they do not know what I have done during the last seven years here: they may also not know that we lost three brothers, two brothers-in-law and one sister-in-law by the Nazis, four of them as you know in various concentration camps last April.

I have so far not sent you the last copy of *The Hibbert Journal*: you may perhaps like to see the article on the 'Two Types of Democracy'.

Yours ever,

List of Books

1. Goethe (especially Faust I and II)
2. Des Knaben Wunderhorn
3. Hölderlin (especially Hyperion)
4. Lessing (especially Nathan der Weise and his philos. writings)
5. Kant (especially Zum ewigen Frieden: Die Religion)
6. Wilhelm von Humboldt (Selected Works in the edition by Felix Meiner)
7. Schleiermacher (Monologen)
8. Heine (especially Gedichte: Reisebilder: Buch der Lieder)
9. Mathias Claudius, Gläubiges Herz (Alfred Kröner Verlag)
10. Schiller (especially Die ästhetische Erziehung des Menschen)
11. Novalis, Hymnen an die Nacht
12. Oxford Book of German Verse (Selection of German poems)
13. Oxford Book of German Prose (Selection of German prose)
14. Stefan George, Deutsche Dichtung (selection of German lyric)
15. Thomas Mann (especially Die Familie Buddenbrock[3])
16. Rilke, Gedichte
17. Hugo von Hofmannsthal, Gedichte (and esp. Tor und Tod)*
18. Burckhardt, Kultur der Renaissance
19. Mommsen, Römische Geschichte
20. Möricke (especially Gedichte)

* MÄRCHEN by J. Grimm

[1] This information appears to be incorrect: see Szabó, *Vertreibung*, pp. 258–9, 368–9.
[2] According to Smend, who reported on the conference of university rectors in the British zone, 26/27 September 1945, the university Göttingen had written to all professors in exile who could be reached to assure them that they remained members of their old university; see Heinemann, *Rektorenkonferenz*, p. 69. Such a message appears not to have reached Leibholz.
[3] The exact title is *Buddenbrooks. Verfall einer Familie*.

Bell to Leibholz, 3 November 1945, BA, N 1334 (typewritten); Bell Papers 40, fol. 341 (carbon)

My dear Leibholz,
I enclose an Order Paper for the House of Lords.

Please note Vansittart's motion for November 20th. I am proposing, as at present advised, to speak on this motion.[1] I found people in the French zone anxious to know what the British and Americans thought of de Gaulle's plan for 'Western Europe'; and I found very high up in the British zone, in Berlin, a regret that de Gaulle had committed himself to such a programme. But what does 'Western Europe' mean? I should be very grateful if you could give me any reflections, which might be useful for a speech. There is no hurry – if you were able to let me have them in say a week or ten days' time.

Yes, your parents did tell me about what the Russians had done in connection with your brother-in-law in Leipzig. They were much worried. I wish there was something that I could do. I take it that what is likely to have happened is that your brother-in-law has been taken to Russia, with promises of excellent treatment if he will work for the Soviet, and an offer to fetch his wife: but it is deplorable. I do hope you will soon have news.

I enclose the text of the resolution of which I spoke in my last letter. It is for some reason marked 'Confidential' by the Education Officer so we must not publish it. But you will be glad to see it.

Yours ever,

[1] Lord Vansittart's motion was postponed until 13 December and finally until 24 January 1946. On 23 October 1945 he still made a long speech about Germany. To this Bell made no answer. See Hansard, H.L. Deb., Vol. 137, cols. 412–40 (23 October 1945).

Leibholz to Bell, 5 November 1945, Bell Papers 40, fol. 342 (typewritten); BA, N 1334 (copy)

My Lordbishop,
Very many thanks for your letter.

I will write to you in greater detail what I think about the plan of 'Western Europe'. I am not perfectly sure whether Vansittart actually wants the same as de Gaulle and advocates the inclusion of Western Germany into Western Europe. If I am not mistaken there are considerable differences. In any case, can Western Europe live by itself? I hope to write a Memo. about 'Europe' for a Birmingham lecture within the next fortnight. Therefore, I should be glad to know when you wish to have my reflections by the latest. Would the 13th or 14th of November suit you?

I am delighted to tell you that the Russians have released Karl Friedrich and that he is back in Leipzig. This is the latest news received today. We are very thankful for his deliverance and I am so very glad to know that this additional sorrow does not afflict my wife's parents any longer: but it seems as if he is not allowed to visit his parents – obviously because the Russians fear that the Americans may take him.

We also had a letter from my wife's mother full of joy and thankfulness for having had the opportunity of seeing you. The parents were deeply moved by your visit.

Thank you also for kindly passing on to me the resolution mentioned in your last letter. I am very sorry to see that what I hypothetically wrote was not well founded because the lines of the resolution are perfectly fair. They could hardly even be fairer.[1] Therefore, please forget what I wrote to you about the approach to the Head of the Educational Branch of the Control Commission. The position seems quite clear. Later on, in case things enter another and possibly more acute stage, I will consult you. For my future decision what to do depends on your advice.

I am enclosing today the copy of a letter by Major Falconer about Dietrich.[2] I know you will like to have it. One point is not correct. Dietrich was not shot but hanged. Falconer, when asked by me on this point, wrote to me in another letter: He should not have been so specific on this point. He obviously wanted to pacify our minds. Therefore, the other version is true. Please forgive the bad state of the enclosed copy. I had made another one for you: but I cannot find it now when I am going to post the letter.

Yours affectionately,

---

[1] But Szabó, in *Vertreibung* (p. 240), questions whether Leibholz really accepted the subordination of restitution to reconstruction in the resolution.

[2] See H.M. Falconer to Leibholz, 1 October 1945, Bell Papers, Vol. 40, fol. 343 (copy); BA, N 1334 (copy)

Bell to Leibholz, 6 November 1945, BA, N 1334 (typewritten); Bell Papers 40, fol. 344 (carbon)

My dear Leibholz,

I was very grateful for your list of books. The text of the resolution of the University Rektors has reached you by now. I am quite ready to take any step which you would like me to take, after reflection, about your resumption of work in Göttingen, for example. I do not know what your wishes are for the permanent future with regard to yourself and your family, in connection with Göttingen. Anyhow, I could start the ball rolling, if you felt you wished to go, say to Göttingen, in the spring.

As to a visit to your parents-in-law, I had a talk with Mrs Bethge, and asked her what she thought her grandparents would think about your coming. She thought it would be most welcome. I told her that they had dissuaded you, and you wondered whether it was because they did not want to encourage anyone to go to Berlin in present conditions. I got Clutton-Brock to follow up my enquiries in a more direct way. He is now in England, and he tells me that there is no doubt that your parents would like you to go. The only fear is that Sabine might worry very much while you were away. That is really the position. You would be welcome, if you could get permission. I do not at all know whether permission would be forthcoming, but I am quite ready to do anything you want me to do.

Yours ever,

Leibholz to Bell, 7 November 1945, Bell Papers 40, fol. 345 (typewritten); BA, N 1334 (copy)

My Lordbishop,

Very many thanks for your letter of yesterday.

After having read the resolution I think it may be better to wait until things have reached a further stage. In the meantime, I have heard that the Society for Protection of Science and Learning is drawing up a list of names of German scholars in this country who might possibly be prepared to consider an offer to go back to Germany. This list is to be passed on to the Educational Branch of the Control Commission. Under these circumstances, it may be better to wait [and see] whether the other side takes the initiative in due course. To judge from the resolution, former posts shall be kept open, although, in my case, it may be argued that it has been filled by Smend who came to Göttingen in 1935 when I retired. I feel that there are so many uncertain factors that I should not press the matter forward at the moment. But I am afraid I shall need your help anyhow.

As to a visit of my parents-in-law I quite agree with all you say. I will try to find a job for Sabine and in case I succeed I shall write to you immediately. Then the position would become much easier.

Thank you for having written to the Secretary of the Royal Society. I am so glad we [did] not post it.

I will write to you about Western-Europe in due course and hope to see you in London on November 14th.

Yours ever,

Leibholz to Bell, 13 November 1945, Bell Papers 40, fols. 346–8 (typewritten); BA, N 1334 (copy)

My Lordbishop,
Unfortunately, the paper I am going to write on the situation in which Europe finds herself today will not be finished before the weekend. Therefore, in order not to be late I will at least let you have these reflections on the question raised by you.

The attempt to set up a central administration for Germany must, in my view, be made, from a European point of view, in order to prevent a final break up of Europe and a division of Europe between West and East. It is frequently said that the administration of defeated Germany is to prove the real touchstone of allied solidarity and of the ability of the Great Powers to act in unison. I agree on that. But, at the same time, we have to ask ourselves today whether such an attempt to act in unison is likely to be crowned with success.

The unity established in Teheran and Yalta was closely connected with the unconditional surrender policy and I think that we agree that this policy was only a formula covering the non-existence of an agreement between the Great Powers concerning the long-term problem of Germany. Potsdam itself is the logical outcome of this policy. What united the Great Powers in Potsdam was, in truth, the common desire to apply Power politics, and the essence of the Potsdam agreement is to be seen in the frontier – and reparation – clauses.[1] Beyond that, there is no real agreement and the use of the term democracy in all these documents means nothing as Russia and the West understand fundamentally different things by this term. I have tried to make this clear in the article in *The Hibbert Journal*[2] I sent you some time ago.

Of course, there may be new agreements on these lines (i.e. lines of Power Politics) in future. But, in my view, this time will come one day when it will no longer be possible to come to such an agreement because, from the point of view of Power Politics, Germany will not attract the interest of the Great Powers. You know, my Lordbishop, that I fundamentally differ from all those who hold the view that in the present age power alone is a sufficient basis for an agreement among the 'Big Three'.³ I am even convinced that if the Western Powers should be prepared to abandon Eastern Europe (i.e. first the countries incorporated into Russia, secondly the countries belonging to the Russian sphere of interest, thirdly the Russian-occupied part of Germany) as is frequently advocated by the 'realists'; unity among the Great Powers would not be established.⁴ The distrust of each other, the suspicion would remain. It would remain because, at least in the present age, the spirit is stronger than power and because we have to deal in the East with a fundamentally different conception of life and of the nature of man than in the West. To judge from the course [the] political development has so far taken the events seem to me to have shown the correctness of this view.

For this very reason I should also not be in favour of the recent suggestion made by Crossman⁵ and others that in order to remove Russian suspicion the Western powers should perform a social and economic revolution in the West and South of Germany just as the Russians have done in the East and thus fundamentally change the social structure of German society.⁶ Neither am I in favour of an offer to share the secret of the atomic bomb. For both, a complete reconstruction of German society and sharing the secret of the atomic bomb would not overcome the mutual distrust of the Great Powers. Such steps would not establish that unity of spirit which is necessary to eliminate war and to create a new international order. They would only weaken the position of the Western countries. They would appease Russia for the moment without securing her sincere collaboration.

I mention all this only in order to show that – in spite of the necessity to make all possible attempts to come to an agreement with the Russians and to set up a central German administration – ªI fear thatª all these attempts will fail in the end. Of course, there may be tactical concessions on the Russian side and these concessions may be hailed as a true compromise, as 'progress' etc. in this country. But a couple of months later people will again have revised their judgement just as they have done with regard to Potsdam. In my view, unity and understanding among the Big Three will ultimately not be established until either the West has accepted the Eastern conception of life or the East the Western one.⁷

I admit that these considerations may well prompt the heart to complete dismay and cause people to say that I wish to encourage or perpetuate existing dissensions. I need not tell you that nothing is further from my mind than this. I think a politician must face the last realities and nothing is gained by wishful thinking in Politics. Wishful thinking has always only worsened the situation and led from disappointment to disappointment. I wonder whether e.g. *The Times* is really in earnest in maintaining the view that the breakdown of the Foreign Minister[s] conference is the result of the work of mischief-makers or war-mongers.⁸

What are the practical consequences resulting from this view? I should say that at the same time when trying to set up a central German administration an active Western policy should be pursued, a policy of the good neighbour as Bevin said in his last speech in the House of Commons. This may at least save Western Europe. But I differ from Vansittart ᶜand obviously also from Bevinᶜ in so far as he obviously wishes to combine an anti-German and anti-Russian policy.⁹ This seems to me beyond the power of this country. Further, Western Europe cannot live by itself. It cannot exist without at least Central Europe i.e. Germany and Italy. Therefore, my conclusion is that such a Western policy must include Germany as a whole or if this not be possible at least the Western and Southern parts.

The objection that it is not possible to pursue a constructive policy in the West and South of Germany when at the same time the attempt shall be made to come to an agreement with the Russians with regard to Germany as a whole does not seem to me to be well founded in face of the fact that the Russians have their unilateral policy in the Eastern-occupied zone. Why should the Western powers not do the same in the West and South of Germany? Indeed such a policy seems to me the only way to face the threat from the East and, ultimately, to put the Germans in a position to make a stand when the Eastern part of Germany, under Russian communist leadership, will make a bid for political unification of Germany as a whole.[10] You have certainly noted that the communists in the East and West of Germany always stress the necessity of having a united Germany in closest friendship with the Soviet Union (Cf. *The Times* of Nov. 13th). A Western Germany, however well administered, provides no alternative to this threat. This is why, from the British and European Point of view, (real British interests seem to me to coincide with European interests) something similar should be done in the West, including the Western and Southern part of Germany.[11]

There remains the question as to what the Germans will ultimately prefer, a united Germany under communist leadership all in close 'friendship' with Russia or (as a united Germany under Western leadership can hardly be visualised) a divided Germany, the Eastern part belonging to the Russian sphere of influence and the Western part to that of the Western countries. You know, my Bishop, that I myself am thinking in primarily ideological terms, but it is difficult to say how the bulk of the German population will react to such an alternative – especially at a time of great despair and distress when the national issue will be combined with the ideological one.[12]

Seen from this angle, I am in the long run probably more in sympathy with de Gaulle's proposal than with that of Vansittart and Bevin. But the motivation is a different one: De Gaulle has made his suggestion as it seems for primarily nationalistic reasons in order to give his country some imaginary security. I myself am not antipathetic to it for ideological reasons in order to save Western Europe. And I should come to this conclusion only if it is proved that the Great Powers have finally failed to come to an understanding. As I have tried to point out I am convinced that, in the end, the attempts to secure understanding will fail. But this does not seem to justify de Gaulle's suggestion *now*. For this would strengthen Russia's position in the East and weaken that of the Western powers. It may be argued that the Western powers can already do nothing in the Russian occupied areas today. This may be true. But there is a big difference as to what is actually happening today and what is recognised as just and legitimate by the Western countries. Further I should say that, in any case, Western Europe should *ultimately* include the whole of Western and Southern Germany (not as de Gaulle says only the Ruhr and Rhine areas).

I offer you these reflections in all humility. I fear you will not like them and you may be perfectly right in doing so. But as you asked me I was perfectly frank and I may say that what I tried to point out is the provisional result of my present thoughts however inadequate, [a]on the issue in question.[a]

Yours ever,

1. This and the following sentence are marked by a black line in the margin.
2. Gerhard Leibholz, 'Two Types of Democracy', reprinted in *Politics and Law*, pp. 37–48.
3. This sentence is marked by a black line in the margin.
4. The last part of the sentence is marked by a black line in the margin.
5. Richard Crossman (1907–74), Labour politician, had been responsible for the German Section of the Political Warfare Executive under Robert Bruce Lockart throughout the war. In the newly formed SHAEF (Supreme Headquarters of the Allied Expeditionary Force) he became Chief of Operations of the Psychological Warfare Division. In 1945 he became an MP.
6. The middle of this sentence is marked by a black line in the margin.
7. Marked by a black line in the margin.
8. Marked by a black line in the margin.
9. Marked by a black line in the margin.
10. Marked by a black line in the margin.
11. Marked by a black line in the margin.
12. Marked by a black line in the margin.

Bell to Sabine Leibholz, 23 November 1945, BA, N 1334 (typewritten)

My dear Sabine,

Mrs Bell ᵃsends her love: and Iᵃ was very glad to get your letter and most touched by what you say about my visit to your parents.

This is a very short line to say that I will gladly write to the Military Government about your sister-in-law,[1] if you will give me full information about her name and last known address, or where she can be traced now. Also could you tell me what would be the grounds on which the Oberpräsident would be able to give her a states pension? Would she be entitled to it on the ground of her husband's profession, and the fact that he was a victim? What was his profession, and where did he live?

Please tell your husband that I have read the *Hibbert Journal* article with much gratitude: and also that the Vansittart motion about Western Europe has been postponed until December 13th. But there is to be a two-days debate in the House of Lords on Foreign Affairs, on Tuesday and Wednesday this coming week. And the Archbishop of Canterbury is calling attention to distress in Central Europe in the House of Lords on December 5th.[2]

Yours very sincerely,

1. That is Emmi Bonhoeffer, Klaus's widow.
2. Hansard, H.L. Deb., Vol. 138, cols. 341–98 (here cols. 341–8), (5 December 1945).

Leibholz to Bell, 28 November 1945, Bell Papers 40, fol. 349 (typewritten); BA, B 1334 (copy)

My Lordbishop,

I do not know whether one should not inform Schacht's counsel in Nuremberg of the fact that Dietrich mentioned him to you as involved in the plot as early as in June 1942 and that you put his name in your memo. passed on to the government a month later. I think it was very wise to omit his name in *The Contemporary*, but I feel that for truth's sake the fact should become known to the Court. I heard on the wireless that Gisevius[1] will act as one of Schacht's witnesses. But G. was (as far as I know) a Gestapo man in former times; therefore, I do not know whether his evidence will have real weight for the judges. Schacht was an ambitious and perhaps dangerous man, but he was certainly not a criminal or a man who wanted war. Of course, I do not know what you think about my suggestion. ªOf course, I do not know whether you can take such a step in the position you hold.ª But I felt that I should submit it to you for consideration.

The last issue of the *Christian News-Letter* reproduced Niebuhr's article.[2] When I had to write to the Editor[3] I added that I felt that she had not yet done justice to Dietrich. This is obviously the reply.

Have you seen Dietrich's poem WHO AM I? in the November issue of the Bulletin?[4] Frankly, neither the translator nor I had agreed to its publication in the Bulletin because we wanted to publish it first in a proper English periodical. But we cannot help it. It seems to us that the translation has been very well done. But you can certainly judge it better than we. Leishman is the translator of Rilke's and Hölderlin's poems into English. To judge from the correspondence he must be a remarkable personality.

Yours affectionately,

---

[1] Hans Bernd Gisevius (1904–74) in 1933 joined the Political Police of Prussia and was assigned to the newly formed Gestapo. In 1936 he was transferred to the Reich Ministry of Interior where he joined other political opponents of the Nazis, especially Hans Oster, becoming one of the central figures of the attempted plot in 1938. In 1939 he was conscripted into the German intelligence service and sent as Vice Consul to Zurich. Here he worked as liaison between the resistance and the American Office of Strategic Services (OSS) headed by Allen W. Dulles and the British Political Warfare Executive in Bern. After 20 July 1944 he managed to escape to Switzerland.

[2] Reinhold Niebuhr, 'The Death of a Martyr', originally published in *Christianity and Crisis* 5, 11/1945, pp. 6–7.

[3] Kathleen Bliss had succeeded J.H. Oldham as editor of the *Christian News-Letter* earlier that year.

[4] Christian Fellowship in Wartime, *Bulletin* N° 24, November 1945.

Bell to Leibholz, 30 November 1945, BA, N 1334 (handwritten)

My dear Leibholz,

Very many thanks for your letter. I don't think I can *ex proprio motu* approach counsel for Schacht and say D. mentioned him as in the plot. I think Gisevius's evidence will be important as he is now, at any rate, regarded as a prime authority on the plot. I hope we shall get a good report of what G. *says* – and generally get light on the plot.

No, I had not seen D's poem in the Bulletin till you wrote. It is admirable. It might have been better in a weekly – but you can't *rely* on a weekly taking a poem.

Please thank Sabine for her information and tell her I will do what I can. I enclose Hansard for first day of Lords debate.[1] I have no spare copy of the second day. But Lord Chancellor Jowitt[2] (on 2nd day) I was interested to see (and I heard him) turned down 'the idea of a *Western bloc* – which rather connotes some other kind of bloc – an Eastern *bloc* – ... is not one which finds favour with us at all'.[3]

Yours affly,

[1] Hansard, H.L. Deb., Vol. 138, cols. 17-66 (5 December 1945).
[2] Sir William Jowitt (1885-1957), Labour politician and MP (1922-31, 1937-46) and lawyer, became Baron in 1946, Viscount in 1947, and 1st Earl Jowitt in 1951. He was Lord High Chancellor of Great Britain in the Attlee governments, 1945-51.
[3] See Hansard, H.L. Deb., Vol. 138, cols. 68-75 (here col. 73) (5 December 1945).

Leibholz to Bell, 4 December 1945, Bell Papers 40, fol. 350 (handwritten); BA, N 1334 (copy)

My Lordbishop,

Very many thanks for your letter. I *fully* understand what you say about Schacht.

Thank you also for Hansard. Of course, I have read once again your impressive speech[1] with special interest, and I think your approach to the problem is more statesmanlike and realistic than that of all the 'realists'. I agree that the new international order must be based on the acceptance of the moral law, and I even think that nationalism will not present an insurmountable obstacle for attaining this aim. The difficulty as I see it seems to me to be that the moral law as you and we understand it is fundamentally different in the East from that in the West. And seen from a realistic angle, why should the Russians accept our moral law after having conquered half of Europe? If they do so they would become a Western country. Unfortunately, I see no sign which points in this direction. Of course, I fully understand that this state of affairs is not being discussed in public today. But I am not perfectly sure whether those responsible for Foreign Affairs in the Western countries visualise the gravity of the spiritual issue, which is the root of all trouble today. You have certainly noted that the Russians have flatly refused the plan for a World state as advocated by Bevin[2] and to a certain degree by Eden. In fact, they cannot accept it. It would result in a basic change of the structure of the Russian state and would imply the loss of the war, as far as it was conducted on ideological lines, ªfrom the Russian point of view.ª

As to the idea of a Western block, which was turned down by the Lord Chancellor I think that Bevin is, in point of fact, in favour of it, even if he does not like to name it so. I think there can hardly be made a case against this idea as the Russians are just doing the same. The last[3] proof for this is given by the newest events in Yugoslavia.[4]

Yours affectionately,

[1] Hansard, H.L. Deb., Vol. 138, cols. 51-6, abridged in Raina, *Bishop George Bell: House of Lords Speeches*, pp. 91-4.
[2] Ernest Bevin (1861-1951), trades union leader and Labour politician. In the wartime government he served as Minister of Labour, but his most important role came as Foreign Secretary in the new Labour Government, 1945-51. He vigorously opposed Communism, and lent strong support to the creation of NATO.
[3] Copy: real.
[4] After the victory of the communists under Tito in the elections of 11 November the Yugoslav Parliament (the Skupština) proclaimed the Federativa Narodna Republika Jugoslavija on 29 November 1945.

Leibholz to Bell, 22 December 1945, Bell Papers 40, fol. 355 (handwritten)

My Lordbishop,
Now that Christmas is coming again our hearts and thoughts go out to you again to thank you for all you have done for Dietrich, for Dietrich's family and for ourselves in this year. Although it has brought us peace again, it has been the most sorrowful and distressing year in our life. We feel strongly that God wanted the blood of the innocent victims to wipe out the guilt of His creatures.

In any case, without your helping hand everything would have been much harder and more grievous. Your friendship has made it easier for us to bear the burden imposed on us. For this we wish to thank you especially this year.

With all good wishes for a happy Christmas to you and Mrs Bell, also from my wife and the children.

Yours affectionately,

Bell to Sabine Leibholz, 22 December 1945, BA, N 1334 (handwritten)

My dear Sabine,
This brings you and your husband and children my affectionate remembrance and best wishes for peace and goodwill this Christmas. Alas! I know what sad thoughts it will bring as well – and how your heart will go out to your parents and family and your country. You will like to hear that I have a message via Mr Waddams[1] (on the British Council of Churches delegation) from Pastor Bethge about Maria von Wedemeyer:

'She is at present studying at the University of Göttingen & Bethge is most anxious that she should later be able to come to England for a year's study if possible, preferably at a University here. Perhaps you would consider the matter. Nothing further was asked of me except to convey this request'.

I shall of course, when the time comes, be ready to do what I can. But *at present* she does not seem to come under any of the categories named by Mr Ede in H[ouse] of C[ommons] on November 13.[2] I have been looking at those categories again, to see if any of your family might be able to come here under their shelter. Perhaps your husband would look at them too and let me have any comments. My last news from Sir Alexander Maxwell[3] (this week) is that the Home Office is still waiting to hear from Germany how far the Control Commission can implement the Home Office proposals.

You will be glad to hear that so far about £ 40 has come in response to my appeal for a memorial fund to Dietrich.

I am glad to be giving a talk on the German BBC at 5 p.m. tomorrow[4] – same series as Gerard's! I hope you may hear and approve.

There is much discussion it seems in Germany about the Stuttgart declaration – also in Switzerland.[5] And about the Abp. of Canterbury's broadcast to Germany of Nov. 28.[6] I wonder what Gerard's views on Stuttgart are? I am thinking of writing something about it all – not so much Stuttgart as this problem of responsibility – ours as well as theirs.[7] Asmussen[8] and others are looking for a reply from Britain or the World

Council. Alas! There is so little time to do all these things. May I please ask you to accept for the Leibholz family the enclosed Christmas present, to be spent as you please – but use a bit for joy!

I saw H. von Trott and Werner Koch again last week.

God bless you all – and dear Dietrich – and your family in Germany.

Your affectionate,

---

1. Herbert Montague Waddams (1911-72) was General Secretary of the Church of England's Council for Foreign Relations, 1945-59. As an authority on the Scandinavian churches and on Russian Orthodoxy he actively participated in theological dialogue between these Churches. With Bell he had collaborated on the publication of a collection of the writings of Bishop Berggrav: *With God in the Darkness and Other Papers by Eivind Berggrav, Bishop of Oslo, Illustrating the Norwegian Church Conflict* (London, 1943).
2. The Home Secretary, James Chuter Ede, had named six categories of admission to the UK in the House of Commons on 13 November 1945; see Hansard, H.C. Deb., Vol. 415 (13 November 1945), cols. 1923-4.
3. Sir Alexander Maxwell (1880-1963) was permanent under-secretary at the Home Office 1938-48.
4. Bell, 'Christianity and the European Heritage'. Christmas Broadcast to Germany, 23 December 1945 in Bell, *The Church and Humanity*, pp. 177-82.
5. The discussion about the Stuttgart Declaration of Guilt (18/19 October 1945) encompassed a wide range of strongly held views, some repudiating it as a political statement based on an acceptance of collective guilt in the manner of Article 231 of the Versailles Treaty, and others – like Karl Barth – criticizing it for being insufficiently self-critical. For all of this see Martin Greschat (ed.), *Die Schuld der Kirche. Dokumente und Reflexionen zur Stuttgarter Schulderklärung vom 18/19. Oktober 1945* (Munich, 1982); also Gerhard Besier and Gerhard Sauter, *Wie Christen ihre Schuld bekennen* (Göttingen, 1985).
6. See Greschat, *Die Schuld von Kirche*, pp. 126-7.
7. See Bell's draft of Archbishop Fisher's letter to Theophil Wurm, Bell Papers, Vol. 9, fols. 396-7, and 'A Letter to my Friends in the Evangelical Church in Germany' (14 February 1946), published in *The Church and Humanity*, pp. 183-93, here pp. 190-1.
8. Hans Asmussen (1898-1968) was prominent member of the Confessing Church. In 1943 Bishop Wurm had brought him into the Württemberg church. At Treysa in 1945 the church leaders elected him to head the new Church Office of the EKD. Before long he became critical of the church politics of Karl Barth and Martin Niemöller, particularly following the Darmstadt declaration of 1947. In 1948 he was relieved of his post as president of the church office and not re-elected to the Council.

Leibholz to Bell, 23 December 1945, Bell Papers 40, fols. 351-2 (handwritten); BA, N 1334 (copy)

My Lordbishop,

Your message to Germany has very much moved me. I am deeply grateful for *all* you said and the translation was very excellent. I feel sure that your message will give untold people comfort and new hope in life. What you quote from Barth in the recent *News-Letter* applies to no one as much as to you and it is this simple fact which explains why you hold such a unique position in the Germany of today.

Sabine has just written to you and I feel like she does. I thank you so much for your friendship and goodness.

As to Stuttgart, I approve, of course, as a Christian, the Stuttgart Declaration. But, from the political point of view, it seems to me that it was not very wise and I should probably have hesitated to accept it, simply because it lends support to the mistaken view that the last war was primarily a nationalistic war. The fact that it was waged by the Allies as a nationalistic war in the last few years could not affect its basic character. You know, my Lordbishop, I stick firmly to this view. If this be correct the Stuttgart declaration makes no sense politically. Now, we have the somewhat grotesque picture that the German nation as a whole refused to accept the responsibility for the war in a nationalistic conflict (1914–18) but that the Church accepts the responsibility of the whole nation in a primarily ideological conflict. From a political point of view, this seems to me bad: for it makes it very difficult to maintain the differentiation between Nazis – and non-Nazis. I fear that the far-reaching political implications of this declaration were not fully realized in Stuttgart.

Once again, many thanks for all the goodness you have again shown us this Christmas and all the best wishes to you and Mrs Bell

Yours affectionately,

Sabine Leibholz to Bell, 23 December 1945, Bell Papers 40, fols. 353–4 (handwritten); BA, N 1334 (copy)

My dear Lordbishop,
Your letter arrived this morning and I feel strongly that I must thank you by return for all your good wishes for peace and good will. It is the very Christmas for which Dietrich had prayed and hoped. Now we will have to celebrate it without him – and the peace he and our brothers and friends had in mind has not yet come to this world.

How good of you, my Lordbishop, to send us such a kind gift. It is very welcome, as we are trying everything possible to help my parents and the family in Berlin. Thanks to the kindness of friends in the Control Commission we are still able to send many a parcel, hoping that they will thus come through the winter. Thank you also very much for the good news about the Memorial fund in honour of Dietrich.

As to Dietrich's fiancée we heard of this plan some time ago, but Gert wrote to Bethge at that time, that this does not seem to him technically possible for the time being, and that therefore he did not wish to approach you in this matter. He said that it would be wiser to wait for a year or so until it would be possible to overcome the present difficulties. Actually Gert thinks that nothing can be done now. (He also thinks that there may be other difficulties as the German Abitur[1] is not accepted here as a basis for reading.) We feel sure that the people in Göttingen will do what they can for her, and that she will enjoy her readings there too.

When Gert read the Ede's statement he found out that it would only apply to my parents. Actually we asked them how they think about it, and they wrote to us that as much as they would love to come over, they could not well leave my sisters now, as their health is very poor. But they added that the situation may well be different in spring, and therefore we very much hope to get them over for a visit at that time. If you would then lend us your help, it would be very good of you and highly valuable. – Gert will write to you about Stuttgart. – We have just heard your most encouraging and inspiring broadcast. I feel that it was the real Christmas gift for the German people and I am looking forward to hearing it again at 8.45.

May God be with you and with Mrs Bell in the New Year.

Yours most grateful and affectionately,

[1] The final public examinations sat by German school pupils before admission to university.

Bell to Leibholz, 29 December 1945, BA, N 1334 (typewritten)

My dear Leibholz,

I was much touched by your letter and Sabine's letter. What you said about my broadcast was an immense gratification. I hear today from the B.B.C. that they have had quite a number of letters from Germans in England to a similar effect, and they are expecting letters from Germany when the post arrives.

The B.B.C. has now asked me to do something of a similar length and spirit for Niemöller's birthday, on January 14th or 15th, and I expect I shall have a try.[1]

By the way, I forgot to tell Sabine that I had written to the Control Commission about the pension for Klaus's widow. I will of course let you know any news I get.

Now I am daring something on a rather larger scale, in which I badly need your help. I have been thinking during the last week or two that there ought to be something much more vigorous and encouraging and recognising of the stand of the Confessing [sic] Church – something indeed, which echoes what you said with regard to Stuttgart, though not in terms commenting on that. So I have drafted, in a very rough form, a 'Letter to my Friends in the Evangelical Church in Germany'. I should like to send it to Germany quite quickly, and to have it published in England as a World Council pamphlet. But as you will appreciate, everything turns on what the letter contains. I don't want to say things that are unnecessary or untrue, and I want to remember the different minds of the readers into whose hands such a letter might fall. I want to say no word which cannot be substantiated. So here is the first shot at such a letter. Could you read it with a clear and critical eye, and let me have your views? Please don't hesitate to cross things out, to question things, or to add things. My only object, if I am to write such a letter, is to make it as useful as possible. I should be particularly grateful if I could have the letter back with your comments by Friday morning. If you would like to see me, with the comments in your hand, I could gladly see you at the Athenaeum on Friday, say at 12.30, when we might have lunch together. I would of course pay expenses.

Yours ever,

[1] Martin Niemöller was born on 14 January 1892.

1946

7 January	Austria is reconstituted and divided into four zones directly occupied by the Soviet Union, Britain, the United States and France.
10 January	The first meeting of the United Nations Organization takes place in Methodist Central Hall in London; a week later the first meeting of the United Nations Security Council takes place in Church House, Westminster.
22 February	George Kennan writes his Long Telegram from Moscow.
5 March	Winston Churchill warns of an 'Iron Curtain' falling across the new Europe.
1 October	The conclusion of the trials of Major War Criminals.
15 October	Hermann Göring commits suicide at Nuremberg before execution; a day later ten convicted war criminals are hanged.
9 December	The first of twelve war crimes trials undertaken by the United States begins in Nuremberg. These will go on until 13 April 1949.

Leibholz to Bell, 1 January 1946, Bell Papers, *Vol.* 220, fols. 176–8 (typewritten)

My Lordbishop,
Very many thanks for your letter and having kindly written to the Control Commission on behalf of Klaus's widow. I am not surprised to see from your letter that the B.B.C. had a number of highly appreciative letters and, no doubt, they will get more as soon as the post from Germany reaches them. Your Christmas message was one of hope and comfort and what this means in the present stage in which the German people finds itself you probably know better from your own experience than I.

I read your 'letter to your friends in the Evangelical Church in Germany'[1] at once because I have to go to a Conference for Theological Students to [sic] Birmingham today for a couple of days. (John Baillie, Edinburgh[2] and I have to speak and it is the problem of power which I have to deal with.) Your 'Letter' follows up the line of your Christmas message in a still more vigorous and inspiring way, and, no doubt, it will have far-reaching and deep repercussions in the whole of Germany.

Apart from a few corrections made in the Ms. I offer you in all humility the following comments for consideration:

First, the passages marked ªe.g.ª by me on page 3 seem to me ªperhapsª to give in some ways too rosy a picture of the stand the Confessional Church as a whole made against the former regime in Germany and do not seem to me quite compatible with what yourself say on page 7. We know that among those who joined the Confessional Church ᶜin due courseᶜ there were many who welcomed National Socialism at its beginning and voted for it in 1933. I ᶜevenᶜ think that only a minority of the later Confessional Church was originally opposed to National Socialism. Further, it is true that the Confessional Church dealt with matters of 'order, justice, the persecution of Jews and the rights of man'. But as far as I know she did this only occasionally. I mention this because I imagine that those who are hostile to Germany as a whole, and consequently to the Confessional Church, could argue that the picture has been oversimplified and that the facts do not fully bear it out.

Secondly, what you say on page 7 about the tendency among German theologians to move away from the community and to draw a sharp frontier between the Gospel and the State seems to me perfectly true and the crux of the whole problem of the Church in Germany. On the whole, the present composition of the Evangelical Council does not seem to me to give a guarantee that the Church will become really 'politically-minded'. And yet the Church has to become fully aware of her political task if she is to be a creative force also in this world. True, to judge from Treysa and Stuttgart, Niemöller has obviously changed his former view that the Church has not to interfere in Politics, and others may have done the same. But I feel you should press this point still more and give a stronger lead in this respect, because the further fate of the German Church seems to me to depend on a revolutionary change in the whole outlook of the Church towards Politics. I should add that this is not an interference from outside but simply the Christian interpretation of the martyrdom and death of those Christians (theologians and lay-men) who gave their lives to eliminate the former political regime in Germany (I myself hope to be able to expound this view in greater detail before long). Such an insertion would be possible on page 1. 1 (behind command) or on page 11 l[ine]. 9. (behind party).

Further, I should like to submit to you for consideration the suggestion to associate yourself (page 9) in one way or another with what the Pope said in his last Christmas Eve broadcast a few days ago: 'Who can say "I am free from sin"? Those who exact today the explanation of crimes and the just punishment of criminals for their misdeeds should take good care not to do themselves what they denounce in others as misdeeds and crimes. Totalitarianism infects the community of nations, renders them incapable of guaranteeing the security of individual peoples, and constitutes a continual menace to war.' Of course, I do not know whether you wish to go so far as the Pope did.³ But I feel strongly that a word on these things would not only greatly be appreciated throughout Germany, but would also still more enhance the preparedness of the German Church and perhaps of the whole nation to follow your lead and advice.

As to the question of the guilt of the German people as a whole I do not wish to reduce the gravity of the German guilt but I should not go so far as you do on page 7. I should not say that the Nazis are Germans, and that you are also Germans, and, therefore, you have to bear the same shame that comes to all Germans because of the guilt of the Nazis. In the prisoner of war camps I have often to deal with this question. Anti-Nazis who were often in prisons and concentration camps can simply not understand why they are responsible for the crimes of the Nazis. I myself think that man is only responsible for what he has done⁴ or omitted to do. To make people responsible for that of which they are individually not guilty seems to me to be only possible on a racialist or nationalist basis. The fact that the Anti-Nazis are Germans would only be sufficient if the war had been a primarily nationalistic one. You know, my Bishop, that I do not share this view. Just as I cannot make the Jews as a whole or another people responsible for terrorist outrages of some of their members I cannot make a minority responsible for the outrages being committed by the majority. Justice is individual and concrete. (Nobody, e.g., holds the Amery family responsible for the treason committed by one of the members of the family).⁵ The principle to make a race or nation as whole responsible for the doings of some of its members (even if they form the majority) is a political principle, which I could only accept (as a historical fact) in a racialist or nationalist age.

I have only mentioned the points on which I thought you may possibly like to have my comments. Otherwise I fully agree. Your 'Letter' seems to me more statesmanlike and constructive than what the professional statesmen are doing today and I was struck by many important points you made (e.g. by your reference to the peculiar character of the German people and by what you say about forgiveness.)

You know, my Bishop, that I love to meet you whenever I have the chance of getting hold of you. But the Conference at Birmingham does not come to a close before Friday and, therefore, it will be difficult to be in London at that day. But I hope to be there Monday next. In case you happen to be in London on Monday and you are not ᶜyetᶜ engaged I should love to have lunch with you where and when you like.

By the way, as to the Fund, which has been collected by you in memory of Dietrich do you not think it wise perhaps to keep it in this country for the time being until things have become more settled in Germany? I know that my wife's father thinks in the same lines.

If you redraft your 'Letter' I should very much like to see it again.

I am enclosing a stencilled copy of another lecture.⁶ Perhaps you may care to have a look at it. It does not seem to me suitable for publication because in it things are being said which I feel cannot freely be discussed today. I hope I am too pessimistic.

With all good wishes

Yours ever,

---

1. 'Letter to my German Evangelical friends' – with many other statements – Bell Papers, Vol. 220, fols. 179–81. See the printed version of 14 February 1946: 'A Letter to my Friends in the Evangelical Church in Germany', in: Bell, *The Church and Humanity*, pp. 183–93.
2. John Baillie (1886–1960) was Professor of Divinity at Edinburgh University, 1934–56, widely read theologian and Moderator of the General Assembly of the Church of Scotland 1943–4.
3. The quotation of the Pope and the following sentence are marked by a blue line in the margin. The quotation is used in the printed version of the text in *The Church and Humanity*, pp. 190–1.
4. Instead of 'I am […] for what I have done'.
5. John Amery, a tragic figure, was a British fascist executed on 19 December 1945, after pleading guilty to charges of treason. He had tried to recruit a British force to fight for the Axis powers during the war. Amery was a son of the leading Conservative MP Leo Amery, whose speech in the Norway debate in the House of Commons in May 1940 was widely seen as a precipitation of the fall of the Chamberlain government. John's brother was the future Conservative MP, Julian Amery.
6. Not preserved.

Bell to Leibholz, 3 January 1946, BA, N 1334 (typewritten)

My dear Leibholz,

I am most grateful for your letter and for the fullness of your comments, which I greatly appreciate. I shall do a revise and will send it along to you. I am trying to catch the post now. This is only to say that I quite understand that you cannot be in town tomorrow, and alas, I cannot be in town on Monday.

Very many thanks also for your Address, which I shall read.

Yours ever,

ᵃI agree re. Pope.ᵃ

Leibholz to Bell, 4 January 1945 (1946), Bell Papers 40, fol. 356 (handwritten)

My Lordbishop,

Many thanks for your letter. I am glad to know that you think my comments may be useful to you and I am looking forward to the revised copy.

I still feel sorry that I did not see you today – all the more as things developed in Birmingham yesterday so that I could possibly have managed to come to town today. But I did not know this beforehand. If you fix another day, suitable to you, and perhaps in connection with the revised 'Letter', I should be *delighted* to come up to town to see you.

I am enclosing Balfour's letter¹ with many thanks for having allowed us to see it. It sounds quite hopeful.

Yours affectionately,

[1] Lieutenant General Sir Philip Balfour (1898–1977) joined the Control Commission in Germany in 1945 and then became Director of Civil Affairs for the Military Government, British Army of the Rhine (BAOR) in 1946. He was appointed General Officer Commanding 53rd Division later in that year and then General Officer Commanding 2nd Division in 1947. Two years later he became General Officer Commanding-in-Chief, Northern Command.

Bell to Leibholz, 13 January 1946, BA, N 1334 (handwritten)

My dear Leibholz,

Very many thanks for the poems – also your letter. [1]

The Athenaeum can't give us lunch on Tuesday early – and I have to take a wedding in *Vere Street* 2.15. So I am reserving places in St. Ermin's Hotel, Caxton St. near S. James Park Station. Please meet me there (instead of Athenaeum) a little before 12 – we can have a good talk before lunch.

Yours ever,

[1] *Time and Tide* had published two poems by Bonhoeffer, translated by J.B. Leishmann, on 12 January 1946.

Leibholz to Bell, 16 January 1946, BA, N 1334 (copy)

My Lordbishop,

It was a great joy for me to see you yesterday and it was so very nice to have lunch with you. Please accept my best thanks for all your kindness.

The paragraph I had in mind yesterday when we talked about Niemöller's letter[1] runs as follows (in an interview with Chaplain Ben L. Rose[2]):

Will you give the reasons for your offer to serve in the German Navy?

'It was certainly not for the reason that I wanted to fight Hitler's war for him, and most assuredly not with any idea of trying to redeem myself with the Nazis. I was thinking only of my people and my country. At that time I saw three possibilities ahead for Germany: 1, total defeat, which would be bitter for Germany; 2, total victory for the Nazis, which would [be] even bitterer for Germany, and 3, to fight on in the hope that the Nazis might be thrown out of government and a negotiated peace reached. It was on the latter that I pinned my hopes. If the latter occurred, and I had good hopes that it might, I did not want to be in prison but wished to be free in order that I might do my part for the future of my country. I was also moved to this offer by the fact that my three sons were being drafted into the Army and I felt that the place of a father is by the side of his sons.'[3]

The second reason seems to me more plausible than the first one under 3).

I am also enclosing the copy of Dietrich's letter mentioned yesterday. What Dietrich says on God being in this world and on God's suffering from this world[4] seems to me very profound. I am not a theologian: but does this idea not represent something new in traditional theological thinking? In any case, it is an idea which often occupied his mind and I myself am thinking on similar lines. Is not his suffering a part of God's suffering in this world? What he says about the French pastor seems to me to apply to him. I think it would be worthwhile having this passage translated into English. Rupp would certainly do it. If so, it would be very good of you to let me have a copy. The enclosed is the only one left to us. But it will be published in the book, which is going to be published in Switzerland.[5] It will come out this month.

I am enclosing the remainder of what was left for you on the table yesterday.

Once again, many thanks

Yours affectionately,

P.S. By the way, I wrote the letter (not Sabine) referred to in the News-Special containing Dietrich's poem. Its re-production is not fully correct; there is one mistake.

[1] Martin Niemöller to Bell, 31 October 1945, partly cited by Bell, *The Church and Humanity*, p. 186.
[2] The Military Chaplain Ben Lacy Rose (1914–2006) served as Presbyterian chaplain in the U.S. Army during the Second World War. After pastoral services he was professor of pastoral leadership and homiletics at Union Theological Seminary in Virginia, 1956–73.
[3] Ben L. Rose, 'As Niemoeller Sees Germany's Future', in *The Christian Century*, vol. 62, 1945, cols. 1155–7, here col. 1156.
[4] Bonhoeffer to Bethge, 21 July 1944, in *DBW* 8, pp. 541–2.
[5] *Das Zeugnis eines Boten. Zum Gedächtnis von Dietrich Bonhoeffer* (Abteilung für Wiederaufbau und Kirchliche Hilfsaktionen des Oekumenischen Rates der Kirchen, Geneva, 1945).

Bell to Leibholz, 21 January 1946, BA, N 1334 (typewritten), Bell Papers 40, fol. 358 (carbon)

My dear Leibholz,

It was a great joy to see you in London last week and to have such a good talk. Thank you also for your letter and the postal order. I am sending you your expenses for the journey, with many thanks.

But the purpose of this letter is to send you my revised version of the 'Letter'. It seems to me now much too long. I shall work over it again, and shall probably have to cut out some of the quotations and take away some of what I fear are repetitions in the argument. But I send it to you by an early post, hoping that you will be kind enough to look it over with a very critical eye, and mark the MS with your comments, deletions etc. And of course I should be most thankful if you could tell me the points in the 'Letter', which are put in a wrong way, or might be put in a better way for German readers. I also enclose my original version.

Reading it through again, I am wondering whether the introductory paragraph is desirable, i.e. the account of my own pre-war contacts. I don't want the 'Letter' to be too long, and I don't want the effect on the reader to be wearing. I should also be glad if you would look at the logic of the argument. I am not sure, after working over the text so continually, that I have left the argument as lucid as it ought to be, and whether I have flowed on from one point to another. Particularly in the last five or six pages, I fear I have gone rather in and out of the question of responsibility – ours and theirs, and to co-operation in a common task.

Yours ever,

Bell to Leibholz, 21 January [1946], BA, N 1334 (handwritten)

My dear Leibholz,

I return Dietrich's poem with many thanks. It is very moving. And yet the poems printed in *T[ime] & Tide* and *New English Weekly* I like even better.

Yours ever,

Leibholz to Bell, 23 January 1946, Bell Papers 220, fol. 183 (typewritten)

My Lordbishop,

I hasten to return your Ms. with my thanks for having allowed me to read it. I have looked it over with a very critical eye, perhaps with a too critical eye. But I know that you want me to do rather too much than too little and I have tried to comply with your wishes.

May I suggest that you, my Bishop, read the paper as it stands now. I wonder how it will strike you. I have deleted all the passages, which do not seem to me urgently necessary, especially repetitions, but also personal recollections. The paper has thus lost something of its attractive personal character. ªBut it has perhaps gained in another way.ª If you should wish to shorten the Ms. still further I think it would be possible to make further cuts in the first five pages.

I have also put things in another order and you will find even important arguments at another place. I do not know, whether you like these changes. The attempt may well prove a failure and in this case please accept my apologies.

I am not quite happy about the sentence: 'History shows all too many people in Germany possessed by a lust of power.' I have left it but suggest that you perhaps put it in a little milder form. Either (omitting 'history shows'): All too many people are possessed by a lust of cruelty' or History shows that, on the one hand, people were inspired by high[1] motives for humanity but that, on the other hand, all too many people in Germany were possessed by a lust for cruelty ...' [2]

Some of the points you make in your paper are very excellent. I have not seen them somewhere else. I also like the way in which you put your argument: you press your point as if you were a judge and in spite of this you are not compromising.

Many thanks for the cheque. May I say that the fare was only about 13/. You have thus heavily overpaid my actual expenses.

Thank you also for returning Dietrich's poem. It may well be that Leishman's translation is not so good as that of the other poems. The German version would probably strike you more.

Please forgive my asking you for kindly returning the copy of *Horizon*,[3] which I have to return to Prof. Kahle[4] to whom it belongs. Have you seen Spender[5] in the meantime?

Yours ever,

---

[1] Instead of 'the highest'.
[2] See the printed version, pp. 189–90. 'History shows that, while a great number of Germans have been inspired by the highest ideals for humanity, too many have been possessed by a lust for cruelty, to which others weakly succumbed.'

³ *Horizon: A Review of Literature and Art*, an influential journal edited by Cyril Connolly and published between 1940 and 1949. Its contributors included many of the leading writers and artists of the day.
⁴ Paul E. Kahle (1875–1964) was Lutheran pastor, eminent orientalist and theologian, in exile in Oxford after emigrating to Britain in 1939. After the war he returned to Germany.
⁵ Presumably the writer and poet Stephen Spender (1909–95).

Bell to Leibholz, 24 January 1946, BA, N 1334 (handwritten)

My dear Leibholz,

You could not have done me a greater service than you have done about my German letter. The revised version is an immense improvement of the version I sent you. More crisp, and with a steadier and more convincing appeal. And when it goes to the printer, I expect you will find that it embodies nearly all of your corrections and improvements. Rudolf Hess's letter, on re-reading, does not contain any sentence really quotable in our context: and in that case it is probably better to leave him out altogether, unless I say after 'enemy and traitor to the N.S. State' ['] as a letter from the D[eputy] F[ührer] R. Hess written to me come [sic] after N's arrest made abundantly plain.'¹

In haste – and with renewed thanks.

Yours ever,

Sir Arthur Streeter writes to me that Clutton Brock has permission to go to Berlin for a month (to start with).

Grüber² will be here for February 1–14.

I have not yet heard from Spender.

¹ See the mention of 'the Deputy Führer Rudolf Hess' in the printed version, p. 184. N is Martin Niemöller.
² i.e. the Berlin pastor Heinrich Grüber.

Leibholz to Bell, 25 January 1946, Bell Papers 220, fol. 186 (typewritten)

My Lordbishop,

This is only to thank you very much for your letter and to tell you how greatly I enjoyed it. You can hardly imagine how happy I am whenever you think that I can be of a little use to you. I also found that the 'Letter' in its more compressed form had a stronger appeal to the reader, but, of course, I was not sure. As to Hess' letter I fully agree with that you say. I should leave it (or only mention it in the form suggested), if it does not contain a new argument.

Today there is a fine letter about Dietrich in the *Time and Tide*. I sent Dietrich's poem 'Who am I' and 'Stations on the road to freedom' to Spender. Perhaps he may like to see them.

Yours ever,

P.S. I suppose Clutton Brock will let us know before leaving this country for Berlin. In any case, he meant to do so.

Bell to Leibholz, 1 February 1946, BA, N 1334 (typewritten)

My dear Leibholz,
Here is a proof of my 'Letter'. I should be most grateful if you would scrutinise it and return it. Please send it to the Athenaeum, where I shall be on Monday, and the rest of next week.

Yours ever,

Bell to Sabine Leibholz, 2 February 1946, BA, N 1334 (handwritten)

My dear Sabine,
This brings you my affectionate birthday greetings, in which I join in love for Dietrich as well. He has gone on, as a torchbearer, both for Germany and for mankind: and by his death, I am convinced, he has liberated many and will liberate many more. But it is hard to be without him. These have been sad years for you, and I know how much your parents and your sisters and whole family must be in your thoughts and prayers. May God grant this coming year may bring some light to the darkness, and some fragment of peace to your country and to Europe. We must each help one another – not forgetting that we are 'compassed about with so great a cloud of witnesses'. [1]

Love to the family

Yours & Dietrich's affectionately,

[1] The Epistle to the Hebrews, Ch.12 v. 1 (KJV).

Leibholz to Bell, 3 February 1946, Bell Papers 40, fols. 288-9 (handwritten); BA, N 1334 (copy)

My Lordbishop,
You know how sincerely I pray that you may have many happy celebrations of the day of your birth. It is the first time that we cannot celebrate Dietrich's birthday together with yours and Sabine's. And yet Dietrich will not be far from us on that day. If he were with us, no doubt, he would wholeheartedly join us in thanking you for all the love you have shown him and us again in the last year. I frequently feel that the blood Dietrich has given for us all has made our friendship different from similar human ties. It is difficult to define it. But it seems to me as if Dietrich's martyrdom has become an integral part of our friendship. This is why your friendship has such a unique significance and meaning for me.

Your 'letter to your friends in the Evangelical Church in Germany' makes excellent reading. The additions you have made seem to me very good and I feel sure that the 'Letter' as it stands is a brilliant piece of Christian statesmanship and I have no doubt that it will deeply impress and inspire all those concerned in Germany.

I have only made a few little technical corrections. The only additional suggestion I should like to make is that you may consider the omission of the brackets: 'A Churchman should be free to belong to any party'. Of course, it is true. But I stopped there when I read your last draft and I stopped again there yesterday. Or perhaps one could add: 'in any party, which is not anti-Christian in character'.[1]

I suppose that Bethge would be delighted and honoured to get a copy of the 'Letter' from you.

May I ask you kindly to accept the enclosed booklet on Natural Law, which may interest you. It is a by-product of our group-work. I myself am only responsible for the 'spheres of application': I wrote part I on Politics.[2]

It seems as if the postal position in Berlin has become more awkward in the course of the last few weeks. Up to now we have been able to send Sabine's parents, sisters and their children food parcels through our friends every week; but it seems as if this will also become more difficult now.

Once again, all good wishes to you and Mrs Bell

Yours affectionately,

[1] See the printed version, p. 192.
[2] See Leibholz, 'Politics and Natural Law', in: A.R. Vidler and W.A. Whitehouse (eds.), *Natural Law. A Christian Re-consideration* (London, 1946), reprinted in *Politics and Law*, pp. 20–3.

Sabine Leibholz to Bell, 3 February 1946, Bell Papers 40, fol. 358 (handwritten)

My Lordbishop,
I am sending you my very best wishes for your work during the coming year. May God always give you the strength to carry out the great tasks which He has laid upon your shoulders.

It is so hard and sad to think, that a year ago Dietrich was still among us on our common birthday – but he is so still in spirit.

Please give my love to Mrs Bell.

Yours affectionately,

Bell to Leibholz, 9 February 1946, BA, N 1334 (handwritten)

My dear Leibholz
Very many thanks to you and Sabine for your letters on my birthday. With you I feel that Dietrich's life and death is a very intimate part of, and gives a very special quality to, our friendship. I have just got from Rupp an English translation of Dietrich's words (supplied by Bethge – and now returned to you). I enclose it. I think it is good. The words themselves are very moving. Thank you Sabine also very much for 'Das Zeugnis eines Boten' – I am very happy to have it with its excellent photograph of Dietrich and shall read it at [intervals] with the help of a German dictionary. Thank you too very much for 'Natural Law', which is sure to be very good and clear and shall be read by me with care.

Grüber's visit has been a great success. He is fine for Monday night. I have seen a good deal of him. I have arranged for an interview between him and the Chancellor of the Duchy of Lancaster¹ on Tuesday morning. Once again: warm remembrances, thanks and affections to you both and all

Yours affectionately,

Grüber likes my 'Letter' and takes it to Berlin on Thursday or Friday.

---

¹ An ancient position of state, in modern times usually held concurrently with another office. At this time the office-holder was the Labour MP John Hynd (1902–71), who was also Minister for Germany and Austria.

Bell to Leibholz, 15 February 1946, BA, N 1334 (handwritten)

I am so glad you are having a change at Gordonstoun.

My dear Leibholz

I enclose 2 *proof* copies of my Letter. It has been translated into German, under Rieger's supervision, by the BBC who will radio it on February 24 and March 3 in two parts. There is a chance of its being printed in the *Christian News-Letter* of March 5. Also by the S.C.M. giving it their imprint. Both have to await the decision of their Boards next week. I am extremely grateful for all the help you have given me in it. Grüber is taking it in German and English to Berlin. And I am through him sending copies to Frau Bonhoeffer and Bethge. I can of course send you more if you want them. It won't be *published* in England till after March 3.

Please thank Sabine for her letter and tell her I will make inquiry as she wishes.

Yours affly,

Leibholz to Bell, 25 February 1946, Bell Papers 40, fol. 292 (handwritten); BA, N 1334 (copy)

My Lordbishop,

This is only to thank you very much for your last letter and the two proof copies you kindly sent me. Your 'letter to your friends in Germany' seems to me to make excellent reading and I feel sure that the German Church leaders will also have greatly appreciated your 'Letter'. You will certainly have heard something about the reaction to your 'Letter' at Geneva¹. – It is good of you to think of sending two copies to my wife's mother² and to Bethge. If you could possibly spare two further copies I should like to have them for circulation among friends. The translation part of which I heard on the wireless yesterday was also good.

I have read in *The Times* of today the resolutions adopted by the W.C.o.Ch. at Geneva³. I am very glad to see that the Council adopted a resolution urging the victorious powers to revise their present plans which meant that Germany would have °either to live from charity or that willing would have° to die from starvation. There are already many signs, which point to the stirring of a new nationalism in Germany today. You will probably have heard about these things. It is a long story and it cannot be told in a short letter. But one can observe the same tendencies – even in prisoners of war camps and the fact that the anti-Nazis are treated by the War Office like the Nazis contributes to this development. The lack in vision and imagination on part of the War Office is amazing.

Yours affectionately,

[1] Copy adds: 'on Germany'.
[2] Copy: 'brother'.
[3] Copy adds: 'on Germany'. See *Minutes and Reports of the meeting of the Provisional Committee of the World Council of Churches held from February 21st to 23rd, 1946; the constitutional documents of the WCC* with an Introduction by W. A. Visser 't Hooft (Geneva, 1947).

Bell to Leibholz, 13 March 1946, BA, N 1334 (typewritten)

My dear Leibholz,
I have just received a reply from General Balfour about your sister-in-law. I am afraid it is disappointing. If there are any material facts which you think could with any hope of profit be still put forward for Mrs Emmi Bonhoeffer[1], tell me, and I will send them on. But it does not look to me very hopeful. General Balfour writes very sympathetically, and indeed I found him most sympathetic when I saw him in Bünde[2]. Please send me his letter back, with any comments. Of course you can take a copy if you wish.

In replying to General Balfour I will bring forward the case of your sister-in-law Ursula Schleicher. I have Sabine's letter giving particulars of arrest and execution. But could you give me the full Christian name and full details about what form of Government official he was?

Yours ever,

ᵃCould I have the translation by *Rupp* of Dietrich's words back. I sent you the original!ᵃ

[1] Emmi (Emilie) Bonhoeffer (1905–91), née Delbrück, the wife of Klaus Bonhoeffer.
[2] Bünde, a little town 20 km north of Bielefeld, was the residence of the Education and Religious Affairs Branch of the Control Commission for Germany/British Element. Bell had visited Bünde during his visit to Germany in October 1945.

Bell to Leibholz, 15 March 1946, BA, N 1334 (typewritten)

My dear Leibholz,
Many thanks for your letter and for telling me about Rüdiger Schleicher. Do you want me to wait for a little more information about Mrs Bonhoeffer, or shall I write straight away about Mrs Schleicher?

Thank you very much for Dietrich's poem and Rupp's translation, and your article in the *Guardian*,[1] which I had already read, and which I like enormously.

Yours ever,

[1] Gerhard Leibholz, 'Dietrich Bonhoeffer', in the Anglican weekly *Guardian*, 8 March 1946, p. 114.

Leibholz to Bell, 28 March 1946, Bell Papers 40, fol. 359 (typewritten); BA, N 1334 (copy)

My Lordbishop,

We were extremely delighted to have your gift for Sabine's family this morning. Very many thanks indeed for it. I really think that there is hardly anything in the Germany of today that is such a blessing as these parcels are. Sabine's father wrote to us some time ago that Sabine's mother (who as the result of the enormous outer and inner strain of the last few years was so weakened that she periodically lost her memory for some time last year) is now again much better and has made good progress and he attributes this recovery to the parcels we are actually sending every week since August last. And the other members of the family are also better – in spite of the general seriousness of the food position. Payne[1] who called on us when he was last on leave here advised us to go on because thus there is a well-founded hope that they would come safely through the winter. Sabine has thus a new job. Now we are even able to buy things which have so far been beyond our power, and, in addition, we can recover in the next few weeks and then go on with new strength. I need not tell you that we share the delight of the whole family and, unless the donor of this generous gift does not want to be named I should very much like to thank him direct and give him some further particulars so that he may share the joy of us all.

Thank you also very much for what you say in the second paragraph, especially for the kind support with regard to the stipend from the Christian Council.[2] As to the further future plans I feel sure that the time will come when the authorities will approach us and then I will try to arrange with your help, my Lordbishop, a visit to Berlin and Göttingen for Sabine and me.

When I was last at Beaconsfield I heard from Koeppler[3] that you would come one evening in the course of the next few weeks to talk to the prisoners. It would be very good of you. In this connection, there may perhaps be – if you do not mind – an opportunity of mentioning me towards Koeppler and your doing this spontaneously would certainly impress him. I suppose I shall go there in the following terms but nothing has been fixed so far. – By the way, the same applies to the German section of the B.B.C. (Lindley Fraser,[4] Graham,[5] Gregory[6]). If they should ask you one day for advice or suggestions there might perhaps be an opportunity of mentioning me for giving some further talks in future, e.g. about Christian Politics, Christianity and International relations, The Essence of Democracy (I lectured on this subject in Balliol some time ago and hope to finish a book on this subject one day), the rule of law, The totalitarian State and The Christian doctrine, I imagine that a German audience would like such subjects, but I myself do not like to submit these suggestions to them for consideration: you will certainly understand this.

Please do not misunderstand me. There is no urgency in what I am writing. And I have a rather bad conscience to mention all this at all. On the other hand, I feel a much greater responsibility now and feel I should do something more than before to meet the demands – all the more as Bethge's and Karl Friedrich's* possibilities in Germany are limited.

With renewed thanks

Yours ever,

* He is in the Eastern zone and has himself a big family.

¹ Captain Sigismund Payne Best (1885–1978) was a British Secret Intelligence Service (SIS, more commonly known as MI6) agent during the First and Second World Wars. As head of Section Z in the Netherlands, Best was captured by the Gestapo in the Venlo Incident on 9 November 1939. He was liberated in Tyrol by German troops and handed over to the 5th U.S. Army on 5 May 1945.
² See Bell to H. Carter, Christian Council for Refugees, 1 April 1946, Bell Papers, Vol. 40, fol. 360: application for the extension of the stipend. The British Methodist Henry Carter (1874–1951) was the head of the WCC Department of Reconstruction, responsible for refugees and displaced persons; see Henry Carter, *The Refugee Problem – Europe and the Middle East* (London, 1949).
³ Sir Heinz Koeppler (1912–79) was born in Posen but educated in Germany; he migrated to Britain in 1933 and became a student and then Fellow at Magdalen College, Oxford. Naturalized in 1937, he taught German to British troops before becoming an officer in the Political Intelligence Department in 1940, transferring to the Political Warfare Executive in 1943. After the war he turned a Prisoner-of-War camp at Wilton Park, near Beaconsfield in Buckinghamshire, into a centre to educate Germans in the meaning and value of democracy. In international understanding Koeppler found his raison d'être. In 1951 'Wilton Park' was transferred to Wiston House in West Sussex where it became a home to an ongoing programme of international conferences held under the aegis of the Foreign Office.
⁴ Lindley Macnaghten Fraser (1904–63), Scottish academic, was recruited by the BBC in 1940 to join its German service. Believing that the service could play a valuable part in the rebuilding of post-war Germany he resigned his chair at Aberdeen in 1945. He was appointed director of the German service in 1947 and head of German programmes in February 1948. In Germany itself he was widely respected.
⁵ David Graham (1912–99) became a regular member of the German News Talks Department of the BBC in 1939. In post-war Germany and in the emerging Cold War, Graham's determination both to condemn Stalinism and reprove the western allies could spark controversy. He later became an executive of the BBC's Russian language programme and then deputy chief of the East European Service.
⁶ Unidentified.

Sabine Leibholz to Bell, 11 April 1946, Bell Papers 40, fol. 362 (handwritten); BA, N 1334 (copy)

My dear Lordbishop,

I was very much moved by what you wrote to me about Dietrich on the first anniversary of his death. It has greatly helped me on this sad day, when I felt the separation from my parents and the other family so very acutely. Pastor Bethge held the Memorial Service for Dietrich in the Dahlem Church on Tuesday, and I am hoping to get the text of his sermon soon. We listened in to the broadcast by the B.B.C. and I found it very beautiful. The poems and documents of Dietrich were read well, very simply and unpretentiously – just as Dietrich would have liked it.

Today I had a letter from USA, by a former pupil of my father,¹ who writes that Memorial Services for Dietrich were held in New York under the sponsorship of Niebuhr and Tillich. He further writes 'that 3 articles of the Bishop of Chichester were published – in German – in the New York "Staatsbürgerzeitung", which by the way I am going to send to your family.' I suppose it is your 'Brief an meine Freunde in der Ev. Kirche i. D.', which was published in three parts?² I thank you, my Lordbishop, very much for sending us the 'Letter'. I was now able to read it in peace. The German listeners and readers of your 'Letter' must have found immense encouragement and comfort in the spirit that permeates it! The only thing which struck me, when reading it, was that it would perhaps have been better to have the 'you' (when addressing the Germans) translated into 'Sie' instead of 'Ihr', as it is a letter and not a sermon. In a letter 'Sie' reads better, I mean it does not sound so much as if it was coming from a superior to a subordinate. I asked my husband and he felt so too. But it is such a small matter, and perhaps more a matter of taste.

I feel I must also thank you, my Lordbishop, very much for the gift you have sent us for the family-parcels. It was very good of you and will be a great help.

With kindest regards to Mrs Bell and to you
Yours affectionately,

---

[1] Paul B. Jossmann (1891–1978) studied at the clinical department of psychiatry at the Charité in Berlin under Karl Bonhoeffer, but due to his 'non-Aryan' descent migrated to the United States and to a career at the Veterans Administration Outpatient Clinic in Boston.
[2] This was in fact Bell's article, 'The Background of the Hitler Plot'.

Leibholz to Bell, 19 April 1946, Bell Papers 40, fols. 363–4 (typewritten); BA, N 1334 (copy)

My Lordbishop,

A few days ago Sabine's father wrote to us that Klaus, although entitled to a pension according to the terms of his appointment, was probably not an official. Therefore, I suggest that we do not follow up his case now. But it would be very kind of you if an opportunity should arise to write to General Balfour on Mrs Schleicher's behalf. Here the position is far more favourable as there is no doubt that her husband was a civil servant of the Reich. She has so far not been granted a pension simply because she is domiciled in Berlin (British Zone). Had she been in the free British Zone or the American Zone she would receive a pension without difficulty.

Rieger wrote me that he is in contact with you about the future treatment of the prisoners of war. He also told me that he had consulted Dr E. Wolff[1] in this matter and that Wolff has come to the conclusion that as a result of the treatment of Germany the view must be maintained that war has actually come to an end and that the Allies are legally bound to repatriate the prisoners if they wish to act in accordance with the spirit of the Convention of Geneva. I have now read what Wolff has put down in his paper and should like to add that I myself do not accept the conclusion to which Wolff has come. A 'subjugation', which alone would justify such a conclusion in international law is not possible without annexation and as an annexation of Germany has neither taken place nor is it planned we cannot speak of a subjugation. Germany has been occupied but not annexed. The conditions under which the occupation has taken place are very harsh and probably exceed the traditional limits of an occupation. But this fact does not make an occupation a subjugation. Apart from that, from a political point of view, the opinion that Germany has been subjugated – if accepted – would make the German situation worse than it is already and the political disadvantages would by far outweigh the possible advantages which could accrue to prisoners of war from such an interpretation.

In passing, I feel sure that neither Sir Cecil Hurst nor any British authority would be prepared to accept this view, which seems to me incompatible with the established facts.

In my view, the solution of this question should be sought by appealing to political, humanitarian and moral standards. If reconstruction work has to be done in this country, say, during the next two years a decision should be made whether the work should have a punitive or compensatory character. If the first be the case it would be just that the work would be done by 'ardent Nazis' like members of the S.S. etc. In the latter case it would be just that the burden would be laid on the German people as a whole. I have no doubt that at a time when Allied policy is directed, by implication, at the creation of a vast unemployment in Germany concerning millions of people two – or three – hundred thousand people would easily come forward and volunteer for the work – especially if the living conditions were better than in Germany and the people were not treated as prisoners and subject to the control of the War Office. I myself feel that the British government would gladly accept such a solution as they would exactly get what they want without the trouble, which I fear otherwise can hardly be avoided in the long run. Today the prisoners feel that they are not justly treated, first because there is no differentiation between Nazis and anti-Nazis and, secondly, because they consider their permanent occupation here a kind of slave work without seeing a plausible reason why just they have been selected to do this job.

I wonder whether you have seen the article THE NAZI GRIP ON GERMANY in the last issue of *The Observer*. What a difference from the situation last year when almost all visitors and observers came back from Germany with the impression that Nazism was dead. But 'if free elections were to be held now, 70 or 80 per cent of the people would vote Nazi' in the British Zone. The tremendous failure of British official policy could hardly be better demonstrated than by this reaction. I myself am not surprised at this development. How can Germany be re-educated if there is no sensible long-term policy which is constructive and gives the people hope for a better future? Under these circumstances how can the churches and the universities fulfil their task?

I am enclosing the last issue of *Time and Tide* with another poem by Dietrich and a copy of *Christianity and Crisis*.[2] I suppose, you may like to see Leiper's introductory article.

With renewed thanks
Yours ever,

---

[1] Ernst Wolff (1877–1959) was a respected lawyer at Berlin who had migrated to Britain in 1938. Here he worked as lawyer and chairman of a commission examining the possible terms of a peace treaty. Nominated by Bell, he also became chairman of a commission to reform German law. Wolff returned to Germany in 1947 and became the presiding judge of the Supreme Court in the British zone.

[2] *Time and Tide* published Bonhoeffer's poem, 'Christians and Unbelievers' on 13 April 1946, translated by Geoffrey Winthrop Young. *Christianity and Crisis* published Bonhoeffer's poem 'Who am I', translated by J. B. Leishmann, on 4 March. The ecumenist Henry Smith Leiper was a natural supporter of Bonhoeffer's growing reputation.

Bell to Leibholz, 26 April 1946, BA, N 1334 (handwritten)

My dear Leibholz,

Very many thanks for your letter of 19th, and Dietrich's beautiful and noble poems in *Time and Tide* (excellently translated) and *Christianity & Crisis* (also very good). I do hope a real sheaf of his poems will be gathered.

Mrs Bell and I are away in Somerset till Monday. So I don't know whether you have got Gen. Balfour's letter or 1 about Klaus? If I have I will write as you suggest.

Yes, I read the *Observer*'s most outspoken article 2 Sundays ago. And today's *Telegraph* with the account of Gisevius at Nuremberg. I wonder whether it will come out in the evidence that the conspirators tried to get at Eden etc in 1942? and whether it would be useful for me to call attention to the non-responsiveness of the Govt. in a letter to the *Times*? i.e. whether it would *do good* just now or better wait.

Yours ever,

Bell to Leibholz, 27 April 1946, BA, N 1334 (handwritten)

My dear Leibholz

I omitted Bethge's letter. I could send £50 or £75 of the Dietrich fund to Maria if desired and *if it can be arranged through Switzerland*. Can it?

I hope to see *Lilje* in Town on Wednesday – he will be here for the Bible Society meetings. I shall be at *Athenaeum* Tu. & Wed. nights.

Yours ever,

Bell to Leibholz, 23 May 1946, BA, N 1334 (handwritten)

My dear Leibholz,

This morning the Cantate by Dr. Rosen has arrived from 184 PW Camp,[1] and I am writing at once to acknowledge and thank. I am greatly touched by the gift.

Now I want your help informing me about this very camp. A friend of mine sent me this month a strong complaint of the feeding conditions in this camp and of the 'inhuman' actions of the Commandant Co[lonel] Clarke: petty tyrannism, and semi starvation. My friend knew a 32 yr. old POW from Hamburg, who had stayed with her before the war while her son has stayed in Hamburg with his parents. The daughter (i.e. brother of the English student of the same age) visited the camp in April, and heard complaints of the food. I had composed a letter to a very humane MP at the War office who deals with POW release etc – and has helped me a lot. But I am holding up this letter for a few days as I think you, having been recently in the camp, can advise me as to whether you have had any complaints, and what is your own impression generally. Of course I should not quote you. It would be a help if you could let me know early this coming week.

All best wishes for Whitsuntide. When do you leave? And I hope the girls will manage all right!

Yours ever,

[1] Llanmartin Camp in Monmouthshire.

Bell to Leibholz, 3 June 1946, BA, N 1334 (handwritten),

Private

My dear Leibholz,

A line to say I am going to Berlin for 3 or 4 days on June 10: to see about Religious Affairs. If possible I will see your parents-in-law.

Yours ever,

Leibholz to Bell, 5 June 1946, Bell Papers 40, fol. 365 (typewritten); BA, N 1334 (copy; handwritten draft on the back of Bell's letter)

My Lordbishop,

It is very good of you to think of visiting Sabine's parents, if possible. Please give them our special love and tell them that our main concern is how we can meet them as soon as possible. Perhaps it may be wise to ring them up before you are calling so that they know that you are calling and can give you a message for us. Their telephone number is 320801.

Perhaps there may be a chance of talking about our meeting them. I tried last autumn to get for Sabine and myself permission to visit them on compassionate grounds, but I was not successful. Although the whole position has hardly changed, in the meantime, there was a reply to a question in the House of Commons about two months ago (made by Mr. Hynd) to the effect that the Control Office would consider 'compassionate' cases on their merits in due course.[1] The question referred to an English Lady who wanted to see her blind mother in Hamburg. As our case seems to me very strong (especially if you would kindly lend me your help) I suppose that, ultimately, permission could be secured. The remaining difficulty, however, is transport, as we should not have as civilians the necessary official backing and might not be able to get to Berlin. We should also not have ration cards and, therefore, we might be a heavy burden for Sabine's parents as there is no surplus food. In spite of these difficulties I am thinking of trying it again if there should turn up no other way of seeing Sabine's parents.

On the other hand, Sabine's parents fall under the government scheme and we asked them a couple of months ago whether they would not possibly be prepared to risk the journey (by air or by car from Berlin to Oynhausen and from there to Dover by train). Then they would be able to recover here from the enormous strain and they could stay here as long as they like. There would also be the advantage of their seeing the children whom we could not take with us for a visit. But it seems as if they do not feel strong enough to risk the journey.

On the other hand again they asked us in one of their last letters whether we could not possibly meet in Switzerland. Of course, we should be able to overcome all difficulties and to secure an invitation for them. But what I should like to know is whether there is a chance of transport for them from Berlin to Switzerland. It seems to me to be easier to come from Berlin to this country than to Switzerland. But I should start with preparations for a visit to Switzerland immediately if Sabine's parents would prefer this. I hope we could take the children with us to Switzerland. Friends would help us to finance the journey and as far as Sabine's parents are concerned the expenses would be easily covered by the American fund now administrated in Geneva.

Sabine would love to send a small parcel to her parents. But we are not sure whether you take again Rupp with you. If so, would you perhaps drop us a line so that we can get into contact with her?

In the meantime, I have had some letters from Göttingen, among them a letter from the Dean of my former faculty (by the way, a former Nazi[2]) saying that they would be pleased to have me back, but the competent British and German educational authorities have shelved the whole matter in face of the present difficulties[3] (just as they have done with all other cases: Karl Barth is only a visitor at Bonn for three months[4]). I myself do not wish to press the matter as the situation is far more complex and intricate than most people realize in this country. I wrote to Tomkins about it in reply to a question and I will write to you more fully as soon as I myself see clearer in this matter.

Do you know Dr. Grimme[5], a religious socialist and adviser to the British educational authorities in cultural affairs? He is expected to be here in about ten days. You may care to meet him. Although I do not know him personally I feel that he is a first-class man with a very clean record. He was minister in Prussia until 1932.

I was at Beaconsfield one day after you left. The prisoners were greatly impressed by you and the whole atmosphere of that evening. They liked your lecture very much.

You will especially be in our thoughts when you are leaving for Berlin in a few days' time.

Yours ever,

---

[1] See Hansard, HC Deb., Vol. 420, col. 1862 (20 March 1946).
[2] Hans Welzel clearly made some concessions to Nazi ideology in his writings; see Günther Stratenwerth, 'Hans Welzel', in: http://www.enzyklopaedie-rechtsphilosophie.net/inhaltsverzeichnis/19-beitraege/83-welzel-hans#I (accessed 24 March 2016).
[3] In a private letter in November 1945 Leibholz's former colleague, Richard Passow, had asked if Leibholz would like to return to his Chair. But Leibholz preferred to wait for an official invitation from the university itself. In consequence, on 29 March 1946 the faculty proposed that Leibholz succeed Georg Erler, who had earlier been dismissed as a Nazi. In May Minister Grimme, who had himself, on 8 March, written to Leibholz, ordered the necessary steps for his re-appointment and visited Leibholz in Oxford. See Wiegandt, *Gerhard Leibholz*, pp. 565–6; Szabó, *Vertreibung*, pp. 383–5.
[4] After the war Karl Barth lectured as a guest professor at Bonn during the summer terms 1946 and 1947, but he did not wish to return to the university as a full-time appointment.
[5] Adolf Grimme (1889–1963) was German Social Democrat. A follower of Carl Heinrich Becker, Grimme was the last minister of education and the fine arts in Prussia until the *Preußenschlag* in 1932. In 1942 he was arrested in view of his connections to members of the 'Red Orchestra' resistance group and sentenced to three years in prison. Even so, his own activities in the resistance remained unknown to the Gestapo. On 15 September 1945 he reported – without success – the Nazi judge Manfred Roeder to the Allied authorities in connection with his involvement in the processes against the 'Red Orchestra', Dietrich Bonhoeffer and Hans von Dohnanyi. After the war he became a member of the parliament of Lower Saxony in Hannover and he was, until November 1948, Minister of Science.

Leibholz to Bell, 7 June 1946, Bell Papers 40, fol. 366 (typewritten); BA, N 1334 (copy)

My Lordbishop,

Just a line to thank you very much for your telegram, Sabine sent you a parcel by return yesterday so that I hope that it will have reached you by to-morrow. We have a bad conscience to trouble you with the matter, on the other hand, you know how things actually stand in Berlin, and, therefore, we thought we should accept your very kind offer.

I am also enclosing a letter Sabine has just written to her parents in Berlin and it would be very kind of you if there were a possibility of passing on this letter to them. I myself should be very glad if Bethge would possibly give you some more copies 'Auf dem Wege zur Freiheit'. I need them rather urgently for translation-purposes. There is also a plan to bring the poems out in a little book in this country and the United States and for this purpose also we should like to have some further copies (three would do).

I wonder what your reaction was to Churchill's speech in the House of Commons?[1] I myself suppose that the Labour Government will have to accept these lines in due course. The tragedy as it seems to me is only that this policy has not been pursued towards Germany during and after the war (unconditional surrender policy and non-fraternisation) and that Churchill himself is mainly to blame for the former unconstructive nationalistic trend of policy, which was bound to be a failure before it was actually applied. Thus immense harm has been done and the good will of millions of people has been perverted and frustrated. The danger seems to me now that the new policy will again make no basic differentiation between Nazis and anti-Nazis and thus ultimately favour the revival of the Nazi-spirit. Of course there are many other implications of the new policy: but you are just leaving and I do not wish to trouble you just now with what I am thinking.

With all our good wishes for your journey

Yours affectionately,

---

[1] See Hansard, HC Deb., Vol. 423, cols. 2011–33 (5 June 1946).

Bell to Sabine Leibholz, 14 June 1946, BA, N 1334 (handwritten)

My dear Sabine

Just back. I saw your parents and the whole family for an hour and a half in a very happy leisurely way on Monday, full of tender inquiries for you all: and they seemed pretty well. Your father working regularly as (professor or) physician, receiving rations of 'heavy worker'. I showed them Gerard's letters – they would of course be very glad to see you in Berlin – and you need not worry about rations – they could manage. 'Not impossible' for them, your parents to come to England though they shirk a little from it. They can't go to Switzerland unless they stay *for 1 year*, on the programme for recuperation from illness. It would need very special efforts to go to Switzerland for short periods.

They gave me banker's papers, which they said would give G. much pleasure about finance.

I saw the Chief of the Division concerned with pensions, told him about Dr. Schleicher: and he has promised to do his best.

Yours affly,

Sabine Leibholz to Bell, 17 June 1946, Bell Papers 40, fol. 367 (handwritten).

My dear Lordbishop,

I am exceedingly glad that you have been in Berlin and that you found time to see my parents and the family. It is such a comfort to know that you obviously found them working much better than in autumn. Many thanks, my Lordbishop, for sending me their letters, photos and papers and for taking my parcel along to them. It was very good of you! If only there were a chance for us to see them soon. My father is now 78 years and I fear that he is working much too hard. He has always hoped that old-age would bring him the time to sit down peacefully at his writing-table, and to write down the results of his long experience as (medically) and of his research. But it seems that he is still very much heeded as a consultant and as a teacher and has no time to write. –

Yesterday Grimme came to Oxford and gave report about education in Germany.[1] I also heard that Prof. Smend hopes to come to Oxford in August. We wonder whether he is coming together with Niemöller. It will be good for Gert to meet him.

Hoping that you, my Lordbishop, have had a fruitful time in Berlin

Yours affectionately,

[1] Grimme spoke with Leibholz about his return to Göttingen; see Szabó, *Vetreibung*, p. 385.

Bell to Leibholz, 18 June 1946, BA, N 1334 (typewritten)

My dear Leibholz,

I shall be at Oxford on Sunday, staying with the Vice-Chancellor, at the President's Lodging, Corpus.[1] I am preaching the University Sermon. I suggest that you, and Sabine if possible, should come round to the President's Lodging on Sunday morning, say at 11.30, and we could have a talk.

I enclose a copy of a letter to Mrs Schleicher, for purposes of information.

Yours ever,

[1] i.e. Sir Richard Livingstone. Henrietta Bell's brother.

Leibholz to Bell, 20 June 1946, Bell Papers 40, fol. 368 (typewritten); BA, N 1334 (copy)

My Lordbishop,

We are greatly delighted to see from your letter that you will be here next Sunday and we are very much looking forward to coming to the President's Lodging, Corpus and to having a talk with you there at 11.30 after the university sermon at St. Mary's.

Have you seen the article on the 20th of July in the current issue of the *New Statesman*? As far as I know, Major Gwynne[1] who called on Mrs v. Dohnanyi some time ago, is its author. This explains why she is mentioned in the article.

I have had a letter from Gisevius. In it Mrs v. Dohnanyi and her murdered husband have been heavily attacked and as it seems to me in a very unfair way.*[2] I mention this because I gather from the same letter that Gisevius is sitting on one of the Committees of the World Council and that he expects to come to this country at the beginning of August. As Hans von Dohnanyi was at the same time Dietrich's closest political collaborator this seems to me to be a rather strange coincidence.

I hope that there may also be a chance on Sunday of shortly talking to you on my own future. The position is that, against my hopes, the Christian Council has so far renewed the grant for half a year only. Although I trust that, ultimately, the Council will reconsider its decision in due course and comply with Tomkin's application I am now trying to find some supplementary means. This is all the more urgent as the grant by Magdalen College has now come to an end as a result of general decision.

As to Germany the whole matter has so far not come up, as the British authorities have shelved it. None of my colleagues here and at Cambridge has been asked by them to return (although a number of applications has been submitted to them by the universities) and none has gone. But even if it comes up many things have to be considered. Our position is very different, for instance, from that of Karl Barth who has gone to Bonn for a term or so. Barth is Swiss and this means that he is practically not much affected by the general misery in Germany. He can go back to Basel at any time he likes and his family remains in Switzerland. Further, he and his family have not really suffered from the Nazis (apart from the fact that he moved from Bonn to Basel) and, therefore, he has not to face the responsibilities we have to bear towards our large family. Actually, I do not yet know how things will, ultimately, develop. I am looking forward to Smend's visit at the beginning of August: for I hope to hear from him more about the actual state of affairs at the Universities, especially Göttingen. In any case, I wish to make the final decision in freedom, because only a free decision seems to me to have a moral value. This is why I have now started looking round for something else. I am enclosing a copy of Dawson's letter to Pakenham[3] who, however, told me that he has resigned his academic activities here and has no longer any academic contacts of weight. He advised me to contact Lindsay whom I approached and asked as to whether there would not be another chance of getting a grant (possibly in connection with the Rockefeller Foundation or the Oxford Press), which would enable me to go on with my work. If this were not possible I suggested some lecturing for the university or some tutorial work in Politics as I have heard that there is a shortage of tutors in Politics. So far I have not heard from him, and he may well have forgotten the whole matter. But this is the present state of affairs about which I should very much like briefly to talk to you also.

Yours ever,

* Dr. John told me that G. had some obscure connections with the Gestapo in 1933 and that many people never trusted him fully.

[1] John Nevile Wake Gwynne (1905–81) joined the British Army in 1939 and in 1941 joined the Special Operations Executive (SOE). In 1945–8 he was Officer in Charge of Religious Affairs in the Control Commission of Germany.
[2] Hans Bernd Gisevius (1904–74) had made Hans von Dohnanyi responsible for the papers which had been found by the Gestapo at Zossen. The discovery had led to the imprisonment and death of many conspirators. See Gruchy, *Daring, Trusting Spirit*, p. 153.
[3] See Dawson to Lord Pakenham, 3 May 1946, BA, N 1334; Bell Papers, Vol. 40 (II), fol. 369. Francis 'Frank' Pakenham (1905–2001) was before the war a lecturer in politics at Christ Church, Oxford, but after military service he became Labour politician in 1940. In 1945 he became 1st Baron Pakenham. Two years later he was appointed deputy Foreign Secretary, with special responsibility for the British zone in occupied Germany, a position which placed him outside the Cabinet. In May 1948 he became Minister of Civil Aviation. A conspicuously principled, though unpredictable, figure he later adopted many public campaigns as Lord Longford.

Leibholz to Bell, 4 July 1946, Bell Papers 40, fol. 370 (typewritten); BA, N 1334 (copy)

My Lordbishop,

I have just learned from a letter by Dr. E. Wolff that he sent you his exposé concerning the legal status of German prisoners of war in this country and that you have in mind to take part in the debate in the Lords on July 11.

Perhaps you may care to know, in this connection, that the Executive Committee of the National Peace Council will probably publish a pamphlet on this question soon and that the suggestions which I have submitted to them in this matter will probably be accepted by them.

My suggestions, as far as the short-term issue is concerned, have been the following:

1. Fixation of a date when prisoners of war will be allowed to return so that the prisoners know how long they will have to stay in this country. They suffer especially from the fact that they do not know when they will probably return to Germany and some have even expressed the view that they will never be repatriated.
2. The prisoners (as far as they are not 'ardent Nazis') should be granted the same privileges as Italian 'co-operators'.
3. An early repatriation of those prisoners-of-war who are urgently needed in Germany for political or other reasons should be affected as quickly as circumstances allow.

I myself attach a special importance to the second suggestion because, from a psychological point of view, it is only by greater freedom that the prisoners of war would gain the feeling that they are not simply 'slave workers'. As far as I can judge from my own experiences, these privileges would have a tremendous effect on them and would at the same time enable them to learn something of the British way of life. This point seems to me all the more important as letters of those who were repatriated some time ago have now arrived at the camps, telling their former fellow-prisoners that they should go slow and not press the authorities to be repatriated *now*.

As to the long-term issue I suppose I wrote to you about it in greater detail in one of my last letters. What I said there seems also to be supported by the trade unions in Germany. I have submitted the same suggestions to the N.P.C. for consideration.

John to whom I sent Gisevius' letter commented on it, as I expected. He says: What a travesty and irony that just a man like Gisevius, a former 'Gestapomann', sits on a Committee of the World Council of Churches. But he is (among the Germans) not the only former Nazi who has now become a member of the new Committees of the W.C.

It was such a pleasure to see you and Mrs. Bell a fortnight ago.

Yours ever,

ᵃP.S. Have you seen the enclosed from the current issue of *The Fortnightly*?ᵃ

Bell to Leibholz, 12 July 1946, BA, N 1334 (typewritten); Bell Papers 40, fol. 371 (carbon)

My dear Leibholz,

Very many thanks for your letter. Your points about prisoners of war were very useful. I enclose a copy of *Hansard*. The debate[1] was rather rushed, at the end of a heavy afternoon, and the Government answer came in the middle, instead at the end.

You will be glad to hear that I telegraphed to Visser 't Hooft, advising against Gisevius coming to England for the World Council, and Tomkins has withdrawn the application for a visa, on the list he sent to the Foreign Office.[2]

Yours ever,

P.S. 16th July. I enclose a letter which has just come from General Balfour. Perhaps you would let your sister-in-law know how the matter stands. Naturally if you think there is any point I can make in reply, I shall be glad to do so. Please send the letter back.

[1] Debate on Employment of Prisoners of War in Hansard, HL Deb., Vol. 142, cols. 377–401 (11 July 1946); Bell's speech cols. 397–400.
[2] See Bell to Visser 't Hooft, 6 July 1946, in Besier, *'Intimately associated for many years'*, pp. 325–6.

Bell to Leibholz, 20 July 1946, BA, N 1334 (typewritten)

My dear Leibholz,

Many thanks for your letter. I cannot understand how it is that my letter to Mrs Schleicher failed to reach her through Miss Bailey. But I am glad you sent her a copy. I should be glad of any information and reflections you can send me, which I can pass on to General Balfour. I wonder if you can give me any *examples* of the payment of pensions rights in the British Zone?

No, I have not seen Dulles' articles in *Life*, or William Billett's book,[1] but I should very much like to. I will see if they are obtainable at the Athenaeum ᵃ, where I shall be on Tuesday + Wednesday nightsᵃ.

By the way, I have not mentioned you to anybody in connection with my telegram to Visser 't Hooft advising against sending Gisevius here. I shall see Visser 't Hooft in ten days' time.

You will be glad to hear that I have just received a letter from Ian Colvin[2] in Berlin, to say that he has been able to visit Göttingen, and has arranged that Fraulein von Wedemeyer will be in a position to continue her studies. He speaks of being in England shortly, and hoping to visit me. His address [in] England is: 17 Linfield Road, Wimbledon, S.W. 19 – 'To wait arrival'.

Yours ever,

[a]Have you seen: Schlabrendorff's book *Offiziere gegen Hitler*?[a3]

[1] Untraced, curiously. William Billett is not an author catalogued by the British Library.
[2] Ian Goodhope Colvin (1912–75) was correspondent for the *News Chronicle* in Berlin before the war, he had been expelled from Germany in 1939. A man of many connections, after the war Colvin became a leading foreign correspondent for the *Daily Telegraph*. He would also go on to write an authoritative study of Sir Robert Vansittart: *Vansittart in Office: An Historical Survey of the Origins of the Second World War, based on the Papers of Sir Robert Vansittart* (London, 1965).
[3] Fabian von Schlabrendorff, *Offiziere gegen Hitler* (Zürich 1946). Schlabrendorff (1907–80) was a lawyer and early opponent of the Nazis. The senior officer and anti-Nazi, Henning von Tresckow (1901–44), had made his cousin his aide-de-camp in the staff of Army Group Centre in 1942. His main duty had been to connect the planning of the Tresckow circle of resistance with the centre in Berlin. After the plot of 20 July 1944 Schlabrendorff was arrested and tortured but he did not betray names of the conspirators. It was only because Roland Freisler, the presiding judge of the People's Tribunal, died during a bombing attack on the court on the day of the trial against Schlabrendorff that his case was – crucially – postponed. In March 1945 he secured an acquittal in consequence of the torture that he had suffered but he was transferred to a concentration camp and, finally, was among the hostages of an SS transport to Tyrol where they were freed. In the summer 1945 he was interned and interviewed by the Americans on the Isle of Ischia. The result was this book, written with the assistance of Gero S. von Gaeverntiz, the first report of by survivor of the resistance to be published. It was published in Britain as *Revolt against Hitler: The Personal Account of Fabian von Schlabrendorff* (London, 1948).

Leibholz to Bell, 24 July 1946, Bell Papers 40, fol. 372 (typewritten)

My Lordbishop,

Many thanks for your letter.

Thank you also for not having mentioned me to anybody in connection with your telegram to Visser 't Hooft. For I should like to spare Sabine's sister in Bavaria further trouble. She wrote in her last letter that she is being attacked and slandered by Gisevius whose intended visit (after Dietrich's and her husband's death) she refused because of his former strange behaviour. I myself do not yet know the details but to gather from his letter, there is no doubt that statements of his, which can be checked by me are incorrect and incompatible with the facts. All the ambitious men who have themselves no clean records like Gisevius and Gerstenmaier who do all in their power to push themselves into the foreground at the cost of those who have given their lives had better be silent.

On the other hand, I liked the article in *The Observer* last Sunday.[1] I also hope to receive Schlabrendorff's book from Switzerland in a few days' time. My friends say that it is very well done. You probably know that Schlabrendorff is a cousin of Dietrich's fiancée, and that he was together with him in Flossenbürg.

We are very glad to hear that the fund which has been collected by you in memory of Dietrich has enabled Ian Colvin to arrange the continuation of Maria v. Wedemeyer's studies. It is very good indeed of you. I will write to Colvin and hope to see him in due course. What I feel is only that £100 are worth much more in Germany today than 4.000 RM (i.e. the official rate). On the average, this amount is being paid for 800 cigarettes, which are worth £4. This is why we have arranged with Cockburn[2] in Switzerland not to send money to Germany but only cigarettes (the real currency), food, clothes, medical supplies and why I advised Maria v. Wedemeyer to accept in cash only the amount that is needed *now* as a transfer at a much better rate could certainly be arranged in due course. But I do not know whether my advice has not come too late. Today I read in a newspaper that 20 million marks have been found with soldiers coming back to this country. This shows that the Mark, however big the nominal amount, has no real value at all.

I shall write to you again as soon as I have heard from Berlin. – By the way, we had a letter from Sabine's mother about two weeks ago. She told us how greatly all enjoyed your visit on Whitmonday and how pleased they were to see you.

Yours ever,

---

[1] This was probably 'Secrets of the July 20 Plot, by a Student of Europe', The Observer, 21 July 1946, p. 4, cols. 3–5.
[2] James Hutchison Cockburn (1882–1973), former Moderator of the Church of Scotland (1941–2), had in March 1945 become Senior Secretary of the Department of Reconstruction and Inter-Church Aid at the WCC in Geneva. See Harold Fey (ed.), *A History of the Ecumenical Movement*, Vol. 2 1948–68 (London, 1970), pp. 204–9.

Bell to Leibholz, 27 July 1946, BA, N 1334 (typewritten); Bell Papers 40, fol. 373 (carbon)

My dear Leibholz,
Many thanks for your letter. I have a spare copy of the Schlabrendorff book, which I can let you have if you like. I have also heard (yesterday) from Mrs Schleicher, giving me answers to various questions, and I propose to write further to General Balfour or Brigadier Heyman telling him what she says.

Meanwhile I have received, though I don't quite know how it reached me, a document from a German of the name of Schubert. I sent it to Mrs Wiener[1], who has written a brief summary: but it looks to me as though there is more in it than the summary suggests, and especially in connection with the Hitler Plot. Perhaps you would have a look at it, and give me any counsel?

Yours ever,

---

[1] Possibly one of the three daughters of Alfred Wiener.

Bell to Leibholz, 29 July 1946, BA, N 1334 (typewritten)

My dear Leibholz,

One of my Examining Chaplains, The Rev. J.N.D. Kelly,[1] sends me the enclosed letter. I suggest that you should get into touch with him *at once*. I have told him that you may be doing so, in case you wish him to see Dietrich's fiancée, or make any enquiries at Göttingen.

Yours ever,

[1] John N.D. Kelly (1909–97) was Oxford biblical and patristics scholar whose books on Early Christian Creeds (1950) and Early Christian Doctrines (1958) became standard works for theological students. His essential academic home was for many years St Edmund's Hall (1951–79), but he had become a canon of Chichester in 1948 and remained such until 1993.

Leibholz to Bell, 30 July 1946, Bell Papers 40, fols. 374-5 (typewritten); BA, N 1334 (copy)

My Lordbishop,

Thank you very much for your two letters. I will try to see the Rev. J. D. Kelly before he leaves Oxford on the 2nd of August.

Thank you also very much for kindly sending me the book on William Temple.[1] I am delighted to have it. I have read what you wrote about him with the greatest interest and much admiration. No doubt, Temple was one of the rare personalities of our time who combined an extraordinary intellectual and spiritual power with vision, imagination and real human greatness. By the way, much of what you say applies to you to a not lesser degree. – I feel that this is the kind of book that should be translated into German. There is so much in it that is of highest actuality and significance just for the situation in which Germany finds itself today. If you do not mind and were good enough to let me know Canon Baker's address I should only be too glad to submit to him this suggestion for consideration.

I am enclosing the paper you sent me. I have read it and I suppose that you will have noted that its author is Trott zu Solz's brother.[2] There is some new material in it, but the points he makes are rather casual and based on personal experiences. He rightly stressed the view that the German opposition movement is much more than a revolt of disappointed and disgruntled generals. – In addition to that, the present trend of Allied policy towards Germany is bitterly resented, especially the lack of truly differentiating the Nazis from the Non-Nazis and anti-Nazis. It is rather difficult to make a suggestion as to what to do with this kind of paper. As far as it deals with the events of July 20 you may consider sending it to somebody who is interested in them. I am thinking of Hahn or Major Gwynn or [Otto] John who would certainly be glad to read the paper, because he is just writing something on these events. As far as the paper deals with politics I feel that all more or less sensible people agree today on the necessity of urging the government to pursue a more constructive policy towards Germany.

I hope to receive a few copies of Schlabrendorff's book from Switzerland in a few days' time. If not, I shall write to you again. I was told that it is mainly identical with a Ms. I read in Scotland last February. Strange as it may sound the circulation of this book is not permitted in Germany (probably because of glorification of the officers' caste). Therefore, we shall have to send it to Germany.

Dietrich's fiancée wrote to us that she is very happy to have received from you (via Colvin) RM 3.000 (i.e. the equivalent of £75 at the official rate) and thus to be able to continue her studies. She asked for your address and, no doubt, she will write to you as soon as she has received Sabine's letter. I have written to Colvin to the effect that if there were a left remainder, say, of £25 it would perhaps be wiser to transfer it in kind (e.g. in cigarettes). Thus it would be possible to secure about RM 15.000 or even more for £25 and to utilize in a much more effective way the fund you have so generously put at Maria v. Wedemeyer's disposal.

Last week I visited the Generals near Bridgend.[3] Among others, I met General Blumentritt[4] who had just come back (with Rundstedt) from Nuernberg. He told me that Brauchitsch[5] and Halder do not think Gisevius to be trustworthy. His statements, they added, were not compatible with the facts. On the whole, I could get on quite well with them, although I was frank and explicit in the lectures.

I am enclosing the latest issue of the *New English Review*. You will find there the last poem, which Dietrich wrote.[6] It is the last written word we have received from him. It was composed in the Prinz Albrechtstr. during heavy air raids.

Yours ever,

---

[1] A.E. Baker, *William Temple and His Message* (Harmondsworth, 1946). To this Bell had contributed a lengthy memoir.
[2] Heinrich von Trott zu Solz (1918–2009) served during the war as officer, but deserted on 26 August 1944, the day of the execution of his brother, Adam.
[3] The Island Farm Camp, outside Bridgend in South Wales, formerly Camp 198 and the largest prisoner-of-war camp in Britain. After March 1945 it had been re-designated Special Camp Eleven for 160 of the most senior German officers captured in Western Europe since D-Day in June 1944. Many of them were later tried at Nuremberg.
[4] Günther Blumentritt (1892–1967), promoted to major general in January 1942, was closely connected with Rundstedt.
[5] Walther von Brauchitsch (1881–1948) had followed W. v. Fritsch as Commander-in-Chief of the Army in 1938. A cautious, ambivalent and even ambiguous, figure, Brauchitsch had opposed Hitler's annexation of Austria in March 1938 and the subsequent intervention in Czechoslovakia. In November 1939 he had accepted that Hitler must be overthrown, but only if he ordered the invasion of France. After the fall of France in June 1940 he was promptly promoted to field marshal, but after the army's failure to take Moscow – and a serious heart attack – he was dismissed as Commander-in-Chief on 19 December 1941. After the war Brauchitsch was imprisoned at the Island Farm camp. He died on 18 October 1948 in a British-controlled military hospital in Hamburg, before he could be prosecuted.
[6] Dietrich Bonhoeffer, 'New Year 1945', translated by Geoffrey Winthrop Young, in the *New British Review*, August 1946, Vol. XII No 2, p. 122.

Leibholz to Bell, 16 August 1946, Bell Papers 40, fol. 376 (typewritten)

My Lordbishop,

Just a line to tell you that in reply to a letter written to Mr. Colvin about two or three weeks ago I had a telephone call from him this morning. I gather from it that the equivalent of the RM 3.000 is £60. This is a better exchange than I feared it would be. Thus a remainder of £40 could still be transferred later on. I asked Mr. Colvin that if this sum is to be transferred in due course, he should do all in his power to secure the best possible exchange under the circumstances and Mr. Colvin promised me to do this. I thanked him for his help.

This does not seem to me to exclude the possibility of setting apart from the remainder of the fund a certain amount of, say, £10 for a transfer in kind (cigarettes etc.) if you, my Lordbishop, wish to do this. Such a transfer could be affected either by Mr. Colvin or Sabine. I mentioned in my last letter that such parcels are highly valued in Germany today. When I saw Niebuhr in London yesterday we agreed that, under the present circumstances, it might be wiser not to transfer the fund in cash because of the very relative and doubtful value of the Mark.

Once again, very many thanks for the generous initiative you have taken in this matter. You could not pay better honour to Dietrich's memory.

Yours ever,

Bell to Leibholz, 17 August 1946, BA, N 1334 (handwritten)

My dear Leibholz

I have just received this disappointing reply from General Balfour about Mrs Schleicher. Please (copy if desired and) *send it back to me*, with advice. I must anyhow acknowledge it at once, and can if necessary reply more fully later. It would obviously be an advantage if I would make some *answer* now. I suggest (without prejudice!)

1. Mrs S. be asked to apply to a denazification board
2. Mrs S. accept social insurance ...
3. I express strong hope that compensation scheme for victims of 1944 plot be pressed forward.

Maas[1] tells me he saw you both in Oxford.

Yours ever,

[1] Hermann Ludwig Maas (1877–1970) was a protestant pastor at Heidelberg, committed democrat, ecumenist and pacifist; insistent on the solidarity of Jews and Christians, Maas became a leading rescuer of Jews and 'non-Aryans'. Because of his ecumenical connections in London and in Geneva Maas was able to work with a number of rescue organizations to get visas for non-Aryan Protestants to emigrate. As a member of the Confessing Church, he worked closely with the 'Büro Grüber' in Berlin. It was at the instigation of the Nazi regime that in 1943 the Superior Church Council of the Baden Church forced him out of office. In 1944 he was sent to a forced-labour camp in France. In 1945 he returned to his work as a pastor in Heidelberg. In 1950 he became the first non-Jewish German to be officially invited to the newly formed state of Israel. On 28 July 1964 Yad Vashem recognized Maas as one of the *Righteous Among the Nations*.

Bell to Leibholz, 22 August 1946, BA, N 1334 (typewritten)

My dear Leibholz,

Many thanks for your letter. You put your points most forcibly, and thus enable me to write a strong letter to General Balfour, both supporting Mrs Schleicher's claim, and incidentally trying to show that you really cannot expect to get results if you work in that way. It is all the sadder, as General Balfour, who is fundamentally a very sound man, simply does not know the line of country.

I think you had better let Mrs Schleicher make her own decision about applying to the denazification committee. It may be one of those technical steps the taking of which might help towards a favourable decision – if she can bear to do it. I will of course let you know what General Belfour replies.

Yours ever,

P.S. I have dictated the above letter to you before dictating my letter to General Balfour. But you will see that I say to him that I would on his recommendation advise Mrs Schleicher to follow the suggested procedure. I thought I would not in this letter quote the instances, which you give me about the Göttingen ardent Nazis, as it might put the C.C.[1] too much on the defensive. But I should like to make a list of such cases, and present them in due course. If you can give me any more, I should be grateful – and also if you can tell me how to collect others.

---

[1] i.e. Control Commission

Leibholz to Bell, 22 August 1946, Bell Papers 40, fol. 377 (typewritten); BA, N 1334 (copy)

My Lordbishop,

Just a line to congratulate you on, and to thank you for, your wise and fine letter in *The Times* of yesterday. It is extremely well balanced it seems to me that its arguments can hardly be disputed.

As to your suggestion you may care to know, my Bishop, that I frequently discussed it with the prisoners and that it[s] practicability was never questioned. To gather from my own experiences I even do not doubt that a considerable number of young prisoners would prefer to stay in this country for a limited time, under the conditions described in your letter. If the suggestion be carried out and co-operation be secured British needs would be met and German wishes be taken into account and thus the first really constructive attempt be made to reconcile the nations, especially if some re-educational work were combined with the practical work of the Germans. I very much hope that transport and similar difficulties will not deter the authorities from carrying out this suggestion.

By the way, I have heard from a reliable source that Russian and German uniforms are being produced in factories in the Russian-occupied Zone.

Yours ever,

Bell to Leibholz, 30 October 1946, BA, N 1334 (typewritten); Bell Papers 40, fol. 378 (carbon)

My dear Leibholz,

I spent over an hour with the Bonhoeffers on Sunday.[1] They were full of enquiries about Sabine and yourself and the children, and they much appreciated your gift. Both parents seemed in good health: they assured me that they were. Mrs Schleicher was pale, but she seemed well. The Bethges were all right, and the children (though I did not see the latter, as it was too late for them). I was also delighted to meet for the first time Sabine's eldest brother from Leipzig, who was cheerful, and said he was getting on quite well in the Russian Zone, and had no difficulties placed in the way – but he is in fact probably changing his appointment for a Professorship in Berlin. It is a question of accommodation in which he can live in Berlin.

I told them of the possibility of your getting over in the Spring, which of course they welcomed, should it turn out to be feasible. They asked me to send you and Sabine and the children their best love.

We had a very profitable and illuminating tour. I thought the situation was worse than a year ago, both physically and psychologically: but this is only a short line sent at once.

With my love to Sabine and the children,

Yours affectionately,

P.S. I was fortunate enough to see Maria von Wedemeyer. Her mother lives at Bunde, and hearing I was at Herford for conferences, Maria found out my movements, and came to a party. I liked her very much. She is very keen, and seems happy at Göttingen. She says she hopes for an academic career, if she can rise to it on the intellectual side.

One more point – Martin Niemöller and his wife arrive on Sunday, and will be in England for two or three weeks.

[1] In October 1946, Bell as chairman of the delegation of British churchmen visited Germany to study the Church situation and to take counsel with Church leaders in the British Zone and in Berlin. 'The delegation spent three nights at each of the following centres: Düsseldorf, whence Cologne and Bonn were also visited; Bad Salzuflen in Westphalia near Herford, where conferences were held; Hamburg, from which the delegation also went to a conference near Kiel; and Berlin.' See 'The Task of the Churches in Germany. Being a Report from a Delegation of British Churchmen after a visit to the British Zone October 16th–30th, 1946, Presented to the Control Office for Germany and Austria, London' (SPCK, 1947), p. 4.

Bell to Leibholz, (undated, but 22 December 1946), BA, N 1334 (handwritten)

My dear Sabine,

This brings our very best wishes to you all for Christmas & 1947, which I hope will bring better things for the family and the future. I was so glad to hear from Pastor Bethge[1] of his happy time with you at Oxford – also of the good condition (comparatively) of your parents in Berlin. It must have been for you, and will be for them, a wonderful comfort to have this personal embassy from Berlin to Oxford.

God bless you all

Yours affly,

[1] Eberhard Bethge visited Bell, Leibholz and others on his journey to Britain made under the aegis of bishop Otto Dibelius in Berlin; see Gruchy, *Daring, Trusting Spirit*, pp. 102–3.

Bell to Leibholz, 26 December (1946), BA, N 1334 (handwritten)

My dear Leibholz,

Many thanks for your letter, and Marianne's excellently designed Christmas card. I am staying with Livingstone at Corpus Wednesday – Friday for a niece's wedding. I should very much like a talk with you and to see Sabine and the girls if possible. I could come to your house on Thursday about 11. Would that be convenient? Perhaps you could send a message to Corpus.

I enclose

1. letter from Brüning[1], on which I shd. like your comments when we meet
2. two offprints of articles, in case I have not sent them before.

Yours ever.

---

[1] Heinrich Brüning (1885–1970), eminent German Centre Party politician, who had served as Chancellor, 1930–2. He fled Germany in 1934 via the Netherlands and settled first in the United Kingdom, and then, in 1935, in the United States. In 1937 he became a visiting professor at Harvard University; between 1939 and 1952 he was the Lucius N. Littauer Professor of Government at Harvard. In 1951 he returned to Germany.

1947

1 January	The British and American zones in Germany are united.
12 March	President Truman announces the Truman Doctrine.
5 June	George C. Marshall presents his European Recovery Program.
11 June	A new American directive (JCS 1067) begins to encourage economic development in those parts of Germany occupied by the western powers.
September	The Soviet Union creates COMINFORM.

Leibholz to Bell, 2 January 1947, Bell Papers 40, fols. 379–80 (typewritten); BA, N 1334 (copy)

My Lordbishop,

May I thank you once again warmly for having so kindly arranged Bethge's journey to this country. His visit was a great joy to us. It was a wonderful experience – just before Christmas – to have this first envoy from Berlin here with us – after all that has happened in the course of the last nine years. After what he said it seems that the parents and the family are, in fact, slightly better off during this winter than during the last one and he added that this is mainly due to the regular arrival of the parcels from this country and the United States and you can imagine that Sabine who has devoted most of her time to this work during the last 15 months is not [a] little proud of this achievement – especially in face of the fact that, on the whole, things are going rather from bad to worse in Germany.

In the meantime, I have written to the Control Office in London asking them to allow Sabine and me to go to Germany for a visit to Berlin and Göttingen.

As far as Sabine is concerned my application has been based on compassionate grounds. I have stated the facts with regard to the family and added that they will probably find in all Germany no family who has suffered more direct at the hands of the Nazis (because of their 'free' activities against the regime) than the Bonhoeffer family. It seems as if a few applications on these grounds have recently been granted and, therefore, I trust that they will comply with my request, especially if you would kindly lend us your help in this matter.

As far as I am concerned I was asked by the Control Commission some time ago whether I should consider to go back to Göttingen and to take over my former chair. Neither the family (including Sabine's parents, brother and sisters) nor our friends and my colleagues inside and outside Germany have so far advised us to do so without strong reservations. They have all urged us not to make a more final decision without having seen for ourselves what the position is like. Therefore, I have asked the Control Commission to allow me (before making a more final decision) to *visit* Göttingen and Berlin and to give at the universities there some lectures for which I have been asked. By the way, I have also been asked (unofficially) to give some lectures at the Evangelical Academy and the Confessional School in Berlin when I should visit this place.

On the whole, the Control Office in London does not seem to be very much in favour of *visits* to Germany by Germans under the present circumstances. But as Schweitzer's case[1] shows they make exceptions and as the reasons stated by me in the application seem to me plausible I trust that they will grant my application, especially if you would also support me in this respect.

What, under these circumstances, I should very much like to ask you, my Lordbishop, is to write a letter to the Control Office in London and to stress in it two points:

First, the fact that Sabine's case is unique – as far as compassionate grounds are involved.

Secondly, as far as I am concerned, that (please excuse my saying this) you think that it would also be in the British interest, from a higher *political* point of view, if it were possible to arrange the *visit* as applied to by me and to allow me to give some lectures at the institutions mentioned in Berlin and Göttingen. The course of lectures would deal with: The Totalitarian State and the European Conception of Life.

I should be most happy if you would approve of the procedure suggested and I should be most grateful to you for any help by you in this matter.

In case you decide to write a letter to support me, my Bishop, you know much better than I to whom it would be the best to address such a letter to make it most effective. But it would perhaps be wise to send a copy of your letter to the Department to which I wrote (i.e. Control Office for Germany, 75, Carlisle Mansions, G.1.c. Carlisle Place, London S.W. 1.) and perhaps also to the Control Officer in Göttingen who is dealing with my case (Major Bird,[2] Control Officer for the University of Göttingen, Göttingen, B.A.O.R.). My own letter was dated December 19, 1946 (Ref. of the Control Office RL 45/G). If the Department to which I wrote would not get a copy of your letter I fear that the different departments may treat the case in a different way and thus come to different conclusions.

I thank you once again for all the friendship you have shown to us again during the last year and wish you and Mrs Bell, also on behalf of Sabine and the children, a very happy New Year.

Yours ever,

---

[1] The theologian Carl Gunther Schweitzer (1889–1965), who had lived in exile in Britain since 1939, returned to Germany in 1947.

[2] Geoffrey Bird was University Officer in Göttingen 1945–50; afterwards he moved to Hannover as Deputy Chief Education Officer for the Niedersachsen province. Like other such officials he earned a succession of titles, first University Control Officer, later University Education Control Officer and, after 1947, University Education Officer. These were not military officers, but civil servants in uniform working under the Control Commission. Often relatively young graduates, most also studied in Germany. They had the task of 'helping the process of material and academic reconstruction' at the Universities, as Bird himself wrote. See G. Bird, 'The Universities', in Arthur Hearnden (ed.), *The British in Germany: Educational Reconstruction after 1945* (London, 1978), pp. 146–57; here p. 146. See too David Phillips, 'Introduction: The Work of the British University Officers in Germany', in Manfred Heinemann, *Hochschuloffiziere und Wiederaufbau*, pp. 11–40, and also other contributions to that volume; also David Phillips, *Investigating Education in Germany: Historical Studies from a British Perspective* (London, 2016), p. 122.

Bell to Leibholz, 5 January 1947, BA, N 1334 (handwritten)

My dear Leibholz

I am delighted that Bethge's visit was so happy and fruitful especially as a channel of recommunication! Also it is very good to hear that the Bonhoeffers, thanks largely to Sabine's parcel system, are *better* this winter than last. I am very sorry indeed that your application for permission [for such] a short visit to Germany has been rejected. I will gladly help in any way I can. But I strongly advise against a second application *now*. Much better wait two or three months. And while the case for both is individually strong: I think if you had a *special invitation* from a University to lecture, there would be far more chance of success for you alone, sorry as I am, if you both applied. Schweitzer and Emmerich[1] both went alone. Ehrenberg (though he is *married*) goes alone too.[2] A specific task – lectures in a given place, discussions, inquiries into prospects of work – would be [wise] to put forward when you apply again. But if you apply *now* (with whatever external support) they would be almost certain to turn you down.

My advice therefore is

1. wait 2 months
2. ask permission for yourself alone.

Later Sabine might have [a] better chance applying alone.

Yours ever,

---

[1] Kurt Emmerich and his wife left Britain in February 1947.
[2] Invited by Martin Heilmann, head of the Volksmissionarisches Amt at Gladbeck, Hans Ehrenberg and his wife had returned to Westphalia in January 1947. But Ehrenberg did not get his old parish at Bochum; instead he was employed in mission work. See Jens Murken, '"Vieles könnte ich in einem bitteren Ton sagen". Hans Ehrenbergs missglückte Reintegration in den Dienst der westfälischen Kirche. Aus der Sicht der Archivquellen', in Manfred Keller and Jens Murken (eds.), *Das Erbe des Theologen Hans Ehrenberg: Eine Zwischenbilanz* (Berlin, 2009), pp. 132–41.

Leibholz to Bell, 13 January 1947, Bell Papers 40, fols. 381–2 (typewritten); BA, N 1334 (copy)

My Lordbishop,

Very many thanks for your letter.

I think you are perfectly right in saying that we should treat the Berlin journey quite separately from the planned visit in Göttingen. In fact, with regard to the Berlin journey the Control Office has referred me to the Military Permit Office, which has to deal with all cases 'on compassionate grounds'.

As to my suggestion that I should like to visit Göttingen and to give some lectures during my stay there I should only be too glad if it were possible to follow your advice and to wait for a couple of months before making a new approach to the Control Office. But I fear that my case is more complex than, and quite different from, that of Schweitzer and others. The point is that the Control Commission took the initiative and asked me on behalf of the Educational Branch of the Control Commission whether I should consider going back to Germany where they offered me a post at Göttingen. By doing so they complied with a request of the Law faculty at Göttingen made in November or December 1945.[1] I received the letter in August 1946 and not until I was asked again by the Control Office about six weeks ago did I ask them to allow me to visit Göttingen. I did so because there was none among all those whom I have consulted in this matter (including the members of my wife's family, my trustworthy friends and colleagues in Germany and most of my friends who have visited Germany after the war) who had not strongly advised me not to come to a more final decision until I had visited Germany and seen for myself what the position is like there. Niebuhr and others have even urged me not to go to Germany for good, under the present circumstances, after all that has happened to our family. He spoke of 'self-destruction', which we should avoid and when coming back from Germany he wrote to me as follows:

'With regard to your problem as to whether to return to Germany, they (the family) took the position, which everybody else in Germany does, which is that those who are out ought not to come in under the present hopeless situation.'

In spite of this advice I have made the attempt to visit Göttingen. I consider the negative decision of the Educational Branch of the C.C. a bureaucratic and unfriendly act. Even under normal circumstances it was a matter of course in Germany to visit the place where one was called to. How much more this is necessary today when the decision is of vital importance with far-reaching implications esp. for the children, I need not stress.

The situation created by the uncooperative attitude of the Control Commission is unpleasant: I fear that if, under these circumstances, I follow your advice, my Lordbishop, this would practically come up to a rejection of the offer made me. I myself feel that I should make a new suggestion to them to the effect that I should be prepared to go to Göttingen next summer term and to act there as 'guest-professor' hoping that it may thus be possible to come to a more definite decision in the course of the summer. I also trust that Sabine would be allowed to come with me for the whole term. Another colleague of mine at Oxford (Pringsheim[2]) whose case is not as strong as mine has not had the slightest difficulty to make such an arrangement with the French authorities with regard to his and his wife's visit to Freiburg. If the Educational Branch of the C.C. would also refuse this second suggestion and thus further prove to be unfriendly then I fear that I must refuse the offer. They cannot ask me for something that almost everybody says I should not do. Of course, I should be very sorry, but no other choice would be left to me and I should have to see whether I can make an arrangement as suggested to the Educational Branch of the B.C.C. with one of the other occupation authorities.

I do not know how you feel about all this, my Lordbishop. I myself feel that it would be a great help if I could perhaps send in to you my application and if you would perhaps find it possible to write a supporting letter. Lindsay wrote a letter a few weeks ago asking me whether I should like him to do anything about getting me to Germany to lecture (of course, without repatriation). Therefore, I suppose that he would also be prepared to support such an application.

Please forgive me for being so lengthy. But I felt I should try to explain the situation more fully. I know that Ehrenberg has taken another line. But his case seems to me to be very different from our case in many respects,

Yours ever,

[1] See Leibholz to Bell, 5 June 1946, note 3.
[2] Fritz Pringsheim (1882–1967) was professor of Roman Law at Freiburg University. In 1935 he had lost his chair because of his Jewish descent. In 1939 he emigrated to Britain where he worked as tutor and lecturer at the University of Oxford. Pringsheim won back his Chair in 1946, but he only returned to Freiburg in 1951. See Tony Honoré, 'Fritz Pringsheim', in Jack Beatson and Reinhard Zimmermann (eds.), *Jurists Uprooted. German-speaking Émigré Lawyers in Twentieth-century Britain* (Oxford, 2004), pp. 205–32.

Leibholz to Bell, 15 January 1947, Bell Papers 40, fol. 383 (handwritten)

My Lordbishop,

I am dictating this letter to my wife, as I am laid up with sciatic neuritis. May I add to my last letter, that I met one of the officials of the Control Office last Monday (in London) and that I gained the impression there that the Educational Branch of the C.C. at Norfolk House considers itself only a 'postman' between Göttingen and myself and is not interested at all in the case as such.

For instance when I asked whether they would provide accommodation in Göttingen they were very vague about it, as [though] Göttingen were a very crowded place; or when asked whether I should get a re-entry permit – I mentioned to the official some people who have got theirs, – they said: no; when asked whether there would be a possibility of transferring part of my salary to this country to maintain the children they said: no; etc. etc. When asked why they were making the offer as unattractive as possible, they said that they had only to observe the general rules laid down. Practically they do not care. They did not even forward my application to Germany as I had asked for, but refused it here straight away. Perhaps they have not even read it properly.

In my view this uncooperative attitude can only be changed if the head of the Educational Department of Norfolk House would be made to take a personal interest in the case. The head is Major James Mark[1], and I am afraid he will only do so, either if you would possibly be prepared to support the application mentioned to you in my last letter, or, and this seems to me even better now, if you would kindly write a letter of recommendation to him, pointing out that I could be of some use also from the British point of view with regard to future co-operation. Perhaps you would not mind mentioning our preparedness to go to Göttingen next summer term and that we hope to come to a more final conclusion there.

We hope to get Sabine's brother over to this country soon. We had news that his health is very much impaired, and that he has had bad heart-attacks as a result of the strain of work under present conditions. Therefore we have contacted his special colleagues here, and I am glad to say that we now seem to have succeeded in so far as he will now be invited to lecture here and stay with us.

With all good wishes

Yours ever,

---

[1] Demobilized in April 1946, James Mark (who had a doctorate from Cambridge) was for over a year civil servant in the Education Branch of the Control Commission for Germany and Austria. Thereafter he was for nine months Private Secretary to Lord Pakenham, at that time Chancellor of the Duchy of Lancaster. In the spring of 1948 he joined the Treasury. See James Mark, 'The Art of the Possible. The British and German Universities, 1945–1948', in: Heinemann (ed.), *Hochschuloffiziere und Wiederaufbau*, pp. 71–8.

Bell to Leibholz, 22 January 1947, BA, N 1334 (typewritten)

My dear Leibholz,

Very many thanks for your letters. I hope you are better now. I am afraid sciatic Neuritis is a very painful thing.

It seems to me that the best thing would be for me to have a talk with Major James Mark (whom I know). The whole matter does seem to have been treated in an extremely red-tape way. I will see what I can do.

Yours sincerely,

Leibholz to Bell, 23 January 1947, Bell Papers 40, fol. 387 (typewritten)

My Lordbishop,

Thank you very much for your letter and intention to see Major James Mark on my behalf. I am still confined to bed but I hope that it will not be too long until I am up again. This kind of Neuritis is very painful indeed.

I am enclosing [a] copy of a letter by Major Bird, the Univ. Educ. Control Officer of Göttingen.[1] He seems to me (unlike the London Control Office) highly co-operative, helpful and really interested in the job he is doing and I myself have little doubt that I could easily settle matters with him on the spot provided he has power and is being backed up by Norfolk House. In any case, the letter may be helpful if you see Major Mark in due course.

I myself think to approach Major Mark after you have seen him [sic]. So far I have not told you that Sabine has never fully recovered from the blows her family has suffered. This is why I cannot leave Sabine behind for a longer period and I am afraid my application must include Sabine. She is in urgent need of some medical attention and this is an additional reason why we should like to see Sabine's father as soon as possible. But please do not refer to this passage if you, my Lordbishop, write to me back [sic].

If I do not succeed with my application I think we could manage to go to Berlin direct – Sabine on compassionate grounds and I in response to a call of the University in Berlin, which has offered me a chair there and has asked me whether I should not like first to come as a guest for one term. As far as I know Norfolk House has nothing to do with the Berlin-university.

I also follow up other plans: but I do not wish to bore you, my Lordbishop, with all the details. I confidently hope that something will eventually come out of them in the course of this year provided I can get rid of my neuritis and can rely on your friendship and advice as I could up to now.

Yours ever,

[1] See G.C. Bird to Leibholz, 16 January 1946 (1947), Bell papers 40, fol. 387: 'I have talked to the Dean of the Faculty and to the Rector and can assure you that they are greatly looking forward to you coming as a guest for one semester. They are also anxious that you should give lectures on political science and similar subjects.'

Bell to Leibholz, 3 February 1947, BA, N 1334 (handwritten)

My dear Sabine,

This is just to bring you affectionate greetings and remembrance of Dietrich[,] brother and my dear friend[,] on our common birthday. Slow though the harvest seems in these tragic post-war years the work which he did is bound to bear more and more fruit, and may God give us the mercy of being here on earth still to taste something of it.

I shall be in Town next week for the Church Assembly, and then hope to see James Mark and discuss Gerhard's and your visit to Germany with him. It is the kind of matter about which a conversation is worth many letters.

I am also taking up the repatriation of POWs on February 12 in the House of Lords; and on February 11 meeting a few MPs in the H. of Commons (together with Mr Ian Wilson from Bunde)[1] about the Report of the Delegation of British Churchman to Germany last October (I will send G. a copy of the Report[2]). It is very difficult to make an *impression*, leading to action! And the fact that representations, letters, press, and speeches *seem* to go on for so long without much visible reaction helps one to see how easy it is in a totalitarian state to become passive!

Well, I hope that Gerhard is recovered now – and you and the girls are entirely well?

Yours affectionately,

---

[1] William Iain Girwood Wilson (born 1912), Scottish theologian who served as military chaplain, 1939–46. In 1946–7 he was assistant director of the Religious Affairs Branch in Bunde and in 1948 secretary responsible for Germany in the Department of Reconstruction and Inter-Church Aid of the WCC.
[2] See Bell to Leibholz, 30 October 1946, Note 1.

Leibholz to Bell, 3 February 1947, Bell papers 40, fol. 388 (typewritten); BA, N 1334 (copy)

My Lordbishop,

Today my thoughts go out again to you, my Lordbishop, to wish you many happy returns of the day. Please, kindly excuse my type-writing: but I cannot yet write my letters myself.

With regard to Norfolk House I have been told, in the meantime, that it is quite a general experience that the London office is interested in a case only if it is pointed out to them that British interest is also involved in it. Only then are they prepared to change their indifferent red-tape attitude. This is all the more surprising as the educational authorities (British) in Germany seem to approach the problems in question, from a much more constructive point of view. But it seems as if Norfolk House has the last word.

The result of this policy of Norfolk House is that thousands of refugees who would be prepared to play their part in Germany today are prevented from doing so (especially all those with dependent children) because the only offer made them by Norfolk House, namely repatriation without any concessions, is unacceptable to them. This explains why according to my information so far only about 250 people have been repatriated and that among them no family with dependent children can be found.

After what we have heard from Berlin it seems that Niemöller's visit has not had the results which one had hoped for in Germany.[1] We are told that the State Department has been overwhelmed with letters protesting against further visits of Germans to the

United States. Even Dibelius' visit to the States seems to have been affected as a result of this reaction.

Once again, all good wishes to you for a new happier year and many thanks for all the kindness you have shown me again during the last year

Yours ever,

---

[1] Niemöller's visit to Britain was effectively a private one; he came as Bell's guest because the British Government would not permit a public appearance. By contrast, during his stay in the United States he gave a series of lectures and sermons. Here Niemöller appealed for penitence and reconciliation while also drawing attention to the reality of starvation in occupied Germany. Such themes were contrary to the spirit of revenge which was powerful in some influential circles of American society, and not least represented by Eleanor Roosevelt. See Schmidt, *Martin Niemöller*, pp. 189–91; Bentley, *Martin Niemöller*, pp. 188–90.

Bell to Leibholz, 8 February 1947, BA, N 1334 (typewritten)

My dear Sabine,

Ever so many thanks for your letter and that from your husband. I do appreciate this mutual correspondence very much.

Will you tell Gerhard that I am hoping to see Major Mark this coming week in town to take up the whole proposal with him.

I wonder what are the sources of your information about Niemöller's visit to U.S.A. I heard from Dr. Leiper that there had been criticisms to start with, but that now he was most acceptable. I hope the latter is true.

Yours ever,

Bell to Leibholz, 15 February 1947, Bell Papers 40, fol. 389 (carbon)

My dear Leibholz,

I saw Mr Mark at Norfolk House yesterday. He was very friendly and wanting to help. Norfolk House have got a general rule against visits for the purpose of seeing about a permanent setting down. On the other hand, if you were to put your request as one for permission to go to Göttingen as a guest lecturer, just on its own merits, that would be a quite different matter.

As to Sabine, he said it was very difficult to get permission for a lecturer to take his wife out to Göttingen. The only ground on which permission could be obtained for such a visit to Germany would be a compassionate ground, and these grounds were so restricted as to make permission in the ordinary way unlikely. But he advised that you should write to him at Norfolk House, putting the facts before him, and asking (1) for permission to go out as a guest lecturer: (2) for permission for your wife also to go out, stating the case from the compassionate point of view as strongly as you can. I showed him Major Bird's letter. I think it would be a good thing if you sent a copy of that yourself.

Mr Mark told me that he believed permission for your wife's brother (he thought it was her father) to come to England (somebody in Manchester had been interested) was through, or practically through. This statement he volunteered.

I enclose *Hansard* of Wednesday's debate.[1] Let me know if I can help further

Yours ever,

---

[1] Hansard, H.L. Deb., Vol. 145, cols. 561–608; Bell's motion and speech on the repatriation of Prisoners-of-War, ibid., cols. 561–8 (12 February 1947).

Leibholz to Bell, 18 February 1947, Bell Papers 40, fols. 390–1. (typewritten); BA, N 1334 (copy)

My Lordbishop,

I am most grateful to you for your letter and for the trouble you have kindly taken on our behalf to see Mr Mark. You have done me a really great service by this. I shall do what you have advised me to and make a new application to Mr. Mark and, of course, keep you informed of how things will go.

Thank you also for *Hansard*. What you have said in the Debate you have initiated is most impressive and moving and, on the whole, I feel that your motion pressed the matter a great deal forward in the right direction. Especially your argument that if there is a need for additional foreign labour in this country the right way to deal with this demand is to send the prisoners home if they want to go and to appeal for volunteers in Germany to come over seems to me unanswerable. In face of the fact that today millions of Germans want to emigrate, under whatever conditions (even Schlabrendorff, the author of the Book 'Offiziere against Hitler' [sic] and Dietrich's friend; he was together with him at Flossenbürg wants to leave Germany) such an offer would certainly have a great appeal. – I am also glad to see that you raised the screening-procedure. What I have heard confirms what you have said. Those who knew best to camouflage themselves got A and many who deserved A or B got C. I once wrote to the Control Office because a man who was sentenced to death by the Nazis (this sentence was squashed by the General v. Hase who was later executed) was screened C. He was then re-screened and has now been repatriated. No doubt, only Germans can screen them in a proper way.

If you could still spare a copy of your book 'The Church and Humanity' I should be delighted to have one. I was very glad to see that you decided to bring out in this book the speeches which you made in the Lords, together with certain articles and sermons on some crucial questions. The book is a monument of which the whole Church can be proud. Beyond that, it has a special personal value for me because it reminds me of the time in which our minds were frequently preoccupied with the same questions. (The internment of Aliens, Germany and the Hitlerite State, Occupation in Germany, Background of the Hitler Plot etc.)

The reports coming out of Germany are terrible. Our family writes with great sorrow of the growing attitude against the occupation authorities. I also heard from an (anti-Nazi) colleague in Marburg that he is just as isolated as he was at the beginning of the

Nazi regime. Another colleague was even threatened because of his pro-British attitude. I fear that people who go back to Germany now, under the present circumstances, have either to become nationalistic again with all that such a nationalism implies or they have to run the risk of being again treated as 'traitors'.

With regard to Niemöller our information came from Pastor Dress in Berlin. He wrote to us that the Americans in Berlin had told him that Niemoller's visit to the United States had had 'disastrous' effects as far as Germany herself was concerned. But, no doubt, Leiper can form a much more balanced judgement on the reactions of Niemoeller's visit than the Americans in Berlin, who, I am glad to say, must have been misinformed.

Once again, many thanks

Yours ever,

Bell to Leibholz, Good Friday (4 April) 1947, BA, N 1334 (handwritten)

My dear Sabine,

I have been reading Dietrich's copy of the *Imitation*,[1] which your parents gave me, today: and my thoughts inevitably turn to him and you in these early April days and the anniversary of April 9. Of course I constantly think of him anyhow: but it is more special just now.

I had a letter recently from Fraulein von Wedemeyer asking me to help a friend of his and hers to get entrance into Göttingen University – a von Bismarck. And I gather that my letter to Major Bird (from his reply to me) was likely to succeed. Has Gerard any news of his visit yet? I am off for 10 days to USA on April 15, meeting of the Provisional Ctee. of the World Council: back on April 26.

I hope you and the children are well. These days are full of melancholy, and the German news is depressing. If G. has time I should greatly like to know (before April 15) what he thinks might be done by the British Government (or at Moscow) or even by the Provisional Committee in the existing situation, when so many bad decisions have been made and over so long a time.

Yours affectionately,

[1] This copy of *The Imitation of Christ* remained with Bell for the rest of his life and was given by Henrietta Bell to the Dietrich Bonhoeffer Church in Forest Hill after his death. It remains a cherished possession of the church there today.

Leibholz to Bell, 8 April 1947, Bell Papers 40, fols. 392–5 (typewritten)

My Lordbishop,

Many thanks for your extremely kind letter to Sabine who will write to you herself.

May I briefly report on the situation [and] how it has developed, in the meantime: We have been told on the telephone by a Mr Kingsley who has been dealing with our case that our application concerning ᶜa visit toᶜ Göttingen has been granted[1] and needless to say we are most grateful to you. There is, however, still a difficulty, which I hope may be overcome with your help. It concerns the conditions attached to the permission. I have been told that we have to make our own arrangements with regard to accommodation etc. in Göttingen and that we have even to pay the fare in £sterling. As far as Sabine is concerned this seems to me perfectly in order. With regard to me they have come to the same conclusion (namely that from their point of view, the journey is a purely private one) because I took the initiative in the matter. If Norfolk House would have approached me in the same matter, no doubt, they would have made all the necessary arrangements on my behalf. The result seems to me rather absurd as I am being paid here by Norfolk House when I go to POW camps or to Wilton Park. But is it not much more in the British interest to give lectures to [a] thousand and more German students on Politics and International Affairs at Göttingen than to give lectures here – all the more as I feel somehow that there is hardly a German either in this country or the United States who could properly do just this specific job. Mr Kingsley, a former German refugee who is now naturalised and is working under Major Mark, will say that the Germans will settle the matter. But even if they do so I do not know whether they will be able to secure accommodation and, apart from that, payment in mark[s] does not mean anything today as one cannot exchange it and can only buy with it the German rations. Even the French are prepared (I could give the exact facts) to pay at least the fare and to secure Unra[2] food when people are prepared to visit German universities in the French zone.

I feel that Mr Kingsley would reconsider the position if he had a letter, which shows that the planned visit to Göttingen also lies in the *British interest*. I feel all the more so as I know that the Control Office is just looking for lecturers for the universities in the British Zone and is prepared to make all the necessary arrangements for them. Of course, I do not know whether you, my Lordbishop, feel able to write an additional letter to Major Mark or Mr Kingsley emphasizing this point. If so, it would greatly help me and put me in a position to write to Norfolk House again and to ask them for a reconsideration of the terms attached to the permission (at least as far as fare, accommodation and Unra is concerned). I do not quite see why things – difficult as they are for me, from a financial point of view, (I have to meet my commitments here and, in any case, to make the necessary arrangements for Sabine) – should become more difficult by dealing with my case in a way which puts me in a position which is worse than that of any English or German visitor who goes to Germany under a scheme from Norfolk House.

We will also do everything in our power to combine the journey to Göttingen with a visit to Berlin. Sabine's father has rather urgently asked us to do so and I fear that we shall need your help in this connection too. I trust that it will not be difficult to secure the permit for Sabine after it has been granted for Göttingen and we have secured medical evidence that Sabine's mother is 'dangerously ill'. With regard to me I am thinking of making use of an offer made by Berlin university to come as a guest professor next term and to lecture on International Law there. As Berlin University is under Russian control Norfolk House has probably not to deal with it and I have been advised by Mr Lindsay jun.[3] and a friend in the Foreign Office to approach Mr. CREIGHTON in Berlin. They told me that he might be interested to have at Berlin

University somebody who is known here. I do not know what you feel about that. In any case it might well be that I have also to ask you for help in this matter after your return from America.

As to the general situation I do not think that something constructive will come out of Moscow.[4] Some people say that the Russians are so weak that they have to make concessions. But I very much doubt it and it might be better not to come to an agreement than to come to an agreement, which (like that of Potsdam) will prove to be unworkable from the beginning. Thus it will come to the division of Germany (one of the reasons why I think that we must now speed up our visit to Berlin), although I feel sure that this so-called alternative solution is no solution at all. The struggle for German unity will only enter a new phase. The Russians will act, no doubt, with firmness, vigour and cleverness and I hope that the Western powers will do the same and use their trumpcard and not recognize the Eastern frontiers. Unfortunately, this country (unlike Russia) is very much handicapped by its obligations towards France (*Saargebiet*, coal deliveries, Ruhr-question).

I think that the Provisional Council should stand

1. for Europe as a spiritual unity
2. for a reaffirmation of the principles of the Atlantic Charter
3. for German unity within Europe
4. for a German Constitution accepted by the German people (by a plebiscite or a National Assembly) with reservations on demilitarisation, human rights etc. The question 'Unified or Federal Germany' is a question of secondary importance which, in my view, could be left to the Germans. I feel that Mr Bevin's opposition to Molotov's suggestion that the German people should be allowed to hold a plebiscite on this question was most unfortunate
5. for the revision of the Eastern frontiers

I fear I have not yet thanked you for the copy of *Christianity and Humanity*[5] you kindly sent me some time ago. I wrote to you in a former letter that this book would be especially dear to me and, in fact, it is so. It is a wonderful book full of wisdom and the Christian statesmanship. It is a book which I also highly value, from a personal point of view. For it covers a period when I was privileged [in] discussing with you some of the topics dealt with in your speeches and essays.

I was delighted to see the article in *The Observer* last Sunday. Its author knows you very well indeed and has pictured your profile with great understanding and love.[6]

I am enclosing a copy of the last issue of the *New English Review*. You may care to have a look at a new version of Dietrich's Stations on the Road to Freedom. I wonder whether you like it.

Our thoughts and wishes will accompany you when you go to America next.

Yours affectionately,

---

[1] Leibholz does not mention that the Faculty and the relevant authorities were impatient in view of Leibholz's delaying his return for almost a year. He had written to the British authorities in London (see Leibholz to Bell, 2 and 13 January) and made his application for his visit on 8 March (see the

letters from the Control Office for Germany and Austria to Leibholz, 3 April 1947, Bell Papers 40, fol. 397). On the same day Grimme had written that Leibholz must make his decision without a visit to Göttingen beforehand, otherwise the Chair would be filled by another candidate. In reaction to Leibholz's answer to this, R. Smend, now Dean of the Faculty, and the Curator, Helmut Bojunga, decided that Grimme should invite Leibholz for a series of guest lectures. It was in consequence of this that Leibholz and his wife received an entry permit from the British authorities. See Szabó, *Vertreibung*, pp. 385–7, an account which does not acknowledge the confusions of Norfolk House.
2   UNRRA: United Nations Relief and Rehabilitation Administration, established in 1943 by the member-states of the anti-Hitler coalition to provide aid for the populace of the countries liberated from German, Fascist and Japanese occupation.
3   Michael Francis Morris Lindsay (1909–1994) would in 1952 become 2nd Baron Lindsay of Birker.
4   The Fifth Conference of Ministers of Foreign Affairs of the Allied Powers held at Moscow (10 March–24 April 1947) led to the division of Germany and in many ways inaugurated the Cold War. Here the newly appointed American Minister of Foreign Affairs George C. Marshall presented the European Recovery Program while on 12 March President Harry Truman proclaimed the Doctrine of the Containment of Communism (soon known as the Truman Doctrine) to 'support free peoples who are resisting attempted subjugation by armed minorities or by outside pressures'. Molotov's proposal of free elections and a central government in Germany failed because of the question of reparations.
5   i.e. Bell's book *The Church and Humanity, 1939-1946* (London, 1946).
6   See *The Observer*, 6 April 1947, p. 6, cols. 2–3. This is a very sympathetic interview indeed. No author is named. In 1948 the paper would have a new editor: David Astor, a personal friend of Adam von Trott and an admirer of Bell.

Sabine Leibholz to Bell, 8 April 1947, Bell Papers 40, fol. 398 (handwritten); BA, N 1334 (copy)

My dear Lordbishop,

It was very good of you to write to me in these sad days, which are bringing back to my mind the suffering of Dietrich, the brothers and friends so very acutely. I am reading in the *Nachfolge* a great deal and I do hope the translation – which seems to be hard – will soon be finished.

During the last days we have been speaking for hours about the years of war in Germany and the 20th of July and have heard more about the happenings after the collapse. Mrs Solf had rung me up and came to see me with her daughter.[1] She knows my family and she and her daughter have gone through terrible pains, and have borne it very bravely. Yesterday they told me that they hope to see you today. – It is a very sad thing that members of the resistance movement in Germany are now widely being looked upon as 'traitors' by the ordinary people. Also the widow of my brother Klaus, heard people saying about her own children: 'Well, those children of course are not to be blamed that their father was a traitor.' Things have been very bad in Berlin as we all know, even my father, who would never exaggerate anything, writes of many deaths due to starvation and freezing. To see such intense suffering without being able to help is the hardest trial for them.

Thank you so much, my Lordbishop, for helping us with the visit to Göttingen. Gert will be writing more fully about it.

I was so glad to read about the Service you held for the prisoners-of-war, and I did like the article about you in the Observer on Easterday.

With very kind regards to Mrs. Bell and to you

Yours affectionately,

[1] Johanna (Hanna) Solf, *née* Dotti (1887–1954), the centre of a circle of non-Nazi intellectuals meeting in Berlin during the war. Together with her daughter Lagi Countess Ballestrem (1909–55) she had been one of those betrayed by a Gestapo informer after a birthday party held for the educationalist Elisabeth von Thadden in September 1943; see Gerhard Ringshausen, *Widerstand und christlicher Glaube angesichts des Nationalsozialismus* (2nd ed., Berlin, 2008), pp. 441–81.

Leibholz to Bell, 8 April 1947, Bell Papers 40, fol. 396 (typewritten)

My Lordbishop,

In addition to my letter of yesterday may I enclose a copy of Mr Kingsley's letter just received.[1]

The conditions attached to the permission are exactly as stated in my letter. I think that no British or German visitor (e.g. I am thinking of Schweitzer or Rieger) has gone over on similar unfavourable conditions and I feel that Norfolk House has come to this decision because I approached them first in this matter and that it was thus impossible to press the point that the visit (as far as I am concerned) also lies in the British interest. How strange the conditions are follows e.g. from the fact that I am even being asked to pay the return fares from here to Göttingen in English currency – even as far as the railways run through Germany (and although, for instance, the fare of all civilians coming from Germany to Wilton Park is being paid by the Government).

In par. 4 of the enclosure it is noted that no facilities regarding accommodation etc. have been requested by me. In fact, I have not specially mentioned these points because I was told over the telephone by Mr Kingsley that no such facilities could be granted.

I am most grateful to you, my Lordbishop, for all help you have kindly given us. I myself am thinking of writing to Mr Kingsley as soon as possible i.e. as I have received your advice.

Yours ever,

[1] See the letter from the Control Office for Germany and Austria, Norfolk House, to Leibholz, 3 April 1947, Bell Papers 40, fol. 397.

Bell to Leibholz, 10 April 1947, BA, N 1334 (typewritten); Bell Papers 40, fol. 400 (carbon)

My dear Leibholz,

I got Sabine's letter and yours this morning. Please thank Sabine very much for what she says. I am also most grateful for your words about the Provisional Committee, as well as about my book. Thank you too for sending me the *New English Review*. I have not yet read the version of Dietrich's Stations, but I shall do so.

I write at once because I thought I had better speak to Major Mark on the telephone. The position is this:

1. In principle there is much to be said for Norfolk House financing visits from guest lecturers to German Universities. The suggestion has been made incidentally, but

has not been considered from the point of view of policy at present. Mark says that now would be quite as good a time as any to raise it, and the best way would be for me to write a formal letter to Mr Hynd or to the Deputy Secretary, Mr Dean. But he says that this would have to be taken up with the Treasury, and it would undoubtedly mean a good deal of delay, even a month or two.
2. Major Bird, the Education Officer at Göttingen, has told Mark that they are fully expecting you both at Göttingen and have made special concessions for you while there, and, he believes, would put you in the way of accommodation i.e. on the German basis. Mark said that if you were now making an application for financial assistance, he would have to warn Göttingen University, as all the arrangements are on top, and there would be a good deal of disappointment, which might be awkward from their point of view.
3. I have arranged with Mark that I will put this before you and see what you decide. This must be affected by the dates you have in view, which I do not myself know. Also, have you any estimate of the cost of the journey, and the expenses, which would be attached to a visit if it had to be paid for from non-Governmental sources? If non-Governmental sources could be found, from our Committee, or in some other way, that might be a solution. But tell me your views.
4. Mark, after checking with Kingsley, did not know about your proposal for a visit to Berlin. There is a very big difficulty here – in transport. The only way is by sealed train from Bad Oeynhausen to Berlin, and he seemed to think that there would be a good deal of difficulty in getting permission. He did not think that a letter to Mr Creighton[1] in Berlin would be much use (though I know him quite well myself). I think the most substantial ground, so far as you are concerned, would be the *definiteness* of the offer from the Berlin University to come as a guest Professor. Let me know about this.

Yours ever.

---

[1] Creighton was responsible for the department of religious affairs in the British military government.

Bell to Leibholz, 10 April 1947, BA, N 1334 (typewritten); Bell Papers 40, fol. 401 (carbon)

My dear Leibholz,

Yesterday I received from Norfolk House a letter about pensions to officers. I should very much like to answer this with facts, if available, especially concerning the amount of the industrial assurance rates, the scale of war pensions before cancellation, and how they compare with pensions to civil servants.

Do you think you could let me have these facts by Monday? If you can't, just send me a line to that effect, and I will give a provisional acknowledgement. But any facts you can get during the next fortnight, so that I may have them on my return, would be most welcome. I should however like to have Mr Wilberforce's document itself back on Monday, to take with me to U.S.A.

I enclose also a letter from a German Vice-Admiral, R. Engel.[1]

Yours ever,

ªI had a good talk with Frau Solf & daughter on Tuesday.ª

---

[1] Rear Admiral Siegfried Engel (1892–1976) was held in Camp 11 in Bridgend from January 1946 to 1948.

Leibholz to Bell, 12 April 1947, Bell Papers 40, fols. 402–6 (typewritten)

My Lordbishop,

I am deeply grateful to you for having phoned Mark and written me by return. It is extremely good of you and of enormous help.

In the meantime, you have certainly received the copy of Mr Kingsley's letter, which speaks for itself. I myself wrote to you how I feel about the conditions which, in fact, put me (as a newcomer to Göttingen) even in a worse position than the residents of Göttingen who all probably have at least some supplementary sources of their own. (A friend of mine who knows Mr Kingsley told me that he belongs to that group of refugees who have retained their resentments. In fact, his first question over the telephone concerned the number of 'my' English passport and his second one 'my' naturalisation. I told him that so far I have not made an application for naturalisation. This may explain the reaction.)

Under these circumstances, I should very much like to ask you to write the formal letter to Mr Hynd or Mr Dean you kindly offered to. I have burdened the Committee so often that I do not feel it fair to make a claim on the generosity of the Committee when it is simply the business of the Government resp. of Norfolk House to put things right and to reconsider the position. Such a letter by you, my Lordbishop, would certainly also have the strong support of Lindsay who asked me some time ago whether I have done something about getting to Germany to lecture or whether I should like him to do something in this matter.

As to the time of my going I think that at least a month or even more will elapse until I shall have finished all the necessary arrangements with regard to the journey and to the children. I must also write to make enquiries whether the German local authorities at Göttingen are really in a position to secure accommodation (I was informed by the Mayor of Göttingen some time ago that it would be very difficult to do so) and what kind of lectures the university wishes me to give there. In addition, we have just had a letter from Sabine's brother saying that he hopes to be here at about the 15th of May.

I was interrupted and am now writing from Hereford.[1]

Of course, I shall ask him to see whether he can manage to come at a little earlier date. But as he needs the permission of the Russians, of the British authorities and of the university I feel a little doubtful whether he will be able to arrange this. In any case, we feel strongly that we should meet him here before leaving Oxford for Göttingen. May I mention this only for your *personal* information.

I am sorry to gather from what Mr Mark says that Göttingen will be a little disappointed about the delay. But as Norfolk House wants me to make all our arrangements by myself I fear the delay is unavoidable in any case. By the way, it is not unusual for German universities that lectures start at a later date and I shall see to it that I make up for the lost time so that the students will not suffer from it.

As to Berlin I had not mentioned this to Norfolk House in order not to complicate the matter. I had made an application to Princess Gardens[2] in February and they told me that there must be medical 'evidence of the serious illness of the person to be visited'. This medical evidence is now in my hands. There was in the answer a P.S., which runs as follows:

'At present, seeing to the large number of applications only one person can be granted permission to travel on each compassionate case.
If, however, applicants are to wait a while, the situation may become easier.'
I feel somewhat that the P.S. does not sound too unfavourable.
I have also been asked by the Rector of Berlin University whether I should be prepared to take over the chair of International Law at the Berlin University and the Dean of the Law Faculty in Berlin has expressed the hope that I should come first as a guest-professor to Berlin and that they would do all in their power to arrange the lectures if I wish to give them. I should send you the letter if you wish to have this.

You know, my Lordbishop, you could not give Sabine's parents greater joy in all their suffering than by lending us your help in seeing them i.e. in combining the visit to Göttingen with that to Berlin in one way or another. Otherwise the hope, which keeps them really alive, may vanish. Sabine's father is 79 years old and has just broken his shoulder and Sabine's mother is not well at all. My original idea, which may have been perfectly wrong, was to make the necessary arrangements in this respect direct with the Military Permit Office at Princess Gardens hoping that a supporting letter by you and Mr Creighton would be very helpful. I thought that Norfolk House has not to deal with 'compassionate cases' and with Berlin University. Sabine seems to me to have something like a claim on this visit and I myself have hoped to manage this visit with your help on the basis of the Berlin-invitation and of the P.S. mentioned in the letter by the Mil. Permit Office. But Norfolk House may, of course, even better have a portion to help than the Mil. authorities. All this does not change the priority of Göttingen and we shall go ahead with making the necessary arrangements in this respect hoping that a way may be found that we can visit Berlin at the time when we shall be in Germany.

As to your question, my Lordbishop, concerning pensions of officers. I made enquiries yesterday as I myself am not informed of the details of the different pension schemes in Germany. I discussed the matter with somebody who is working in the Institute of Statistics here and another reliable gentleman.

After what I have been told old age and invalidity pensions amount to about 35 or 40 R.M. per month (with 20 R.M. allowance for each child). The industrial Accident Insurance rates are about double or even treble as high as the old age pensions and leave room for a more individual treatment of the case. The scale of war pensions before cancellation was very high as a result of the fact that the Nazis considerably increased them. They were considerably higher than those paid under the Weimar constitution, although even at that time the pensions of officers were higher than the pensions to civil servants. A Major's pension e.g. under the Weimar Constitution amounted to about 550 Reichsmark plus children allowance (40 R.M. each child) and the Reichsmark under the Weimar Constitution had a higher value than the Mark today. The average pension takes a general amount to about 800 or 1000 Reichsmark. But the higher ranks have certainly received still higher pensions.

I shall try to make further enquiries if you wish me to do so. In this case I will let you know, my Lordbishop, the results before your return from America.

Once again, very many thanks for your invaluable help

Yours affectionately,

[1] This section of the letter is handwritten.
[2] The address of the Military Permit Office (see following).

Bell to Leibholz, 27 April 1947, BA, N 1334 (handwritten)

Please return

My dear Leibholz

I have just come back from USA; and send you the copy from CCG.[1] *Please tell me what you decide, as soon as you can.* Does it not look as though it will be best to stick to the plan, if you wish to get out, with your wife, soon!

Yours ever,

[1] See Foreign Office (G. Jenkins) to Bell, 24 April 1947, Bell Papers 40, fol. 408.

Leibholz to Bell, 28 April 1947, Bell Papers 40, fols. 409–10 (typewritten)

My Lordbishop,

I am delighted to know that you are back in this country. Sabine told me that she heard over the wireless that you were among the passengers who crossed the Atlantic in a new record tempo. We only hope that you are not too tired and over-worked and that the meeting of the Provisional Council was, on the whole, a success.

May I shortly report to you on the situation as it has developed, in the meantime?

1. I have received good news from the Military Permit Office at Princess Gardens. They have granted my application to combine the Göttingen journey with our proposed compassionate visit to Berlin. They have promised me to give permission, not only Sabine but also me, to proceed from Göttingen to Berlin on compassionate reasons. We are very glad about this decision.
2. I was in London last Friday to speed up the matter and also to see Kingsley who asked me over the telephone to come and see him when I be in town.

The impression I have gained from the discussion with him is not favourable. He complicates every situation and makes difficulties when – and wherever possible. His 'correct' line is that the case can only be dealt with on a general line. And yet if I have [been] granted to go to Berlin it is undoubtedly against the general rule. It is simply an act of good will. The same applies to Sabine if she is allowed to go to Göttingen. This decision is simply the result of your personal action with Major Mark. What I felt was that one could get on much better with any real Englishman than with this type of man who is a naturalised refugee and cannot overcome his resentments.

   a. I was told that I could possibly go on the usual English scheme. In this case journey, accommodation and food would be provided and the fee would be £1 a day. But Kingsley added that in this case I should only be allowed to go for two or three weeks and that Sabine would then not be allowed by his office to accompany me even in a private capacity. I do not see why she would not be allowed to do so, if authority has been given by the same office for her to go to Göttingen for a much longer time. Apart from that I feel somehow that the 'Göttinger' would be very much disappointed if I should only come for two or three weeks.
   b. I was told that when I should stay in Göttingen for a longer time I could also be accommodated in the 'English' way if I should be prepared to pay £1 daily. Unfortunately, I cannot afford this.

3. It thus remains with the proposal about which I wrote to you. When questioned about the letter you, my Lordbishop, kindly wrote to Mr Dean. Kingsley said that five or six months would elapse until a decision would be reached (Major Mark spoke of one or two months) and that a favourable decision would not be probable. Even if so, the decision could not be applied to my case because such a decision would have no retrospective effect. Thus I am still expected (what seems to me rather absurd) to pay the return-fare in £ sterling, to book my own accommodation in Göttingen and to get German rations. When I mentioned that even the practice of the French is more generous and that at least they pay the fare and UNRA rations he said that what the French do is of no concern to Norfolk House.

It seems to me bad that such a man is practically in charge of such a department.

Under these circumstances, there is, in my view, only room for the following alternative:

Either it is possible to reach a decision at a higher level on an individual basis. Pakenham, who I suppose is a friend of yours, may well be prepared to overrule K[ingsley]'s decision. You know better than I that Pakenham is a Christian, friendly to refugees and that he was a lecturer in Politics in Christ Church and, therefore, knows something about the relevance of the matter concerned. He also knows something about me as Christopher Dawson wrote to him on my behalf some time ago.[1] He also attended a lecture of mine at Wilton Park about six or eight weeks ago.

If you, my Lordbishop, feel that such an action would overdo the matter in question, what else can be done? I have written to Tomkins asking him whether he would possibly be prepared to make an application to the Christian Council for Refugees for an extension of the grant for at least half a year so that I should be able to meet my commitments here when I am in Germany and can make a start again when I shall be back and I should be grateful to you for your support.

As to the journey itself I made enquiries with Cook. The return journey would cost about £ 20 per person (Second class: without sleeper: there is no third class).

The position needs a clarification before long: Yesterday I got a telegram from Göttingen asking me when I should come and I have written to them that I hope to be able to come in the second half of May – provided all the necessary arrangements can be made up till then. We also feel strongly that we should now take the first and perhaps last chance of seeing Sabine's parents and alone for this very reason we should do all in our power to make the journey possible.

By the way, as to Berlin Kingsley said that he could not give permission to lecture there. The Russians would have first to make an application to Norfolk House. In my view, this is again an unnecessary complication as the University in Berlin acts under Russian authority and with its consent. But I think as the question stands now it is better not to follow up this matter but to wait until we are in Berlin. If there should be an opportunity of giving some lectures in Berlin during August I will talk it over with Creighton. K. also said that I should never get the permission to go to Berlin on compassionate reasons and he was surprised to see that, in the meantime, permission has been granted.

It would be very good of you to let me know what you think can or should be done in this matter.

[a]With many thanks[a]
Yours ever,

P.S. Please forgive this rather untidy letter today. But I am not quite well today.

[1] See Leibholz to Bell, 20 June 1946.

Leibholz to Bell, 29 April 1947, Bell Papers 40, fol. 411 (typewritten)
URGENT.

My Lordbishop,
Although the letter I wrote to you yesterday evening is partly out of date as a result of the letter you have got from the Control Office, in the meantime, I leave it as it stands and am enclosing it herewith.

I myself thank you very much for the note. Time is pressing and, therefore, if you do not come to another conclusion as a result of my letter I think we should stick to the original plan. As to the conditions attached to the permission to go to Göttingen I can only say that I never broached this question: I was simply told by Kingsley over the telephone that no facilities with regard to accommodation etc. could be granted and that there is no prospect of granting the application if I should not be prepared to make my own arrangements and to pay the fare in £ sterling. My answer was that if this be so no choice is left to me and that I should have to put up with these conditions. This does not prevent me from saying that these conditions seem to me to be rather absurd – especially with regard to [the] fare, and are quite unusual.

As things stand the matter is now a financial question and I have written on it in the enclosed letter. I very much hope that there is still a way out of these difficulties. I should be most grateful to you.

Yours ever,

Bell to Leibholz, 30 April 1947, Bell Papers 40, fol. 413 (carbon)

My dear Leibholz,
Many thanks for your two letters of 28th and 29th April. I agree that it is much best to stick to the original plan, and I am writing to Sir Gilmour Jenkins to that effect.[1] I am telling him that I have been in touch with you, and that the original plan stands. I take it that you will at once tell the Control Office yourself that you wish to go, and with the necessary steps taken for both of you.

Tomkins is away. But I am talking up the matter of the grant, so it is not necessary for you to take action on that at the moment.[2] Somehow or other the financial problem must be solved. You must let me know of any difficulty.

I am very glad indeed to hear that all is in order for you both to go to Berlin. But I suggest that you should take the matter of the journey to Göttingen up at once, so as to get there in May.

Yours ever,

[1] See Bell to Jenkins, 30 April 1947, Bell Papers Vol. 40, fol. 414. Sir Thomas Gilmour Jenkins (1894–1981), senior civil servant who was promoted in 1946 to Permanent Secretary of the Ministry of Shipping. In 1947 he joined the Foreign Office, but later returned to the Ministry of Transport as Permanent Secretary (until 1959).
[2] See Bell to Franz Hildebrandt, 30 April 1947, Bell Papers Vol. 40, fol. 412.

Leibholz to Bell, 4 May 1947, Bell Papers 40, fol. 416 (typewritten)

My Lordbishop,
Very many thanks for your letter.
The Control Office has been informed that the original plan stands and that we wish to go. This does not mean that the Control Office will take any further steps in this matter as would probably have been the case if the future plan of which Sir Gilmour Jenkins wrote to you had already been put into operation. The Control Office has given authority for us to go to Göttingen and beyond that they consider the journey as a private one and accordingly we have to make all the necessary arrangements with regard to the journey, accommodation food etc. by ourselves, which does not make things easy. For instance, I have just received a letter from Smend that so far no room has been found for us in Göttingen. But in spite of these difficulties I hope to do some

good in Göttingen and we must do everything in our power to get to Berlin. You, my Lordbishop, could give Sabine's and Dietrich's parents no greater joy in their age than by helping us in making this journey possible.

By the way, I hope to give some lectures in Berlin, in any case, at the Kirchliche Hochschule, which invited me to come a few months ago. Bethge will make further arrangements with regard to other Christian bodies which are situated in the English and American Zones. This might help to facilitate the solution of the financial question.

Yours ever,

Leibholz to Bell, 18 May 1947, Bell Papers 40, fol. 417 (typewritten)
URGENT.

My Lordbishop,
Yesterday I got our travelling-papers (with re-entry permit and Military Permit for Göttingen and Berlin). Unfortunately, these things take a longer time than I anticipated, although I have been pressing the authorities all the time. But as you know, my Lordbishop, Kingsley does not lend me a helping hand in this matter and, therefore, I cannot help it. Just the same I am afraid will repeat itself with the travel arrangements. If the Control Office would make the necessary arrangements it would only take a couple of days. But I have been told to make the necessary arrangements with Cook and, of course, this will certainly take a fortnight or so. In any case, I shall see in London to-morrow what can be done in this matter to speed it up.

As to the financial position I am extremely grateful to you for what you have done. Without the extension of the grant of the Christian Council the visit to Göttingen and the plan to go to Berlin afterwards would not materialise. The grant is of enormous help to me to make the necessary arrangements here for the children when we shall be away (probably three months). We shall leave the children by themselves. This is certainly not the ideal solution, but, under the given circumstances, we have not found a better one.

The travel-expenses will amount to £ 45 for both of us (Oxford-Hannover-Göttingen-Berlin and return). So far I have secured £ 25 and I am still looking for the remainder. I do not know whether the fund collected by you, my Lordbishop, last year has, in the meantime, been exhausted. If not, would it perhaps be possible that I take something out of it and put the equivalent in Reichsmark (or even more, if possible) on a special account for the Bonhoeffer-family or Maria v. Wedemeyer so that they can dispose of this amount when you give instructions accordingly. Thus one could perhaps cut both ways. In this case I should report to you on the arrangements made on my return. If this not be possible, would you perhaps allow me to take the matter up with the Committee? I am very sorry for all the trouble, although I myself feel that in so far as my journey to Göttingen is concerned the difficulty is due to the unobliging intransigence of Mr Kingsley.

We have been informed via the Foreign Office that Sabine's brother is expected to-morrow in this country and we hope to meet him at Harwich or London to-morrow-morning. You can imagine how greatly we are looking forward to seeing him. The last time we met him was Whitsun 1939 just before the whole tragedy took its course.

I am just coming back from a big officer's camp at Newport (No. 184). They asked me to write to, and ask, you whether you have received the musical composition dedicated to you and written by a Mr Rosen together with an orchestra consisting out of [sic] sixty officers. They said that it was very difficult to get it through and they did not feel sure whether you actually got it at all.

Yours ever,

Bell to Leibholz, 22 May 1947, Bell Papers 40, fol. 418 (carbon); BA, N 1334 (typewritten; only the second part of the sheet)

My dear Leibholz,

I am very glad things have gone forward all right for your journey. I gladly send you £20 as an advance from the Bonhoeffer Fund.

I am much interested to hear that Sabine's brother is expected. I should very much like to see him if he is going to be any length of time in this country. Perhaps you will encourage him to write to me – or tell me where I can write to him?

No, I have not received the musical composition from Camp No. 184 of which you speak. I am much interested to hear about it.[1]

Yours ever,

[a]Can you tell me any facts about *generals* now charged or sentenced for war crimes.[2] I have full particulars about *Mackensen*.[3] What of Kesselring[4]?[a]

[1] Bell did receive this composition by the German conductor Hans Waldemar Rosen (1904–1994); see Bell to Leibholz, 23 May 1946. But, most regrettably, the copy has not been traced and seems at some point to have slipped out of the Bell archive. In 1948 Rosen would migrate to the Republic of Ireland.
[2] For Bell's engagement in the question see the critical study of Tom Lawson, in *The Church of England and the Holocaust: Christianity, Memory and Nazism* (Woodbridge, 2006), chapter X; also 'Bishop Bell and the Trial of German War Criminals', in Andrew Chandler (ed.), *The Church and Humanity*, pp. 129–48. For a response to Lawson see Andrew Chandler's review of the first of these in the *Journal of Ecclesiastical History* and also Chandler, *George Bell* (Grand Rapids, MI/Cambridge, UK, 2016), pp. 135–8.
[3] See Bell's letters relating to the case of Eberhard von Mackensen (1889–1969) in Bell Papers Vol. 49, fols. 13–15.
[4] Albert Kesselring (1885–1960) was in 1940 promoted to field marshal; he was responsible for the Ardeatine massacre on 25 March 1944 which was carried out by Mackensen as commander of the 14th Army; see Kerstin von Lingen, *Kesselrings letzte Schlacht. Kriegsverbrecherprozesse, Vergangenheitspolitik und Wiederbewaffnung. Der Fall Kesselring* (Paderborn, 2004).

Leibholz to Bell, 24 May 1947, Bell Papers 40, fol. 419 (typewritten)

My Lordbishop,

Very many thanks for your kind letter and for sending me the cheque. I shall make the best possible arrangements and shall write to you again when we have come back to this country.

We hope to go to Göttingen on the 6th or 7th or 8th of June. This was the earliest possible date we could book when we were in town last Monday. We might even go earlier if other bookings should be cancelled.

Of course, Sabine's brother will write to you (his arrival was delayed for 36 hours)˙. He very much hopes to see you. He will stay with us until next Tuesday and then go to Manchester as the university there has sponsored his invitation. We are delighted to have him here.

As to the German Generals charged and sentenced for war crimes I wrote to John who has been at Bridgend for a couple of weeks and has 'screened' the generals.[1] I asked him to send you the particulars. I could also write to the Generals myself but I fear that the censor would not pass on such a letter to them.

I am sorry to see from your letter that you have not yet received from Camp 184 the musical composition of which the men told me. It seemed to me as if the Commandant of this Camp did not like the idea and made some difficulties. In any case, I shall let them know that so far the composition has not reached you.

Yours ever,

ª˙ as soon as he knows when he will be in townª

[1] In July 1946 his department of the Political Information Department (PID) came under control of the Control Commission for Germany and Austria (CCGA) and Otto John became responsible for screening the German officers and generals.

Leibholz to Bell, 25 May 1947, Bell Papers 40, fol. 420 (typewritten); BA, N 1334 (copy)

My Lordbishop,

I am delighted to hear from you that the *Cantate* has ultimately reached you. Therefore, I shall not send off the letter written to the German interpreter-office yesterday.

As to the Camp I myself have not met the Commandant. But I was told that he is very unpopular even among the British officers. He is obviously very strict and militarist-minded. Special indignation has been aroused by the fact that officers when going for a walk have been stopped by sergeants who acting on behalf of the Commandant publicly searched the pockets of the officers for food, cigarettes etc. As to the *Cantate* sent to you it was also difficult to get it through as the Commandant did not seem to like the idea. Only Dr. Rosen was allowed to send the opus while it was meant to be offered you as a gift from the Camp-orchestra (or even from the whole Camp). The camp-leader (General Bruns)[1] told me that there were more complaints and that he wanted to resign, as, under the given circumstances, the war office could not be properly informed and a re-education was made impossible. I cannot say anything definite on the feeding-conditions. The officers seemed to me well fed.

In this connection, may I call your attention to another point concerning the generals. About a third of the generals have been informed by the war office that their names have been listed either as war criminals *or* as witnesses in trials concerning war-trials, or as persons who would possibly be in a position to give valuable information in such trials, or as members of organisations declared criminal by the Court in Nuremberg. Those concerned do not even know today to which group they belong. All attempts to get more detailed information from the War Office in the course of the last six months have failed. This procedure is considered an intentional cruelty causing something like a mental torture.

We hope to go to Göttingen in about a fortnight's time, but possibly earlier: in any case we have booked the earliest possible date available. As our military permit contains the clause 'Holder to Provide own food, transport and Accommodation' and I suppose that at the instigation of Mr. Kingsley no support whatsoever will be given us by the Control Office I should [be] *very* grateful to you for a letter, which would enable us to get more easily into contact with the British authorities and to find the necessary support, which [we] might urgently need. In any case, I shall write to you again before our leaving.

Yours ever,

---

[1] Major General Walter Bruns (1891–1957) had been captured on 8 April 1945 and was a prisoner-of-war from 9 January 1946 to 5 February 1948 in Island Farm Special Camp 11. But it should be noted that there was another Major General Walter Bruns (1889–1967), held as a prisoner-of-war from 8 May 1945 to 6 September 1947.

Leibholz to Bell, 29 May 1947, Bell Papers 40, fol. 421 (handwritten)

Very Urgent
My Lordbishop,

I have just been informed by telegram that we are expected to leave Oxford for Göttingen on the 1st of June. Therefore, could I possibly get your letter by Saturday. I should be most grateful to you as Kingsley has done *nothing* to make things easier for us, under the present difficult circumstances, and your letter would be a great help for us.

I have told the children that in an emergency case they should write to you and we know that in such a case you will help them. But I very much hope that everything will be all right.

We can best be reached (also by telegram or telephone) c/o Major G. C. Bird, Univ. Educ. Control Officer, University of Göttingen, HQ. MIL. Gov. Land Niedersachsen, att. HQ Mil. Gov. Kreis Gp. Göttingen, 126 HQ. CCG. BAOR.

Sabine gives you her special love.
God be with you and us.

Yours affectionately,

Bell to Leibholz, 30 May 1947, BA, N 1334 (typewritten); Bell Papers 40, fol. 422 (carbon)

My dear Leibholz,

I hope the enclosed commendation will be of use to you. Please do not hesitate at any time to invoke my aid if you think I can be of any assistance whatever. I am delighted that the children should let me know if they are in need of any advice or assistance.

But please let them write to me at an early date – whether they need any assistance or not – when they have heard from you that you have arrived.

I do hope that your visit will be fruitful in very many ways. I am sure that not only will your whole family be delighted to see you, but many other friends will rejoice. It cannot fail to be a time of mixed feelings for you, as you go back to Germany, and there will be much sorrow: but may God keep and protect you both, and make the way for the future plan.

Give my love to Sabine, and please ask her to give my love to her whole family – and a special message to Miss Wedemeyer. If there is anything that you or they need while you are away, I will of course try to do what I can. Will any of the family be handicapped for lack of the parcels, which you have been accustomed to send – or in any other way?

I note your address. I shall be very thankful to get letters, with any reflections, from you, as you have opportunity.

Yours affectionately,

Bell's letter of recommendation, 30 May 1947, Bell Papers Vol. 40, fol. 423 (carbon)

It gives me great pleasure to write this letter of introduction and warm commendation in favour of Professor G. Leibholz and his wife. They are particular friends of mine: I have known them since 1939, when they came over to England. I should be most grateful for any assistance that could be given to them by Military Government and by C.C.G. (British Element) during their stay in the British Zone and in Berlin.

Professor Leibholz is a well-known authority on International Law and Political Science, and is now revisiting Göttingen University and also paying a visit to Berlin University. Mrs Leibholz is the sister of Pastor Dietrich Bonhoeffer, whom I knew for many years before the war. Pastor Bonhoeffer was a prominent member of the Confessional Church and a very active opponent of the Nazis, who paid for his opposition with his life, being one of the victims of the July 20 Plot.

I should be most grateful for any sympathy shown to Professor and Mrs Leibholz, who have my warm friendship and whole-hearted confidence.

Bishop of Chichester.

Leibholz to Bell, Oxford, 31 May 1947, Bell Papers 40, fol. 424 (typewritten)

My Lordbishop,

Just a line before our leaving to thank you warmly for your letter, which has just arrived. It is a great comfort to us as so far we have never left the children by themselves. I trust that they will manage all right – provided there is no emergency case. In any case, the children are delighted to know that they may write to you if something should happen that they cannot master.

With regard to the parcels for the family we have made some arrangements with American friends who we felt are in an easier position to help during the period of our absence.

All is a little bit overwhelming but perhaps it is quite good that there is no time left for reflection, which would make things so much more difficult.

Thank you also very much for the recommendation-letter, which I trust will be of an enormous help to us. I thus hope to get permission for us to travel from Hannover to Berlin in a military train and to avoid the Russian control, which otherwise seems to be unavoidable.

I hope to be able to write to you from Göttingen.

Once again many thanks for all the help you have given us. We fully realize that without it there would not have been the chance of going to Göttingen and Berlin and of combining the lectures with the hope to see Sabine's parents and whole family. Let us hope that things will go according to plan. We shall bear in mind what we owe you when we meet those whom we love and we shall think of you.

Yours affectionately,

Bell to Leibholz, 29 June 1947, BA, N 1334 (handwritten)

My dear Leibholz,

You and Sabine will be glad to hear that I found Marianne & Christiane well and happy when I paid them a surprise visit on Wednesday (24th) when I went to Oxford for the Ch[rist] Ch[urch] Gaudy. They gave me good news of you both, and of your lectures: and told me roughly what you found in Germany, and the difficulties, material and others, with which Germans have to contend.

I was very glad to meet your b.-in-law the scientist – and had a good long evening with him at the Athenaeum.

I was vy glad to hear how much your lectures[1] are appreciated by the students! and also to have news of Maria.

I have arranged (provided the Government give the time from legislation business) to open a debate on British Zone conditions, and the *urgent need* of making a Peace Treaty on Tuesday, on July 30. I have seen Pakenham, and he will I think be glad of such a debate.

Now I should greatly value your help once again, on points that should be made both *re* conditions in the British Zone, and the Peace Treaty itself.

As to the latter: Potsdam says 'No separate Treaty' – and to *advocate* a Treaty for West-Germany as preferable to indefinite continuance of the present uncertainty etc. would be a grave step. What is your view? And with whom could a Treaty be concluded? I mean, what Germans? Short of a treaty, what could Britain, America (and France) determine (supposing Russia still refuses to co-operate) for the Western Zones? and [illegible] what form could their policy take? decrees? and in what order should such a policy or policies be put? How, for example, would you act if you were Bevin in the present circumstances?

I should like to make a constructive speech; after setting out the unsatisfactory present facts. I should enormously value your help, *facts and arguments*. All the better if you could let me have them by say July 22.

Yours ever,

---

[1] The first lesson of Leibholz's lecture *Politische Probleme der Gegenwart*, given on 11 June, was published: 'Wiederbegegnung' in *Göttinger Universitätszeitung*, No. 14, 20 June 1947, pp. 1–3.

Bell to Leibholz, 14 July 1947, BA, N 1334 (typewritten); Bell Papers 40, fol. 425 (carbon)

My dear Leibholz,

I am wondering whether you got my letter telling you of the debate in the House of Lords, which I am opening on July 30th.[1] If you have done, this is likely to cross a reply from you – but I don't want to run a risk.

I am almost anxious for your opinion about peace between Germany and the Allied Powers, and the kind of line that it would be really useful and practicable to take. I suppose the main problem is, can I and should I urge that a peace settlement is so necessary for Europe's sake that if Russia still stands out the Western Powers should make peace with Western Germany?

I should be on very dangerous ground if I advocated a fully-fledged treaty of peace with Western Germany irrespective of Russia, after the pledge not to make an independent peace. But what is there, short of a fully-fledged treaty, which would bring some settlement and some future? Further, what are the main ways in which the Potsdam Agreement has been broken – especially by Russia but also by the British?

In the *Observer* next Sunday – the anniversary of the Plot – an article is appearing by me on Germany's Underground.

Yours ever,

---

[1] The subject of which was the repatriation of prisoners-of-war: see Hansard, HL Deb., Vol. 151, cols. 745–6 (30 July 1947).

Leibholz to Bell, 16 July 1947, Bell Papers 40, fol. 426 (handwritten)

My Lordbishop,

This is just a line to ask you kindly to forgive me for not having written to you before. I had in mind to send you my comments as early as a couple of days ago. But the conditions of life and the daily works are rather overwhelming in these days and, therefore, I have not yet quite finished them. But I shall see to it that you get them by the 22nd of July and thus I hope I shall still be in time.

Yours affectionately,

P.S. Sabine and I are most grateful to you for having called on the children three weeks ago when you were in Oxford for the C.C.G.[1] one day. It was extremely kind of you and we are delighted to know that you have seen the children and have found them well and happy.

Sabine gives you her special love.

My Memo. will be sent to you by Air Mail.

[1] i.e. Christ Church Gandy.

Leibholz to Bell, Göttingen, 19 July 1947, Bell Papers 40, fols. 427–30 (typewritten); BA, N 1334 (copy)

My Lordbishop,

I hope you have received the note I sent you the day before yesterday. I am terribly sorry to be so late with my comments, but one is simply overwhelmed here with work and the difficulties of the daily life and, therefore, unfortunately, too little time is left to concentrate on the things, which really matter. But still I hope you will get the letter in time by the 22nd of July.

Without dealing with my personal experiences I shall simply give you my impressions, which might be useful in connection with the forthcoming debate which you have arranged to take place on the 30th of July. Of course, I can only base my comments on the experiences made in Göttingen, but conditions in Göttingen are, on the whole, better than in the remainder of the British zone and, therefore, I think that what I am going to say about Göttingen also applies to a more or lesser degree to the rest of the British zone.

The overwhelming impression by which one is struck is that people are living here in a state of hopelessness, despair and despondency. This state has caught so intensively the souls and minds ᵃof peopleᵃ that most of the latter hope somehow that the conflict between West and East, which they think is inevitable, might bring in the end some relief to them and improve their present plight. They argue that as things stand today they cannot go on for long, and, therefore, the sooner the conflict would come the better would it be for Germany in the end.

It is not difficult to see the reasons for this state of affairs:

First, there is as you know the food crisis. I think it is no overstatement to say that it is not possible to live on the average ration unless one belongs to those who

a. either live in the country or have special friends among the farmers or are able to grow some additional food by themselves or
b. live on the Black Market or
c. are able to exchange property for food or
d. live on parcels sent to them by friends abroad regularly.

On the whole, children and the girls are in a better position to bear the hardship than the men who cannot live on this diet. The man in the street, the students and the old people, are obviously very badly affected ᵃby this crisis.ᵃ

Secondly, there is the general economical crisis. As you know the general economical situation has gone from bad to worse in the course of the last two years. F[or]. i[nstance]. there [...][1]

[It is] perhaps interesting to mention in this connection that it is very difficult to find people willing to serve on the German denazification committees, simply because these people fear that they would be punished for their activities later on.[2] It is also not a quite uncommon experience ᵃtodayᵃ that anti-Nazis shut their windows before they start to speak frankly about what they are thinking. Thus I myself have little doubt that Adolf II, if he could only make his appearance, would receive a tremendous welcome by the great majority of the German people today.

Considering this state of affairs it is not surprising to see that ᵇtheᵇ people simply do not believe in what is being told them about the British people, their good will and their own plight. F[or] i[nstance], they roar with laughter when news films are being shown in which they are being told that Germans coming to England as guests are being received with great kindness, friendliness and hospitality. On the whole, they believe things which are apt to compromise the British. For example, they are completely convinced that butter, sugar, vegetables, fruit are being exported to England and it seems to me ᵃevenᵃ urgent to ask the Government whether such an export has really taken place. I have heard many a detailed story about these things [are] ᵃsupposedᵃ to go on all the time that it would be very useful to extract the truth from the Government in this respect.

This reaction of the German people is perhaps not so surprising if we bear in mind the political mistakes made during and after the war by the Allies, including Great Britain, especially the unconditional surrender and non-fraternisation policy. It was actually predictable and was foreseen. You know better than I that the Allies let their great chance slip from their hands when they came to Germany as victors (in a nationalistic war) and not as liberators as they were expected to come by the majority of the people after the propaganda of the BBC.

On the whole the situation seems to me very serious and alarming, although not ᶜyetᶜ hopeless:

With regard to the food position the United States must be pressed again and again by Britain who cannot help herself in this respect to do more and to include the Western zones into the Marshall project, which I think is also being planned. Today, the integration of the Western zones is not only necessary for humanitarian but also for political reasons.

With regard to the general economic situation I suggest to press home the questions raised above and especially to ask the Government whether they are prepared to put a stop to the activities of those economic groups which rather prefer to support Germany by import of the cost of the English taxpayer than to give her economy a chance of recovery. As long as Germany cannot compete with other countries on the world market the present deplorable state of living cannot be improved over[3] here.

Further, would it not be possible to leave the whole import and export business to the Germans and just to tell them how much coal and currency they have to export to the Western countries.[4] Today people say[5] that they (the Germans) would be by far better off if they were only allowed to take their chance and to manage things by themselves and ªthatª it is only the British who prevent the Germans from making a success out of their work.[6] When it is being pointed out to them that they get much food from Britain they answer that the British are being compensated by what they are exporting from Germany and by what they have taken away from her when they occupied her. Today nobody says 'thank you' for anything that is being done for the British zone by Great Britain. Let the Germans try to manage their own economic affairs by themselves.[7] Then the whole psychological situation would fundamentally be changed. Such a change would give a decisive stimulus to the German public and revive German initiative. Then they would learn what they really owe to the British and that they themselves cannot master the situation, even if they have not to pay reparations for the time being and not to take into account British import interests.

On the other hand, under the present circumstances I should not press the point to give the German administration a wider power to act in [any] other but the economic field. I even think that one has rather ᶜalreadyᶜ gone too far in this respect. The nationalistic reaction in the German administration shows itself in many ways today and tends to become even stronger every day. A sort of passive resistance can be seen everywhere and the British can practically do very little about it as they have no power to act but only the right to control German affairs.

With regard to the 'Vertrauenskrise' (crisis of confidence), which is of no less far reaching importance than the economic crisis, I feel strongly that something should also be done in this respect. Today British and German live quite a separate life. True, something is being done to overcome the present deadlock by discussion-groups, occasional lectures etc.[8] But the effect of all these efforts is almost nil. There is an air of unreality and artificiality behind all these contacts, partly as a result of the deterioration of the general situation and of the nationalistic reaction on the German side, partly as a result of a wrong approach to the German problem as a whole. It is simply not possible to solve this question with a kind of paternalism under the motto: 'We must set the Germans thinking again'. It is not enough to treat the Germans as natives and to tell them how things ought to be handled. It is necessary to meet them as equals. Today people ask: what is the meaning of all our talking? I feel sure that if no change takes place in this attitude people will *completely* lose interest in these contacts.

From a technical point of view, I think it would be a good idea ªin this connectionª to set up public relation officers or something like that under the central office at Berlin or Bünde. These officers ought first to have the task to enlighten the German public on all relevant economic facts (especially food, coal etc.) using newspapers, wireless, posters and offering special premiums to everybody able to prove the incorrectness of the facts stated.

Secondly they should also lay down the general principles which should guide the British officials as how to handle the German problem, from a psychological point of view, and how to approach the Germans in a more creative way. Thirdly, and this seems to me the most important political task, they should show the Germans that there is hope for them in a new Europe on a Western basis in future.⁹ As the political situation has developed in the course of the last few months it does not seem to me unduly difficult to show persuasively that there is no need for the Germans to despair and to be without hope and that it is only a new nationalistic attitude that might destroy Germany's future. Actually, I have tried within the limited scope of my work here to deal with it on those lines trying to show that, under the present circumstances, a new radical nationalism is nothing but the expression of a nihilistic attitude and of despair and that this kind of nationalism is⁰ not only reactionary but also unable even to solve one of the vital German and European problems in a constructive manner. No doubt a great effort will be needed on the British side to arrest this destructive nationalistic trend. Everything will depend on the standard and qualifications of those who are in charge of these offices and of their advisers who must possess ingenuity and a real knowledge of German affairs and of the working of the German soul.

I am afraid to have to post the letter now. Its remainder will follow to-morrow.

Yours ever,

P.S. Please kindly excuse the many slips. But the typist cannot write English properly.

---

1. The following sheet is missing.
2. The sentence is marked by a black line in the margin.
3. Copy: out.
4. This and the next sentence are marked by a black line in the margin.
5. 'people say' instead of 'the general argument is'.
6. The sentence is marked by a black line in the margin.
7. This and the next sentence are marked by a black line in the margin.
8. Such meetings were organized by the University Officer.
9. The second half of the sentence is marked by a black line in the margin.

Leibholz to Bell, Göttingen, 20 July 1947, Bell Papers 40, fols. 431–3 (typewritten); BA, N 1334 (copy)

My Lordbishop,

I hope you have received my two letters (one of these containing p. 1–9 of the Memo. was posted to you by airmail yesterday). Here is the remainder of the report ᵃcontinued from page 9.ᵃ

A close co-operation with the German authorities might even be of special value in this connection, because the latter (unlike the British authorities) are subject to ᵃopenᵃ criticism, (for instance, by questioning the Government in the parliamentary bodies and in newspapers) and because thus a way would have been opened of challenging official statements without running the risk of being involved in a trial with all its unpleasant implications.

Finally, a word on denazification about which everybody is complaining. No doubt, the whole question has been mishandled, first because it has been dealt with on the basis of a questionnaire, which will never provide a satisfactory basis for a fair and just decision. It would have been much better to have had entrusted reliable anti-Nazis with this task. True, denazification is today an essentially German affair, but, unfortunately, the denazification committees are composed of people who are often either corrupt or consist of former criminals who claim to have been in concentration camps for political reasons or of communists who use the committees to follow up their political anti-Western aims.¹ I already mentioned in my last letter that other ªsuitableª people who might have been found to serve on these committees have refused to do so for fear of what might happen to them later on.

The result of mishandling this whole question is that, on the one hand, ᶜveryᶜ many Nazis have been left at large or even in their jobs and that, on the other hand, anti-Nazis who have become members of the party under pressure have to face great difficulties. In any case, it seems to me a gross exaggeration when even people say that denazification, as a whole, has been too strict in the British zone. In the faculty, for instance, to which I am attached as guest and to whose tasks it belongs to educate the German youth there are about six former Nazi members and a couple of former nationalists and the position in the other faculties is not better. And this is typical of the whole situation.

I add that the embitterment of the anti-Nazis goes back not only to the wrongly handled denazification business but also (and even more) to the lack of discrimination between Nazis and non-Nazis by ᶜthe official policy ofᶜ Military Government, for instance with regard to the requisition of houses of the civil population. ªIt has very often happened that houses and flats of anti-Nazis have been requisitioned, while the Nazis could stay in their homes undisturbed.² This especially has produced a great deal of ill feeling.ª

I do not think that these things can be put right again. The failure of this policy has practically resulted in drawing together Nazis and anti-Nazis and I think that even the bad type of Nazis who have justly been excluded from public life today will make their bid to play their part again in politics and in other spheres of public life in due course. The anti-Eastern trend of the time will further this dual agreement³ and help to wipe out the distinction between Nazis and non-Nazis in future. However, this distinction must constantly be borne in mind and emphasised by the Western powers, if it is not only to have historical value before long. I think it is time to stress for important political and ideological reasons (otherwise Russia could justly complain of the Western countries using fascist elements against her) that the distinction between Nazis and anti-Nazis will remain the basis to future British policy in Germany.

By the way, the situation is especially bad in the churches. I hear again and again of people who have justly been removed from office that they have found a refugium [sic] in the churches and I do not feel very happy about this alarming trend within the churches.⁴

As to the question of [a] separate peace treaty I think that such a treaty will be the necessary consequence of a break with Russia. I myself think that it will not come to a formal break until November unless the conference will not come off at all. Therefore I do not quite know whether the time is already ripe to broach the question of a fully-fledged treaty as early as on the 30th of July? Has the formal break already gone so far? I have not followed up in detail the recent political events and, of course, you can judge the situation much better than I from London.

However this might be, I myself have little doubt that, in the end, we shall be faced with two Germanys, with two German governments, with two separate peace treaties, with two capitals etc. If it comes to that I think that the West must be emphatically

[sic] in stressing the fact that the division of Germany is only provisional and only takes place because Russia has broken the Potsdam agreement and has not created the German economic unity which is one of the essential terms of the whole treaty. It must be said (just as Russia will do) that Germany will be united again in due course. Then the West must try to make for its own sake its zones a going concern and ᶜmake themᶜ for the Eastern zone as attractive as possible. I think that both West and East have their special economic, political, and ideological trump cards (I am thinking f[or]. e[example]. of the Eastern frontier, of the American loan, of the economic integration of the Western Zones into Europe, of the idea of a European confederation) ᵃwhich must fully be used. No doubt, the struggle for Germany between West and East will then enter its decisive phase.ᵃ Its outcome will I think decide, by implication, the fate of Europe.

As to the peace treaty itself I admit that there are great advantages in putting it in force by degree. Such a procedure would enormously quicken the winding up of the present ᵃpathologicalᵃ state of affairs and greatly help to normalise it. On the other hand, in following this procedure one runs the risk of being denounced by the political parties, which would be only too glad thus to be able to get rid of the responsibility for the peace settlement. It will, in any case, not be easy to find a representative government willing to sign the forthcoming peace treaty, and we should ask ourselves in earnest whether we should burden democratic parties with the political responsibility for the forthcoming peace settlement.

On the other hand, if one comes to the conclusion, as I think one should, that it would be much better to have a German signature under the peace treaty (just as the S.E.D.[5] will sign it in the East) the best solution seems to me to ask the people themselves after signature of the treaty by a German government to ratify it. Approval by Parliament would not be sufficient. It would only lead to discredit parliamentary institutions. In spite of the present situation the people would ratify the peace treaty, simply because they believe (and justly) that a peace treaty would be a great step forward in normalising the relations between the nations, and would greatly help to end their present misery. Such a plebiscitary act seems to me to be the best guarantee against using the future peace settlement as a weapon against democracy on Western lines.

With regard to the question as to who is to form the German government I myself suggest to enlarge the competence of the bizonal agencies and to extend their authority from the economic side to the political one. It will come to this development, in any case, and by the time when the peace settlement has to be concluded the right moment will have come to do this and to broaden the sphere of action of the bizonal agencies.[6]

From a technical point of view, another possibility would be to conclude[7] the peace treaty with the governments of the different 'Länder' (Bavaria etc.). But such a procedure would greatly complicate the whole business. Six treaties would have at last to be concluded. It would also run against the trend of time, which favours concentration (with disintegration) of political and economic power in Germany. This is why I also am very sceptical about the Western plan to federalise Germany.

If it should be too early to discuss the possibility of a fully-fledged Peace treaty[8] the question of a Preliminary Peace at least should be raised so that all the various war regulations concerning e.g. the Trade with the Enemy would be annulled.

Please accept my sincere apologies for the many mistakes and corrections made in the letter. If enough time were left the letter would be written again. Unfortunately, time is too short and the letter must be posted. I feel that many remarks are rather casual and fragmentary and I do not know whether they might be useful to you at all.

We hope to go by military train to Berlin on the 24th of July and if there should be no hitch we hope to be in Berlin on the morning of the 25th. Miss Bailey will certainly pass on letters or telegrams to us. Her address is Miss M. C. Bailey, 831 HQ CCG, MG, HQ, BTB., Berlin-area, BAOR. But it must be made urgent, as otherwise some time might elapse until the post might reach us. Perhaps you have got a better address.

Once again please forgive all the inadequacies of the letter,

Sabine gives you her special love.

Yours ever,

The letter would become too long if I should make the attempt to write to you on more personal thoughts today.

---

[1] Sentence marked with black line in the margin.
[2] A notorious example was the requisition of Professor Max Planck's house for the British Army in 1946. But reports of this case promptly led the British Prime Minister, Clement Attlee, to intervene.
[3] Instead of 'dual agreement' the copy has: 'development'.
[4] Sentence marked with black line in the margin.
[5] The Sozialistische Einheits Partei had been established in April 1946. It would become the party basis for the German Democratic Republic when it was founded in October 1949.
[6] The following final page is written by hand; typewritten in copy.
[7] Copy: 'consider'.
[8] The copy adds: 'to'.

Bell to Leibholz, 22 July 1947, BA, N 1334 (typewritten); Bell Papers 40, fol. 434 (carbon)

My dear Leibholz,

Very many thanks for your letter of the 16th July received yesterday.

I am sorry to say that Mr Bevin has just sent me a message urgently requesting that the debate should not take place on July 30th, owing to the extremely delicate situation now prevailing. It will therefore be postponed till October. I am very sorry to have given you this trouble.

I enclose a copy of my article in Sunday's *Observer*.[1] I am also sending you by separate post a copy of the Nuremberg Trial Penguin.[2]

My love to Sabine,

Yours affectionately,

(Dictated by the Bishop but not personally signed).[3]

---

[1] 'July the Twentieth, by the Bishop of Chichester', in *The Observer*, 20 July 1947, p. 4, cols. 3–5. A copy is in the Bell Papers, Vol. 47, fol. 451.
[2] R.W. Cooper, *The Nuremberg Trial* (Harmondsworth, 1947).
[3] Only in the carbon copy.

Bell to Leibholz, 25 July 1947, BA, N 1334 (typewritten); Bell Papers 40, fol. 435 (carbon)

My dear Leibholz,

Your long and extremely valuable letter of the 19th July arrived on Wednesday. I read it with the greatest gratitude and interest. It is very constructive, besides pointing out the great urgency and the great dangers of the situation.

I have asked Lord Pakenham, in response to a request from him for point[s], if he would really draw up a properly considered statement of policy for the British Zone, or rather of British policy on a bi-zone basis, both for home affairs and (limited) foreign affairs – especially trade. He is now unfortunately ill. But I will let you have any news.

Yours ever,

Sabine Leibholz to Bell, Berlin, 21 August 1947, Bell Papers 40, fols. 436–7 (handwritten)

My dear Lordbishop,

Today we had a letter from Marianne telling us that you had to have an operation and I hasten to tell you how very sorry we are about it. We had hoped that you were enjoying a restful holiday somewhere now and now we hear that you are ill! We do hope that you are not in pain, and that you will be feeling much better when this letter arrives.

We are now living with our parents here. I found my mother very much changed and aged, but my father much better than I expected. My mother had just broken her arm, but apart from this the whole family is in fairly good health. – I like it much better in Berlin than in Göttingen. It looks that [sic] there is no anti-British feeling here, which you meet in Göttingen nearly everywhere, and this hatred makes life in Göttingen very difficult. We are having a very interesting time here and shall have to tell you a great deal, when we are back in England.

Our daughters are getting alone quite well. Marianne has just taken finals and she got a 'second'. Last Sunday we heard a very good sermon by Barth, who is just here for a week.[1] – Next Sunday we shall have the baptism of Eberhard Bethge's third child.[2]

The whole family is joining in the very best wishes for your recovery, my Lordbishop. Gert sends his special love.

Yours affectionately,
Sabine

[1] See Eberhard Busch, *Karl Barth's Lebenslauf: Nach seinen Briefen und autobiografischen Texten* (Zurich, 2005), pp. 358–9.
[2] This was Sabine, born in June 1947.

Bell to Leibholz, 26 August 1947, BA, N 1334 (handwritten)

My dear Leibholz,

Very many thanks for your and Sabine's letters and good wishes. I am very glad also to get your news and to know that your visit to Göttingen and Berlin has been fruitful:

besides being much interested to know of the difference in feeling between the Zone and Berlin. How glad your children will be to see you back in Oxford – and how eager they will be to hear all your news! I do hope you left the parents in reasonably good health: though I can well understand the change in them which the last 9 years have made. I long to hear your news also – both personal and general, political and social and church: and how the future seems to you – both in your own personal case and for Germany & Europe.

My operation (for hernia) was extremely well performed. It took place on August 2 in Hove. After a good spell in bed I left the nursing home on August 20 – and am taking things easy at Chichester. But Mrs Bell and I are off to Pembrokeshire on Friday for about 3 weeks holiday quite away from the diocese, and I hope from work! An operation takes much out of you – it is not only the body which is wounded, for that can be more quickly healed, but the energy within is affected – and they say I shan't recover *full* strength for a couple of months! But I am glad it is over – and I am sure it was wise to have it done. Mrs Bell also needs a rest! *She* is taking a delegation of churchmen to Germany for 3 weeks on October 6 – to make contact with the German churchwomen (Protestant & Catholic). I know she hopes to include Berlin in her visit – though not all the members may manage it. The Religious Affairs Branch is planning it. I am so glad the Bonhoeffer money was useful. I hope Maria Wedemeyer is well. And all the nephews, nieces, grandnephews and -nieces, brother and sisters. My love to all of you.

Yours affectionately,

I shall very much want to see you – but no chance of being in town for a month. Anything you have time to write would of course be much valued.

Leibholz to Bell, Oxford, 2 September 1947, Bell Papers 40, fols. 438–41 (typewritten); BA, N 1334 (copy)

My Lordbishop,
I am overjoyed to find your letter on my return with the good news of your recovery. No better news could have awaited us here. When we first heard from the children that you had to undergo an operation the news came to us as a great shock in Berlin, but now that all is over we are greatly relieved from our anxieties and we are very thankful to Him for all He has done to you and us during the time of your illness.

We ourselves left Berlin about a week ago and after a rather adventurous journey safely arrived in Oxford three days later. I must frankly confess that we were delighted to be home again and to find our children well and happy.

All the members of the Bonhoeffer-family, especially the parents, have asked us first to thank you very much for all the help you have given us in arranging the journey, which without your help would not have been possible at all and, secondly, to convey to you their very best wishes for a speedy recovery. We have met the whole family – either in Göttingen or in Berlin – and you can imagine what this has meant for us. Apart from Sabine's mother who is not as well as we should have liked to find her we found all in reasonably good health thanks to the regular flow of parcels from abroad.

Especially Sabine's father who is nearly 80 is almost unchanged and full of energy and vitality. That we were allowed to see them again after nine years and after all that has happened in the meantime was a wonderful experience and a special gift, which we cannot value highly enough.

The money you, my Lordbishop, gave me and Marianne from the Bonhoeffer fund during our absence has been [a] great help. It has enabled Marianne to help Dorothee Schleicher during her stay in this country and to continue to send parcels to Berlin where we passed them on to Sabine's parents with whom we stayed there. In addition, the money made it possible to arrange a holiday for the Dohnanyis and Bethges. Mrs v. Dohnanyi with her three children came from Munich to Göttingen to stay there for a month and [the] Bethges are going to leave Berlin for a holiday during these days. They all needed a rest rather urgently.

I should be delighted to see you one day after your return from Pembrokeshire. On the whole, what I wrote to you in the Memo. still holds good, although it needs some supplementing after our stay in Berlin and what we heard about the Russian Zone there – as far as Politics, Economics and Church affairs are concerned. If I should make a written report at an earlier date I shall, of course, send you a copy of it.

Today I only wish to say a word about the personal implications of our visit to Germany. I was told that it was a full success and pleased the Germans as well as the British. But all this does not alter the bitter reality that if one is pro-British in Germany today, and wants to stand for one's convictions, one can only live as a German in the British Zone if one is prepared to live in isolation and does not mind being considered a Quisling and traitor by the great majority of the German people. The isolation would be complete as, in practice, the British do not make a differentiation between Nazis and non-Nazis, but simply differentiate between Germans and British. Thus I should lose the confidence of the British educational authorities without gaining the trust of the Germans. I already noted in the Memo. that nationalism and National Socialism and Anti-Semitism are not dead at all in the Western Zones. One notes it everywhere and the elections in the different German elections are mere sham elections.

Friends who think on the same lines as we do have frequently voiced the view that if the British clear out of Germany one day they will have to suffer severely for their pro-British and Western attitude. Some of them even think that they will be ᶜthe first to beᶜ hanged when such a change should take place. I feel strongly that, under these circumstances, to go back to Germany for good comes up to a kind of self-destruction, which has no real meaning. Therefore, I have told my colleagues in Göttingen (and Berlin) that I should be prepared to do all in my power to collaborate with them in future and to come back again next year but that I feel unable to give up my permanent residence in this country. Faculty and university (the Senate) in Göttingen have gladly agreed to that at a special meeting and pressed the government to make arrangements with me on the basis of a gentlemen['s] agreement.[1] In practice, this means that they do not mind my being naturalised here and that I would get a guest-professorship in Göttingen, which would enable me to go to Göttingen whenever I like to do so.

This plan has the full backing of the British educational authorities in Göttingen. They think, and as it seems to me rightly, that a visit to Germany on a 'German' basis, as our visit was, is connected with such a strain with regard to food, accommodation, transport and all the other technicalities and involves such a great financial sacrifice that one cannot be asked to repeat the experiment. A naturalisation would make all these things much easier.

I wish to take this step also in the interest of the children who have been brought up here. After all we have seen it seems to me utterly irresponsible to take our daughters (against their will and explicit wishes) to the infested [infected?] moral atmosphere in Germany who [sic] is more or less a great slum today. On the other hand, I cannot leave my children here as this would imply a legal split up of the family with incalculable implications – quite apart from the fact that Christiane is still entirely dependent on me.

I add that this plan meets with the full approval of Sabine's family. Sabine's eldest brother will in the end probably leave Germany himself with his family and go either to America or to this country. He belongs to those scientists who are urgently needed in these countries and who have not the possibility to work properly in Germany, under the present circumstances.

I myself think that I could easily get priority with regard to my application for naturalisation. I gave lectures at Oxford during the war and have worked after the war for the Intelligence Department of the Foreign Office, for Norfolk House and the B.B.C. I even hope to get top priority so that the naturalisation might go through quickly. The British education officer at Göttingen told me that he would press the Home Office to put things through as quickly as possible as a British interest is involved in the case.

As to the financial position I realize that as a result of the naturalisation the grant so far made me at your instigation comes automatically to an end. But this would be the case, at any rate. As things have developed as a result of the inflationary trend in this country this grant is only a part of my income and I must see to find a more permanent position here within the next year or so. I trust that the fact of naturalisation will give me a new chance in this respect – especially if I should be prepared partly to work in Germany in future. In addition, I am making arrangements to get some of our valuable furniture, which has been saved to this country, and thus we should be provided with a reserve in case of emergency.

I myself consider it a privilege of taking this step [sic] and only regret not to have taken it at an earlier date. Actually Niebuhr advised me to take it more than a year ago. I have waited to see first by myself how things have developed. You know, my Lordbishop, that I am primarily thinking on ideological lines and I feel strongly that as things have developed I can serve the purpose I have in mind better this way round. This step also is in accordance with our feeling. When we arrived at Dover we felt again happy and at home.

Under these circumstances would you please kindly let me know if you were prepared to vouch for my loyalty and character. I should be most grateful to you if you could possibly reply soon. As soon as I get it I will write to Christopher Dawson, Lindsay and Hodgson whether they would also be prepared to sponsor my application.

Sabine gives you her special love.

We very much hope that you will find the rest you need to regain full strength again.

Yours affectionately,

P.S. Please kindly remember us to Mrs. Bell. If Mrs. Bell should include Berlin in her visit please kindly give her the address of Sabine's parents who would no doubt be delighted to see her there.[2]

---

[1] See Szabó, Vertreibung, pp. 388–9.
[2] Henrietta Bell travelled to Germany in the second half of October with a visit to Berlin for a few days at the end of that month.

Bell to Leibholz, 5 September 1947, BA, N 1334 (handwritten)

The Globe Hotel, Angle, Pembrokeshire

My dear Leibholz,

I have just got your most interesting letter, forwarded from Chichester, and hasten to reply that I should be delighted to be your sponsor (or one of them) in applying for naturalisation. More than that, now that you have and Sabine have both had the opportunity of going to Germany, and seeing your family and your University colleagues and other friends, and have their unanimous counsel and advice to be naturalised, after examining all possibilities on the spot I am very glad your decision is what it is. And I earnestly hope that the combination of work in Germany with work in England, and a permanent basis of some kind in this country, may be soon and successfully accomplished. I am very glad to read what you say about the Göttingen university people and the British educational authorities.

I am sure you must have been very happy in getting back to your home and children. I was greatly interested in all your letter contained, and very grateful for the things from the Bonhoeffers. And I hope to hear more *viva voce* before long. My own recovery is vy good. I am in Pembrokeshire for another week – and go home about September 21. We have our car, and shall stay at one or two places en route. Do you know if the POW camp – officers – which you I think have visited from time to time in S. Wales, is open? I *know* that the Bridgend camp was recently closed. I don't know whether I shall have the opportunity – but if any where near any *special* POW camp I might go and see. But I cannot be at all sure. If you know, and cd. send me a line to Angle with address and name of commandant and special people, I shall be grateful.

My love to Sabine & the girls. And all best wishes for speedy naturalisation. You know that if there is anything I can do to help you at any time I shall be only too glad. I shall give my wife the Bonhoeffer address.

Yours affectionately,

Leibholz to Bell, 11 September 1947, Bell Papers 40, fol. 442 (typewritten)

My Lordbishop,

I am greatly delighted to have your extremely kind letter with the very good news that you feel much better. You know how happy and thankful we are for it.

Further, of course, I am *most* grateful to you for your willingness to be one of my sponsors (in fact, my first and main sponsor) in applying for naturalisation. All you say in your letter has made me very glad. You know how much time I have needed to come to a decision. But after having seen for myself what the position is over there I feel very strongly that the decision taken is the right one in every respect and will greatly help me in future to further work of understanding between the two countries.

I am enclosing today the naturalisation form and ask you very kindly to return it after having signed No. 1 of the References. Then I shall pass it on to the other sponsors. I have been told that if one gets priority the naturalisation could be through in about two or three months' time. A personal letter by you later on will, I feel sure, greatly help to speed up the matter and I shall write to you again as soon as I have posted the application together with the application for priority.

As to POW camps you might possibly visit I heard yesterday that somebody has just got from the General's camp a letter from which he concludes that the camp has not yet been closed down. In any case, the address of this camp No. 11 is Island Farm Camp, Bridgend, Glamorgan, Tel. Bridgend 541. – The address of the other officer-camp, which dedicated a musical composition to you some time ago, is Lamartin Camp (No. 184), Newport, Mon., Tel. 71216. – There are two other (non-officer) camps, which you might pass on your return to Chichester and were occasionally visited by me. They are Camp 263, Leckhampton Court Camp, CHELTENHAM, Glouc., Tel. Cheltenham 52363 and Camp No. 37, Sudeley Castle Camp, Winchcombe, Cheltenham, Glos., Tel. Winchcombe 118. It seems as if there is some regrouping of the camps going on just now. I do not think that the camps mentioned will be affected by these organisational changes because the men were used for some farm work. But it might be wiser to ascertain by telephone whether they are still at the above mentioned places.

I am still making further enquiries and shall give you further addresses if I succeed in getting them. Unfortunately, I do not know the names of the Commandants who are in charge of the camps. It is difficult to find them out, especially as there have frequently been changes in the staff personnel.

Sabine and the children give you her [sic] special love. By the way, did I write to you that Marianne got a good second.

Once again, *very* many thanks and please kindly remember us to Mrs Bell.

Yours affectionately,

Bell to Leibholz, 13 September 1947, BA, N 1334 (handwritten)

My dear Leibholz

I return the Application, duly signed, with pleasure. (Haven't you forgotten to put *place* of your children's birth in?)

I am very glad all is now in train. I hope you get a priority all right.

We leave Angle on Monday – then with one or two short visits hope to get home on Tuesday 23rd.

Don't bother about POW camps. It is clear I shall not be able to manage any visit.

Yours affly,

Bell to Leibholz, 24 September 1947, BA, N 1334 (dictated; handwritten, but only signed by Bell)

My dear Leibholz,

I enclose some letters and other documents from a certain Colonel Böhm-Tettelbach[1], who has written to me before. You might like to cast your eye over them before I send them back. But I don't fancy they are of much importance or that the writer is very notable.

Yours ^aalways^a sincerely,

---

[1] Lieutenant Colonel Hans W. Böhm-Tettelbach, a friend of Hans Oster. He wrote to Bell on 12 June 1947 with translated extracts from a diary. See Bell Papers, Vol. 47, fol. 291. See Hans Böhm-Tettelbach, 'Ein Mann hat gesprochen' in *Rheinische Post* 10 July 1948; also Klemperer, *German Resistance against Hitler*, pp. 100–1.

Leibholz to Bell, 29 September 1947, Bell Papers 40, fol. 443 (typewritten); BA, N 1334 (copy)

My Lordbishop,

I return herewith the letter and documents from Colonel Boehm-Tettelbach with many thanks. It was very kind of you to send them to me and I have read them with interest. Although I do not think that the author of the documents is very original it seems to me that what he writes reflects the present state of the German mind rather correctly. In fact, the many mistakes which have been made have created a very bitter hatred and people in Germany believe today that not by words, but by deeds the British want nothing else but the utter ruin of Germany. I do not know whether you have seen quoted in Mr. Stokes'[1] letter to the Editor of *The Times* the words of a very senior official of the C.C.G.[2] who said to his assembled staff: 'Gentlemen, your job is so to destroy German industry that it can never rear its head again.' This is exactly what the Germans believe and fills them with hatred and makes any 're-education' impossible. I myself think that the list of firms due to be dismantled in the British Zone (which is said to comprise about 900 plants) will give – when published – a knock-out to German morale.

I also think that the writer calls rightly attention to the fate of the General Baron von Gersdorff who is still a Prisoner of war although he tried to kill Hitler during an inspection of the Zeughaus in Berlin in 1943.[3] This is absolutely mad but a consequence of the general practice that a general is always wrong even if he has tried at the risk of his life to murder the tyrant. Is it perhaps not possible to ask the colonel for the address of General Gersdorff so that something can be done for him. I know that the story is true.

Yours ever,

---

[1] i.e. Richard Stokes MP. See Leibholz to Bell, 15 July 1944, note 6.
[2] Control Commission for Germany.

[3] Major General Rudolf-Christoph Freiherr von Gersdorff (1905–80), an American Prisoner-of-War in 1945–7. For his engagement in the resistance and his assassination attempt of 21 March 1943, see Hoffmann, *Widerstand, Staatsstreich, Attentat*, pp. 333–60; for Gersdorff's autobiography see *Soldat im Untergang* (Frankfurt/M., 1977).

Leibholz to Bell, 21 October 1947, Bell Papers 40, fol. 447 (typewritten)

My Lordbishop,

Just coming back home I find your very kind letter and I hasten to say that I am most grateful to you for having written to the I.St.S.[1] and especially also for the personal gift you enclosed.[2] I feel somewhat ashamed by it, but, in spite of this, I must confess I very much enjoyed it. I have not informed Büsing[3] about our new plan with regard to Marianne as after experiences made I thought it would be better so.

Sabine's father asked me in his last letter to send you his warmest greetings and best wishes and to tell you how very glad he is to have heard from us that you feel much better and have recovered from the operation. I hope that he and Sabine's mother will have the opportunity of seeing Mrs Bell during her stay in Berlin at their home.

We do not quite know whether we should advise Sabine's family to leave Berlin and to go to the West. If you should have heard that the Western Powers are prepared to leave Berlin after a failure of the November Conference[4] would you please kindly let me know. I myself am inclined to think that simply for reasons of prestige the Western powers will not leave Berlin. For its occupation stands for much more than simply the occupation of a big city. It has somewhat a symbolic significance today. It means that the Western powers are not prepared to accept the division of Europe for good.

With renewed thanks and all good wishes

Yours affectionately,

[1] International Student Service.
[2] On 15 October Leibholz wrote to Bell (Bell Papers 40, fol. 444) concerning the future of his daughter Marianne after her Diploma of Education and asking Bell for help in securing sponsorship by the Church of England Committee and the International Student Service. Accordingly, Bell wrote a supporting letter to Miss Harrison of the I.S.S. (Bell Papers 40, fol. 445) and answered Leibholz on 17 October (Bell Papers 40, fol. 446) enclosing £ 5 as a personal contribution to Marianne's fees.
[3] Wolfgang Büsing (1910–94) studied theology 1930–4. After his first examination in the Confessing Church, in 1935, he became curate in a parish of Berlin and a member of the theological seminary under the Bonhoeffer's leadership in Finkenwalde. With the help of Franz Hildebrandt he became curate at the German-Lutheran St. Georg Church at London in 1936 and in 1938 married Erika Danckwarth who was, according to the Nazi Nuremberg laws, 'Half-Jewish'. After taking his second examination in Berlin Büsing returned to London and in 1938 the Committee for Non-Aryan Christians of the Church of England appointed him pastoral counsellor of 'non-Aryan' Christian refugees in London. In 1940–9 he was vicar of Christ Church, Spitalfields, London. In 1949 he and his family emigrated to Canada. See Ludwig and Röhm, *Evangelisch getauft*, pp 68–9.
[4] The Fifth Conference of Foreign Ministers of the Allied Powers took place in London from 25 November to 15 December 1947.

Leibholz to Bell, 4 November 1947, Bell Papers 40, fol. 448 (typewritten); BA, N 1334 (copy)

My Lordbishop,

I have just heard from the World Council of Churches that the Board of Management of the Christian Council for Refugees at its next meeting on Friday, November 7th, will deal, among others, [sic] with the question of the renewal of my grant of £25 per quarter, until such time as I become a British subject. I hope and trust that the latter will be the case in a few months' time. As the Church of England Committee has reduced its grant by a third it would be a great help if the C.C.R. came to a positive decision. I should have dropped this line to Büsing who (as Secretary of the Church of England Committee) is a member of the C.C.R. But as you know, my Lordbishop, I am not sure whether he will support my case so warmly as I think he should. Therefore, it would be very good of you to drop a line to Mr Salway[1] in this matter. I should be very grateful to you.

With regard to the application for naturalisation I should like to mention something that you probably do not know and [which] might possibly expedite the procedure. As is generally known Hitler planned the invasion of this country in August 1940 and it was decided on August 27 that landings were to take place in four main areas (Folkestone, Dungeness, Bexhill, Brighton). But then two things happened. First the R.A.F. defeated the German Luftwaffe and secondly the German Intelligence Service produced reports that there were 20 British operational divisions in Southern England and a further 19 in reserve. The official version is that the German Intelligence Service was deceived by British Propaganda. What is not yet known is that the German Intelligence Service was very well informed about the true position in which Britain found herself in 1940 and that the reports were intentionally falsified to prevent Hitler from invading this country. Three men were responsible for these reports: one of them was Dohnanyi (husband of my wife's sister).[2] All three were executed: two of them together with Dietrich at Flossenbürg. There are only very few people who know the full story. They have told me that they must be silent because considering the present state of affairs in Germany they would be considered the worst type of traitors and I need not elaborate what this means today in Germany. I mention this story today because I suppose you will be consulted by the Home Office in due course and I could imagine that the background of a family which applies for naturalisation – if referred to – might also contribute to expediting the procedure – provided you feel it right and expedient to do so.

Yours affectionately,

---

[1] Unidentified.
[2] Leibholz's sources here remain mysterious. The story is not corroborated by other sources and not mentioned in the extant literature.

Bell to Leibholz, 5 November 1947, BA, N 1334 (handwritten)

My dear Leibholz

Many thanks for your letter. I will drop a line to Salway. I am raising the question of Germany & the November Conference in the Lords on November 12.[1] Any views you care to send me will be quickly received: and I shall of course consult your long letter written for the postponed debate in the summer.

A point I specially want light upon is the future structure of Germany. If a federal system, how much should be reserved for the central government (if any), and which would be the federal units?

Yours ever,

I note what you say about the 1940 invasion and yr brother-in-law.

[1] See Hansard, HL Deb., Vol. 152, cols. 587–97, 644–6 (12 November 1947).

Bell to Leibholz, 13 November 1947, BA, N 1334 (handwritten)

My dear Leibholz

I was most grateful for your letter from Stratford-on-Avon, with points for my speech. They are of much value, and emphasise what I found in my re-reading of your Göttingen letter for the July debate. The budget crowded out any place in print in the *Times* & *Manchester Guardian* today. But the debate went well. There was a full House, and a *crowded* gallery, with many unable to get in. And the atmosphere of the House was sympathetic. In fact I perceived a real change in the attitude – and others present commented on it afterwards, with congratulations. Lilje was there and much pleased.[1]

Yours ever,

[1] Lilje visited London on the way back from Edinburgh where the university theological faculty had honoured him as Doctor Divinitatis honoris causa on 5 November 1947.

Leibholz to Bell, [1]7 November 1947, Bell Papers 40, fols. 449–50 (typewritten); BA, N 1334 (copy, date is corrected to 17)

My Lordbishop,

Many thanks for your kind letter and my congratulations on your masterly statesmanlike speech in the Lords last Wednesday. I am delighted to hear that in spite of the Budget you had a full House and a most sympathetic hearing. I am also very glad to see from the debate that you were strongly supported by some of those who took part in the debate. I especially liked what the Bishop of Sheffield said in addition to what you called the psychological crisis in Germany today.[1]

Your suggestion to set up a provisional political regime for a unified Germany seems to me of great importance because it really provides a definite plan coming from the West, which meets the needs of Germany as well as of Europe. I myself have not raised this question in my letter because I take it that the Russians will not (and as it seems to me cannot, from their point of view) accept it: for its acceptance would imply the loss of Eastern Germany and I am afraid they will not make this concession. In so far I am more pessimistic, but, of course, I do not know in [sic] how far you have taken a more optimistic line for simply political reasons considering the special political circumstances under which the debate took place. But even if the Russians say 'NO' I think it is very valuable that the proposal has been made. It is only a pity that Pakenham has not given it sufficient attention in his reply on behalf of the Government.[2]

By the way, I was heavily reproached by some people coming from Germany for having said as I also did in my letters to you that the great majority of the German people resent the English today and that there is much nationalism in the British zone. They do not question the facts but take the line that these things should not be referred to in this country. I only mention this in order to show how difficult and complex the situation has become for those who wish to state the facts if they are non-British.

Mosley's re-appearance in public seems to me a very serious matter.[3]

Yours affectionately,

---

[1] Leslie Hunter (1890–1983) was the second bishop of Sheffield from 1939 to 1962; founding member of the British Council of Churches; see Hansard, H.L. Deb., Vol. 152, cols. 610–2 (12 November 1947).
[2] Ibid., cols. 618–43.
[3] After spending his first two years of post-war liberty as a Wiltshire farmer the former leader of the British Union of Fascists, Sir Oswald Mosley (1896–1980) was about to set up a new party, the Union Movement. This was a noisy, but short-lived, affair which Mosley himself soon abandoned in favour of a spell in Ireland, before settling in France (as neighbours of the Duke and Duchess of Windsor).

Bell to Leibholz, 26 December 1947, BA, N 1334 (handwritten)

My dear Leibholz

Mrs Bell and I are most grateful to you and Sabine for your good wishes. The beautiful crucifix arrived on Christmas Eve, and I do want to thank you most warmly for the gift, and the thought behind it. I am greatly touched not only that you should send it, but that you should have brought it from Germany. Both my wife and I am struck by the beauty and feeling of the carving; and we like it, its origin, and its meaning greatly.[1] This New Year is I fear only too likely to be a crucial year. We both greatly value your friendship – for itself and for the links it brings with it. I trust that this coming year may bring you personally all you hope for.

Our love to the girls, and to Sabine

Yours affectionately,

---

[1] This cross has not been traced to any private collection.

Leibholz to Bell, 29 December 1947, Bell Papers 40, fols. 451–2 (typewritten), BA, N 1334 (copy, without the concluding, personal section)

My Lordbishop,

I expect that the outcome of the London Conference has not surprised you.[1] As it seems to me it was the unavoidable consequence of the attempt, which could not succeed, namely to settle a primarily ideological conflict by methods of power politics. London has thus only proved that Yalta and Potsdam were based on a misinterpretation of the meaning of history in the 20th century.

What, of course, we most fear is the loss of Berlin, which I fear cannot be avoided in the long run and its far-reaching personal implications for Sabine's parents and the other members of her family. It might be that the Americans and British will try to get out Sabine's brother and his family but we are not sure whether he will leave the parents behind, who would not go. [The] Bethges also urgently wish to leave Berlin but I am afraid there is no opening. Thus the situation is very disturbing.

I also very much doubt whether the system of balance of power which the Western Powers hope to secure following the division of Germany will work. For ideologies are dynamic and transcend stationary barriers created by this system, which belongs to the age of the nation-state. In this connection, the situation in Greece is terribly alarming.[2] I have read somewhere that people in Italy and France fear similar developments in their countries. But how much more must this development be expected in Germany where a communist sponsored Government need not be created artificially but is the natural result of the division of Germany. National unification of Germany (in the service of Russian totalitarianism) will be the slogan. This means that the Western powers if they do not want to quit Germany as a whole must no less intensively propagate Germany's unity (in the sense as described by you in the last debate in the Lords on this matter) and possibly fight for it. This might well mean that the struggle between Russia and the Western powers might take on the character of a civil war in Germany. In this connection, the rumour that Paulus is ready for action on Russian orders is worthwhile to be remanded.[3]

In addition to that, there are a few personal things I should like to ask you, my Lordbishop.[4]

First, with regard to pending naturalisation I wonder whether an official from the Home Office has already called on you. If not, it would be very good of you (if this were technically possible) perhaps to stress that you would welcome my naturalisation as quickly as possible as I hope to do some work in connection with [the] Educational Branch of the Control Commission in the near future and this work depends on naturalisation. So far I have not asked the Education Department at Göttingen to undertake anything because I fear that misunderstandings might arise when they say that I am thinking of revisiting Göttingen University as guest professor. For I have been told that the Home Office only wants to naturalise people who have no closer contacts with Germany now and in future. Therefore, much depends on how things are put in this matter.

Further, may I ask you, my Lordbishop, kindly to send me a letter of introduction to the Dean of Oriel Mr Collins[5] or to write to him direct? Within a framework of 'Christian Action' Mr Collins is making preparations of different kinds for meetings, conferences, lectures, which are to be held resp. [sic] given next year and in which German universities are involved. I feel I might perhaps be helpful in this matter in one way or another all the more as I am the only refugee lecturer at Oxford who has revisited German universities after the war for a couple of months and hopes to do the same in future. So far I have not met Mr Collins and, therefore, I should be very grateful for such a letter.

There is a last question I should like to raise. I have been approached by the Rector of Göttingen University asking me whether it would not be possible to help them in getting back the university auditorium building, which is now being occupied by the College of the British Army of the Rhine (since 1945). This building (the biggest of its kind and providing more than 25% of all available lecture rooms at Göttingen) is, in fact, urgently needed for the 5400 students especially for those who read theology, law, economics, greats⁶ etc. They say that no proper teaching is possible without this building, which is only being used for about 300 Britishers ᶜtodayᶜ who do not even claim to be students. There were negotiations going on aiming at sharing the use of the building so that the Germans should be in a position to make use of the building after 5 o'clock in the evening but these negotiations have suddenly broken off and come to nothing. Thus I have been pondering over what to do and what I should like to ask you in this connection is whether you, my Lordbishop, would possibly be prepared to accept a letter written by me in greater detail on this matter and pass it to Robert Birley⁷ for consideration? I feel a sharing of the building by British people and German students might even help to create valuable contacts. But I do not know how you feel.

Please kindly forgive the undue length of this letter and once again our best wishes for you and Mrs Bell for the coming year.

Yours affectionately,

---

[1] The Fifth Conference of Foreign Ministers of the Allied Powers in London ended on 15 December prematurely without a consensus about the German question.

[2] Since 1946 civil war had been going on between communist and democratic powers in Greece, but the British government had ended its engagement with the conflict in March 1947. It was in this context that President Truman had provided a guarantee of help for the democratic forces which became known as the Truman Doctrine.

[3] Friedrich Paulus (1890-1957), Commander-in-chief of the 6th Army, which lost the battle of Stalingrad. On 31 January 1943, the day of the capitulation and his capture by the Soviet Army, Hitler appointed him Field Marshall. As their highest-ranking prisoner Paulus had no alternative but to play a role in the psychological warfare of the USSR, but he only joined the association of German officers (BDO), which was linked with the National Committee for Free Germany (NKFD), in August 1944. After Paulus's testimony at the Nuremberg Trials he wished to return to the Soviet Zone of Germany, but in the Western world rumours about a possible Paulus-Army, a German Liberation Army, broke out in 1947/8. In such a way did the fate of Paulus illustrate the developing narrative of the new Cold War. See Torsten Dietrich, *Paulus. Das Trauma von Stalingrad. Eine Biographie* (Paderborn, 2008), esp. pp. 359-60, 364.

[4] The following text not in the copy.

[5] John Collins (1905-82) was Chaplain of Oriel College at Oxford, 1937-48; later famous as Canon of St Paul's Cathedral, founder of *Christian Action* and leading figure in the Campaign for Nuclear Disarmament.

[6] i.e. Classics. Leibholz has appropriated the title used at Oxford.

[7] Sir Robert Birley (1903-82) was appointed Headmaster of Charterhouse in 1935. In 1947 he had become Educational Advisor to the Control Commission for Germany/British Element. In 1949 he was appointed Headmaster of Eton, where he remained until 1963. Birley would contribute

an introduction to the first English edition of Annedore Leber's *Conscience in Revolt: Sixty-four Stories of Resistance in Germany 1933–1945* (London, 1957). After a period as visiting Professor at Witwatersrand University, South Africa, he became Professor and Head of Department of Social Science and Humanities at City University London in 1967.

Leibholz to Bell, 29 December 1947, Bell Papers 40, fol. 453 (handwritten)

My Lordbishop,

Sabine and I are most grateful to you for your very kind letter and the good wishes you and Mrs Bell are sending us for the New Year. We are delighted to know that you and Mrs Bell like the crucifix. It expresses better than words can do what we feel just today at the appearance of the New Year, which I fear will be one of the most difficult years we have so far had to have. But however things may develop, we know that your friendship and all that it stands for will last and you know how deeply grateful we are for being granted this privilege.

I am enclosing a letter, which was written before your letter arrived.

Yours affectionately,

Bell to Leibholz, 31 December 1947, BA, NL 1334 (typewritten); Bell Papers 40, fol. 450 (carbon)

My dear Leibholz,

I am just off to Malvern Wells for a week's rest: but before I go I must send this brief line in answer to your important letter of the 29th December.

1. I agree about the disturbing implications of the possible and not too improbable loss of Berlin – not least for Sabine's family. We must think more about this. The political situation is most distressing.
2. I have had no call from the Home Office about your naturalisation. I will think about the advisability of a personal appeal by me to Sir Alexander Maxwell.[1] I made it recently on behalf of somebody else, and Maxwell said he was very sorry but he could not now depart from the order in which applications had come in, owing to the great difficulty incurred by making exceptions. I think perhaps the matter might be better handled in connection with Birley, and the next point.
3. Yes, do please send me a letter in greater detail about Göttingen University auditorium; and I will gladly send it on to Birley.
4. I enclose a letter of introduction to the Rev. L.J. Collins.

Yours affectionately,

[1] Sir Alexander Maxwell (1880–1963) was permanent under-secretary at the Home Office 1938–48.

1948

25 February	The Communists take control in Czechoslovakia.
10 March	The death of Czech foreign minister, Jan Masaryk.
3 April	President Truman signs the Marshall Plan.
21 June	The Deutsche Mark becomes the currency of the western zones of Germany.
24 June	Soviet forces blockade Berlin. The Berlin Airlift begins on 28 June.

Leibholz to Bell, 7 January 1948, Bell Papers 40, fols. 454–5 (typewritten); BA, N 1334

My Lordbishop,

I am most grateful to you for your kind letter of December 31st and for the enclosed letter to Mr. Collins. I do hope you have had a good week's rest at Malvern Wells.

I wonder whether you have seen the article on Greece by a Student of Europe in the last issue of the *Observer*. It seems to me to be a fine and, on the whole, correct analysis of the situation, although I think it can hardly be compared with that in 1936 when Hitler marched into the Rhineland because Russia and her satellites are in a much stronger position today than Hitler was in 1936.

I am also still thinking about what you said in the Lords in November concerning the necessity of creating German unity on a Western and European pattern. The more I am thinking about that the more do I feel the very importance of the point made by you. For as things stand today it seems to me that, from a tactical point of view, the Russians are in a better position than the Western powers. The Russians really want German political unity (of course, dominated by the Russian Unity party) while the Western powers are somewhat half-hearted in this respect paying lip-service to German unity, but not really wanting it. This especially applies to France, but to a certain extent also to the Americans and to a trend in this country. Behind that there is the belief that a divided Germany is weak and powerless and, therefore, no longer a danger to the world. But such an attitude makes things much easier for the Russians. No doubt, all Germans who are prepared to accept the partition of Germany, even if they genuinely recognise its necessity, will be regarded as separatists, collaborators and traitors. This makes the situation very difficult for the Germans. I think the Ministerpresidents of the German Länder have rightly refused to consent to the setting up of a new State in Western Germany. If the partition is inevitable, as I think it is, the partition must be imposed on, and executed by, the Germans, but they cannot accept it of their own accord. In addition the Western Powers must call I feel for German unity no less loudly and clearly as [sic] the Russians do in their Zone today.

I am enclosing a more formal letter about the Göttingen auditorium university building. If you agree with it it would be very good of you to pass it on to Birley[1] for consideration.[2]

This might at the same time offer an opportunity of asking him whether he would kindly write to the Home Office a supporting letter for expediting the procedure of my naturalisation in case you feel that a personal appeal by you to Sir Alexander Maxwell is less advisable after the experiences recently made.

May I give you a few facts in this connection:

The application for naturalisation and for granting priority was made three months ago[3] and the advertisement in the newspaper appeared in the Middle of November. The delay with regard to the interview is due to the fact that there are many applications for naturalisation in the Oxford area and that there are only a few officials who are able to deal with them. The granting of formal priority only means that the applications are being dealt with but in this stage there is no longer a distinction between priority and non-priority cases. In 1945 and 1946 this was quite different as at that time only priority cases were being dealt with, while non-priority cases were not being handled at all.

On the other hand, I have heard from I believe a reliable source that even today applications are being dealt with more quickly if the applicant wants to get abroad and the journey is being considered to be in the British interest, and it seems to me that, from this special point of view, something might be possible [and might] be done quite successfully. I hope to spend again the next summer term at Göttingen-university as *guest*-professor provided I am naturalised before then. As you know, my Lordbishop, I was in this capacity at Göttingen last year lecturing there on INTERNATIONAL LAW, BRITISH INSTITUTIONS, and POLITICS. When leaving Göttingen the university Control Officer Major Bird told me that he considers my coming back to Göttingen as a *guest* very much lying in the British interest and that he would gladly be prepared warmly to support such an application as far as he is concerned. So far I have not approached him because I feel ªstronglyª that a letter by you or by the Educational Adviser in Berlin has much more weight with the Home Office than a letter by the university control officer at Göttingen. I may perhaps add in all humility that I myself felt that I had the right approach psychologically towards the Germans and that felt quite useful in reconciling the British and German point of view. May I further add that I was the only former full university professor who went over to the British Zone to teach again Politics and International Law and Relations for a couple of months as *guest* professor and that I hope to do so in future in case I shall be naturalised and get the necessary British backing.

Please forgive my being lengthy and accept my most sincere thanks

Yours affectionately,

---

[1] See Bell to Birley, 9 January 1948, Bell Papers 40, fol. 456.
[2] The following text is not in the copy.
[3] In the margin is added, by hand: My Reference number is L10258 (R.601)

Bell to Leibholz, 3 February 1948, BA, N 1334 (handwritten)

My dear Sabine

This is to bring you my affectionate best wishes for your birthday, with loving thoughts of Dietrich. It is a deep bond between us, and I shall never cease to think of and care for Dietrich. I am vy glad to hear (last week) from the SCM that a translation of *Nachfolge* is well on the way, with a memoir by Gerard: I am to write a brief foreword in due course.[1]

I have not yet heard from R. Birley, about Göttingen University – and so have waited before tackling the approach to the Home Office about priority. But of course I'm ready to do anything wanted – only I feel Mr Birley's backing[,] from the angle of the British Zone[,] would be more effective than mine.

I hope the girls are well, and both of you.

Yours affectionately,

[1] See the fragment of a letter of Bell to Leibholz, BA, N 1334 (handwritten): 'I am very glad Dietrich's book is accepted by SCM.' Gerhard Leibholz, 'Memoir of Dietrich Bonhoeffer', in Dietrich Bonhoeffer, *The Cost of Discipleship* (London/New York, 1948); reprinted in Leibholz, *Politics and Law*, pp. 139–53.

Leibholz to Bell, 12 February 1948, Bell Papers 40, fol. 458 (typewritten)

My Lordbishop,

Thank you very much for kindly letting me see Mr Birley's letter, which I am returning herewith.[1]

I have had my interview concerning naturalisation today. The file will now go to Chichester after Hodgson, Micklem and Dawson will have been called upon in the course of the next few days. I think that considerable further delay would be avoided by a letter from you, my Lordbishop, (addressed to the Detective Department (or Scotland Yard) Police Main Station, St. Aldates, Oxford) in your capacity as sponsor.[2] I think that in this case the file would be directly returned to the Nationality Division of the Home Office. Of course, I do not know how you feel about this suggestion. But I thought I should submit it to you for consideration.

Of course, it would be a great thing if it were possible to take the opportunity of combining the letter qua sponsor with the attempt to speed up the whole procedure. One might mention that for professional reasons an early naturalisation would be greatly valued. One might add that I made a special application for priority and that this application could perhaps [be] duly taken into account in this connection. Further, Marianne will be 21 by the end of June. We should have to go through the whole procedure with regard to her if further considerable delay occurs.

But I suggest that we do not mention in this connection my intention to revisit Göttingen university as guest-professor because this plan might easily cause some misunderstanding on the part of the Home Office. Their policy seems to me to be to discourage closer connections with Germany (even as a guest-lecturer) after naturalisation.

Please accept my most sincere thanks for all help you feel possibly able to give me in this matter.

Yours affectionately,

P.S. Sabine's parents hope to celebrate their golden wedding in March and Sabine's father his 80th birthday. We are very sorry that we shall not be able to be with them in these days.

[a]The Ref. Number of my file is: L 10258 (R. 601)[a]

[1] See Birley to Bell, 28 January 1948, Bell Papers 40, fol. 457.
[2] See Bell to the Detective Department, 17 February 1948, Bell Papers 40, fol. 459

Leibholz to Bell, 28 February 1948, Bell Papers 40, fol. 460 (typewritten)

My Lordbishop,

This is a just a line to ask you, my Lordbishop, whether, in the meantime, you have had a call from the Home Office concerning naturalisation. The sponsors here were called upon about a fortnight ago. In any case, it would be very kind of you to drop me a line when people have come to see you so that I know how things are getting on. For I am still hesitating to take further steps until I know more definitely how things will probably go.

The events in Czechoslovakia[1] have taken the turn I anticipated long time ago when quite different views prevailed in this country. Which country will be the next? And Berlin? We shall thus have a new Refugee Problem.

Yours affectionately,

[1] After the resignation of 12 ministers from the Centre parties on 20 February the communists forced President Beneš to appoint the new government of Klement Gottwald on 25 February.

Bell to Leibholz, 1 March 1948, BA, N 1334 (typewritten)

My dear Leibholz,

I have had no call from the Home Office concerning naturalisation. I wrote as I promised, but have had no reply. I will certainly let you know when they do come to see me.

Yes, the Czech events are tragic. If only the Western governments had taken a different line long ago, and if even now they could only make up their minds in a strong Western way! I am taking part in the debate in the House of Lords on Wednesday.[1]

Yours ever,

[1] See Hansard, HL Deb., Vol. 154, cols. 346–52 (3 March 1948).

Bell to Leibholz, 23 March 1948, BA, N 1334 (typewritten)

My dear Leibholz,

Just a line to let you know that I am going to Berlin next week, April 1 – 5. I felt, in view of recent events especially this last week-end, that I wanted to see some of my friends there.[1] I rang up the Foreign Office yesterday, and they are giving me every facility. If there is any message I can take to the Bonhoeffers, let me know. I shall be at the Athenaeum on Wednesday before starting.

ᵃA happy Easterᵃ

Yours ever,

[1] On 20 March 1948 the Supreme Head of the Soviet Military Administration in Germany, Marshal Wassili Sokolowski (1897–1968), left the Allied Control Council for Germany. This concluded the work of the Control Council.

Leibholz to Bell, 28 March 1948, Bell Papers 40, fol. 462 (typewritten)

My Lordbishop,

In addition to my last letter addressed to Chichester I am enclosing a few letters to the family in reply to a letter just received from Sabine's mother and it would be very good of you to take them with you unless they cause you undue trouble. It seems so as though they all are very busy in preparing the celebration of the 80th birthday of Sabine's father – happily ignoring all that is happening in the political field.

By the way, if you happen to talk to Mr Birley it might perhaps be possible to mention my name in this or that connection. A fortnight ago I met his liaison officer Guy Wint and had an opportunity to discuss with him some of the problems of German education. He had also seen the Control Officer of Göttingen University and promised me to approach the Home Office to accelerate naturalisation. In fact, things are moving and I hope that naturalisation will be an established fact in about a fortnight's time. I also promised Mr Wint to write a memo. on German university reform about which I am expected to talk over the wireless on April 23: he will pass it on to Mr Birley.

Once again, our very best wishes for your visit to Berlin and greatly looking forward to having you back in a week's time.

Yours affectionately,

Leibholz to Bell, 28 April 1948, Bell Papers 40, fol. 461 (typewritten)

My Lordbishop,

I am very glad indeed to say that, in the meantime, our naturalisation has become an established fact and I wish to thank you very warmly for all the help you have kindly given us again in this matter.

Yesterday I had a letter from Grimme (Hannover) urging me to spend again the summer term at Göttingen as guest-professor. In fact, I applied to the Education Department of the Foreign Office about a month ago for authorisation for Sabine and myself to spend again this term at Göttingen. I pointed out that the Rector and the Law faculty at Göttingen University have pressed me to come over as a guest and that the British Control-officer of the university warmly welcomes this invitation.

I added that I myself am prepared to accept this invitation provided that Sabine is also authorised to go, as was the case last year and provided that they would give me all possible support. When I met Miss Maclean at the Foreign Office last Friday I told her that the Göttingen people are prepared to accommodate us and that the university will settle the financial question during my stay over there, but that the least I must ask of the Government is that they pay the fare as I cannot be expected to do this out of my own pocket. I was told by the Educ[ation]. Department that they are greatly interested in my projected visit but that they cannot commit themselves at the moment, as they must make inquiries about the technical possibility of financing this visit.

Considering the fact that hundreds of Germans are coming to this country at the cost either of the British Government or other British agencies I have written to Mr Bird (University Control Officer at Göttingen) pointing out that the payment of the fare by the Government is a condition of our coming to Göttingen at the end of May or at the beginning of June.

I should very much like to ask you, my Lordbishop, whether you would mind writing to Mr Bishop who is in charge of [the] Educ. Department or to somebody else whom you know there and pointing out that you have heard of our projected visit to Göttingen and that you wish to ask him to do all in his power to give us all available facilities. Perhaps it might be possible to mention in such a letter two points, which I myself cannot make:

1. that the initiative for the projected visit has come from the German side and that it is important, also from the British point of view, to have people over there who at the same time enjoy the full confidence of the Germans and have the ability of approaching them in a very direct and frank way.
2. that I am expected to fill at Göttingen the post of a professor of Politics and Public Law and International Relations and that it might be of considerable importance in future to have just a professor in these subjects over there.

I imagine that such a letter will greatly speed up the matter and lead the people ᶜover thereᶜ at the Foreign Office to take the initiative and to settle things quickly.

I should be very grateful indeed if you felt able to comply with my request.

Yours affectionately,

P.S. I noted in my application that Sabine will act as my secretary and that I cannot meet the daily difficulties in Germany without her help. I also mentioned that I hope to proceed from Göttingen to Berlin in August to give a course of lectures there at the university as I have been asked for.

Leibholz to Bell, 29 April 1948, Bell Papers 40, fol. 463 (typewritten); BA, N 1334 (two different copies)

My Lordbishop,

Just a line, in addition to my last letter, to say how very glad I am to see your letter in today's *Times* and how very much I wish to thank you for it. The issue at stake in Berlin could not have been stated in better and more impressive terms. I wish to associate myself fully with every word you have written and I only hope that the Government also realizes the enormous importance Berlin has today for the whole of Europe. It is this battle, which is being fought out today in Berlin by the Western powers and the Germans who – as it seems to me – act in so far as their allies and no longer as their enemies.

By the way, I have had a letter from the Göttingen university authorities this morning saying that the most important university buildings are still all being occupied by the College of the Rhine Army. I suppose that Mr. Birley has not written to you more fully in this matter as he hoped to do when he confirmed [receipt of] your letter in January. Do you feel, my Lordbishop, one could possibly ask him whether his enquiries in this matter have led him to a decision in this respect or another? In this case, I should gladly be prepared to write to you another letter.

Yours affectionately,

Bell to Leibholz, 29 April (1948), BA, N 1334 (handwritten)

My dear Leibholz

I am delighted to hear you are all naturalised British subjects. Welcome to you all!
I will certainly write to the F.O. about Göttingen on the lines you suggest.[1]

Yours ever,

[1] See Bell to Bishop, 5 May 1948, Bell Papers 40, fol. 464.

Leibholz to Bell, 30 May 1948, Bell Papers 40, fol. 465 (typewritten)

My Lordbishop,

I am afraid I have not yet thanked you for your last kind note and the enclosed letter by Mr Bishop. As things stand now I think we shall leave Oxford for Göttingen on the 9th of June. Our address will be c/o G.C. Bird, British University Control Officer, HQ Land Niedersachsen c/o Sub Office GÖTTINGEN, 126 HQ CCG, BAOR 30. We expect to stay in Germany for about two or three months and we hope you [will] allow us to tell the children as we did last year that in a case of emergency they may turn to you.

With regard to the children themselves we feel strongly that we should make a last attempt to bring the children to the grandparents who have not seen them for ten years. I gather from the letter from the Military Permit Officer that favourable consideration will probably be given to their applications but that compassionate visits are restricted to 14 days. I have written to him as shown in the enclosure and if it does not cause you too much trouble it would be very kind of you perhaps to attach a letter to my own and to ask him whether it would not be possible to consider the special circumstances of the case (about which he was informed by me in a previous letter) and the difficulties of the journey and to allow Marianne and Christiane for this reason to stay in Germany for about four or six weeks.

Please kindly forgive my raising another question concerning my personal future after return from Germany. I have applied for a Professorship of Political Science to be filled by the British Council by the 1st October, 1948. But I was asked in the application form to give the nationality of both my *parents* at *birth* and, therefore, I take it for granted that I shall not get the post, although I noted that before Naturalisation I was offered a chair of Political Science (and Law) by six German universities (Berlin, Göttingen, Heidelberg, Munich, Mainz, Frankfurt).[1]

In the meantime, I have also met Cole[2] and it might be that I shall lecture again here next term. But, of course, from a financial point of view, such a lecture course is only a burden and provides no basis whatsoever for the future. What I am thinking of in this connection is whether you would perhaps possibly be prepared to write to Lindsay asking him whether now that I have been naturalised and have refused all the offers mentioned it might not be possible to offer me a Readership or Senior Lectureship within the framework of the Faculty of Social Sciences. I realize that Lindsay cannot make the necessary arrangements himself but I gathered from the talk with Cole that there are obviously plans to enlarge the Faculty of Social Sciences in [the] not too distant future and, in fact, Cole vaguely discussed the possibility of a Readership in Political Sociology. What I think would be of great value is if at your instigation Lindsay would talk to Cole about the matter and cause him to give it further serious consideration.

In addition, to show my 'usefulness', which I myself cannot emphasise, one could perhaps point out that there is hardly in this country a scholar who is better informed about German political institutions and theory and that considering the fact that things are moving in the direction of including Western Germany into a Western European organisation it might be worthwhile considering to make use of me under this aspect as long as I am available. There are people here who specially deal with France, Italy, the Balkans, Russia etc. but as far as I can see there is nobody who is dealing with the German Problem. Just as I am trying to interpret British Institutions to German students I think I could talk to English Students on the German problem: and strange to say the interest of students here in the German problem seems to me sincere and great.

I have a very bad conscience that I write all this to you, especially as I really think very humbly of my work: but I must in some way try to face the future and I do hope that a solution might be found on the basis mentioned or a similar one.

With very many thanks

Yours affectionately,

---

[1] On 19 April 1948 the ministry at Hannover confirmed Leibholz's position as emeritus with a permanent visiting professorship and an obligation to lecture in every second semester; see Szabó, *Vertreibung*, p. 389.

[2] Presumably the historian G.D.H. Cole (1889–1959) was at this time Chichele Professor of Social and Political Theory at Oxford.

Leibholz to Bell, 2 June 1948, Bell Papers 40, fol. 467 (typewritten)

My Lordbishop

Many thanks for having kindly written to Lindsay.[1] I have just had a letter from him saying that he would like to see me before I go, in connection with the German university reform.

You may care to know that a new Protestant Youth House which has been set up in Berlin has been named Dietrich Bonhoeffer House. Dibelius addressed the audience at the inauguration ceremony. Unfortunately, Sabine's parents could not attend the ceremony because her father had a severe heart attack at that time. This is one of the reasons why we were keen on getting the children over.

In the meantime, we have also heard that two streets in Germany have been named after Dietrich.

We shall probably be away for three months.

Yours ever,

[1] See Bell to Leibholz, 1 June 1948, Bell Papers 40, fol. 466; Bell to A.D. Lindsay, 1 June 1948, ibid., fol. 466ʳ; Lindsay to Bell, 18 June 1948, ibid., fol. 468. On Lindsay's interest in Germany and in German universities see Drusilla Scott, *A. D. Lindsay*, A Biography (London, 1971), pp. 296–8.

Bell to Leibholz, 4 June 1948, BA 1334 (typewritten)

My dear Leibholz,

Many thanks for your letter. I am deeply interested and moved to read what you say about the Dietrich Bonhoeffer House in Berlin – though sad that Professor Bonhoeffer could not be at the opening ceremony.

I wrote to Lord Lindsay at the beginning of the week, and have had the enclosed interim reply.[1]

Yours ever,

[1] See A.D. Lindsay to Bell, 18 June 1948, Bell Papers 40, fol. 468: 'he does not think there is much chance of there being anything here that would suit him'.

Bell to Leibholz, 22 June 1948, BA 1334 (typewritten)

My dear Leibholz,

I wrote to the Master of Balliol, who has been in touch with Cole about you. Cole 'likes and admires' you; but I am afraid he does not think there is much chance of there being anything in Oxford that would suit you – as hopes of expansion of social studies have been rather cut down. I am very sorry – but there it is.

[a]All best wishes for your visit to Germany and greetings to the Bonhoeffers.[a]

Yours ever,

Leibholz to Bell, 24 September 1948, Bell Papers 40, fol. 470 (typewritten); BA, N 1334 (carbon, without the last section)

My Lordbishop,

Efforts are being made in Germany to set up a British-German Society[1] and I have been asked to approach in this country those who would probably be inclined to join such an organisation, which is to represent the most important strata of society. I think that time is rather rapidly moving towards a setting up of such a society and that we should support this plan. But before going ahead I should be glad to know what you yourself feel about this plan and whether you would be prepared to support it.

I myself have been thinking of approaching, among others, Lindsay, Beveridge, Gilbert Murray, Arthur Salter[2], Ernest Barker, Hodgson, Micklem, Raven[3], Henry Carter[4], Tomkins, Collins, Dodds[5], Oldham, Christopher Dawson, Benians[6], Cole, Sorensen[7], Stokes, Templewood. These (apart from the last two mentioned) I have met before. I should be glad to know how you feel about the names suggested and to have further names of those who you feel would like to join such an organisation the avowed aim of which would be to secure a mutual understanding between, and a reconciliation of, the two nations. I fully realize the great difficulties (especially in Germany), which have to be overcome if the aim mentioned is to be attained. But I feel strongly that at least the attempt should be made and a platform be found on which political as well as non-political activities should be conducted. I imagine that such a body would be able to render valuable services, especially in the political field after [a] Western government has been set up.

I note that most of the Germans who have already joined this planned organisation are well known to me. Of course, the fruitful work of such a society presupposes that there will be no war in the near future. But must [it] not be our working hypothesis that there will be none?

We came back from Germany last month. But we were not able to go to Berlin to see Sabine's parents as the necessary visas for Sabine and our daughters were not available. Of course, Sabine's parents were very much disappointed and simply could not understand why there was no way of seeing their grand-children after ten years' time and after all that has happened. But I am glad to say that they seem to be fairly well, although they are anxious about what the next winter will have in store for them all. Especially they fear the lack of fuel: I am just trying to relieve their situation in this respect and have just written to Niebuhr in this connection.

Yours ever,

1   The German-dominated Anglo-German Association had its first meeting in March 1949 in Wittlar; in 1950 the Königswinter Conference followed, chaired by Robert Birley. The British-German Association (BGA) was founded in 1951.
2   Arthur Salter (1881–1975) was appointed Gladstone professor of political theory and institutions at Oxford University in 1934, and a fellow of All Souls College. He became Parliamentary Secretary to the Ministry of Shipping in 1939, heading the British shipping mission to Washington from 1941 to 1943. In 1944 he was appointed deputy director-general of the United Nations Relief and Rehabilitation Administration. He became 1st Baron Salter in 1953.
3   Charles Raven (1885–1964) was Anglican priest and influential theologian, pacifist, scholar of Christian Socialism and of the relationship between religion and science. He had become Regius Professor of Divinity at Cambridge in 1932 and Master of Christ's College, 1939–50.
4   Henry Carter, who died in 1951, was a prominent Methodist and, like Charles Raven, a pacifist.
5   Eric Robertson Dodds (1893–1979), Irish classical scholar who had become Regius Professor of Greek at Oxford University in 1936. In 1946-7 he was President of the Association of University Teachers. For his interest in Germany see his planning for the re-education of Germany in Phillips, *Investigating Education*, pp. 89–104; see too E.R. Dodds, *Missing Persons. An Autobiography* (Oxford 1977).
6   Ernest Alfred Benians (1880–1952) was British academic and historian; Master of St John's College, 1933–52 and Vice-Chancellor of the University of Cambridge, 1939–1941.
7   Reginald William Sorensen (1891–1971) was Unitarian minister and Labour Party M.P. between 1929 and 1964. In 1964 he became Baron Sorensen.

Bell to Leibholz, 27 September 1948, BA, N 1334 (handwritten)

My dear Leibholz

I am delighted to know you are safely back – and I hope the journey and the time spent in the Zone was profitable. I am vy. sorry indeed you could not get the visas to Berlin.

I have had a vy. busy summer with the World Council of Churches[1] following Lambeth.[2] I have been elected Chairman of the Central Committee of the World Council. At the moment Mrs Bell and I are ending a fortnight's holiday – in Cumberland. But I am deeply interested in your proposal. But I am myself involved in negotiations for a similar project with Lord Henderson[3]. I suggest waiting till we see what Henderson says to my proposal, and am hoping to see him again in October. I am also seeing Sholto Douglas[4] and shall see Pakenham who is very sympathetic.

Yours ever,

I will write after seeing Henderson.
You want more *MPs* than your list has.

1   The First Assembly of WCC took place in Amsterdam from 22 August to 4 September 1948.
2   The Eighth Lambeth Conference of bishops of the Anglican Communion took place in July–August 1948.
3   William Watson Henderson (1891–1984) was Labour politician. He served in Attlee's Labour government as a member of the Air Council from 1945 to 1947 and as Joint Under-Secretary of State for Foreign Affairs from 1948 to 1951. He had become 1st Baron Henderson in 1945.
4   William Sholto Douglas (1893–1969) was senior commander in the Royal Air Force during the Second World War. Promoted to rank of Marshal in the RAF, he had become the second commander of the British Zone of Occupation in Germany in May 1946. In 1948 he retired and became 1st Baron Douglas of Kirtleside. He was chairman of British European Airways from 1949 to 1964.

Leibholz to Bell, 2 October 1948, Bell Papers 40, fol. 471 (typewritten); BA, N 1334 (copy)

My Lordbishop,

I was delighted to hear from you again and to learn that you and Mrs Bell are now on a fortnight's holiday. I should have written earlier but I knew that you have been extremely busy this summer in connection with the Lambeth and Amsterdam Conferences and I did not want to intrude on your time.

I am also delighted to hear that you have been elected Chairman of the Central Committee of the World Council. No better election could be made which is at the same time a sign of the deep gratitude felt by all the Churches toward you for the work you have done for them for so many years.

How very encouraging to know that you have also been thinking of setting up an organisation similar to that one about which I wrote to you in my last letter. Of course, there is no room for overlapping organisations and, therefore, I shall now wait until I have heard from you again and know more about your own plans. I think and I hope you agree that there is no harm for people in Germany going ahead with their plans in the meantime. Among others, they have approached Lilje, Grimme, Arnold[1], Geiler[2], Frings[3] (who, by the way, has refused on the ground that he cannot join a political organisation). They have also written to some individual people here, but rather at[4] random: these have partly accepted like Gilbert Murray and others, but most of them wish first to have more information about[5] those who are backing the project in this country and in Germany. This is why they asked me to step in and to help them and as I myself feel that something should be done in this direction I should gladly be prepared to comply with their request provided that there is no overlapping and I have secured your full support.

So far the people in Germany themselves seem to think of a primarily private organisation. But I feel strongly that a new edition of G.E.R.[6], valuable as such an organisation may be, will not meet the requirements, under the present circumstances. At least some official backing will be necessary as otherwise the tasks such a society would have to fulfil could not properly be performed, simply because the means are not available to make such an organisation work efficiently. I myself feel that it will not be too difficult to secure this support in face of the importance and urgency of this plan.

My list was very provisional: I also thought of Pakenham but was not sure whether an active Minister can join such a society, which has special political aims.

I felt that my stay in Germany was very profitable: this applies especially to the time I spent in Göttingen as guest-professor. I have just written at request [sic] an exposé on the new planned constitutional charter for my friends who are sitting in Bonn and hope to finish the job before long.[7] I have also been invited by the Board of Faculties[8] to give a lecture-course this term.

Yours ever,

P.S. I have seen today Goebbels Diaries. No better proof could be found for our thesis that the doctrine of Unconditional Surrender needlessly prolonged the war and that Vansittart was music for Goebbels' ear.[9] May I quote from him:

'The fellow Vansittart is really worth his weight in gold to our propaganda. After the war a monument ought to be erected to him somewhere in Germany with the inscription: "To the Englishman who rendered the greatest service to the German cause during the war."'[10]

Goebbels does not get tired in saying that Vansittart has made it very easy for him to toughen and strengthen German resistance.

---

[1] Karl Arnold (1901–58) was Christian socialist, co-founder of the Christian Democratic Union and the trade unions in the Rhineland in 1945. From 1947 to 1956 he served as deputy leader of the state of North Rhine-Westphalia.

[2] Karl Geiler (1878–1953) was Mannheim lawyer and former member of the DDP, the German Democratic Party. Geiler had lectured in commercial law at the commercial college at Mannheim and also at Heidelberg University from 1929 to 1939. In October 1945 the Military Government for Germany, United States appointed Geiler leader of Grand-Hessen at Wiesbaden. In 1946 he returned to Heidelberg University, which appointed him professor of international law. In 1948-9 he served as rector of the university.

[3] Josef Frings (1887–1978) served as Archbishop of Cologne between 1942 and 1969. He was elevated to the cardinalate by Pope Pius XII in 1946.

[4] Instead of 'with any' this becomes 'rather at' in the copy.

[5] Copy: concerning.

[6] German Educational Reconstruction was a voluntary organization officially founded under the presidency of Eleanor Rathbone and, since 1946, Sir Ernest Barker. Its main focus was originally on the preparation of the return of German refugee educationists to post-war Germany but later on it changed to the interchange of German and British subjects. The organization was disbanded in the mid-1950s; see Jane Anderson, '"GER": A Voluntary Anglo-German Contribution', in: Hearnden, *The British in Germany*, pp. 253–67.

[7] Since 1 September 1948 the Parliamentary Council had been discussing the new Constitution of the Federal Republic of Germany in Bonn. It was accepted on 8 May and published on 23 May 1949. See Leibholz, 'Die Struktur der neuen Verfassung' (1948), in his collection, *Strukturprobleme*, pp. 63–70.

[8] Copy adds: here. Probably one of the three Conferences of the Faculties of Law at Cologne in 1949.

[9] On the accusation that Vansittart's speeches and writings had assisted Goebbels, see Robert Vansittart, *The Mist Procession: Autobiography* (London, 1958), pp. 141–4.

[10] Louis P. Lochner (ed.), *Goebbels Tagebücher* (Zürich, 1948), p. 312.

Bell to Leibholz, 19 October 1948, BA, N 1334 (typewritten); Bell Papers 40, fol. 472 (carbon)

My dear Leibholz,

I saw Lord Henderson last week. He was more reserved on the subject than when I saw him at the beginning of his taking office. He said that he thought the Foreign Office would be in sympathy with a good scheme for a social centre in London; but that it could not take the initiative (that I naturally did not expect.)

But I saw Lord Douglas (Sholto Douglas) the next day. He was much more active and energetic in the matter, and is taking counsel with some members of Parliament, and will let me know the result. I will keep you informed. Meantime I should advise a waiting attitude on your part.

Yours ever,

Leibholz to Bell, Oxford, 21 October 1948, Bell Papers 40, fol. 473 (typewritten); BA, N 1334 (copy)

My Lordbishop,

Thank you very much for your letter and for kindly telling me of the results of your talks with Lord Henderson and Lord Douglas last week. I have followed your advice and taken no further action in the matter and shall go on taking a waiting attitude until I hear again from you. I have advised my opposite number in Germany accordingly who, in the meantime, has again written to me saying that his efforts as far as the Germans are concerned are going well and that he has also had a letter in which General Sir B. H. Robertson[1] says that he has learned with interest of the intention to found a society for the promotion of Anglo-German relations. He adds that he has the cause of Anglo-German understanding very much at heart and that he welcomes every effort to bring about closer contacts and that he will be glad to consider any request for assistance in specific points, which may arise.

Yours ever,

---

[1] Brian Hubert Robertson (1896–1974) was restored to the Active List in 1945 as a substantive Major General, he became a lieutenant general in the following year and a full general in 1947. From 1945 Robertson had been the Deputy Military Governor in the British Zone and from 1947 to 1950 Military Governor and British member of the Allied Control Council for Germany.

Verso: Sabine Leibholz to Bell (handwritten; typewritten in BA,N1334)

My dear Lordbishop

Maria von Wedemeyer has just asked me to tell you that she is engaged to be married to Paul Werner Schniewind, son of the Professor of Theology in Halle.[1] He is studying law in Göttingen and reading for his degree there, so we know him quite well and like him very much indeed. His right arm is crippled as a result of the war. Maria is just gone to Bryn Mawr College USA for one year where she got a scholarship.[2] – My parents have just written that Dietrich's and Klaus's portraits have been hung up in Charlottenburg-Town Hall. Both my parents are fairly well and full of confidence.

It would be so nice seeing you again if your way leads you to Oxford! Please give my love to Mrs. Bell.

Yours affectionately,
Sabine

[1] Julius Schniewind (1883–1948) was widely read New Testament scholar whose activities on behalf of the Confessing Church and as a public opponent of the National Socialist state led to a chequered academic career between 1933 and 1945. In 1945 he was restored to his Chair at Halle. His son Paul-Werner (* 1923) married Maria von Wedemeyer in 1949. The marriage ended in 1956.
[2] At Bryn Mawr College Maria von Wedemeyer studied mathematics. She was awarded an MA in 1950.

Sabine Leibholz to Bell, 2 November 1948, Bell Papers, Vol. 42, fol. 125 (handwritten)

The address is:
M. v. Wedemeyer
Bryn Mawr College
Bryn Mawr/ Pensia. U.S.A.
I was very glad to have your letter. Today we received the first copy of Dietrich's 'The Cost of Discipleship'.
Sabine

Bell to Leibholz, 16 November 1948, BA, N 1334 (handwritten)

My dear Leibholz,
Your letter reached me (forwarded) today – Thursday: and I am *greatly* helped by it. I am trying to compose a speech this evening quietly in the Club. It is very difficult.
    It was such a pleasure to see you and Sabine on Wednesday.

                                                                        Yours affectionately,

Leibholz to Bell, 26 December 1948, Bell Papers 40, fol. 476 (handwritten)

My Lordbishop,
I feel strongly I must also thank you for your letter to Sabine who will write to you herself. Sabine's father was indeed one of the few men whose passing has made the world poorer – in a quite literal use of the word.[1] The great thing was that the underlying force of his wisdom was his goodness and that this goodness was united in him with an aristocratic noble-mindedness and attitude, with an untiring preparedness to help others, with an incorruptible sense of honour and fairness. And in addition I loved his moving human unassumingness, his simplicity, this faithfulness and then there was his ability to differentiate with certainty the essential things from the non-essential, his reliableness of judgement, which was so entirely independent of all criteria (as e.g. success) on which most people somewhat depend in their judgements and which was based on a true appreciation of the real values in life. Yes, he was a man of unique great human and intellectual gifts and I myself feel as if I have lost my father for the second time.
    The day we have had for the first time from Sabine's mother a letter, which very much reminds us in its spirit and language of Dietrich's poems. Where there is so much love as in this family the suffering will take no end.

We shall listen to your broadcast on Christmas Eve. I myself gave the last four talks there (under the Heading, *Europe alive*) and I have also made arrangements for broadcasting some extracts from Dietrich's *Ethics* during seminary (every Friday).

My I just ask you what has come out of the contacts you have made with regard to the project about which we had some correspondence in September & October. You wrote to me last in October when saying that you met Lord Henderson and Lord Douglas. You told me that you would let me know the results of his taking counsel with some members of Parliament. In any case, following your advice I have taken a waiting attitude since I received your letter.

By the way, Marianne hopes to join the editorial staff of S.P.G.[2] next August. Thank you for what you have written to that.[3]

---

[1] Karl Bonhoeffer had died on 4 December 1948. He was 80 years old.
[2] The Society for the Propagation of the Gospel in Foreign Parts. In 1948 its editorial secretary was E.H. Ward.
[3] See Bell to Ward, 28 October 1948, Bell Papers 140, fol. 475.

1949

4 April	NATO is established.
11 May	The Soviet blockade of Berlin ends though the airlift continues until September.
23 May	the 'Bizone' in Germany unites with the French zone to create the Federal Republic. The new capital city is Bonn.
29 August	The Soviet Union explodes its first atomic bomb.
15 September	Konrad Adenauer becomes the first Chancellor of the Federal Republic.
7 October	The creation of the German Democratic Republic out of the Soviet-controlled zone. Its capital will be East Berlin. On 11 November the Soviet Union concedes partial sovereignty to the new Communist state.

Bell to Leibholz, 29 July 1949, BA, N 1334 (typewritten)

My dear Leibholz,

Very many thanks for your kind letter of good wishes and congratulations on the very generous action taken by the Theological Faculty of Goettingen University.[1] I do most highly appreciate this honour, and I look forward greatly to receiving it.

I have not actually heard anything officially from the Faculty or the University. But I have seen it announced in various English papers. I have also heard from Pastor Menn[2], so presumably it has been announced in Germany.

My wife and I are going to Australia on August 5th.[3] So the official communication may come when we are away. But I just want to thank you most warmly for your congratulations.

All best wishes.
Yours sincerely,

---

[1] On 25 June 1949 Bell was awarded an honorary doctorate of the (protestant) theological faculty by Göttingen University.
[2] Wilhelm Menn (1888–1956) was head of the Ecumenical Central Office of the Evangelical Church in Germany in Frankfurt/M between 1946 and 1956.
[3] This tour would include visits to New Zealand, Tasmonia, India then Rome. The Bells returned home on 9 December 1949.

1950

11 May A speech by the French politician Robert Schuman inaugurates the new European Community.
25 June North Korea invades South Korea precipitating a conflict with an international coalition operating under a mandate from the United Nations.

Bell to Leibholz, 21 January 1950, BA, N 1334 (typewritten)

My dear Leibholz,

I have a letter from Bishop Wurm about von Neurath[1], which I send you herewith. Obviously nothing can be done with the government until after the Election.[2] But I should be glad of your comments. I am sending you the German text; and I am sending the English text to Lord Hankey for his comments.[3]

Yours ever,

[1] Konstantin von Neurath (1873–1955) was German Minister of Foreign Affairs, 1932–8. In 1939 Hitler had appointed Neurath Protector (Reichsprotektor) of Bohemia and Moravia, but he relinquished this position for political reasons in 1941. In 1946 the Nuremberg Trial sentenced him to a term of 15 years in prison, but in 1954 he would be released for health reasons with the agreement of the Soviet Union. See Bell's speech in the House of Lords in Hansard, HL Deb., Vol. 174, cols. 477–83 (21 November 1951).
[2] The British general election was held on 23 February 1950.
[3] Lord Hankey had become the most prominent critic of the continuing trials of war criminals in a succession of interventions, not least in the House of Lords. In 1950 he would publish his book *Politics, Trials and Errors* (London, 1950). Hankey's reputation as a judge of affairs has not prospered in the hands of the historians, but as a diarist he remains impressive.

Bell to Leibholz, 11 February 1950, BA, N 1334 (typewritten)

My dear Leibholz,

I am extremely grateful for your letter about von Manstein[1] – and also your letter today about von Weiszäcker.[2]

I am seeing Professor Courvoisier[3] in Geneva in a week's time; and Liddell Hart in town on Wednesday. All you say about von Manstein is very much to the point.

Please thank Sabine very much for her birthday letter, and for her second letter. I sent the birthday telegram before I got her letter (which came by the second post): so I had not forgotten. I am sorry I did not write on February 3rd.

Yours ever,

[1] This letter is lost. But see Tom Lawson, 'Bishop Bell and the Trial of German War Criminals', in Chandler, *The Church and Humanity*, pp. 340–1. About the cases of the Generals Erich von Manstein, Gerd von Rundstedt and Walter von Brauchitsch Bishop Hanns Lilje had written to Bell on 15 September 1948, LKArch. Hann, L3, II, 32, cited by Siegmund, *Lilje*, p. 261: 'It would have the most unfortunate psychological repercussions in the German public if something should happen to them during the time of their detention. [...] A speedy and positive solution of the problem seems to me to be unavoidable in the interest of both our nations.' After the Nuremberg Trial Manstein was again sentenced by a British Court at Hamburg in 1949 to 18 years in prison, later on shortened to 12 years. Since Otto John's time as a screener of the Control Commission for Germany and Austria he was in touch with the case of Manstein and took part at the trial at Hamburg; see Gieseking, *Fall*, pp. 52–4. Half a year ago a memorandum of the POW Commission of the WCC had discussed the situation of Manstein and his comrades and informed Lilje. See Alex Wunderlich, 'Hanns Lilje und der Umgang mit NS-Verbrechern', in: Heinrich Grosse et al. (ed.), *Neubeginn nach der NS-Herrschaft?* (Hannover, 2002), pp. 187–99, esp. 190–1. Did Lije write to Bell? Manstein was released in 1953.
[2] Ernst Freiherr von Weizsäcker (1882–1951) was Secretary of State of the Foreign Ministry between 1938 and 1943 and Ambassador to the Vatican, 1943–45. Weizsäcker had played an important part in providing some freedom and opportunity for active resisters at the Foreign Ministry but historians

continue to place him in a grey area between the categories of resistance and complicity. For his case see Bell to President Truman, 19 May 1949, Bell Papers 49, fol. 379. In 1949 the Nuremberg Trial sentenced Weizsäcker to 5 years in prison. In October 1950 he was released as part of a general amnesty.
[3] Jaques Courvoisier (1900–88), since 1939 Professor of Church History at Geneva University.

Bell to Leibholz, 29 March 1950, BA, N 1334 (typewritten)

My dear Leibholz,

Very many thanks for your letter about Germany. I am naturally in agreement with you. I do not know what sort of repercussions Churchill's speech[1] will have in Germany, but he has got something to get over. But I do wish it were possible to get more vision and more imagination into the Foreign Secretary's mind. I expect there will be a debate in the House of Lords after Easter. If so, I shall try to say something.

All good wishes.

Yours affectionately,

[1] See Hansard, HC Deb., vol. 472, cc. 1280–99 (16 March 1950). Here Churchill had argued that an increasingly confident 'Western Germany' should be allowed to contribute to 'the general framework of defence' of European frontiers against the Soviet threat.

Bell to Leibholz, 3 April 1950, BA, N 1334 (typewritten)

My dear Leibholz,

Many thanks for your letter. There is to be a debate in the House of Lords on Foreign Affairs, opened by Lord Salisbury, on 9th May. I shall hope to be there, and I shall put my name down to speak.[1] But of course whether I get the chance will depend on how high up in the list of speakers my name is placed. For I have an appointment that evening in Sussex. I am afraid I shall not be able to come to Germany this summer. I have to go to a meeting of the World Council of Churches in Toronto.[2]

All good wishes.

Yours affectionately,

[1] Lord Salisbury did not open a debate in May 1950, but Bell's interest was probably in the fate of German prisoners in Russia; see his motion and speech in Hansard, HL Deb., Vol. 167, cols. 465–8 (23 May 1950); also in Raina, *Bishop George Bell: House of Lords Speeches*, pp. 128–32.
[2] In July 1950 the third annual meeting of the WCC's Central Committee at Toronto would adopt a resolution on the war in Korea and a statement on *The Church, the Churches, and the World Council of Churches*.

1951

18 April   The Treaty of Paris creates the European Coal and Steel Community.
10 October   President Truman announces the Mutual Security Act.

Bell to Sabine Leibholz, 15 February 1951, BA, N 1334 (handwritten)

My dear Sabine

Thank you so much for your letter, which crossed mine. I was glad to hear your news of the visit to Germany in the summer. But I was very sorry to hear the news of your dear mother's death on February 1st of which the printed announcement has just reached me. I know how greatly you and your brother and your sisters, and all the members of her large family, will feel her loss. But what gratitude you and all her children, living and departed must feel, and feel to the end of your days for having been blessed with a Mother so brave, so full of faith, and so unfailing in her care and love for them, and for their father, and for those whom they married, and for all who are added to the great household. It was a great privilege for me to know her – and I shall ever remember her, and her goodness, at our successive meetings from 1945 onwards. There was something both Christian and old Roman about her. Profoundly Christian she still recalled something of the fine heroic Roman matron, strong, resolute, as well as tender and completely forgetful of herself. She was a wonderful mother, and wife: and must have done marvels for the upholding of your father's courage, and of that of your brother Dietrich and your other brothers and sisters and yourself. A great example to the present, and the coming generation! May God give rest to her soul, after all her sorrows: and comfort to all of you.

Yours affectionately,

Bell to Leibholz, 15 February 1951, BA, N 1334 (handwritten)

Do you come to Wilton Park, now moved to Sussex?[1] I visited it on 24 Jan.

My dear Leibholz

I take the opportunity of the accompanying letter to Sabine to write and say you how glad I should be to have your appreciation of the present international situation, especially on the German and European side. There is a debate on Foreign Affairs in the Lords on February 28, which I hope to attend, and may *possibly* speak at. What an extraordinary turn round there has been in British policy to Germany 1945–1951. It makes one rub one's eyes. Schutz told me before Christmas that Vansittart openly confessed at a lunch of Foreign Press correspondents that the speeches he had been making about Germany for years were completely wrong, and his policy completely mistaken![2] And the Government has of course completely changed its tune, and implicitly must acknowledge that its interpretation of the situation was utterly mistaken. A British friend, whose judgement I respect, describes it as a 'cynicism' or [what] is likely to be taken as such by many people in Germany. I wonder whether you view it in this way? and whether you can set down turning points, or significant dates, in British and Allied post-war policy, which it would be useful to bring out in a speech?

I wonder further what you think of the release of certain war criminals? Or of the pressure on the British Govt. to follow the American example? (I have just had a [renewed] appeal from Bishop Wurm on behalf of von Neurath[3] though his case is one for the *four* powers).

I enclose a copy of 'Letter to the Churches' composed by the Exec. Ctee. of the World Council of Churches at its last meeting near Paris.[4] You might be interested.

Yours always,

---

[1] See Leibholz to Bell, 8 April 1947, note 2. Wilton Park had now become an executive agency of the Foreign and Commonwealth Office. This new status involved a move to Wiston House in West Sussex in January 1951.
[2] See the last sentence of Vansittart, *The Mist Procession*, p. 550: 'Mine is a story of failure but it throws light on my time which failed too.'
[3] For Bell's correspondence on behalf of Neurath see Bell Papers Vol. 48, fols. 113, 121, 155.
[4] The Executive Committee met at Bièvres near Paris in January 1951 and agreed a new 'Letter to the Churches', appealing against the accumulation of armaments.

Leibholz to Bell, 18 February 1951, Bell Papers 40, fol. 477seq (typewritten); BA, N 1334 (copy)

My dear Bishop,

Very many thanks for your letter. I am so glad to have heard from you again and to learn that you might possibly speak at the next debate on Foreign Affairs in the Lords.

I am very much impressed by what you say about Vansittart's change. The bad thing is that his views only reflected those of the then government and that they have had such a disastrous effect on the whole political development. I think that the whole mess we are in today is simply the result of the policy which was supported by Vansittart and his friends at that time. All the other mistakes made after the war (as, for instance, disarmament and annihilation of Germany's and Japan's political and military[1] power) are nothing but conclusions drawn from this basic grave mistake. This mess is also not due to a tragedy (as Niebuhr says) but simply to man's stupidity and lack in political insight and constructive political thought. Had Eisenhower told the Germans in 1945 what he has told them today things would have taken quite a different turn – at least as far as Germany is concerned.

As to the international situation I feel the whole position has become so intractable and awkward because the initiative lies entirely with the Russians and because nobody really knows whether they will act and, if so, when. Sometimes I am reminded of the position of Switzerland during the last war. Just as she had to thank the Führer at that time for not having °invaded their country we have to thank Stalin for having not yet° invaded the West-European countries and thus for having unleashed world war No. III.

I wonder whether it will be really possible to live for a long time in the presence of two conflicting political systems, and whether war can be postponed for a long time. Of course, we could still avoid war if we would follow Gandhi and take the radical pacifist line. This might sound defeatist and unheroic. But who knows whether the Koreans would have not preferred communism to what has been going there since June, 1950. And it is this attitude, which is also not unpopular in Germany today and which finds its expression in sayings like the following: It is 'better to be alive under Communism than to be dead under the Americans'. This does not mean that Western-Germany is not Western-minded today. I think she has impressively voted for the West in all elections held since 1945. But this attitude does not prevent many Germans (and other people) from thinking in terms of a tactical neutrality i.e. of a pure escapism.

Of course, one can tell them that one must make a stand for what one thinks is right and true and good and that one must defend the way of life in which one believes and that death might be better than a life, which is no real life. This is the Adenauer- and Kirkpatrick[2]-line (by the way K.'s speeches have not always been very fortunate): but there are many Germans who have become rather sceptical.

These Germans have spent up to ten years in the army and prison camps and simply wish to live and to survive. It is these people who make the futile attempt to 'reassure' themselves against the day of Russian invasion and who take no part in Politics and do not support the demand for German rearmament simply because they believe they would be allowed by the Russians to go on unmolested if Germany were to be 'liberated' by the East. These people can point out that other countries like Switzerland and Sweden do not want to be involved either in a third potential world war and that Britain herself has not taken a clear-cut moral decision in the Far East when China invaded Korea. In addition, Demilitarisation was one of the main war aims of the Allies and the whole re-education-policy was bent on eliminating German militarism and making the Germans a peace-loving nation. Among these Germans there also are many who have had bad experiences with the Allies after 1945 and, therefore, have a special grudge against them. The stupid handling of the denazification policy, dismantling, the Heligoland affair[3] etc. have had their effect.

In addition, there is the nationalistic argument. People say that so far no equality has been granted to Germany and that one cannot expect them to fight for and with the Allies as long as Germany has not[4] secured an equal status. They also point out that an Eastern invasion would at least secure national unity and would prevent Germans from killing each other. These men like Niemöller, wittingly or unwittingly, play into the hands of the Russians.

Further, the Germans know as we do that there are only 30 divisions on the one side and 105 divisions on the other and that, therefore, they can only fight a rearguard action for the allies and in doing so lose everything. Moreover, they fear that a German rearmament now might just provoke the Russian action which the Western powers wish to avoid.

I think these are the main arguments which one can hear in Germany today and to meet them I think the following line should be taken:

1. Support of the Adenauer Government: i.e. full equality, which has to be granted in due course, in any case, should be granted soon. It is time that matters today.
2. One should stress that the West stands for German unification in the same way as the East and that the Western powers will do all in their power (short of war) to achieve this aim. But at the same time they should state that they prefer a divided Germany to a unified Germany under communist rule.
3. One should point out that the Germans cannot expect the Allies to defend Western Germany if the Germans themselves cannot make up their minds to make a contribution to the common cause.

4. One should tell the Germans again and again that the conclusion to be drawn from what has happened in Korea is that weakness rather than strength is provocative, from the Russian point of view, and that in a case of Russian invasion the Germans would automatically have to fight for a cause which they detest.

Apart from taking this line I should impress on the Government the necessity of sending as many divisions to Germany as can be spared under the circumstances: This would show the Germans that the Western Powers are in earnest when they talk of the defence of Western Germany and would make it easier for them to make a contribution of their own. They would feel that then at least they would have a chance of survival. Such a decision would also lie in the British interest. For Western Germany is an integrated part of Europe and I do not think that Europe can live without Germany. Germany's fate is also Europe's fate, in which Britain is vitally interested.

After what one can read in the papers and after what Eisenhower has said in America it seems that, from a technical point of view, German rearmament cannot start until 1952. If this be so this might considerably help to overcome the present difficulties. For up to then the Germans will have made up their minds and made their contribution – provided the above policy is vigorously pursued: French fears of revival of German militarism might be allayed and the Russians might be deprived of a pretext for war.

Of course, from a point of view of home policy, German rearmament is not to be welcomed, for it will strengthen again the power of the old military caste and – what is worse – the Nazi spirit, which tends to become stronger every week. I could give you many illustrations. But I fear the letter would be too long and I think it could not be helped as foreign policy has priority before home policy.

Only one last word to the war criminals. I think that it was right to release Krupp and the other industrialists.[5] I think that, on the whole, they are not much worse than their colleagues in other countries and British reaction seemed to me to have been too noisy. But that men who were in charge of concentration camps have been released seems to me very bad and the German propaganda in favour of the remission of the death sentences passed on those criminals who were responsible for the death of hundred of thousands of innocent people is simply disgusting.

By the way, I have just read a German paper that the man who acted as prosecutor in Dietrich's trial at the concentration camp of Flossenbürg a few hours before Dietrich's death has been acquitted of complicity in murdering him (and four other fellow-prisoners) – obviously because this man complied with the Nazi-law.[6] He has only been sentenced to three and a half years imprisonment for other crimes committed. In this trial the president of the Nazi Court,[7] which sentenced Dietrich to death said as witness before the Court that Dietrich had to be sentenced to death because he contacted like-minded people abroad during the war. This man has been denazified in Nuremberg and is a solicitor there. This is 'justice'.

Yours always,

P.S. I have not been in Wilton Park recently and I do not know its new surroundings.

I also fear that the case of Neurath is a difficult one because it is one for the four powers.

1. Crossed out in the original, but not in the copy.
2. Sir Ivone Augustine Kirkpatrick (1897–1964) was British diplomat who served as the British High Commissioner for Germany in Bonn 1950–3, and then as the Permanent Under-Secretary of State for Foreign Affairs until 1957.
3. After the war Heligoland was a prohibited area used by the RAF for bombing. On 20 December 1950 two students occupied the island and hoisted the flags of Germany, Heligoland, and the European Movement International. Although they were promptly removed, the episode provoked a public movement of protest. In January 1951 the German parliament demanded unanimously that the island be re-opened, but it was only in March 1952 that the British Government did so.
4. Copy adds: been.
5. Alfried Krupp von Bohlen und Halbach (1907–67), the last owner of the Friedrich Krupp Company, had in 1948 been sentenced at Nuremberg to 12 years in prison and the confiscation of his property. On 31 January 1951 the American High Commissioner for Germany, John Jay McCloy, reprieved him in view of a report by American lawyers. McCloy also reprieved a number of other war criminals, particularly industrialists.
6. SS Standartenführer (Colonel) Walter Huppenkothen (1907–78) was prosecutor of Hans von Dohnanyi in the Sachsenhausen concentration camp on 6 April 1945 and, on 8 April, of Dietrich Bonhoeffer and other conspirators in Flossenbürg concentration camp; see Bethge, *Dietrich Bonhoeffer*, pp. 1034–6. In 1955 he was sentenced to seven years imprisonment, but one year later exonerated.
7. SS Sturmbannführer (Major) Otto Thorbeck (1921–76) was appointed the chief judge of the SS and police court in Munich in 1941. In 1955 he was convicted by a court of assizes in Augsburg for assisting in the murder of Hans von Dohnanyi and other resisters and was sentenced to four years imprisonment. On 19 June 1956 the Federal Court of Justice of Germany exonerated him on grounds that the killings were 'legal' because the Nazi regime had the right to execute 'traitors'.

Bell to Leibholz, 21 February 1951, BA, N 1334 (typewritten)

My dear Leibholz,

Very many thanks for your interesting letter, which I found extremely useful. I will write again either before or after the debate in the Lords next Tuesday.¹

I saw something in the *Times* or the *Telegraph* the other day about the prosecutor at Flossenbűrg, and wondered whether it was the same who prosecuted Dietrich. It is indeed a tragic reflection on [the] modern conception of Justice.²

Yours sincerely,

1. See Hansard, HL Deb., Vol. 170, cols. 629–722; Bell's speech: cols. 692–9 (28 February 1951).
2. The district court 'Munich I' acquitted Walter Huppenkothen on 16 February 1951. This seemed to Leibholz 'like scorn'. See Leibholz to the Curator of Göttingen University, 21 February 1951, in Szabó, *Vertreibung*, p. 391.

Bell to Leibholz, 14 March 1951, BA, N 1334 (typewritten)

My dear Leibholz,

Many thanks for your letter. I am particularly interested in what you tell me about Captain Best and Dietrich. I wonder whether his letter is in English, and if so, whether I could have the privilege of reading it – and returning it to you? I should like to see what he said. Captain Best wrote to me in 1945 saying he wanted to see me, but then I think he was ill, and so we never actually met. He and R.H. Stevens (whom I have seen many times) apparently did not get on at all with one another,¹ and were of a quite different temperament: so I am afraid I have not myself made any recent effort to make contact with Best.²

I am glad you approved the arguments in my speech in the House of Lords. The debate was a very unsatisfactory one, because it was crossed at every point by the really irrelevant issue of the American supreme naval commander. It was really too bad to interject that into a debate on foreign affairs.

I wonder what the Russians are up to? Their attitude does seem extraordinary. If they really want a conference, how can they imagine that its main point should be the remilitarization of Germany?

Yours ever,

---

[1] After the war Captain Sigismund Payne Best accused Major R. H. Stevens of co-operation with the Gestapo in Sachsenhausen concentration camp. They had both been captured in the Venlo Incident in November 1939.

[2] For something of this tangled narrative see Andrew Chandler, 'The Death of Dietrich Bonhoeffer', in the *Journal of Ecclesiastical History*, Vol. 45, No. 3, July 1994, pp. 448–59.

Bell to Leibholz, 17 March 1951, BA, N 1334 (typewritten)

My dear Leibholz,

Very many thanks for sending me Captain Best's letter, which I return. I have read it with great interest. It was very good to see what Best said about Dietrich and the impression he made upon him and others.

I am very much interested to hear about the offer you have received to accept a post as judge in the German Supreme Court. I am sure that those who know Germany and the German law would be clear that the German authorities, in making the offer, have acted very wisely in the interests of their country. But obviously there are many circumstances to take into account so far as you are concerned, and you are the best judge of them.

You might like to see, if you haven't seen it already, the accompanying memorandum (which I don't want back). It is a sort of questionnaire on European issues – largely the work of André Philip.¹

ᵃNo need to reply.ᵃ

With all best wishes to you and the family,
Yours ever,

---

[1] André Philip (1902–70) was a leading member of the Free French (and 'interior minister') during the Second World War who conceptualized possibilities of a European integration in 1943; member of the French Section of the Workers' International; finance minister in the French government, 1946–7.

Leibholz to Bell, 11 November 1951, Bell Papers 40, fol. 479 (handwritten)

My dear Bishop,

This is just a line to say that we have returned from Germany. But I think we shall only stay here for about a fortnight. For, in addition to the professorship I am holding in Göttingen I have decided to accept the membership of the Supreme Constitutional Court in Western Germany. This part had unanimously been offered me by Parliament in Bonn about two months ago and I feel it difficult to refuse the offer – in face of the very important powers the Court is called upon to wield in Germany in future and which are more far-reaching than those of the Supreme Court in the United States and the Dominions.[1]

I am glad to say that arrangements have been made with the German authorities and with the Home Office that my status as a British subject will not be affected. My permanent residence will remain in Oxford.

Christiane has been very seriously ill recently – but she has been given us back and you can imagine how we feel.

We do hope that you and Mrs Bell are perfectly well. Should you happen to come to town within the next ten days and to have time to see me I should try to meet you there.

My wife gives you her love.

With kindest regards from us all

Yours ever,

---

[1] When in March 1951 the Minister of Justice had invited Leibholz to accept an appointment to the newly created Court he refused due to his continuing obligations in Göttingen. Leibholz later relented and on 4 September was elected for a term of four years. His appointment was very likely supported by Eugen Gerstenmaier, at that time chairman of the Parliament's judicial election committee. See Donald P. Kommers, *Judicial Politics in West Germany* (Beverly Hills, 1976), pp. 122, 126.

1952

30 June   The end of the European Recovery Program ('The Marshall Plan').
2 October   The British government explodes its first atomic bomb.
1 November   The United States tests the first thermo-nuclear bomb.

Bell to Leibholz, 23 June 1952, BA, N 1334 (typewritten)

My dear Leibholz,

I was extremely interested to get your letter, and to know that the second edition of 'The Cost of Discipleship' has come out.[1] I am also very glad that the 'Papers and Letters' are to be translated, and published in the autumn.[2]

My wife and I are both well, and hope that you and Sabine and the family flourish.

All you say about the great constitutional issue before the Court is of deep importance. I feel very much for you and your fellow Judges, and for all those most nearly involved.

Yours ever,

---

[1] A second edition of Bonhoeffer's *The Cost of Discipleship* had been published by the SCM Press in London in 1951.

[2] Eberhard Bethge had published a selection of Bonhoeffer's letters and papers from prison under the title *Widerstand und Ergebung* in 1951. The English translation by Reginald H. Fuller was published under the title *Letters and Papers from Prison* (SCM Press, London) in 1953.

1957

The launching of the Sputnik satellite into space on 4 October inaugurates a new era in Cold War rivalry while a nuclear arms race between the American and Soviet states intensifies.

Bell to Leibholz, 15 February 1957, BA, N 1334 (typewritten)

My dear Leibholz,

Very many thanks for your letter and for your greetings, which reached me on my birthday; and for what you tell me about Otto John. I am much interested in the copies of the letters, which you sent. I do hope that something may happen, which will lead to John's early release.[1] I should be very glad to hear more about the circumstances when an opportunity occurs.

With all best wishes,

Yours ever,

[1] On 3 December 1950 Otto John became president of the newly founded Bundesamt für Verfassungsschutz, that is the Secret Service of the Federal Republic of Germany, a decision that was confirmed on 13 December. But what followed was extraordinary. On 20 July 1954, after the annual commemoration of the German resistance against Hitler in Berlin, Wolfgang Wohlgemut, whom John regarded as a friend but who was in fact a spy of the KGB, drove him across the border to East Berlin. Some days later John was paraded by the government of the German Democratic Republic as an opponent of the politics of Adenauer and of the re-militarization of the West. Between 24 August and 12 December he was held in the hands of KGB in the Soviet Union. He left East Berlin and reached West Berlin with the help of a Danish correspondent. Immediately he was arrested and sentenced by the Federal Supreme Court on 22 December 1956 to four years in prison. He was released on 27 July 1958.

Bell to Leibholz, 13 April 1957, BA, N 1334 (handwritten)

My dear Leibholz

I am busy preparing my lecture at Göttingen (May 15) on my Stockholm Conversations.[1] I wonder whether you have information about the actual channel through which Dietrich himself came? My belief is that he came as a courier (for this occasion) on the way to Norway with a despatch for the German military or political authority there, and was commissioned by the Foreign Office. I suppose that 'Foreign Office' covers many possibilities. Would Canaris be one of them? (I should not mention Canaris, unless information was undeniable – but is any one particular organisation or government-agency identifiable?

It is clear that Schönfeld's visit was quite independent in *arrangement* and origin: though the coincidence was fortunate.

Yours ever sincerely,

Dietrich does not seem to have had much (if any) personal acquaintance with von Trott, although von Trott knew other members of the family.

[1] Awarded an honorary doctorate of the Theological Faculty of Göttingen University on 15 May 1957, Bell gave a lecture, 'The Church and the resistance movement', which he repeated at Bonn University on 16 May. It was 15 years after Bell's conversations with Bonhoeffer and Schönfeld in Sweden and his second such treatment of the subject. See letters of invitation from Eberhard Bethge and others, Bell Papers 61, fols. 19–21.

Leibholz to Bell, 21 April 1957, Bell Papers 61, fol. 64 (handwritten)

My dear Bishop

Having just returned to Karlsruhe[1] I find your letter and hasten to answer it.

As far as we know Dietrich's visit to Stockholm was formally covered by the Foreign Office[2] (probably via v. Trott who was known to him just as well as to us and other members of the family[3]) for the official purpose mentioned in your letter. Substantially, of course, his visit was inspired and organised by the group round Dietrich i.e. my brother-in-law v. Dohnanyi, Oster and Canaris. I think no other organisation or government agency can be identified beyond that. In order to be safe we shall write to Mrs v. Dohnanyi who we think might know more than we on the concrete arrangements. Should we get more reliable news on the question raised I shall re-write to you. Bethge might know more too.[4]

I had been in contact with the Bundespräsident, the German Embassy in London and the Göttingen Rector in order to secure that your visit will become a full success and satisfy you. I am informed about the program and should only like to know when you arrive in Hannover on Tuesday. I suppose that you will proceed by car from Hannover to Göttingen on the same day. I shall take leave from the Court and travel with Sabine to Göttingen in order to be with you on these days until you leave Göttingen for Bonn.

Greatly looking forward to seeing you soon

Yours ever,

P.S. By the way, you asked for Marianne's address in one of your last letters. Here it is: 5a, Porchester Terrace, London W.2

---

[1] Elected in 1951, and re-elected in 1955 and 1963, Leibholz served as a judge at the Constitutional Court of Justice in Karlsruhe and also as a visiting Professor in Göttingen. In the spring of 1957 he received an invitation from the Faculty of Political and Social Sciences of Cologne University but the Minister of Science of Lower Saxony managed to retain him. In September that year Leibholz was appointed to a new regular Chair for Political Sciences and General Theory of State. His work as a judge in Karlsruhe ended in 1971.

[2] It has become clear that the arrangements were made by Canaris's office; see Bethge, *Dietrich Bonhoeffer*, p. 851.

[3] Trott was well known to Klaus Bonhoeffer, but Dietrich Bonhoeffer did not become acquainted with him until September 1939, and then through Trott's connections with his friend Hans Bernd von Haeften; see Bethge, *Dietrich Bonhoeffer*, p. 753.

[4] In fact, Bethge was informed and collected Bonhoeffer from the airport on his return from Sweden; see Bethge, ibid., p. 853.

Bell to Leibholz, 27 April 1957, BA, N 1334 (typewritten); Bell Papers 61, fol. 68 (carbon)

My dear Leibholz,

Very many thanks for your letter and for the information it gives. I look forward to hearing the result of your enquiries from Mrs v. Dohnanyi. But I have heard from Dr Gerstenmaier[1] in a way which makes it clear that Schönfeld came from the Kreisau circle. When Dr Gerstenmaier met Schönfeld at the Tempelhof aerodrome on his return from Stockholm, he was as surprised as anybody to see Dietrich with him.

It is very good of you to take so much trouble in connection with my visit. The programme is that I arrive at Hannover* at 12.45 on Tuesday, May 14th, and am taken by car to Göttingen. I lecture at Göttingen on the evening of Wednesday, May 15th. On Thursday, May 16th I travel from Göttingen to Bonn by car, and repeat the lecture that evening at Bonn University. On the evening of Friday, May 17th I am dining with Dr Gerstenmaier. I am seeing the President at 11.30 on Saturday morning, May 18th, and then go to Cologne in time to catch the plane for London (which takes off at 15.45).

Many thanks for giving me Marianne's address. I will do my best to get into touch with her.

I look forward very much to seeing you and Sabine.

With all warm remembrances,

Yours very sincerely,

[*] ªI gather that Bishop Lilje meets me at the aerodrome.ª

[1] See Gerstenmaier to Bell, 24 April 1957, Bell Papers 61, fol. 65: 'Betr. Zusammenhang zwischen den Reisen von Bonhoeffer und Schönfeld nach Stockholm, so glaube ich, daß diese Reisen unabhängig voneinander stattgefunden haben. Ich erinnere mich noch, daß ich Schönfeld, als er von Schweden zurückflog, auf dem Flughafen Tempelhof in Berlin abgeholt habe und dabei zu meiner Überraschung auch Bonhoeffer begegnet bin, der mit dem gleichen Flugzeug ankam. Jedenfalls hat der Kreisauer Kreis, mit dem Schönfeld damals zusammengearbeitet hat, vorher von der Reise Bonhoeffers nach Stockholm nach meiner Erinnerung keine Kenntnis gehabt.' For the riddle of the two emissaries see Bethge, *Dietrich Bonhoeffer*, pp. 851–2.

Leibholz to Bell, 2 May 1957, Bell Papers 61, fol. 72 (typewritten)

My Lordbishop,
Many thanks for your letter.

In the meantime, Mrs v. Dohnanyi has confirmed what I wrote to you in my last letter. i.e. Dietrich was formally backed by the Foreign Office to do – I suppose – what you mentioned in your former letter. Materially, he went to see you in complete understanding with v. Dohnanyi, Oster and Canaris. I cannot say whether the initiative rested with Dietrich alone or with his friends. I suppose the idea was common to all.[1] I fear it will be difficult to get the details of the plan as it was elaborated since nobody who participated in drafting the plan is alive today.

I gather that Bishop Lilje will meet you at the aerodrome in Hannover. We shall travel by car from Karlsruhe to Göttingen on Monday afternoon or Tuesday morning and shall get into touch with you on Tuesday afternoon to make further arrangements. In any case, we should be delighted if you would dine with us on Tuesday evening. I probably wrote to you that we moved from Göttingen to Karlsruhe a few months ago. Therefore, I suggest to you that we dine at a third place and then withdraw to our apartment after dinner.

We greatly look forward to seeing you soon.
With our very best wishes,

Yours ever,

[1] Evidently it was Bonhoeffer's idea to meet Bell; see Bethge, *Dietrich Bonhoeffer*, p. 851.

Bell to Leibholz, 11 May (1957), BA, N 1334 (handwritten)

My dear Leibholz

Many thanks for your letter. I don't know what the possibilities are on Tuesday! I should love to dine with you if it is possible. Lilje meets me at the airport. I lunch at 2 with the Minister-President (and Lilje) and am driven to Göttingen, where I stay, with my Chaplain Robert Miln, at *Hotel Gebhard*.

Professor Weber[1], Theaterstr. 14, Telephone 22614 is the Dean, making arrangements.

I don't think anything is planned for the evening. But neither do I know when the car takes me from Hanover to Göttingen. Sorry to be so vague. Marianne is here, looking blooming. Looking forward to seeing you and Sabine.

Yours ever,

---

[1] Otto Weber (1902–66) was professor of Reformed Theology at Göttingen University since 1934; Dean in 1939–45 and again in 1957/58; Rector in 1958–9. Though a disciple of Karl Barth Weber was also a follower of Emanuel Hirsch, had joined the Nazi Party and the *Deutsche Christen* in 1933 and was appointed Reformed member of the governing body of the German Evangelical Church under Reich Bishop Ludwig Müller. The scandal of the Sportpalast rally in Berlin in 1934 caused Weber to distance himself from the movement, but he remained a representative of the National Socialist German Lecturers' Association and his book *Bibelkunde des Alten Testaments* (1935) presents some anti-Semitic expressions. See Vicco von Bülow, *Otto Weber (1902–1966). Reformierter Theologe und Kirchenpolitiker* (Göttingen: 1999).

Bell to Leibholz, 20 May 1957, BA, N 1334 (typewritten); Bell Papers 61, fol. 112 (carbon)

My dear Leibholz,

First of all let me repeat my deep sympathy with Sabine and yourself over the loss of her eldest brother.[1] It was a real distress and its suddenness brought the sorrow home all the more keenly.

I do want to thank you and Sabine most heartily for your kindness to my chaplain and myself during our days at Göttingen. I was deeply impressed by the audience in the Aula, and by the manifest sympathy and attention with which my lecture was heard.[2]

I should be much interested to hear whether the news contained in the lecture was much reported in the German press. Here *The Times* had a very full account – and also *The Manchester Guardian*. Other papers gave good extracts, though I have not seen many of the papers.

I had a very happy time at Bonn. The lecture was given in a big room holding, they say, 600. It was estimated that there were at least 500 present, the great majority students. There was a very distinguished audience of senior people, including the Rektor (a Catholic), who was most welcoming, and Prelat Kunst[3], and Dr Gerstenmaier. I was also very glad that Peter Schönfeld was there. He is [Hans] Schönfeld's eldest boy, aged 28, and has just started in the Foreign Office. General ªTresckow'sª widow[4] was there, and thanked me warmly afterwards. Mr Cecil was there and Professor Potter from the Embassy.[5] Professor Rothfels, who is said to be a very good historian of the resistance movement, from Tübingen, spoke to me afterwards.[6] He was deeply interested in the new material, which my lecture contained, and thought it very important. He wants to use it in a new edition of his History on which he is busy.[7]

I had lunch on Friday with Prelat Kunst, and met various State Ministers – Home Affairs, Refugees and Vice-President Carlo Schmidt.[8] Prelat Kunst invited his Catholic colleague.[9] Both of them I had met at Herford or Cologne in 1946. Then on Friday evening I went to dinner with Gerstenmaier and met Adenauer, who was very friendly. He told me how pleased he was with Harold Macmillan's visit.[10] There were various other people there, including your friend Strauss[11] from the Ministry of Justice and General Huisinger[12].

On Saturday morning I saw President Heuss.[13] I had asked the Foreign Office representative who made the arrangements beforehand how long he would give me – expecting a quarter-of-an-hour. He said one hour! So I went to the interview well prepared, and had a most interesting time. The President was extremely friendly and courteous, entered into conversation very easily, and enabled me to have a full talk about displaced and stateless persons, and others, a talk, which was continued when the hour was over (some French parliamentarians having arrived) with one of his officials expert in the question, who promised to go thoroughly into the points I had made.[14]

Before leaving the President I asked about Otto John. I was very glad I did so. The President was obviously very much upset by John's departure to the Eastern Zone. It had come immediately after Heuss had seen him. He was also particularly annoyed because the sensation of John's disappearance completely obscured his own speech on the Tenth Anniversary of the 20th July.[15] He had seen the judgement, but was expecting to study it carefully. There were various complications in the whole matter. He could not express any opinion at present as to whether John had been kidnapped or had gone voluntarily. I gather that you saw Heuss about a year ago and talked about this matter, and he, I think, had been expecting a follow-up by you. I am sure he would like to hear from you, and probably to see you. I told him that I had met John in England. He had seen him on three or four occasions himself, but did not feel he could size him up.

Again with very many thanks and affectionate remembrances to Sabine,

Yours ever,

---

[1] Karl Friedrich Bonhoeffer died on 15 May 1957 at Göttingen.
[2] 'The Church and the resistance movement' – Lecture given by Bishop of Chichester on Conversations with two German pastors in Stockholm, May 1942, given at Göttingen University, May 15, 1957, and at Bonn University, May 16, 1957, Bell Papers 61, fols. 1–18; subsequently published in the Anglo-German journal, *The Bridge*, November 1957, pp. 3–17 and also the *Wiener Library Bulletin* Vol. 11, 1957, Nos. 3–4; a revised German version: 'Die Ökumene und die innerdeutsche Opposition', was published in *Vierteljahreshefte zur Zeitgeschichte* 5, 1957, pp. 362–76.
[3] Prälat (prelate) Hermann Kunst (1907–99), the first authorized representative of the Evangelical Church in Germany at the new seat of Government of the Federal Republic in Bonn, 1950–77, and also Bishop to the Army, 1957–72.
[4] Erika ('Eta') von Tresckow, née von Falkenhayn (1904–74), married Henning von Tresckow in 1926. After the war she lived in Göttingen.
[5] Cecil is unidentified. Professor Simeon Potter (1898–1976) was Professor of the English Language and Philology at the University of Liverpool, 1945–65. Potter was an ally of Sir Heinz Koeppler at Wilton Park.

6   Hans Rothfels (1891–1976) appointed to the chair in History at Königsberg University in 1926, a position which he lost in 1934 because of his Jewish descent. In September 1939 he emigrated to Britain and in 1940 became guest professor at Brown University in Providence, Rhode Island, in the United States. In 1948 he published the first historical study of the German opposition to Hitler. After his sixtieth birthday he returned to Germany and to a Chair in modern history at Tübingen University. As chairman of the advisory council of the Institute for Contemporary History (Munich) and, after 1953, co-editor of its journal, he became a leading figure in the development of this new field of research.
7   See Hans Rothfels, *Deutsche Opposition gegen Hitler* (Krefeld, 1949; enlarged edition Frankfurt/M., 1958); see his prefatory remark to Bell's article, 'Die Ökumene', pp. 362–3.
8   Carlo Schmid (1896–1979) was Professor of Political Science at Frankfurt University and a Social Democrat politician, member of the Federal Diet, 1949–72, and vice-president, 1949–66, 1969–72.
9   Prälat Wilhelm Bühler (1891–1958) was member of the cathedral chapter of Cologne; he played a dominant role in maintaining the interests of the churches at the consultations of the parliamentary council in 1948/9. After 1950 he was authorized representative of the Conference of Catholic Bishops to the government in Bonn.
10 Harold Macmillan (1894–1986) was British Conservative politician and Prime Minister, 1957–63. Macmillan visited Germany on 8 May 1957.
11 Walter Strauß (1900–76) was a founder of the CDU in Berlin in 1945; he served as secretary of state in the Hessian state ministry, 1945–7, and in the Ministry of Justice of the Federal Government, 1949–63.
12 Adolf Heusinger (1897–1982) was army officer in both world wars and finally lieutenant general. He knew something of the plans of the resistance but did not participate. In 1950 he became an adviser to the Federal Government in the Petersberg discussions with the Allied Powers and in 1953 head of the military department of the Amt Blanck, the precursor of the Ministry of Defence. Consequently he was chairman of the Military Management Team (Militarischer Führungsrat) of the new Federal Defence Army (Bundeswehr), 1955–7. In June 1957 he was appointed General and first Inspector General.
13 Theodor Heuß (1884–1963) was leading liberal German politician who served as the first President of the Federal Republic of Germany, 1949–59.
14 See Bell to Otto Dibelius, 21 May 1957, Bell Papers 61, fol. 273.
15 See Theodor Heuss, 'Bekenntnis und Dank', in Forschungsgemeinschaft 20. Juli (ed.), *Gedanken zum 20. Juli 1944* (Mainz, 1984), pp. 31–50; the speech was made on 19 July 1954 in the Auditorium Maximum of the Free University at Berlin. The father of the wife of Otto John, Lucie, was a friend of Heuss. On 1 August 1953 she had written asking him to intervene in the case of her husband. This did not move him. See Gieseking, *Der Fall Otto John*, pp. 121, n. 3; 136. In 1958 she tried again; see ibid., p. 143, 15. It was unknown to Bell and Leibholz that from 1954 the Organisation Gehlen (from 1956 the Bundesnachrichtendienst, Federal Intelligence Service) had intrigued against Otto John as head of the Secret Service, reporting to Konrad Adenauer alleged contacts with the Communists who had been members of the wartime 'Red Orchestra' organization. See Gerhard Sälter, *Phantome des Kalten Krieges. Die Organisation Gehlen und die Wiederbelebung des Gestapo-Feindbildes, Rote Kapelle,* (Berlin 2016), pp. 449–60.

Leibholz to Bell, Le Collège d'Europe, Bruges, 26 May 1957, Bell Papers 61, fol. 128–9 (handwritten)

My dear Bishop,

Your very kind letter has just reached me in Bruges.¹ Please accept our very best thanks for all you have said in it. Sabine has not yet quite recovered from the new blow she has suffered. Her own heart seems to be affected. Therefore, we are together in Bruges.

I myself am delighted that your visit to the Federal Republic was such a great success. It seems to me that it could hardly have been greater. I had written to the editors of the *Frankfurter Allgemeine* to inform the German public about your visit in a proper way. A few days ago they did so by publishing the essence of your lecture in full.[2] I am very glad they did so and I am enclosing a copy of the article – in case you should not yet have seen it. Marianne who is with us here in Bruges told us of the accounts in *The Times* and *The Manchester Guardian*. She will let us have them as soon as she is back in London.

By the way, I understood from what the Rector said in Göttingen that the President of the Federal Constitutional Court (i.e. the 'German' Supreme Court of the United States) sent you a telegram in which he heartily welcomed and thanked you for all you have done to protect justice and law. I wonder whether you have, in fact, received the telegram. I should imagine that he would be glad just to get a line [from] you saying that you enjoyed it.

I am delighted that you had such a good and long talk to the President. He himself wrote to me two days ago about your visit and said how glad he was to have seen you – in spite of his recent illness and the fact that he had just returned from an official visit in Turkey.[3] He obviously greatly enjoyed your visit. I am very grateful to you for having broached the John question. On the basis of the President's letter and of what you have kindly written to me about the contents of your talk to him I shall now be able to approach him in this matter in the near future. I am glad to have this possibility now.

I know well a number of people you have met in Bonn. Especially I am glad that you had a talk to Dr. Rothfels who is one of the German historians of the German resistance movement. He told me some time ago that he would be glad to see you in Bonn. No doubt, your account and the new material you have produced will be important for the new edition of his book.

During your stay in Göttingen I did not mention to you that the present Dean of the Theological Faculty Weber was under the regime of the former Reichsbischof Müller a church minister for the Reformed Church and that the present Rector of Göttingen University (Werner Weber[4]) also came into conflict with the Confessional Church. They both were on the wrong side. I think you ought to know this now. It filled me with deep satisfaction that in their official capacity they had to welcome you. They must have felt very much ashamed about their former attitude after your lecture.

With affectionate greetings from both of us,

Yours ever,

---

[1] From 1953 Leibholz gave guest lectures on comparative constitutional law at the College of Europe in Bruges, which awarded him an honorary professorship in 1970.
[2] *Frankfurter Allgemeine Zeitung*, 22 May 1957.
[3] Heuss was invited to Turkey on 5–13 May 1957.
[4] Werner Weber (1904–76) was German jurist, member of the Nazi Party since 1933 and member of the Academy of German Law since 1936. In 1931 he had been a consultant to the Prussian Ministry of Science and Art. After 1934 this became part of the Reich Ministry of Culture. Weber worked in the religious department and in the departments of national education, music and nature conservancy until he retired because of political differences in 1937. In 1935, he had been appointed to a Chair in public law at the Berlin business school, in 1942 he secured another at Leipzig University, and in 1948 another at Göttingen University, where he became Rector, 1956–8.

Leibholz to Bell, 11 November 1957, Bell Papers 40, fol. 480 (handwritten)

My dear Bishop,

I am enclosing a copy of the petition of pardon for Otto John put before the President of the Federal Republic a month ago.[1] I think you might be interested in seeing it, since you talked to the President about the whole affair.

As far as I know, the President, from the human point of view, seems to be inclined to comply with the petition.[2] On the other hand, he seems to be afraid of the potential political implications resulting from an act of grace, which would give Otto John his liberty again. It is obviously a highly delicate issue and my impression is that the President is rather nervous, although, on the whole I should think that the petition will be granted in the end.

I myself have had many talks on this matter in the course of the last few months. E.g. I had talked to the Minister of Justice and the Minister of Home Affairs[3] and their Secretaries of State and they all have promised me to support the enclosed petition warmly. Unfortunately, in the meantime, Schäffer has replaced the former Minister of Justice. In July and August I also had some correspondence with the President himself. My original intention was to collect some signatures of well-known people inside and outside Germany with a view to their supporting the petition. I have now abandoned this plan because I have been told, that in the tense atmosphere the President might feel to be under pressure by such an action and that the opposite effect might result from it.

In any case, I feel strongly I should inform you about the state of affairs and I wonder how you feel about it. There is not the slightest doubt that Dietrich and his brothers would most strongly ask for his early release. Otto John was a close friend of Klaus and was well known to Dietrich too. This fact alone proves his basic honesty. Further I am firmly convinced that the verdict, which has sentenced Otto John, is not based on sound assumptions.[4] But as I say I do not know whether it is wise under the circumstances, to take any action. Should you consider it I think it would be better *not* to mention my name. For the President knows that I have been operative behind the scene[s] all the time to secure the release of John and it might be detrimental (for the reasons stated above) to any potential action you might consider to undertake.

I was very glad indeed to see your lecture delivered at Göttingen published in full in English and German. It has been given the wide publicity it deserves.

With our very best wishes

Yours ever,

---

[1] See 'Gnadengesuch für Otto John', 11 October 1957, Bell Papers 40, fols. 481–8.
[2] A rather different impression of Heuss's position is given in Gieseking, *Fall*, pp. 502–4.
[3] The Federal Minister of Justice was Hans-Joachim von Merkatz (DP), 16 October 1956–29 October 1957, followed by Fritz Schäffer (CSU) in consequence of the formation of Adenauer's third cabinet. The Federal Minister of Home Affairs was Gerhard Schröder (CDU), 1953–61; for his position in the case see Gieseking, *Der Fall Otto John*, ibid., pp. 512–4.
[4] See the criticisms of Klaus Schaefer, *Der Prozess gegen Otto John* (Marburg, 2009), and the assessments of the opinion in Gieseking, *Fall*, pp. 359–61.

Bell to Leibholz, 18 November 1957, Bell Papers 40, fol. 489 (carbon)

My dear Leibholz,

I am greatly interested in getting your letter about Otto John. I wonder what the President said when you wrote to him? He seemed so annoyed with Otto John himself, when I mentioned John to him – but anxious to get in touch with you about him. You say that he is rather nervous as to intervention. I wonder whether Mrs Otto John would agree to getting in touch with me? I think she is in London, but I don't know where.[1]

I do hope that you and Sabine are well. I enclose a cutting from *The Manchester Guardian* about my lecture, which will interest you. I am glad that it caused such widespread interest in our two countries.

Yours ever,

[1] Lucie John had been living in Hampstead since May 1955 (Gieseking, *Der Fall Otto John*, p. 142), but she often travelled back to Germany to support her husband.

Leibholz to Bell, 25 November 1957, Bell Papers 40, fol. 490 (handwritten)

My dear Bishop,

Many thanks for your good letter. I trust Mrs John will contact you as you have suggested. But I wish to warn you of her in so far as a result of what she has gone through she is very excitable and not fully reliable in her statements. This makes things so very difficult for us.

Nevertheless, I have decided today to write a letter to the President. Its copy is enclosed.[1] Should you decide to act I may leave it to you whether or not you wish to refer to my letter.

Yours ever,

[1] Leibholz to Heuss, 28 November 1957, Bell Papers 40, fols. 491seq. (copy): 'Das Vermächtnis unserer Geschwister und Schwäger Dietrich, Klaus und Karl-Friedrich Bonhoeffer zwingt uns, das Gnadengesuch zu unterstützen, das der Anwalt von Otto John vor einigen Wochen an Sie gerichtet hat. [...] Zusätzlich darf ich nur auf die schweren rechtlichen Bedenken hinweisen, die ich – jedenfalls für meine Person – gegen die Schlüssigkeit des Indizienbeweises habe, auf Grund dessen Otto John (am 22.12.1956 durch 3. Strafsenat des BGH) verurteilt worden ist. Diese Bedenken sind so schwerwiegend, daß mir persönlich das Urteil – und zwar gleichgültig ob Otto John entführt worden ist oder freiwillig in die Ostzone gegangen ist – als ein Fehlurteil erscheint.'

Leibholz to Bell, 7 December 1957, Bell Papers 40, fol. 493 (typewritten)

My dear Bishop,

I am enclosing a copy of the letter of the President for your further information.[1]

I gather from the letter that the President seems to be inclined to grant Otto John's release from prison by an act of Grace in due course. I only hope that the decision will be taken before Christmas.

It might be better not to take further action in this matter so that the President might not get the impression to be put under some kind of moral pressure.

Mrs Jones [John] does not seem to me quite in balance at the moment. Therefore, it might be better for you that she does not contact you now.

With good wishes from us all,

Yours ever,

---

[1] Heuss to Leibholz, 2 December 1957, Bell Papers 40, fol. 494.

Bell to Leibholz, 16 December 1957, BA, N 1334 (typewritten); Bell Papers 40, fol. 495 (carbon)

My dear Leibholz,

Very many thanks for your letter of the 7th December, with a copy of that from the President, which is certainly promising.

Mrs John rang me up from London the other day, wanting to see me. She seemed rather distressed. I said that I was quite willing to see her, but would she let me have a memorandum first. She has not in fact sent a memorandum. It looks to me as though your advice, that friends abroad should hold their hand, is very wise.

I do hope that you and Sabine and the two daughters will have a very happy Christmas.

Yours ever,

Bell to Leibholz, 19 December 1957, BA, N 1334 (typewritten)

My dear Leibholz,

I am sending you a copy of the Wiener Library Bulletin, Vol. XI, Nos. 5 – 6, 1957 –, which has just been sent to me by the Editor. It contains a strong criticism of my Lecture, with a brief reply by myself, for which I was asked at the time (some months ago).[1]

I am particularly interested in the editorial comments on the situation – and the Editor's conviction that there is a new and different Germany.

Yours ever,

---

[1] Sidney Salomon, '"The Church and the Resistance Movement" Bishop of Chichester Criticised, and Dr. Bell's Reply', in *The Wiener Library Bulletin* 11, 1957, p. 38, and also the editorial, 'The Rebels of July were Symbols of a New Germany', ibid., p. 39.

Leibholz to Bell, 21 December 1957, Bell Papers 40, fol. 496 (typewritten)

My dear Bishop,

Very many thanks for your letter of December 16th.

I am enclosing a copy of a further letter from the President, which I have not yet answered.[1] I have interpreted the letter in a sense that the President is willing to release O. John but he cannot act [as] he likes to because he cannot secure the counter-signature of the Minister of Justice. On the other side, I understand from what I have heard that the Minister of Justice is prepared to counter-sign the decision of the President provided that he takes the initiative and responsibility for the step he has in mind. I do not see 'through' the controversy at [the] moment and it seems to me as if the Chancellor who does not seem very sympathetic with an early release of O. John[2] will be consulted either by the President or by the Minister of Justice.

Mrs John has been in Germany and has seen her husband. She told us over the telephone that the health of her husband is very bad: on the other hand, the doctor who is in charge of the prison thinks that O. John is 'alright'. Therefore, I do not quite know what the actual position is at the moment.

In spite of all these difficulties I hope and trust that it will be possible to overcome them before long, although I am very sorry indeed not to have been able to secure his release now.

With our very best wishes for a happy Christmas,

Yours ever,

[Verso, handwritten]

P.S. I have just received the copy of the Wiener Library Bulletin you kindly sent me. I think your short letter is very good and the Editorial comments are to the point and well balanced. Many thanks for letting me have it.

---

[1] Heuss to Leibholz, Richter am Bundesverfassungsgericht, re the Gnadengesuch of Otto John, 9 December 1957, Bell Papers 40, fol. 497.
[2] On the position of Konrad Adenauer see Gieseking, *Der Fall Otto John*, pp. 490–2.

Bell to Leibholz, 31 December 1957, BA, N 1334 (typewritten); Bell Papers 40, fol. 498 (carbon)

My dear Leibholz,

Very many thanks for your letter and the copy of that from President Heuss. I shall be very much interested to hear what happens, and if President and Minister of Justice come to an agreement. I have refrained from writing personally to the President, for I don't think that much would be gained if I did. But I am of course willing to do anything that would really help, if you will let me know.

With the best wishes to you and Sabine ªfor 1958ª,

Yours ever,

1958

10 November   The Soviet premier Nikita Khrushchev initiates the second Berlin crisis by demanding that British and American forces withdraw from the city within six months.

Leibholz to Bell, 20 May 1958, BA, N 1334 (carbon)

My dear Dr. Bell,

I do hope that you and Mrs. Bell have settled down in the meantime and that you have had a beautiful trip to Greece.

Today I am writing to you to bring up a matter of urgency rather under pressure of time. I should like to ask you if you would kindly be prepared to write to the Bundespräsident, Dr. Heuss, Bonn, Bundespräsidialamt, and to say that you had heard that Dr. John has not yet been released up to now and that, therefore, you feel compelled on Christian and humanitarian grounds to join the ranks of those who plead for his very early release from prison ªconsidering the fact that he played an active part in the German resistance movement which was re-establishing Gy. as a moral power in the world.ª

I have had the opportunity of talking twice to the Attorney General of our Commonwealth[1] and what I say now is, of course, strictly confidential: The Attorney General himself is very much concerned over the fact that Otto John has not yet been pardoned and he is moved in his conscience and has pleaded with Heuss himself. He fears that this pardon might again be unduly delayed by the political time-table as a result of unrelated political events and that only through your intervention these obstacles might now be removed so that John might be finally released. As things stand it seems to me of no use that I should personally act again in this matter. Therefore, it would not be good to refer to me in your letter. It would not further our common purpose. If you felt able to act now John might be released before Whitsun. I feel strongly that the whole affair tends to become alarming and more than perturbing ªall the more as John's guilt has never been proven.ª

With our very best wishes and kind regards,

As ever

Yours affectionately,

[1] The Attorney General at the Federal Court of Justice between 1956 and 1961 was Max Güde; see Schaefer, *Der Prozeß gegen Otto John*, pp. 166–8.

Bell to Leibholz, 23 May 1958, BA, N 1334 (typewritten)

My dear Leibholz,

Your letter of 10th May has reached me after some wandering, due to my change of address,[1] but apart from that it was not possible to answer it at once because I was taken rather seriously ill a month ago in Oxford with a thrombosis, and had to spend a fortnight in the Radcliffe Infirmary. I am, however, making a good recovery and am hoping to move into our new home, as above, in the next fortnight.

I am glad to write to Dr Heuss on behalf of Dr. John, and enclose a copy of my letter. Your own strong support, and what you have told me in strict confidence of the Attorney General, weigh very much with me.

With all affectionate remembrance to Sabine and your daughters and yourself, in which my wife joins.

Yours affectionately,

ªI expect to be at the Lambeth Conference July 3 – August 7 and at the Central Committee of the World Council of Churches August 18 – 30 at Denmark.ª

[1] Bell had retired on 31 January 1958 and he and Henrietta had moved to a new home in Canterbury, where he had been Dean, 1924–9.

Bell to Leibholz, 4 June 1958, BA, N 1334 (handwritten)

My dear Leibholz,

I enclose the reply received from the Bundespräsidialamt. I hope perhaps Dr. Heuss will write later on his return from Canada.[1] Please let me have the reply back in due course.

Yours affectionately,

[1] Heuss made state visits to Canada, 28 May–3 June, and to the United States, 4–23 June 1958.

Bell to Leibholz, 14 July 1958, posted 18 July, BA, N 1334 (typewritten)

My dear Leibholz,

I have today received a reply from President Heuss dated July 8th, and send a copy herewith.[1]

Please let me have any news in due course and also tell me what you think of the prospects.

ªLove to Sabine and the girls.

I am in the bonds of the Lambeth Conference, a prisoner till August 10. On August 18 my wife and I go to Nyborg Strand until September 1, for a meeting of the Central Committee of the World Council of Churches.

Yours affectionately,

I have no secretary any more! Hence spelling.ª

[1] See Heuss to Bell, Bonn, 8 July 1958, BA, N. 1334 (copy): 'Mit kaum einer Sache habe ich mich persönlich so intensiv zu beschäftigen gehabt und beschäftige ich mich noch. Es sind ja in dem Problemkreis dadurch, daß Johns "Partner", wenn ich so sagen darf, Dr. Wohlgemuth, in der Zwischenzeit verhaftet wurde, neue rechtspolitische Situationen entstanden.' John was reprieved on 26 July 1958; after serving two-thirds of his four-year term. It was hardly an act of mercy since the legal costs were not rescinded and the pardon was made condition to John desisting from publishing any account of his case. See Gieseking, *Fall*, p. 413; Schaefer, *Der Prozeß gegen Otto John*, p. 305. Otto John would campaign for a retrial for the remainder of his life. A more credible act of mercy with regard to his financial situation followed, but only in 1986, from Federal President Richard von Weizsäcker; see Schaefer, *Der Prozeß gegen Otto John*, pp. 313–14.

Leibholz to Henrietta Bell, 4 October 1958, Bell Papers 387, fol. 127 (handwritten)

Dear Mrs Bell,

We have just heard the news of the bishop's death. –

We need not tell you how terribly grieved we all are and how deeply we feel with you in your bereavement. With the Bishop we have lost the most faithful and best friend we have had in the English speaking world.

Today our thoughts go back to the time when we left Germany and found a second house in England arriving to the never moving friendship and kindness at all he has shown us again and again throughout the years of sorrow and want. Especially I remember the time when I was allowed to be associated with him whenever he was going to re-examine the German question during the war. At that time I learned to admire again and again not only his humanity and Christian steadfastness but also his political wisdom and statesman-like instinct. How glad we were to meet him last year in Göttingen in May when we found him quite unchanged and as lively as ever and the people of Germany tried to express their thanks to him for all his goodness.

What made him unique was that he put into action the spirit which moved him and commanded his conscience. The World has become poorer by a really great man. We can only comfort ourselves by the thought that we have to thank him for having granted us the privilege of setting up a bond of friendship which shall last forever and death cannot destroy.

God bless you.

With all our love, also from Marianne and Christiane,

Yours ever Sabine & Gerhard Leibholz

Appendices

Appendix 1

A review by Gerhard Leibholz of George Bell's *Christianity and World Order* (Penguin Books, Harmondsworth, 1940), first published in *Christian Fellowship in Wartime*, Bulletin of 15 February 1941.[1]

Under this heading the Bishop of Chichester has recently published a most admirable and illuminating book. It deals with vital and central issues of the present world crisis and contains a variety of wonderfully penetrating observations to the spiritual and moral causes which have given effect to the disintegration of today's world. It analyses the nature and the growth of the totalitarian state, the conditions of Western civilization and the position of the Christian Church in the modern world. It puts forward the answer of Christianity to modern secularism. The problem of the Christian Church and the modern state, the nature of the present war and the relations of the Universal Church to the several Christian communities are considered. It advocates a growing collaboration among all Christians in the world as the only possible basis on which a new world order can be reconstructed and Western civilization can be saved from destruction.

This is not the place to give a detailed review of the book. The bulk of deep reflections in this stimulating study is too large to be dealt with. Such a book has to be read and not to be taken in by second-hand information. The following lines are limited to a few issues, especially from the political and sociological point of view.

The book is not only that of a Christian, but also of a politician. This is not accidental considering that, in the long run, politics and Christianity are connected with each other. If the ecclesiastical world conferences of Oxford, Edinburgh and Madras have laid down that the Church must be truly a church, it means that the Universal Church as Una sancta is not a mere idea but a reality which reaches into the realities of life here below. 'The Church has been called into existence by God not for itself but for the world' (*The Churches Survey Their Task*, 1937, p. 45). It is among the most ancient duties of the church also to take care that the earthly life is carried on in a Christian fashion and that the Christians who live and work in this world apply the principles of their faith to the actual problems of life. This can be done by the church only if it is conscious of its political task. Therefore, it is the duty of the church to influence the supreme decisive objects of the state and also those functions of the state which define its specific substance and its concrete existence.

This political task of the church is not objectively limited. There is no sphere of life which can refuse this claim of the church. This applies to men's life, property and work,

---

[1] This text was reprinted in Gerhard Leibholz, *Politics and Law* (Leyden, 1965), pp. 133–8. Certain typographical errors have been corrected but all matters of presentation, including the use of upper cases, have been preserved.

as well as to their family, leisure and thought. Christian influence has to permeate every department of life according to the last pronouncement of the Confessional Church in Germany before the outbreak of war: 'The Christian faith is not a private matter nor does it occupy some particular part of the life and heart of man. God's word claims the whole man.'

It is one of the numerous merits of the book that its author stresses again and again how impossible it is 'to separate Christianity from the ordinary, natural world' (p. 36) and 'all private and public affairs must come under God's control' (p. 142). In other words, the political claim of the church has somehow an all-embracing character. It tends to re-order the whole human life by the power of the Word and the spirit of God. It applies to the life within a national community as well as to the life between the nations. The conception that politics and especially international politics have nothing to do with Christianity, but much more with immorality (a German proverb says 'Politics ruin the character') is completely unacceptable for a Christian and the Churches. Christianity does not desert the cause of civilization in this sphere. On the contrary, Christianity has to connect its moral standards to the life of nations as well. In fulfilment of this duty the Church should not hesitate, in case of need, to conduct an open war with the powers of the world.

It is one of the most disastrous errors, especially of Lutheranism, to have failed to perceive the basic importance of this fact. The Protestant church on the continent already ceased to a large extent in the era of liberalism actively to influence policy. The failure of the churches in Germany can be traced back to this conception of Lutheranism. National-Socialism had just to continue on the same line. National-Socialism knew far better than the Church itself that its claim against the Churches of not being political and being merely spiritual did not mean anything else but the death-warrant for the church itself. A division of tasks between Church and State so that the political world and responsibility belongs to the state and that the church has to limit itself to the teaching of God's Word does completely misrepresent the real task of the Church. For it is impossible to keep religion out of public life. The Church cannot live in self-contained seclusion and limit its activities to the proclamation of the Gospel. It would be like destroying somebody by a kind of gradual suffocation. It is not surprising therefore, that in Germany – apart from the Confessional Church – a misrepresented Lutheranism was in a position to accept with a number of reservations the National-Socialist dogma and to cease thereby to be a truly Christian Church.

The claim of the Church for a 'totalitarian' policy does not mean that it should replace the state and take over its functions. In contrast to the Church 'the distinctive character' of the State's activity ... is the power of constraint, legal and physical' (*The Churches Survey Their Task*, p. 87). Further, the church has no detailed interest in the conduct of the social activities of man. The Church has too deep a knowledge of the corruption of mankind and if the insufficiency of all human institutions to qualify as Christian a certain kind of community, a constitutional system or an interstate system. As the author says 'Christianity does not identify itself with any programme purely social or political' (p. 142). Or as Dr Oldham says 'The question whether Christianity has a specific programme to offer to society must be answered with a decisive No.'

The conclusion is: there is no Christian state. Take the latest example: the Austrian state under Dolfuss. The claim of the church for an all-embracing policy only implies that the whole policy of the State is governed by the eternal values of the Gospel and that the whole life of society is powerfully affected and moved by Christian faith and morality.

This relation between Christianity and politics demands a living and active Christianity. This is also emphasized by the Bishop: 'We have to live the Christian life' (p. 144): 'There is only one way of maintaining Christian principles, that is, by applying them' (p. 102) and that 'should begin now – and not after the war' (p. 148).

This call for immediate action, however, is necessary, if the great chance the Church has to-day is to be successfully taken. Only in listening to this call, a new birth of the community as a living spiritual order is possible.

What are the conditions for such a new birth? Firstly, it 'involves a revolution in the Church-life itself' (p. 147). The serious premonitions of the Bishop to the Church are of no less importance than the thesis that 'the organised Christian Church has failed to live up to the principles and teachings of its master' (p. 137) and 'to present men with the spectacle of unflinching belief in God and unlimited love of the Neighbour' (p. 105). If we have to practise Christianity, first of all, 'a vigorous educational policy must take place within the Church itself' and 'ministers must take their start from the activities of the common life itself and reorientate them to God from within' (p. 57).

Furthermore, the Church ought to know in claiming its leadership that the masses are incapable of forming independent judgements of any kind. This inability of the masses can be traced back to the fact that the political emancipation of the mass-man has been completed at a time when the development of the spiritual and moral powers of men has not kept pace with the astonishing improvements in the technical and scientific sphere. As the Bishop says 'On the one side you see incredible advances in mechanical invention: but on the other side a crying ignorance of human nature, resulting in failure of man to keep pace with the machine.' In particular, K. Mannheim in his books has shown that industrialization has by no means led to an increase of substantial rationality. The spiritual independence and critical faculty of the individual and with it the general morality and rationality of the average man have been degraded rather than exalted by the rapid industrial expansion. The saying of Goethe: 'When the masses fight, they are respectable, but their opinions are not delectable' applies to the twentieth century as well. The totalitarian states, much quicker to realize political issues, have noticed it at a much earlier stage than the liberal democracies of the pre-war time with their belief in continuing progress. The elite and not the masses stamp the history of nations.

If the Christian fellowship in the Church is a reality, the Church must, first of all, be in touch with the most urgent social needs of the present time; for 'the social problem is intimately related to the central religious problem of our time' (Demant). The great Commandment 'Love your neighbour as yourself' has, therefore, to be applied practically. 'The social order is an unnatural order – a radical disorder which requires a radical cure' (p. 73). Then the Christian Church will be able to regain contact with the lower classes who have become dissociated from the church through sheer lack of interest in a subject which seems to be quite irrelevant to their every-day life. The task of the churches to play a leading part in achieving social justice is the more urgent as the churches – at the time of appearance of social contrast – bound themselves too largely to the ruling social system. It is important and encouraging to know that responsible leaders of the Church as, for instance, the Archbishop of Canterbury, the Archbishop of York and the Bishop of Chichester admit the special urgency of this question.

The Church of to-day has the great chance of reconstructing a new world order and of saving western civilization from destruction because it only has the moral capacity to overcome the new conceptions of life, and, at the same time, to meet the totalitarian States on the same political grounds. If the Church is alive enough to-day, it will be in a position to fill up the religious vacuum that the withering economic epoch has left behind. To a large extent, mankind of to-day lives in a despairing, skeptical, nihilistic world. There is a longing for a new substance of society. As the Bishop says, there is a human hunger for a true religion. The totalitarian states with their capacity of understanding political realities attempted to settle this longing by means of quasi-religious substitutes. But this can only be a temporary matter. Neither any class feeling nor the doctrine of race will make masses stop in their religious feelings, even if one makes those phenomena into gods and gives them a quasi-religious homage.

That the masses in the totalitarian states are not content with those religious substitutes offered to them is illustrated most clearly by the fact that the masses must always be kept going. Only in this way it is possible to make the masses unconscious of that vacuum in which they live. This explains why the totalitarian states are compelled to be dynamical and not static.

The totalitarian states with their mystical deification of race, state and class do not stand for anything other than the fact of continuing the secularizing process which began as early as in the Renaissance and in Humanism with the revival of Roman Law, of the Aristotelian philosophy, of ancient art and literature, then passing through the age of enlightenment and of natural law where religion already was regarded as a dark force. Further, as the author remarks, rationalism and still more the era of industrial progress have also been 'the eras of increasing scepticism, criticism and doubt' (pp. 21, 22). The process of secularization reached its climax in the sphere of politics in liberal Democracy itself. This explains why modern culture and Democracy have moved more and more away from Christianity and are to-day almost entirely divorced from its Christian context. Therefore, the Bishop can say: 'Christian belief and morality are no longer the basis of western civilisation. That civilisation has lost its basis. It is no longer religious, but secular' (p. 23).

This makes it clear why Christianity cannot be identified with Western civilization, and Christianity and humanism cannot be practically equalized. It was, therefore, not by accident that at the time of emergence of the bourgeoisie in the eighteenth and nineteenth centuries the secularizing process together with the liberation of reason led to some conflict with Christianity and that at that time the Christian Churches were often the rallying point for action against the forces of enlightenment, rationalism and humanism.

On the other side, we cannot overlook the fact that the conception of man in Western civilization is based on Christianity and historically due to the Christian religion and that the increasing secularization in the totalitarian states has called in question the basic principles of humanism, rationalism and political liberalism no less than those of Christianity itself. The secularization of Christian thought was formerly still bound to Christianity by a belief in the unity of the human species and spirit, but now it is just this decisive belief which is questioned by the new radical secularization and the increasing materialism of modern thought. For instance, the appeal to nature and race in Germany of to-day is opposed to the appeal to reason as well as to Christianity. This fact explains why Christianity and modern Western civilization hold common ground to-day and why Christian civilization has been called Christian.

This fact gives also its decisive stamp to the present conflict. As it has been justly called, the present conflict is a war between two principles or two attitudes towards life. It springs from the clash of fundamental ideals, as was expressed in the last Royal proclamation on 21 November 1940.

Certainly, the present conflict has been given a colouring of nationalism too. This country is also fighting for its own safety. But even this question is only part of a still wider and more important issue. 'It is something which is bigger than the Empire we are fighting for' (Dr. Hill). Hitler was quoting these issues when he said in one of his latest speeches: 'We find ourselves in the midst of a struggle in which more is at stake than the victory of one country over the other. It is indeed a conflict between two worlds.'

The present war has been justly called, therefore, a revolutionary war or an international war or an international civil war. It is a war of ideas on a scale the world has not seen since the Reformation. It depends on the outcome of this present conflict whether it will be possible to uphold the traditional conception of what constitutes the good life for man and the standards of Christian morality on which Western civilization and culture depend.

The author of the book is one of those men who with clear sight and political instinct have seen the spiritual character of the present conflict and have drawn the consequences out of this understanding courageously and boldly.

One of these consequences is 'that the West does not desire to crush Germany' (p. 95). 'The West must aim at rebuilding the Christian civilisation of Europe upon planned co-operative lines, based on justice and truth. In a peace to come, each nation must play its contributory part' (p. 88) [This is a mistake: Bell's text contains no such quotation.]. This demand runs the risk of becoming unpopular the longer the war continues and the more difficulties arise as a result of the conflict. Already to-day the chorus of voices increases which demands to impose on Germany the same kind of treaty which Germany would like to impose on the Allies. Actually, one adopts, herewith, the National-Socialist ideology which people are claiming to fight and one suffers a deep moral defeat.

Only if we rightly perceive the meaning of the present conflict will an increase of a new common ethos be possible which is the essential condition of any new world order. The ideological cleavage between the liberal Democracies, Western civilization and Christianity on the one side, and the principles of the totalitarian States on the other cannot be overcome to-day. A new order of Europe does not ask for 'schemes or constitutions or blue prints, but a new spirit, a conversion of human persons' (p. 102). Not before a new homogeneity and a new standard of civilization common to all confederated states is gained, an international organization which deserves to be called international order will be possible.

Appendix 2

Sabine Leibholz-Bonhoeffer remembers the first visit to Chichester, in January 1939. An extract from *The Bonhoeffers: Portrait of a Family*.[1]

In January 1939 we received an invitation from the bishop of Chichester, a close friend of Dietrich. He invited us to spend a weekend with him and to bring the children, too. The bishop was fifty-five years old. He had been educated at Westminster and Oxford and had formerly been an Oxford don. During the 1920s he had been dean of Canterbury, and since 1929 bishop of Chichester. Later he became a member of the House of Lords. In his earlier days he had also been engaged in social work, and had taken a special interest in homes for the working classes. Through his friendship with my brother he had become better informed than anyone else in England about the church's struggle in Germany, and he supported the Confessing Church in its conflict with the Nazi regime. He was a strong supporter of all movements that promoted the unity of the churches and the collaboration of all creeds in international and social matters.

These were pleasant days. The old palace and the splendid chapel, the fine garden with its well-kept lawns, the walls overgrown with creepers, the great high rooms with their open fireplaces where Mrs. Bell and the bishop received us so charmingly – everything was quite new to us and very interesting. When tea was brought we were still alone with our hosts in the drawing room. The children sang for them the first English Christmas carols they had learned. Evening prayers were held in the chapel as early as six o'clock, and this, too, made a great impression upon the children. Afterwards at dinner there were several more guests. Suddenly I saw before me the face of someone I knew, though it was much altered. It was an acquaintance of my younger days, a neighbour during my early childhood, the son of a lawyer from Grűnewald who had subsequently become a lawyer himself. His head was shaved completely bald, and he had just been released from a Nazi concentration camp with a warning not to tell what had happened to him. Here he was, still afraid to talk because of the warning, although he was now in Chichester! Of course, we had much news to exchange. He intended to go still further and emigrate to the United States with his wife and children.

Dinner took place at a long and wonderful table with well-trained servants to attend to our needs. After this we reassembled in the drawing room where we read *Antony and Cleopatra*, the various parts being distributed among the company. The beauty of the English language, which is so often contested in Germany, overwhelmed me.

---

[1] First English edition published by Sidgwick and Jackson in 1970. A second edition of the book, prepared by F. Burton Nelson, was published by Covenant press, Chicago in 1994 (pp. 100–1).

The next morning at seven o'clock a housemaid knocked and brought us two pretty trays from which emanated a wonderful aroma of morning tea. Intending to offer us biscuits, she opened the biscuit box that stood on our bedside table. We had not realized the purpose of this pretty box and, to our shame, had already eaten the biscuits the evening before as a bedtime snack. So she departed in astonishment to replenish the box, brought us our shoes, drew back the curtains, and wished us good morning. After morning service in the chapel, breakfast was prepared. The bishop himself handed us our plates of porridge and cream, and later bacon and eggs that had been placed hot on the sideboard. Mrs. Bell poured the tea, and a maid brought fresh hot toast and orange marmalade. A huge log fire was blazing in the largest fireplace I ever saw in England, but even so it was rather cold in that gigantic old dining hall. The conversation turned upon the struggle of the church, ecumenism, and the problem of finding posts for the refugee pastors.

Bibliography

Alfred E. Baker, *William Temple and His Message*, Harmondsworth: Penguin, 1946.
Jack Beatson and Reinhard Zimmermann (eds), *Jurists Uprooted. German-speaking Émigré Lawyers in Twentieth-century Britain*, Oxford: Oxford University Press, 2004.
George K. A. Bell, *Christianity and World Order* (Penguin Special), Harmondsworth: Penguin Books, 1940.
George K. A. Bell, *The Church and Humanity (1939–1946)*, London: Longmans, Green & Co., 1946.
George K. A. Bell and Herbert Waddams, *With God in the Darkness and Other Papers by Eivind Berggrav, Bishop of Oslo, Illustrating the Norwegian Church Conflict*, London: Hodder & Stoughton, 1943.
James Bentley, *Martin Niemöller*, Oxford: Oxford University Press, 1984.
Gerhard Besier, 'Selbstreinigung' unter britischer Besatzungsherrschaft. Die Evangelisch-lutherische Landeskirche Hannovers und ihr Landesbischof Marahrens 1945–1947, Göttingen: Vandenhoeck & Ruprecht, 1986.
Gerhard Besier, Hartmut Ludwig and Jörg Thierfelder (eds), *Der Kompromiß von Treysa*, Weinheim: Deutscher Studien Verlag, 1995.
Gerhard Besier, *'Initimately Associated for Many Years': George K.A. Bell's and Willem A. Visser 't Hooft's Common Life-Work in the Service of the Church Universal – Mirrored in their Correspondence*, Newcastle: Cambridge Scholars Publishing, 2015.
Gerhard Besier and Gerhard Sauter, *Wie Christen ihre Schuld bekennen: Die Stuttgarter Erklärung 1945*, Göttingen: Vandenhoeck & Ruprecht, 1985.
Eberhard Bethge (ed.), *Dietrich and Klaus Bonhoeffer, Auf dem Wege zur Freiheit. Gedichte und Briefe aus der Haft*, Berlin: Verlag Haus und Schule GmbH, 1946.
Eberhard Bethge, *Dietrich Bonhoeffer. Theologe – Christ – Zeitgenosse*, 9th ed., Gütersloh: Gütersloher Verlagshaus, 2005.
Eberhard Bethge and Ronald C. D. Jasper (eds), *An der Schwelle zum gespaltenen Europa. Der Briefwechsel zwischen George Bell und Gerhard Leibholz 1939–1951*, Stuttgart: Kreuz Verlag, 1974.
Eberhard Bethge, Renate Bethge and Christian Gremmels (eds), *Dietrich Bonhoeffer: A Life in Pictures*, translated by John Bowden, London: SCM Press, 1986.
Dietrich Bonhoeffer, *Gesammelte Schriften*, edited by Eberhard Bethge, vol. 1, Munich: Christian Kaiser Verlag, 1958.
Dietrich Bonhoeffer Werke, edited by Eberhard Bethge, et al., 17 vols., München-Gütersloh: Christian Kaiser Verlag, 1986–96.
Dietrich Bonhoeffer Werke (DBW) 4: Nachfolge, edited by Martin Kuske and Ilse Tödt, Gütersloh: Christian Kaiser Verlag, 1989.
Dietrich Bonhoeffer Werke (DBW) 16: Konspiration und Haft 1940–1945, edited by Jørgen Glenthøj, Ulrich Kabitz, Wolf Krötke and Herbert Anzinger, Gütersloh: Christian Kaiser Gütersloher Verlagshaus, 1996.

Dietrich Bonhoeffer Werke (DBW) 8: Widerstand und Ergebung, edited by Eberhard Bethge, Renate Bethge and Christian Gremmels, Gütersloh: Christian Kaiser Verlag, 1998.

Dietrich Bonhoeffer Werke (DBW) 15: Illegale Theologenausbildung: Sammelvikariate 1937–1940, edited by Dirk Schulz, Gütersloh: Gütersloher Verlagshaus, 1998.

Armin Boyens, *Kirchenkampf und Ökumene 1939–47*, Munich: Christian Kaiser Verlag, 1973.

Charmian Brinson, 'Please Tell the Bishop of Chichester' George Bell and the Internment Crisis of 1940, *Kirchliche Zeitgeschichte/Contemporary Church History*, vol. 21, pp. 287–99, 2008.

Vicco von Bülow, *Otto Weber (1902–1966). Reformierter Theologe und Kirchenpolitiker*, Göttingen: Vandenhoeck & Ruprecht, 1999.

Eberhard Busch, *Karl Barths Lebenslauf: Nach seinen Briefen und autobiografischen Texten*, Zurich: Theologischer Verlag Zurich, 2005.

Andrew Chandler, 'The Death of Dietrich Bonhoeffer', *Journal of Ecclesiastical History*, vol. 45, no. 3, pp. 448–59, July 1994.

Andrew Chandler (ed.), *The Church and Humanity. The Life and Work of George Bell, 1883–1958*, Farnham: Ashgate Publishing, 2012.

Andrew Chandler, *George Bell, Bishop of Chichester: Church, State and Resistance in the Age of Dictatorship*, Grand Rapids: William B. Eerdmans, 2016.

Ian Colvin, *Vansittart in Office: An Historical Survey of the Origins of the Second World War, based on the Papers of Sir Robert Vansittart*, London: Hamish Hamilton, 1965.

Russell W. Cooper, *The Nuremberg Trial*, Harmondsworth: Penguin Books, 1947.

Philip Coupland, George Bell, the Question of Germany and the Cause of European Unity, 1939–1950, in: Andrew Chandler (ed.), *The Church and Humanity*, pp. 109–28, Farnham: Ashgate Publishing, 2012.

Anne Deighton, *The Impossible Peace: Britain, the Division of Germany and the Origins of the Cold War*, Oxford: Oxford University Press, 1990.

Torsten Dietrich, *Paulus. Das Trauma von Stalingrad. Eine Biographie*, Paderborn: Ferdinand Schöningh, 2008.

Eric R. Dodds, *Missing Persons: An Autobiography*, Oxford: Oxford University Press, 1977.

Harold Fey (ed.), *A History of the Ecumenical Movement, Vol. 2: 1948–1968*, London: SPCK, 1970.

Franklin L. Ford, 'The Twentieth of July in the History of the German Resistance', *American Historical Review*, vol. 51, no. 4, pp. 609–26, July 1946.

Matthew Frank, *Expelling the Germans: British Opinion and Post-1945 Population Transfer in Context*, Oxford: Oxford University Press, 2007.

Rudolf Christoph Freiherr von Gersdorff, *Soldat im Untergang*, Frankfurt am Main: Ullstein, 1977.

Erik Gieseking, *Der Fall Otto John. Entführung oder freiwilliger Übertritt in die DDR*, Göttingen: Göttinger Verlag, 2005.

Jørgen Glenthøj, *Dokumente zur Bonhoeffer-Forschung 1928–1945*, Munich: Christian Kaiser Verlag, 1963.

Martin Greschat (ed.), *Die Schuld der Kirche. Dokumente und Reflexionen zur Stuttgarter Schulderklärung vom 18/19. Oktober 1945*, Munich: Christian Kaiser Verlag, 1982.

Heinrich Grosse and Hans Otte (eds), *Neubeginn nach der NS-Herrschaft?* Hannover: Lutherischer Verlagshaus, 2002.

John W. de Gruchy, *Daring Trusting Spirit: Bonhoeffer's Friend Eberhard Bethge*, London: SCM Press, 2005.

Lord Hankey, *Politics, Trials and Errors*, London: Pen in Hand Publishing, 1950.
Arthur Hearnden (ed.), *The British in Germany: Educational Reconstruction after 1945*, London: Hamish Hamilton, 1978.
Peter Hoffmann, *Widerstand, Staatsstreich, Attentat. Der Kampf der Opposition gegen Hitler*, 3rd ed., Munich: Piper Verlag, 1979.
Manfred Heinemann (ed.), *Nordwestdeutsche Hochschulkonferenzen 1945–1948*, Hildesheim: Verlag August Lax, 1990.
Manfred Heinemann (ed.), *Hochschuloffiziere und Wiederaufbau des Hochschulwesens in Westdeutschland 1945–1952, vol. 1: Die Britische Zone*, Hildesheim: Verlag August Lax, 1990.
Ronald C. D. Jasper, *George Bell. Bishop of Chichester*, London: Oxford University Press, 1967.
Manfred Keller and Jens Murken, *Das Erbe des Theologen Hans Ehrenberg: Eine Zwischenbilanz*, Berlin: LIT Verlag, 2009.
Klemens von Klemperer, *German Resistance against Hitler. The Search for Allies Abroad 1938–1945*, Oxford: Oxford University Press, 1992.
Donald P. Kommers, *Judicial Politics in West Germany*, Beverly Hills: Sage Publications, 1976.
Tom Lawson, *Bishop Bell and the Trial of German War Criminals: A Moral History*, Kirchliche Zeitgeschichte/Contemporary Church Histor, vol. 21, pp. 324–48, 2008.
Annedore Leber, *Conscience in Revolt: Sixty-four Stories of Resistance in Germany 1933–1945*, London: Vallentine, Mitchell, 1957.
Gerhard Leibholz, *Die Gleichheit vor dem Gesetz*, Berlin: Liebmann, 1925; 2nd enlarged ed., Munich and Berlin: C.H. Beck Verlag, 1959.
Gerhard Leibholz, *Strukturprobleme der modernen Demokratie*, Karlsruhe: Müller Verlag, 1958.
Gerhard Leibholz, *Politics and Law*, Leyden: A.W. Sythoff, 1965.
Sabine Leibholz-Bonhoeffer, *The Bonhoeffers: Portrait of a Family*, London: Sidgwick and Jackson, 1971; new ed., Chicago: Covenant, 1994.
Sabine Leibholz-Bonhoeffer, *Vergangen – erlebt – überwunden*, Gütersloh: Gütersloher Verlagshaus, 1976.
Kerstin von Lingen, *Kesselrings letzte Schlacht. Kriegsverbrecherprozesse, Vergangenheitspolitik und Wiederbewaffnung. Der Fall Kesselring*, Paderborn: Ferdinand Schöningh, 2004.
Louis P. Lochner (ed.), *Goebbels Tagebücher*, Zürich: Atlantis, 1948.
Hartmut Ludwig and Eberhard Röhm (eds), *Evangelisch getauft – als "Juden" verfolgt. Theologen jüdischer Herkunft in der Zeit des Nationalsozialismus. Ein Gedenkbuch*, Stuttgart: Calwer Verlag, 2014.
Reinhard Mehring, *Carl Schmitt. Aufstieg und Fall*, Munich: C.H.Beck Verlag, 2009.
Friedeborg L. Müller, *The History of German Lutheran Congregations in England, 1900–1950*, Frankfurt am Main: Peter Lang, 1987.
Sigismund Payne Best, *The Venlo Incident*, London: The National Book Association, 1950.
David Phillips, *Investigating Education in Germany. Historical Studies from a British Perspective*, Abingdon – New York: Routledge, 2016.
Peter Raina (ed.), *Bishop George Bell: House of Lords Speeches and Correspondence with Rudolf Hess*, Frankfurt am Main: Peter Lang, 2009.
Gerhard Ringshausen, *Widerstand und christlicher Glaube angesichts des Nationalsozialismus*, 2nd ed., Berlin: Litt Verlag, 2008.

Holger Roggelin, *Franz Hildebrandt. Ein lutherischer Dissenter im Kirchenkampf und Exil*, Göttingen: Vandenhoeck & Ruprecht, 1999.
Hans Rothfels, *Die Deutsche Opposition gegen Hitler*, Krefeld: Scherpe, 1949; enlarged edition, Frankfurt am Main: Fischer, 1958.
Gordon Rupp, *Martin Luther: Hitler's Cause – or Cure? A Reply to Peter Wiener*, London: Lutterworth, 1945.
Gordon Rupp, *I seek my Brethren. Bishop George Bell and the German Churches*, London: Epworth Press, 1975.
Gerhard Sälter, *Phantome des Kalten Krieges. Die Organisation Gehlen und die Wiederbelebung des Gestapo-Feindbildes, Rote Kapelle*, Berlin: Links, 2016.
Klaus Schaefer, *Der Prozß gegen Otto John*, Marburg: Tectum, 2009.
Fabian von Schlabrendorff, *Offiziere gegen Hitler*, Zurich: Europa Verlag, 1946.
Dietmar Schmidt, *Martin Niemöller – Eine Biographie*, Stuttgart: Rowohlt Verlag, 1983.
Drusilla Scott, *A. D. Lindsay. A Biography*, Oxford: Blackwell, 1971.
Jörg Später, *Vansittart. Britische Debatten über Deutsche und Nazis 1902–1945*, Göttingen: Vandenhoeck & Ruprecht, 2003.
Anikó Szabó, *Vertreibung, Rückkehr, Wiedergutmachung. Göttinger Hochschullehrer im Schatten des Nationalsozialismus*, Göttingen: Vandenhoeck & Ruprecht, 2000.
Sir Robert Vansittart, *The Mist Procession: Autobiography*, London: Hamish Hamilton, 1958.
Alec R. Vidler and Walter A. Whitehouse (eds), *Natural Law. A Christian Re-consideration*, London: SCM Press, 1946.
Clemens Vollnhals (ed.), *Die evangelische Kirche nach dem Zusammenbruch. Berichte ausländischer Beobachter aus dem Jahr 1945*, Göttingen: Vandenhoeck & Ruprecht, 1988.
Manfred H. Wiegandt, *Norm und Wirklichkeit: Gerhard Leibholz (1901–1982): Leben, Werk und Richteramt*, Baden-Baden: Nomus, 1995.
Manfred H. Wiegandt, 'Gerhard Leibholz (1901–1982)', in: Jack Beatson and Reinhard Zimmermann (eds), *Jurists Uprooted. German-speaking Émigré Lawyers in Twentieth-century Britain*, Oxford: Oxford University Press, 2004.
Peter Wiener, *Martin Luther: Hitler's Spiritual Ancestor*, London: Hutchinson, 1944.
Arthur P. Young, *The 'X' Documents: The Secret History of Foreign Office Contacts with the German Resistance 1937–1939*, London: André Deutsch, 1974.

Index

Addison, Christopher   127, 127 n.2
Alfred E. Baker   184, 351 n.1
American Consul General   28
American Journal of International Law   22
American Round Table Conference   206
Anschütz, Gerhard xi
Allied nations conference   72
Allied powers conference   123, 250 n.1
Anti-Nazi government xix, 62, 63, 87, 175
Anti-Nazi revolution xix, 62, 63, 89
Armitage, John   73 n.1
Arnold, Karl   419 n.1
Aryan paragraphs x
Asmussen, Hans   321 n.8
Astor V, John Jacob   184 n.2
The Atlantic Charter of the Western Powers xix, 21, 58 n.1, 65, 74, 87, 88, 94, 112 n.5, 154, 156, 183, 191, 193, 195, 211, 252, 282, 368
Attlee, Clement   283 n.1, 297 n.4, 297, 319 n.2, 391 n.2
Aubrey, Melbourn Evans   297 n.2

Badoglio, Pietro   195, 195 nn.5–6, 211, 225
Baillie, John   325, 327 n.2
Balfour, Philip   328 n.1, 335, 338, 347, 349, 352, 353
Barker, Ernest   41, 42 n.1, 175 n.4, 183, 183 n.2, 184, 416, 419 n.6
Barlett, Vernon   184 n.1
Beatson, Jack xi n.2, 360 n.2
Beck, Ludwig   227, 227 n.1, 228 n.1, 229, 238, 292 n.5, 294, 295
Bell, George K. A. ix, x, xiv n.17, xvii n.27, xxv, xxvii, 6 n.1, 10 nn.1–2, 17 n.3, 132 n.1
Benians, Ernest Alfred   417 n.6
Bentley, James   258 n.2, 364 n.1
Bergstraesser, Arnold   23, 23 n.3

Bermuda Conference of British and American leaders   123
Besier, Gerhard   xiv, xvii n.27, 10 n.2, 31 n.2, 68 n.1, 198 n.2, 207 n.1, 208 n.4, 262 n.2, 278 n.3, 280 nn.1–2, 289 n.4, 292 n.1, 301 n.1, 321 n.5, 347 n.2
Best, Sigismund Payne   309 n.4, 337 n.1, 434 n.1
Bethge, Eberhard   xiii n.12, xvi n.23, xxvii, 4 n.1, 6 n.3, 19 n.4, 22 n.2, 92 n.2, 93 n.5, 133 n.2, 149 n.1, 205 n.7, 211 n.2, 214 n.2, 216 n.2, 221 n.1, 266 n.1, 270 n.3, 275 n.1, 276 n.4, 285, 285 n.4, 286 n.1, 287, 288 n.1, 299, 300, 301, 303–5, , 307 nn.1–2, 313, 320, 322, 329 n. 4, 333, 337, 343, 354 n.1, 378, 433 n. 6, 437 n.2, 439 n.1, 440 nn. 2–4, 441 n.1
Bethge, Renate   xiii n.12, 211 n.2, 307 n.1
Beveridge, William Henry   xvi, 39 n.1, 416
Bevin, Ernest   315, 316, 319, 319 n.2, 383, 391
Bidault, George   242 n.2, 243
Bielenberg, Peter   279 n.2
'Big Three' conference   195 n.2
Bird, Geoffrey   358, 358 n.2, 362, 362 n.1, 366, 371, 381, 408, 412, 413
Birkett, William Norman   10 n.6, 130
Birley, Robert   404 n.7, 405, 408 n.1, 409 n.1, 411, 413, 417 n.1
Black Record   xviii, 64 n.1, 101, 101 n.3
Blumentritt, Günther   351 n.4
Böhm, Hans   286 n.1, 398, 398 n.1
Bonhoeffer, Christine   xi, 93 n.8
Bonhoeffer, Dietrich   ix, x, xiii n.12, xvi, xvi n.23, xxi, xxv, xxvii, 4, 4 n.1, 6 n.3, 10 n.1, 13, 49, 59 n.2, 92 n.2, 93 n.5, 94 n.8, 133 n.2, 149 n.1, 150, 183 n.6, 207 n.3, 211 n.1, 214 n.2, 215 n.1, 254, 258 nn.3, 5, 262 n.1, 271, 273, 274 n.3,

275–6, 276 nn.4, 6, 277, 279, 283–4, 286 n.1, 287, 288 n.1, 288–92, 294–5, 299, 301, 305, 307, 307 n.1, 308, 309, 313, 317–8, , 320, 321–2326, 328, 329 n.5, 331–3, 335 n.1, 337, 339, 340, 342 n.5, 349, 351, 351 n.6, 362, 366 n.1, 369, 382, 400, 404 n.3, 408, 409 n.1, , 415, 429, 432, 433 n.6, 434 n.2, 439–40, 440 nn.2–3, 441 n.1, 446, 447 n.1, 463
Bonhoeffer, Emmi   289 n.2, 317 n.1, 335, 335 n.1
Bonhoeffer, Karl Friedrich   282 n.5, 309 n.1, 312, 443 n.1, 447 n.1
Bonhoeffer, Klaus   xi, xxiv, 205, 205 n.4, 207 n.3, 270 n.3, 271, 274, 274 n.3, 275, 276, 276 n.1, 279, 284, 285, 287, 288 n.1, 289 n.2, 291, 292, 304 n.4, 309 n.1, 335 n.1, 338, 340, 369, 440 n.3, 446, 446 n.4, 447 n.1
Bonhoeffer, Sabine   x, xi
Boyens, Armin   8 n.1, 10 n.4, 98 n.1, 100 n.1, 110 n.3, 247 n.1
Brailsford, Henry Noel   113, 114 n.4, 116, 197 n.1
Brauchitsch, Walther von   351 n.5, 426 n.1
Breckenridge Long, Samuel Miller   55, 55 n.1
Brilioth, Yngve   107, 108, 132, 135, 138, 139, 143
Brinson, Charmian   10 n.1, 145 n.1
The British Empire Economic Conference   58 n.3
British policy think tank   73 n.2
Brock, Guy Clutton   268 n.1, 269, 285, 289, 299, 302, 306, 313, 331
Brüning, Heinrich   xxv, 238 n.5, 355 n.1
Bruns, Walter   380, 381 n.1
Bühler, Prälat Wilhelm   444 n.9
Busch, Eberhard   392 n.1
Butler, Harold B. 81, 86, 101, 103, 259
Butler, Rohan d'Olier   64 n.2
Buxton, Dorothy Frances   42 n.3, 83

Cadogan, Alexander   297 n.5, 298
Caldwell, Peter C. xi n.3, 4
Cambridge Conference   104
Canaris, Wilhelm   291, 292 n.4, 439, 440, 441

Carr, Edward Hallett   91 n.1, 102–3, 303
Casablanca Conference   xxi, 123, 130
Cathedral, Dunblane   190 n.3
Catlin, George Edward Gordon   250 n.3
Chamberlain, Houston Stewart   3, 5, 100 n.5, 103 n.1, 238 n.1, 327 n.5
Chandler, Andrew   x n.1, xxi n.54, 10 n.1, 211 n.1, 379 n.2, 426 n.1, 434 n.2
Chandler, Edgar H. S. 30 n.2
Christian Brotherhood conference   93 n.7
The Christian Conception of Freedom   xiv
Christian Fellowship in Wartime   xvi, xviii n.35, 22 n.3, 133, 258 n.4, 318 n.4, 457
Christianity and World Order   xvii, xvii n.27, xviii, xviii n.35, 36, xix n.37, xx n.50, 17 n.3, 19 n.1, 61 n.3, 166 n.2, 457
'Christianity, Politics and Power'   xvi, 22 n.1, xix, xix n.43, 95, 97 n.4, 105 n.1, 107 n.1, 109
'Christianity, Totalitarianism and Democracy'   22
The Church and the Resistance Movement   xxiv, 439 n.1, 443 n.2, 448 n.1
Church Commission for International Friendship   31, 32 n.1
'The Church's Function in Wartime'   xvii
Clarke, Richard W. B.   113, 114 n.6, 340
Cockburn, James Hutchinson   190, 190 n.3, 349 n.2
Coffin, Henry Sloane   43 n.2, 45–9, 90
Cole, G.D.H.   414, 414 n.2, 415, 416
Collins, John   403–4, 404 n.5, 405, 407, 416
Colvin, Ian Goodhope   348 n.2, 349, 351–2
Conference of Catholic Bishops   444 n.9
Conference of the Lutheran Pastors of German Speaking Congregations   80 n.1
Cooper, Alfred Duff   179 n.4
Cooper, Russell W. 391 n.2
Corpus Christianum   xiv
Coupland, Philip   17 n.3, 244 n.2
Courvoisier, Jaques   427 n.3
Crimea Conference   261 n.4, 262, 265
Cripps, Isobel   243 n.3

Cripps, Richard Stafford 133, 133 n.3, 238 n.1, 239, 240, 240 n.1, 243 n.3, 244, 248, 255, 255 n.1, 256
Croce, Benedetto 195 n.5
Crossman, Richard 317 n.5
Curtis, Lionel George 120 n.2, 183 n.1, 239 n.1, 240, 250

Dalberg-Acton, John 283 n.2
Darmstaedter, Friedrich 73, 73 n.4, 74
Darré, Richard Walther 99 n.2
Davies, Joseph Edward 205 n.5
Dawson, Christopher xvi, xix, xx n.50, 114 n.1, 116, 131 n.1, 132 n.3, 135, 136 n.2, 137, 215, 230, 232, 233, 244–7, 277, 283, 346 n.3, 375, 395, 409, 416
de Gruchy, John W. 285 n.4
Deighton, Anne 283 n.5
Delbrück, Emmi xi, 288 n.2, 333, 335 n.1
Delbrück, Justus xi, 289 n.2
de Madariaga y Rojo, Salvador 109, 110 n.5
Dibelius, Otto 287, 288 n.4, 299, 300, 354 n.1, 364, 415, 444 n.14
Diehl, Heinrich Johannes 45, 45 n.1
Dietrich Bonhoeffer Werke (DBW) 6 n.3
Dietrich, Torsten 271–6, 276 n.6, 277–9, 283–4, 286 n.1, 287, 288 n.1, 288–95, 299, 301, 305, 307, 307 n.1, 307–9, 313, 317, 318, 321–2, 326, 328, 331–3, 335 n.1, 337, 339, 340, 342 n.5, 349, 351, 351 n.6, 362, 366 n.1, 369, 382, 400, 404 n.3, 408, 409 n.1, 419, 432, 433 n.6, 433, 434, 439–41, 440 nn.2–3, 441 n.1, 446, 447 n.1, 463
Dodds, Eric Robertson 417 n.5
Dohnanyi, Hans von xi, xiii, xxi, 84 n.8, 93 n.8, 149 n.1, 205, 205 n.6, 207, 211 n.1, 238 n.1, 275–6, 279, 284, 289, 291–2, 299, 342 n.5, 345, 346 n.2, 394, 400, 433 nn.6–7, 440–1
Douglas, William Sholto 417 n.4, 419, 420, 422
Dress, Walter 83 n. 1, 302 n. 2, 307, 366
Drucker, Peter Ferdinand 136 n.1
Drummond, James Eric 128 n.5
Dulles conference 167
Dumbarton Oaks conference 201, 249, 250 n.1, 266 n.2, 269

Dun, Angus 19, 20, 24–37, 43, 47, 48, 54, 56
Dunlop, Alexander 40 n.3

Eden, Anthony xxi, xxii, xxxi n.55, 75 n.2, 81, 88, 97, 98, 100, 100 n.1, 101 n.1, 110, 113, 114, 116, 117, 119, 120, 130, 147, 148, 164, 178, 179, 182, 183, 184, 212, 213, 227 n.1, 229, 229 n.2, 230, 231, 242 n.3, 244, 248, 271, 293, 294, 319, 340
Edinburgh World Conference on Faith and Order 68 n.3
Ehrenberg, Hans xvii n.27, xvi n.25, 10 n.3, 12 n.2, 13 n.2, 15 n.2, 36 n.2, 359, 359 n.2, 360
Ehrenberg, Paul 36 n.1
Ehrenström, Nils 107 n.3, 240 n.3
Eidem, Erling 92 n.3, 94 n.9, 148
Eighth Lambeth Conference of bishops of the Anglican Communion 417 n.2
Eliot, Thomas Stearns 15 n.4
Emerson, Herbert William 49 n.2, 53
Emmerich, Kurt 202 n.2, 209, 215, 216, 359 n.1
Engel, Siegfried 372, 372 n.1
Equality before the Law xi
Ewing, Alfred Cyril 257 n.3, 258, 259
Executive Committee of the Universal Christian Council for Life and Work ix

Falls, Cyril Bentham 214 n.2
Fey, Harold 247 n.2
Fichte, Johann Gottlieb xi
Fifth Conference of Ministers of Foreign Affairs of the Allied Powers 369 n.4
Flew, Robert Newton 305 n.4
Foot, Michael 248 n.4
Ford, Franklin L. 302 n.1
Forell, Birger 174, 174 n.2, 215, 301, 301 n.1
Fraenkel, Heinrich 107 n.4, 108, 110, 113
Franck, James 23, 23 n.3
Frank, Matthew 282, 284, 300 n5, 307 n.1, 316, 346 n.3, 351
Fraser, Lindley Macnaghten 336, 337 n.4
Freie Deutsche Bewegung (FDB) 108 n.1, 204 n.2, 220

Freisler, Roland   270 n.2 n.3, 348 n.3
Freudenberg, Adolf   211, 212 n.1, 270 n.3, 275, 277, 279
Friedrichsen, Anton   89 n.1
Frings, Josef   419 n.3

Gaevernitz, Ruth   262 n.3
Garbett, Cyril Forster   296 n.1
Gascoyne-Cecil, Robert Arthur James   59 n.1, 128 n.4
Geiler, Karl   419 n.2
German refugees   23, 50, 78, 85
German resistance, destruction of   xxi–xxii
Gersdorff, Rudolf Christoph Freiherr von   398, 399 n.3
Gerstenmaier, Eugen   133 n.2, 240 n.4, 241 n.6, 276, 276 n.1, 277, 278 n.3, 278, 279, 284, 285 n.3, 289, 289 n.4, 290, 307, 348, 435 n.1, 440, 441 n.1, 442–3
Gierke, Julius von   xiii
Gieseking, Erik   278 n.2, 426 n.1, 444 n.15, 446 n.2, 446 n.4, 447 n.1, 449 n.2, 452 n.1
Gisevius, Hans Bernd   318 n.1, 340, 345, 346 n.2, 347–8, 351
Glenthøj, Jørgen   151 n.4
Gobineau, Arthur de   98, 100 n.4
Goerdeler, Carl   187 nn.1–2, 229, 231, 233 n.7, 236, 238, 238 n.4, 273 n.3, 288, 290 n.1, 291, 292 n.5, 294–6, 296 n.1, 296
Goerdeler, Reinhard   187 n.1
Goltz, Rüdiger Graf von der   93 n.4
Gooch, George Peabody   239 n.2, 240, 242, 293, 295
Graham, David   336, 337 n.5
Gremmels, Christian   xiii
Greschat, Martin   321 nn.5–6
Griffin, Bernard William   295 n.3
Griffiths, Cuthbert   xiv, 20 n.1
Grimme, Adolf   340 n.5
Grosse, Heinrich   426 n.1
Grotius, Hugo   40, 41 n.1, 145, 146
Grüber, Heinrich   296, 297 n.7, 331 n.2, 333, 334, 352
Gutmann, Franz   xiii
Gwynne, John Nevile Wake   335, 346 n.1

Hahn, Kurt   272 n.1, 273, 283, 299, 350
Halder, Franz   227, 228 n.2, 351
Hankey, Maurice   127, 128 n.8, 220, 221, 426, 426 n.3
Hase, Karl   232 n.4
Hase, Paul von   231, 232 n.3 n.4, 283, 285, 291, 294, 365
Hastings, Francis   251 n.2
Hearnden, Arthur   358 n.2
Heckel, Theodor   17 n.5, 240 n.4, 276 n.7, 279, 280 n.3, 298 n.2
Heinemann, Manfred   307 n.1, 311 n.2, 358 n.2, 361 n.1
Held, Heinrich   301 n.2
Henderson, William Watson   417 n.3
Hertz, Friedrich (Otto)   179 n.6, 259 n.1
Hess, Rudolf   98, 99 n.1, 331 n.1, 331
Heusinger, Adolf   444 n.12
Heuß, Theodor   444 n.13
Hildebrandt, Franz   6 n.3, 16, 16 n.4, 17 n.6, 29 n.1, 71 n.1, 73 n.5, 79, 80 n.5, 113, 140 n.1, 213 n.8, 272 n.3, 375 n.2, 397 n.3
Hitler, Adolf   ix, xxiv, 3, 5, 23, 24, 25 n.3, 59, 61 n.4, 62, 74–5, 87, 88, 92 n.2, 93, 94 n.8, 99 n.1, 107, 111–3, 116–9, 119–20, 119 n.1, 124, 127 n.4, 133 n.1, 139 n.2, 144 n.1, 148 n.2, 149, 150, 154, 156, 161, 163, 164 n.3, 170, 176, 181, 187 n.1, 191–2, 199, 201, 218, 222–5, 229–30, 232 n.2, 237, 237 n.1, 239 n.1, 240, 244, 244 n.4, 248 n.1, 254, 259, 260, 263, 271, 272, 279, 281, 282, 283 n.2, 288, 291, 292 n.3, 293, 294, 295, 296, 296 n.7, 304 nn.1–2, 351 n. 5, 365, 398, 400, 404 n. 3, 407, 426 n.1, 439 n, 444 n.6, 461
Hoare, Samuel   103 n.1, 249
Hodgson, Leonard   xvi, xix, 68 n.2, 3, 79–84, 86, 95, 97, 267, 395, 409, 416
Hoffmann, Peter   223 n.1, 232 n.2, 399 n.3
Hopf, Konstantin   12 n.2, 29 n.1
Hughes, Llewelyn   278 n.4
Huizinga, Johan   248, 249 n.2
Hunter, Leslie   307 n.1, 402 n.1
Huppenkothen, Walter   433 nn.6, 2
Hurst, Cecil James Barrington   14 n.2, 41 n.1, 338

'Idea of Democracy'   xi
Israel, Wilfrid   120 n.2, 129, 166, 166 n.4, 352 n.1

Jacks, Lawrence Pearsall   206, 207 n.1, 221 n.1, 283
Jasper, Ronald C. D.   x n.10, xxvii, 6 n.1, 19 n.4, 22 n.2, 149 n.1, 205 n.7, 211 n.1, 216 n.2, 221 n.1, 266 n.1, 286, 305 n.2
Johansson, Harry   107, 107 n.2, 108, 151 n.2, 152
Johnson, Mordecai   23, 23 n.1
Jossmann, Paul B.   338 n.1
Jowitt, William   319 n.2

Kahle, Paul E.   330 n.4
Kaiser, Jakob   139 n.2, 290 n.1, 292, 307 n.2
Kaiser Wilhelm Institute for Foreign and Public International Law   xii, 23 n.4, 39 n.2, 223 n.1
Kauffmann, Alfred   20 n.3
Kauffmann, Kurt   173 n.2
Keller, Manfred   359 n.2
Kelly, John N.D. 351 n.1
Kelsen, Hans   29 n.1
Kesselring, Albert   379 n.4
Kessler, Friedrich   39 n.2
Keynes, John Maynard   114, 128 n.7, 198, 199 n.1
Kirkpatrick, Ivone Augustine   431, 433 n.2
Kittredge, Tracy Barrett   33 n.1, 35, 38, 46
Koch, Werner   283 n.2, 284, 321
Koeppler, Heinz   336 n.3, 443 n.5
Kommers, Donald P.   435 n.1
Königswinter Conference   417 n.1
Kramm, Hans Herbert   80 n.1

Lafitte, François   42 n.4
Lambeth Conference   417 n.2, 452
'Law for the Restoration of the Professional Civil Service'   xii, 23 n.3
Lawrence, Frederick Pethick   219 n.3
Lawson, Tom   379 n.2, 426 n.1
Leibholz, Hans   50 n.1
Leishman, James Blair   309 n.7, 318
Lewis, Clive Staples   96, 96 n.3
Liddell Hart, Basil Henry   220 n.2, 426
Life and Work movement   ix, 13 n.1, 92 n.3, 151 n.3

Lilje, Johannes 'Hanns'   240, 241 n.5, 300, 340, 401, 401 n.1, 418, 426 n.1, 441, 442
Lindsay, A.D.   xvi, xix, 40 n.3, 4, 98 n.2, 110, 213 n.7, 244, 345, 360, 367, 369 n.3, 372, 395, 414, 415 n.1, 416
Lindsay, Michael Francis Morris   369 n.3
Livingstone, Richard Winn   344 n.1, 355
Lochner, Louis P.   128, 129 n.2, 419 n.10
Loewenstein, Karl   23, 24 n.4
London Agreement   111
London Conference   403
Ludwig, Hartmut   10 n.3

Maas, Hermann Ludwig   352 n.1
McFarlane, Kenneth Bruce   96 n.2
Mackie, Robert C. 150, 151 n.1, 152
MacMichael, Canon Arthur William   214 n.3
Macmillan, Harold   443 n.10
Mairet, Philipp   309 n.6
Malicious Practices Act   x
Mannheim, Karl   xvi n.25, 73 n.4, 183, 183 n.4, 184, 419 n.2, 459
Marahrens, August   278 n.2, 296, 301 n.1
Maritain, Jacques   xix, 67, 68 n.4
Maxwell, Alexander   320, 321 n.3, 405 n.1
Mehring, Reinhard   xii n.7, 9, 10, 11
Meiser, Hans   300 n.1
Menn, Wilhelm   424 n.2
Micklem, Nathaniel   xix, 80 n.2, 215 n.2, 216, 217, 409, 416
Milford, Humphrey Sumner   40, 40 n.1, 4, 41, 42, 80, 167, 167 n.1, 172
Ministers of Foreign Affairs conference   189 n.3
Minshall, Thomas Herbert   113, 114 n.5, 197 n.1
Moscow Conference   123, 189, 191, 193, 194, 195, 206, 215, 368, 369 n.4
Müller, Friedeborg L.   202 n.1, 204 n.1, 442 n.1
Müller-Sturmheim, Emil   179, 179 n.5
The Munich settlement   3
Murken, Jens   359 n.2
Murray, Gilbert   245 n.8, 256, 416, 418
mutual aid, agreement of   5
mutual assistance agreement   21, 112 n.1

'National Law' conference   107
National Socialism and the Church   xvii, xvii n.28, 6 n.2
National Socialist Lecturers Association   xii
National Socialist movement   ix
Neurath, Konstantin von   426 n.1, 429, 430 n.3, 432
Niebuhr, Reinhold   xiv, xix, 15 n.1, 22, 23 n.2, 25, 26, 28, 29, 166, 166 n.2, 194, 216, 218, 228, 230, 299, 318 n.2, 337, 352, 359, 395, 416, 430
Niemöller, Martin   25, 25 n.3, 83 n.1, 187 n.3, 189, 233, 234, 258 n.298, 298 n.2, 300, 321 n.8, 323 n.1, 325, 328, 329 n.1, 331 n.1, 344, 363, 364 n.1, 366, 431
Niesel, Wilhelm   301 n3
Neutrality Act   5

Oakeshott, Michael   110 n.2
Oldham, Joseph Houldsworth   xvii, xix, xxii, xxiii n.61, 13 n.1, 15 n.5, 40 n.4, 44, 59, 60 n.1, 94, 182, 193 n.4, 244 n.2, 246, 246 n.2, 289, 299, 318 n.3, 416, 458
Onslow, Richard William Alan   143, 144 n.7
Operation Torch   72
Opie, Redvers   51, 96 n.1
Ottawa Conference   57
Oxford Conference   58 n.2, 109, 110 n.4, 190 n.2, 286 n.1

Pakenham, Francis   346 n.3
Paton, William   xiv, xix, 13 n.1, 17, 23 n.2, 24–6, 29, 30–9, 43, 43 n.1, 44, 44 n.1, 45–6, 48–9, 51–5, 60, 61 n.1, 4, 63, 66, 76–80, 90, 91, 91 n.1, 100 n.1, 104–6, 140 n.1, 150, 174, 186 n.1, 260, 260 n.3
Peace Aims Conference   98, 98 n.2, 100, 101, 112, 113
Philip, André   434 n.1
Phillips, David   358 n.2
political and economic planning   42, 73 n.2, 204 n.5
post-war conference of Protestant church leaders   298 n.2

Potsdam agreement   314, 384, 390
Potsdam Conference   xxiii, 254, 279–282, 283 n.1
Potter, Simeon   443 n.5
Pretzel, Raimund   85 n.1
Pringsheim, Fritz   360 n.2

Quick, Oliver Chase   xix, 80 n.3, 83, 97, 166, 166 n.2, 208 nn.1, 3

Rabel, Ernst   22
Raina, Peter   132 n.1, 141 n.1, 266 n.3
Rathbone, Eleanor Florence   11 n.4, 419 n.6
Raven, Charles   417 nn.3–4
Restoration of Civil Service Law   x, xii, 23 n.3
Rheinstein, Max   23, 23 n.3
Ringshausen, Gerhard   xxi n.54, 258 n.3, 370 n.1
Robertson, Brian Hubert   420 n.1
Rockefeller Foundation   xv, 23 n.2, 29, 30 n.2, 32, 33–40, 33 n.1, 42 n.1, 43, 44, 46, 48, 49, 52–5, 70, 345
Rodhe, Edvard Magnus   92, 92 n.4
Roggelin, Holger   6 n.3, 17 n.6, 71 n.1, 73 n.5, 80 n.5, 213 n.8, 274 n.3
Röhm, Eberhard   10 n.3, 13 n.2, 202 n.1, 204 n.1, 226, 227 n.2, 399 n.3
Rommel, Erwin   119 n.1
Rose, Ben Lacy   329 nn.2–3
Rosenberg, Alfred   98, 100 n.3
Rothfels, Hans   444 nn.6–7, 445
Routh, Guy   190 n.4
Rowse, Alfred Leslie   128, 129 n.4, 246 n.1, 259, 259 n.2
Rundstedt, Gerd von   231, 233 n.8, 351 n.4, 426 n.1
Rupp, Ernest Gordon   258 n.4, 272, 278, 280, 286, 305, 305 n.3, 306, 329, 333, 335, 342

Salter, Arthur   296 n.6, 417 n.2
Sälter, Gerhard   444 n.15
Salter, James Arthur   297 n.6, 415, 416 n.2
Sauter, Gerhard   321 n.5
Schacht, Hjalmar   187 n.2, 236, 290, 293, 318–9
Schaefer, Klaus   446 n.4, 451 n.1, 452 n.1

Scheel, Klaus   205 n.4, 446 n.4, 451 n.1, 452 n.1
Scheliha, Rudolf von   126 n.3, 148, 148 n.2
Schleicher, Kurt von   160, 164 n.3
Schleicher, Rüdiger   207 n.3, 274, 275, 276 n.1, 284, 287, 291, 292
Schmid, Carlo   443, 444 n.9
Schmitt, Carl   xii, xii n.7–11
Schniewind, Julius   276 n6, 421 n.1
Schönfeld, Hans   107 n.2, 132, 133 n.2, 139 n.2, 151 n.3, 152, 276, 290 n.1, 293–6, 439, 439 n.1, 440, 441 n.1, 442
Schumacher, Ernst Friedrich 'Fritz'   113, 114 n.7
Schweitzer, Carl Gunther   358 n.1, 359, 370
S.C.M. Conference   283
Scott, Drusilla   415 n.1
secularization   xvii, 156, 460–1
Sforza, Carlo Graf   195 n.4
Simpson, Esther   41 n.3
Simpson, John Hope   8, 9 n.1, 14 n.2, 38–40, 41, 190
Smend, Rudolf   304 n.3
Smith, Herbert Arthur   110 n.6
Snowden, Ethel   212 n.3
Sokolowski, Wassili   410 n.1
Sorensen, Reginald William   417 n.7
Southern, Richard William   187 n.4, 236
Spender, Stephen   330 n.5, 331
Stokes, Major Richard   222 n.5, 398 n.1, 416
Strauß, Walter   444 n.11
Strong, Tracy   102 n.2, 185, 188 n.1, 240
Sutz, Erwin   6 n.1, 30 n.2, 106 n.1, 107 n.2
Szabó, Anikó   309 n.1, 311 n.1, 313 n.1, 342 n.3, 344 n1, 369 n.1, 396 n.1, 414 n.1, 433 n.2

Tehran Conference   123
Temple, William   xix, xx, 45 n.2, 110 n.4, 125 n.1, 128 n.6, 133 n.1, 138, 140 n.1, 141, 141 n.1, 196 n.2, 350, 351 n.1
Thierfelder, Jörg   202 n.1
Thoma, Richard   xi
Thorbeck, Otto   433 n.7
Tillich, Paul   15 n.1, 216, 217 n.2, 337

Tomkins, Oliver   299 n.4, 342, 347, 376, 377, 416
totalitarianism   xvii, xx, xxi, 68, 136 n.1, 162, 304, 326, 403
Toynbee, Arnold J.   xix, 190, 191 n.1
Treysa conference   305 n.6
Triepel, Heinrich   xi
Trott zu Solz, Adam von   100 n.1, 120 n.2, 127 n.3, 129 n.4, 237, 238 nn.1–2, 239, 240, 245 n.6, 279 n.2, 369 n.6
Trott zu Solz, August von   238 n.3
Trott zu Solz, Heinrich von   278 n.1, 349 n.2
Truman Doctrine   369 n.4, 404 n.2

unconditional surrender   xxi, 123, 128, 129, 130 n.1, 145, 153, 154–7, 159, 161, 164, 165, 173, 182, 185, 185 n.1, 187, 188, 188 n.1, 192, 193, 195, 212, 220, 225, 244, 252, 255, 260, 280, 281, 303, 314, 343, 386, 419
United Nations   106, 111–12, 147, 154–6, 160, 162, 167–73, 178, 180, 191, 222, 250 n.1, 251, 282, 303
United Nations Charter   266 n.2, 289 n.5
United Nations Conference on International Organization   266 n.2
United Nations Relief and Rehabilitation Administration (UNRRA)   369 n.2
Universal Christian Council for Life and Work   ix
university rectors conference   309 n.1, 311 n.2
Unwin, Stanley   42 n.2, 43–7

van Dusen, Henry Pitney   15 n.2, 30 n.1, 31–9, 42, 44, 46, 47 n.1, 49, 52, 54, 55, 56, 59, 60, 65–7 70, 75–9, 90, 90 n.2, 91, 95
Vansittart, Robert   xviii, 64 n.1, 68 n.1, 73, 101 n.3, 119, 122, 127, 128, 132 n.1, 135, 137, 138–9, 142, 143, 144 n.5, 174, 175, 178, 179, 214–5, 216 n.2, 217, 220, 222, 224, 240, 248, 269, 272, 296 n.1, 296, 312, 315–7, 348 n.2, 419, 419 n.9, 429, 430 n.2, 430
Vidler, Alexander R.   xvi, xvi n.25–6, xix, 80, 80 n.4, 81–2, 84, 86, 97, 107 n.1, 208 n.5, 249 n.3, 333 n.2

Visser't Hooft, Willem   xiv, xiv n.17, 18, 9, 10 n.2, 13 n.1, 16 n.1, 19, 25, 32 n.2, 37, 37 n.2, 38, 61 n.4, 100 n.4, 148–50, 166, 186, 189, 189 n.2, 206, 206 n.1, 207, 207 n.1, 208, 208 n.4, 209, 214, 214 n.2, 234, 247 n.1, 262 n.2, 278 n.3, 279, 280, 280 n.1, 287, 289 n.4, 290, 292 n.1, 301, 305 n.2, 307, 335 n.3, 347, 347 n.2, 348
Voigt, Frederick Augustus (Frank)   167 n.2, 204, 212, 212 n.6, 213, 232, 233 n.11, 256, 265, 265 n.1
Vollnhals, Clemens   305 n.2
von Bohlen und Halbach, Alfried Krupp   290, 292 n.2, 433 n.5
von Bülow, Vicco   442 n.1
von Klemperer, Klemens   92 n.2, 244 n.4
von Lingen, Kerstin   379 n.4

Waddams, Herbert Montague   321 n.1
Walker, Patrick Gordon   113, 114 n.3, 197 n.1
Wannsee conference   72
Warren, Avra M.   90, 90 n.1
WCC Conference   304 n.2, 249
Weber, Otto   442 n.1
Weber, Werner   445 n.4
Wedemeyer, Maria von   276 n.6, 303, 306, 310, 320, 351, 354, 378, 420, 421 nn.1–2
Wegner, Arthur   15 n.3
Weizsäcker, Ernst Freiherr von   426 n.2, 452 n.1
Wergin, Kurt   207 n.3
Westmann, Knut Bernhard   89 n.1

Whitehouse, Walter A.   xvi n.26, 208 n.5, 331 n.2
Wiegandt, Manfred H.   xi n.2, xii, xii n.10, 4, 342 n.3
Wiener, Peter   304 n.1, 305 n.5, 349, 349 n.1, 443 n.2, 448, 448 n.1, 449
Winant, John Gilbert   97 n.2, 98, 102, 103, 104, 230
Wingfield-Digby, Stephen Basil   289 n.3, 297 n.1
Winterhager, Jürgen   279 n.1, 283, 284, 286, 289
Wirmer, Josef   238 nn.4–5
Witzleben, Erwin von   229, 230 n.1, 238, 293, 295
Wolf, Erik   304 n.2
Wolff, Ernst   339 n.1
Wolfgang Büsing   399 n.3
World Council of Churches   viii, xiii, xix, xxiii, xxiv, 25, 66 n.2, 96, 151 n.3, 247, 247 n.2, 297 n.2, 335 n.3, 347, 400, 427 n.2, 430, 452
Wurm, Theophil   240, 241 n.7, 288 n.4, 296, 298, 300, 305 n.5, 306, 321 nn.7–8, 426, 429

The Yalta conference   254, 261 n.4, 263, 265, 303, 314, 403
Yorck von Wartenburg, Peter Graf   133 n.2, 232 n.5
Young, Hubert Winthrop   137 n.7
youth conference at Fanø   80

Zabriskie, Alexander C.   43, 43 n.3
Zimmern, Alfred   190, 190 n.2

www.ingramcontent.com/pod-product-compliance
Lightning Source LLC
Chambersburg PA
CBHW070005010526
44117CB00011B/1435